Beguiling Guidance

Études sur le Judaïsme Médiéval

Fondées par

Georges Vajda

Rédacteur en chef

Paul B. Fenton

Dirigées par

Phillip I. Lieberman
Benjamin H. Hary
Katja Vehlow

VOLUME 101

The titles published in this series are listed at *brill.com/ejm*

Beguiling Guidance

Zechariah Alḍāhirī's Sefer Hamusar, a Hebrew Maqāma from 16th-Century Yemen

By

Adena Tanenbaum

BRILL

LEIDEN | BOSTON

Library of Congress Cataloging-in-Publication Data

Names: Tanenbaum, Adena author
Title: Beguiling guidance : Zechariah Alḍāhirī's Sefer hamusar, a Hebrew maqāma from 16th-century Yemen / by Adena Tanenbaum.
Other titles: Sefer hamusar
Description: Leiden ; Boston : Brill, [2026] | Series: Études sur le Judaïsme Médiéval, 0169-815X ; volume 101 | Includes bibliographical references and index.
Identifiers: LCCN 2025019010 (print) | LCCN 2025019011 (ebook) | ISBN 9789004733794 hardback | ISBN 9789004733787 ebook
Subjects: LCSH: Ḍāhrī, Zachariā, approximately 1505-approximately 1583. Sefer ha-musar. | Maqamah, Hebrew.
Classification: LCC PJ5050.D28 Z99 2026 (print) | LCC PJ5050.D28 (ebook)
LC record available at https://lccn.loc.gov/2025019010
LC ebook record available at https://lccn.loc.gov/2025019011

Typeface for the Latin, Greek, and Cyrillic scripts: "Brill". See and download: brill.com/brill-typeface.

ISSN 0169-815X
ISBN 978-90-04-73379-4 (hardback)
ISBN 978-90-04-73378-7 (e-book)
DOI 10.1163/9789004733787

For my Mother

פִּיהָ פָּתְחָה בְחָכְמָה וְֽתוֹרַת־חֶסֶד עַל־לְשׁוֹנָהּ׃

She speaks with wisdom
and the teaching of kindness is on her tongue.
(Proverbs 31:26)

Contents

Acknowledgments IX

Introduction 1

1 Literary Dimensions: *Maqāma, Musar*, Narrative and Poetic Techniques 42

2 Travel in Many Guises: Journeys Real and Imagined 165

3 A Distinctive Sense of Self: Transregional Contacts with Jews in the Land of Israel 239

4 Representations of Muslims: Perspectives on the Dominant Faith 291

5 Didacticism or Literary Legerdemain? Philosophy, Ethics, and the Picaresque 346

6 A Conduit for Kabbalah: Belles-Lettres as a Medium for Mysticism 375

7 The Urge to Be Immortalized: Auto-Epitaphs, Eulogies, and the Afterlife of *Sefer hamusar* 429

Bibliography 461
- Bibliographic Abbreviations
- Primary Sources
- Secondary Literature

Index of Hebrew Poems 539
General Index 541

Acknowledgments

My initial encounter with Yehuda Ratzaby's long out-of-print edition of Zechariah Alḍāhirī's *Sefer hamusar* occurred with the acquisition, many years ago, of a used copy from the library of A.S. Halkin. Still occupied at the time with completing my doctoral dissertation, I placed the large book bound in green cloth and its original 1965 dust jacket on a shelf, with the intention of returning to it at a later date. When I finally began to dip into it, I was mesmerized by the work's beguiling tales, its elegant, ornate Hebrew, and its distinctive Yemenite coloration. As a graduate student I had been privileged to read medieval Judeo-Arabic texts with Professor Ratzaby, whose enthusiastic textual glosses drew on realia from his childhood in Yemen as well as the living tradition of Yemenite Jews in Israel. The same blend of erudition and lived experience informs his annotations to *Sefer hamusar*. Alḍāhirī's inquiring mind and refined literary sensibilities, his concurrent rootedness in 16th-century Yemen and receptivity to external developments piqued my curiosity. The more I read, the more I became convinced that *Sefer hamusar* deserved a broader audience.

All translations of Alḍāhirī's poetry, rhymed prose, and biblical exegesis in this book are my own. Translations of biblical verses are drawn mostly from The Jewish Publication Society's *Tanakh* (Philadelphia, 1985), although on occasion I have used the Revised Standard Version, and at times have modified both of these to reflect, or set off, his reading of a particular passage. For citations of rabbinic literature I have used the Soncino Press translations of the Babylonian Talmud (London, 1935–1952) and Midrash Rabbah (London, 1939). Where secondary sources in Hebrew have existing English titles I have endeavored to use them; otherwise the Hebrew title is given in transliteration. Hebrew names have generally been given in their Latin forms (Judah, rather than Yehudah), and hyphens have been omitted from Jewish family names, even if Arabic in origin (Alḥarizi, rather than al-Ḥarizi). I have, however, retained certain forms as they appear in bibliographic references.

This book has benefited from the help of colleagues and teachers who have generously shared their expertise, whether in response to queries or in reading earlier versions of individual chapters. For their invaluable insights and suggestions I am grateful to: Reuven Ahroni ז״ל, Ahmad Al-Jallad, Sean Anthony, Menashe Anzi, Tova Beeri, Haggai Ben-Shammai, Snezjana Buzov, Michelle Chesner, Jonathan Decter, Dana Fishkin, Daniel Frank, Bruce Fudge, Yossi Galron, Matt Goldish, Jane Hathaway, Brad Sabin Hill, Elisabeth Hollender, Elliott Horowitz ז״ל, Moshe Idel, Ruth Langer, Tzvi Langermann, Raphael Loewe ז״ל, David Malkiel, Uri Melammed, Vera Moreen, Ester Muchawsky-

Schnapper, Ophir Muentz-Manor, Alan Mintz ז״ל, Ayelet Oettinger, Bilal Orfali, Maurice Pomerantz, Michael Rand ז״ל, Jim Robinson, Joseph Sadan ז״ל, Raymond Scheindlin, מורי ורבי Bernard Septimus, Stefan Sperl, Michael Swartz, Yosef Tobi, David Torollo, Alan Verskin, Mark Wagner, David Wasserstein, Elliot Wolfson, Yosef Yahalom, and Joachim Yeshaya. Thanks are also due to the series editors of *Études sur le Judaïsme Médiéval*, Paul Fenton, Phillip Lieberman, Benjamin Hary, and Katja Vehlow, and to the outside readers who took the time and trouble to review the manuscript. It was a pleasure to work with the professional team at Brill: Katelyn Chin, Senior Acquisitions Editor, and Katerina Sofianou, Associate Editor, as well as with Marlou Meems, Production Editor, TAT Zetwerk. I thank them for their congeniality and support at every stage of publication.

For their gracious, expert assistance, I thank Yael Okun of the Institute for Microfilmed Hebrew Manuscripts of the National Library of Israel (formerly the Jewish National and University Library), Jerusalem; Ofra Friesel, Zmira Reuveni, and Shai Chazan of the NLI; and Lyudmila Sholokhova, Curator of the Dorot Jewish Collection of the New York Public Library. For his unfailing willingness to obtain materials, no matter how out of the way, and for drawing my attention to relevant new publications, I am deeply grateful to Yossi Galron, Jewish Studies Librarian at The Ohio State University. Without his tireless and unstinting help, this project would not have been possible. My thanks to Gillian Steinberg for her exceptional editing and to Alexander Trotter for his meticulous indexing. Final preparation of the manuscript was generously supported by the Department of Near Eastern and South Asian Languages and Cultures, the Melton Center for Jewish Studies, and the Division of Arts and Humanities at The Ohio State University. My warm thanks to Morgan Liu, Chair, and Naomi Brenner, Acting Chair of NESA; to Hannah Kosstrin, Director of the Melton Center; and to Dana Renga, Dean of Arts and Humanities.

Portions of several chapters of this book appeared in preliminary form as independent articles. Chapter 3 substantially revises ideas previously presented in "Of Poetry and Printed Books: Cultural Contacts and Contrasts Between the Jews of Yemen and the Land of Israel in Zechariah Aldahiri's *Sefer Hamusar*," *JSQ* 12/3 (2005): 260-280. One section of Chapter 4 appeared as "Polemics Real and Imagined in Zechariah Aldāhirī's *Sefer Hamusar*," in *Giving a Diamond: Essays in Honor of Joseph Yahalom*, edited by Wout van Bekkum and Naoya Katsumata (Leiden: Brill, 2011), 243–263. I have adapted Chapter 5 from "Didacticism or Literary Legerdemain? Philosophical and Ethical Themes in Zechariah Aldahiri's *Sefer Hamusar*," in *Adaptations and Innovations: Studies on the Interaction between Jewish and Islamic Thought and Literature from the Early Middle Ages to the Late Twentieth Century, Dedicated to Professor Joel*

L. Kraemer, edited by Y. Tzvi Langermann and Josef Stern (Leuven: Peeters Publishers, 2008), 355–379. Preliminary, unrevised versions of Chapter 6 and 7 appeared respectively as "Kabbalah in a Literary Key: Mystical Motifs in Zechariah Aldahiri's *Sefer Hamusar*," *JJTP* 17/1 (2009): 47–99 and "The Urge to be Immortalized: Zechariah Aldahiri's Poetic Epitaphs for Himself," in *Studies in Arabic and Hebrew Letters in Honor of Raymond P. Scheindlin*, edited by Jonathan Decter and Michael Rand (Gorgias Press, 2007), 181–210. I thank the publishers of these journals and Festschriften for permission to use this material. My thanks also to Ester Muchawsky-Schnapper for permission to reproduce the map from her catalogue, *The Yemenites: Two Thousand Years of Jewish Culture* (Jerusalem, 2000), and to Matt Carissimi and Madeleine Fix of the Ohio State University Library Technology Center for digitizing the image.

While working on this book I had the opportunity to present some of my research at conferences sponsored by the Ben Shalom Center for the Study of Yemenite Jewry at the Ben-Zvi Institute in Jerusalem; at the *Faces of the Infinite* Conference sponsored by the British Academy and the School of Oriental and African Studies (SOAS), London; at a conference in New York on "Shared Cultural Values of Jews and Muslims in Yemen and Beyond" sponsored by the American Sephardi Federation, the Princeton Institute of Semitic Studies, and the E'eleh BeTamar Association for Yemeni Jewish Heritage in Israel; at the Shalom Spiegel Institute of Medieval Hebrew Poetry at the Jewish Theological Seminary; the Medieval Hebrew Poetry Colloquium at Harvard University, sponsored by Brandeis University, The Real Colegio Complutense, and Harvard's Center for Jewish Studies; and at KU Leuven with the support of the European Association for Jewish Studies. I am grateful to all of these institutions and for the valuable feedback I received from colleagues on these occasions.

Over the course of this project my family has been patient and supportive. My husband, Daniel Frank, has always been helpful with bibliographic queries and has kept an eye out for colloquia and publications pertaining to *yahadut teiman*. Our daughter, Naama Frank, has provided all sorts of delightful distractions; כִּשְׁמָהּ כֵּן הִיא. My brother, Michael Tanenbaum, has encouraged me throughout. My sister, Susie Tanenbaum, has been unfailingly generous with her time and sage advice. My mother, Helga Weiss, has been my anchor and moral compass. Through her devotion to family and community, and her belief in the dignity and potential of every human being, she has been a constant source of inspiration. This book is dedicated to her in love and boundless gratitude.

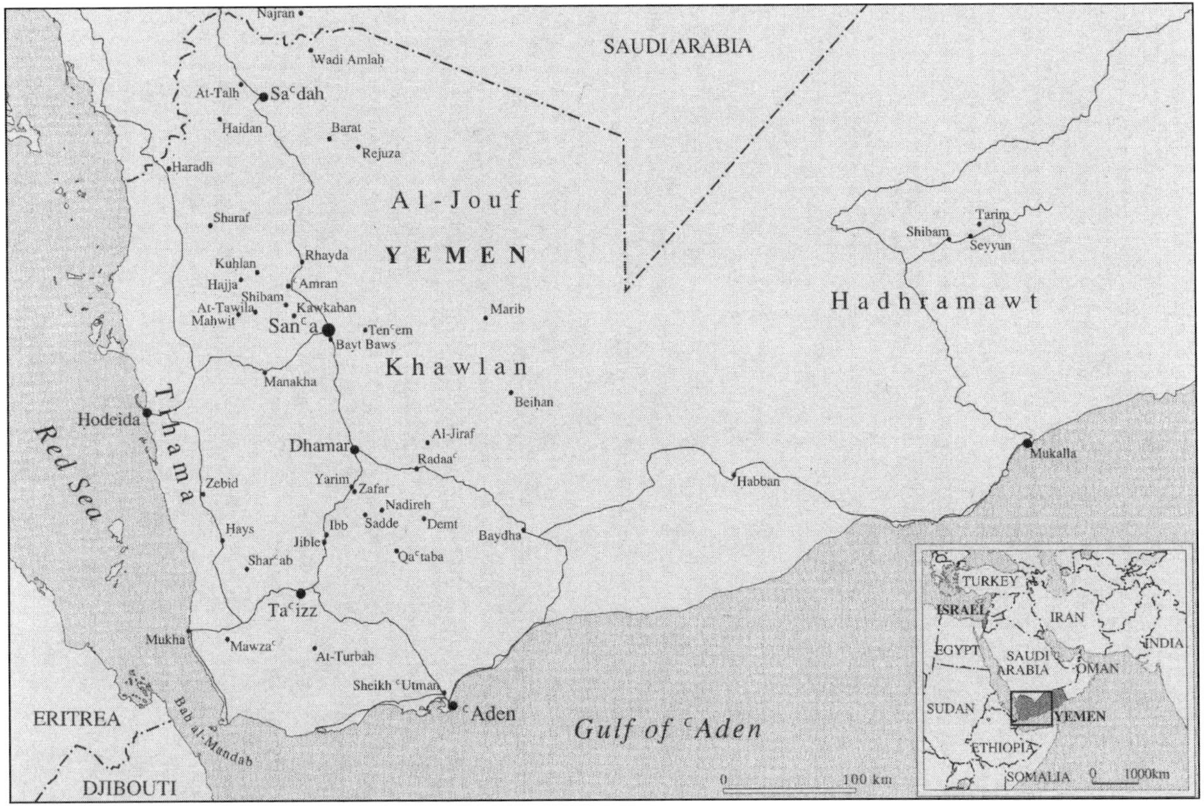

Locations of Jewish communities

COURTESY OF DR. ESTER MUCHAWSKY-SCHNAPPER

Introduction

Sefer hamusar, the only Hebrew picaresque *maqāma* known to us from Yemen, takes its readers on a journey both physical and spiritual, with tales of wandering and adventure throughout the Muslim East and an offer of spiritual ascent via kabbalistic study. In elegant rhymed prose interspersed with formal poems, *Sefer hamusar* interweaves travel accounts, folk tales and trickster stories with moral instruction, interreligious polemic, philosophical discourse and kabbalistic themes. It revolves around the escapades of two invented and itinerant characters—a gullible narrator and rogue hero—who beguile us with their tales of disguise, deception, and swindling by means of brilliant rhetorical display. But these stories of imposture are at odds with the work's aspiration to moral guidance, and the tension between the two prompted its author, Zechariah Alḍāhirī, to cast *Sefer hamusar* in a pious and consolatory light. Alongside its levity, a melancholic, elegiac tone surfaces repeatedly throughout the book's forty-five self-contained chapters as the Yemenite Jewish protagonists convey the debilitating effects on their community of crushing historical developments and repressive political conditions. Its tales unfurl against the backdrop of the short-lived 1567 Zaydī overthrow of the Ottomans in Ṣanaʿā, in whose wake the men of the Jewish community, Alḍāhirī included, were imprisoned and subjected to forced labor by the reascendant Zaydīs. This distinctively Yemenite Jewish coloration sets *Sefer hamusar* apart from any of its predecessors in the Hebrew or Arabic *maqāma* traditions.

Zechariah Alḍāhirī is hardly a household name. He is a bit of a cipher even for specialists in Jewish Studies and is virtually unknown outside of a small circle of experts in Yemenite Jewish literature and history. Certainly, he and his community deserve to be better-known: a 16th-century polymath and presumptive traveler, Alḍāhirī left behind an impressive corpus of writings, lived through momentous historical events, and endorsed new modes of spirituality and textual production that would leave their mark on Jewish life in Yemen. He was an accomplished author and prodigious reader who moved with ease between Hebrew poetry and Arabic belles-lettres, popular folklore and the demands of cultivating religious law, biblical exegesis, philosophy, and kabbalah. Attuned to aspects of Islamic religious law, he responded boldly to Muslim anti-Jewish polemics and was profoundly sensitive to the needs of his community. The cultural hybridity of his *curriculum vitae* in and of itself should pique our curiosity. Yemenite Jewry of the 14th–16th centuries boasted many fine scholars who combined formidable expertise in the exact sciences, Islamic and Jewish philosophy, Hebrew Bible and exegesis. But only Alḍāhirī penned an imaginative Hebrew *maqāma* in the classical Arabic mode.

 | DOI:10.1163/9789004733787_002

In addition to *Sefer hamusar*, Alḍāhirī's extant writings encompass an anthology of homonymic rhymes called *Sefer ha-ʿanaq* (Book of the Necklace); a *dīwān* of poems; a Torah commentary informed by both Maimonidean rationalism and kabbalah called *Ṣeidah la-derekh* (Provision for the Road); and glosses on Maimonides' laws of ritual slaughter. Other works, which have not survived, are known to us by name. Alḍāhirī was enchanted with the Hebrew language, was intimately familiar with the medieval Hebrew poetry of al-Andalus, and had an impressive command of Arabic belles-lettres. He composed approximately 270 poems, half of which appear in *Sefer hamusar*. The remainder are found in *Sefer ha-ʿanaq*, his *dīwān*, and Yemenite prayer books (*takālīl*; sng. *tiklāl*). Alḍāhirī was a respected religious scholar and a bibliophile who wrote poems in praise of books and their authors. He was also, notably, a key conduit for the transmission of kabbalah to Yemen, a development that was facilitated by the advent of printing—though no Hebrew press was ever founded in his native land—and which had dramatic ramifications for Yemenite Jewish life. Across the Jewish world, the emergence of Hebrew printing led to the creation of a transregional Jewish culture that challenged the authority of time-honored local customs.[1] This was certainly the case in Yemen, where the arrival of kabbalistic works, printed prayer books of the Sephardi rite of the Land of Israel, and Joseph Karo's newly and broadly authoritative code of law, the *Shulḥan ʿarukh* (1565), effected lasting, not uncontroversial changes in venerable Yemenite Jewish traditions. Considering the breadth of his achievements and the recognition he garnered within his own community, it is surprising how little contemporary mention of Alḍāhirī has survived and that he has languished in near oblivion for so long. His neglect is all the more remarkable, given that he was one of Yemenite Jewry's two outstanding poets in the late medieval period and that his are some of the only extant Yemenite Jewish writings from the 16th century.[2]

Beguiling Guidance is the first full-length study of *Sefer hamusar* and the only critical examination of the intersecting worlds Alḍāhirī inhabited as they are refracted through the picaresque prism of his *maqāma*. It highlights the intercultural nexus that *Sefer hamusar* represents by inviting the reader into Alḍāhirī's teeming, richly embroidered and multi-layered fictional world of Jews and Muslims and Islamicate cultural ideals adapted across confessional

1 See, e.g., Ruderman, *Early Modern Jewry*, 99–125 *passim*.

2 On Alḍāhirī's oeuvre see Ratzaby's Introduction to *Sefer hamusar*, 44–45 and idem, *Toratan she-livnei teiman*, 44–48. A lost work called *Sefer ha'apiryon* is also attributed to Alḍāhirī; see Jerusalem ms. Michael Krupp 364, f. 85[a]–88[a] and Tobi, *Yemenite Jewish Manuscripts in the Ben-Zvi Institute*, p. 141, #223.

lines.[3] Through this lens, it aims to call attention to the vast and varied cultural output of pre-modern Yemenite Jewry, still relatively unfamiliar to English-language readers, and to situate that creativity within its broader contexts. Apart from my own publications, the existing literature touching on *Sefer hamusar* is in Hebrew. While indebted to the insights and textual work of earlier scholars, this book seeks to apply a fresh reading to Alḍāhirī's *maqāma*. Previous scholarship has read *Sefer hamusar* through a positivist lens, as a travelogue that can be mined for concrete historical "facts," or as autobiography with a thin overlay of fictive garb. *Beguiling Guidance* takes a more holistic and theoretically informed approach, addressing both literary and social-historical issues. It reads Alḍāhirī's narratives in light of current literary critical scholarship on the Arabic and Hebrew *maqāma* and on storytelling and performativity in the *Arabian Nights*, and offers original translations of extended passages and poems. It analyzes the work as a bountiful repository of intellectual history, approaches its travel narratives as composites of fiction and fact, and uncovers a distinctive Yemenite Jewish sense of self in Alḍāhirī's representations of Jewish and Muslim Others. *Sefer hamusar* has remained relatively untapped for such purposes, and there is much to say regarding these deeply enmeshed strands. Where earlier scholarship was bent on surgically extracting the work's historical threads from Alḍāhirī's tapestry, we can relish the captivating mélange of moral instruction and entertainment, seriousness and jest, Judeocentricity and shared Islamicate cultural ideals reflected in Alḍāhirī's tales of trickery, travel, learning, and lore.

Beguiling Guidance contextualizes *Sefer hamusar* by reading it as an artifact of Yemenite Jewish culture informed by broader 16th-century historical and intellectual currents. From the perspective of literary history, it situates Alḍāhirī's *maqāma* in relation to the Arabic and Hebrew literary models and antecedents that nourished it—foundational *maqāmāt* of Eastern Muslim provenance on the one hand and of Iberian and Italian Jewish origin on the other. More synchronically, it discusses aspects of the work that shed light on the particular social, political, and interconfessional milieus in which it was conceived and executed and to which it owes its formation. In reevaluating the ways *Sefer hamusar* has been read until now, this book also attempts to illuminate some larger methodological issues in the study of pre-modern Yemenite Jewry and its cultural production. To that end, it is attentive to changes in the historiography of Yemenite Jewry and the presentation of its inner life and

3 The term 'Islamicate' was coined by Marshall Hodgson "on the analogy of 'Italianate,' 'in the Italian style,'" to refer to shared cultural ideals that cut across religious traditions in the Islamic world; see Hodgson, *The Venture of Islam*, 1:59.

literary/artistic creativity over time, due to gradual shifts in the cultural and ideological commitments of scholars from the 19th century into the first decades of the 21st.

1 Historical Context

Sefer hamusar is entertaining and inventive, and is crafted with unmistakable skill in accordance with the aesthetic conventions of the *maqāma* genre. Nonetheless, its stylized form and prosody should not obscure its composition at a particular historical juncture and within a distinctive Jewish culture. While it is not clear how aware he was of contemporaneous developments in the wider, global arena, Alḍāhirī lived in an era of discovery, empire, and slave trade; enhanced mobility and contacts; the diffusion of ideas, printed books, and manuscripts; orthodoxies and heterodoxies; and transitions, transformations, and innovations affecting an increasingly interconnected world. Despite serious reservations about reading the work primarily as a repository for historical facts, we would be remiss if we did not acknowledge that Alḍāhirī's *maqāma* marks a definitive moment in Yemenite Jewish history and letters. Unlike most earlier Hebrew rhymed prose narratives, *Sefer hamusar* does not retreat from direct engagement with historical circumstances, albeit from an exceedingly Judeocentric point of view. Quite clearly, its brimming universe of comic and tragic incidents furnishes glimpses of larger political, communal, and cultural developments, even if its protagonists view the world primarily through a more circumscribed lens. Various episodes unselfconsciously entwine the historical and the domestic, the global and the local.

Sefer hamusar is written against the tumultuous background of the 1567 Zaydī overthrow of the Ottomans in Ṣanaʿā following the death of Suleiman the Magnificent (1566) and its reversal with the dispatch of a large-scale Ottoman military expedition from Egypt in 1569 to retrieve the province. As such, it provides a sense of the ebb and flow of Yemenite Jewish fortunes resulting from the rivalries, cleavages, and struggles among different ruling factions. It articulates a particularly vehement Jewish animus toward the Zaydī Muslim *imāms*—political rulers and religious leaders—and Imām al-Muṭahhar in particular, who, with the takeover from the Ottomans, had imprisoned the men of the Ṣanaʿā Jewish community, which traced its existence back to antiquity.[4]

4 No archival document that would shed light on this incident has been unearthed. Zaydī legal sources mention relatively few cases involving Jews; see Tobi, "Sifrut ha-halakhah ha-zaydit

The incident is framed entirely in archetypal biblical terms, and, apart from one or two vague references to al-Muṭahhar's successor, who may have been an Ottoman proxy from a rival Zaydī faction ("the King of the South"; cf. Daniel 11:5–6), there is no meaningful mention of the Ottomans.[5]

The Zaydīs were (and are) a branch of Shīʿī Islam descended from supporters of the unsuccessful revolt of the fifth Shīʿī *imām*, Zayd ben ʿAlī, in 740 C.E. against Umayyad rule (and hence called "fivers").[6] In Yemen, the Zaydīs were a recurrent force to contend with from the ninth century well into the 20th. As Jane Hathaway has observed, "Yemen's isolation relative to the central Islamic lands has historically made it an attractive haven for sectarian offshoots of normative Sunni Islam."[7] Pre-modern Yemen was beset by Sunnī, Ismāʿīlī, and Zaydī dynasties carving out regional centers of power and vying for the allegiance of indigenous tribes from the ninth century on.[8] The land was not only divided into outlying tribal districts and more urban centers. With Yemen's rugged terrain of highlands—a mountainous interior of jagged peaks and narrow fertile valleys—surrounded by narrow coastal plains, including the arid Red Sea littoral of the Tihāma, the natural boundaries that separated parts of the population from one another ensured that no one dynasty ever gained centralized control over the entire land.[9] In the twelfth century, the Sunnī Ayyūbids invaded from Egypt, conquered almost the whole of Yemen, and ruled from the

ke-maqor le-toldot yehudei teiman" and idem, "Information on the Jews of Yemen in Arabic Writings from Yemen." Greidi maintains that Imām al-Muṭahhar sent the Ṣanaʿā Jewish community into exile while imprisoning its prominent members, among them Alḍāhirī; see *Peʿilut ve-zikhron ishim*, p. 70.

5 On the 16th-century Zaydī-Ottoman conflict, see Blackburn, "The Collapse of Ottoman Authority in Yemen," and Hathaway, *The Arab Lands under Ottoman Rule 1516–1800*, 53–54.

6 See: Crone, *God's Rule*, 99–109; Haykel, *Revival and Reform in Islam*, 5–10; Madelung, "Zaydiyya"; Serjeant, "The Zaydis"; and Schmidtke, "The History of Zaydī Studies: An Introduction."

7 Hathaway, "The Mawzaʿ Exile at the Juncture of Zaydi and Ottoman Messianism," 111.

8 On ruling dynasties and their centers of power see: Dresch, *Tribes, Government, and History in Yemen*, 158–197 *passim*; idem, "Imams and Tribes: The Writing and Acting of History in Upper Yemen"; El-Shami and Serjeant, "Regional Literature: The Yemen," 443–445; Serjeant, "The Interplay Between Tribal Affinities and Religious (Zaydī) Authority in the Yemen"; and Tobi, *The Jews of Yemen*, 34–47 and 142–156. On Yemeni history up until the first Ottoman conquest see Hathaway, "The Forgotten Province: A Prelude to the Ottoman Era in Yemen."

9 On the historical division of the land into the well-defined geographical regions of Upper and Lower Yemen (divided by the Sumara mountains just south of Yarīm), the Western Mountains, and the Tihāma, see Haykel, *Revival and Reform in Islam*, 3–4. The natural barriers that created a landscape isolating blocks of population also gave rise to regional linguistic differences; see Gluska, "Language," p. 144.

south, which was the richest agricultural region (1173–1229); their success in putting an end to all local dynasties except the Zaydīs north of Ṣanaʿā ensured that, with their departure, the Sunnī (Shāfiʿī) Rasūlid dynasty ushered in a period of relative stability (1229–1454). The Rasūlids made Taʿizz their capital and concentrated their power in the southern coastal region, turning Zabīd into a focus for Sunnī autonomy in the Tihāma coastal plain. Instability returned with the rise of the local Yemeni Ṭāhirid dynasty (1454–1517), also centered in the south, while the Shīʿī Zaydī *imāms* remained on the scene for centuries, exercising control from strongholds in the north (particularly Ṣaʿadah) and, intermittently, from Ṣanaʿā in the central plateau (897–1962), an area home to some of the larger Jewish communities.[10] Most Muslims were aligned with one tribe or another. Outside of areas of Zaydī control, Jews also lived in over a thousand villages among the Yemeni tribes, who protected them in a network of patron-client relations. Whereas Yemeni Muslims could travel safely only within the territory where they had tribal connections, Jews "were not perceived as security threats [and] could cross tribal boundaries in relative safety."[11]

The Ottomans, defenders of Sunni Islam, established their first foothold in Yemen with the occupation of Aden in 1538–1539, followed by the conquest of Taʿizz and Ṣanaʿā in 1547, but even they never succeeded in controlling all of Yemen. Hathaway writes that

> Zaydi doctrine … calls for a living, active imam who defends the community militarily, if necessary. This religious impulse, combined with the Zaydis' seven-hundred-year domination of Yemen's northern highlands, made the Zaydis a constant threat to Ottoman control of the province.[12]

10 Information on Jewish life in Yemen during Ṭāhirid rule is scarce; see Tobi, "Jews of Yemen"; idem, "Information on the Jews of Yemen"; and idem, *Studies in Megillat Teman*, 71. The city of Ṣaʿadah was a center of Zaydī learning and home to an important Jewish community going back to geonic times; see Ratzaby's Introduction to *Sefer hamusar*, pp. 38 and 45–46. Ṣaʿadah produced eminent rabbis and served as a spiritual center for the Jews of northern Yemen; see Bar-Maoz, "Social Tension Between the Sanaʿa Community and Other Communities."

11 Verskin, *A Vision of Yemen*, 20 and 100–109, and Goitein ed. and trans., *Massaʿot ḥabshush—Ruʾyā al-yaman*, 51–61. See also Verskin, ibid., p. 40 regarding social stratification under tribal law. On the social hierarchies in Upper Yemen (17th–20th centuries) see Haykel, "Dissembling Descent, Or How the Barber Lost His Turban," 205–208 and idem, *Revival and Reform in Islam*, 4–5. On the status of the Jews in the tribal regions of Northern Yemen see Tobi, *The Jews of Yemen*, 142–156.

12 Hathaway, *The Arab Lands under Ottoman Rule*, 53.

The tempestuous period of the first Ottoman occupation (lasting until their ouster by the Qāsimīs in 1635) had been preceded by a consolidation of Zaydī influence, which was, however, soon undermined by disunity and internecine wars that left the Zaydīs vulnerable to Ottoman expansionism.[13] (In 1525, a Turkish admiral in the Red Sea reported to the Ottoman authorities that the flourishing province of Yemen "has no ruler" and deserves to be "a fine *sanjak*" whose conquest would facilitate taking India.[14]) The initial 1538–1539 Ottoman invasion of Yemen—in response to Portuguese incursions into the Red Sea, the Indian Ocean, and India—had provoked local Zaydī resistance, which considerably reduced Ottoman control. But the Ottomans retook the province in 1569, eroding the political influence of the Zaydī Imām al-Muṭahhar, at whose hands, following the short-lived but consequential overthrow of Ottoman rule in 1567, Alḍāhirī and the men of the Ṣanaʿā Jewish community had been incarcerated, possibly on suspicion of sympathizing with the forces of the Ottoman occupation.[15] Even though Alḍāhirī's poetic complaints of Yemeni Muslim oppression rely on familiar, non-specific biblical tropes, he actually mentions al-Muṭahhar once by name and several times by the epithet *ha-ḥigger* (*al-arʿaj*, "the lame one"; the Imām was congenitally lame in his left leg).[16] One might have expected Alḍāhirī to be positively disposed toward the Ottomans, insofar as their victory promised relief from Zaydī oppression and could easily have been framed in apocalyptic terms. But he hardly mentions them, and, despite his characters' extensive travels, they show no awareness of the maritime conflict between the Ottomans and the Portuguese.[17]

---

13 See Ahroni, *Yemenite Jewry*, 82–86; Serjeant and Lewcock, *Ṣanʿā: An Arabian Islamic City*, 70–72; Blackburn, "The Era of Imām Sharaf al-Dīn Yaḥyā and his Son al-Muṭahhar," and idem, "The Ottoman Penetration of Yemen."

14 For the document attributed to Selman Reis (d. 1528), see Ozbaran, "A Turkish Report on the Red Sea and the Portuguese in the Indian Ocean (1525)."

15 See: Blackburn, "The Collapse of Ottoman Authority in Yemen"; Serjeant, *The Portuguese Off the South Arabian Coast*; idem and Lewcock, *Ṣanʿā*, 70–72; Hathaway, *A Tale of Two Factions*, 64–66 and 79–93; and idem, *The Arab Lands under Ottoman Rule*, 53–54. Hathaway points out that in the face of al-Muṭahhar's rebellion, the Ottoman struggle to retain Yemen proved "extremely costly and draining."

16 See Blackburn, "The Era of Imām Sharaf al-Dīn Yaḥyā and his Son al-Muṭahhar." Throughout Quṭb al-Dīn Muḥammad al-Nahrawālī's pro-Turkish chronicle of the 1569–1571 Ottoman campaign and Zaydī resistance, al-Muṭahhar is referred to (in Clive Smith's translation) as "the lame," "the charlatan cripple," etc.; see *Lightning Over Yemen*.

17 For a 19th-c. view of the Ottomans as redeemers, see Ḥayyim Ḥabshush's chronicle, ed. Qāfiḥ, "Qorot yisrael be-teiman," 249.

2 Medieval versus Early Modern

A word is in order here about the use of the designation "early modern" in connection with sixteenth-century Yemenite Jewry. Alḍāhirī occupied different temporalities: *Sefer hamusar* responds to an effectively medieval political constellation within Yemen while also reflecting newer cultural realities and material transformations taking hold outside of Yemen. These novel developments, which often came to Alḍāhirī's attention via Jewish communities in other lands, are characteristic of the early modern era. Historically, due to its strategic location, Yemen was central to the international Indian Ocean trade. Until the Portuguese onslaught of the sixteenth century, the port of Aden was an entrepôt for goods from the Far East or India headed for the Mediterranean via the Red Sea or overland caravans to Egypt.[18] Yemenite Jews maintained strong ties with their far-flung coreligionists, whether through trade, epistolary exchanges, the import of books, visits of emissaries, or migration to and from Yemen for mercantile purposes.[19] Despite Yemen's relative insularity, Yemenite Jews were not immune to the effects of the dramatic material, political, economic, and cultural transformations affecting the larger world between 1500 and 1800, which are viewed as hallmarks of the early modern period in the historiography of western Europe. As Sheldon Pollack has written,

> Few deny that over the three centuries up to 1800 the world as a whole witnessed unprecedented developments: the opening of sea passages that were global for the first time in history and of networks of trade and commodity production for newly globalizing markets; spectacular demographic growth (the world's population doubled); the rise of large stable states; and the diffusion of new technologies (including gunpowder and printing) …

But as Pollack argues with regard to India, modernity is "additionally, or exclusively, a condition of consciousness," and it is not necessarily helpful to assume that the western European model of early modernity is uniformly applicable

---

18 See Margariti, *Aden & The Indian Ocean Trade.*

19 See: Serjeant, *The Portuguese Off the South Arabian Coast*; Abir, "International Commerce and Yemenite Jewry: 15th to 19th Centuries"; and Bar-Maʿoz, "Hishtarshut ha-qabbalah be-teiman." Geniza documents reveal ties with other Jewish communities in earlier centuries; see Goitein and Friedman, *India Traders of the Middle Ages*. See also Tobi, "Teiman ve-yerushalayim" and Qāfiḥ, "The Ties of Yemenite Jewry with the Jewish Centers."

elsewhere, particularly as it pertains to intellectual history.[20] As the only sizeable religious minority in Southern Arabia, Yemenite Jewry in many respects retained its fundamentally medieval characteristics well beyond the sixteenth century, both internally and in its legal status vis-à-vis Yemeni Muslims, whether as *dhimmīs* under the Zaydī *imāms* or as protégés (*jīrān*) of tribal patrons in the rural territories outside of Zaydī control dominated by tribal sheikhs.[21] Well into the 20th century, the Zaydī legal system remained founded on religious law, such that the discriminatory restrictions imposed upon Jews by the medieval *dhimma* were enforced by the Zaydī rulers into modern times. Yemen's economy was based on agriculture; the Muslims farmed while the Jews were artisans and craftsmen who supplied the Muslims with a broad range of services and manufactured goods. Significant technological and economic change came to Yemen only in the 19th century as the result of the 1839 British colonization of Aden (fuelled by Aden's enhanced strategic value in the age of steam) and the 1872 Ottoman occupation of central Yemen (facilitated by the opening of the Suez Canal in 1869).[22]

Internally, within the Jewish community, the sixteenth century saw no instantaneous, dramatic break with earlier traditions of science, Jewish religious scholarship, or communal authority, but seeds of change were planted that would contribute to certain striking challenges to established norms in the seventeenth and eighteenth centuries.[23] In this regard, the medieval/early modern distinction is artificial for sixteenth-century Yemen, and the periodization that applies to the history and thought of Italian Jewry, for example, is not necessarily applicable to Yemenite Jewry. But material, political, economic, religious, and cultural innovations emanating from elsewhere (Hebrew printing, which facilitated the import of the *Shulḥan ʿarukh*, kabbalah, and printed prayer books; voyages of discovery; Portuguese mercantilism; the expansion of the Ottoman Empire) did affect Yemen during Alḍāhirī's lifetime. Since they

20 See Pollock, *Forms of Knowledge in Early Modern Asia*, 1–16. I thank Asad Ahmed for calling this work to my attention. On the academic debate over the use of the term "early modernity" for a post-medieval, pre-modern historical period (in place of Renaissance and Reformation in European historiography), see also Starn, "The Early Modern Muddle" and Goldstone, "The Problem of the 'Early Modern' World."

21 See Dresch, *Tribes, Government, and History in Yemen*, 118–123 and Serjeant, "The Interplay Between Tribal Affinities and Religious (Zaydī) Authority in the Yemen."

22 See, e.g., Klorman, "Yemen"; but see also Sadan, "The 'Latrines Decree.'" On imperial encounters between the Ottomans and the British in the Red Sea region, see Kühn, "Shaping and Reshaping Colonial Ottomanism," 318–320.

23 See, e.g., Tobi, "Challenges to Tradition: Jewish Cultures in Yemen, Iraq, Iran, Afghanistan, and Bukhara," and idem, *The Jews of Yemen*, 48–84.

would ultimately introduce discontinuities into areas of spiritual and communal life (and, more immediately, would disrupt the Mediterranean trade in which Yemenite Jews had been active for centuries), applying the term in a qualified way may prove useful to flag the "connections, contacts, and conversations over time and across specific localities" that David Ruderman has emphasized in his synthetic study of early modern Jewry.[24]

3 Authorial Sensibilities

Alḍāhirī was shaped by the intellectual flowering of late medieval Yemenite Jewry (14th–17th centuries), which was nourished by the exegetical, philosophical, and scientific creativity of Jewish communities across the Islamic world and beyond. The transfer of knowledge facilitated by the Indian Ocean trade to which Yemen was central also exposed Yemenite Jewish scholars to ideas of non-Jewish provenance from India, Iran, and Egypt.[25] Alḍāhirī's impressive range owed much to the broad Judeo-Arabic *paideia* Yemenite Jewry had inherited from the "Golden Age" of Andalusian Jewry (10th–12th centuries), with whose outstanding poetic, exegetical, halakhic, and philosophical works he engaged in his own writings. Within the Yemenite tradition, he can be situated between the 15th-century savants whose Judeo-Arabic writings were profoundly immersed in philosophy, science and the Maimonidean corpus, Bible and rabbinic literature (Ḥoṭer ben Shelomoh, Zechariah ha-Rofé, Moshe ben Yosef al-Balīda, and David [Alu'el] ben Yeshaʿ Halevi) and the universally venerated 17th-century kabbalistic poet and exegete Shalem Shabbazi, whose ascent reflected the turn toward kabbalah that began in the sixteenth century.[26]

---

24 See Ruderman, "Why Periodization Matters: On Early Modern Jewish Culture and Haskalah." In his *Early Modern Jewry*, Ruderman expands upon his argument that it is possible to identify "larger patterns of cultural formation affecting early modern Jewry as a whole" without effacing the specificities of local Jewish cultures; see esp. pp. 1–21 and 207–226. See also Kaplan, "Introduction," in *The Posen Library* vol. 5.

25 See Langermann, *Yemenite Midrash*, xvii–xxx; idem, "Cultural Contacts of the Jews of Yemen"; and idem, "Maḥshevet hodu be-qerev yehudei teiman."

26 On Alḍāhirī's prolific 15th-century predecessors, whose work often took an exegetical approach to biblical, rabbinic, and Maimonidean texts, see: Tobi, "Ketav-yad ḥadash ha-kollel ḥibbureihem shel rabbi ḥoṭer al-dhammārī ve-rabbi zekharya ha-rofé"; idem, "Piyyut le-rabbi moshe al-balīda"; Blumenthal, *The Commentary of R. Hoter Ben Shelomo to the Thirteen Principles of Maimonides*; idem, *The Philosophic Questions and Answers of Hoter Ben Shelomo*; Langermann, "Saving the Soul by Knowing the Soul"; idem, "*Sharḥ al-Dalāla*: A Commentary to Maimonides' *Guide* from Fourteenth-Century Yemen"; idem, *Yemenite*

In tandem with *Sefer hamusar*, Alḍāhirī's other extant works can help us to reconstruct his intellectual biography, if not precise dates and places. But these writings can also frustrate attempts to divine Alḍāhirī's authorial sensibilities due to the distinct modes of expression he adopts in different genres. The tone of his Torah commentary is at times so grave and prescriptive that it is difficult to recognize in *Ṣeidah la-derekh* the often lively and even mischievous author we know from *Sefer hamusar*. Nor does his penchant for expounding the laws of ritual slaughter allow us to glimpse the more inventive, animated, lyrical, and whimsical sides of his writerly personality that come across in his rhymed prose narratives. (Abdelfattah Kilito writes that soon after the publication of al-Ḥarīrī's *Maqāmāt*, it was alleged that he was not their author because his style in the *Maqāmāt*, already distinct from al-Hamādhānī's, differed from that of his own earlier writing.)[27]

Yet we need not assume that Alḍāhirī was deliberately addressing audiences of radically opposed spiritual and intellectual inclinations. His picaresque protagonists in *Sefer hamusar* proudly lay claim to all of his own writings; they recite panegyric poems for *Ṣeidah la-derekh* and select kabbalistic, exegetical, and halakhic works by other authors; they advocate kabbalistic and philosophical study, and they endorse particular kabbalistic doctrines and rituals. All of this indicates a holistic rather than sharply bifurcated conception of his oeuvre and intended readership. Like the Andalusian Jewish polymaths who preceded him by four centuries, Alḍāhirī was at home in both the classical Hebrew and Arabic literary traditions, perhaps even to a greater degree than his immediate predecessors and successors in Yemen. Apart from his own testimony that he consciously modeled *Sefer hamusar* on the early twelfth-century *Maqāmāt* of "the incomparable" al-Ḥarīrī, there is ample textual evidence of his direct access to al-Ḥarīrī's masterpiece in the original Arabic.[28] Apparently, he was also familiar with the Arabic writings of the renowned littérateur Abū ʿUthmān ʿAmr b. Baḥr al-Jāḥiẓ of Baṣra (776–868).[29] But Alḍāhirī did not restrict himself to elevated, classical Arabic or strictly literary sources: he also produced

---

Midrash, 269–279 *passim*; Havatselet ed. and trans., *Midrash ha-ḥefeṣ*; and Tobi, "Rabbi david yeshaʿ ha-levi (Yemen, 15th century)."

27 "But must a writer be condemned to the stranglehold of a single style, and never permitted to write differently?" See Kilito, "Foreword: In Praise of Pretense," in Cooperson, trans., *Impostures*, x. Stylistic judgments are, of course, subjective; of *Ṣeidah la-derekh* Moshe Zadock writes that, "from a literary perspective, its style is easygoing and simple relative to that of *Sefer hamusar*"; see *Maḥshevet yisrael be-teiman*, 57.

28 See Ratzaby, "The Influence of al-Ḥariri Upon Alḍāhiri."

29 On Alḍāhirī's translations from Arabic see *Sefer hamusar*, 18–20. On his use of a tale that appears in the writings of al-Jāḥiẓ see p. 19, n. 9.

Hebrew translations of Yemeni Arabic folk poems and aphorisms and drew liberally on a rich corpus of Arabic folk tales that he may well have encountered in oral form.[30] The complexity of his authorial preferences is reflected in the way he combines literary conservatism with boldness, and adherence to religious norms with intellectual independence. He found compelling and meaningful Hebrew models in Andalusian verse and the *Taḥkemoni* of Judah Alḥarizi (d. 1225) but also expanded and turned a contrafactual technique into a hallmark of Yemenite Hebrew poetry. A strict halakhist, Alḍāhirī nevertheless made extensive, unacknowledged use of the *Maḥbarot* of Immanuel of Rome (c. 1261–1335) precisely when the work was banned for its pointed eroticism by no less a halakhic authority than Joseph Karo.[31] In short, his authorial tastes are marked by a much greater degree of intellectual curiosity and eclecticism than has hitherto been acknowledged, and his expansive vision is difficult to pigeonhole.

4 Distinguishing Features of *Sefer hamusar*

In crafting *Sefer hamusar*, Alḍāhirī added his own distinctively Yemenite touches—literary techniques, settings, realia of everyday life, references to historical events and political circumstances—that conjure a unique world and render his *maqāma* quite unlike any of its predecessors. In embryonic form—and almost incidentally—his belletristic narratives subtly anticipate actual historical shifts, new departures, and discontinuities in the learned and literary culture, liturgical practices, and inter-communal ties of Yemenite Jewry that would come to the fore a century later: the gradual eclipse of philosophy by kabbalah as a framework for Jewish religious thought; the "discovery" of Yemenite Jewry by rabbinic emissaries sent from the Land of Israel to far-flung and "exotic" Jewish communities of the East; and the eventual displacement of earlier versions of the Yemenite liturgical tradition with the arrival of printed prayer books containing the Sephardi rite of the Holy Land. These gradual transformations resulted not only from internal dynamics, but also from

---

30 See Ratzaby, "Sheloshah shirim meturgamim me'ito shel rabbi zekhariah al-ḍāhirī."

31 See *Oraḥ ḥayyim* 307:16. On the impact of Karo's works on Yemenite Jewry see, e.g.: Ratzaby, "Rabbi yosef karo vihudei teiman"; Gaimani, "The Penetration of Rabbi Yosef Karo's Literary-Halakhic Work to Yemen"; for speculation that Alḍāhirī himself may have been instrumental in transmitting the text see pp. 120–124; see also idem, *Temurot be-moreshet yahadut teiman be-hashpa'at ha-shulḥan 'arukh ve-qabbalat ha-ari*; and Tobi, "Shulḥan 'arukh le-rabbi yosef karo le'umat mishneh torah le-ha-rambam be-teiman."

changes associated with the early modern period and sixteenth-century innovations in spiritual, communal, and material culture in other parts of the Jewish world: the great kabbalistic revival in Safed; an international fundraising campaign for communities and institutions in the Land of Israel; and the increased availability of affordable prayer books printed in Italy and the Ottoman Empire, primarily for domestic markets. But there is no sense of abrupt rupture; if anything, *Sefer hamusar* suggests the coexistence of these incipient innovations with continuities in religious sensibility and liturgical practice, the types of scholarly literature being written, the modes of their transmission, and internal communal autonomy.

5 Literary Continuities and New Departures

On the literary level, *Sefer hamusar* exhibits continuity, deliberate classicizing, and even conservatism vis-à-vis earlier exemplars of the Hebrew *maqāma*. At the same time, it breaks new formal and thematic ground. This simultaneous embrace of the old and the new highlights the limited utility of a rigid, somewhat artificial distinction between "classical" and "post-classical" that has been applied to the *maqāma* genre.[32] Alḍāhirī explicitly modeled his work on Alḥarizi's *Taḥkemoni* as well as on the early twelfth-century *Maqāmāt* of Abū ʾl-Ḥasan al-Ḥarīrī of Basra (d. 1122), who gave the Arabic *maqāma* its definitive form. Though he does not mention them by name, he also drew on the late tenth-century *Maqāmāt* of Badīʿ al-Zamān al-Hamadhānī (d. 1008), who pioneered the genre in Arabic, and the *Maḥbarot* of Immanuel of Rome, a work replete with sonnets, sexual innuendo, and Italian Renaissance ideals. It is useful to locate *Sefer hamusar* within the extended tradition of Arabic and Hebrew literary *maqāmāt*, but I do not concur with the scholarly tendency to brand Alḍāhirī an epigone simply because his aesthetic sensibilities and modes of expression hark back to "classical" models of the *maqāma* and the prescriptive poetics of the Andalusian school of Hebrew poetry. When it is framed purely in terms of slavish "imitation," that judgment is inaccurate, nor does it do Alḍāhirī justice, since he borrowed selectively from, and engaged creatively with, his strikingly diverse sources of literary and learned inspiration.[33] Recent studies

32 Cf., e.g., Pomerantz, "The Play of Genre: A *Maqāma* of 'Ease after Hardship' from the Eighth/Fourteenth Century and Its Literary Context."

33 On the widely held view among 19th- and early 20th-century Western European scholars that Middle Eastern Jewish poetry was a second-rate imitation of classical Andalusian Hebrew poetry, see Yeshaya, *Medieval Hebrew Poetry in Muslim Egypt*, 4–7 and *passim*.

have reevaluated the assumption that an epigone is by definition second-rate, inferior to his or her predecessors, allowing us to appreciate the dynamic role of such successor figures in the development of Jewish culture.[34] While *Sefer hamusar* does tread some familiar ground, its recourse to kabbalistic ideas on the one hand and its covert use of Immanuel's subversive *Maḥbarot* on the other distinguish it from its Hebrew antecedents.[35]

6 Kabbalah and Philosophy

Sefer hamusar draws on theosophical ideas from the *Zohar* and other works of classical kabbalah as well as a generous sampling of contemplative and theoretical themes derived primarily from the geonic-Andalusian Jewish philosophical tradition. Yemenite Jews revered Maimonides, and, like earlier Yemenite Jewish intellectuals with access to the Maimonidean corpus, Alḍāhirī takes for granted that philosophical discourse is an accepted and desirable mode of expressing religious thought. Yemenite Jewish thinkers read Maimonides' injunction to "accept the truth from whatever source it comes" (*isma' l-ḥaqq mi-man qālahu*) as a mandate for rational inquiry, which allowed them to draw on a wide range of speculative sources.[36] Unlike the anti-philosophical stance of certain earlier Spanish and contemporary Italian kabbalists, Alḍāhirī's quest to uncover sacred truths often moves so fluidly between philosophical and mystical modes that the boundaries between the two appear to be fairly porous.[37]

For varying positions on the nature of Alḍāhirī's contribution, see Wagner, *Like Joseph in Beauty*, 163–164.

34 See Berger and Zwiep, eds., *Epigonism and the Dynamic of Jewish Culture*.

35 Isaac Ibn Sahula's rhymed prose *Meshal ha-qadmoni* (13th century, Castile) contains the earliest quotations from *Midrash hane'elam*, part of the Zoharic corpus. But scholars have varied as to whether the work reflects kabbalistic tendencies. Unlike *Sefer hamusar*, it does not make explicit reference to the doctrine of the ten *sefirot*. See Ibn Sahula, *Meshal Haqadmoni: Fables from the Distant Past*, xvii–xviii; Scholem, "Kabbalat r. yiṣḥaq ben shlomo ben avi sahula ve-sefer ha-zohar"; idem, "Ha-ṣitut ha-rishon min ha-midrash ha-ne'elam"; Liebes, "How the Zohar Was Written," 87; and Lachter, "Spreading Secrets: Kabbalah and Esotericism in Isaac ibn Sahula's *Meshal ha-kadmoni*." Matti Huss has identified criticism of kabbalists in Ibn Zabara's *Sefer sha'ashu'im* and Jacob ben Elazar's *Sefer ha-meshalim* for directing prayer to an intermediary entity on the grounds that it smacks of Christian belief; see his "Criticism of Kabbala in Hebrew Rhymed Narratives."

36 See Gorfinkle, ed. and trans., *The Eight Chapters of Maimonides on Ethics*, 35–36 and Hebrew/Judeo-Arabic, p. 6. On the diversity of genres considered legitimate sources of sublime truth, see Langermann, *Yemenite Midrash*, xvii–xxx.

37 Cf.: Gottlieb, "Shem Tov Ibn Shem Tov's Path to Kabbalah"; Idel, "Jewish Thought in

The conviction of an underlying unity among his metaphysical sources is also evident in the exegetical approach he adopts in his esoteric Torah commentary, *Sefer ṣeidah la-derekh*, where, alongside the *Zohar* and other classical kabbalistic works (*Maʿarekhet ha'elohut, Shaʿarei orah*), he draws on Maimonides' rationalistic *magnum opus, The Guide of the Perplexed*.[38] Presumably, due to their culturally specific modes of reception and interpretation of kabbalistic materials, Yemenite Jews did not see a rigid dichotomy between rationalism and kabbalah—a binary opposition that is, to a certain extent, the legacy of 19th-century Western European Jewish historiography—until a bitter controversy, fueled in part by contact with "enlightened" European Jews but also by its larger Islamic religious and political context, erupted in early twentieth-century Ṣanaʿā.[39] Through the protagonists of *Sefer hamusar*, Alḍāhirī champions the cultivation of kabbalah, whose broader reception in Yemen dates only to the first decades of the sixteenth century, concurrent with the great mystical revival centered in Safed in the Land of Israel. The Yemenite Jewish readership to whom he introduces arcane kabbalistic ideas appears to have been largely uninitiated. In Yosef Tobi's estimation, Alḍāhirī's engagement with kabbalah made him a pivotal figure in the intellectual history of Yemenite Jewry, marking a turning point vis-à-vis the school of thought that culminated with his most illustrious and prolific predecessor, the late fifteenth-century David ben Yeshaʿ Halevi (also known by his pseudonym, Alu'el). An ardent Maimonidean, exegete, lexicographer, and scholar of astronomy, Alu'el penned a key philosophical midrash, *al-Wajīz al-mughnī* (The Sufficient Compendium), as well as a small corpus of poems and brief rhymed prose narratives. According to Tobi, Alḍāhirī wrought a decisive change in Yemenite Hebrew poetry—which until then had been "an extension" (*sheluḥah*) of the Andalusian school—as one of two known poets who forged a link with the kabbalistic poetry of Safed, paving the way for the emergence of the seventeenth-century school of Shalem

Medieval Spain"; idem, "Particularism and Universalism in Kabbalah, 1480–1650"; Dweck, *The Scandal of Kabbalah*, 101–126; and Bonfil, *Rabbis and Jewish Communities in Renaissance Italy*, 270–298.

38 *The Guide* has, ironically, been characterized as having "formulated a vision of Judaism in conscious opposition to" proto-kabbalistic elements in Judaism; see Kellner, *Maimonides' Confrontation with Mysticism*, 2–32.

39 On the multiple factors inflaming the kabbalah controversy, see: Wagner, "Jewish Mysticism on Trial in a Muslim Court: A Fatwā on the 'Zohar': Yemen 1914"; idem, *Jews and Islamic Law in Early 20th-Century Yemen*, 83–90; Klorman, *Traditional Society in Transition*, 20–69; Ratzaby, "Le-toldot ha-maḥloket ʿal ha-qabbalah bikhillat ṣanaʿa"; and idem, "*Dardeʿim: minhagim u-massorot.*" For 17th- and 18th-century precursors, see Gaimani, *Temurot be-moreshet yahadut teiman*.

Shabbazi.[40] As I argue below, there is reason to be skeptical about Alḍāhirī's first-hand knowledge of Lurianic kabbalah, although he clearly had a hand in importing pre-Lurianic kabbalistic theosophy and literature to Yemen, and helped to inaugurate the turn toward kabbalah whose apotheosis is marked by Shabbazi's vast quantity of kabbalistic verse.[41]

7 Receptivity to Printed Books

The innovation of Hebrew printing resonated with Alḍāhirī even though there was never a Hebrew press in Yemen, where an age-old manuscript culture continued to thrive. But Hebrew books printed in Italy and the Ottoman Empire circulated in Yemen, imported by rabbinic emissaries from the Land of Israel or by European or Ottoman Jewish merchants.[42] Once obtained, scarce printed books were often copied by hand. The newly emergent print culture of the 16th century makes its way into Alḍāhirī's fictionalized narratives. In overlapping accounts of the emissary Rabbi Abraham Ashkenazi's visit to Yemen, the protagonists express unqualified delight that he has brought a shipment of Hebrew books with him on his fundraising mission, and in a few poetic lines couched in biblical language, they marvel at the technology of the printing press and its democratization of learning.[43] Together with the work's notable preoccupation with books and their authors, these enthusiasms differentiate *Sefer hamusar* from better-known Hebrew rhymed prose narratives that antedate the invention of Hebrew movable type. The receptivity of Alḍāhirī's protagonists to the idea of printed books is noteworthy, given that the medium facilitated the transmission of liturgical rites, legal codes—particularly the *Shulḥan ʿarukh*—

40 On David (Alu'el) ben Yeshaʿ Halevi see: Ratzaby, *Toratan she-livnei teiman*, 35–41; idem, "David ben yeshaʿ ha-levi," (but note that the article mistakenly conflates him with a similarly-named later figure); Tobi, "Rabbi david ben yeshaʿ halevi"; idem, "Rabbi yiṣḥaq wannah ve-hitḥazzqut ha-ʿissuq ba-qabbalah"; and Langermann, *Yemenite Midrash*, 273–279. Langermann, who calls Alu'el one of the figures "of greatest interest for the intellectual history of Yemeni Jewry," explains that the numeric value of the name Alu'el is equivalent to that of David; see ibid., p. 273.

41 Yemenite authors at the beginning of the 17th century were still addressing basic concepts of classical kabbalah; see Hallamish ed., *The Kabbalah in Yemen at the Beginning of the Seventeenth Century*, 9–11; Baumgarten, "Netivot ha'emunah le-rabbi yiḥye ḥarāzī"; and Chapter Six below.

42 For the effect of these developments on Jewish communities in the Ottoman Empire (outside of the Land of Israel), see Hacker, "The Intellectual Activity of the Jews of the Ottoman Empire During the Sixteenth and Seventeenth Centuries."

43 These issues are discussed more fully in Chapter Three below.

and kabbalistic ideas that were "agents of change" and in subsequent centuries would give rise to polarizing controversies within Yemenite Jewish society.[44]

8 A Unique Case?

To the best of our knowledge, there are no other Hebrew *maqāmāt* from Yemen comparable to *Sefer hamusar* in conception, artistry, panoramic scope, or intellectual breadth. Exceedingly partial antecedents exist in the form of three brief or fragmented rhymed prose texts ascribed to David ben Yeshaʿ Halevi, the late fifteenth-century scholar of philosophy, halakhah, and science. (Two of these, didactic or cautionary tales aimed at ritual slaughterers, may originally have been part of the same work.) Two later didactic and devout works, Yiḥye ben Abraham Ḥarāzī's kabbalistic *Netivot ha'emunah* (The Paths of Faith; late 17th or 18th c.) and Saʿadya Manṣura's consolatory *Sefer ha-maḥshavah* (The Book of Thought; second half 19th c.), claim direct descent from Alḍāhirī's *maqāma*, though neither truly resembles it.[45] It is not entirely clear why *Sefer hamusar* is the only Hebrew *maqāma* of its kind known to us from Yemen. What allowed Alḍāhirī, an uncompromising religious scholar in other respects, to cultivate the often irreverent picaresque model with relative equanimity when other Yemenite authors seemingly could not? The usual answer is that he was a traveler who was not only exposed but also receptive to a wide variety of influences and therefore not averse to appropriating and adapting ideas, practices, or genres that resonated with him.[46] There may be something to this: Alḍāhirī presents his characters' peregrinations as a quest for knowledge, and his stories link mobility with the diffusion of learning. Although there is no inherent reason to doubt Alḍāhirī's mobility, it is worth bearing in mind that the travel in *Sefer hamusar* is related on the authority of a fictitious narrator, such that the lines between the actual and the fabricated are artfully blurred. Technically, it is his narratorial persona who en route seeks to gain halakhic competence and kabbalistic wisdom on the one hand and *musar* (amusing and instructive stories, choice folktales, moral exempla, and proverbs) on the other. Of course, the picaresque *maqāma* was hardly a novelty in the sixteenth century; if anything, its appropriation and modification make Alḍāhirī something of a neoclassicist. Nor would he have had to travel to gain access to the works of Alḥarīzī or al-

44 See, e.g. Ratzaby, *Bem'agloth Temān*, 74–77.

45 On these antecedents and successors see below, Chapter One and Tanenbaum, "Hidden Gems: The Hebrew *Maqāma* from Yemen."

46 See e.g., Ratzaby, *Bem'agloth Temān*, 116.

Ḥarīrī: there is manuscript evidence for their reception in Yemen. In brief, we do not know whether the unique status of *Sefer hamusar* is due to matters of literary taste; whether the picaresque paradigm offended the austere religious or moral sensibilities of Alḍāhirī's predecessors and successors; or whether *Sefer ha-musar* stands alone because no manuscripts of comparable texts have survived or yet come to light.

Although *Sefer hamusar* is largely *sui generis*, I would argue that it is more than just a curio. It is rather a revelatory work of seeming paradoxes, internal tensions, and intriguing contrasts from which we can learn a great deal about the inner life, deep intelligence, and broad intellectual makeup of its author, and infer something about his imagined community of readers, even if we lack sufficient evidence to determine that Alḍāhirī's intellectual biography and wide-ranging interests were characteristic of a larger cohort of his contemporaries. It is, of course, tempting to view *Sefer hamusar* as evocative of a period and its shared *mentalité*; to see in it a microcosm of the aesthetics, disciplines, and ideas that preoccupied the literate, scholarly class of its time and place. It is appealing to treat *Sefer hamusar* as a case study rather than as the product of an exceptional author, possibly a transitional figure, who was unusually attentive to intellectual developments elsewhere in the Jewish world as well as at home.[47] But in the absence of corroborating literary or documentary sources, it is difficult to ascertain whether Alḍāhirī is representative of even a small, select group of Jewish authors in his native land, although it is clear that his ideas were not formed in a vacuum and that, at some level, *Sefer hamusar* is the product of cultural dynamics affecting sixteenth-century Jews in Ṣanaʿā and, perhaps, other urban centers. As Natalie Zemon Davis remarked, "an extreme case can often reveal patterns available for more everyday experience and writing."[48] Alḍāhirī's fictional protagonists mention epistolary exchanges with eight different sages from various parts of Yemen who, according to Ratzaby, were real-life contemporaries who had turned to the author for halakhic guidance, although one is praised for his profound knowledge of esoteric matters and another for his expertise in astronomy. While some of these individuals apparently also wrote poetry, there is no evidence that any of them produced a work akin to *Sefer hamusar*.[49] Fortunately, we now know quite a bit about the expansive intellectual commitments of Alḍāhirī's predecessors and near contemporaries, thanks to the works of Yemenite biblical commentary, halakhah, midrash, liturgical poetry, philosophical thought, science, and kabbalah from

47 See, e.g., Lepore, "Historians Who Love Too Much."

48 See Davis, *Trickster Travels*, 11.

49 See Ratzaby's Introduction to *Sefer hamusar*, 45–46.

the fourteenth through seventeenth centuries that have been uncovered and analyzed in recent decades by Y. Tzvi Langermann, Yosef Tobi, Yehuda Ratzaby, and others. This wealth of creativity in other genres contrasts sharply with the relative paucity of extant *maqāma* texts. So, too, the profusion of Yemeni Arabic *maqāmāt* utterly dwarfs the modest number of those in Hebrew, no matter how broadly we define the genre.[50]

The scarcity of such texts has been attributed to a cultural discomfort with, and therefore repudiation of—or at best indifference to—"secular" literature.[51] Ratzaby maintains that *Sefer hamusar* was altogether anomalous; a belletristic book in a corpus otherwise devoted almost entirely to sacred or metaphysical matters; a lone literary *maqāma* in a sea of Yemenite exegetical, legal, liturgical, philosophical, and scientific writings.[52] The label "secular" is, of course, not entirely adequate in characterizing the content of the work, for alongside tales of trickery and deception, *Sefer hamusar* is full of messianic calculations, pious laments over Yemenite Jewish suffering, and celebrations of sacred Hebrew works and their authors. But the rubric, which applies at least as much to function as to substance, is invoked to distinguish Alḍāhirī's *maqāma* collection from the *piyyutim*, midrashim, commentaries, and halakhic works used in synagogue or study circles, which were not intended to have the same entertainment value. In classifications of Yemenite poetry, even chaste poems written to gladden the hearts of bridegrooms are considered secular because they lack a formal liturgical function. Ratzaby observed that there were relatively few extant manuscripts of *Sefer hamusar* (likely no more than twenty, most of them late, from the 18th–20th centuries), which led him to conclude that the work was not widely copied or circulated among Yemenite Jews until more modern times due to its perceived frivolity. He maintained that, despite its ebullient creativity and rich biblical idiom, *Sefer hamusar* seems never to have gained

50 There is nothing remotely comparable in Hebrew to al-Ḥibshi's two substantial anthologies of Yemeni Arabic *maqāmāt*, each well over 400 pages; see his *Maqāmāt min al-adab al-Yamanī* and *Majmūʿ al-maqāmāt al-yamanīyah*. See also Saitta, "Notices de manuscrits de *maqāmāt* yéménites de la période postclassique, 1ère partie–2e partie."

51 See, e.g., Ratzaby's Introduction to *Sefer hamusar*, 21–22 and Tobi, "Yemenite Poetry and its Relationship with Sefardi Poetry," esp. 313–321.

52 On the types of works preserved in Yemenite mss., including a vast literature in philosophy and the exact sciences, see Tobi, *Yemenite Jewish Manuscripts in the Ben-Zvi Institute*; Langermann, *The Jews of Yemen and the Exact Sciences*; idem, "Manuscript Moscow Guenzburg 1020: An Important New Yemeni Codex of Jewish Philosophy"; and idem, *Yemenite Midrash*, p. xvii: "Philosophical midrash is the richest and most enduring literary accomplishment of Yemenite Jewry during the fourteenth to early sixteenth centuries, the golden age in the intellectual history of that community."

full admission to the Yemenite Jewish literary canon; in the following century, it was eclipsed by the celebrated kabbalistic verse of Shalem Shabbazi and his circle. While concurring that the work had had relatively low visibility in its day, Shalom Medina highlighted its *high* proportion of *piyyutim*, spiritual, and ethical content, none of which can be considered "secular" in the modern sense of the term, and posited that its restricted circulation was more likely due to internal censorship. *Sefer hamusar* was suppressed, according to Medina, because of its forthright critiques of Islam which, had word gotten out, would have brought disaster upon all the Jews of Yemen.[53] By contrast, Shelomo Dov Goitein saw the existence of nine or ten manuscripts as an indication of the work's popularity, and Uri Melammed has remarked that, unlike Alḍāhirī's *Sefer haʿanaq*, which is extant only in a unique manuscript, the multiple manuscripts of *Sefer hamusar* suggest that it must have circulated more widely.[54] Interest in the work appears to have revived in the 19th century. But given the paucity of evidence regarding its readership closer to its time of composition, it is difficult to determine how representative of 16th-century Yemenite Jewish literary tastes *Sefer hamusar* might have been. Despite his erudition and the esteem in which he appears to have been held, we lack information as to whether Alḍāhirī had disciples or even a circle of like-minded colleagues. Nevertheless, *Sefer hamusar* is richly suggestive for our understanding of the broader intellectual, spiritual, and historical developments affecting the Yemenite Jewish community and, as such, deserves fuller exploration.

9 Earlier Perspectives on *Sefer hamusar*

At a time when 19th-century Yemenite Jewish authors such as Saʿadya Manṣura (d. c. 1880) and Ḥayyim Ḥabshush (1839–1899) had by no means lost sight of Alḍāhirī's *maqāma*, a modest miscellany of readers outside of Yemen were just beginning to discover it.[55] The earliest phase of critical scholarship in the

53 See Medina, "Sefer hamusar, mahadurat ratzaby."

54 On the book's reception among Yemenite Jews see Ratzaby's Introduction to *Sefer hamusar*, 21–23. Cf. "Sheloshah shirim meturgamim," where Ratzaby says it is doubtful that more than ten copies were preserved among Yemenite Jews. For Goitein's comment, see "A Yemenite Poet on Egypt of the xvith Century," p. 27, n. 3. Uri Melammed conveyed his view in a personal communication (December 18, 2006). I am unaware of any evidence that *Sefer hamusar* circulated outside of Yemen prior to the modern period.

55 See Verskin, *A Vision of Yemen*, 67–68 and n. 19; Goitein, ed. and trans., *Massaʿot Ḥabshush*, 6–7; and Manṣura, *Sefer ha-galut ve-ha-ge'ulah*, 129.

West was undertaken by a clutch of European Hebraists and bibliographers whose curiosity was piqued when they encountered *Sefer hamusar* in manuscript. Confronted with its exceptionally varied content and form, seemingly generic title, and often incomplete manuscripts, their treatments of the work were of necessity selective, calling to mind the parable of the blind men and the elephant. In some instances, this was due to the fragmentary nature of the available material; in others, it resulted from a narrow interest in a particular aspect of the work. From 1886 until 1965, no one undertook to collate the manuscripts and publish the text in its entirety, even after complete copies had come to light. During those eight decades, the slender sheaf of publications relating to *Sefer hamusar* focused primarily on piecemeal textual transcription and attempts to reconstruct Alḍāhirī's biography.

Prior to Yehuda Ratzaby's complete, annotated edition of 1965, a handful of scholars and learned enthusiasts each published individual chapters of the Hebrew text with little or no commentary, at times choosing to excise the embedded poems, thereby depriving readers of fuller insight into the author's lyrical side. Most of them read *Sefer hamusar* as a factual travel account, quarrying it for precious biographical, historical, and geographical information while downplaying the significance of its fictional and literary content. Few of these readers were willing to acknowledge that the work's hybridity was integral to its very conception and precisely what made it so captivating—that its ornate language and full compass of trickster tales and folk legends with their patently fantastic elements were more than mere frippery obscuring the work's hard data. There was a pronounced tendency toward *quellenforschung*, with some scholars content to identify borrowings from Arabic literature and folklore. Those who focused exclusively on tracing the sources of tales and motifs left the reader with the misleading impression that the work was at best derivative. A lack of originality was also implied by the oft-repeated and unqualified assertion that *Sefer hamusar* was composed "in imitation of" Alḥarizi's *Taḥkemoni*.[56] Despite such constrained perspectives and the absence of sustained literary analyses, these contributions laid the groundwork for subsequent research by publishing the texts, attempting to locate Alḍāhirī in a larger literary-historical context, and calling attention to an unduly neglected work. As such, they are valuable, even if current research would do well to reconsider their underlying assumptions.

---

56 See, e.g.: Neubauer, "The Literature of the Jews of Yemen," 618 and idem, *Catalogue of the Hebrew Manuscripts in the Bodleian Library*, 1:841.

Methodological approaches to *Sefer hamusar* evolved in accordance with changes in the cultural and ideological commitments of 19th- and 20th-century scholars and technological advances that gradually facilitated greater access to manuscript material. Early 19th-century adherents of the *Wissenschaft des Judentums* (the "scientific" study of Judaism) conceived a powerful attraction to medieval Jewish life in the Islamic world out of complex motivations that were in part apologetic, relating to their own struggles to gain admission into non-Jewish society. Later in the century, this scholarly preference was reinforced when previously unknown Hebrew and Judeo-Arabic manuscripts from Yemen and the Cairo Geniza came to light in European libraries and private collections.[57] Interest in Yemenite Jewish sources was kindled following the publication of Jacob Sapir's travelogue *Even Sapir* (1866–1874), which details manuscripts the Lithuanian-born *maskil* acquired during his nearly year-long sojourn in Yemen.[58] While enthusiasm was sparked by the discovery that the Yemenites had preserved versions of rabbinic and geonic texts unadulterated by later textual accretions, as well as works previously unknown in the West, the collecting activity of Sapir and other Europeans was fuelled at least as much by the commercial potential of these finds.[59] Notices of Alḍāhirī's *Sefer hamusar* by the eminent bibliographer Moritz Steinschneider (1816–1907) and Bodleian librarian Adolph Neubauer (1831–1907) were part of Herculean undertakings to catalogue Hebrew-character manuscript holdings acquired by major European collections, and for the most part did not include any significant textual transcriptions.[60] The first of the European-trained scholars to publish a complete *maqāma* from *Sefer hamusar* (1894) was the Hungarian-born Ḥayyim Brody (1868–1942), a gifted Hebraist and editor of medieval Hebrew poetry, who in his 20's traveled from Berlin to Oxford where he rejoiced at finding a complete ms. of *Sefer hamusar*, which he hurried to study, so that he might "discover

57 See: Schorsch, "Converging Cognates: The Intersection of Jewish and Islamic Studies in Nineteenth Century Germany"; idem, "The Myth of Sephardic Supremacy"; Marcus, "Beyond the Sephardic Mystique"; Efron, *German Jewry and the Allure of the Sephardic*, 190–229; and Schapkow, *Role Model and Countermodel: The Golden Age of Iberian Jewry and German Jewish Culture during the Era of Emancipation*, 149–199.

58 Sapir, *Even Sapir*. On the mss. see, *inter alia*, 2:174–198, s.v. *divrei ḥefeṣ* ("Precious Items"). For a serviceable English translation of the Yemen section in vol. 1, see Lavon, *My Footsteps Echo: The Yemen Journal of Rabbi Yaakov Sapir*.

59 See Gerber, *Ourselves Or Our Holy Books?*, 28–51 and idem, "Jewish Studies and Its Discoveries of the Jewish Orient." See also Marx, "A New Collection of Mss: A Recent Acquisition of the Library of the Jewish Theological Seminary."

60 See Steinschneider, "An Introduction to the Arabic Literature of the Jews," esp. no. 612 for the entry on Alḍāhirī; Neubauer, "The Literature of the Jews of Yemen," 618; and idem, *Catalogue of the Hebrew Manuscripts in the Bodleian Library*, 1:841–842.

something about the life of its author," who "was previously unknown to us, and [about whom] I have not been able to find anything ... in any printed book." Brody betrays a characteristically *Wissenschaft* antipathy to mysticism as irrational superstition when he dismisses the poems of one of Alḍāhirī's correspondents as "shrouded in gloom and fog" due to their incorporation of kabbalistic ideas, although he is relatively restrained regarding Alḍāhirī's kabbalistic proclivities.[61]

At precisely the same time, Senior (Schneour) Sachs (1816–1892), a Russo-French Hebraist, announced his discovery of the only surviving copy of Alḍāhirī's book of homonymic verse, *Sefer ha'anaq*, in a manuscript belonging to Sachs' student, the collector Baron David Guenzburg. While this was a major find, Sachs spent the lion's share of his notice in an onomastic muddle, puzzling over the relationship between Alḍāhirī's Arabic and Hebrew names and nom de plume, Abner ben Ḥeleq.[62] (In Yemenite usage, the Hebrew names Zechariah and Ḥayyim were interchangeable, and the Arabic Yiḥye—the semantic equivalent of Ḥayyim—was used for either.)[63] Decades earlier, Sachs had written an effusive endorsement (*haskamah*) of *Even Sapir* in which his portrayal of Yemenite Jews was by turns romanticized, patronizing, and downright disparaging. As such, it was—and remains—emblematic of the Eurocentric ambivalences and limitations of some of the most eminent 19th-century Jewish scholars, including those who immersed themselves in the study of Yemenite Jewry.[64]

The manifestation of European Orientalism as a curious amalgam of excessive idealization and disdainful attitudes toward non-Western cultures is very much in evidence in the study of Yemenite Jewry. While they displayed genuine intellectual curiosity regarding the objects of their investigation, *fin de siècle* Jewish scholars also betrayed their Orientalist cultural biases to varying degrees. Scholars shaped methodologically by the Germanic traditions of philology and ethnography, such as the pioneering ethnomusicologist, Abraham Tzvi Idelsohn (1882–1938; Latvia-Jerusalem-Cincinnati)—whose *Dīwān of*

61 Brody, *Maṭmunei mistarim*, Pt. 3, pp. 1–26.

62 See Sachs, "The Riddles of Rabbi Solomon Ibn Gabirol and their Solutions," 100–101; ms. Guenzburg 1306, The Russian State Library, Moscow, IMHM film no. F 48786 (provenance: 16th-century Yemen). The ms. also contains a *dīwān* of Alḍāhirī's poems and his commentary on Maimonides' *Hilkhot sheḥitah*; see Amir, "Shirim ḥadashim mi-dīwān rabbi zekharyah alḍāhirī."

63 See: Gaimani, "Shemot pratiyyim bi-qehillot teiman: meḥqar shemot 'al pi shetarei ketubbah," 59–60; idem, *The Names of Yemenite Jewry*, 146–159; Ratzaby, *Bem'agloth Temān*, 6–9; and Gavra, *Ha-shemot ha-pratiyyim be-qerev yehudei teiman*, 289–290.

64 The *haskamot*, which preface vol. 1, are not paginated.

Hebrew and Arabic Poetry of the Yemenite Jews (1930) includes a handful of Alḍāhirī's poems both attributed and unattributed and mentions *Sefer hamusar* in passing—were swayed by European Romanticism, which regarded the objects of anthropological and folklore study as ancient populations untainted by contact with "civilization." Many subscribed to the notion that the Yemenites embodied the most authentic Judaism going back to pre-exilic times due to their "total isolation" from other diaspora Jewish communities and from Western civilization, a trope that is difficult to square with the visits of rabbinic emissaries and apostate missionaries, not to mention the presence of the Ottomans already in the 16th century and the arrival of scientific expeditions and mercantilists in subsequent centuries. They exoticized the Yemenites for their imagined authenticity but at the same time viewed Yemenite Jewish life as static; condemned Yemenite practices that they considered irrational or backward; and treated contemporary Yemenite Jews with paternalism, condescension, disparagement, and even revulsion.[65]

As the locus of Jewish Studies shifted from Europe to pre-State Palestine, Jewish nationalist scholars affiliated with the Institute for Jewish Studies at the Hebrew University, often referred to collectively as the "Jerusalem School," adopted a reading of Jewish history colored by their ideological commitment to Zionism and the realization of the Zionist dream.[66] Only a few of these European-born and -trained researchers dealt specifically with *Sefer hamusar*, which was for them no more than a minor interest in the service of some larger project. Abraham Yaari (1899–1966) stands out for having superimposed a blinkered Palestinocentric reading on the work. Yaari mined *Sefer hamusar* for texts corroborating the continuous settlement of Palestine by Jews as part of a vast literary project in support of the Zionist argument for the return to the ancestral Jewish homeland and creation of a modern Jewish state. Others who treated the work as a source for historical facts (Walter J. Fischel, S. D. Goitein) did so to extract information on various lesser-known Jewish communities in the East: Fischel on Azarbaijan and the Persian Gulf region, and Goitein on Egypt.[67] Goitein's research in Mandatory Palestine was shaped by

65 See, e.g.: Efron, *German Jewry and the Allure of the Sephardic*, 192–193; Guilat, "The Yemeni Ideal in Israeli Culture and Arts"; and Loeffler, "Do Zionists Read Music from Right to Left? Abraham Tsvi Idelsohn and the Invention of Israeli Music."

66 See Myers, "Was There a 'Jerusalem School'? An Inquiry into the First Generation of Historical Researchers at the Hebrew University"; idem, *Re-inventing the Jewish Past: European Jewish Intellectuals and the Zionist Return to History*, 3–37, 129–150; and idem, "Is There Still a 'Jerusalem School?' Reflections on the State of Jewish Historical Scholarship in Israel."

67 See: Yaari, *Massaʿot ereṣ yisrael*, 196–221, 399; idem, "Sheliḥim me'ereṣ yisra'el le-teiman"; idem, *Sheluḥei ereṣ yisrael*, 256–261; Fischel, "Azarbaijan in Jewish History," esp. p. 20; idem,

Zionist ideology as well as Germanic academic traditions, and his lone piece on *Sefer hamusar* is in keeping with the positivist approach exemplified by Yaari. In a footnote, he indicates his intention (never realized) to edit the entire text.[68] There were also scholars who gravitated to the work's folkloric content (Fischel, Hayyim Schirmann, and, in the 1960's, Haim Schwarzbaum). Fischel's half-hearted publication of the forty-third *maqāma* lacks any meaningful comment on the chapter's extraordinarily strange folktales about Maimonides' birth and early upbringing, and omits its closing poem about the anti-Maimonidean animadversions of Rabad of Posquières.[69] Schirmann, whose early interest in the *maqāma* genre is evident from his doctoral dissertation and first major publication, transcribed the 9th and 10th chapters of *Sefer hamusar*, which feature colorful and involved folktales. To these he prefaced an outline of the work, offering judgments on Alḍāhirī's style, language, and likely appeal, and expressed regret that it had not yet merited a complete and correct edition. He reviewed the existing bibliography and manuscripts known to him and listed the other works in Alḍāhirī's corpus. But even he, the future doyen of medieval Hebrew poetry, stopped short of any literary analysis.[70] Schwarzbaum was most interested from the perspective of comparative folklore and the classification of international folk motifs. He identified the tales embedded in the fourth and fifth chapters of *Sefer hamusar* as variations on recognizable themes from the vast repository of international folklore but made no attempt to discuss their significance within the literary context of Alḍāhirī's *maqāmot*.[71]

In the early years of the *yishuv*, interest in *Sefer hamusar* from within the Yemenite community initially came not from professional academics so much as from bibliophilic and learned lay and rabbinic leaders of the Yemenite Jews

"The Region of the Persian Gulf and its Jewish Settlements in Islamic Times," esp. 216–217; and Goitein, "A Yemenite Poet on Egypt."

68 Goitein's extensive contributions have undergone re-evaluation over the past quarter century; see, e.g.: Frenkel, "The Historiography of the Jews in Muslim Countries in the Middle Ages—Landmarks and Prospects," esp. 48–55; Libson, "'Hidden Worlds and Open Shutters': S.D. Goitein Between Judaism and Islam"; idem, "Shlomo Dov Goitein's Research into the Relationship between the Jewish and Muslim Traditions through the Prism of His Predecessors and Colleagues"; Gerber, *Ourselves Or Our Holy Books?*, 111–197 *passim*; and Wasserstrom, "Apology for S.D. Goitein."

69 Fischel, "Maqāma 'al ha-rambam ve'aviv." But cf. Avishur, *In Praise of Maimonides: Folktales in Judaeo-Arabic and Hebrew from the Near East and North Africa.*

70 Schirmann, "Two Maqamas of Zecharia Aldahiri's Sepher Hamussar."

71 Schwarzbaum, "Leḥeqer arba'ah sippurei 'am besefer hamusar le-rabbi zekharyah alḍāhiri."

in Jerusalem.[72] Moshe Kehati (b. Ṣanaʿā, 1900), son of a goldsmith descended from a renowned rabbinic line, and among the first to qualify as a lawyer in Israel during the Mandate period, published an article in the first series of the Hebrew historical periodical *Zion* in 1928 entitled, "From the Travels of Rabbi Zechariah ben Seʿadya ben Yaʿaqov in the Land of Israel."[73] Noting that there was no printed edition of *Sefer hamusar*, Kehati transcribed the sixth *maqāma* (set in Safed), as well as portions of the twenty-second and twenty-third (set in Jerusalem and Tiberias respectively) from a manuscript in his personal possession.[74] His approach was largely biographical, based on a literal reading of the travel accounts, and reflected a Zionist preference for those episodes that he deemed to be of "enormous importance for the history and life-ways of the Jewish community (*yishuv*) in the Land of Israel in those days."[75] Methodologically, his treatment does not significantly differ from that of earlier and contemporary European-trained scholars. The first series of the academic journal *Zion* had recently been founded (1925) by the Historical and Ethnographic Society of Israel and was "dedicated to the history of Oriental and Palestinian Jewry," in what Amnon Raz-Krakotzkin describes as "a project intended to provide the requisite knowledge for the formation of the new Jewish culture" in the nascent State of Israel.[76] Kehati's selections were obviously tailored to the journal's historiographical platform, although he himself was also a committed Zionist.[77]

The same year, 1928, saw the publication in Jerusalem of Abraham Alnadāf's alphabetical inventory of works by Yemenite Jewish authors, *Sefer oṣar sifrei teiman*, which he included in a slim volume to which he gave the title *Seridei teiman*, "The Remnants of Yemen."[78] Unlike Kehati, who attended university and gained his professional qualifications at European institutions, Alnadāf was an erudite and revered rabbinic figure with an entirely traditional Yemenite

---

72 See, e.g., Langermann's discussion of Yosef Qāfiḥ's entry into the "academic periphery" in "Rabbi Yosef Qafih's Modern Medieval Translation of the *Guide*."

73 "Mi-massaʿo shel rabbi zekhariah ben seʿadya ben yaʿaqov be'ereṣ yisra'el." On Kehati, see Tidhar, *Encyclopedia of the Founders and Builders of Israel*, 9:3320 and Gaon, *Yehudei ha-mizraḥ be'ereṣ yisra'el*, 2:607.

74 Kehati donated his copies of *Sefer hamusar* and *Ṣeidah la-derekh* as part of a larger mss. bequest to Hebrew University's Jewish National and University Library in 1990. Both were copied circa 1930 from older Yemenite mss.

75 Kehati, "Mi-masaʿo shel rabbi zekhariah ben seʿadya," 45–46.

76 Raz-Krakotzkin, "The Zionist Return to the West and the Mizrahi Jewish Perspective," esp. 171–181.

77 The sparse biographical information available for Kehati indicates that he was instrumental in purchasing lands from the Palestinian Arabs for the new state during the Mandate period; see Tidhar, *Encyclopedia*, 9:3320.

78 Alnadāf, *Ḥoveret seridei teiman*.

education. Both, however, worked tirelessly on behalf of the Yemenite community. Alnadāf viewed his independently published *Seridei teiman* as an act of conservation, as well as the fulfillment of "a sacred duty vis-à-vis our brethren in the other Jewish communities, from whom the Yemenites' creativity and rich spirtual assets remain hidden."[79] His inclusion of Alḍāhirī's *Sefer hamusar, Sefer haʿanaq, and Ṣeidah la-derekh* in three discrete entries underscores how integral to the Yemenite canon Alḍāhirī's oeuvre was in the late 19th and early 20th centuries. Unlike Steinschneider, Neubauer, Bacher, and Brody (the last of whom was his exact contemporary), Alnadāf did not have to "discover" or even reclaim Alḍāhirī because Alḍāhirī had never fully disappeared from view. Alnadāf presents *Sefer hamusar* as a book of moral instruction-cum-travelogue, with particular emphasis on the episode set in the holy city of Safed. Still, Alnadāf is happy to remark on the beauty of Alḍāhirī's language and to cast his *maqāma* as a bona fide piece of Yemenite Jewish creativity without any hint of censure despite his own scrupulous piety.

The complete edition that Schirmann had called for in 1936 and that Goitein had contemplated in 1947 was brought to fruition in 1965 by Yehuda Ratzaby (1916–2009).[80] Ratzaby collated four principal mss. of Yemenite provenance that, on the basis of internal evidence, he surmised were all descended from the same progenitor. As his base text, he selected a ms. placed at his disposal by the bibliophile Yaʿish Re'uven Nadāf.[81] He recorded variants from the other three—one in the Bodleian, one in the formidable private collection of David Solomon Sassoon, and one belonging to Shalom Ratsaby that contained many variants and some expansions.[82] In difficult or opaque spots, he consulted two additional mss. belonging respectively to Ḥayyim Yemini and Yosef Qoraḥ, as well as a ms. in the Jerusalem Schocken library.[83] It was not

---

79 On Alnadāf, see also Gerber, *Ourselves Or Our Holy Books?*, 150–157 and 164–166.

80 Ratzaby himself, while working on his complete edition, published three stories from #25, #31, and #17 in little-known journals published by the Yemenite community in Israel during the 1940's and 50's (*Hed Ḥugim*; *Sheluḥot*; and *Maslul*) and a poem about the Talmud from #18 (*Maḥanayyim*) in 1961; see *Sefer hamusar*, p. 23, n. 10.

81 Nadāf was one of the founders of the Yemenite neighborhood Naḥalat Aḥim (1924) in Jerusalem. A 1908 internal census of the Jerusalem Yemenite community lists his occupation as *mesadder bidfus*, a compositor or typesetter, though he also appears to have been an independent printer; see Tobi, *The Yemenite Community of Jerusalem, 1881–1921*, p. 298, no. 341 and Gaon, *Yehudei ha-mizraḥ be'ereṣ yisra'el*, 2:79–80.

82 Oxford ms. Opp. Add. 8° 31 (= Neubauer #2397; highly accurate and the most complete, although missing a colophon) and the former ms. Sassoon 995 (described in *Ohel Dawid*, 2:1021–1033; IMHM #F 9589; the earliest of the mss.) are accessible online. No information is provided for the mss. belonging to Nadāf or Ratsaby.

83 Ms. Jerusalem Schocken 13207, formerly Schocken 68. For a few images and a codicolog-

uncommon for first-generation emigrant families from Yemen to hold private copies of mss. Like Brody in his day, Ratzaby was working before the advent of electronic databases and digitized manuscripts, technological innovations that have since greatly facilitated comparing larger numbers of mss. held in collections around the world.[84] Ratzaby's generous annotation fills in historical background and identifies the sources of intertextual allusions to Scripture, rabbinic literature, medieval Hebrew and Arabic texts of various genres, and Yemenite Jewish proverbs and folklore. Drawing on his intimate, first-hand knowledge of Yemenite Jewish customs, liturgical practices, and daily life, he illuminated the text for a broad spectrum of contemporary Hebrew readers. The edition is prefaced by an informative introduction and was received to critical acclaim. Ratzaby was awarded the prestigious Bialik prize for 1965, only the second time that this recognition was extended to a member of the Yemenite Jewish community. A festive conference, organized by the editorial board of the journal *Afikim*, was framed as an opportunity to raise awareness of neglected Yemenite Jewish cultural treasures within the community and the broader Israeli population.[85]

In 2008, Mordechai Yiṣhari of Rosh Ha'ayin privately printed the text of *Sefer hamusar* on the basis of a manuscript that had been in his family's possession in Yemen.[86] Yiṣhari claimed the author as a forebear since the family surname had originally been Alḍāhirī but was Hebraicized as Yiṣhari—a virtual anagram in Hebrew characters (צ׳אהרי/יצהרי)—when they settled in Israel. He recounts that in his childhood *Sefer hamusar* was read aloud during get-togethers on various occasions and, as a child, he knew two of the episodes virtually by heart: the fifth *maqāma* with its animal tales and the forty-third with its strange folktales about Maimonides. Clearly an enthusiast, Yiṣhari writes of his desire to make *Sefer hamusar* accessible to a broader readership. His contribution was

---

ical description, see Christie, Manson & Woods, *Important Hebrew Manuscripts from the Salman Schocken Collection*, pp. 55–56, no. 15.

84 The Institute of Microfilmed Hebrew Manuscripts [IMHM] had moved to the National Library of Israel in Jerusalem only very recently, in 1963. See https://www.nli.org.il/en/discover/manuscripts/hebrew-manuscripts/about; Richler, "On Editing the Catalogue of the Hebrew Manuscripts in Parma" and idem, "Microfilming the Baron Guenzburg Collection of Hebrew Manuscripts in the Russian State Library in Moscow."

85 See Ar'el, "Kenes ḥagigi le-sefer hamusar," and Amir, "Shirim ḥadashim mi-dīwān rabbi zekharyah alḍāhirī." In his humble acceptance speech, Ratzaby noted that the bibliophile Re'uven Ya'ish Nadāf had offered H.N. Bialik a ms. of *Sefer hamusar* for publication by Dvir, but at the time Bialik was preoccupied with bringing out editions of Andalusian Hebrew poetry. On Bialik's ambivalent attitudes, see Gerber, *Ourselves Or Our Holy Books?*, 147–148.

86 *Sefer hamusar, ha-shirah ve-ha-piyyuṭ le-rabbenu yiḥye (zekhariah) ben se'adya be-rav ya'aqov al-ḍāhirī*, ed. Yiṣhari.

gratefully acknowledged at a special symposium on Alḍāhirī, convened by the Ben-Zvi Institute in the summer of 2014.[87] For the record, however, Yiṣhari's is not a critical edition, and while it is very welcome, it complements but does not supplant Ratzaby's text. Long out of print, Ratzaby's volume was reissued by the Ben-Zvi Institute in 2015 in a limited photo offset edition to mark the 50th anniversary of the original publication.[88]

In recent decades, individual scholars, mostly based in Israel, have worked on literary, kabbalistic, and exegetical facets of Alḍāhirī's corpus within the larger context of the project to preserve and study *moreshet teiman* (the cultural heritage of Yemenite Jewry), although not as part of any formally coordinated initiative to produce a definitive set of texts and studies. At last sight, a critical edition of Alḍāhirī's esoteric Torah commentary, *Ṣeidah la-derekh*, was being prepared under Uri Melammed's supervision from mss. in the Institute for Microfilmed Hebrew Manuscripts and private collections.[89] This must be a daunting proposition, given that *Ṣeidah la-derekh* is extant in countless partial or fragmentary mss., and close to a quarter of the work as transmitted consists of anonymous scribal interpolations that have become part of the text.[90] Until recently, the existing literature on *Ṣeidah la-derekh* was fairly slender; comprising brief treatments by Ratzaby, Moshe Zadock, Shalom Medina, and Shimon Greidi, it was aimed, for the most part, at a learned lay readership.[91] To this list, Otniel Mansur's monograph on Alḍāhirī's exegetical method in his glosses to Genesis can now be added.[92] Uri Melammed and the late

87 "Zechariah Aldahiri and his Literary, Rabbinic, and Historical Oeuvre," June 18, 2014, Jerusalem, Israel.

88 The April 15, 2015 blog page of the "Association for the Cultivation of Society and Culture—The Heritage of Yemenite Jewry" urged readers to sign up for the limited reissue.

89 Uri Melammed, personal communication, Dec. 17, 2006. Alḍāhirī refers to *Ṣeidah la-derekh* twice in *Sefer hamusar*, once in #21 (on Gen. 2:1) and once in #45. This suggests that at least some portion, if not all, of his Torah commentary was complete when he wrote these two *maqāmāt* or that their stages of production were intertwined.

90 The interpolations are generally prefaced by the phrases *ani ha-ḥosheq* (*le-zeh ha-sefer*) or *ve-zot haggahah*. On the phenomenon of scribal interpolation see Beit-Arié, "Publication and Reproduction of Literary Texts in Medieval Jewish Civilization: Jewish Scribality and Its Impact on the Texts Transmitted."

91 See Ratzaby, *Toratan she-livnei teiman*, 45–46; idem, *Sefer hamusar*, pp. 35 and 44; Medina, "Ṣeidah la-derekh le'alḍāhirī"; Zadock, *Maḥshevet yisrael be-teiman*, 57–60; idem, "Ṣeidah la-derekh, midrash filosofi qabbali"; and Greidi's introduction in the *Tāj*; repr. *Pe'ilut ve-zikhron ishim*, 70–74.

92 *Shiṭato ha-parshanit shel rabbi yiḥye al-ḍāhirī*. Mansur discusses the scribal interpolations and the attempts to identify their author(s) on pp. 103–122. See also idem, "Rabbi yiḥye al-ḍāhirī: ha-ḥuṭ ha-meqashsher bein tequfot ha-filosofiya ve-ha-qabbalah be-teiman," and Baumgarten, "Kabbalah and Printing in Yemen."

Efraim Yaakov were working on producing a critical edition of Alḍāhirī's book of homonymic rhymes, *Sefer ha-ʿanaq*, extant only in Guenzburg 1306, the manuscript discovered by Sachs at the end of the 19th century.[93] Over the years, Yosef Tobi has redeemed many of Alḍāhirī's poems from obscurity, publishing and explicating individual texts in academic periodicals as well as in *Afikim*.[94] Privately founded initiatives such as Yosef Qāfiḥ's *Association for the Rescue of the Hidden Treasures of Yemen* (*Ha'agudah le-haṣalat ginzei teiman*) and Yehuda Levi Naḥum's *Initiative to Uncover the Hidden Treasures of Yemen* (*Mifʿal ḥasifat ginzei teiman*) have published ms. fragments as well as complete editions, translations, and studies of otherwise neglected Yemenite texts and documents.[95] A few of these indirectly cast additional light on one facet or another of Alḍāhirī's varied oeuvre, thereby helping to illuminate his versatility as a writer and his capacity to move with ease between different genres, stylistic conventions, and substantive foci.[96]

Scholarship from the end of the 20th and the beginning of the 21st centuries has continued to adduce *Sefer hamusar* in studies of Yemenite kabbalah, in discussions of Yemenite Jewish anti-Muslim polemics, and as evidence for settlement in the Land of Israel. As indispensable and profoundly erudite as these contributions are, they do not significantly depart from the dominant positivist model to ask new questions of Alḍāhirī's text.[97] As newer analytical paradigms are adopted and as additional manuscript works held in private hands or otherwise inaccessible to scholars continue to see the light of day and, ideally are made available through digitization, we will be better equipped to reevaluate

93 See Yaakov, "Liqrat hahdarato shel 'Sefer haʿanaq' le-mari yiḥye al-daheri she-huva la'aḥronah me-russya."

94 For bibliographic details, see Amir, "Shirei rabbi zekharyah Alḍāhirī (bibliographiyah)." On *Afikim* and its advocacy, see Druyan, "Yemenite Jews on the Zionist Altar," 164–167 and Almagor, "Ketav ʿet ʿaṣma'i ve-loḥem: holadeto shel ketav haʿet *Afikim*."

95 See Tobi, "Trends in the Study of Yemenite Jewry," in *The Jews of Yemen*, 277; Yevin, "'Treasures of the Yemen'—a Private Manuscript Collection in Holon"; and Ben-Ari, "Ha-makhon le-ḥasifat ginzei teiman."

96 See Naḥum, "Tefillah le-rabbi zekhariah al-ḍahiri vidiʿot ḥadashot le-toledot mishpaḥto."

97 Studies of Yemenite Jewry that adopt newer theoretical approaches include: Anzi, "Yemenite Jews in the Red Sea Trade and the Development of a New Diaspora"; idem, "From Biblical Criticism to Criticism of the Kabbalah"; Gerber, *Ourselves Or Our Holy Books?*; Fogel, "'These little girls, coming now in their thousands'—Yemeni Women and their Songs as Reflected in Studies by S.D. Goitein"; Guilat, "The Yemeni Ideal in Israeli Culture and Arts"; idem, "The 'Israelization' of Yemenite-Jewish Silversmithing"; Abdar, "White as the Sun—The Language of Dress of Jewish Brides in Yemen in the First Half of the 20th Century"; and idem, "Reflections on Magical Texts on Jewelry and Amulets of Jewish Women and Children from Yemen and Habban."

the ways in which Alḍāhirī's corpus has been read until now and to balance or temper the images of Yemenite Jewry, its textual traditions, and its artistic accomplishments as conveyed by earlier studies. Ultimately, perhaps, instead of occupying an academic niche, the distinctive and underrepresented cultural production of this vibrant south Arabian Jewish community will be integrated into synthetic treatments of the Jewish Middle Ages and Early Modernity, as well as Islamicate Literature, Ottoman Studies, and Indian Ocean Studies.

10 Postscript: *Sefer hamusar* as Auto/biography Manqué?

Like many medieval works governed by literary convention, *Sefer hamusar* both invites and discourages auto/biographical readings. In this respect it might productively be viewed through the lens of "pseudo-autobiography" as outlined by Laurence De Looze, as a work that

> lends itself ... at one and the same time to readings as ostensibly nonfictive autobiography and as narrative fiction without the reader's being able to declare either genre clearly dominant.[98]

Most 19th and 20th-century scholars treated the work as autobiography with a thin veneer of fiction. While this largely outmoded approach is still alive and well, it was particularly characteristic of figures such as Ḥayyim Schirmann who were products of German universities of the early twentieth century. Tova Rosen has remarked that Schirmann's investigations were driven by

> the biographical inclination prevailing then in literary research. In the absence of solid biographical facts about the medieval poets—and based on the romantic assumption that 'poetry is biography,' with no consideration of the fictional dimension—Schirmann drew biographical conclusions from the texts themselves.[99]

Once Alḍāhirī's names were sorted out, many of those interested in him betrayed a deep-seated need to construct a more detailed picture of the author as an individual by extracting from *Sefer hamusar* a reliable chronology of his life and travels. This meant approaching his creative work from the van-

---

98 De Looze, *Pseudo-Autobiography in the Fourteenth Century*, 21 and *passim*.
99 See Rosen and Yassif, "The Study of Hebrew Literature of the Middle Ages," 257.

tage point of history rather than literature. But we should bear in mind that the medieval Hebrew literary tradition limited the specificity of actual historical events by assimilating them to familiar, generic biblical tropes, which lent them a paradigmatic quality. Alḍāhirī's *maqāma* does so in abundance even though it furnishes some specific dates as well. Nevertheless, since portions of his belletristic work resemble personal testimony, and very few traces of his pursuits or ventures remain outside of his literary writings, scholars have typically resorted to identifying the author with the different selves he conjures in *Sefer hamusar*, which is to say with his invented personae or masks. Goitein encapsulated this approach when he insisted that

> each of the two [protagonists] constitute one half of [Alḍāhirī's] own self, which means that the facts recorded about both of them apply in reality to the author.[100]

Almost everyone to date has resisted seeing Alḍāhirī's narrator and rogue-hero as literary constructs and has deliberately overlooked the contrivance in their portrayal. It seems a great pity to reduce each of these characters to nothing more than "one half" of the author and to discount the craft that went into devising their personalities as unreliable narrator and trickster hero. Even if these two are stock figures of the *maqāma* genre and therefore not terribly well developed qua characters, and even though their more sobering episodes have the ring of truth to them, such an approach effectively devalues the literary imagination and masks the author's inventiveness. Throughout *Sefer hamusar*, Alḍāhirī obscures his own voice by projecting it through his imaginary protagonists; to assume that they can be entirely identified with him is to underestimate his literary sleight of hand: ("I have narrated it by means of two men who are strangers to me … [they] … are both concealed and revealed ….").[101] But the identification persists because the potpourri of dates and places offered up in *Sefer hamusar* fills a vacuum left by the dearth of surviving records of sixteenth-century Yemenite Jewry and the patchy details of the author's life.[102] Although it seems to have been the rule, the facile equation of author and personae in

100 Goitein, "A Yemenite Poet on Egypt," 28.

101 Cf. Decter, *Iberian Jewish Literature*, 135–136. Ratzaby confirms that after Alḍāhirī's death, his name became confused with those of his protagonists so that he is not only called Abner but is occasionally also given his fictitious narrator's toponymic ("Yiḥye ha-ṣidoni"); see *Sefer hamusar*, p. 10, n. 6; Sassoon, *Ohel Dawid*, 2:1021; and the former ms. Sassoon 995, IMHM #F 9589, p. 7.

102 See, e.g., the headers at https://wysinfo.com/jewish-scholars-of-yemen/#Dhahiri

the service of historical and biographical reconstruction can still seem striking, coming from scholars who were otherwise often sophisticated readers of 19th and 20th century European literature.

Even if Alḍāhirī's protagonists *are* in part authorial self-projections, scholarly attempts to straiten their free-flowing movements into a tidy itinerary and recalibrate their random chronological references into an orderly timeline only stunt the lively fluidity of his narrative. Imagined journeys entwining observational writing, common knowledge, and literary fantasy are forced to yield reliable geographical records and eyewitness accounts. In the hands of the fact-finders, the casual, intermittent entangling of story and history becomes something far more prescriptive and regimented. Few, if any, of these biographical reconstructions are genuinely critical. There are no careful or nuanced attempts to chart Alḍāhirī's responses to the ideas and techniques, currents and influences that he encountered at various stages of his career to let us see how, as an artist, an intellectual, and a religious scholar in a profoundly traditional society, he worked out a modus operandi that comfortably accommodated his innovative impulses alongside his more conservative leanings.

Yet, Abraham Yaari was anxious to get to the bottom of all the embellishment. When he voiced his frustrations with the flowery rhetoric obscuring Alḍāhirī's descriptions and the lack of chronological sequence in *Sefer hamusar*, Yaari spoke for all those readers hoping to retrieve biographical and historical data from Alḍāhirī's literary artistry.[103] Yaari is perhaps the most zealous ideologue of this highly reductive approach, but his basic instincts have been shared by any number of readers over the past 125 years who have attempted to elicit the historical Alḍāhirī from his textual representations. This reading strategy betrays a utilitarianism set on making *Sefer hamusar* historically useful by imposing on it a certain kind of order.[104] The crux of Yaari's critique is provoked by what he sees as Alḍāhirī's willful disregard for chronicling events in a strict linear fashion. The annalistic chronicle (*taʾrīkh*) had long been a staple of pre-modern Arabic and Islamic writing. And there was a biographical tradition in Islamic historiography; closely related to the *taʾrīkh* genre was the historical diary that integrated personal information about the author into

103 See "Sheliḥim me'ereṣ yisra'el le-teiman," 393–394. Another approach was simply to fill in the gaps with anecdotal touches. For a charming popular account of the work and its author, see Shva, "Masa'ot zekhariah al-ḍāhiri."

104 Cf. Mordechai Pachter's self-confessed compulsion to impose chronological order in editing what he calls R. Elazar Azikri's "diary," as cited in Chajes, "Accounting for the Self: Preliminary Generic-Historical Reflections on Early Modern Jewish Egodocuments," 4–5.

his broader historical account.[105] But *Sefer hamusar* is the product of an artistic imagination and makes little pretense to chronological veracity. Yaari undoubtedly saw the handful of historical figures and miscellaneous dates as proof that Alḍāhirī was trying to establish some historical record of events in tandem with a retrospective summation of his own life and accomplishments. The notices contained in medieval Arabic biographical dictionaries often included a bibliography (*fihrist*; lit. "catalogue" or "index") of the subject's works along with other crucial information about that individual; regardless of whether Alḍāhirī was familiar with the genre, the inclusion of his auto-bibliography in the final *maqāma* likely stems from a similar impulse to ensure his posthumous reputation.[106] But Yaari's irritation with the compound nature of Alḍāhirī's texts and with what he saw as disconnected anecdotes reveals a culturally determined notion of order that Alḍāhirī may simply not have shared. In other words, the chronological reconstructions of latter-day scholars espousing a Western auto/ biographical model, regardless of their own cultural identities, may well misrepresent the way Alḍāhirī viewed his *own* life. In their work on autobiography in the Arabic literary tradition—which is now acknowledged to have been more prevalent in the pre-modern period than previously supposed—Dwight Reynolds and his colleagues have argued compellingly that medieval Muslim texts reflect

> a widespread conceptualization of life as a sequence of changing conditions or states [*aḥwāl* or *aṭwār*] rather than as a static, unchanging whole or a simple linear progression through time. A life consists of stages dictated not merely by one's progression from childhood through youth to adulthood and old age but also by one's changing fortunes ...[107]

Immersed in a Judeo-Islamic cultural milieu, Alḍāhirī may well have held similar assumptions about the shape and texture of one's life as a succession of changing circumstances affecting one's degree of well-being. The Andalu-

105 See Makdisi, "Autograph Diary of an Eleventh-Century Historian of Baghdad."

106 His "urge to be immortalized" is discussed at greater length in Chapter Seven. On the bibliography (*fihrist*) of one's own works, see Reynolds et al. eds., *Interpreting the Self: Autobiography in the Arabic Literary Tradition*, p. 38 and n. 8 and Pellat, "Fahrasa."

107 Reynolds, *Interpreting the Self*, p. 4. See also pp. 2–3, where Reynolds notes that "al-Suyūṭī [a prolific 15th-century Egyptian scholar] does not use a noun for the concept of autobiography but rather a verbal expression, *tarjama nafsahu* or *tarjama li-nafsihi*, which, among several interrelated meanings ... signifies 'to compile a titled work/entry on oneself' or 'to translate/interpret oneself,' in the sense of creating a written representation of oneself ...." See also pp. 42–43.

sian Hebrew poets whom he so admired often lamented the effects of Time (Hebrew: *zeman*; Arabic: *dahr*), conceived as the fateful force controlling life's vicissitudes that caused sudden setbacks and reversals of fortune (belief in which was not seen to contradict one's faith in God's omnipotence). The *maqāma* too invoked this notion of mutability, perhaps nowhere more visibly than in its depiction of the mercurial rogue hero. To do Alḍāhirī's text justice, therefore, requires an acknowledgement of its cultural matrix and characteristic literary strategies. Though Yaari would have preferred consecutive accounts to Alḍāhirī's collages, such expectations would have been methodologically misplaced, both in terms of the author's representation of self and the narrative techniques of the Arabic and Hebrew *maqāma*. In fact, the episodic *maqāma* form with its constantly changing settings and disguises is much more congenial to a non-linear conception of life and its metamorphoses. There is a certain irony in the determination to extract a continuous sequential narrative, however skeletal, from a genre that is, by definition, quite so discursive, digressive, twisting, and turning.

That being said, it is nevertheless clear that Alḍāhirī projected certain realia of his own circumstances onto his two main characters, such that their imaginary exploits are inflected by history. The tribulations of the community are woven into the fabric of the work while scattered bits of documentary evidence are enveloped in rich fictive garb. We would be hard-pressed to deny that there *is* an autobiographical impulse to *Sefer hamusar* as a whole even though it represents only one of the work's several strands. While the Author's Introduction speaks in the first person, most of *Sefer hamusar* deliberately blurs the lines between the author and his invented characters, a teasing literary strategy that makes resistance to the biographical fallacy that much more difficult. The indeterminacy raises a vexing question for modern readers wary of overly simplistic and reductive identifications between author and fictive characters: What, if anything, can be known with certainty about the life of the author who gives his full name as Zechariah ben Seʿadya ben Yaʿaqov Alḍāhirī?[108] *Sefer hamusar* delights in its own artifice and is rife with carefully cultivated

108 Alḍāhirī gives his full name only twice: in his Author's Introduction, *Sefer hamusar*, p. 51, l. 3 and without the *nisbah* in the final *maqāma*, p. 461, l. 46. Ratzaby points the *nisbah* Alḍāhrī (without the medial *i*), and says it derives from the toponym *balad al-ḍāhr*; see *Sefer hamusar*, p. 41 and Sassoon, *Ohel Dawid*, 2:1041. In his entry in the *EJ*, Ratzaby includes the medial *i*; see "Zechariah Al-Ḍāhiri." On attestations of the surname and its variants see Gavra, *Shemot ha-mishpaḥah shel ha-yehudim be-teiman*, 621–624 and Wagner, *Like Joseph in Beauty*, p. 160, n. 69. In the British Library ms. Or 11337, the *nisbah* is omitted in the body of the text, but a marginal note adds: מכונה אלצ׳אהרי. Similarly, in the Bodleian ms. אלצ׳אהרי has been added above his name in a different ink.

ambiguity. Alḍāhirī's artful straddling of the boundaries between realism and fictionality should give us pause. As readers, we are left with the delicate task of navigating between pure invention and the author's self-insinuation into the narrative without being able to determine decisively where one ends and the other begins. At a certain point, it is more productive to explore his constructions of identity rather than to seek out the objective facts of his life.

Still, it may be useful to address some of the essential details of these biographical reconstructions rather than to gloss over them as though undeserving of comment. In order to establish Alḍāhirī's dates, scholars have assumed he was the same age as his personae, who make passing references to age and aging. But elaborate attempts to harmonize these oblique references with disparate dates mentioned in *Sefer hamusar* and *Ṣeidah la-derekh* have only produced chronological straightjackets (a given event "must have occurred between the years x and y").[109] Closer scrutiny of these data suggests that even such particulars as the precise place and date of Alḍāhirī's birth cannot be established with certainty. As Yehuda Amir's careful reassessment of Ratzaby's chronology makes clear, there is no firm basis for placing Alḍāhirī's birth between 1516 and 1519. Ratzaby's calculations were extrapolated from fairly flimsy evidence centering on Chapter 39, where Abner tells Mordecai in a dream that he is now over sixty years old. Ratzaby assumed (a) that this must have been Alḍāhirī's own age at the time and (b) that this chapter was written in 1580 because that date is mentioned in chapters that both precede and follow #39 but are not contiguous to it. Hence the author must have been born sometime before 1520. But given the piecemeal composition of the work, there is no a priori reason to assume with Ratzaby that this entire stretch of chapters was composed at the same time. Amir suggests 1531 as a more likely date of birth by combining Abner's claim in #39 that he is over sixty years old with his remark in the same chapter that he has already been imprisoned for twenty-four years.[110] Since, in his Introduction, Alḍāhirī dates the incarceration following the 1567 Zaydī overthrow of the Ottomans in Ṣanaʿā from 1567/8, he (and/or Abner) would have been over sixty in 1592 and therefore born circa 1531 and imprisoned around the age of thirty-seven. But this too is

109 A characteristically tantalizing if vague statement occurs in #24, where the narrator says that by the time he reached the year 1579, his strength had waned and that "[his] childhood and youth had left [him]." Throughout the book, there are periodic, non-specific references to Mordecai or Abner's accelerated aging and exhaustion due to the extreme privations of imprisonment.

110 See lines 36 and 32 respectively. For Ratzaby's chronology see *Sefer hamusar*, pp. 40–43. On the protracted composition of the work and another attempt to adduce all the relevant dates, see Sassoon's review of Idelsohn and Torczyner's *Shirei Teiman*.

speculative, and Amir concedes that, at the end of the day, all we can really establish with certainty is that Alḍāhirī's *floruit* was in the sixteenth century.[111] The incorporation of historical personages into several of the fictional accounts has also fueled chronological speculation. At the very least, the historical figures Alḍāhirī mentions provide a *terminus a quo* for his dating since he cannot completely antedate the renowned mystic and legal scholar Joseph Karo (1488–1575) or the distinguished kabbalist Moses Cordovero (d. 1570). And while it is an argument *ex silencio*, the absence of any mention of Shabbetai Tzvi, whose mid-17th century advent was so terribly repercussive for Yemenite Jewry, provides a *terminus ad quem*. Despite Ratzaby's suggestions, Alḍāhirī's death date is also still unresolved.[112]

Discussions of Alḍāhirī's place of birth pose similar difficulties. The oft-repeated assertion that he was from Kawkabān (to the north-west of Ṣanaʿā) is only supposition. It is based exclusively on the testimony of the *maskilic* last chief rabbi of Ṣanaʿā, Rabbi Amram Qoraḥ (1871–1953), who saw a manuscript leaf in Alḍāhirī's hand indicating that city as his place of residence. In fact, Qoraḥ suggests that Alḍāhirī may have been a resident of Ṣanaʿā and that, after returning from his travels, he decided to live in Kawkabān. Based on this, Ratzaby writes that he was "from Kawkabān," which subsequent studies then take to mean that Kawkabān was his birthplace.[113] In a series of corrections issued following the appearance of Ratzaby's edition, Shalom Medina speculates that Alḍāhirī was actually from Ṣaʿadah (Diqla) in the north, which was roughly a ten-day journey from Ṣanaʿā, while Yehuda Levi Naḥum writes that Alḍāhirī is buried in Kawkabān.[114]

In truth, we know little of Alḍāhirī's childhood and early youth. Was he born into a rabbinic family? Given his erudition, it is highly likely. The conjecture

111 Amir also notes a scholarly reluctance to entertain the possibility that Alḍāhirī lived beyond the confines of the 16th century so that any attribution to him of works alluding to early seventeenth-century texts has been roundly rejected; see Amir, "The Life of Rabbi Zecharia Al-ḍaheri," p. 460 and nn. 10–12. Nevertheless, Amir points out a text ascribed to Alḍāhirī that suggests that he was still alive c. 1608; see ibid., p. 462 and nn. 24–27 and Yehuda Levi Naḥum, *Miyṣirot sifrutiyot me-teiman*, 184–185.

112 See Amir, "The Life of Rabbi Zecharia Al-ḍaheri"; idem, "Shirim ḥadashim mi-dīwān rabbi zekharyah Alḍāhirī," 125; and Tobi, "Piyyuṭ ḥadash le-rabbi yiḥye al-ḍāhirī," 16. See also Medina, "Sefer hamusar, mahadurat ratzaby," p. 9.

113 As noted by Shalom Medina in "Sefer hamusar, mahadurat ratzaby," p. 8. See: Qoraḥ, *Saʿarat teiman*, p. 5, n. 10; *Sefer hamusar*, p. 41, and cf. Gavra, *Shemot ha-mishpaḥa shel ha-yehudim be-teiman*, p. 621. Efraim Yaakov writes that he was born in Kawkabān; see "Liqrat hahdarato shel 'Sefer haʿanaq' le-mari yiḥye al-daheri," 30.

114 See Medina, "Sefer hamusar, mahadurat ratzaby," ibid. and Tobi ed., *Miyṣirot sifrutiyot mi-teiman*, 188.

that he was a silversmith lends weight to this argument, for Yemenite rabbis were especially prominent in that esteemed profession across the ages, and both his *maqāma* and Torah commentary reflect familiarity with the properties of precious metals.[115] (Yemenite rabbis took seriously the mishnaic enjoinder to earn a livelihood from the work of their hands and not from their rabbinic leadership and took to heart Maimonides' opposition to "an institutionalized and salaried rabbinate.")[116] Alḍāhirī's gloss on the Golden Calf (Ex. 32:3–4) in *Ṣeidah la-derekh* is particularly persuasive when he expresses doubts about how quickly Aaron cast the gold brought to him:

> One has to wonder about this: for we the craftsmen, who habitually engage in this process, when we make a molten vessel, have to wait at least three days before casting it.[117]

Yet other details often rest on fairly slender evidence, sometimes no more than a single, relatively generic line of poetry.[118] The duration and conditions of Alḍāhirī's imprisonment are also unclear, due to discrepancies between the accounts he gives in the Introduction to *Sefer hamusar* and at the end of *Ṣeidah la-derekh*, and to the absence of any archival document that would shed light on the incident.[119] In general, this sketchiness is compounded by the lack of reliable external sources that might help to delineate Alḍāhirī's life. Although Judah Alḥarizi provides only a single chronological detail in his *Taḥkemoni*,[120]

---

115 In #32, lines 117–129 (pp. 371–372), Abner reflects a familiarity with the proportions of metals used in producing objects out of silver. Ratzaby and Goitein point to *Sefer ha-musar*, #15, l. 41 (p. 185), where Abner tells Mordecai that he is earning his livelihood as a *ṣoref* (silversmith) while in prison; see Ratzaby's note to l. 41 and Goitein, "A Yemenite Poet on Egypt of the 16th century," 32.

116 See *Avot* 2:2, 4:5; *Mishneh Torah*, "Hilkhot Talmud Torah" 3:10, and Twersky, *Introduction to the Code of Maimonides*, 5. See also Zadock, "R. Yiḥye Qāfeḥ zal—Tequfato u-mifʿalo," in Yishaʿyahu and Zadok eds., *Shevut teiman*, 166. On rabbis as silversmiths, see, e.g., Klein-Franke, "Jewelry Among the Jews of Yemen" and Guilat, "The 'Israelization' of Yemenite-Jewish Silversmithing." See also Brauer, "Ha-ḥaqlaʾut ve-ha-melakhah eṣel yehudei teiman," in Yishaʿyahu and Zadok eds., *Shevut teiman*, 81–83.

117 Cited in Zadock, *Maḥshevet yisrael be-teiman*, 58–59.

118 See *Sefer hamusar* #27, l. 31 (p. 316).

119 See: Amir, "The Life of Rabbi Zecharia Al-ḍaheri," p. 460, n. 14; Ratzaby, "Sifrut yehudei teiman (bibliographiyah)," *KS* 28 (1952/3), p. 264, no. 27; idem, Introduction to *Sefer hamusar*, p. 35; idem, *Toratan she-livnei teiman*, 45–46; Greidi, Introduction to *Ṣeidah la-derekh* in *Taj ḥamishah ḥumshei torah*; Medina, "Ṣeidah la-derekh le'Alḍāhirī"; idem, "Sefer hamusar, mahadurat ratzaby," p. 8; and Zadock, *Maḥshevet yisrael be-teiman*, 57–60.

120 Michael Rand notes that in Alḥarizi's *Taḥkemoni*, "the date of the visit to Jerusalem [1217]

we now have a biographical entry on him from a Muslim author who was his contemporary.[121] Al-Hamadhānī's biographical details have been illuminated by the substantial corpus of letters (*rasā'il*) he left behind. Addressed to friends, political figures, and potential patrons, these epistles shed light on the author's movements across Iran in search of patronage and have enabled scholars to reconstruct the religious and political affiliations crucial to his gaining support, and to infer the state of his personal finances at various junctures in his career.[122] By contrast, Alḍāhirī left no separate body of correspondence, nor do we have any contemporaneous corroboration for his life story; even 18th and 19th-century Yemenite authors who mention him derive their information from *Sefer hamusar*. At times, Alḍāhirī's mere mention of a historical figure such as Cordovero—to whom his narrator refers once, without claiming to have laid eyes on him—has been sufficient to suggest a personal encounter, which in turn has produced assumptions about the philosophical or theosophical content of his work that do not necessarily stand up under closer scrutiny. Such speculations repeated in the scholarly literature over time tend to lose their initially cautious, tentative formulations and become certainties.[123] But the idea of fiction underlying these interwoven strands of the fabulous, the realistic, and the plausible is more complex than such a reductive reading would allow. *Sefer hamusar* is steeped in artifice, moral tension, and ambiguity, starting with its title and ending with its final blurring of the boundaries between author and personae. Along the way, its picaresque tales and trickster travels are intertwined with mourning, rejoicing, setbacks and small triumphs, a love of learning, and a rich loam of lore. To what degree Alḍāhirī is recounting his life

---

is the sole chronological detail given in the entire work"; see *The Evolution of al-Ḥarizi's Taḥkemoni*, p. 4, n. 5.

121 See Sadan, "Un intelectuel juif au confluent de deux cultures" and "Judah Alḥarizi as a Cultural Junction."

122 See: Rowson, "Religion and Politics in the Career of Badīʿ al-Zamān al-Hamadhānī"; Stewart, "Professional Literary Mendicancy in the *Letters* and *Maqāmāt* of Badīʿ al-Zamān al-Hamadhānī" and idem, "ʿĪsā b. Hišām's Shiism and Religious Polemic in the *Maqāmāt* of Badīʿ al-Zamān al-Hamadhānī." Virtually identical passages in certain of al-Hamadhānī's *maqāmāt* and his letters have prompted Vahid Behmardi to ask whether, since the *Letters* are verifiable, Hamadhānī was in the *Maqāmāt* "disguising certain facts about his real life and the real identity of particular characters … under the cover of fiction"; see "Author Disguised and Disclosed: Uncovering Facts in al-Hamadhānī's Fiction."

123 E.g., "In Safed he was privileged to meet Rabbi Yosef Karo, Rabbi Moshe mi-Trani, and the kabbalist Rabbi Moshe Cordovero." With minor variations, this claim recurs throughout much of the recent literature on Alḍāhirī, including articles which are otherwise meticulously researched. Yaari is often cited as an authoritative source; see, e.g., Werblowsky, *Joseph Karo, Lawyer and Mystic*, p. 140 and n. 4.

from these interlaced threads, to what degree he is self-fashioning, and whether the odyssey he conjures may be a journey that he never took, one thing is certain: the story-telling is immensely engaging and has kept readers guessing for more than four centuries.

11 Chapter Outline

Chapter One (Literary Dimensions) examines the work's aesthetic ideals, narrative strategies, poetic techniques, metapoetic reflections, and performative dimension in light of current literary critical scholarship. Special attention is paid to Alḍāhirī's championing of contrafaction, a type of rewriting or counter-writing of earlier poems—many by the revered Hebrew poets of al-Andalus—that enabled him to put his own distinctively Yemenite stamp on pieces that spoke to him and to shape his own poetic voice.

The arc of this study then moves from the literary to the social-historical:

Chapters Two, Three, and Four (Travel, Self-perceptions, and Representations of Muslims) probe the way Alḍāhirī represents his protagonists' crossing of boundaries and encounters with Others, whether Muslim or Jewish, and how he constructs Yemenite Jewish identity in response to these cross-cultural interactions. In keeping with the more recent turn in literary and cultural studies, anthropology, history, and geography, **Chapter Two** approaches the travel narratives in *Sefer hamusar* as composites of fiction and fact rather than as reliable records of actual journeys and examines the stimuli to travel, the cultural exchange, and the diffusion of texts refracted through these travel accounts. **Chapter Three** probes how, on encountering Jewish "Others" in the Land of Israel, the identifiably Yemenite characters perceive themselves and are perceived by those others as members and practitioners of a distinctive Jewish subculture. **Chapter Four** examines Alḍāhirī's ambivalent representations of Muslims and argues that, by deploying deliberate narrative strategies, he devises fictional alternatives to the inferior social and political status of his people, constructing an audacious and clever Jewish literary identity to foster a sense of communal self-definition and self-legitimation.

Chapters Five and Six focus on intellectual history and explore the effect of weaving philosophical or kabbalistic ideas into diverting and imaginative stories. **Chapter Five** demonstrates how, using subtle ironies and incongruities, Alḍāhirī undercuts the force of seemingly sober philosophical addresses and moral reproofs. **Chapter Six** argues that the lighthearted, belletristic framework of *Sefer hamusar* afforded Alḍāhirī an opportunity to bring arcane kabbalistic theosophy and literature and more recent liturgical innovations to the attention of a largely uninitiated, broader public in Yemen. **Chapter Seven** concludes with the afterlife of Alḍāhirī's oeuvre, both the one he imagined for himself and the one accorded him by posterity. I argue that his strategy of applying his auto-epitaph to his protagonists furnishes a closure device rarely seen in Hebrew and Arabic *maqāmāt* and that it enabled Alḍāhirī to deflect potential criticism of his protagonists' transgressive behavior, bringing *Sefer hamusar* full circle to its opening, where he takes pains to frame it in a pious vein.

CHAPTER 1

Literary Dimensions: *Maqāma, Musar*, Narrative and Poetic Techniques

1 Setting the Scene: Author's Introduction

לְמִשְׁפָּטֶיךָ עָמְדוּ הַיּוֹם כִּי הַכֹּל עֲבָדֶיךָ:

They stand this day to [carry out] Your rulings, for all are Your servants.[1]

Said the lowly Zechariah ben Seʿadya ben Yaʿaqov Alḍāhirī:

Having praised the First Cause and Supernal Thought—He is the blessed God who creates His world *ex nihilo* (out of nought), to Whom all creatures look, duty-bound to give thanks for whatever measure He metes out—I will praise Him in the midst of the congregation and crowd. My heart moved me to tell something of the trials that befell us and the troubles that beset us. We, the community dwelling in Ṣanaʿā, nearly became like sheep without a shepherd—ah! So that future generations might know, I will cry out to them with full throat.

The incidents began, by decree of Him who is perfect of understanding, in the year *ha-shakhaḥ* [5328 = 1567/68 C.E.], "Has God forgotten how to pity? Has He in anger stifled His mercy?"[2] In that year the Ishmaelites prevailed against the Turks and struck them down and locked us in prison, to be trampled and bound. With all this, we paid a heavy tax. Down to our last coin, engulfed in endless night, some despaired and loathed their very lives. Their time was running out. By the first of Av 5329 [1568] he[3] had scattered us to every prison tower and fort—the destitute, the needy, and the poor. We cried, we sighed, young and old, bound in chains of iron, tears flowed from every eye. Some were sent to forced labor, some to grind flour, in hunger and thirst, naked and utterly bereft … craving food, with no one to give them a morsel to relieve their starving bellies. The foes took

1 Ps. 119:91.

2 Ps. 77:10. If the *heh* is construed as five thousand, the alphanumerical value of the opening word, *ha-shakhaḥ* (Has God forgotten?) is 5328, equivalent to 1567/68 C.E.

3 Presumably a reference to Imām al-Muṭahhar.

 | DOI:10.1163/9789004733787_003

their own signs for true signs, for they saw the precious ones clinging to refuse heaps .... We were like dung for the field, we have all become like an unclean thing; we were hotly pursued; exhausted, we were given no rest. Our hope was thwarted, almost lost; there was no one to remove our disgrace.

After this I asked myself, how can I find respite from my trouble and misery when there is no breath left in me? ... To soothe my soul, I wrote a book for all those bitter of spirit. From the depths of my imprisonment I called it *Sefer hamusar*—a book of guidance [and beguilement]—so that all who read it with expression will learn a lesson from the hardships that befell us through our sins and our transgressions .... Apart from this, it will advance knowledge of the Sacred Tongue, which deserves to be enhanced, engraved in our hearts and fluent on all lips .... Perhaps in this will be the balm for our wounds and a tree of life bearing fruit.

Yet I have narrated it by means of two men who are strangers to me, Mordecai ha-Ṣidoni and Abner ben Ḥeleq ha-Teimani, for the numeric value of their names and mine are the same, may God be with me as I declaim.[4] And I have divided the book into chapters (*maḥbarot*) on varied matters; they tell of what befell me while I wandered as a stranger, and when I was in prison among my people—abject in my misery—by means of the two men I mentioned, who are both concealed and revealed, so that the subject should be sweet and pleasing to those who seek it. One man speaks and the other responds, to construct verses of lament and song; one builds battlements of poetry, or memorable *epistolae*, their words a crowning glory, for honor and adornment.[5] All this will be relayed through the two pure ones who are the heroes, they are known for every speech and famed for every flourish. On a word from them we make camp and break camp. They convey delightful amity, the strength of their bond and lasting love. This way was paved by Rabbi Judah Ḥarizi, who spoke in his book through Heman ha-Ezraḥi and Ḥever ha-Qeni. And he learned from the Muslim sage al-Ḥarīrī, surpassing master of elegant style, who flourished among his brothers. Truly there is none like him for eloquence: his honeyed rivers overflow with riddles and flourishes beyond compare;

---

4 The numerical value of the letters that spell Zechariah ben Seʿadya is 443, which is also the numerical value of the names Mordecai ha-Ṣidoni and Abner ben Ḥeleq. Cf. Segal, *The Book of Taḥkemoni*, p. 645.

5 ליסד בתי הקינים והשירים והאחד טירותיהם בונה. או דברי אגרת. לענינים טובים מזכרת. גלה וכותרת. לכבוד ולתפארת. Alḍāhirī is playing here on the dual sense of *bayit* as "house" and poetic "verse," hence the construction metaphor.

> flocks of parables repose in his book. By the light of his intellect he illuminates my night (*ʿaravi*), even though his language was Arabic (*ʿaravi*). Truth lights his way; he has no peer. But the wise man said to his profligate son: "Who is rich? He who is satisfied with his lot."[6] I have come this far to console my sorrowful soul with the meager gleanings that have detached from well-knit works, though I am not a man of words.[7] In truth, I have relied on the maxim of the wise: "Whoever utters song in this world deserves to do so in the next."[8] Hence my praise offering before God: I will acclaim Him in the midst of the congregation and throng. My heart exulted; I will glorify Him with my song.[9]

From the epigraph citing Psalm 119:91 to the *inclusio* enveloping the Introduction in the language and sentiments of Psalm 109:30, this rich collage—all of it rhymed in the original—sets the tone and agenda for what is to come. A dense weave of biblical verse fragments (and one mishnaic phrase) that summon associations with their original contexts is interlaced with medieval philosophical commonplaces (God as the First Cause and Supernal Thought, who creates His world *ex nihilo*) and allusions to recent events in Yemenite Jewish history, so that Alḍāhirī's words are colored with both a timelessness and a real and urgent sense of chronological specificity.[10] Ratzaby sees the invocation of Psalm 119:91 as scriptural support and theological justification for accepting the community's trials and sufferings as divine decree, i.e., as a kind of theodicy. Abraham Ibn Ezra interpreted the verse to mean that the heavens and the earth stand ready as servants to carry out God's ruling since they are invoked in the two preceeding verses and furnish the nearest antecedents to the anonymous verb. But Alḍāhirī's reading may well reflect that of Saʿadya Gaon, who

6 *Avot* 4, 1. Ratzaby suggests that Alḍāhirī cites the proverb from *Avot* to assuage his sense of inadequacy.

7 Per Ratzaby, this is a wistful confession of inferiority vis-à-vis al-Ḥarīrī: Alḍāhirī merely "gleans" the remainders of the more accomplished artist's harvest.

8 bSanhed 91b; the term for "song," *shirah*, is also the Hebrew term for poetry in the Middle Ages.

9 *Sefer hamusar*, pp. 51–53.

10 "For whatever measure He metes out"—cf. mBer 9, 5; "In the midst of the congregation I will exalt Him"—cf. Ps. 109:30 ("I will acclaim him in the midst of a throng"); "that befell us"—cf. Esther 9:26; "like sheep that have no shepherd"—cf. Nu. 27:17; "cry with full throat"—cf. Is. 58:1; "so that future generations might know"—cf. Ps. 78:6. Merely citing the sources of an author's allusions is, of course, highly unsatisfying, since it conveys nothing of the overtones and associations carried by these intertextual references. But to explain them would, in T. Carmi's words, "require a forbidding apparatus of notes and comments;" see *The Penguin Book of Hebrew Verse*, 10.

in his *tafsīr* renders "they stand" as "we stand" (*waqafnā*) and translates *mishpaṭekha* (Your rulings/ judgments) as *sīraka*, "Your path" or "Your way." If, in light of the travails he is about to recount, Alḍāhirī's is a quietist reading, viz., 'We stand this day prepared to follow Your judgment/rulings, for all are Your servants,' it would dovetail with the idea of dutifully giving thanks "for whatever measure He metes out."[11] Though he does not cite it, perhaps he also had in mind the consolation offered by the Psalm's next verse (119:92), "Were not Your teaching my delight, I would have perished in my affliction." The sentiments are surely genuine. And yet, by framing *Sefer ha-musar* as a pious response to communal trauma, the Introduction sounds an apologetic note that reverberates throughout the work as a counterweight to its interludes of levity and tales of transgression. (In his own preface, al-Ḥarīrī had struck a pious and apologetic chord, anticipating criticism of his protagonist's sinful conduct.) At the same time, a contrapuntal thread of aesthetic sensibility weaves its way through Alḍāhirī's Introduction. Couched within his dutiful defense of the work as a source of moral edification is a rudimentary *ars poetica* that touches on questions of genre, narrative technique, language, style, literary models, intended audience, and purpose. Following his lament over the cruel and debilitating incarceration of his community by the local Zaydī rulers of Ṣanaʿā in the wake of their (temporary) overthrow of the Ottomans, Alḍāhirī turns to the nature of the book at hand. He tells us that to soothe his soul and console his coreligionists, he began to compose this work from the abyss of prison. He entitled it *Sefer hamusar* in the hopes that the reader would derive moral instruction (*musar*) from the tribulations visited on the Ṣanaʿānī Jews on account of their many sins, and that in doing so would learn humility before God. But prison, with its wrenching hardships and privations, did not entirely sap him of his creative energy; despite the serious obstacles to writing that he refers to in several of his works, he managed to sustain his literary enterprise.[12] Though it is

---

11 ואלי סירך וקפנא אליום, פאן אלכל עבידך. See Saadya Gaon, *Tehillim ʿim tirgum u-feirush ha-ga'on rabbeinu seʿadyah ben yosef fayyūmī*, p. 256. Literally a path or a way, *sīra* designates a course, rule, mode, or manner of acting or conduct. Qāfiḥ notes that in contexts where *mishpaṭ* has the sense of judgment or ruling, Saʿadya consistently renders it as *sīra*; see the notes to Ps. 81:5, ibid., p. 193. In Islam, *sīra* is used synonymously with *ṭarīqa, sunna, and madhhab,* terms which all have the base meaning of 'a way' or 'a course,' and which figure in Islamic jurisprudence but carry multiple nuances depending on the context; see Lane, *Arabic-English Lexicon*, Pt. 4, 1484.

12 Alḍāhirī alludes to the conditions of his confinement in a postscript to his Pentateuch commentary, *Ṣeidah la-derekh*; see Ratzaby, *Toratan she-livnei teiman*, 45–46. In a brief apology at the end of his unpublished commentary on *Hilkhot sheḥitah*, he frames the work's defects as a casualty of his incarceration; see ms. Guenzburg 1306, f. 63[v]. See also

only implicit, the continuation of his words suggests that the *musar* of the title is also intended as the Hebrew equivalent of the Arabic *adab*. Associated with the sophisticated culture of the medieval courtier or professional secretary, the ideal of *adab* encompassed refined written and conversational skills, including the ability to quote choice anecdotes and proverbs, though over time it came to refer to particular genres of literary creativity, among them poetry and artistic prose.[13] Adab literature often aimed to instruct the reader through diversion. So it stands to reason that hard on the heels of Alḍāhirī's avowed resignation to divine decree come several topoi of the medieval Hebrew *maqāma* literature: the desire to rehabilitate the neglected Hebrew language by drawing the reader to the *maqāma*'s fine use of the Sacred Tongue; a caveat that the author has conveyed his narrative through two decidedly imaginary protagonists who are not to be facilely identified with him despite certain similarities; and a declaration that he has divided the work into discrete *maḥbarot* or episodes incorporating a multiplicity of literary subgenres (poems, epistles, etc.) with a broad array of entertaining and edifying settings and plots.[14] Judah Alḥarizi and Abū 'l-Ḥasan al-Ḥarīrī are the two tutelary spirits who hover over the work. Alḍāhirī acknowledges his indebtedness to Alḥarizi, who blazed the trail with his magnificent Hebrew *maqāmāt* and who, in turn, learned the craft from al-Ḥarīrī, the peerless Muslim master of Arabic eloquence. Alḍāhirī closes with a striking homage to al-Ḥarīrī, which is tinged with regret at his own inability to defend the honor of the Holy Tongue by achieving comparable rhetorical feats in Hebrew.[15] As he voices these feelings of inadequacy, he quietly deploys a virtuosic pun, playing on the phrase *yahel ʿaravi* (Isaiah 13:20, where *yahel* signifies pitching a tent and *ʿaravi* designates an Arab), to yield "he illuminates my night" (*beʾor sikhlo*

Sefer hamusar #15, p. 187, line 86: *eikh yukhal le-ḥabber shirim, veʾafilu be-veit haʾasurim* and the similar sentiment expressed in #2, p. 75, lines 232–234. On medieval prison writing, see Chapter Two.

13 See Roger Allen's Foreword to Kilito, *Arabs and the Art of Storytelling*, vii. The *musar/ adab* equivalence is discussed at greater length below.

14 *Sefer hamusar*, p. 52: *ve-ḥilaqti ha-sefer ha-hu le-maḥbarot/beʿinyanim shonim medabberot. Maḥberet* became the standard Hebrew equivalent for *maqāma*; a particularly felicitous choice, given that the abstract meaning of the root *ḥ-b-r* has to do with joining together, and derived forms of the root include the terms for friend, friendship, and society as well as original literary composition, compilation of written material, and author; see Klar, "ʿArbaʿah shemot sefarim," 246–248.

15 *Sefer ha-musar*, p. 53. Michael Rand has written that the acknowledgement of one's models became a standard feature of the Ḥarīrīan and Ḥarizian *maqāma* tradition; see *Studies in the Medieval Hebrew Tradition* etc., 11–12. Alḍāhirī diverges from the convention as outlined by Rand insofar as he does not boast of his superiority to his models.

yahel ʿaravi; where *yahel* derives from the root *h.l.l.*), which he then pairs with his muted linguistic polemic, "even though his language was Arabic (*ʿaravi*)."[16]

Alḍāhirī's brief, bare-bones outline of his compositional principles draws on Judah Alḥarizi's more fully elaborated Hebrew Introduction to the *Taḥkemoni*, where he conveys the impetus for composing that work. A seasoned translator, Alḥarizi explains that he had been so taken with the artful and exuberant flow of language in al-Ḥarīrī's Arabic *Maqāmāt* that he had initially rendered the work into a suitably elevated Hebrew. (That translation, which has not survived in its entirety, was undertaken while he was still in the Christian realms of Northern Spain or Provence and has come to be known as *Maḥberot Itiʾel*, after the biblical name Alḥarizi gave its narrator.[17]) But he then regretted neglecting his own sacred tongue for a translation from Arabic and was driven to produce an original Hebrew *maqāma* as well, to prove that the Holy Tongue was equal to the task. (He began this project after setting out for the Muslim East.) Ironically, Alḥarizi adopted and mastered a quintessentially Arabic literary genre in order to demonstrate that biblical Hebrew was every bit as elegant, versatile, and expressive as classical or qurʾānic Arabic, which was considered inimitable by Muslims on both aesthetic and theological grounds.[18] Of all the Iberian Hebrew rhymed prose narratives, the *Taḥkemoni* follows the Arabic picaresque *maqāma* model most faithfully. Alḥarizi's adulation for al-Ḥarīrī seemingly knows no bounds until his ambivalence becomes apparent as he abruptly reverses himself to invoke the apologetic idea, much touted among 13th-century Iberian Jewish translators, that Arabic wisdom originates in Hebrew sources: "all his themes are hewn from the Holy Tongue, and most of his precious parables are taken from our Torah."[19] Alḥarizi complains that Ara-

16 Cf. Alḥarizi, *Taḥkemoni*, ed. Yahalom-Katsumata, 542. Al-Ḥarīrī's *Maqāmāt* are praised for their luminous quality in a poetic eulogy by al- Zamakhsharī: "… al-Ḥarīrī's *Assemblies* deserve to be written in letters of gold … they are guided by the light of his lamp." Cited in Kilito, *Arabs and the Art of Storytelling*, 14.

17 The title was coined by the Oxford Arabist Thomas Chenery who published the work in 1872; see Schirmann, *HPCS*, 177–184. Only slightly more than half of his translation has survived in a unique ms.; see Alḥarizi, *Maḥberot Itiʾel*, pp. 4–5 (Hebrew numeration) and Rand, *Studies in the Medieval Hebrew Tradition* etc., p. 47, n. 6 and p. 56, n. 24. Joseph Yahalom and Naoya Katsumata suggest that Alḥarizi might have undertaken the translation for the benefit of Provençal Jewish intellectuals with varying degrees of connection to Arabic literary culture; see Alḥarizi, *Taḥkemoni*, ed. Yahalom-Katsumata, viii.

18 On inimitability (*iʿjāz al-qurʾān*) see von Grunebaum, *A Tenth-Century Document of Arabic Literary Theory and Criticism*, xiii–xxii and Boullata, "The Rhetorical Interpretation of the Qurʾān: *iʿjāz* and Related Topics"; on its polemical applications see Rosenthal, "A Jewish Philosopher of the Tenth Century," 155–157.

19 On this recurrent motif see Alfonso, *Islamic Culture through Jewish Eyes*, 29–30, 49.

bic has lured Jews away from Hebrew and champions the cause of Hebraism; familiar topoi by his time, these concerns are also voiced in the *Taḥkemoni's* first *maqāma* and in his Arabic Introduction to the work.[20] In the latter, Alḥarizi singles out the Jews of the East for their deficient Hebrew; a particular disappointment, given that he had pinned his hopes for Hebrew cultural renewal on the Islamic East following the decline of Andalusian Jewry.[21] While this charge seems plausible in light of the Eastern Jews' Arabic linguistic milieu, Rina Drory has argued that to properly understand Alḥarizi's campaign to rehabilitate Hebrew, one cannot view the *Taḥkemoni* exclusively in its Eastern, Arabic context. Rather, it is also crucial to take into account the impact of the changing cultural ideals that Alḥarizi had internalized in northern Spain before his departure, during the early 13th century, when Arabic cultural influence had declined and Hebrew had begun to assume many of the literary functions previously fulfilled by Arabic.[22]

After sounding these apprehensions, Alḥarizi goes on (rather disingenuously) to assert his originality:

> Of all the things I have mentioned in this book, I have not taken one thing from the book of the Ishmaelite, unless it was [inadventently] through forgetfulness ... all the themes in this book are my own inventions ....

He calls attention to the imaginary nature of his protagonists and underscores the novelty and unprecedented variety of his subject matter.[23] While each of these declarations is a familiar touchstone from prefaces to Arabic *maqāmāt*,

20 Following Alḥarizi's lead, several 13th-century Hispano-Jewish authors in Christian Iberia felt compelled to defend the honor of Hebrew, even though the lure of Arabic culture had waned and their works reflect the heterogeneity of their European cultural milieu. See: Ben El'azar, *Sippurei ahavah*, 13–14; Ibn Sahula, *Meshal ha-qadmoni*, xxviii and 5–19; Levy and Torollo, "Romance Literature in Hebrew Language with an Arabic Twist: The First Story of Jacob Ben El'azar's *Sefer ha-Meshalim*"; Rosen, "The Story of the Crooked Preacher by Jacob ben El'azar"; Yahalom, "A Romance Maqāma: The Place of the 'Speech of Tuvia Ben Zedeqiah' in the History of the Hebrew Maqāma"; Decter, *Iberian Jewish Literature*, 99–213; and Scheindlin, "The Love Stories of Jacob ben Elazar: Between Arabic and Romance Literature."

21 See: Alḥarizi, *Taḥkemoni*, ed. Yahalom-Katsumata, pp. 70–80 and Alḥarizi's Arabic introduction, ibid., p. 55; cited by Rand, *The Evolution of al-Ḥarizi's Taḥkemoni*, 8–9. See also Decter, *Iberian Jewish Literature*, 197–199.

22 See: Drory, *Models and Contacts*, 215–232; Brann, *The Compunctious Poet*, 119–124; and Schirmann, *HPCS*, 188–190 and 214–216.

23 Alḥarizi, *Taḥkemoni*, ed. Yahalom-Katsumata, p. 77, lines 338–342.

Alḥarizi's litany of subjects and genres does not merely parrot an Arabic literary convention. It also intimates that Hebrew—and, by extension, the gifted Hebrew author—too, is fully capable of addressing any topic or literary form:[24]

> Now I have included in this work matter of all manner: anthems for Love's banner, riddles and saws, lore and laws, reflection, censure, the wayfarer's adventure, tales of times past or of death's blast, the grace of every season, the way of reason or treachery and treason, godly wrath and the penitent's path, the beloved's face and hot embrace, wooing and bedding and holy wedding—and divorce as well.
>
> Yes, I tell of teetotalers and drinkers, of warriors and thinkers, spin tales of journeys, of kings and poets' tourneys, prayers and supplication, praise and protestation, the rebuke of the wise and good fortune's demise, the role of Love's gazelles and the cool of desert wells, stint's harsh breeze and beggars' pleas, wind and water, sword and slaughter ....[25]

This extensive catalogue inextricably intertwines two seemingly incongruous types of narrative that also coexist in *Sefer ha-musar*: cautionary and hortatory tales intended as guides to ethical conduct, and mischievous, subversive, and ribald storylines providing diversion and amusement. The idea of the list is clearly inspired by the analogous section of al-Ḥarīrī's paradigmatic Introduction, although al-Ḥarīrī homes in on the rhetorical and stylistic excellence on offer in his *Maqāmāt*:

> In them are mixed the grave and the ridiculous, the rugged and the delicate. Studded with the gems of oratory, salted with the table-talk of cultivated men, and emblazoned with verses of the Koran, they are replete with figures and allegories, proverbs and maxims, literary subtleties and grammatical enigmas, and judgments on disputed points of speech. Nor will they be found deficient in pleasantry and laughter, in epistles ingenuously contrived, in orations gaudily bedecked, or in sermons bedewed with the tears of penitence.[26]

---

24 Drory, *Models and Contacts*, 226–227.

25 Segal, trans. *The Book of Taḥkemoni*, 15–16; for a more literal rendition see Reichert trans., *The Tahkemoni of Judah al-Harizi*, 1:36–37. For the Hebrew see Alḥarizi, *Taḥkemoni*, ed. Yahalom-Katsumata, 75–76.

26 Cooperson trans., *Impostures by al-Ḥarīrī*, p. 5.

Both lists afford a fine illustration of what Abdelfattah Kilito has termed the *maqāma*'s characteristic *pluralité* or *mélange*, noting that the complex *maqāma* incorporates and reworks a number of simpler, smaller, pre-existing genres whose novel use and combination modulates their usual "tone."[27]

Alḍāhirī is rather more laconic in characterizing the contents of his work ("I have divided the book into *maḥbarot* which speak of varied things … verses of lament and poetry … noble words of an epistle …"). But *Sefer ha-musar* also deploys, in new contexts and juxtapositions, an entire arsenal of subgenres with their associated themes and dramatis personae. Folk tales, midrashic stories, sermons, homilies, parables, poetic competitions, letters, riddles, travelogues, dialogues and debates are peopled by itinerant preachers, swindlers, quack doctors, kings, Muslim religious judges, noble Bedouin, religious polemicists, kabbalists, cantors, and a rebuffed bride and duped bridegroom. Nor are Alḍāhirī's sources of literary inspiration limited to those he explicitly mentions. But he readily asserts that his book is governed by the aesthetic conventions of the Arabic *maqāma* as epitomized by al-Ḥarīrī in the eleventh century and as adapted into Hebrew by Alḥarizi at the turn of the thirteenth. Notably, his retention of medieval literary ideals does not mean that Alḍāhirī is impervious to the changing world around him. Quite the contrary, his work reflects varying degrees of awareness of material and intellectual innovations and political upheavals associated with the early modern era, ranging from Hebrew printing and the advent of the *Shulḥan ʿarukh*, kabbalah, and printed prayer-books, to the Ottoman conquest of Yemen.

2 The *Maqāma* Genre

In Arabic literature, the inauguration of the *maqāma* genre is traditionally ascribed to Abu 'l-Faḍl Aḥmad al-Hamadhānī (968–1008), an Iranian virtuoso in Persian and Arabic, poet, and gifted littérateur, who spent much of his career searching for patronage and died at the early age of 40. Already during his lifetime, al-Hamadhānī gained renown for his *Maqāmāt*, a riveting collection of roughly forty to fifty independent stories that are nevertheless linked

27 See Kilito, "Le Genre Séance: une introduction," 51; idem, *Les Séances*, 13; cf. Drory, *Models and Contacts*, 11; idem, "The Maqama," 190; Beeston, "Al-Hamadhānī, al-Ḥarīrī, and the *Maqāmāt* Genre," esp. 128–129; Beaumont, "The Trickster and Rhetoric in the Maqāmāt"; idem, "A Mighty and Never Ending Affair: Comic Anecdote and Story in Medieval Arabic Literature." On generic heterogeneity in al-Hamadhānī's *Maqāmāt*, see Hämeen-Anttila, "The Early Maqama: Towards Defining a Genre."

by virtue of the recurrence of their two protagonists and certain key stylistic and narrative features. This accomplishment earned him the sobriquet *Badīʿ al-Zamān*, "the Marvel of the Age." Al-Hamadhānī's *Maqāmāt* started gaining pockets of attention in al-Andalus and North Africa soon after his death, while in the Muslim East—according to Jaako Hämeen-Anttila, who takes issue with the traditional reception history—al-Hamadhānī's contemporaries and immediate successors did not view him primarily as a *maqāma* author but rather as an exceptionally skilled belletrist and epistolary stylist. Hämeen-Anttila argues that, as a consequence, the *maqāma* did not become a fixed genre until the mid-eleventh century and that al-Hamadhānī only reached the peak of his fame by the latter part of that century, in large measure due to the posthumous praise bestowed on him by al-Ḥarīrī of Basra (1054–1122), the man who brought the genre to prominence and gave it what came to be considered its definitive form.[28] Al-Ḥarīrī's *Maqāmāt* surpassed those of al-Hamadhānī in reputation and canonical status a century after their composition and led to the proliferation of the genre across the Muslim world.[29] The literary form of the Arabic *maqāma* traveled across many regions of the Islamicate world (and ultimately beyond) to become naturalized in different linguistic and confessional milieus. In the West, it took hold in Andalusia in the twelfth century, prompting the composition of new works such as *al-Maqāmāt al-luzūmiyya* by the Andalusian al-Saraqusṭī. Fictional Hebrew rhymed prose narratives began to emerge during roughly the same time frame in early 12th-century Iberia, though the earlier authors did not feel constrained to adopt all the elements of the Ḥarīrīan model. It is only with Judah Alḥarizi's *Taḥkemoni* that we see close adherence to the norms and conventions of the picaresque Arabic *maqāma*.[30] Following

28 See Hämeen-Anttila, *Maqama: A History of a Genre*, 121–147 and idem, "The Early *Maqāma*"; van Gelder, "Fools and Rogues in Discourse and Disguise: Two Studies"; Kennedy, "Reason and Revelation or A Philosopher's Squib"; and Drory, "The Maqama," 193.

29 On the "widespread literary influence" of al-Ḥarīrī's *Maqāmāt*, see, e.g., Kilito, *Arabs and the Art of Storytelling*, 136, quoting Renan, "Les *Séances* de Hariri." For a catalogue of *maqāmāt* by different authors, see Hämeen-Anttila, *Maqama*. On the speed with which they were transmitted from Baghdad to Spain and early evidence of their impact on the Hebrew tradition, see Rand, *Studies in the Medieval Hebrew Tradition* etc., p. 44 and n. 2. Rand writes (p. 47) that: "According to al-Ḥarizi's report, the translation of Ḥarīrī's collection had been attempted before him, but without success, on account of the difficulty of the material."

30 See Decter, *Iberian Jewish Literature*, p. 119: "… there is a curious development in Hebrew writing from a less classical model to one that is more classical, from the innovative to the imitative. Only some of the Hebrew narratives truly seem fully at home in the Arabic *maqama* tradition."

Alḥarizi, the Hebrew *maqāma*—or in some cases, primarily its prosimetrical medium—traversed geo-cultural realms within the Jewish world and was cultivated over many centuries by authors from Italy to Egypt, Greece, and Yemen.

Whether in Hebrew or Arabic, the classical model of the literary *maqāma* is a collection of episodic, self-contained texts written in elevated and effervescent rhymed prose (Arabic: *sajʿ*) with formal, metered poems inserted at key junctures (a phenomenon known as prosimetrum). Typically, each independent chapter (also called a *maqāma*; Hebrew: *maḥberet*) is set in a different location and is unconnected to what has preceded or what follows by any continuous plot line or narrative development. The work is lent unity by the consistent presence of its two main characters, a ubiquitous narrator (Arabic: *rāwī*) and a wandering rogue-hero (a *balīgh*, or eloquent man), and by what Devin Stewart has called the "running gag" that typifies their interactions.[31] Arriving in a given city, the gullible narrator encounters but does not recognize the scheming hero who, disguised differently in each episode, dupes the narrator and onlookers into parting with their money and other material rewards by disingenuously pleading hardship and impressing them with his spellbinding displays of rhetorical brilliance. The rogue-hero constantly reinvents himself and is endowed with a limitless capacity for deception. As Kilito puts it, "[i]n each of his performances he wears a new mask; his identity, provisional and fleeting, is at every instant a borrowing, an impersonation."[32] The dénouement of virtually every episode involves a recognition scene or anagnorisis; often the narrator identifies the hero on the strength of his verbal prowess alone. On occasion, the narrator recognizes his old friend early on and chooses to connive at his ruse rather than give him away, but generally the shape-shifting hero's true identity becomes apparent to him only once it is too late.[33] As Stewart notes, the structure of the *maqāma* is defined by dramatic irony: at the opening of each episode, the unreliable first-person narrator is unaware that he is going to be deceived, although it is obvious to the work's audience, and this repetitive pattern, along with the expectations it engenders, contribute to making the *maqāma* so enjoyable. (The narrator is unreliable both because he lacks omniscience and because he trustingly reports events as conveyed to him by a master of deception.) Variety and suspense are provided by the unpredictability of the constantly changing locales, disguises, and techniques of impromptu verbal showmanship. The open spaces, marketplaces, and crossroads frequented

31 Stewart, "The Maqāma," 145.

32 Kilito, "Foreward," in Cooperson, *Impostures*, xi.

33 On anagnorisis see Kennedy, *Recognition in the Arabic Narrative Tradition* and idem, "Islamic Recognitions: An Overview."

by the trickster hero are thresholds and "places of transition, movement, and license," where clearly defined boundaries are broken down.[34] The hero is at one and the same time an erudite littérateur and an unabashed mendicant who relies on charity inveigled out of an appreciative audience. Literature, deception, and artifice are intertwined not only on the level of the recurrent plotline but also in the rogue-hero's enigmatic narrative techniques and deliberately recherché and often obscure style.[35]

Unscrupulous and protean, the hero resorts to imposture without qualm and, in Arabic *maqāmāt*, often adopts personae from the lower social strata or margins of medieval society: physically decrepit beggars, down-at-the-heel confidence men, quacks, dodgy popular preachers, sellers of charms.[36] Wolfhart Heinrichs observes that part of the appeal of the text is precisely the ironic tension engendered by the incongruity between the narrative's elevated language and "lowlife contents."[37] Similar masks—albeit Judaized—are adopted in those Hebrew *maqāmāt* that adhere closely to the Ḥarīrīan model. Despite the repeated exposure of his deceits, for which he is periodically chastised by the narrator, and in spite of his dubious moral standing, the protagonist of the *maqāma* exerts a raffish appeal and manages to retain an imposing reputation for linguistic virtuosity and sharp wit. Regarding this conjunction, Philip Kennedy has written that the *maqāma* "explor[es] and toy[s] with the idea that eloquence, so prized in medieval Arabic literature, is not commensurate with veracity."[38] While numerous episodes are full of incident, others showcase the hero's sparkling rhetoric and magisterial linguistic games unframed by any plot. Michael Cooperson maintains that the stories and intrigues may be more appealing to modern readers, but it is the verbal performances that were the high point for pre-modern Arabic readers, who were captivated by their panoply of "puns, rhymes, rare words, and far-fetched figures of speech; riddles, anagrams, lipograms, palindromes, word- and sound-play."[39]

Scholars are in general agreement that the *maqāma* was the first avowedly fictional genre in Arabic literature, although it clearly had antecedents and

---

34 Babcock-Abraham, "'A Tolerated Margin of Mess': The Trickster and His Tales Reconsidered," 153.

35 Kilito, "Foreward," in Cooperson, *Impostures*, x.

36 See Kilito, *Les Séances*, 55–70 ("Le centre et la périphérie"); idem, "Foreward," in Cooperson, *Impostures*, x; Jayyusi, *Classical Arabic Stories*, 4–5.

37 Heinrichs, "Prosimetrical Genres in Classical Arabic," 265.

38 Kennedy, "Islamic Recognitions," 40.

39 See Cooperson, *Impostures*, xx and xxxiii.

hardly emerged in a vacuum.[40] The late tenth-century saw a surge in the use of *sajʿ* and a turn toward a more elaborate style in Arabic artistic prose.[41] Accounts of the *maqāma* genre's inception and transmission vary, not least because al-Hamadhānī's extant corpus lacks an Author's Introduction that might have provided information about his models and sources of inspiration.[42] An older, now largely discredited view held that the stylistic virtuosity and rhetorical acrobatics of the *maqāma* overshadowed its narrative content, yielding "a medley of prose and verse in which the story is nothing, the style everything."[43] According to this theory, the *maqāma*, especially in its later, classical Ḥarīrian formulation, was primarily designed to teach professional secretaries arcane vocabulary and eloquent style. Though such a didactic purpose has not been ruled out entirely, this is now considered only one possible factor contributing to the development of the genre. Rina Drory posited that the first *maqāmāt* were produced by al-Hamadhānī as humorous oral improvisations that parodied serious *adab* materials. Intended to serve as comic relief, these extempore pieces were produced at the end of group study sessions. To distinguish them from bona fide educational texts, it was necessary to introduce fictitious characters and acknowledge their fictional nature.[44] Devin Stewart also highlights the inherently humorous and parodic elements of the genre, emphasizing the centrality of mendicancy (*kudya*) to the *Maqāmāt* of al-Hamadhānī who, in his *Letters*, refers to his collection as *Maqāmāt al-kudya* (The *Maqāmāt* of Beggary). A learned study by C.E. Bosworth explores the affinities between the swindling hero and the Banū Sāsān, an "underground guild of professional sham beggars."[45] While not disputing the connection, Stewart frames his analysis in terms of an additional type of begging, "the literary mendicancy practiced by the members of the secretarial class" in medieval Islamic society. Stewart argues persuasively that the silver-tongued hero of al-Hamadhānī's *Maqāmāt* is

---

40 See Beeston, "Al-Hamadhānī, al-Ḥarīrī, and the *Maqāmāt* Genre," 125–129; Richards, "The *Maqāmāt* of al-Hamadhānī"; and Drory, *Models and Contacts*, 11–36.

41 See: Rowson, "The Aesthetics of Pure Formalism" and Fahd et al., "Sadjʿ."

42 Crucial information about the size of the corpus is also missing; later copyists added new materials to Hamadhānī's corpus; see Orfali and Pomerantz: "Three *Maqāmāt* Attributed to Badīʿ al-Zamān al-Hamadhānī"; "A Lost *Maqāma* of Badīʿ al-Zamān al-Hamadhānī?"; and *The Maqāmāt of Badīʿ al-Zamān al-Hamadhānī: Authorship, Texts, and Contexts.*

43 See Beeston, "The Genesis of the *Maqāmāt* Genre," 10, citing Nicholson, *A Literary History of the Arabs*^{2}, 328. Cf. Margoliouth and Pellat, "al-Ḥarīrī": "… al-Ḥarīrī … restricts the scope of the *Sessions* and, neglecting depth, puts all his effort into form." See also Kilito, "Contribution à l'étude de l'écriture 'littéraire' classique: l'exemple de Hariri," 36.

44 Drory, "The Maqama," 190–202 *passim.*

45 *The Mediaeval Islamic Underworld.* On the literary background to the *maqāma* see esp. 1: 96–103.

"also a caricature of the secretary-for-hire, crafting verbal art in myriad ways in order to fill his coffers with funds from less-than-discerning patrons."[46] Underlying the parody, then, is the phenomenon of the freelance secretary or *kātib* who, lacking a regular position, was compelled to search repeatedly for patronage, offering his well-crafted *saj*ʿ (a medium characteristic of the secretarial class) as a commodity in exchange for cash and other emoluments, despite its actual lack of monetary value. From evidence in al-Hamadhānī's collected *Letters*, Stewart infers that the renowned author, active in eastern Iran, found himself in precisely such a predicament.[47]

Scholars have also discerned parodies of Islamic religious literature in al-Hamadhānī's *Maqāmāt*. Many of his episodes open with the set phrase, "ʿIsā ibn Hishām related to us/me …," where the verb of transmission (*ḥaddathanā*; "he reported to us") together with the name of the transmitter, and followed by the text (*matn*) they introduce, are highly reminiscent of the traditional structure of the *ḥadīth* literature with its chain of reliable authorities (*isnād*) authenticating a report of the exemplary sayings and deeds of the Prophet. But, as James Monroe points out, al-Hamadhānī's single-transmitter *isnāds* are—by both Sunnī and Shīʿī criteria—inherently defective, signaling the author's intention to pastiche the *ḥadīth*.[48] *Isnāds* also figure in the short historical or anecdotal narratives known as *akhbār* (sing. *khabar*) and in *adab* literature, especially of a didactic bent, although in such texts the chain of transmission was not necessarily held to standards as rigorous as those applied in *ḥadīth*.[49]

---

46 Stewart, "Professional Literary Mendicancy in the *Letters* and *Maqāmāt* of Badīʿ al-Zamān al-Hamadhānī," 39. On the role of state secretaries as the originators of Arabic artistic prose, see also Schoeler, *The Genesis of Literature in Islam*, 56–60. For the technical skills of the ideal secretary see Bosworth, "A *Maqāma* on Secretaryship."

47 See Stewart, "Professional Literary Mendicancy" and Richards, "The *Rasāʾil* of Badīʿ al-Zamān al-Hamadhānī." On Hamadhānī's far-flung network of patrons, see Rowson, "Religion and Politics in the Career of Badīʿ al-Zamān al-Hamadhānī." Note that Shawkat Toorawa makes a compelling case for the emergence already in the ninth century of a new kind of *adīb* who was unwilling to be tied too closely to patrons; see his "Defining *Adab* by (Re)defining the Adīb: Ibn Abī Ṭāhir Ṭayfūr and Storytelling," and idem, *Ibn Abī Ṭāhir Ṭayfūr and Arabic Writerly Culture: A Ninth-Century Bookman in Baghdad.*

48 See: Stewart, "The Maqāma," 149–150; idem, "Of Rhetoric, Reason, and Revelation: Ibn al-Jawzī's Maqāmāt as an Anti-Parody and Sefer Taḥkemoni of Yehudah al-Ḥarīzī"; Monroe, *The Art of Badīʿ az-Zamān al-Hamadhānī as Picaresque Narrative*, 19–38; Kilito, "Le Genre Séance," 38–44; and idem, *Les Séances*, 127. For a critique of Monroe's contention see Hämeen-Antilla, *Maqama*, 46–48. Kennedy notes that in addition to *ḥadīth*, the *maqāma* parodies "romance, theological discourse, and in certain instances the mythic tales of Shiʿi Imamic hagiography"; see "Islamic Recognitions: An Overview," 40; on this see also Stewart, "ʿĪsā b. Hišām's Shiism and Religious Polemic."

49 See: Kilpatrick, "The 'Genuine' Ashʿab: The Relativity of Fact and Fiction in Early *Adab*

The "counter-genre" aspect also comes across in explanations offered for the term *maqāma*, translated variously as "assemblies" or "sessions," or in French as "séances." A.F.L. Beeston suggested that al-Hamadhānī called his collection of rhymed tales *Maqāmāt*, or "Standings" (from the root *q-w-m*, "to rise, to stand") to distinguish his new, fictional and narrative use of *sajʿ* from the anecdotes in plain prose that had generally been told in *majālis* or sessions "where both narrator and audience were seated." In early Islam, *sajʿ* was the medium of the *khuṭba* (religious homily or sermon), which was delivered by an orator or *khāṭib* whose traditional posture was standing. Hamadhānī's originality lay in part in his adoption of *sajʿ* as the vehicle for his entire narrative composition. By calling his anecdotes *maqāmāt*, he may also have been signaling his innovative use of the linguistic mode characteristic of the "standing" *khāṭib*.[50] Stewart, too, sees the origin of the term as "an ironic inversion of the term *majlis*, literally 'sitting, session, seated assembly.'" Refining the notion of a "counter-genre" to the *ḥadīth*, he sees the *maqāmāt* as a parody of the *ḥadīth*-lecture or *majlis*. *Ḥadīth-majālis* were

> lectures held at regular intervals involving a framed narrative. Like the *maqāmāt*, they appeared in collections of texts each beginning with the phrase *ḥaddathanā*, mentioning the narrator(s) and often including a reference to the specific time and place the lecture was held.[51]

Donald Richards, however, cautions that it may be a mistake to look for one unequivocal meaning for the term, as it has many resonances, starting with "the basic notion of a 'standing forth' and from there it can cover the place, the people, the discourses associated with certain gatherings." Richards notes that for Hamadhānī

Texts"; Bray, "Isnāds and Models of Heroes"; Leder, "Authorship and Transmission in Unauthored Literature"; and Beaumont, "Hard-Boiled: Narrative Discourse in Early Muslim Traditions."

50 See Beeston, "Al-Hamadhānī, al-Ḥarīrī, and the *Maqāmāt* Genre," 127 and idem, "The Genesis of the *Maqāmāt* Genre," 8–9. Daniel Beaumont also links the term to the homily (*maqām*/ *maqāma*); see "The Trickster and Rhetoric in the Maqāmāt," 4–5.

51 Stewart, "The Maqāma," 149 and idem, "Of Rhetoric, Reason, and Revelation." On the broad semantic field of the term *majlis* and the role of *majālis* in Islamic society, see Madelung, "Madjlis," esp. sec. 1: "in Social and Cultural Life." See also Kraemer, *Humanism in the Renaissance of Islam*, 55–60 and *passim*; Orfali, *The Anthologist's Art*, 186–187; Lazarus-Yafeh et al. eds., *The Majlis*; and Brookshaw, "Palaces, Pavilions and Pleasure Gardens: The Context and Setting of the Medieval Majlis."

> a *maqāma* of al-Iskandarī [the rogue-hero] could be his typical 'standing' to deliver one of his hypocritical homilies (itself a *maqām* or *maqāma*), or his 'exploit,' used ironically of one of his typical *kudya* ruses.[52]

Drory has highlighted some of the distinctions between the *Maqāmāt* of al-Hamadhānī and al-Ḥarīrī. She has stressed the public, improvised, and oral aspects of al-Hamadhānī's *maqāmāt*, noting that al-Hamadhānī "apparently did not trouble to arrange for an authorized collection." A century later, however, al-Ḥarīrī was operating with a different notion of 'text,' even though he openly modeled his *Maqāmāt* on those of al-Hamadhānī. Al-Ḥarīrī "composed his [texts] privately, in writing, and presented them in an authorized version of fifty pieces."[53] Unlike al-Hamadhānī, he regarded the work as finalized and therefore inalterable.[54] The language of al-Ḥarīrī's *Maqāmāt* is also more florid, ornate, and recherché than that of al-Hamadhānī's texts.[55] These difficulties gave rise, early on, to numerous commentaries that were transmitted together with the text of al-Ḥarīrī's *Maqāmāt* in written form. (Kilito deems it "perhaps the most explicated Arabic work after the Qur'ān.")[56] The most celebrated of the roughly twenty commentaries is that of al-Sharīshī (d. 1222), *Sharḥ maqāmāt al-ḥarīrī al-baṣrī*, written in Spain. There is no analogue to this phenomenon in the Hebrew *maqāma* literature.[57] Al-Ḥarīrī's fifty episodes became the paradigmatic number associated with the genre, although not all *maqā-*

---

52 Richards, "The *Maqāmāt* of al-Hamadhānī," 92. On the various meanings of the term, see also Brockelmann, "Maḳāma"; Blachère, "Étude sémantique sur le nom *maqāma*"; and Prendergast trans., *The Maqāmāt of Badīʿ al-Zamān al-Hamadhānī*, 11–14. On the relationship between the terms *maqām* (a pious exhortation) and *maqāma* see also Hämeen-Anttilla, "The Early Maqama."

53 Drory, "The Maqama," 191–192. On additions made to Hamadhānī's corpus for many centuries following his death, see Orfali and Pomerantz, *The Maqāmāt of Badīʿ al-Zamān al-Hamadhānī*, 29–51.

54 According to an anecdote cited by Yāqūt al-Rūmī (1179–1229), al-Ḥarīrī had authorized 700 copies of the text during his lifetime; see Drory, "The Maqama," 191 and Heinrichs, "Prosimetrical Genres in Classical Arabic," p. 262 and n. 22.

55 On the stylistic distinctions between the texts of al-Hamadhānī and al-Ḥarīrī, see Beeston, "Al-Hamadhānī, al-Ḥarīrī, and the *Maqāmāt* Genre," 132–133.

56 Kilito, *Arabs and the Art of Storytelling*, 134.

57 On the engagement with al-Ḥarīrī's text through commentary, see also Keegan, "Commentarial Acts and Hermeneutical Dramas"; idem, "Throwing the Reins to the Reader"; and idem, "Digressions in the Islamic Archive." On the presence of commentaries in the earliest mss. of al-Hamadhānī's *Maqāmāt*, see Orfali and Pomerantz, *The Maqāmāt of Badīʿ al-Zamān al-Hamadhānī*, 141–167.

māt composed by subsequent authors have survived in this number, nor do they necessarily conform to his model. Scholars have noted that the order and number of episodes in Hamadhānī's collection varies in the manuscripts that have come down to us; those numbering fifty may be due to Procrustean efforts to make Hamadhānī's oeuvre the same size as al-Ḥarīrī's.[58] Similarly, not all medieval Hebrew rhymed prose narratives hew closely to the precedents set by al-Ḥarīrī and Alḥarīzī. Dan Pagis laments the fact that modern scholarship developed

> a somewhat normative approach which judged various works by their proximity to the maqama proper, occasionally evaluating them as lesser ramifications of the pure genre and evolving a theory of flowering and decline in keeping with this principle.[59]

This tendency is not unknown in traditional scholarship on the Arabic *maqāma*, which has cast the century from al-Hamadhānī to al-Ḥarīrī as the genre's definitive period and has dismissed subsequent developments as deviations from the high-water mark. Even surveys that are not entirely dismissive of later developments still adduce the works of al-Hamadhānī and al-Ḥarīrī as the standard.[60] But more recent studies have shown the application of such a rigid distinction between "classical" and "post-classical"—the latter with its suggestion of "decadence" or decline—to be of limited utility.[61] A long-lived form, the *maqāma* underwent various adaptations in response to new literary environments as it spread across the Muslim world and down the centuries. In general, scholars have observed an expanded definition of the genre from

58 See Richards, "The *Maqāmāt* of al-Hamadhānī," 92–99. Prior to the 19th-century edition published by Muhammad Abduh, "the *Maqāmāt* of al-Hamadhānī was an open corpus that grew as a result of the influence of the larger collection of … al-Ḥarīrī"; see Orfali and Pomerantz "*Maqāmāt badīʿ al-zamān al-hamadhānī: al-naṣṣ wa'l-makhṭuṭāt wa'l-tārikh*"; idem, "Assembling an Author: On the Making of al-Hamadhānī's *Maqāmāt*"; and idem, *The Maqāmāt of Badīʿ al-Zamān al-Hamadhānī: Authorship, Texts, and Contexts*, 29–51. See also Cooperson, *Impostures*, p. 9.

59 See Pagis, "Variety in Medieval Rhymed Narratives," esp. 86–91. Drory cautions that the medievals themselves often did not distinguish between proper *maqāmāt* and other rhymed narratives; see "The Maqama," 199.

60 See, e.g., Brockelmann, "Maḳāma," and Hämeen-Anttila, *Maqama*, 339–346.

61 Thomas Bauer has argued forcefully for abandoning the unhelpful designation "post-classical" as applied to Arabic literature altogether, in light of its tendentious late 19th-century underpinnings. See his "In Search of 'Post-Classical Literature,'" esp. 157, and "Mamlūk Literature: Misunderstandings and New Approaches."

the Mamlūk and Ottoman periods, which includes works designated *risāla* (a rhymed prose epistle), *maqāma, munāẓara* or *mufākhara*; the latter are poetic contests debating the relative merits of two personified objects or concepts, such as rose versus narcissus or pen versus sword.[62] Recognizing the dynamism of Arabic literature, a fresh perspective has applauded the vibrancy of forms and subjects of these later texts, reflecting shifts in the larger Arabic literary culture and the changing expectations of audiences, which were now drawn from a much-broadened social base.[63] Maurice Pomerantz has embarked on a reassessment of Arabic *maqāmāt* from the 14th–16th centuries to show how, in incorporating elements of the popular epic, the Sinbad stories, and other well-loved genres, these later texts are indicative of the increasingly blurred lines, as well as the tensions, between popular and élite literature.[64] It is now recognized that holding up the *Maqāmāt* of al-Hamadhānī and al-Ḥarīrī as a "one size fits all" model fails to take adequate account of later texts exhibiting discontinuities with this paradigm since many of these works are still labeled *maqāmāt* and were considered such by their authors.

62 See Reinink and Vanstiphout eds., *Dispute Poems and Dialogues in the Ancient and Mediaeval Near East*; Alḥarizi, *Taḥkemoni*, ed. Yahalom-Katsumata: Day/Night (#33), Man/Woman (#34), Pen/Sword (#35), Stinginess/Generosity (#36), Sea/Land (#37); and Rand, *Studies in the Medieval Hebrew Tradition* etc., 34. See also: van Gelder, "The Conceit of Pen and Sword: On an Arabic Literary Debate"; idem, "Arabic Debates of Jest and Earnest"; Geries, *A Literary and Gastronomical Conceit*; Heinrichs, "Rose versus Narcissus"; Toorawa, *Ibn Abī Ṭāhir Ṭayfūr and Arabic Writerly Culture*, 87–101; Yosef Tobi, "Šālom (Sālim) al Šabazī's (17th-century) poem of the debate between coffee and qāt"; and Wagner, "The Debate Between Coffee and Qāt in Yemeni Literature."

63 On changes in Arabic literary culture in the Mamlūk period, see Hirschler, *The Written Word in the Medieval Arabic Lands*. On the expanded definition of the *maqāma* in later centuries see, e.g., Stewart, "The Maqama," 157–158 and Saitta, "Notices de manuscrits de *maqāmāt* yéménites de la période post-classique, 1ère partie," and idem, "Le genre séance au Yémen entre tradition et innovation." Typical of this trend is the Yemeni *maqāma* in the form of a debate between the two historic settlements of al-Rawḍah and Bīr al-ʿAzab (located just outside Ṣanaʿā) composed by ʿAbdallāh b. ʿAlī al-Wazīr in a mixture of colloquial and classical Arabic in 1711. A later takeoff of this boasting match by the *ḥumaynī* poet ʿAlī b. al-Ḥasan al-Khafanjī (d. 1766/1767) personifies the two villages as women; see Wagner, *Like Joseph in Beauty*, p. 53 and n. 83 and Macintosh-Smith trans., *City of Divine and Earthly Joys*, p. 13, n. 69.

64 See Pomerantz, "A *Maqāmah* on the Book Market of Cairo in the 8th/14th Century"; idem, "An Epic Hero in the *Maqāmāt*?"; idem, "The Play of Genre"; idem, "Tales from the Crypt: On Some Uncharted Voyages of Sindbad the Sailor"; and idem, "A Maqāma Collection by a Mamlūk Historian."

3 The Idea of Fiction in Medieval Arabic and Hebrew Literature

Well before the emergence of the *maqāma*, Arabic literature was populated by all kinds of short narratives and anecdotes, often presented with an *isnād* or chain of reliable transmitters intended to authenticate materials ostensibly handed down from earlier authorities. These included not only *ḥadīth* traditions about the sayings and actions of the Prophet and his Companions but also pious miracle tales; didactic animal fables of Eastern origin such as those of Ibn al-Muqaffaʿ's (d. 756) *Kalīla wa-dimna*; accounts of salvation compiled in the genre known as *al-Faraj baʿada al-shidda* (Relief After Adversity); and *Ḥadīth khurāfa* or wondrous, bizarre, and amusing stories popularized by *adab* anthologies.[65] At various junctures, theologians, philosophers, or literary critics raised scholarly objections to such stories on the grounds that they contravened basic religious beliefs or did not correspond to the "truth."[66] Stefan Leder notes that in pre-modern Arabic literature, fictional narration is embedded in "factual or allegedly factual, narration," and he explores whether these elements were "ever perceived, and admitted, as fiction in their original context."[67] Rina Drory has argued that, "having developed primarily out of religious motivations, classical Arabic prose is very much occupied with the 'truth' or 'falsehood' of its texts." All prose genres are therefore at pains to prove the veracity, and hence the legitimacy, of their texts by means of attribution to a reliable narrator and chain of transmitters and the incorporation of historical figures as personae and real place names as settings. According to Drory, these techniques are "designed to create the impression of 'actual' reality and to convince the reader of the historicity of [the] texts."[68] Though some scholars have taken issue with Drory's broad application of these criteria, the consensus in the wake of her seminal contributions is that "the bulk of narrative in medieval Arabic lit-

65 See: Fishbein and Montgomery ed. and trans. *Kalīlah and Dimnah: Fables of Virtue and Vice by Ibn al-Muqaffaʿ*; Keegan, "Before and after *Kalīla wa-Dimna*: An Introduction to the Special Issue on Animals, *Adab*, and Fictivity"; Latham, "Ibn al-Muqaffaʿ and Early ʿAbbasid Prose," 50–53; Bray ed. and trans., *Stories of Piety and Prayer: Deliverance Follows Adversity*; and Sadan, "An Admirable and Ridiculous Hero: Some Notes on the Bedouin in Medieval Arabic Belles Lettres."

66 On the various types of anecdotage antecedent to the *maqāma* and objections to them, see: Bonebakker, "Some Medieval Views on Fantastic Stories"; idem, "Nihil obstat in Storytelling?"; Drory, *Models and Contacts*, 37–47; and the introduction to Jayyusi, *Classical Arabic Stories*, 1–35.

67 Leder, "Conventions of Fictional Narration in Learned Literature," 34–35.

68 See Drory, *Models and Contacts*, 11–13 and 37–47.

erature claims to be a literature of fact," due to the development of a normative poetics that discouraged innovation.[69]

In medieval Arabic criticism, entertaining literature that lacked a serious edifying dimension was generally considered of lesser worth. Although there were fictive, sometimes fantastic narrative components embedded in texts classified as historiography, *adab*, or *ḥadīth*, and although fables of Indian, Persian, and Greek origin were translated into Arabic, Arabic literary theory did not conceive a rubric for imaginative fiction per se.[70] It is against this background of distrust of purely imaginative narrative that Drory discusses the introduction of fictionality into classical Arabic literature occasioned by the advent of the *maqāma*. She notes that in their prefaces, the authors of the first *maqāmāt* cautiously call attention to the poetic innovation of the new genre by claiming to have made several salient departures from previous poetic norms. These are: (a) "Creation from the heart," viz., the claim that their stories are completely invented (and not merely reworkings of existing anecdotes or poems); and (b) "Naming the hero and narrator," i.e., declaring that they themselves named their characters, "who otherwise never existed," viz., who were not historical figures. At the same time, the authors of the Arabic *maqāmāt* attempted to anchor their new genre in tradition to lend it legitimacy. This was done by relating the *maqāmāt* to established literary genres such as love poetry and fables, neither of which was obliged to convey reality despite their incorporation of realistic details. Nevertheless, these apologia did not go uncontested in certain quarters. A twelfth-century *Refutation of al-Ḥarīrī's Maqāmāt* took issue with the attempt to identify the fictionality of the *maqāma* with that of animal fables. This in turn prompted a supporter of al-Ḥarīrī to defend his *Maqāmāt* by inventing a biography for the hero, Abū Zayd al-Sarūjī, claiming that he was a historical figure whom the author had met in the Banū Ḥaram Mosque.[71]

---

69 Beaumont, "A Mighty and Never Ending Affair," 139. For reservations regarding Drory's claims, see Kilpatrick, "The 'Genuine' Ashʿab: The Relativity of Fact and Fiction in Early *Adab* Texts."

70 See Rosenthal, "Literature" and Leder, "Conventions of Fictional Narration in Learned Literature." See also Bonebakker, "Some Medieval Views on Fantastic Stories," p. 24 and n. 12, endorsing Wolfhart Heinrichs' conclusion that "Islam is not sympathetic to fiction." And cf. Boyarin, "Placing Reading: Ancient Israel and Medieval Europe," 28–30.

71 See: Drory, *Models and Contacts*, 14–33; Beeston, "The Genesis of the *Maqāmāt* Genre"; idem, "Al-Hamadhānī, al-Ḥarīrī, and the *Maqāmāt* Genre"; and Beaumont, "The Trickster and Rhetoric in the Maqāmāt." Donald Richards notes that al-Hamadhānī's narrator, ʿIsā ibn Hishām, bears the same name as a Ḥadīth scholar who had taught Hamadhānī in his hometown, but perhaps this should be viewed as a pseudo-historical name. See Richards,

Drory draws a subtle but essential distinction between the conceptualization of fiction in the Hebrew *maqāmāt* and in the Arabic works on which they are modeled. By openly proclaiming their fictional nature, the Arabic *maqāmāt* were contravening the literary norm of "faithfully reporting on reality." But in Jewish literary tradition it was customary to relate actual occurrences to a stock of canonical paradigms; to conceal historical realities "behind ancient vocabulary with nonspecific denotations." One instance of this tendency was the assimilation of historical events to familiar, generic biblical tropes in medieval Hebrew poetry. Thus, the challenge for the authors of Hebrew rhymed prose narratives lay precisely in representing reality in a fictional text. When Arabic *maqāma* authors declared in their prefaces that they had named their protagonists, who had otherwise never existed, they were declaring that they had "employed invented, fictional—rather than historical, real—characters." The authors of Hebrew *maqāma* collections took this assertion as "an indispensable part of the *maqāma* model" and regularly reproduced it in their prefaces, apparently without appreciating its original significance. According to Drory, the Arabic authors

> are not denying that their fiction is founded on plausible representation of reality. But when Hebrew writers make the same statements, they are firmly asserting not only that the stories are false, but that they are not even plausible. Numerous variations on the Talmudic saying "[It] never was and never happened, but is only a parable" (bBaba Batra 15a) recur in Hebrew rhymed narratives in order to remind the audience that the stories are imaginary events illustrating a moral or spiritual lesson, not actual reality.

Drory also maintains that Hebrew authors misconstrued the convention of the "naming-of-the-hero declaration as a … device for disguising the identity of the real author." She argues that they understood the fictional hero "as a disguised appearance of themselves in the text, not of some plausibly existing person, as was the case in the Arabic *maqāmāt*." These opposing conceptions of fiction stem, in Drory's view, from differing mental habits and textual tools for the representation of reality in written texts.[72]

"The *Maqāmāt* of al-Hamadhānī." On this see Stewart, "ʿĪsā b. Hišām's Shiism," pp. 7 and 23.

72 See Drory, "The Maqama," 199–205 and idem, *Models and Contacts*, 11–33. A similar distinction is drawn between the status of fiction in the Western European and Hispano-Hebrew

4 *Sefer hamusar*: Structure, Texts, and Paratexts

4.1 *Overall Structure*

Even though it was written in installments, and portions of the work may well have circulated before the collection was finalized, *Sefer hamusar* was clearly conceived as a complete ensemble of *maqāmāt*, collected and organized by the author himself (as he tells us in his Introduction) rather than by a later redactor. That it comprises forty-five episodes is likely on analogy with the fifty of Alḥarizi and al-Ḥarīrī, Alḍāhirī's two acknowledged models. The first ten chapters alone showcase the work's impressively broad range and kaleidoscopic variety of settings, literary subgenres, and narrative devices. Set in Damascus, Ṣanaʿā, Irbīl, Baghdad, Safed, Cairo, Cochin, and Hormuz, they feature travel frames, riddle poems (#1), pious laments (#2), kabbalistic verse (#3), elaborate folk tales (#4, #10), animal fables (#5), a philosophical disquisition (#6), and Muslim-Jewish polemics (#7), not to mention Alḍāhirī's version of a medieval misogynist set-piece involving a duped bridegroom and his rebuffed bride (#8), and an outlandish story of one-upmanship between confidence men of three different faiths (#9). Structurally, the narrator's appearance at the opening of each chapter and his inevitable encounter with the hero produce a predictable pattern that binds the otherwise self-contained episodes together. Apart from that, it is often difficult to discern any continuity between the settings, plots, or narratives of contiguous chapters. The protagonists' movements from one *maqāma's* locale to the next are not determined by any immediate geographic proximity, nor does there seem to be any sequence—chronological or otherwise—to the tales as they unfold. Arguably, the work's unconcern with narrative continuity and its meandering, seemingly random progression on the levels of plot and geography correspond to the rogue-hero's vagabondage and elision of borderlines on various planes, and may be related to the residue of episodic oral narratives in the *maqāma* genre. As in trickster tales of various cultures,

> the trickster's effacing of spatial, temporal and social boundaries is embedded in the very structure of the narrative that violates commonly held parameters such as unity of time, place, and action or plot.[73]

---

literary traditions in Huss, "The Status of Fiction in the Hebrew *Maqama*: Judah Alḥarizi and Immanuel of Rome."

73 Babcock-Abraham, "'A Tolerated Margin of Mess,'" 166–167 and *passim*.

In a few instances, Alḍāhirī reprises a setting or story line—as in Chapters 22 and 35, both involving a study group on the Mount of Olives, or the story of Rabbi Abraham Ashkenazi told with variations in Chapters 24, 25, and 40—but it is difficult to know whether the overlap is intentional or simply due to imperfect editing and hasty assemblage resulting from working fragmentarily. Certainly, *Sefer hamusar* is not unique in this regard: the *maqāma* typically does not display much deliberate internal ordering of its autonomous chapters, and the connective tissue often seems missing. In theory, the reappearance of settings or story lines, or even phrases or objects, may afford the audience the pleasure of recognition when they recur in more than one episode.[74]

And yet, there are periodic hints that Alḍāhirī arranged some of his *maqāmāt* in a specific order. Closer inspection reveals some subtle correspondences between discrete episodes, which suggest a degree of structuring beyond the level of the individual *maqāma*.[75] The unspoken pairing of the contents and functions of the Author's Introduction and final episode (#45), which bookend the work, yields an overarching sense of ordering. Alḍāhirī's Introduction provides a point of entry into the text, setting out its title, genre, contents, and purpose, and introducing his invented characters as the conduit for his narrative: imaginary figures who resemble him in certain ways, yet are, crucially, distinct from him. This complex three-way relationship of author-narrator-hero surfaces for the final time in the forty-fifth *maqāma*, whose account of the protagonists' ultimate meeting concludes with the author stepping in to direct his fictional personae, as if to frame the entire narrative with the reassertion of his authorial prerogative. The episode provides closure to the work by celebrating Mordecai and Abner's lifetime accomplishments in anticipation of their deaths. But, tellingly, it also ascribes the titles of Alḍāhirī's own works to Mordecai and Abner so that it not only brings the cultivated ambiguity between authorial identity and invented personae to a climax but also takes us back full circle to the Author's Introduction where Alḍāhirī first claims to have narrated his tale by means of two men "who are strangers" to him.[76]

---

74 Cf. Pinault, *Story-Telling Techniques in the Arabian Nights*, 16–25.

75 Although nothing as formal as the highly regular internal structure detected in al-Ḥarīrī's *Maqāmāt*: "a number of editions establish at the outset that the work exhibits a discernible thematic and rhetorical structure, consisting of five series of ten episodes each, that the first episode in each cycle is exhortatory (*waʿẓiyyah*), the sixth literary (*adabiyyah*), the fifth and tenth whimsical (*hazliyyah*)." See Kilito's Foreword to Cooperson, *Impostures*, xiii, and *Arabs and the Art of Storytelling*, 136–137. Al-Ḥarīrī's "exhortatory" *maqāmāt* are #1, 11, 21, 28, 31, 41, and 50.

76 For a poignant analysis of al-Ḥarīrī's 50th and final episode, see Kilito's Foreword to Cooperson, *Impostures*, xiv–xv.

A more explicit link is established between Chapters 1 and 2 when the author intervenes in the narrative to manipulate the content and structure of the work. The first *maqāma* sees Mordecai traveling to Damascus, where Abner appears at his door in a bedraggled state, seeking overnight shelter from extremely inclement weather. When Mordecai demands an explanation for Abner's pathetic circumstances, Abner reveals that he was compelled to wander from his previous lodgings following an incident of severe overindulgence; the entire scenario is adapted from the fifteenth of al-Ḥarīrī's *Maqāmāt* ("The Legal").[77] Yehuda Ratzaby argues that the decision to begin the work with an identifiable borrowing from al-Ḥarīrī was tantamount to trumpeting the book's secular, non-Jewish sources of inspiration, a transgression for which Alḍāhirī felt obliged to make amends in the second chapter.[78] According to Ratzaby, this is why the author makes one of his rare appearances at the end of the first *maqāma* and reassures his audience that the next chapter will be about "our *galut*," by which he means the oppressive exile in Yemen. Set in Ṣanaʿā, the second *maqāma* laments this bleak and repressive state of affairs in no less than ninety-eight lines of doleful verse. Altogether, roughly a quarter of the episodes in *Sefer hamusar* are devoted to *galut teiman*, a focus that makes the work distinctively Yemenite. Ratzaby's theory makes certain assumptions—which may well be justified—about the piety of Alḍāhirī's imagined community of readers. But in Chapter 2, Mordecai looks back longingly to Chapter 1, when Abner was in Damascus, not yet beset by the anxiety of imprisonment, and Abner recites a poem in praise of his former tranquility.[79] This not only establishes a chronological sequence but also validates Chapter 1 on the level of the narrative. Moreover, a closer look reveals that Alḍāhirī does not really recant his deftly rendered Hebrew version of al-Ḥarīrī or its prominent placement as the entry point to the body of his work:

> Said the lowly Zechariah ben Seʿadyah: When I had completed the first *maḥberet*, and its proper *meliṣah* was pleasing to all, it occurred to me to mention our *galut* and how the crown has fallen from our head, using the medium of *meliṣah* which is like a budding vine whose blossoms have

77 See al-Ḥarīrī, *Assemblies* 1:185–193 and *al-Ḥarīrī: Maqāmāt Abī Zayd al-Sarūjī*, 69–74. For a detailed comparison with the first *maqāma* of *Sefer hamusar*, see Ratzaby, "The Influence of al-Ḥariri Upon Alḍāhiri," esp. 64–70.

78 See Ratzaby, "The Influence of al-Ḥariri Upon Alḍāhiri," 62. Ratzaby makes a similar claim in the Introduction to his edition, viz. that when Alḍāhirī sensed that certain chapters (e.g., #31) were excessively "secular," he concluded them with a sacred theme in order to rectify his transgression; see *Sefer hamusar*, p. 11, n. 12.

79 *Sefer hamusar*, p. 75, lines 235–240.

> come out, by means of the two men who are related to me in my thoughts, Abner ben Ḥeleq ha-teimani and Mordecai ha-ṣidoni.[80]

He assumes that the polished, elegant style (*meliṣah*) of the first *maḥberet* has wide appeal and that it is no less suitable for lamenting the sufferings of *galut teiman* than it is for rendering the Arabic riddle poems and story line of al-Ḥarīrī's fifteenth *maqāma*. Alḍāhirī does not identify al-Ḥarīrī as the source of his own first chapter, but he does say that in the second he will depict *galut teiman*—a historical condition—by means of his two principal characters, who are notional and imaginary. So, in the interstices between the first two chapters of his book, Alḍāhirī as author has intervened to intimate the connections between them as well as to declare yet again the fictionality of his protagonists and to highlight the work's aesthetic form—in other words, to achieve metafictional aims. By inscribing himself into the narrative, however briefly, he disrupts its normal course and calls attention to its workings. But this type of artful linkage between episodes is rare; nowhere else in the book does the author interpose himself with a promise to re-orient the subject matter of the next *maqāma*.

There are also areas of overlap between Chapters 23 and 24, which are set in Tiberias. In both chapters, Abner officiates—to Mordecai's utter amazement—as *ḥazzan* in the synagogue attended by the patrician head of the Tiberias yeshivah. But they are by no means simple duplications: each of these chapters furnishes narrative threads that illuminate the other. In Chapter 23, Abner has become a kabbalistic adept who, as *ḥazzan*, recites a poem of his own devising that betrays an esoteric view of the Sabbath and intriguingly suggests some familiarity with Solomon Alqabeṣ' kabbalistic hymn "Lekha dodi," a product of the sixteenth-century mystical revival in Safed. When probed, Abner explains that he came to penetrate this mystical, esoteric body of knowledge through assiduous study of several classical kabbalistic texts and avers that "Kabbalah is what raises man from death to eternal life." In Chapter 24, there is not the slightest hint of kabbalistic doctrine; instead, Abner is revealed to be the author of a panegyric epistle to the sages of Tiberias, the likes of whose elegant language its recipients had never seen. This extraordinary missive had accompanied an unusually generous donation from the Ṣanaʿā community in response to a fundraising campaign for the upkeep of the Tiberias yeshivah. Not only do the intertwined narratives of these two chapters highlight different facets of

80 *Sefer hamusar*, p. 63, lines 108–111. Notoriously difficult to translate, the term *meliṣah* in medieval Hebrew writing denotes the stylistic ideal of elegant, rhetorically embellished, and flowery phrasing that interweaves biblical verse fragments, rare words, and word play.

Abner's activities and reception in Tiberias, but Chapters 24 and 25 also figure in the three-part overlapping account of Rabbi Abraham Ashkenazi's fundraising mission to Yemen on behalf of the Tiberians. Despite a complete absence of chronological sequence as the tales unfold, there are distinct imprints here of an editorial hand. One gets the impression that Alḍāhirī deliberately placed these episodes back to back in an attempt to tell a longer continuous story within his patchwork collection.

4.2 *Front Matter: The Structure of Alḍāhirī's Introduction*

There is an element of "streamlining" in Alḍāhirī's front matter, in that it does not include any dedication to would-be patrons, and most manuscripts do not contain a prefatory poem such as those that immediately precede the Introductions of Alḥarizi to the *Taḥkemoni*, Jacob ben Eleazar to *Sefer ha-meshalim*, and Isaac Ibn Sahula to *Meshal ha-qadmoni*.[81] The front matter in *Sefer hamusar* consists exclusively of the Author's Introduction and rhymed prose Table of Contents, both of which contextualize what follows. In structure and content, Alḍāhirī's Introduction broadly conforms to the well-established conventions of the Arabic *muqaddima* or *ṣadr*—a programmatic introduction prefaced to texts of various genres. Originating in the Hellenistic world, the *muqaddima* developed from the ninth century onwards into a literary subgenre that was adopted by Muslim, Jewish, and Christian authors in Islamic lands as a means of laying out the goals and basic principles of a work. Its classic form was characterized by a tripartite structure. This consisted of an opening invocation to God beginning with the *basmala* ("In the name of God, the Merciful, the Compassionate"), often followed by the *ḥamdala* ("Praise be to God, the Lord of the worlds"); a central section that addressed the purpose of the work and the reasons for its composition, its intended audience, its content and generic classification; and a closing section of additional praises.[82] (Naturally, Judeo-Arabic prefaces substituted suitable equivalents for the Qur'ānic *bas-*

81 In the Sassoon ms., the citation of Prov. 8:33 is immediately followed by a brief prefatory poem (likely a scribal addition) announcing that all who read the work will learn *musar* and that in order to appreciate this *musar* properly, one must supplicate God for understanding; see Sassoon, *Ohel Dawid* 2:1021 and IMHM #F 9589, p. 7. See also Kozodoy, "Prefatory Verse and the Reception of the Guide of the Perplexed"; Mondschein, "*ʿIyyunim baḥaruzot ha-petiḥah shel R. Avraham ibn Ezra le-ferusho ha'arokh le-sefer Shemot*"; and Schmelzer, "Shirei petiḥah va-ḥatimah be-sefer 'yeḥusei tanna'im va'amora'im.'"

82 See Orfali, "The Art of the *Muqaddima* in the Works of Abū Manṣūr al-Thaʿalibī (d. 429/1039)"; Frank, *Search Scripture Well*, pp. 8, n. 30; 149; and 252–254; Harvey, "Maimonides and the Art of Writing Introductions"; idem, "The Author's Introduction as a Key to Understanding Trends in Islamic Philosophy"; Freimark, *Das Vorwort als literarische Form in der*

mala and *ḥamdala*.) The sub-genre was naturalized within the Jewish literary canon by Saʿadya Gaon (882–942), who prefaced his many Bible commentaries with Introductions structured on this model. The programmatic introduction was also adopted by tenth-century Karaite authors and later Andalusian Jewish scholars. Provençal and Southern European Jewish authors from the thirteenth century on drew increasingly on the Latin tradition of the prologue, or *accessus ad auctores*, modeled on the Aristotelian prologue.[83]

Alḍāhirī's Introduction parallels the *muqaddima* or *ṣadr* in its effectively tripartite division, as well as in the types of questions it addresses. Praise and the acknowledgment of human subservience to God figure prominently in its opening lines, not only by means of Alḍāhirī's citation of Psalm 119:91 but also through his use of the roots *y.d.h.* (*hodot el, le-hodot lo*, 'to praise' or 'to give thanks') and *h.l.l.* (*ahalelennu*).[84] What is striking is that Alḍāhirī characterizes the Divine in Aristotelian terms ("Having praised the First Cause and Supernal Thought ....") in a preface that otherwise adheres to a traditional idiom, familiar from scripture and the liturgy. But this is the very phrase with which Immanuel of Rome—one of Alḍāhirī's unnamed sources—opens the Introduction to his *Maḥbarot*, and it seems likely that he encountered it there. Though perhaps not typical of belletristic texts, Alḍāhirī's opening acclaim for "the blessed God who creates His world *ex nihilo*" can be traced back to much earlier Judeo-Arabic introductions to speculative works.[85] Consistent with the closing conventions of Arabic prefatory writing, Alḍāhirī also ends with praise for God, forming an *inclusio* by repeating the allusion to Psalm 109:30 ("in the midst of the congregation I will exalt Him") that he had used in his opening lines.[86]

---

arabischen Literatur, 22–68 *passim*; and Almbladh, "The 'Basmala' in Medieval Letters in Arabic Written by Jews and Christians."

83 See Lawee, "Introducing Scripture: The *Accessus ad auctores* in Hebrew Exegetical Literature from the Thirteenth through the Fifteenth Centuries" and Sirat, "Biblical Commentaries and Christian Influence: The Case of Gersonides."

84 As noted earlier, the opening invocation of Psalm 119:91 also provides a pious justification for the sufferings Alḍāhirī is about to recount.

85 It is found, inter alia, in a Geniza fragment of the Arabic introduction to the *Book of Questions on the Unity of God* (*Masāʾil fī ʾl-tawḥīd*) by Dāwūd al-Muqammaṣ, a speculative theologian of the ninth century who had studied with Christian scholars and may have been one of the first Jewish authors to write introductions; see Adler and Broydé, "An Ancient Bookseller's Catalogue," 60–61, cited in Frank, *Search Scripture Well*, p. 252, n. 20.

86 The inclusio is formed by Alḍāhirī's chiastic use of the phrases *ahallelennu ve-tokh qahal vaʿedah* and *u-ve-tokh qahal vaʿedah ahallelennu* (Heb. lines 5 and 44), which echo (or paraphrase from memory) the second half of Ps. 109:30, *odeh adonay be-fi/ uve-tokh rabbim ahallelennu* ("My mouth shall sing much praise to the Lord; I will acclaim Him in the midst of a throng").

Corresponding to the central portion of the programmatic introduction are Alḍāhirī's remarks on the purpose of the work and the reasons for its composition, its title, contents, language, and style. There are also expressions of authorial modesty ("Said the lowly Zechariah ben Seʿadyah ben Yaʿaqov Alḍāhirī," "... meager gleanings ... I am not a man of words ..."), another topos of Arabic prefatory writing.[87] Though he does so obliquely, he effectively classifies the genre of his work by saying (in rhythmical rhymed prose) that he divided the book into *maḥbarot* and by explicitly identifying Alḥarizi and al-Ḥarīrī as his literary models. These remarks also imply that Alḍāhirī envisaged his *maqāma* as an integral whole and organized it himself, which would seem to align with the method of textual production adopted by Alḥarizi and al-Ḥarīrī.[88] (Immanuel's preface contains deliberately contradictory statements about the authorship of the *Maḥbarot*, one of which is that his *Maḥbarot* were not conceived as a self-contained book at all, but were rather pieced together from preexisting poems and stories written over an extended period.[89]) Alḍāhirī's comments regarding the nature and goals of the book make it clear that he is not only working with the formal elements of the Arabic preface but also with *topoi* specifically associated with the Author's Introduction to the Hebrew *maqāma* (i.e., the desire to rehabilitate the Sacred Tongue; the tinge of ambivalence regarding al-Ḥarīrī's expressive brilliance in Arabic; the caveat that his protagonists are fictional; and the catalogue of literary forms and themes employed in his work). That being said, his preface differs markedly from those of Alḥarizi and Immanuel in explaining the inception of his book. Where Alḥarizi engages in grand, quasi-prophetic allegories out of zealousness for the Hebrew language, and Immanuel deploys artful literary stratagems and is consumed by the thought of others plagiarizing his poems, Alḍāhirī's stated point of departure is a desire to chronicle the abysmal misfortunes confronting his people. Presumably, the dissimilarities can be ascribed to the authors' distinct cultural and historical contexts as much as to differences in individual temperament.

87 See Orfali, "The Art of the *Muqaddima*," 183.

88 Unlike these two predecessors, however, Alḍāhirī does not specify the number of *maqāmāt* in his work; cf. Rand, *Evolution*, p. 42.

89 Immanuel contrasts this with Alḥarizi's intention to write a book from the outset, for which purpose he then composed poems. See Immanuel Ha-romi, *Maḥbarot*, p. 5, lines 40–45. On the contradictions in Immanuel's preface, see Huss, "The Status of Fiction in the Hebrew *Maqama*"; Rand, *Studies in the Medieval Hebrew Tradition* etc., 50–55, who notes that this is a disingenuous claim intended to highlight Immanuel's superiority to Alḥarizi; and Bregman, *The Golden Way*, 64, who notes that Dante makes a similar claim. On Immanuel's ambivalences vis-á-vis Alḥarizi and the Spanish Hebrew poets, see Kfir, *A Matter of Geography*, 123–139.

Alḍāhirī's foregrounding of communal trauma also sets his Introduction apart from al-Ḥarīrī's. If al-Ḥarīrī expresses any angst, it grows out of a concern that his *Maqāmāt* are "tainted by the sordidness of the events they describe;" he has no need to mourn the persecution of his people.[90] Alḍāhirī too would seem to have moral qualms about the impious behavior typically depicted in the picaresque *maqāma*. But in adapting this literary form from the dominant Islamic culture, he adds a layer of Jewish diasporic consciousness that goes beyond "linguistic nationalism" and that is, as one would expect, completely absent from his Muslim Arabic paradigm. He uses all the conventions of the *maqāma* form—prosodic, structural, narrative, rhetorical, spatial—to recount, record, and mourn the lingering trauma of the maltreatment to which his politically vulnerable and religiously marginalized community has been subjected, and to offer them hope, moral fortitude, and distraction in the face of their adversity.

4.3 *Alḍāhirī's Introduction as Paratext*

The term 'paratext,' coined in 1981 by the French literary critic Gérard Genette, refers to the ancillary material accompanying a published text that helps to introduce the text to the reader.[91] Genette identified as paratexts the title page, title, author's name, dedication, preface, illustrations, and blurbs that mediate between text and reader and thereby shape a book to present it in a certain light. Though his focus was on modern printed books, the notion of paratext has proven useful in exploring the interpretation and reception of pre-modern texts.[92] Alḍāhirī's Author's Introduction conveys not only the title, genre, and impetus for writing *Sefer hamusar* but viewed as a paratext it also reveals how he wished his audience to receive his work. The book's title and content allow for a multivalent interpretation, but in his Introduction, Alḍāhirī explicitly endorses only the pious, didactic reading. Even the language of the Introduction subtly reveals something of Alḍāhirī's intentions. In and of itself, elevated rhymed prose thick with biblical allusion is conventional and utterly unremarkable in a medieval Hebrew belletristic text. But Alḍāhirī's Introduction is particularly dense with interwoven verse fragments from Job, Lamentations, and

90 See Cooperson, *Impostures*, 6.

91 See Genette, *Palimpsestes*, 9 and idem, *Paratexts: Thresholds of Interpretation*. For critiques see Smith and Wilson, *Renaissance Paratexts*, "Introduction," 1–14.

92 There is quite an extensive literature on pre-modern paratexts; for a sampling, see Hollander et al., *Paratext and Megatext as Channels of Jewish and Christian Traditions*; Smith and Wilson, *Renaissance Paratexts*; Bös and Peikola, "Framing Framing: The Multifaceted Phenomena of Paratext, Metadiscourse and Framing"; and Palmer, "Paratextual Readers: Manuscript Verse in Printed Books of the Long Eighteenth Century."

Psalms. This scriptural diction and imagery, evocative of destruction and exile, inexplicable affliction and questions of theodicy, allows him to assimilate the persecution and forbearance of his people to familiar biblical tropes, thereby suggesting that they are part of a long cycle of suffering but also of redemption. Even the dates of the persecutions are cast according to these themes. Not only does Alḍāhirī single out the first of the mournful month of Av, but he also produces a chronogram using the opening interrogative of Psalm 77:10, *ha-shakhaḥ* (Has God forgotten?), the numerical value of whose letters add up to 5328 (1567/68 C.E.), and the substance of which he reads as a prognostication of the troubles in his own day. In light of the ambiguity at the heart of Alḍāhirī's enterprise, these allusions further serve to frame the work as a "Book of Moral Instruction," lending that reading of the title greater weight than the more irreverent and amusing "Book of Belles Lettres." Of course, it is difficult to gauge the effect these efforts would have had on the work's audience unless they had left behind annotations or a separate account of their reactions. A late example of an intervention made in the name of propriety is provided in the margins of the 18th-century Oxford Bodleian manuscript of *Sefer hamusar*. The anonymous Yemenite scribe who copied this manuscript was discomfited by the self-promoting line with which Alḍāhirī closed an Andalusian-style poem of friendship in Chapter 37. Despite its conventionality in the earlier Hispano-Hebrew poetry Alḍāhirī was emulating, such hyperbolic self-aggrandizement struck this reader of the post-Shabbazian era as distasteful and out of place. To protect Alḍāhirī's reputation, the scribe added a marginal note in which he claimed that he himself had added the two final verses of the poem in praise of *ha-rav ha-meḥabber*, "for such is fitting for a man of his stature, may his memory be blessed."[93] For this scribe, the margins of the manuscript were a site not just for glossing terms or filling in missing words but also for addressing the reader directly and managing the author's image, even if it effectively meant telling a white lie.[94]

4.4 *Alḍāhirī's Rhymed Prose Table of Contents*

In Arabic *maqāma* collections, the independent nature of each chapter is reflected in the convention of naming individual *maqāmāt* either after their contents ("The Lion," "The Amulet,") or geographical setting ("Of Alexandria,"

93 Oxford Bodleian ms. Opp. Add. 8° 31, f. 156ʳ.

94 Ratzaby points out that, ironically, the two verses are of a piece with the rest of the poem so that there is no reason to suspect that they are a later addition. Their originality is also confirmed by their attestation in other mss. of the work, including the Sassoon ms., which is the earliest. See *Sefer hamusar*, p. 11, n. 13.

"Of Mecca"). Al-Hamadhānī gave his *maqāmāt* titles, and though al-Ḥarīrī originally numbered his, they eventually acquired titles as well.[95] Likewise, Alḥarizi gave each *maqāma* in his *Taḥkemoni* a number and a title.[96] While the textual history of the *Taḥkemoni* is quite complicated, one of the two main recensions of the work produced by Alḥarizi himself includes an Arabic rhymed prose Introduction with a Table of Contents that not only assigns each *maqāma* its title and sequential number but also describes its subject matter in an Arabic rhyming couplet.[97] Unlike the *Taḥkemoni*, *Sefer hamusar* does not feature chapter titles, but it does include a Hebrew Table of Contents that provides each discrete episode with a rhymed prose synopsis in keeping with the stylistic medium of the work as a whole. Its physical placement between the Author's Introduction and the text of the first *maqāma* lends the Table of Contents a mediating ("threshhold") function, introducing the reader to the work's topics and settings, twists and turns. Proceeding chapter by chapter, it summarizes each episode in pairs of rhymed phrases, each of which begins with the somewhat prosaic formula, *ha-maḥberet ha-x* (*ha-rishonah, ha-sheniyyah, etc.*) *kollelet* ... ("The first/second, etc. *maḥberet* includes ..."). Occasionally, the second half of the summary is similarly formulaic: *ve-sofah be-* ... ("and it ends with ..."). The wording of the opening formula is more or less a translation of Alḥarizi's Judeo-Arabic, which likely served as a model. (Though Alḥarizi seems the most likely candidate, it is also possible that Alḍāhirī's Table of Contents was partially inspired by indices in printed books that he or a later copyist may have seen.) The Table of Contents appears, with some variations, in most manuscripts of *Sefer hamusar*, including the former Sassoon 995, which is one of the earliest (17th century).[98] In those manuscripts with running headers, it is subsumed under the *"Haqdamah"* ("Introduction") or *"Haqdamat ha-meḥabber"* ("Author's Introduction"), or labeled *"Mafte'aḥ"* ("Index/Key").[99] In Ratzaby's

95 See Cooperson, *Impostures*, p. 10.

96 Abraham Lavi points out that in *Maḥberot Iti'el*, Alḥarizi "tended to hebraize Islamic place names, and the place is, therefore, not necessarily germane to the events occurring there." In that translation, Alḥarizi therefore called his *maḥbarot* "not by the name of the locality, but according to their subject matter." See Lavi, "A Comparative Study of al-Hariri's Maqamat and their Hebrew Translation by al-Harizi," p. 24.

97 See Rand, *Evolution*, p. 30 and n. 14 and pp. 44–47; for the text see Alḥarizi, *Taḥkemoni*, ed. Yahalom-Katsumata, 56–60.

98 It does not appear in NLI ms. Heb 8° 637, an incomplete ms. (18th–19th c. Yemenite script).

99 *"Haqdamah"*: BL Or 11337 and the former Sassoon 995; *"Haqdamat ha-meḥabber"*: JER NLI 8° 2080; *"Mafte'aḥ"*: Oxford Bodleian Opp. Add. 8° 31. On the placement of indices at the front, rather than the back, of early printed European books, and hence their role as a reader's primary port of entry into a book's contents, see Duncan, *Index, a History of the*, 125–127.

edition, it is headed "*Ve-zeh luaḥ ha-maḥbarot*" ("And this is the table of the *maḥbarot*"), which is how it appears in the former Sassoon 995 and the manuscript copied in Ṣanaʿā for Moshe Kehati in 1929.[100] Within fairly well-defined parameters, it seems to both expand and contract: in the British Library manscript (BL Or 11337; 19th-century Yemenite) the Table of Contents is lightly annotated with scribal marginalia in a different hand from the body of the text, while Kehati's 20th-century copy provides only the first half of each synopsis ("the xth *maḥberet* includes …") without their rhyming completions (apart from #45). It is not clear that the Table of Contents originated with Alḍāhirī himself; variations in both form and content suggest that at least some of these recensions were supplied or altered by later copyists. At whatever point in the text's history the Table of Contents was added though, it must then have been replicated repeatedly.[101] If it did not originate with Alḍāhirī but was added by a scribe or copyist, then it can be seen both as a reader's response to *Sefer hamusar* and as a paratext devised by the scribe to provide other readers with a distillation that could guide them into the work's abundance of topics and narratives.

As a gateway into the texts they introduce, the Hebrew digests in Ratzaby's edition and several of the manuscripts may strike one as providing an oblique account of a given *maqāma's* contents and seem to be more rhyme-driven than intent on providing a fully descriptive outline of each episode. Some are so nondescript as to give no inkling of the raucous carryings-on in a particular tale: "The eighth *maḥberet* includes the author's marriage in the land of Kush," or "The seventeenth *maḥberet* includes the tale of the ass and the Muslim judge …." Both of these episodes are laced with intrigue, deceit, cruelty and pathos, though one would never know from their anodyne descriptions, which may be due to missing cola or scribal attempts to sanitize them. Conversely, in other instances the précis alludes, without any trace of condemnation, to transgressive behavior masked by elegant rhetorical display: "The ninth *maḥberet* includes the exploits of the three partners, a Jew, a Christian, and a Muslim, with wonderful tricks and refined words." In chapters such as the first, the fourteenth, or the nineteeth, where Alḍāhirī adapts a storyline from al-Ḥarīrī or al-Hamadhānī, there is no mention of the fact, but there is often an indication when a chapter borrows an Arab folktale (#41, e.g.), and the authors of the Andalusian Hebrew poems to which Alḍāhirī composes contrafactions or responses (e.g., #17, 19, 22, 26, 31) are almost always named. Other summaries

100 Jerusalem ms. Heb. 8° 6748.

101 Of the mss. I have been able to consult, it appears in the following: BL Or 11337; Oxford Bodleian ms. Opp. Add. 8° 31; Jerusalem ms. Heb. 8° 6748; JER NLI 8° 2080; and the former Sassoon 995; on the latter see Sassoon, *Ohel Dawid* 2:1021.

explicitly identify the author as the chapter's protagonist. In some cases, this identification is so implausible that it would have to be the work of someone other than Alḍāhirī. As noted, in Ratzaby's edition, the highly conventionalized story of Abner's ill-fated nuptials in Cochin is presented as though it were an account of Alḍāhirī's own wedding: "The eighth *maḥberet* includes the author's marriage in the land of Kush." In this version, the second half of the rhyme is missing, but Ratzaby does not comment on this omission. He does provide a variant reading found in the Oxford manuscript: "The eighth *maḥberet* includes a marriage that befell the author, about which he speaks, and he was strengthened." Far more intriguing is the British Library manuscript, which Ratzaby did not consult. Here the synopsis of #8 is omitted from the body of the text altogether but is supplied in the margin by a different hand. It conveys the broad outlines of the plot quite faithfully and consists of two full rhyming couplets that identify Abner as the actor in the escapade:

> *Ha-maḥberet ha-ḥet ʿinyan massaʿ avner leʾereṣ hodu ve-kush medabberet/ ve-nisuʾav ʿim ishah zeqenah u-sheḥorah ve-hi mitnakeret/ veʿal yedei taḥbulat shigaʿon az nimlaṭ mimena/ ve-sofah shir she-shalaḥ eleha.*
>
> "The eighth *maḥberet* recounts Abner's journey to India and his marriage to an old, black and alienated [alienating?] woman. By feigning madness, he escapes from her. And it ends with a poem that he sends to her."[102]

Other occurrences of the author-protagonist conflation occur in the synopses of chapters long viewed by scholars as autobiographical: "The thirty-ninth *maḥberet* mentions retroactively the author's exile, return, and imprisonment, and how he regrets having left the Land of Israel ..."; "The forty-fifth *maḥberet* declaims a eulogy for [of?] the esteemed author, of blessed memory, for Mordecai the Sidonian and Abner ben Ḥeleq the Yemenite ...." Nevertheless, the wording of this last précis also suggests it was written or augmented by someone other than the author.[103] By contrast, the more serious content tends to be more accurately conveyed: "The second *maḥberet* includes lamentations and dirges, with supplications and wailing ..."; "The third *maḥberet* includes praise for the knowledge of kabbalah, for it is the goal of all praise ..."; "The thirtieth *maḥberet* includes poems on the exile ...." And there are periodic attempts to identify the moral virtue illustrated by a particular *maqāma* (e.g., visiting

102 BL Or 11337, f. 2^r. For an analysis of this rather disturbing *maqāma*, see Chapter Two.

103 Ratzaby nowhere comments on this possibility.

the sick in the fourth *maqāma*). The Table of Contents concludes with a citation of Proverbs 8:33 (*shimʿu musar va-ḥakhamu veʾal tifraʿu*; "Heed discipline and become wise; Do not spurn it").[104] Ratzaby comments that this verse, with its mention of *musar*, serves as a fitting epilogue to the Introduction. Placed immediately before Chapter One, this exhortation to upright behavior is effectively another paratextual effort that serves to present as a "Book of Moral Instruction" a work that begins rather irreverently. The unresolved creative tension between these two moral poles is a driving factor throughout the work and is encapsulated in the double meaning of its title.

4.5 *The Work's Title: Musar and Adab*

Like other paratexts, a book's title can shape one's expectations of its contents by eliciting associations with a long-standing tradition.[105] A reader unfamiliar with Alḍāhirī's *Sefer hamusar* might be forgiven for assuming that it is yet another in a long line of medieval Jewish works belonging to the genre of *sifrut ha-musar* (ethical literature), many of which bore the anodyne titles *Sefer hamusar, Iggeret musar* (Epistle of Moral Instruction), *Tokheḥot musar* (Ethical Exhortations) *or Shevet̩ musar* (Rod of Chastisement). By calling his book *Sefer hamusar*, Alḍāhirī clearly intended to summon up this venerable tradition of contemplative, often prescriptive, often philosophically informed ethical treatises or collections of wisdom literature by respected Iberian and Provençal Jewish scholars of the twelfth through fifteenth centuries and their North African and Eastern Mediterranean heirs.[106] Themes, motifs, and principles from this corpus offering ethical guidance and models for exemplary conduct made their way into other genres and formats as well. Though not as common, there were also poetic or literary works called *Sefer hamusar*: in his *maqāma* evaluating the Hebrew poets of al-Andalus (*Taḥkemoni* #3), Alḥarizi lavishes two couplets of praise on a dignitary of Judah Halevi's generation named Isḥaq Ibn Krispin, author of one *Sefer hamusar*, a book in which "all of the poems are

---

104 It is omitted in the Bodleian ms.

105 Cf. Shevlin, "To Reconcile Book and Title, and Make 'em Kin to One Another: The Evolution of the Title's Contractual Functions."

106 For a sampling see: Abraham Bar Ḥiyya, *Sefer hegyon ha-nefesh o sefer ha-musar*; Joseph Ibn Caspi, *Sefer ha-musar ha-niqra yoreh deʿah*; Joseph Ibn Aqnīn, *Sepher musar, Kommentar zum Mischnatraktat Aboth*; Habermann ed., "Rabbi Shem Tov Falaquera's *Iggeret ha-Musar*"; Samuel Benveniste, *Sheloshah sefarim niftaḥim: Sefer ha-musar, Sefer orekh yamim*; Solomon Alami, *Iggeret musar*; Ephraim ben Joab ben Moses of Modena, *Sefer hamusar*; and Judah Khalaṣ, *Sefer ha-musar, ʿesrim peraqim beʿinyenei ha-miṣvot ve-ha-tefilot, musar u-middot*.

delightful and wise."[107] In addition, Alḥarizi describes his own work as *maḥberot musar ḥamishim*, "fifty *maqāmāt* of moral instruction," at the beginning of his Hebrew prefatory poem to the *Taḥkemoni*.[108] It is also worth noting that *Sefer hamusar* was the alternate title of *Mishlei heʿarav* (Sayings of the Arabs), a thirteenth-century Hebrew ethical compilation of unknown authorship claiming to be a translation from Arabic, which consisted of fifty prose chapters interspersed with Andalusian-style poems.[109]

Early *maqāma* collections in Arabic and Hebrew were not necessarily given a single dedicated title. Michael Rand notes that neither al-Ḥarīrī's nor Alḥarizi's bears a proper title, though in the latter case, "this fact has become obscured by the popularity of the name *Taḥkemoni*" (from the root *ḥkm*, "to be wise"; cf. 2 Sam. 23:8), which seems to have become attached to the work only with the publication of the *editio princeps* in the late 16th century. In both his Hebrew and Arabic Introductions, Alḥarizi refers to his work simply as "this book" or "this dīwān," just as he refers to the work of al-Ḥarīrī as *sefer ha-yishmaʿeli(m)*; "the book of the Ishmaelite(s)."[110] Alḍāhirī too, refers to the *maqāma* collection of each of these two predecessors only as "his book." By contrast, he explicitly names his own book *Sefer hamusar*, which, despite its generic ring, deliberately underscores the idea of moral guidance that resurfaces at key intervals throughout the work. The ethical reading of the title which first appears in the Author's Introduction acquires additional weight in the final chapter when Abner eulogizes Mordecai as the author of *Sefer ha-musar ve-ha-ḥokhmah/ le-naʿar daʿat u-mezimah*, "The Book of Moral Instruction and Wisdom which offers the young knowledge and foresight." Here the allusion to Proverbs 1:2–4 draws an implicit parallel between Alḍāhirī's *maqāma* collection and that bib-

---

107 Alḥarizi, *Taḥkemoni*, ed. Yahalom-Katsumata, p. 113, lines 246–247: *U-migdoleihem ha-sar ha-tifsar/Rabbi Yiṣḥaq ben Krispin baʿal sefer ha-musar/ve-hu sefer kol shirav ḥashuqim/ veʿinyanav metuqim*. The text differs slightly in the published versions that antedate Yahalom and Katsumata's edition; see e.g., *Taḥkemoni*, ed. Toporowsky, p. 45: *U-meʾaṣilei sefarad hayyah ha-sar ha-gadol Rabbi Yiṣḥaq ben Krispin baʿal sefer ha-musar/ ve-hu sefer asher kol shirav ḥamudim/be-yad ha-sekhel ṣemudim/ve-hayu leʾaḥadim*; Steinschneider speculated that this was the same Yiṣḥaq who translated the ethical-sapiential *Mishlei ʿarav* from Arabic; see Fleischer in Schirmann, HPCS, p. 221 and Torollo, "Wisdom Literature in Judeo-Arabic."

108 See Rand, *Evolution*, p. 42. For the poem see Alḥarizi, *Taḥkemoni*, ed. Yahalom-Katsumata, p. 63, l. 7.

109 On the provenance and transmission history of *Mishlei heʿarav*, see Torollo, "Wisdom Literature in Judeo-Arabic," and idem ed., *Mishle he-ʿarav: la tradición sapiencial hebrea en la Península Ibérica y Provenza, s. XII y XIII.*

110 See Rand, *Evolution*, 42–43, who also notes that Immanuel of Rome refers to Alḥarizi's book generically.

lical wisdom book, perhaps again with the intention of legitimizing its more picaresque aspects. This is not to suggest, however, that Alḍāhirī is in any way disingenuous when he states his intention to provide ethical guidance. He invokes the lessons to be learned from the 1567/68 persecutions with great sincerity, just as he earnestly frames the work as a means of consoling his "sorrowful soul" and as "a praise offering before God." But there is at base a moral tension inherent in the very conception of the *maqāma*, going back to its classical Arabic prototypes, of which authors from the time of al-Ḥarīrī on were well aware, and which they sought to mitigate by comparing their works to animal fables or other types of edifying stories.

The complicated interplay between the claim that *maqāmāt* inculcate moral virtues and their equally fundamental impetus to entertain, often by depicting unscrupulous or transgressive behavior, is subtly encapsulated by the multivalence of the term *musar*, which became the medieval Hebrew equivalent of the Arabic *adab*. By choosing a title that could be understood in disparate ways, Alḍāhirī intimates the multiple aims but also the paradoxical dynamics and ambiguities of his *maqāma* collection. In biblical Hebrew, the term *musar* (derived from the root *y.s.r.*) signifies moral instruction, discipline, reproof, chastisement, or castigation. This sense is exemplified by the citation of Proverbs 8:33 just before Alḍāhirī's first *maqāma* and is more closely associated with Proverbs than any other biblical book. Alḍāhirī's explicit interpretation of his title in an ethical and didactic vein ("so that all who read it ... will learn a lesson") frames the book as a salutary and morally instructive work. This was a common concern among *maqāma* authors: as mentioned, al-Ḥarīrī had issued a prefatory apology for his *Maqāmāt*, in which he defensively insisted that the work did not contravene the Law or mislead, and compared its didactic potential to that of exempla or fables, in an effort to neutralize the morally indefensible, antinomian behavior of his protagonist.[111] But the biblical *musar* acquired a vastly extended semantic range when medieval translators from Saʿadya Gaon on rendered it as *adab* in Arabic, gradually giving the Hebrew term a broad signification that it did not originally possess. As the Hebrew equivalent of the Arabic *adab*, *musar* retained its biblical sense but also took on an entire array of cultural meanings derived from medieval Islamicate society. The term *adab* acquired multiple senses over time, making it difficult to define. Bilal Orfali has observed that modern attempts at defini-

111 For a refreshing take on al-Ḥarīrī's prefatory apology, see Kilito, *Les Séances*, 248–259 ("Le menteur professionel"). Drory argues that the authors of Arabic *maqāmāt* turned to animal fables as a way of legitimizing the fictionality of their own compositions; see *Models and Contacts*, 24–27.

tion nearly always exclude some aspect that medievals would have considered *adab*.[112] In light of the term's manifold meanings, Patricia Crone cautions that "it has to be explained before it can be translated." Hence,

> *adab* often refers to praiseworthy characteristics [social, moral, cognitive] instilled by education .... The word has several related meanings, as do the English terms 'culture' and 'literature' with which it mostly overlaps ....

With its emphasis on upright conduct, refined manners, and wide knowledge, *adab* most closely approximates the Greek *paideia*.[113] The basic early meaning of *adab* appears to have been "proper behavior or conduct," particularly in conformity with the norms of a given social group. But beyond that, *adab* came to designate both a curricular and a social ideal, for it then emphasized the study of disciplines deemed necessary for inculcating the proper behavior specific to a particular profession or class.[114]

Broadly speaking, by the tenth century, *adab* was the urbane, genteel, and literate culture of the *adīb*—the Abbāsid courtier or gentleman or professional secretary—who was expected to express himself felicitously and to have a general knowledge of a formidable array of disciplines rather than rigorous scholarly mastery of any one field. For courtiers and professional secretaries who relied on patronage from the political élite, *adab* education was focused on philologically based disciplines and belles-lettres as a means of achieving the elegant expression required for drawing up official correspondence and the refined manners necessary for success in courtly circles; what Shawkat

112 See Orfali, "A Sketch Map of Arabic Poetry Anthologies Up to the Fall of Baghdad." Orfali cites Wolfhart Heinrichs to the effect that, by the tenth century, the term *adab* had acquired three main significations: (1) good and correct behavior, (2) the genre referred to as "*adab* literature" in modern scholarship and which usually encompasses compilations of quotable sayings, and (3) the body of literary and linguistic knowledge presented by "*adab* disciplines."; see p. 29, n. 1. Regarding Joseph Sadan's discussion of the relationship between oral and written *adab*, see Orfali, ibid., p. 31.

113 See Crone and Moreh trans., *The Book of Strangers: Medieval Arabic Graffiti on the Theme of Nostalgia*, 168–176 and Khalidi, "Adab Hand at Work."

114 The literature on *adab* is vast; see, e.g. Heath, "Al-Jāḥiẓ, *Adab*, and the Art of the Essay"; Kilpatrick, "Adab"; Kraemer, *Humanism in the Renaissance of Islam*, 10–11; Sadan, "Adāb—règles de conduite, et ādāb—dictons, maximes, dans quelques ouvrages inédits d'al-Thaʿālibī"; Bonebakker, "Early Arabic Literature and the term *Adab*"; von Grunebaum, *Medieval Islam: A Study in Cultural Orientation*, 250–257; Gabrieli, "Adab"; and Pellat, "Variations sur le thème de l'adab." On storytelling as a component of *adab*, see Toorawa, "Defining *Adab* by (Re)defining the Adīb." See also Kilito, *Les Séances*, 71–74.

Toorawa has referred to as "writerly culture."[115] Accordingly, the *adab* curriculum centered on the study of poetry, artistic prose, grammar, lexicography, and rhetoric, though it might also take in the essentials of history, ethics, philosophy, and political theory, as well as astronomy and astrology.[116] Knowledge of these fields was essential to advancing one's standing in courtly and lettered circles, where competition for patronage was fierce and displays of eloquence and the ability to quote choice anecdotes and proverbs or aphorisms were the *sine qua non* of polite conversation and graceful writing. As Wolfhart Heinrichs notes, "the practice of *muḥāḍarah* (having the apposite quotation at one's fingertips) is an informing principle of *adab*."[117] In such an élite milieu, *adab* demanded adherence to courtly propriety and polite etiquette, and as such entailed moral virtues and ethical norms of comportment in addition to linguistic mastery, stylistic grace, and refined manners.[118] Over time, therefore, the term *adab* was applied not only to a set of social and cultural aspirations, and to the educational program required to achieve them, but also to the disciplines it was necessary to master. In a more restricted sense, *adab* came to refer to genres of literary creativity—epistles, anthologies, biographical writings, and perhaps most notably, poetry and artistic prose.[119] The impulse to anthologize was characteristic of *adab*, and along with producing such collections, *adab*

115 In his reevaluation of "the transition from a predominantly oral and aural literary culture to an increasingly textual, book-based, writerly one," Toorawa notes that "*adab*, in its meaning of 'writerly culture' ... developed *after* the arrival of paper, the rise of a scribal class, and the development of the notions that equated literacy and eloquence with refinement ...." He has argued that the accessibility of books in 9th-century Baghdad facilitated a certain autodidacticism in *adab* disciplines; see Toorawa, *Ibn Abī Ṭāhir Ṭayfūr and Arabic Writerly Culture*, 1, 9–10, and 123–129.

116 For practically-minded students of *adab*, the science of the stars held the key to the proper course of human behavior; see Safran, "Baḥya ibn Paquda's Attitude toward the Courtier Class," 162–165.

117 See Orfali, "A Sketch Map," 30–31. On the prominence of aphorisms in Arabic and Hebrew *adab* literature, see Ratzaby, "Adab Maxims in Medieval Literature" and Torollo, "Wisdom Literature in Judeo-Arabic."

118 As Crone notes, *adab* was used in both a descriptive and a prescriptive sense; the latter "predominates in well-known book titles such as *adab al-kātib* or *adab al-mulūk* or *adab al-wuzarā'*, where *adab* stands for the social, moral, or cognitive attributes to which secretaries, kings, or viziers should aspire"; see *The Book of Strangers*, p. 168. The latter category includes the genre known as Mirrors for Princes; the prescriptive sense was also used by Sufis in works known as *adab al-ṣūfīya*.

119 For this more restricted definition of the term see: Bonebakker, "*Adab* and the Concept of *Belles-Lettres*." On the generic classification of *adab* by medieval Arabic literary critics, see Arazi, "L'*adab*, les critiques et les genres littéraires dans la culture arabe médiévale."

authors regularly drew upon a reservoir of pre-existing texts—proverbs, anecdotes, poems, sermons, fables—in their own original compositions.[120] There was often a didactic aspect to works associated with the *adab* genre, many of which were marked by frequent digression and asides, eclecticism and changes of tone, in an attempt to sustain interest and instruct the reader through diversion. In Andalusian Jewish literature, these characteristics come to the fore in Moses Ibn Ezra's two major Judeo-Arabic prose works, one on poetics, *Kitāb al-muḥāḍarah wa'l-mudhākara* (The Book of Conversation and Discussion), and one on "the meaning of figurative and literal language" in the Bible, *Maqālat al-ḥadīqa fī ma'na 'l-majāz wa 'l-ḥaqīqa*.[121] *Adab* literature could confound the boundaries of the solemn and the comical, the sincere and the facetious, the staid and the lighthearted. This was certainly true of the hugely entertaining rhymed prose *maqāma* with its humorous vignettes revolving around the schemes and foibles of its mercurial hero. The *maqāma* educated while amusing, blending gravity with mirth, didacticism with witty playfulness, and moral and intellectual edification with tales of knavery.

The gradual shifts in the semantic range of the term *adab* in the dominant culture are refracted through Jewish writings from the Islamic East and Andalusia, where the various meanings of the term were mapped onto its designated Hebrew equivalent, *musar*. Exhortations to pursue *musar* recur throughout the biblical book of Proverbs. In his Judeo-Arabic translation and commentary on Proverbs, Saʿadya Gaon consistently renders *musar* as *adab*, understood primarily as proper, moral conduct and the ethical discipline instilled by instruction. This, as we have seen, was the basic early meaning of *adab*, although by Saʿadya's time in Abbāsid Baghdad it had acquired broader, literary significations as well. The book of Proverbs often pairs *musar* with wisdom, and in his comments on Proverbs 1:1–2 Saʿadya sharply differentiates between the two. Locating moral discipline in his epistemological hierarchy, he identifies *adab* as the vehicle for training a person's lower instincts and proverbs or parables as the medium for doing so:

> when the intellect wants to discipline [a person's] nature [*qaṣada ta'dīb al-ṭabʿ*] it presents in proverbs [or parables] that which is clear to the intellect but obscure to one's natural impulses … therefore … the text says, "[the proverbs of Solomon …] for learning wisdom and discipline

120 See Drory, *Models and Contacts*, 11.

121 See Fenton, *Philosophie et exégèse dans* Le Jardin de la métaphore *de Moïse Ibn ʿEzra*, 30–31, 36.

> (*ḥokhmah u-musar*)." For wisdom is what is revealed and clear to the intellect. And *musar* is *al-ʾadab* by means of which one's natural impulses are disciplined and reigned in ....[122]

Saʿadya again translates *musar* as *adab* in the sense of proper conduct inculcated by instruction when rendering Proverbs 1:8, "My son, heed the discipline of your father (*musar avikha*), and do not forsake the instruction of your mother (*torat immekha*)." But in his comments on the following verse (Prov. 1:9), which continues the injunction, "for they are a graceful wreath upon your head, a necklace about your throat," Saʿadya enlarges on this meaning, endowing *adab* with an intellectual component and more than purely utilitarian value:

> the intention is that knowledge and religious faith (*al-ʿilm waʾl-dīn*) together make up *adab*, and that as *adab* they serve to adorn an individual in both worlds [i.e., this world and the next].[123]

Proverbs 5:11–12 reads, "And in the end you roar, When your flesh and body are consumed,/ And you say, 'O how I hated discipline (*musar*) and heartily spurned rebuke.'" In his gloss, Saʿadya cautions against the rejection of ethical guidance and castigation, which leaves one devoid of wisdom. He explains that these verses evoke

> the regret of the wicked and rebellious individual when worldly pleasures are no more, and only sins remain ... and he regrets that he is lacking in wisdom (*ʿadam al-ḥikma*), as it is written ... "O how I hated discipline (*musar/adab*)," and that he rebelled against those who reproved him, as it is said (v. 13), "I did not pay heed to my teachers."[124]

Regarding Proverbs 15:33, *yirʾat adonai musar ḥokhmah* ("The fear of the Lord is the discipline of wisdom ..."), Saʿadya translates *musar ḥokhmah* as *adab al-ḥikma* and comments that

> by means of this he [Solomon] informs us that there is no fear [i.e., fear of the Lord cannot be achieved] other than by means of wisdom

122 See Saadya Gaon, *Mishlei ʿim tirgum ufeirush hagaʾon rabbeinu seʿadyah ben yosef fayyūmī*, 23.

123 Ibid., 26–27.

124 Ibid., 56.

> (*bi'l-ḥikma*) and that by means of which it disciplines (*wa-mā tu'addibu hīya bīhī*) and guides an individual.[125]

In these few citations, Sa'adya's notion of *adab* is generally subsidiary to wisdom. Apart from these epistemological considerations, his conceptualization of the term seems to be restricted to moral virtues and proper conduct inculcated by instruction, even though in the Baghdad of his day *adab* already incorporated the refined and highly literate culture of the *adīb*. Stimulated by his interaction with Islamic culture, Sa'adya had pioneered many of the disciplines that would reach maturity in 11th-century Spain, adapting the ideals and techniques of Islamic philosophy, exegesis, speculative theology, linguistic studies and poetics. But it seems that he did not subsume mastery of these fields or refined expression in his understanding of *adab*.[126]

The amplified sense of *adab*, encompassing the curricular and social ideals of elegant style, graceful form, good upbringing, and courteous manners is, however, evidenced in the writings of the Andalusian Jewish literati and their critics. As Bezalel Safran demonstrates in his now classic study, the Jewish courtiers' emulation of their Muslim counterparts was the object of sharp criticism by the Saragossan Jewish pietist Baḥya Ibn Paquda (2nd half of the 11th century) in his *Kitāb al-hidāya ilā farā'iḍ al-qulūb* (Book of Direction to the Duties of the Heart). Concerned with serving God with one's inner being as well as through external observances, Baḥya condemned the Jewish aristocrats' pursuit of *adab* and the self-consciously refined culture of the *adīb* as utterly superficial and spiritually bankrupt. His reading of *adab* as an entire *paideia* leading to an urbane lifestyle in élite circles was transferred onto the term *musar* without discarding the latter's more limited sense of moral discipline in Judah Ibn Tibbon's Hebrew translation of Baḥya's work (*Sefer ḥovot ha-levavot*), which circulated widely and was highly influential among non-Arabophone Jews for more than half a millenium.[127] The amplified sense of *musar* also occurs throughout the poetic corpus of the broadly educated and highly literate Andalusian school. Samuel Hanagid (993–1056) clearly enjoyed his prestige as a seasoned statesman and soldier, a respected and powerful communal leader, and one of the foremost Talmudic authorities of his day.[128] As an

125 Ibid., 117.

126 See Schlossberg, "Hashpa'at sifrut ha-adab 'al rav Sa'adia ga'on."

127 See Baḥya Ibn Paquda, *Kitāb al-hidāya ilā farā'iḍ al-qulūb*, 171, 395; *Sefer ḥovot ha-levavot*, ed. Zifroni, 217, 493; and Safran, "Baḥya ibn Paquda's Attitude toward the Courtier Class," esp. 157 and 185, n. 12.

128 Samuel bore the title *Nagid* ("Prince") as regional head of the Maghrebi community and

Andalusian courtier and aesthete with a passion for elegance and eloquence, he was also a consummate *adīb* who recognized the political utility of commanding "the understanding of the Greeks" and the "wisdom of the Arabs" and a polished Arabic style that would open doors in the corridors of the powerful.[129] His affinity for wisdom literature and aphorisms is manifest in the titles of the three anthologies that make up his *dīwān*, *Ben Tehillim* (After Psalms), *Ben Mishlei* (After Proverbs), and *Ben Qohelet* (After Ecclesiastes). And while *Ben Mishlei* and *Ben Qohelet* enlarge upon the sapiential themes of Proverbs and Ecclesiastes, they also draw directly on Arabic *adab* sources that had in turn naturalized wise dicta on virtues and vices and cautionary tales from India, Persia, and Greece.[130] So when Samuel invokes *musar* in his verse, he does so in the fullest sense of the term. In a poetic exchange, the Nagid salutes his fellow poet Isaac Ibn Khalfon as an adept in *musar* (and Torah), but also as a brother in *musar*, "Aḥi musar u-var torah."[131] The compound *aḥi musar*, like *benei musar*, is an Arabism, meaning one who is proficient in or cultivates *musar*, but it also suggests a kind of fellowship. Accordingly, in one of his gnomic couplets in *Ben Mishlei*, the Nagid declares all *benei musar* a distinctive kinship group that overrides genealogical differences:

> "He who has no wealth to share with the poor—let him share his words, for kind words are generosity.
> And *musar* is the kinship among the *benei musar*, even though they are separated by lineage."[132]

In a broken-hearted lament over the passing of his brother Joseph, Moses Ibn Ezra (c. 1055-after 1138) praises his sibling's many outstanding virtues. He too was an *aḥi musar*, in this case, the poet's biological brother, but also a brother in *musar*, upright in conduct, faithful and wise, whose pen spun silk embroidery.[133] And though one might not think to find the worldly, literate culture

its supreme representative before the government. See Schirmann, *HPMS*, 183–256; idem, "Samuel Hannagid, The Man, The Soldier, The Politician"; Weinberger, *Jewish Prince in Moslem Spain*, 1–17.

129 Cf. "Shemu'el qademah yoshev keruvim," in *Diwan Shemu'el Hanagid*, ed. Jarden, 1:58, vv. 22–26.

130 See Ratzaby, "Adab Maxims in Medieval Literature"; idem, "Limqorot ben mishlei u-ven qohelet"; Levin, "Le-ḥeqer ben mishle shel rabbi shemu'el ha-nagid."

131 "Aḥi musar u-var torah," in *Diwan Shemu'el Hanagid*, ed. Jarden, 1:181, v. 1.

132 "Asher ein lo rekhush," in *Diwan Shemu'el Hanagid*, ed. Jarden, 2:20, no. 45. See also Decter, "The Jewish *Ahl al-Adab* of al-Andalus."

133 "Ḥaradah laveshah tevel," in *Moses Ibn Ezra, Secular Poems*, ed. Brody and Pagis, 1:117–120, esp. vv. 21–25.

of the *adīb* cast as a divine benefaction, that is how it appears in Ibn Ezra's extensive philosophical and cosmological poem, "Be-shem el asher amar." The longest of Ibn Ezra's poems (164 lines), "Be-shem el" prefaces his philosophically informed treatise on "the meaning of figurative and literal language" in the Bible, *Maqālat al-ḥadīqa*, by celebrating the totality of God's creation with a survey of the cosmos and the beings of the sublunar world, culminating with human beings, who alone are endowed with a pure soul and an intellect. Ibn Ezra acknowledges God for endowing man with speech and mastery of the Holy Tongue. This divine munificence not only allows man to comprehend the visions of God's prophets but also to cultivate what is effectively a full, culturally hybrid *adab* program of etiquette, linguistic prowess, and stylistic refinement that encompasses the Hebrew language; Arabic sayings, themes, and elegant expressions; the social virtues of advice, understanding, and eloquence; "and the *musar* of the language of Greece, its proverbs and riddles."[134] The Andalusians naturally associated speech with the capacity for reason: the medieval philosophers viewed speech as an external manifestation of the thought process—an idea reflected in their use of the Arabic term *nātiq* and its Hebrew equivalent *medabber* to denote "rational."[135] But these lines also reflect Ibn Ezra's valorization of his broad education as a littérateur and acknowledge the Greco-Arabic contributions to the courtier poets' *paideia*.[136] The aphoristic aspect of the *adab-musar* correspondence figures here both as "Arabic sayings" and as Greek "proverbs and riddles." It also comes across in Judah Alḥarizi's rendering as *Sefer musrei ha-pilosofim* of Ḥunayn Ibn Isḥāq's (809–873) *Ādāb al-falāsifa* (Apothegms of the Philosophers). A popular work by the ninth-century translator, philosopher, and physician, *Ādāb al-falāsifa* conveys the wise sayings of ten ancients, including Socrates, Plato, and Aristotle, Pythagoras, Hippocrates, and Galen.[137] The *adab-musar* terminological equivalence is also found in *Maḥberot Iti'el*, Alḥarizi's translation of

---

134 ויודה לשם אמרו/ בפיהו להגבירו/ בהשכל לשון קדשו/ וחזיון נבואותיו
ומדבר יהודית ה-/מדובר עלי אפניו/ ועז מאמר ערב/ ומעניו וצחותיו
סעדו במועצה/ ובינה ובמליצה/ ומוסר לשון יון/ משליו וחידותיו

135 The equation is Greek in origin; *logos* denotes both the word by which the inward thought is expressed and the inward thought, or reason, itself.

136 "Beshem el asher amar," in *Moses Ibn Ezra, Secular Poems*, ed. Brody and Pagis, 1:243, vv. 131–133. Elsewhere Pagis wonders whether this section marks a transition to self-description; see Pagis, *Secular Poetry and Poetic Theory: Moses Ibn Ezra and His Contemporaries*, 248–252.

137 See: Griffith, *Hunayn Ibn Ishaq and the Kitab Adab al-falasifa* and Loewenthal ed., *Sefer Musre Haphilosophim Aus dem Arabischen des Honein ibn Ishak.*

Maqāmāt al-ḥarīrī.[138] And the *adab* penchant for pithy gnomic sayings is on display in the 44th *maqāma* of the *Taḥkemoni*, a miniature anthology of what are described in Alḥarizi's Arabic Table of Contents as *amthāl adabīyya* (*adab* proverbs).[139]

For Jewish literati in eleventh- and twelfth-century Islamic Spain, the courtly context of the *adab* curriculum was especially relevant, but the *musar-adab* equivalence persisted long after the disappearance of that political and social reality. Capitalizing, therefore, on the manifold shades of meaning encompassed by the medieval Hebrew term *musar*, Alḍāhirī must have expected his more worldly readers to recognize that his title promised a belletristic narrative brimming with entertaining energy and mischievous, occasionally transgressive content, as well as a staid and respectable, instructive, and edifying book of cautionary and hortatory tales. The ostensible incongruity was rich with potential and not without precedent: Alḥarizi had described his spirited *Taḥkemoni* as *maḥberot musar* while offering up a menu of both raucous entertainment and loftier, more inspirational fare. As Devin Stewart has noted, the energy devoted to frivolous topics and the triumphs of the "bad guy" in the classical Arabic *maqāma* "created a moral tension which neither escaped, nor sat very easily with, many medieval authors," hence their tendency to apologize in some fashion for the morally questionable material contained in their texts.[140] Judging from his strategic deployment of key paratexts at the beginning and end of his work, Alḍāhirī too seems to have been keenly aware of the apparent discrepancy between his sober stated goal of providing uplift and his hero's frequently immoderate, ethically indefensible behavior. Though he sought to soften the blow by presenting his work in a pious light, the moral ambiguity is evident throughout *Sefer hamusar* and is embodied in the deliberately cultivated multivalence of its title. Still, there is no need to construe the meanings of *musar* in Alḍāhirī's title in binary terms, as strict didacticism versus lax diversion. *Sefer*

---

138 *al-Ḥarīrī: Maqāmāt Abī Zayd al-Sarūjī* (#22, "Of the Euphrates"), p. 104, l. 3: *li'adabihim*, which is rendered as *le-musaram* in *Maḥberot Iti'el*, p. 181 and *'im musaram* in *Sefer ha-musar* #33, p. 373, l. 7. Alḍāhirī sets this *maqāma* in a town of scholars on the Euphrates that he calls Qiryat Sefer ("Town of the Book").

139 Alḥarizi, *Taḥkemoni*, ed. Yahalom-Katsumata, p. 57, l. 63. For additional citations illustrating the various meanings of *musar*, see Ben Yehuda, *A Complete Dictionary of Ancient and Modern Hebrew*, 4:2849–2851.

140 See Stewart, "The Maqāma," 154–157. Note also David Stern's remark, "While authors of *maqama* collections may have piously claimed that their compositions served the purposes of moral instruction, their sophisticated morality is usually as qualified as the rest of reality represented in these clever narratives"; see "Introduction," *Rabbinic Fantasies*, 27.

hamusar is both a book of ethical and religious guidance and amusing *adab* literature, which in its very essence also recommends a broad educational ideal. Alḍāhirī's narratives reflect a command of classical Jewish disciplines (Bible, exegesis, rabbinic literature) as well as grammar, rhetoric, poetry, and stylistics; an easy familiarity with wisdom literature, proverbs and folklore; and a reasonable knowledge of medieval Jewish philosophy and ethics, religious polemics, and classical kabbalah. The example of this disciplinary diversity, resulting from genuine authorial interest and intellectual curiosity, might not be lost on Alḍāhirī's community of readers.

The multi-hued senses of *musar/adab* run like a thread throughout the work, knitting together what appear to be the unrelated sections of individual *maqāmāt*. The notion of *musar* as moral instruction figures prominently in several episodes. In the story framing Chapter 11 (strikingly similar to that of Chapter 32), Mordecai reports that he longed to hear words of rebuke so that he might be saved from the pit and become a man of honorable character. His soul would then "walk in the paths of *musar*" until he became habituated to comporting himself uprightly. His yearnings are (ironically) fulfilled when Abner appears in the guise of a fire-and-brimstone preacher who delivers a spellbinding public repudiation of worldly desires and pursuits. Elsewhere, the narrator's travels are motivated by a search for *musar* in the sense of maxims and edifying stories. In these instances, Mordecai seeks out choice folktales, anecdotes, and proverbs on his journeys in a quest for knowledge that is reminiscent of the famous (if spurious) *ḥadīth* urging believers to "Seek knowledge even as far as China."[141] He pursues *musar* overland and across seas; in urban centers, port cities, and bucholic rural settings; amidst surging crowds in public squares and markets; in sacred spaces, synagogues, *batei midrash*; in prison, and even a caravanserai. His sense of mission recalls ʿIsā ibn Hishām, the narrator of al-Hamadhānī's *Maqāmāt*, whom Stewart describes as "a well-to-do merchant and aspiring scholarly dilettante who travels to the major cities of Syria, Iraq, and Iran to engage in trade and collect poetry, rare literary anecdotes, and words of wisdom from the past."[142] At other times Mordecai arms himself with such wisdom before embarking on particularly dangerous travel. On a sea trip from Sidon to Egypt that is fraught with perils, Mordecai says, "I took *musar* with me as a provision for the road," imbuing the term with

141 *Ṭalabu 'l-ʿilm wa-lau fī sīn*; see, e.g., Goldziher, *Muslim Studies*, 2:164–180 *passim* and Kraemer, *Humanism in the Renaissance of Islam*, 24–25. Kraemer remarks that al-Hamadhānī's *Maqāmāt* gave literary expression to the itinerancy that was a way of life for merchants, intellectuals, and roving mendicants in medieval Islamic society.

142 Stewart, "ʿĪsā b. Hišām's Shiism and Religious Polemic," 22.

an almost talismanic aspect but also possibly reflecting an idiom found in al-Ḥarīrī, *adab yustazādu*, or *adab* taken as provision for the road.[143] Mordecai's longings for knowledge, refined expression, poems, legends and wise adages are often inseparable from his yearnings for his beloved friend, Abner ben Ḥeleq, who is in his eyes the genre's most accomplished practitioner, if not its very embodiment. For Abner, the deployment of *adab/musar* is a lifeline since he relies on the recognition and remuneration he receives for his incandescent speeches and luminous literary performances, his witticisms and accomplished word play. In Chapter 25, he tells folktales of non-Jewish provenance to illustrate verses from the Book of Proverbs and informs the wise men of Sidon that he has always sought words of *musar* so that he will be beloved by all and kings will bring him tribute.[144] And it is the concept of *musar* in all its nuances that ties together the several portions of Chapter 14, which at first blush seem to be a bricolage of unrelated material. In the central section of that *maqāma*, a ravenous Abner attempts to barter his rhetorical skills and broad expertise in "the sciences and the arts" for food, but the local Syrian Jews, whose sin of parsimony is compounded by their tenacious philistinism, will have none of it. To the protagonists' dismay, the youth they accost explains that his compatriots do not care at all for *ḥokhmat ha-musar*. They guard their worldly goods jealously and bear a provincial, ill-bred hostility to all spiritual and cerebral endeavors. Foiled attempts to offer *adab* as a commodity in exchange for food or other tangibles are a common feature of the *maqāma* literature and were apparently a reality of the literary mendicancy of the *adīb*, such that al-Hamadhānī wrote in his *Epistles*:

> Time has embarked on a war against *adab*, proclaims Abū ʾl-Fatḥ. Though it rhymes w/ gold (*dhahab*), *adab* has none of its prestige or power. In the market, *Adab al-kuttāb* of Ibn Qutayba, the poems of Shammākh … are not a currency one can exchange. Nor can one barter the Qurʾān, the *ḥadīth*, jurisprudence, or grammar for clothes, perfumes, bread and meat.[145]

---

143 *Sefer hamusar* #12, p. 165, line 4. For *adab yustazādu* see *al-Ḥarīrī: Maqāmāt Abī Zayd al-Sarūjī*, p. 75 (the 16th *Maqāma*; *al-maghribiyyah*). The usage is pointed out by Klar in "ʿArbaʾah shemot sefarim," p. 249, n. 59. Although the Arabic root زود does not seem to be attested in the tenth form (Chenery translates *yustazādu* as though it were from the root زاد, "scholarship that might be gotten in increase"), Klar cites as a parallel a verse by Moses Ibn Ezra which suggests that it might have been taken as a cognate for הצטייד.

144 *Sefer hamusar* #25, p. 298, ll. 258–260.

145 Cited by Kilito, *Les Séances*, 72.

Then again, in Alḍāhirī's Chapter 14, the narrative twist of the closing ten lines is as unexpected as it is comical. Abner orders a meal far more lavish than he can afford and then abandons the hapless Mordecai to face the unpaid shopkeeper. The ruse is adapted from al-Hamadhānī's "Maqāma of Baghdad" (#12), perhaps via Alḥarizi's adaptation in the twenty-first *maqāma* of the *Taḥkemoni*.[146] Though *Sefer hamusar* embraces the general contours of the picaresque *maqāma*, one could hardly know before delving in that these incongruously decorous and indecorous, ethically instructive and freewheeling aspects of *musar/adab* are latent in Alḍāhirī's seemingly straightforward title.

5 Stylistic and Narrative Techniques

5.1 *Rhymed Prose as Narrative Medium*

The narrative portions of *Sefer hamusar* are composed in carefully crafted rhymed prose, a medium that, while not as highly structured as poetry, carries its own constraints and challenges. The style is elaborate and the language evocative; constructed of biblical diction and imagery, it is suffused with wordplay and scriptural verse fragments cleverly lifted out of context. Despite its archaic locutions, the mannered diction would not have sounded out of place to Alḍāhirī's audience: florid classical Hebrew was regularly used by Yemenite Jews for a wide range of genres, including formal epistles, rabbinic writings, and even chronicles of anti-Jewish persecutions.[147] Like that of his models, Alḍāhirī's elevated prose is arranged in successive pairs of balanced, rhymed, and rhythmic phrases, each of which forms a complete thought or syntactic unit. In contrast with the monorhyme that characterizes much of classical Arabic and Andalusian Hebrew poetry, and unlike the complex pattern of the strophic poem (*muwashshaḥ*), the end-rhymes in the prose sections change after every pair of rhymed cola (aa/bb/cc).[148] When the final word in both halves of a rhymed pair of phrases has the same morphological pattern—e.g., *yaduʿa/qavuʿa*; *ahavtihu/ḥaqaqtihu*—the additional assonance and internal rhymes produce an even richer sense of euphony or aural harmony. The net result is a profusion of rhymes cascading from a series of rhythmic cadences,

146 See Tanenbaum, "Of a Pietist Gone Bad and Des(s)erts Not Had: The Fourteenth Chapter of Zechariah Alḍahiri's *Sefer hamusar*."

147 See, e.g. *Toledot yehudei teiman mikhitveihem*, p. 53 (re. the Mawzaʿ exile of 1679) and pp. 178–181 (re. the 1851 persecutions in Ṣanaʿā).

148 Every so often, there is a triad (aaa) rather than a pair of rhymes.

to which the ear becomes accustomed. The effect is markedly auditory, and something is lost if the text is not read aloud. Thomas Chenery, who translated al-Ḥarīrī's *Maqāmāt* in the 19th century, noted this strong sense of writing for the ear when he imagined that "the people loved to listen to the mingled rhythmical prose and verse as they were half chanted by the reciter."[149] Al-Ḥarīrī himself valued rhymed prose (*saj*ʿ) for its persuasiveness, which he linked to the superiority of the sense of hearing over other modes of sensory perception.[150] As noted, the rhymed prose medium of the Arabic *maqāma* had roots in oral composition and popular oratory, going all the way back to the oracular utterances of pre-Islamic diviners. Al-Ḥarīrī's exceptional achievement in his *Maqāmāt* was to stretch the limits of this medium to its most ornamental, refined, and recherché. Alḍāhirī's boundless admiration for al-Ḥarīrī's mastery of elegant, scintillating, and rhetorically ornate style sets a high standard for his own creativity: "Truly there is none like him for eloquence: his honeyed rivers overflow with riddles and flourishes beyond compare ...." But it is Judah Alḥarizi's singularly exquisite and resonant Hebrew, with its aural effects and archaizing biblical diction, that Alḍāhirī adopted as his principal model. The language of *Sefer hamusar* is largely biblical, but Alḍāhirī is not constrained by the earlier Andalusian ideal of strict biblical classicism and draws freely on rabbinic and medieval Hebrew as well as talmudic Aramaic in his search for a suitably versatile and expressive linguistic medium. While his prose is not as extravagantly ornamented as Alḥarizi's, it is robust and rich with artful allusions and puns, Arabisms, and Hebrew neologisms, as well as rabbinic citations and Aramaic phrases.[151] By lodging bits of canonical diction, whether verbatim or slightly altered, in sometimes surprising contexts, Alḍāhirī achieves a striking array of effects, whether decorative, rhetorical, humorous, or implicitly exegetical.[152] Nevertheless, there does not appear to be any Hebrew *maqāma* convention for representing distinctions in the textures and phrasing of spoken language. Alḍāhirī does not attempt to simulate different spoken styles and never shifts to a register of Hebrew that might be understood to suggest "colloquial" speech or an everyday demotic level of diction. This is left to the auditor or reader/reciter's imagination. Even when the narrator conveys the speech

149 Beeston, "The Genesis of the *Maqāmāt* Genre," p. 10.

150 See Stewart, "Professional Literary Mendicancy," p. 43. On the rhyming patterns in al-Ḥarīrī's *Maqāmāt*, see Hämeen-Antilla, *Maqama*, 156–158.

151 For an evaluation of his language and style, see Ratzaby's Introduction, *Sefer hamusar*, 13–14. In keeping with his affinity for aphorisms, quite a few of the rabbinic dicta he quotes are from *Pirqei avot*; see e.g. pp. 53, l. 41 and pp. 78, l. 32.

152 See Tanenbaum, "The Uses of Scripture in Zechariah Alḍāhirī's *Sefer hamusar*."

of minor characters from widely disparate walks of life, there is no attempt to identify the speaker's class or social status or to parrot regional variations in pronunciation by spanning linguistic registers. Nor do Abner's diction or speech patterns waver from his characteristically elevated and flowery Hebrew, even when he poses in vastly divergent guises. (Of course, Hebrew was not a naturally spoken language in the 16th century.) Perhaps most striking is that the speech of identifiably Muslim characters is also couched in undifferentiated Hebrew rhymed prose. Ross Brann has highlighted this narrative technique known as "impersonated artistry," which allows non-Jewish figures to "behave and speak as members of their confessional community even though their discourse is rendered in perfectly elegant medieval Hebrew."[153] A rare exception, if indeed intentional, occurs in the ninth *maqāma*, where a concentration of Arabisms (lexical and syntactical) in the Muslim thief's Hebrew speech is perhaps intended to simulate his speaking Arabic, although it still does not convey his lowlife status.

Beyond its ornamental function, the difficult style of the *maqāma* is integral to the genre's *modus operandi*. The most illustrious *maqāma* authors were masters of artifice, who used deception and illusions not only as elements of the plot but also as literary devices. Apart from the series of ruses and changing identities that fool the other characters, but which the reader often sees through, there is another variety of deception at work in the text, specifically aimed at the audience or readership. These are stylistic or rhetorical tricks that the author employs as a way of keeping the reader or listener engaged but also as a comment on the potential of language to obfuscate as much as to reveal or to generate aesthetic pleasure. In classical Arabic and biblical Hebrew, a single word can have two dissimilar, even opposite meanings, leaving the *maqāma's* audience to determine which is—or whether both are—intended.[154] Words or images with an ostensibly positive valence may, through intimation or complex interrelationships with other texts, provoke more troubling associations. The genre's heavily allusive, intertextual prose often conceals its implicit meaning, requiring the reader or auditor to delve beneath the surface of the text to get at its deeper sense. Alexander Elinson has remarked that

> The self-consciously ornate language ... place[s] both the protagonists and the audience in the unenviable position of trying to understand a text that is obstinately elusive .... Linguistic style is the means by which the

153 See Brann, *Power in the Portrayal*, p. 147 and n. 35, who cites Leicester, *The Disenchanted Self*, p. 4.

154 Cf. Kennedy, *Recognition in the Arabic Narrative Tradition*, 260–263.

> protagonists and the audience are forced out of their familiar surroundings, and thrust into a text that aims to trick and deceive.[155]

Language becomes a means of obstruction. Stewart has written that

> Perhaps most disturbing for many pious readers, the classical *maqāma* suggests that language in general, and the Arabic language in particular, the language of Scripture, can be put to excellent use as a means of deception, subterfuge and fraud.[156]

Even rhyme can be harnessed for this strategy of deception, as it "creates the impression of a basic equivalence between the two [rhyming words]" but may actually juxtapose opposing terms and thus further the author's cunning verbal scheme.[157]

The audience is also confronted with verbal trickery and acrobatics when the author challenges himself to write with constraints: palindromic epistles or poems that can be read forwards and backwards with the same meaning; poems that can be read horizontally or vertically; lipogrammatic passages from which the author consistently omits a certain letter or letters of the alphabet, and so on. Al-Ḥarīrī excelled at these contortionist maneuvers, penning passages that alternate words made up entirely of dotted Arabic letters with words consisting entirely of undotted letters (#6 and #26), for example.[158] In #28 ("Of Samarqand"), the constraint is to compose a Friday sermon containing no dotted letters. Michael Cooperson explains that "this means using only thirteen of the twenty-eight letters of the Arabic alphabet," leading to the exclusion of "almost all the common prepositions, second- and third-person imperfect verbs, and many other exceedingly frequent features of the language."[159] In #16 ("Of the Maghreb"), the challenge put to the narrator and scholars meeting in a mosque is to improvise palindromes of increasing length. Between them, they manage sentences of only three to six words and are roundly trounced by the rogue hero who produces a five-line poem that retains its sense whether read forwards or backwards.[160] In #46 ("Of Aleppo"), there are various poetic con-

155 Elinson, *Looking Back at al-Andalus*, 58–60.

156 Stewart, "The *Maqāma*," 154.

157 Cf. Stewart, "Professional Literary Mendicancy," p. 43.

158 The titles in Chenery's translation are #6: "Of Marāgha" or "The Diversified"; #26: "The Spotted."

159 Cooperson, *Impostures*, 248.

160 Chenery, *The Assemblies of al-Ḥarīrī*, p. 194; Cooperson, *Impostures*, 135.

straints, including verses consisting of near anagrams.[161] Even outside of his *Maqāmāt*, al-Ḥarīrī wrote a pair of epistles, in one of which every word contains the letter *s* and in the other the letter *sh*.[162]

This partiality for playing with language by imposing additional restrictions on one's writing has inevitably drawn parallels with the mid-20th-century Oulipo (Ouvroir de Littérature Potentielle), a group of mathematicians and writers devoted to intricate explorations of form in literature. One of the best-known members of the group, Georges Perec, was a master of complex constraints involving semantic substitutions, homophone games, resegmented words, palindromes, and lipograms.[163] Perec was not simply interested in word games, however; much of his stunningly varied corpus addresses heart-wrenching historical realities, including some of the worst atrocities of the twentieth century. His 1969 novel, *La disparition*, is written without the letter "e," which in French is pronounced the same way as the pronoun "eux," meaning "them." The title alludes not only to the disappearance of the most common letter of the alphabet but also to the French bureaucratic term for missing persons presumed to be dead, which is all Perec was able to glean about his mother who perished in Auschwitz, having last been seen alive in the Drancy transit camp in 1943.[164]

In an essay on Perec and al-Ḥarīrī, Kilito explores a Borgesian reference to the eleventh-century Arab author in a non-existent academic study by a fictional character in Perec's *La Vie mode d'emploi* (Life: A User's Manual). Noting Perec's familiarity with al-Ḥarīrī's propensity for word games and constrained writing, he draws certain analogies between the two authors and suggests that al-Ḥarīrī might even be termed an *oulipien avant la lettre*.[165] What Kilito does not mention is Perec's attraction to the alphabetic/alphanumeric permutations of the Kabbalists (*gemaṭria*—determining the alphanumeric value of words; *notarikon*—treating each word of the Bible as an acronym;

161 Cooperson, *Impostures*, 429–439.

162 Kilito, *Arabs and the Art of Storytelling*, 132. Cf. Alḥarizi, *Taḥkemoni*, ed. Yahalom-Katsumata, pp. 296–298, where in response to a challenge, Hever includes the letter *resh* in every word of a section of rhymed prose and its embedded poem, and pp. 298–299, where he then complies with the request to omit the letter *resh* from every word. In his *Maqāmāt al-Luzūmiyya*, al-Saraqusṭī adheres "beyond the call of duty" to the constrained rhyme scheme of the renowned poet, Abū 'Alā' al-Ma'arrī (973–1057); see Monroe, ed. and trans., *Al-maqāmāt al-Luzūmīyah*, 43–44.

163 See Magné, "Transformations of Constraint."

164 Perec's poignant life story and major contributions to Oulipo are recounted in Bellos, *Georges Perec: A Life in Words*.

165 Kilito, *Arabs and the Art of Storytelling*, 131–139.

and *temurah*—the notion that Scripture is "an anagram that encodes … the name of God" or "a cryptogram whose code is the Alphabet"), and the links between these esoteric letter manipulations and the lipogram, "a work in which one compels oneself strictly to exclude one or several letters of the alphabet."[166] Perec presumably would have been pleased by the Yemenite Jewish penchant for the alphabetic code known as *atbash*, in which the first letter of the alphabet is substituted for the last, the second letter for the second to last, etc. The *atbash* code is frequently used for proper names in Yemenite Hebrew literature, such that Ḥazmaq was regularly substituted for the name Saʿīd.[167]

There are numerous instances of codes, puzzles, and constrained writing in *Sefer hamusar*: *gemaṭriot*; *notarikon; atbash* and other alphabetic substitutions; poems of longing for an absent friend that hint at his name with a numerical riddle; substitute names for cities (Uzal for Ṣanaʿā, Diqla for Ṣaʿadah); anagrams (*meʿon tanim* for *teiman*); and polemically charged puns (*zeidim* for the Zaydīs). Some of these devices were widely used in Yemenite Jewish writing but presumably would still have required Alḍāhirī's audience to pause for a moment.[168] A truly recondite hybrid alphabetic substitution occurs in a panegyric for an individual named עדו בירב ישע who is addressed as זקף בי רב טרס, where זקף is in *atbash*, but טרס is the result of using the letter of the alphabet immediately preceding the one it is encoding. In the sixth *maqāma* Mordecai refers euphemistically to his beast of burden as רומ״ח ("spear" or "lance"), the reverse of חמור. The 28th *maqāma* includes a long piece in question-and-answer format that centers around the device of *notarikon*, with a designated word in the first line of each couplet followed by a biblical verse whose acronym it is.

---

166 Perec, "History of the Lipogram."

167 Some less familiar examples are: חתכי = סאלם, בביץ = שלומה, מסמת = יחיא.

168 For the identifications of Uzal and Diqla (Gen. 10:27), see e.g., *Sefer hamusar*, p. 64, l. 5 (#2) and p. 187, l. 90 (#15). Ratzaby writes that the usage follows the Yemenite recension of Saʿadya Gaon's *tafsīr*. In his commentary *Neveh shalom* on Gen. 10:27, the last chief rabbi of Ṣanaʿā, Rabbi Amram Qoraḥ (1871–1953), writes that Saʿadya was actually opposed to translating biblical toponyms with Arabic equivalents and issued an explicit injunction against doing so in his commentary on Job. The substitution occurs only in later versions of the *tafsīr*, due to scribal interpolations that were subsequently replicated. As an illustration, Qoraḥ cites Netan'el ben Yeshaʿya's 1329 *Nūr al-ẓalām*; see *Sefer keter ha-torah, ha-tāj ha-gadol*, 1:66–67 and Qāfiḥ, ed. and trans., *Nethanel ben Yeshaʿya, Nur al-ẓalām* (*Ma'or ha'afelah*), p. 74. In a *tāj* dated c. 1800, the *tafsīr* substitutes Dhamār, Ṣanaʿā, and Ṣaʿadah for the biblical Hadoram, Uzal, and Diqla; see NLI Ms. Heb. 24° 6881, openings 25–26. See also Beit-Arié, "'Emunah yoṣrah eṣlo amanah,'" 44–45. For some unusual toponyms in *atbash*, see the annotations to David (Alu'el) ben Yeshaʿ Halevi's *Maqāma on Luck in Livelihood and on Good Intention* in Naḥum, *Ḥasifat genuzim mi-teiman*, 170–171.

But some of the acronyms only work when the words of the biblical verse are read from last to first. When Alḍāhirī augments poems composed by others, he often sets himself more stringent rhyming requirements in order to "improve" upon the original and make it more euphonious. And when he translates riddle poems from Arabic, he has to find clever equivalents in style and substance to make them work in Hebrew. His third *maqāma* is devoted to kabbalistic themes, but embedded within it is a rich lode of constrained writing which, on the surface, has nothing to do with kabbalah. This interlude is inspired by Chapter 8 of the *Taḥkemoni* (#7 in Yahalom-Katsumata), itself a reworking of al-Ḥarīrī's seventeenth *maqāma* ("The Reversed"). In this inset, a guest at a feast given by Abner says that he had found a precious, eloquent passage (*meliṣah yeqarah*) in Arabic that could be read forwards and backwards while retaining the same meaning. In light of its form and themes, he requests a similarly reversible Hebrew composition, specifying that it should lash out at a man he had considered a faithful friend but who repaid his kindness with evil. Mordecai improvises an enigmatic prose passage that intially praises but then curses the addressee with lacerating and scornful words. When read backwards, the letters produce exactly the same words as when read forwards. This is followed a few lines later by a brief poem, each individual line of which can be read right to left or left to right with the identical meaning. But it functions as a sort of automatic palinode, insofar as the first half of each line lauds an ideal patron while the second hemistich vilifies such an individual.[169] David Simha Segal has pointed out that al-Ḥarīrī's original is a reversible letter regarding the virtues of the ideal nobleman, which conveys essentially the same message when read in either direction, whereas Alḥarizi adds a constraint so that when read backwards, his letter recants what it says when read forward; "the paean's contents and tone both are reversed with backward reading."[170] When he then produces a brief palinode, each couplet conceals a volte-face, acclaiming the anonymous patron when read forward but disparaging him when read backward. Alḍāhirī's poem is something of a hybrid in that each individual line produces the same words whether it is read right to left or left to right, but at the same time the first half of each line is laudatory while the second half cancels the praise. This skillfull display inspires yet another guest to request a poem that can be read horizontally and vertically, specifying that it should emulate a piece by the 13th/14th-century Adanī poet Abraham ben Ḥalfon. Abner obliges

169 *Sefer hamusar*, pp. 83, l. 117–p. 84, line 142.

170 See Alḥarizi, *Taḥkemoni*, ed. Yahalom-Katsumata, 153–160 (#7 in their edition) and Segal, *The Book of Taḥkemoni*, 86–92 and 468–472 (commentary). Cf. *Maḥberot Immanu'el* #11, p. 204, ll. 206–210. Note that Immanuel's retraction is achieved by resegmenting the words.

with eight lines asking God to redeem and avenge His people who languish in exile. The solemnity of the poem itself marks something of an about-face from the preceding tone and themes.[171]

Alḍāhirī's palindromes are arguably not as clever and sophisticated as Alḥarizi's since the physical act of reading them backwards does not, in itself, bring about a retraction of the content. Yet his decision to insert this interlude into a chapter on kabbalah is significant even if the poems were pre-existing and in need of a frame. All these reversals—in form, rhetoric, tone and substance—intimate that things are not quite as they appear and that, unlike the divine world, the material world and the human relationships it houses are highly mutable. There is certainly an element of irony in the fact that, following his handsomely rewarded improvisations, Abner suddenly repudiates the pursuit of such trivial verbal games on the grounds that the sages consider them worthless. Instead, he advocates engagement in serious intellectual endeavors and immersion in kabbalah, for kabbalistic study is the true key to man's ultimate felicity, which is entirely spiritual. Why, then, embed these intensely playful tricks, some of whose content is mean-spirited, in an episode largely concerned with the kabbalistic conception of paradise and the inner workings of the sefirotic system? Was the goal simply to divert with unrelated material so as not to overburden the audience with weighty kabbalistic matters? Was it to forge a connection, not explicitly articulated, with the alphabetic manipulations of the kabbalists? Perhaps. But the text's return to the question of theosophical insight raises the possibility that the themes of reversal and mutability are also invoked metaphorically to point beyond the inserted set-piece and link it with the loftier considerations that surround it.

5.2 *Anagnorisis*

In the *maqāma*, masks are the order of the day. The deliberate use of textual opacity and enigmatic literary devices is closely aligned with the hero's repeated dissimulation and self-reinvention. Identities are notoriously fluid. In many chapters of *Sefer hamusar*, the mischief-making Abner—a wandering bard, adventurer, and downright impostor—turns up in a given location in one of numerous disguises in order to exploit the generosity of trusting strangers who unfailingly succumb to his trickery. When he appears amidst surging crowds, creating a commotion, or in the less populous surroundings of the synagogue or study house, he is frequently watched but not recognized

171 "Elohim meraḥem ve-noqem ve-qanna," *Sefer ha-musar*, p. 85, lines 153–160. The poem is listed without attribution in Davidson, *Thesaurus*, 4:80.

by his friend Mordecai, who has come upon him fortuitously. The reader is never quite sure whether Abner has one real identity and several disguises or whether, in his serpentine fashion, he simply dons and sheds various personae. In a Judaized version of the Ḥarīrīan repertoire of masks, Abner poses variously as a brilliant yeshiva student, a kabbalist, a near-shipwreck master of incantations, a quack purveyor of nostrums, a superb cantor, an anti-Muslim polemicist, and a fire-and-brimstone preacher. His ruses, so successful in fooling bystanders as well as the narrator, are always effected by means of well-turned words: poetic improvisations, versified riddles, flowery epistles, rousing homilies and sermons, stirring debates, absorbing philosophical discourses, and affecting prayers. As a rule, Abner reveals himself to Mordecai only at the dénouement of each escapade. Often he then recites a poem of self-revelation that puns on his name and serves as the episode's *envoi*. Periodically, a given *maqāma* departs from this formula insofar as the narrator discerns early on that he has stumbled on his old crony. It is usually Abner's remarkable eloquence that gives him away rather than any physical characteristics. Sometimes Mordecai rebukes Abner once he is unmasked, either for his moral hypocrisy or for having been reckless. In other instances, he recognizes Abner in both senses of the word, not only uncovering his identity but also commending him as a supremely gifted poet and stylist. In still other scenarios, Mordecai sees through Abner's imposture soon after their encounter but intuits that he would prefer to keep his identity concealed from mesmerized onlookers. In such instances, Mordecai effectively becomes his accessory. Paradoxically, none of these discoveries entirely resolve the vexing question of who is who since the metamorphic Abner so frequently impersonates someone else that it is often difficult to discern an unwavering core to his personality.[172]

On a structural level, the recognition scene or anagnorisis functions as a counterweight to the inherent instability and fluctuation of the protean hero's identity. Anagnorisis is a central component of Aristotle's *Poetics* and has been a key element of narratives in many cultures through the ages, often quite independently of the *Poetics*.[173] A narrative convention of the *maqāma*, the recogni-

172 For a detailed taxonomy of recognition scenes in Hebrew *maqāmāt* written in the Ḥarīrīan/Ḥarizian tradition, see Rand, *Studies in the Medieval Hebrew Tradition* etc., 67–81. For al-Ḥarīrī's *Maqāmāt* specifically, see Zakharia, *Abū Zayd al-Sarūǧī, imposteur et mystique*, 193–212.

173 See Kennedy and Lawrence, Introduction to *Recognition: The Poetics of Narrative*, 6: "the early Arabic translations and commentaries of Aristotle's *Poetics* did not understand his work to be essentially about narrative; rather they took it to be a treatise on logic .... Nonetheless, many of the categories of Aristotle's *Poetics* can shed light on aspects of Arabic (Islamic) narrative literature and storytelling generally ...."

tion scene provides an expected, reliable closure mechanism that exposes the impostures and sleight of hand deployed by the rogue-hero to defraud the narrator and other characters. Structurally, it also completes the formulaic frame to those episodes that open with a seemingly accidental encounter between the narrator and unrecognized hero and close with their separation. But anagnorisis can be more than a narrative device associated with the final unveiling of identities. Applying the insights of Terence Cave's seminal work on anagnorisis to the *maqāma*, Philip Kennedy argues that recognition stories are not just about disclosure of the rogue's deception or plot reversal; they can also play a meta-textual role by prompting reflection on the nature of fiction itself. Kennedy cites Cave's discussion of Western literature to the effect that

> in the Aristotelian tradition of antiquity, anagnorisis is ... a focus for reflections on the way fictions as such are constituted, the way in which they play with and on the reader, their distinctive markers as fiction—untruth, disguise, trickery, 'suspense' or deferments ...[174]

Building on Cave's contributions, Kennedy and Marilyn Lawrence observe that while, according to Aristotle, anagnorisis effects a transformation from ignorance to knowledge, the revelations it affords are in fact "barely credible" or rational or stable, such that "what recognition so often discloses is that knowledge itself is precarious."[175] For *maqāma* audiences, therefore, anagnorisis may provide clarification and a sense of resolution with regard to plot or structure. But it can also expose the fabricated nature of fiction, whose multiple levels of meaning introduce an element of uncertainty into one's experience of the text.

5.3 *Framing Devices*

By definition, *maqāma* collections are not enveloped by one continuous, overarching story comparable to the outer frames of the *Thousand and One Nights* or Chaucer's *Canterbury Tales* or Boccaccio's *Decameron*. In those works, an external framing story lends coherence to, and is regularly interrupted by, a series of inserted stories (which often enclose tales within tales): Shahrazād delays her execution by storytelling for a thousand and one nights; a group of pilgrims on their way to Canterbury passes the time by telling each other tales; ten high-born friends who have fled Florence during the plague take turns

174 Cave, *Recognitions: A Study in Poetics*, p. 46, cited in Kennedy, *Recognition in the Arabic Narrative Tradition*, 246.

175 Kennedy and Lawrence, Introduction to *Recognition: The Poetics of Narrative*, 3.

telling stories on a set theme over ten days.[176] There is no analogous unifying "umbrella" narrative to which we return at the beginning of each discrete chapter of *Sefer ha-musar*. Nevertheless, if we view the external frame as a narrative strategy facilitating movement from one story into the next, it is possible to identify several devices in the *maqāma* that produce a comparably connective effect.[177] Just as the continuous outer frame serves to link its enclosed tales but does not determine their nature, there are occasional narrative or stylistic devices that loosely link some or all of the self-contained chapters in *Sefer ha-musar* without dictating their content. The most all-encompassing of these is the continuing presence of narrator and hero, which provides an element of commonality between otherwise independent episodes. And the narrator's opening of each chapter furnishes a context for the embedded tales that ensue. In *Sefer hamusar*, this internal frame or "boxing tale" for each *maqāma* usually takes the form of a brief travel account whose formulaic predictability ("Said Mordecai the Sidonian, 'I journeyed from No Amon to Mount Hermon'"; "Said Mordecai the Sidonian, 'I journeyed from the land of *Metim* to the land of the *Ḥittim*'") serves on the rhetorical level to bind the independent episodes together, even if each escapade unfolds in a different locale. So, too, thematic linkages between certain groups of tales weave a web of subtle interrelationships between the work's ostensibly autonomous chapters. The most far-reaching of these thematic ties is furnished by the leitmotif of *musar* in all of its shades of meaning. As the moral and theological lesson prescribed in the Author's Introduction, *musar* provides the project with an overall purpose or organizing principle.[178] And as the entertaining folktales and anecdotes peppered throughout the work, *musar* in the sense of *adab* yields the pleasantly diverting material interwoven into that scaffolding. The juxtaposition of a solemn framing device with the droll and seemingly random tales embed-

176 See: Van Leeuwen, *The Thousand and One Nights: Space, travel and transformation*, 6; "Frame Story," in Marzolph and van Leeuwen, eds., *The Arabian Nights Encyclopedia*, 2:554–556; Reynolds, "A Thousand and One Nights: a history of the text and its reception," 273–275; Stephan, Introduction to Ḥannā Diyāb, *The Book of Travels* 1: xxiii–xxvi; Gittes, "The Canterbury Tales and the Arabic Frame Tradition"; Mallette, "The Hazards of Narration: Frame-Tale Technologies and the 'Oriental Tale'"; Fajardo, "The Frame as Formal Contrast: Boccaccio and Cervantes"; Potter, "The Function of Framing in the *Decameron*"; Almansi, *The Writer as Liar: Narrative Technique in the Decameron*, 1–18 ("Narrative Screens"); and Forni, "The Decameron and Narrative Form."

177 See Haring, "Framing in Narrative."

178 On the tremendous variety encompassed by the term "frame tale," see, e.g., Irwin, "What's in a Frame? The Medieval Textualization of Traditional Storytelling." On thematic patterning as a unifying device, see also Pinault, *Story Telling Techniques in the Arabian Nights*, 22–25.

ded in many of the individual *maḥbarot* suggests that storytelling is not only a vehicle for edification and moral guidance but also a way of easing the despair brought on by the persecutions described in the Introduction and select chapters of *Sefer hamusar*. Such beguiling narratives had the power to draw readers and listeners out of their quotidian concerns and transport them to other worlds.

Alḍāhirī also weaves subtle links between *maḥbarot* by clustering several chapters with similar topics. Assuming that these groupings are not coincidental, they too suggest that he took pains to organize portions of *Sefer hamusar*, despite having written it fragmentarily. The fourth *maqāma* introduces the first of the work's many tales with themes and motifs recognizable from the vast repertoire of international folklore, and the fifth features animal fables attested with numerous variants in the oral lore of the medieval Islamic world and India.[179] Chapters 8 and 10 are two of the only *maḥbarot* in *Sefer hamusar* that incorporate material with bawdy or erotic overtones. Chapters 16, 17, and 18 all include praise for medieval Hebrew books and their authors. Toward the end of the work (Chapters 34, 36, 38, and 41) there is a clutch of folktales that hold up the exemplary behavior of "Arabs" as object lessons for Alḍāhirī's Jewish audience. In a related strategy, Alḍāhirī occasionally "balances" certain features of two otherwise independent chapters.[180] We have already mentioned the explicit balancing of Chapters 1 and 2, occasioned by the author himself intervening in the narrative. To make amends for opening the book with a scatological tale adapted from the non-Jewish al-Ḥarīrī, Alḍāhirī devotes Chapter 2 to a pious lament over *galut teiman*. Chapters 9 and 10 are even more subtly counterpointed. In Chapter 9, a chest is the conduit for Abner's ruse, enabling him to lay claim to a deposit of valuables which he never made. In Chapter 10, an elaborate casket allows a virtuous young woman to reclaim her rightful inheritance from a crooked judge with whom it had been deposited in good faith. Chapter 16 features books and righteous sons whereas Chapter 23 ends with the story of a precious book entrusted to an unworthy son who allowed it to be stolen.

The *maqāma* technique of nesting one story within another allows Alḍāhirī to produce a layered narrative structure that adds nuance to a given chapter's

179 See Schwarzbaum, "Le-ḥeqer arbaʿah sippurei ʿam be-sefer ha-musar le-rabbi zekharyah alḍāhirī." Schwarzbaum also notes parallels in the *Mishlei shuʿalim* (Fox Fables) of Berakhia ha-Naqdan (late 12th-early 13th-c.), but does not think Alḍāhirī necessarily derived his material from Berakhia or any other written source, for that matter.

180 Cf. Gittes, "The Canterbury Tales and the Arabic Frame Tradition," 165–166.

inserted tales.[181] By enclosing individual chapters in internal frame stories or boxing tales, Alḍāhirī is able to interlace several narrative threads, allowing different narrative levels to intersect with one another. Parallels or contrasts between frame stories and their embedded tales are often revealing. As Philip Kennedy has noted in regard to the *Arabian Nights*, "a story will often mirror, whether inversely or otherwise, the cognitive structure and thematic development of the story that contains it."[182] For instance, in *Sefer hamusar* the central tale of Chapter 36 concerns a noble and selfless Bedouin named Taḥkam. Framing this account is an embryonic story (told by Mordecai as narrator) that contrasts blameless Jews with "debauched and depraved" Muslims. The pairing of this frame story with the inner tale of Taḥkam hints at additional moral disparities since the ignoble Muslims mentioned in passing in the frame serve as implicit foils for the unimpeachable Taḥkam. At the same time, the frame story sets up Proverbs 18:16 ("A man's gift eases his way/And gives him access to the great") as an enigmatic motto that only becomes intelligible once we have read the inserted story of Taḥkam.

5.4 *Alḍāhirī's Fictional Characters*

Al-Hamadhānī's silver-tongued hero may originally have had some basis in reality as a caricature of the freelance secretary or *kātib* trapped in a perennial search for patronage, and his narrator may have loosely parodied the *rāwī* or oral transmitter of *ḥadīth* and other genres. But by Alḍāhirī's time, the ubiquitous narrator and eloquent rogue-hero had been stock *maqāma* characters for centuries. These fictional figures embodied recognizable human types, and although never particularly well developed or highly individuated in the *maqāma* literature, they nonetheless exerted appeal.[183] In those Hebrew rhymed prose narratives closest to the Ḥarīrīan model, these conventional-

181 On the use of this technique in Hebrew rhymed prose narratives see Pagis, "Variety in Medieval Rhymed Narratives" and Yahalom, "The Function of the Frame Story in Hebrew Adaptations of the Maqāmāt."

182 Cf. Kennedy, "Islamic Recognitions: An Overview," 33. See also Pinault, *Story Telling Techniques in the Arabian Nights*, 16–30.

183 Though he draws heavily on the *maqāma* literature for his study of the medieval Islamic underworld, C.E. Bosworth portrays these types as more than just fictional imaginings: "… there are indications that a teeming underworld existed at the lower end of pre-modern Islamic society, ….entertainers and mountebanks of diverse types, beggars of differing degrees of ingenuity, quack doctors, dentists and herbalists …. These practitioners … were only a level or two below the widespread class of popular preachers and religious storytellers, who were … easily tempted to play upon the credulousness of the masses and to exploit them for financial gain or for the achievement of prestige and influence." See Bosworth, *The Mediaeval Islamic Underworld*, vol. 1, IX–X, and Berkey, "Storytelling,

ized characters were repurposed to fit a Jewish context while retaining the defining features of their original, stereotypical roles. As a pair of itinerants, one of whom tells the story and is one of its two central players, and the other of whom thrives on having an audience for his role playing and disguise, Mordecai and Abner fit the traditional mold in many respects. But Alḍāhirī also tailors his protagonists to the historical specificities of his *maqāma* just enough to render them identifiable as 16th-century Yemenite Jews. Apart from the two principals, the other dramatis personae in the *maqāma* are minor characters who are rarely differentiated. In *Sefer hamusar*, Rabbi Abraham Ashkenazi and the unnamed head of the Tiberias yeshivah make cameo appearances, but even they are fairly two-dimensional. We have no real sense of Rabbi Abraham the *shadar*: is he gruff? overbearing? mild-mannered? austere? Only one well-known historical figure briefly appears as himself—the legendary Joseph Karo, who allows himself to be dazzled by Abner's confident philosophical disquisition on the soul; a few others are mentioned in passing but do not actually appear. The remainder of the supporting cast is made up of nameless onlookers, guests at feasts, worshippers, and anonymous crowds.

In contrast with Alḥarizi, who declares in his Hebrew introduction that his protagonists are entirely imaginary, Alḍāhirī's more cryptic prefatory remarks on the fictionality of his protagonists seem to retain some of the ambiguities of his Arabic models. According to al-Ḥarīrī, his predecessor al-Hamadhānī attributed the composition of his *Maqāmāt* to the hero, Abū l-Fatḥ al-Iskandarī, and their narration to ʿĪsā ibn Hishām, "*both of whom are unknown* (*majhūl*)." Of his own *Maqāmāt*, al-Ḥarīrī states, "I have dictated all of it [as though it came] from the tongue of Abū Zayd … and I have ascribed its narration to al-Ḥārith ibn Hammām."[184] The closest Alḍāhirī comes to attributing the composition of *Sefer hamusar* to one of his characters is in the epitaphs that conclude the work. But in his Introduction, he does say that he has "narrated it by means of two men *who are strangers to me*." His choice of words recalls al-Ḥarīrī's description of al-Hamadhānī's protagonists as "unknown." Stewart has indicated that "unknown" may be a way of signalling their fictionality although it may also reflect the assumption that Ibn Hishām and al-Iskandarī were actual historical figures to whom references have simply not been preserved in the historiographical tradition.[185] Then again, even the compulsion to identify *maqāma*

Preaching, and Power," 60–61. For a 13th-century manual of trickery and scams see al-Jawbarī, *The Book of Charlatans*.

184 See Rand, *Studies in the Medieval Hebrew Tradition* etc., pp. 45–47 and n. 5.

185 See Stewart, "ʿĪsā b. Hišām's Shiism," p. 23. Cf. Drory, "The Maqama," 199–205.

protagonists with real people is tied up with attitudes toward fiction, inasmuch as it betrays a discomfort with the idea that they might simply be products of the author's imagination.[186]

Lexically and conceptually, however, Alḍāhirī's comments echo Alḥarizi even more directly. Toward the end of his Hebrew Introduction, Alḥarizi makes a categorical statement regarding the invented nature of *maqāma* protagonists:

> All the epistles in this book I have composed/ and have crafted [as though they came] from the tongue of Heiman ha-ezraḥi/ and I have constructed them in the name of Ḥever ha-qeini/ even though not one of them lives in our generation/ and everything that I have said in their names 'never was and never happened, but is only a parable' (bBaba Batra 15a)/ *for such is the rule of all those who create maḥbarot: they must be composed [as though they came from] the tongue of strangers.*[187]

Alḍāhirī's remarks are rather more laconic and elliptical; nevertheless, his oblique language suggests that over the course of the three centuries since the *Taḥkemoni*, the authors of the Hebrew *maqāma* tradition had still not developed a critical discourse or technical vocabulary for discussing fictionality. But he also seems to play with the reader in a different way from Alḥarizi, who states up front that he has invented everything in his book but has projected the narratives through his characters' voices. By contrast, Alḍāhirī is somewhat more elusive, oscillating between distancing himself from, and identifying himself with, the literary personae he has created:

> I have narrated it by means of two men who are strangers to me ... the numeric value of their names and mine are the same ... the two men ... are both concealed and revealed ...

His equivocality may owe something to his familiarity with the *Maḥbarot* of Immanuel of Rome (c. 1261–1335), a work that postdates the *Taḥkemoni* and was also one of Alḍāhirī's sources, albeit unacknowledged. *Maḥberot Immanuel* fuses elements of the medieval Iberian Jewish literary tradition with poetic forms, stylistic conventions, and cultural allusions drawn from the world of Renaissance Italy. Despite the glaring dissimilarities in cultural context and

186 See Cooperson, *Impostures*, 455: "Abdelfattah Kilito has argued that the search for a real person behind Abū Zayd is a response to the uneasiness generated by an avowed fiction (Kilito, *Séances*, 125–133) ...."

187 See Alḥarizi, *Taḥkemoni*, ed. Yahalom-Katsumata, 78–79.

authorial temperament, the *Maḥbarot* furnished Alḍāhirī with significant literary precedents for elements of *Sefer hamusar*, and there is no question that he knew Immanuel's work well. Immanuel draws a highly ambiguous line between himself as author, his fictitious namesake who narrates the work, and the unnamed Prince, his patron and partner in crime. In the work's first Introduction, Immanuel is troubled by the appropriation and misquotation of his poetry by others and is advised by the Prince to collect all of his poems and artistic prose in a book on the model of the *Taḥkemoni*. In accordance with Alḥarizi's paradigm, the Prince urges Immanuel to devise an imaginary character, the Prince, who will function as his fictional collaborator:

> take up your parable as though you had a partner / who poses questions to you and to whom you reply / and who replies to you when you pose questions to him. / Give him a new name, / invented as a figment of your imagination./ *Now I have never composed poetry, / nor have I etched eloquent phrases with the stylus of my mind. / Make me a partner in your book / and attribute to me some of your parables and poems.* / And though the poems and stories that will be attributed to me will not redound to my glory, / I have chosen to be your friend and companion / and to have my name etched on the tablets of your book for all eternity.[188]

In this first Introduction, Immanuel claims exclusive authorship of all the contents of his work. Even though some of them are ascribed to the Prince, the Prince explicitly says that he has never composed poetry or rhymed prose. Yet, strikingly, in the second Introduction, Immanuel's patron is credited with having inspired and even authored much of the work's contents. Unravelling the threads of Immanuel's intentionally enigmatic treatment of his authorial relationship with his two protagonists is well beyond the scope of the present work (and has already been treated with tremendous insight elsewhere).[189] Suffice it to say that whatever Alḍāhirī may have taken away from Immanuel's two Introductions may have helped to shape his terse pronouncements on the role of his personae in the compostion and narration of *Sefer hamusar*. At the end of his first *maqāma*, there is another instance of authorial equivocality on this matter:

> Said the lowly Zechariah ben Seʿadyah: When I had completed the first *maḥberet*, and its proper *meliṣah* was pleasing to all, it occurred to me

188 Translated by Rand, *Studies in the Medieval Hebrew Tradition* etc., p. 53. Italics added.
189 See especially Chapter 5 of Rand, *Studies in the Medieval Hebrew Tradition* etc., pp. 94–134.

> to mention our *galut* and how the crown has fallen from our head, using the medium of *meliṣah* which is like a budding vine whose blossoms have come out, by means of the two men who are related to me in my thoughts, Abner ben Ḥeleq ha-teimani and Mordecai ha-ṣidoni.[190]

Here there is a subtle ambiguity to the idiom *ʿalah ʿal libbi*, which in theory could be read either as an act of deliberate agency ("I thought to do x") or as an idea that comes to one unexpectedly, as if from outside ("it occurred to me that I ought to do x"). The former reading is better suited to the idea that Alḍāhirī felt a pressing need to atone for opening his book with a plot borrowed from al-Ḥarīrī; the latter seems to convey less urgency, particularly as Alḍāhirī would like to mention the *galut* using the unhurried and carefully cultivated medium of *meliṣah*. And there is a parallel open-endedness in the passive construction "by means of the two men who are related to me (*ha-meyuḥasim elay*) in my thoughts (*be-hegyoni*)," as though the two personae through whom he will channel his eloquent lament over the historical *galut* are both the products of his invention and somehow independent of him.

5.5 *Authorial Voice*

These equivocations regarding Alḍāhirī's authorial relationship with his two invented protagonists facilitate the deliberate masking of the author's own views, a rhetorical strategy typical of the *maqāma*. While he confesses to an affinity between his voice and theirs, the fiction of two characters who are distinct from each other as well as from the author is maintained throughout the work. Alḍāhirī obscures himself by dividing his voice between the narrator and the hero, neither of whom can be wholly identified with him. And yet he intermittently conflates his identity with that of his personae. In his Introduction he tells us, "I have divided the book into chapters on varied matters; they tell of what befell *me* while I wandered as a stranger, and when *I* was in prison among my people—abject in my misery—by means of the two men I mentioned, who are both concealed and revealed …," while in the final chapter he ascribes the titles of his own literary and exegetical works to them.[191] Scholarly readers of *Sefer hamusar* have assumed that Abner is Alḍāhirī's mouthpiece or stand-in, whether he publicly disputes a Muslim on theological matters, com-

---

190 *Sefer ha-musar*, p. 63, lines 108–111. אמר הצעיר זכריה בן סעדיה ... אז עלה על לבי לזכור גלותינו ... על פי שני האנשים המיוחסים אלי בהגיוני אבנר בן חלק התימני ומרדכי הצידוני.

191 This fiction also occurs roughly halfway through the book, in chapter 21, when Abner advises Mordecai to consult Abner's Pentateuch commentary *Ṣeidah la-derekh* for further explanation of an esoteric riddling poem he has just recited.

poses a letter of unparalleled elegance to the communal leaders of Tiberias, or gets married on a visit to India. Yet, from a literary perspective, the rogue hero's realities are not a priori those of the author. Abner, "the father of all ruses," is not a trustworthy figure but rather a poseur who passes for what he is not and tells contrived stories to listeners whom he dazzles and deludes. His truth claims are therefore suspect. To say that Abner and Mordecai "are both concealed and revealed" is to convey metaphorically their vacillating relationship to, and representations of, the truth. As first-person narrator, Mordecai is gullible, reporting what he hears from Abner, much of which is fabricated. Moreover, as the author of these fictions, conveying what Mordecai has transmitted from Abner, Alḍāhirī himself is subject to doubt. In a sense, none of them is beyond reproach. Abdelfattah Kilito has explored the moral tensions attendant upon the use of *hikāya*, the attributed discourse. He writes that the *maqāma* author gives the illusion that it is not he who speaks but other beings who are, nevertheless, of his invention. So the author is not speaking in his own name; rather, he attributes, fraudulently or fictively, his own speech to someone else. The author "pretends" to convey what he hears from the narrator, who in turn transmits the speech of the rogue hero. The resulting ambiguity is a sort of imposture; the author effaces himself by dissimulating his voice. He transfers it to his imaginary characters who acquire, through this rhetorical trickery, an autonomy and a presence they would otherwise not have, producing an illusion in the reader that speaks to the nature of fiction itself.[192]

5.6 *Delineation of Characters*

Like a good deal of Western literature prior to the rise of the 18th-century novel, the medieval *maqāma* is far from realist fiction; its characters are not intended as one-of-a-kind individuals endowed with highly specific personalities but as recognizable types (the Itinerant Storyteller; the Popular Preacher; the Incantation Whisperer; the Mendicant Poet, etc.) whose roles could be performed by interchangeable actors in *maqāmat* composed by different authors.[193] *Maqāma*

192 See Kilito, *Les Séances*, 125–133 ("Les fictions du *je*") and 248–259 ("Le menteur professionel"), esp. 251. And cf. Leicester, "The Art of Impersonation: A General Prologue to the Canterbury Tales," 165–166: "… the voices of the text create the characters and the narrator. Only by treating the pilgrims as the products, rather than the producers, of their tales can we construct their personalities. Similarly, we must construct the poet from his poem. The general narrator is not a naïve 'Chaucer the pilgrim' but a complex and sophisticated impersonator who withholds himself and directs us to the roles he plays in order to create himself as fully and complexly as possible in his poem."

193 Cf. Kindley, "The People We Know Best." In his Yemeni travelogue of 1884, the European Jewish explorer and Arabist Eduard Glaser mentions a striking real-life analogue to the

authors were not concerned with their characters' dynamic development. Arguably, the rogue hero lacks a core self and is effectively the sum total of all his role-playing. The lack of specificity is evident with regard to the protagonists' external as well as internal traits. Outwardly, we are given very little sense of a character's physiognomy or telltale characteristics. Abner's appearance is much more changeable than Mordecai's, yet Alḍāhirī gives us only the barest of physical details, most of which are isolated belongings or garments related to the role he plays in a given episode: as a kabbalist he wears a bloated turban (#3); as a savvy trader he has 30 caravan loads of goods (#19) or enjoys comfortable trappings in his lodgings; to bring a specious suit against a Muslim trader in front of a Muslim judge he dresses as a merchant from Muslim lands (#9); as an itinerant preacher he is prematurely aged due to his former incarceration and forcible exile (#11); at the end of the book he is bowed with age and leans on a staff (#45). The bodily deterioration due to imprisonment is delineated already in Mordecai's eyewitness account in the second *maqāma*: Abner is forced to draw water for the king from underneath the prison tower; his clothes are bedraggled, his legs are shackled, and he is bent over and surrounded on all sides by guards. This is one of the more detailed accounts of his physical state; the unusual degree of precision suggests an interweaving of the life with the works. Yet we are not told much about Abner's disguises in some of the more dramatic encounters: as a brilliant student in Karo's Safed yeshivah; as the anti-Muslim polemicist in a public disputation in the streets of Cairo; or as an avowedly Jewish thief competing with a Muslim and a Christian counterpart in a Mosul marketplace. Moreover, Mordecai rarely describes his own physical condition, as though he were merely a disembodied conduit for relaying Abner's feats.

5.7 *Character Development*

Internally, the protagonists in a *maqāma* show no real signs of transformation over the course of the work. Unlike characters in other odysseys, they do not return from their journeys noticeably changed. Apart from their multiple visits to the Land of Israel, Mordecai and Abner rarely comment on any epiphanies sparked by their encounters.[194] These generalizations are largely true of

itinerant entertainer, known as the *dawshān*: "in South Arabia a kind of clown who goes to the houses of the prosperous seeking tips in exchange for flattery, etc. He belongs to the *Ahl Khums*, the pariah class." See Glaser, "My Journey Through Arḥab and Ḥāshid," 1.

194 On the external narrative stance in earlier Muslim narrative discourse, cf. Leder, "Conventions of Fictional Narration in Learned Literature," 37–38 and Beaumont, "Hard-Boiled: Narrative Discourse in Early Muslim Traditions."

Sefer hamusar even though it is framed as a morally instructive work and contains poetic exhortations to look deep inside, to know one's soul, and to repent, and periodically invokes the rabbinic notion that this world is a mere passageway to the next. The one exception, perhaps, resides in the final *maqāma*, where Alḍāhirī's two personae confront their mortality, engage in a sort of stock-taking of their accomplishments, and express an urge to be immortalized through their works. Yet even here it is not clear that the characters undergo a profound self-reckoning or that their journeys can be read in an allegorical sense. On the fictional plane, the work certainly closes on a moral high note. But the final episode also serves as a vehicle for the author to undertake a retrospective summation of his life's work, more akin to the *fihrist* in certain Arabic autobiographical subgenres than to a closing transfiguration of his personae.[195]

The use of the two protagonists to convey opposing sides of an argument is another indication of how abstractly the author of a *maqāma* could view his characters. Alḍāhirī notably pits his protagonists against each other to reflect critically on the moral and literary merits of emulating, appropriating, and modifying poems by other authors. This was a practice (*jawāb*/ *muʿāraḍa*) in which he freely engaged but regarding which he apparently had certain qualms. He externalizes these ambivalences by having Mordecai and Abner each advocate one of the two conflicting sides in his inner struggle. As Uriah Kfir has persuasively shown, Immanuel deployed this device throughout his *Maḥbarot*, using the Prince to champion the supremacy of Iberian Hebrew poetry and his fictional namesake (Immanuel) to challenge the Spanish poets' exceptionalist claims to poetic hegemony. Immanuel's conflicted attitudes toward the Andalusian school and their pretensions are externalized by means of this "dialogical technique." Through the verbal sparring of his protagonists, it becomes clear that he holds the Iberians in high esteem but indignantly rejects their claims to monopoly over literary achievement.[196]

And yet, the emotional ties between Alḍāhirī's two main characters have a warmth and an immediacy that strike a genuine and universal chord, capable of moving the reader. Mordecai always refers to Abner in extremely affectionate terms; *aḥi ve-reʿi* (my beloved brother), *alufi u-meyudaʿi* (my companion, my friend). Describing their close-knit relationship in his Author's Introduction, Alḍāhirī writes, "They convey delightful amity, the strength of their bond and lasting love." The two intimates echo and contradict and amplify one another:

195 See Reynolds, *Interpreting the Self*, p. 38 and n. 8.
196 Kfir, *A Matter of Geography*, 127.

"One man speaks and the other responds, to build verses of lament and song." Abner has an instinct for theatricality; he can be imperious and quirky while Mordecai is more guarded. Yet there is a palpable sense of kinship and innate sympathy between them and true devotion to one another, whether in farcical or truly dire circumstances. When Abner bitterly regrets his rash marriage in Cochin, it is Mordecai who devises his escape scheme. When Abner is in prison, Mordecai has ominous dream visions; when Abner is reckless, Mordecai beseeches him not to expose himself to danger. They share their quiet grief and sense of loss over Abner's incarceration and the tragic events affecting the Jews of Yemen, whether natural disasters—floods and famines—or ill treatment at the hands of the Zaydīs. Unless they are conniving to hide their identities from onlookers, they are quite demonstrative when reunited after a lengthy separation. When reunited, they always embrace and kiss, albeit without overt suggestion of homoeroticism.[197] *Sefer hamusar* reflects the specific mores of Yemenite Jewish male society; the world Alḍāhirī conjures is, like that of most medieval Arabic and Hebrew *maqāmāt*, overwhelmingly androcentric and homosocial. As Shawkat Toorawa has written,

> The idea of voyage, too, may be read as the manifestation of homosocial desire .... voyages are undertaken ostensibly in the quest for knowledge, but the company of other male scholars lies on this route, which leads away from the heterosexual environment of the hearth, and toward the exclusively male environment of the mosque, the *madrasa* (college of law) and the *ribāt* (Sufi retreat).[198]

In the work's closing *maqāma* (#45), where the audience anticipates that after so many seemingly fortuitous encounters, the narrator and hero will finally undergo a permanent separation, Mordecai telegraphs his distress at the idea of their bond being broken, saying, "When I heard Abner's words, *I held him fast and would not let him go* (Canticles 3:4)." Neutralizing the hint of homoeroticism engendered by the intertextual allusion, he expresses his love and

197 See, e.g., Ratzaby's comment, p. 341, n. 45 that Abner's kissing Mordecai on the mouth when they are reunited was "according to the custom of the inhabitants of Yemen." The broader implications of this customary expression of homosocial desire are beyond the scope of the current study.

198 Toorawa, "Language and Male Homosocial Desire," 262, n. 5. Tova Rosen's valuable feminist critique of the "homotextuality" of the *maqāma* and its objectification of women is only partially applicable to *Sefer hamusar*, due to its relatively chaste contents compared with a work like *Maḥberot Immanuel*. See Rosen, *Unveiling Eve*, 124–148.

profound admiration with a blessing, effectively deifying Abner by applying to him biblical verses originally predicated of God.[199]

5.8 *The Protagonists' Names in Arabic and Hebrew Maqāmāt*

In homage to his predecessor, al-Ḥarīrī patterned the names of his principal characters after those devised by al-Hamadhānī in such a way that they have similar component parts and rhyme with their models. Al-Ḥarīrī's narrator is al-Ḥārith Ibn Hammām, after al-Hamadhānī's ʿIsā Ibn Hishām, and al-Ḥarīrī's trickster hero is Abū Zayd al-Sarūjī, after al-Hamadhānī's rogue protagonist, Abū ʾl-Fatḥ al-Iskandarī. Down the centuries and in various lands, post-Ḥarīrīan *maqāma* authors repeatedly harked back to this pattern of *kunya* (Abū *x*) + *nisba* (the toponymical adjective indicating one's place of origin or residence, e.g., al-Iskandarī) for the rogue hero figure and *ism* (given name) + *nasab* (patronymic; Ibn *x*) for the narrator. Curiously, each of these models omits the two standard onomastic elements out of which the other is composed. Stewart has commented on this anomaly:

> The fact that ʿĪsā b. Hišām's *kunya* is missing, when it is so prominent in the case of the trickster, Abū ʾl-Fatḥ, suggests that the reader is supposed to notice its absence and to attempt to figure it out.

Explaining that Ibn Hishām's name recalls that of ʿAmr Ibn Hishām (d. 624), an arch-enemy of the Prophet, whose *kunya* was ironically inverted from Abū ʾl-Ḥakam ("the Father of Wisdom") to Abū ʾl-Jahl ("the Father of Ignorance"), Stewart suggests that the reader was intended to supply al-Hamadhānī's Ibn Hishām with the *kunya* Abū ʾl-Jahl and pick up on the intimation of the narrator's ignorance. Similarly, the absence of a toponymical *nisba* parallel to the hero's al-Iskandarī should have sparked the recognition that the text of the *Maqāmāt* designates Ibn Hishām as a native of Qum, and therefore "his natural *nisba* would have been *al-Qummī*," though it is never used. (Based on his origin in Qum, Stewart makes a persuasive case for identifying ʿIsā Ibn Hishām as a Twelver Shiʿite, and for reading al-Hamadhānī's *Maqāmāt* as "an attempt to satirize Shiʿi values and practices.")[200] At the same time, Ibn Hishām's combination of given name and patronymic "establishes a relatively fixed identity … that is missing in the case of Abū ʾl-Fatḥ, [who lacks a given name, and therefore]

199 Michael Rand discusses the emotional impact on the reader of the relationship between narrator and hero and "the knowledge that their accidental encounters will one day cease;" see Rand, *Studies in the Medieval Hebrew Tradition* etc., pp. 45 and 68.

200 Stewart, "ʿĪsā b. Hišām's Shiism."

whose identity is not stable."[201] Philip Kennedy has also discussed the protagonists' names. Citing Abdelfattah Kilito, Kennedy points out that the *nisba* of al-Hamadhānī's hero, al-Iskandarī, identifies Abū 'l-Fatḥ as a native of Alexandria, but since there were many ancient towns by that name, his place of origin is uncertain. Rather than relating him to a fixed place, the *nisba* al-Iskandarī may suggest that he comes "from everywhere and anywhere," thereby "accentuat[ing] the themes of travel, vagrancy and mutability," which became central to the *maqāma* genre. By contrast, the associations with the Mesopotamian town of Sarūj, home to al-Ḥarīrī's trickster, are more specific: the city fell to the Franks in 1101, marking the transition between the rule of Islam and that of the infidels. So the *nisba* al-Sarūjī also serves as a reminder of the world's mutability and instability, as well as of the trickster hero's liminal status.[202]

The "complementary incompleteness"[203] of these naming patterns inevitably calls attention to the contrasting and complementary traits al-Hamadhānī assigns his two central characters, whether in social status, degree of literary accomplishment, or the way each one relates to the truth. Where his narrator ʿĪsā is a successful merchant, Abū 'l-Fatḥ is a mendicant and a swindler whose changing personae are drawn from the lower social strata or margins of society; where ʿĪsā dabbles in scholarship and collects *adab* texts and sayings on his travels, Abū 'l-Fatḥ is an eloquent littérateur and stylistic virtuoso; where ʿĪsā is gullible, Abū 'l-Fatḥ is shrewd and crafty. In a similar vein, Kilito highlights the moral counterweight that al-Ḥarīrī's mostly irreproachable narrator, al-Ḥārith Ibn Hammām, provides for his trickster, Abū Zayd al-Sarūjī, who is not a model of virtue, even though in his periodic guise as holy man he delivers edifying discourses and conducts himself as a man of integrity (all of which is part of a ruse).[204]

201 Ibid., p. 4.

202 Kennedy, "The *Maqāmāt* as a nexus of interests," 156–157. Kennedy notes that the fall of Sarūj forms the backdrop to al-Ḥarīrī's forty-eighth *maqāma, al-Maqāma al-Ḥarāmiyya*, which was apparently the first that he composed; see al-Ḥarīrī, *Assemblies* 2:163. Cf. Stewart, "ʿĪsā b. Hišām's Shiism," p. 6, who sees a similar symbolism in the *nisbas* of both rogues: "the *nisba* al-Iskandarī refers instead to Alexandretta ... Near Antioch in northern Syria, this territory had been conquered by the Byzantines just decades before al-Hamaḏānī wrote the *Maqāmāt* .... Both al-Iskandarī and al-Sarūǧī are thus inhabitants of the borderlands between the Islamic states of the central Middle East and the territories that had recently been conquered by Christian forces. They are both men of dubious allegiances, potential apostates or renegades, who use their liminal origin in order to take advantage of others."

203 Stewart, "ʿĪsā b. Hišām's Shiism," p. 4.

204 Kilito, *Les Séances*, 248–259 ("Le menteur professionel").

Following this blueprint, the authors of subsequent *maqāmāt* devised names for their characters that to some degree reprised the earlier symbolism, whether through wordplay or intertextual allusion. In the Islamic West, the twelfth-century Andalusian al-Saraqusṭī (d. 1143), author of *al-Maqāmāt al-luzūmiyya*, named his narrator al-Sā'ib ibn Tammām, which rhymes with al-Ḥarīrī's al-Ḥārith b. Hammām and, as Stewart notes, "refers to the narrator's lack of purpose, for *al-sā'ib* means 'stray, lost, [or] wandering.'"[205] Several centuries later, during the Mamlūk sultanate, an Eastern author named Ibn Abī Ḥajalah (d. 1375), whose patronymic means "partridge," or "mountain quail," included ten *maqāmāt* in an anthology of his own work entitled *Manṭiq al-ṭayr* (The Conference/Speech of the Birds). Maurice Pomerantz, who has brought this work to light, has elucidated the clever punning in the names devised by Ibn Abī Ḥajalah for his protagonists, which not only rhyme with those of al-Ḥarīrī, but also play on the avian motif suggested by the author's own name. Pomerantz writes that Ibn Abī Ḥajalah "refers to his *maqāmāt* as ten feathers (*rīsh*) in the *Manṭiq al-ṭayr*":

> These are 'the feathers' which I attributed in my *māqāmāt* to Abū r-Riyāš the trickster (*ṣāḥib kayd*) who stands in for Abū Zayd [as-Sarūǧī]. And as-Sāǧiʿ b. Ḥamām who stands in the place of al-Ḥāriṯ b. Hammām.

Pomerantz explains that:

> … Like many authors of *maqāmahs*, Ibn Abī Ḥaǧalah invents the names of his protagonists to signal his indebtedness to al-Ḥarīrī. Ibn Abī Ḥaǧalah also uses the names to signal his own authorial persona. Punning on his avian family connection, he names his narrator, al-Sāǧiʿ b. Ḥamām, "Cooer son of the Dove." To his trickster figure, he gives the name, Abū r-Riyāš, "the one having many feathers," perhaps evoking thereby the variability of the trickster.[206]

Another Mamlūk-era collection of *maqāmāt* that Pomerantz has discussed, *al-Maqāmāt al-Jalāliyya* by al-Ḥasan b. Abī Muḥammad al-Ṣafadī (fl. first quarter of the 14th c.),

> is comprised of thirty *maqāmāt* that describe the meetings of the narrator Ṯāmir b. Zammām and the trickster character, Abū Fayd al-Luǧūǧī. The

205 Stewart, "The *Maqāma*," p. 151.
206 Pomerantz, "A *Maqāmah* on the Book Market of Cairo," 181–182.

> names of the two characters rhyme with those of the two protagonists of the *Maqāmāt* of al-Ḥarīrī: Ḥāriṯ b. Hammām and Abū Zayd al-Sarūǧī. … The name … Ṯāmir b. Zammām (lit. "sower, son of the one who bridles") is a meaningful variation on the meaning of Ḥāriṯ b. Hammām ["tiller, son of one beset by cares"]. Similarly, Abū Fayd al-Luǧūǧī resembles Ḥarīrī's Abū Zayd al-Sarūǧī, exchanging the notion of increase (*zayd*) for benefit (*fayd*).[207]

The idea of Everyman seems implicit in many of these names, as if to say that the protagonists are ordinary, flawed human beings who represent all mankind despite the extraordinary circumstances in which they often become enmeshed.[208] This motif is evident in the idea that the *nisba* al-Iskandarī hints at coming "from everywhere and anywhere." It is also driven home by the oft-quoted gloss of the celebrated commentator Abū l'Abbās al-Sharīshī (d. 1222) on the name of al-Ḥarīrī's narrator, Ḥārith Ibn Hammām, in which he cites a *ḥadīth* of the Prophet to the effect that Ḥārith and Hammām were the most truthful of names "because every man is a *ḥārith* (one who tills the earth or toils for his bread), as well as a *hammām* (one beset by cares)."[209] Though he veers from one behavioral extreme to another, there are intimations of universality in the name of al-Ḥarīrī's rogue hero as well. Michael Cooperson writes that,

> "Zayd" may allude to the figure of the same name used in examples in grammar books: "Zayd struck 'Amr," for example, has a resonance similar to "See Spot run" for American English speakers.[210]

As befits a swindler, *zayd* derives from the root meaning "to increase or augment." Enticing, too, is the correspondence set up by the rhyme between the generic term for the shape-shifting hero, *ṣāḥib kayd* (one who engages in ruse, artifice, or cunning) and Abū Zayd, the artificer par excellence.

If the onomastics in Arabic *maqāmāt* follow the leads of al-Hamadhānī and al-Ḥarīrī, the names of the principal characters in Alḥarizi's *Taḥkemoni* and those Hebrew *maqāmāt* most faithful to it are biblicized analogues which

---

207 Pomerantz, "A *Maqāma* Collection by a Mamlūk Historian," 641.

208 Cf. Stewart "'Īsā b. Hišām's Shiism," p. 6.

209 Al-Sharīshī's gloss on al-Sarūjī's name is discussed by Cooperson, *Impostures*, p. 10; Hämeen-Anttila, *Maqama*, 155; and Pomerantz, "A *Maqāma* Collection by a Mamlūk Historian," p. 641.

210 Cooperson, *Impostures*, p. 10. See also Hämeen-Anttila, *Maqama*, 155.

with great ingenuity preserve elements of the formal patterns and symbolism of the Arabic names but rely on a web of meaning intelligible to an audience immersed in Hebrew scripture. By means of clever wordplay and intertextual allusion, Alḥarizi's names gesture toward key *maqāma* motifs such as the eloquent rogue's vagabondage and rhetorical virtuosity. Ḥever ha-Keni and Heman ha-Ezraḥi both consist of a biblical personal name followed by a gentilic analogous to the Arabic *nisba* (which in Heman's case also functions as an epithet). Ḥever ha-Keni, who is the counterpart of al-Ḥarīrī's Abū Zayd al-Sarūjī—and appears already as such in *Maḥberot Iti'el*, Alḥarizi's Hebrew translation of al-Ḥarīrī's *Maqāmāt*—is the namesake of a figure from Judges 4:11 who "had separated from the other Kenites, descendants of Hobab, father-in-law of Moses, and had pitched his tent at Elon be-Ṣaʿananim, which is near Qedesh." (His wife, Jael, is renowned in her own right.) Alḥarizi has cleverly exploited the resonances of this verse to drive home the central *maqāma* theme of wandering and displacement: the toponym Ṣaʿananim is derived from the triliteral root *ṣ.ʿ.n*, which conveys roving, roaming, migration, nomadism, or being uprooted from one's place. In his fourth *maqāma*, al-Ḥarīrī uses a cognate Arabic root to convey departure.[211] Moreover, Ṣaʿananim corresponds to al-Ḥarīrī's Sarūj, which shares its three root letters with the Arabic for "saddle" and so affords the trickster Abū Zayd a fine opportunity for a pun invoking the idea of travel ("in Sarūj I was reared, and in the saddles [*al-surūj*] I got my training").[212] Finally, Ḥever's gentilic (ha-Keni) further alludes to his itinerancy since the biblical Kenites were nomadic. There is some suggestion that their eponymous ancestor was Cain, who was condemned by God to become a fugitive and a wanderer on the earth (Gen. 4:12).[213]

In contrast with the almost relentless intimations of displacement in Ḥever's name, Heman's epithet, ha-Ezraḥi denotes an indigenous person. The root *z-r-ḥ* yields the associated verb *zaraḥ*, "to rise from the soil," which, as Jonathan Decter points out, underscores Heman's profound rootedness in his native land of Sefarad.[214] (Ironically, though, a related sense of the root is used by Alḥarizi in a context of *deracination*, when he says in his Introduction that after completing his translation of al-Ḥarīrī's *Maqāmāt*, he fled the West and *zaraḥti*, "I

---

211 Lavi, "The Rationale of al-Ḥarīzī in Biblicizing the Maqāmāt of al-Ḥarīrī," 286; see also Decter, *Iberian Jewish Literature*, 29–30.

212 Lavi, "The Rationale of al-Ḥarīzī," 287.

213 Cf. Lavi, "The Rationale of al-Ḥarīzī," 284–287 and idem, "A Comparative Study," pp. 13–15. See also Decter, *Iberian Jewish Literature*, 128–129, and Segal, *The Book of Taḥkemoni*, 637–645.

214 Decter, *Iberian Jewish Literature*, 129.

shined" in the East.[215]) Heman's name also calls up associations with wisdom and poetry: in Scripture, the authorship of Psalm 88 is attributed to Heman ha-Ezraḥi, while in 1 Kings 5:11, Heman is a wise man with whom Solomon is compared. Psalm 88 is designated as a *maskil*, a literary work wisely wrought. Moreover, in a genealogy of Levites in 1 Chronicles 6:18, another Heman is called *ha-meshorer*, the singer or poet. The threefold association with Sefarad, wisdom, and poetry suggests that Alḥarizi channeled portions of his own persona through Heman.[216] By means of copious wordplay and punning on the resonant root *ḥ-b-r*, he also endowed Ḥever with some of his authorial traits. Ḥever is a friend (*ḥaver*) to Heman, to whom he vaunts his unparalleled ability to compose (*le-ḥabber*). Much like Alḥarizi, author of *maḥbarot*, he enagages in the act of authorship (*ani Ḥever meḥabber x*), joining together (*aḥabber*) scattered, unruly prose into orderly and beautifully balanced poetic compositions.[217]

In *Sefer hamusar*, the names Alḍāhirī bestows on his protagonists synthesize the patterns devised by al-Ḥarīrī and Alḥarizi, with a biblical personal name (Abner, Mordecai) followed by an adjective relating to a place-name (*ha-teimani, ha-ṣidoni*).[218] Reversing the Arabic precedents, the hero Abner has a patronymic (*ben Ḥeleq*) while the narrator Mordecai does not, which preserves a disparity between the two names, if not exactly the "complementary incompleteness" of the Arabic onomastics. It is likely no coincidence that Abner is a near-rhyme with Ḥever: both are bi-syllabic with alliteration in *bet* and *resh* and assonance in the second syllable, while the trisyllabic ben Ḥeleq/ ha-Keni share a *qof* and some vowel harmony.

Abner's given name conjures up some of his most salient characteristics. A biblical name, Abner is a variant of Abiner, meaning 'my father is Ner,' or 'my father is a lamp.'[219] The duplicity of the biblical Abner ben Ner is under-

215 Lavi, "A Comparative Study," pp. 18–19. *Mizraḥ*, meaning East, where the sun rises, is another derived form of the root.

216 Segal, *The Book of Taḥkemoni*, 643–644; Decter, *Iberian Jewish Literature*, 129.

217 See: Segal, *The Book of Taḥkemoni*, 639–643; Decter, *Iberian Jewish Literature*, 129; and Lavi, "A Comparative Study," pp. 13–14. The Hebrew *ḥibbur* and *nifrad* (or *meḥubbar* and *meforad*) render Arabic terms for poetry and prose respectively, *naẓm* (lit.: order, arrangement) and *nathr* (scattering, dispersal). Conversely, the transformation of prose into poetry was called *ʿaqd* (lit: solidifying) and poetry into prose *ḥall* ("dissolution"); see Heinrichs, "Prosimetrical Genres," p. 269.

218 It is conceivable that the Hebrew הצידוני is meant to recall the Judeo-Arabic אלצ׳אהרי, given the several similarities in their graphic representation. (Or, per Medina, Alḍāhirī's origins in Ṣaʿadah.) If so, the association would further augment the conflation of protagonists and author resulting from Alḍāhirī's adoption of his characters' names as pseudonyms.

219 See *BDB*, 4.

scored in II Samuel 3:25, where Joab reproves King David saying, "Don't you know that Abner son of Ner came only to deceive you, to learn your comings and goings and to find out all that you are planning?" Though Alḍāhirī never comments on it, the allusion to light in Abner's name is deliberately ironic since he is far more given to obfuscation than to transparency and has a penchant for imposture. The antiphrastic reading of his name obtains throughout much of the work, with plays on 'Abner' and 'light' already in the first *maqāma*, which unfolds under cover of darkness. When a man knocks at the door seeking shelter from the elements, Mordecai kindles a candle. Since the man does not divulge his identity, it is only with the aid of the lamp that Mordecai recognizes him as Abner. The scenario implies that Abner is less illuminating than his name would suggest. Nevertheless, further on in the chapter Abner's name is linked with his ability to shed light on convoluted legal riddles. The pun on light may also allude to his shimmering language, which is used in no small measure to deceive others, just as the name al-Sarūjī "coincidentally shares three letters with the Arabic root *s-r-j*, making it usable for playing games with such words as *sarj*, saddle, and *sirāj*, lamp."[220] Only the final line of *Sefer hamusar* seems to credit Abner with true illumination—a striking closure device that has Mordecai blessing him with a biblical verse originally predicated of God: "May the mighty and awesome One bless you, for with you is the fountain of life, by your light do we see light (Psalm 36:10)." But overall, the ever-changing Abner luxuriates in his ability to go incognito while Mordecai is generally put out when he arrives in an unfamiliar location and is not recognized as deserving of hospitality. Only rarely does he intentionally obscure his identity, conspiring with Abner to remain nameless while exploiting the unsuspecting victims of a joint hoax.[221] Abner's patronymic too intimates that he is a master of trickery and deception. Derived from the root meaning 'smooth,' the name Ḥeleq alerts us to Abner's disarming deployment of his silver tongue to swindle and defraud. In the fourteenth *maqāma*, Abner dupes his own boon companion. When Mordecai finally realizes that he has been hoodwinked, he is disgusted with himself for having been taken in by Abner's smooth speech, *ḥaliqut amarav*.[222] In rabbinic literature, the consonantal spelling *h.l.q.* occurs in certain instances of the rhyming moniker Ḥillaq u-Billaq, which Jastrow glosses as "fictitious names for

220 Cooperson, *Impostures*, p. 19.

221 See, e.g., *Sefer hamusar* # 3, pp. 82–83, lines 110–116.

222 *Sefer hamusar*, p. 182, line 87. *Heḥeliq amarav* and *heḥeliq lashon* are biblical idioms for "smooth talking"; cf. Prov. 2:16 and 28:23. For *ḥalaqot* as smooth, seductive speech, see Isa. 30:10; Ps. 12:3–4; and Dan. 11:32. For *ḥalaqlaqqot* as trickery or deceit, see Dan. 11:21.

any men (similar to our 'Tom, Dick, and Harry')."[223] While it is etymologically far-fetched, it is tempting to associate this non-specific name with a character who constantly sheds and transforms his identity as well as with the Everyman motif, and perhaps with the themes of strangeness, estrangement and deracination so central to the picaresque *maqāma*. If read as "portion," as in the biblical *ḥeleq ve-naḥalah* (inheritance), *ḥeleq* plays on Abner's preoccupation with material reward and perhaps alludes to his concern with his reputation for posterity, which comes to the fore in the final *maqāma*.

6 The Role of the Formal Poems

6.1 *Prosimetrum*

As noted, the *maqāma* is a mixed-form, prosimetrical genre, meaning that formal poems are interspersed throughout the prose narratives. By the time of al-Hamadhānī (2nd half of the 10th century), Arabic literary culture had long included prose stories intermingled with poems (e.g., the allegedly historical accounts known as *ayyām* or *akhbār alʿarab*) but had historically held poetry in much higher esteem than prose.[224] Arabic literary critics prized poetry's aesthetics of perfectly placed words, compression, symmetry, and the musicality of its quantitative meters that could best be appreciated when recited aloud. The emergence of the *maqāma* marked the culmination of a process whereby medieval scribes and literati moved from a strict division of labor—the one exclusively cultivating ornate prose and the other highly embellished poetry—to mastery of, and equal facility in, both media. The *adab* anthologies produced during this period—offering selections of poetry, prose, aphorisms and epistles—repeatedly move between the two types of discourse, regularly breaking off to cite poems before returning to the prose discussion at hand. In the *maqāma*, the inset poems often fulfill particular functions vis-à-vis the narrative. Sometimes the inserted poems are integral to the story, as when the hero is challenged to improvise a poem on a particular theme with the promise of reward (although it is always possible that the story was constructed around the poem).[225] At other times a poem recapitulates or comments on the preced-

223 See Jastrow, *Dictionary* 1:161, s.v. Billaq, citing Hullin 19a: "I know no Ḥillak and no Billak (I know of no authorities or individual opinions), I only know a tradition," and Sanhedrin 98b: "shall Ḥillak and Billak (any persons indiscriminately) enjoy it?"

224 Much of this paragraph is indebted to Heinrichs, "Prosimetrical Genres in Classical Arabic."

225 Scholars have speculated that the poems sometimes inspire the surrounding narrative

ing rhymed prose text rather than continuing the narrative or advancing the plot. In such cases, the poems play second fiddle to the prose; their principal purpose is to embellish and lyricize the narrative rather than move it forward. Discussing one of the best-known prosimetrical texts that is not a *maqāma*, Wolfhart Heinrichs has drawn an apt analogy between the role of the poems inset in the stories of the Arabian Nights and that of illustrations, since "they both pick out one moment in the story-line as a still."[226] Among the diverse functions fulfilled by the 170 poems in al-Ḥarīrī's *Maqāmāt* is the provision of closure. One type of closure poem serves as "the crowning end to a sermon or harangue" given by the rogue hero when posing as a preacher. Closure is also provided at the end of more than half of al-Ḥarīrī's *maqāmāt* by means of a poetic envoi in which the disguised hero reveals his identity and justifies his ruse before departing the scene. Heinrichs writes that in these instances, "the sequence prose-poetry is rarely reversed ... and probably felt to be climactic."[227]

In *Sefer hamusar*, as in other Hebrew *maqāmāt*, poems inserted into the prose narrative are regularly introduced with formulaic phrases that serve as transition markers. These phrases signal a change in voice as well as in expressive medium, since Mordecai typically delivers the prose narration while Abner recites most of the poems embedded in it. Abner's poetic performances are introduced by one of two biblical formulae phrased in the third person, either, *va-ya'an va-yomar*, "he replied, saying ..." or *va-yissa meshalo* (*va-yomar*), "he took up his parable/theme (and said ...)."[228] Although Abner usually declaims, periodically the narrator does so. In those instances, he substitutes the first person variant, *va'a'an va'omar*, "*I* replied, saying ...." A scriptural set phrase, *va-yissaʿ meshalo* occurs in Numbers 23–24 where it prefaces Balaam's stirring prophecies. The polyvalent term *mashal* can be difficult to translate; in biblical and rabbinic literature it signifies a proverb, parable, or allegory. Medieval exegetes and literary critics applied the term to figurative or metaphorical expression.[229] The gnomic overtones of *va-yissa meshalo* no doubt carried over to the Hispano-Hebrew *maqāmāt*, whose authors framed their works as "quasi-prophetic revelations," claiming to have composed their books in accord with a

---

rather than the other way around, particularly in the more rhetorical episodes where nothing much happens on the level of the plot, see, e.g., Pagis, *Change and Tradition in the Secular Poetry*, 204–212.

226 Heinrichs, "Modes of Existence of the Poetry in the Arabian Nights," 530.

227 "Prosimetrical Genres in Classical Arabic," 267.

228 The phrase *va-ya'an va-yomar* recurs in varied contexts throughout Scripture; see, e.g., Gen. 18:27; Ex. 4:1, 19:8; Zech. 3:4, 3:6; Job 4:1; 6:1.

229 See Cohen, *Three Approaches to Biblical Metaphor*.

command from on high; a heavenly commission.[230] Presumably over time *vayissa meshalo* no longer actively evoked the topos of poet qua prophet. But it became a fixture of the *maqāma* literature, where it preserved a vestigial link between poetry and prophetic utterances as the conventionalized header for an inset poem.

Other set phrases mark the flow in the opposite direction, which is to say that they signal the resumption of the prose narrative following a versified interlude. At the conclusion of nearly every poem Abner recites, the narrator registers his (and/or the crowd's) admiration for the scintillating verbal display. These reactions are prefaced by the transition marker *amar ha-maggid*, "said the narrator," followed by some variant on "when I (or: they) heard Abner's words and poems, I (they) marveled at his electrifying brilliance and the eloquence of his speech." Once this routine praise is uttered, the plot resumes. The phrase *amar ha-maggid* is likely the Hebrew equivalent of the Arabic *qālā al-rāwī* ("the storyteller said") or *qālā ṣāḥib al-ḥadīth* ("the master of the tale said").[231] In his *Story Telling Techniques in the Arabian Nights*, David Pinault cites a study linking the recurrence of these phrases in manuscripts of the *Nights* to the oral provenance of the stories recorded in the manuscripts. Pinault observes that such phrases tend to appear at transition points, often between the conclusion of a poem and the resumption of the prose narrative. He notes that in some manuscripts these phrases are written "in disproportionately large characters" or in a different ink from the surrounding text, suggesting that they may originally have been visual markers for reciters, alerting them to "an imminent change in narrative voice."[232] In the extant mss. of *Sefer hamusar*, most of which are quite late (18th–19th c.), the poems are set off visually from the prose in several ways. They are either centered or transcribed in two vertical columns, with space between the two hemistichs of each line to mark the caesura, in accordance with poetic convention. By contrast, the prose runs straight across the page. Though in some manuscripts it is minimal, the additional white space around the poems as well as in between hemistichs facilitates spotting the verse. In the 19th-century British Library ms., the poems are written in large and beautiful, clear square characters, whereas much of the rhymed prose is in a somewhat smaller semi-cursive hand. In the 18th-century

230 This device was employed by Judah Ibn Shabbetai, Judah Alḥarizi, Joseph Ibn Zabara, Isaac Ibn Sahula and Shem Tov Falaquera; see Pagis, "The Poet as Prophet in Medieval Hebrew Literature." It was a topos of Arabic *maqāmāt* as well; see Kilito, *Arabs and the Art of Storytelling*, 1–17.

231 See the extensive discussion in Huss, "The 'Maggid' in the Classical 'Maqama.'"

232 Pinault, *Story Telling Techniques in the Arabian Nights*, 13–14.

Bodleian ms., only the poems have vowel points, and they are also copied with an obvious caesura between the stichs. In both of these mss., the transition markers (*va-yissaʿ meshalo*, *va-yaʿan va-yomar*, etc.) are either given their own line and centered above the first line of the poem, or, if on the same line as the preceding prose, a generous space is left between the end of the last prose sentence and the phrase signaling the start of a poem.

6.2 *Poetic Varieties*

The poems occurring at key junctures in every chapter of *Sefer hamusar* are formally and thematically varied and range from two lines of gnomic verse to just over one hundred lines. The work includes 137 Hebrew poems, the vast majority of which are Alḍāhirī's original compositions. Also included are his hallmark contrafactions—emulations, appropriations, and responses to the poems of others—as well as some Hebrew renderings of Arabic poems.[233] Alḍāhirī's literary tastes tend toward the classicizing, favoring the "canonical" rhyme schemes and quantitative metrics of the Andalusian school of the 11th and 12th centuries. These formal features lend the poems a sense of movement and symmetry. But he does not hesitate to use prosodic models with a more archaic feel as well. Some of his longer pieces lamenting the *galut* or supplicating God for forgiveness are structurally and formally more akin to the classical *piyyut* that antedated Andalusian poetry. Often, they are marked by full alphabetic acrostics and the syllabic meters of liturgical poetry or have no meter whatsoever. Some employ the ancient rhetorical device of *shirshur* or anadiplosis, which links the strophes by opening each new stanza with the final word of the preceding one.[234] There are poems that closely resemble a long line of venerable *piyyutim* like the *ʿavodah*—an early Palestinian genre that flourished well into the Andalusian period—whose preambles recount the nation's sacred history, surveying creation, the succession of the patriarchs, the exodus from Egypt, and the revelation on Mt. Sinai.[235] But in Alḍāhirī's hands, such pieces acquire medieval coloration, whether by means of the philosophical and cosmological commonplaces that he takes for granted or the complaints deploring Muslim oppression that weave their way in and out of so much of his verse. The-

233 On the latter see Ratzaby, "The Influence of al-Ḥariri Upon Alḍāhiri" and idem, "Sheloshah shirim meturgamim."

234 Cf. *sharsheret*, "chain." See the poem "Zeraʿ ʿaniyah ṣahali," in Tobi, "Shenei piyyuṭim ḥadashim le-rabbi zekharya alḍāhirī." On *shirshur* see, e.g., Yona and Pasternak, "Concatenation in Ancient Near East Literature, Hebrew Scripture and Rabbinic Literature" and Münz-Manor, "Studies in Figurative Language Of Pre-Classical *Piyyut*," 135–141.

235 See Swartz and Yahalom, *Avodah: An Anthology of Ancient Poetry for Yom Kippur*, 1–42.

matic shifts occur particularly in his lengthier poems which, as a result of their hybridity, defy strict generic classification according to the dictates of Andalusian poetics. Their movement between sets of themes is on the whole much more free flowing than that of the earlier Arabic and Hebrew *qaṣīdas* with their prescribed transitions. Alḍāhirī's rhyme schemes are either monorhymed or strophic, though he often adds internal rhymes and other flourishes that lend the poetry additional aural density and musicality. Ratzaby calls attention to his periodic preference for the Andalusians' vocalic rhymes that level out the difference between *qamaṣ* and *pataḥ*, *ṣere* and *segol*, despite the time-honored Yemenite tradition of pronunciation that distinguished between these vowels. (On the other hand, he sees a reflection of the author's Ṣanʿānī accent in his rhyming *segol* with *pataḥ*).[236] Most of the formal and prosodic characteristics of Alḍāhirī's poetry would have been familiar to his audience, having been naturalized in Yemenite *dīwāns* and the *dīwāns* of other Eastern Jewish communities.[237]

The Hebrew secondary literature refers to the more prayerful, sermonic, and penitential poems in *Sefer hamusar* as *piyyutim*. But apart from the actual *piyyutim* that Abner improvises when serving as *ḥazzan* in Tiberias, these pieces are not designated for liturgical use in the fictional narrative, and only a few were subsequently adopted for that purpose in real life. Yemenite *dīwāns* included a wide array of poems designated as *piyyutim* that were not intended for use in the statutory synagogue prayers but rather in extra-liturgical or paraliturgical settings: weddings, circumcision ceremonies and other communal celebrations, pre-dawn penitential vigils, and recitations following the statutory prayers.[238] Alḍāhirī's devotional or pietistic poems often develop the themes of their surrounding prose texts. Much like the poem serving as the culmination of a sermon in al-Ḥarīrī's *Maqāmāt*, there are hortatory poems whose penitential motifs and censure of the material world (*dhamm al-dunyā*) furnish a finale to Abner's sermons. When, in the eleventh *maqāma*, he appears in tattered clothes as a fire-and-brimstone preacher urging renunciation, his spellbinding oratory persuades Mordecai and the gathered crowds to take to heart his pious admonitions to repudiate worldly desires and pursuits. Abner's asceticism is

236 See Ratzaby's Introduction, *Sefer hamusar*, 14; Tobi, "*Tséré* (E vowel) and *Ḥolam* (O vowel) in Yemenite Jewish Pronunciation"; and Yaʿakov, "Yemen, Pronunciation Traditions."

237 For antecedents, see, e.g., Tobi ed., *Abraham Ben Halfon: Poems*.

238 See Tobi, *Abraham Ben Halfon*, 49–69 and 218–220; idem, "Poetry and Society in the Works of Abraham Ibn Ḥalfon"; and Ratzaby, "Piyyuṭei teiman: bibliografiyah," who explains that such extra-liturgical poems are also found in a dedicated "*Shirot ve-tishbaḥot*" section at the end of the *tiklāl*, whereas actual *piyyutim* are found in the *tiklāl* sections headed "*Seliḥot*," "*Seder ha-raḥamim*," and "*Tokheḥot u-vaqqashot*."

viewed as serious and sincere—not only by the credulous Mordecai but also by much of the secondary literature—since, unlike al-Ḥarīrī's Abū Zayd, who is often caught drinking in the tavern, he is never exposed as a hypocrite or sinner at the end of his jeremiads. And yet, there are some ever so subtle suggestions of cynicism and lack of contrition on Abner's part. His urgent exhortations to repentance are followed by a confession that seems heartfelt, yet it is not without a hint of the mercenary:

> Accept these words *gratis* from him who has acquired them with his heart's blood. For how many troubles have afflicted me because I did not act properly? I have become an example for the many ... take me as a sign, it should suffice you that I have sunk appallingly. Take reproof from me now (*ve'attah kaḥ musar mimenni*), before you seek me and find I am gone.

Abner rebukes his listeners for indulging their baser appetities and amassing material goods whose value is ephemeral and holds himself up as an example of what not to do. And yet, the fact that he urges acceptance of his advice *be-ḥinnam* (free of charge) implies that, under other circumstances, he might have expected remuneration. What is more, following his rousing homily, he returns home with his entourage and crows about the efficacy of his sermon, which prompted the crowd to mass repentance and rebuke of one's neighbor. It is precisely at this point that the anagnorisis occurs, the narrator having pursued him. When Mordecai asks why his old friend has prematurely aged, Abner explains that, "for some years we have been in the hands of cruel oppressors," who had imprisoned him in their tower and subjected him to hard labor. Crying out with a bitter soul, he recites a long, mournful poem expanding on these themes. Yet it is the succinct couplet at chapter's end that best encapsulates the thrust of his sermon and allows Abner to depart, formally closing the episode:

> Seek truth, cast away sins, and to my words attend;
> Woe to him whose evil deeds anger the Lord but pander to men.[239]

Abner's poems in praise of the Torah, the Talmud, and medieval exegetical and philosophical works and their authors also reprise the themes of the narratives in which they occur. The same is true of his openly polemical poems against

239 See "'Anenei dim'i shequdim," pp. 162–163 and "Emet baqqesh ve-hashlekh ha-meradim," p. 164.

Islam, his petitions to God for redemption, his poems of messianic speculation, and his kabbalistic verse. The preponderance of such overtly Jewish sensibilities has led scholars to view *Sefer hamusar* through the prism of its religious orientation, at times at the expense of its picaresque features, although Ratzaby himself attributed its poor reception to precisely those aspects of the work that marked it as secular. Shalom Medina, on the other hand, placed *Sefer hamusar* in an intermediate zone "between sacred and secular" (*bein qodesh le-ḥol*), noting that 31 out of its 45 chapters contain some form of moral instruction, penitential poems, prayer-like supplications, or praise for religious scholars and their works.[240] A glance at the incipits in Ratzaby's index of poems does give the impression that they are heavily weighted toward the devotional. Certainly, the prominence of religious concerns is more marked in *Sefer hamusar* than in most Iberian Hebrew *maqāmat* of an earlier era and can presumably be ascribed to the historical moment, political, religious, and intellectual milieu in which the work was conceived and executed.[241]

The impetus to read *Sefer hamusar* through a pious lens is encouraged by Alḍāhirī himself in his paratexts. No doubt it is also fueled by the fact that he does not cultivate all of the secular genres for which the Andalusians were celebrated and that those he omits are precisely those that, viewed from a somewhat reductive perspective, might be expected to give the most offense to a conservative religious sensibility. In medieval Hebrew poetry the label "secular" is not entirely adequate and applies at least as much to function as to substance. The secular poetry introduced by the Andalusian Hebrew poets had been inspired by Arabic courtly models governed by the conventions of the exceedingly mannered modernist (*muḥdath*) school that had originated in the Abbāsid East. This highly stylized Hebrew verse was entirely external to the realm of the liturgy and fulfilled an array of social functions quite remote from the world of the synagogue. Courtly poems were renowned for their celebrations of erotic love, the beauties of nature, the pleasures of wine-drinking, and the joys of friendship as well as for their meditations on the evanescence of these fragile, sensual delights. Although these themes frequently overlapped, they were explored in discrete genres, each with its own body of conventional motifs.

The secular genres in *Sefer hamusar* include outpourings of longing for a faraway friend; panegyrics; versified riddles; complaints about the vicissitudes and capriciousness of Time (i.e., fate); contemplative pieces; aphoristic poems; and

240 Medina, "Sefer hamusar, mahadurat ratzaby," p. 11.

241 See, e.g., Tobi, "Yemenite Poetry and its Relationship with Sefardi Poetry," 319.

poems of invective and self-promotion, all of which were part of the extended Andalusian repertoire. Some of the riddle poems are translations from the Arabic; their solutions are often drawn from the realia of everyday life, such as the two doors of the main entrance to a Yemeni house or the brush for applying kohl to the eyes. There is often overlap between the friendship poems and panegyrics; the protagonists address heartfelt tributes to scholarly friends in distant Yemeni cities, whom they yearn to see and whose verse and sagely writings they praise.[242] Broadly construed, the panegyrics are not solely for individuals and have less of a political subtext than most: they celebrate well-known books and their authors—Maimonides' *Mishneh torah* and *Guide*; Obadiah of Bertinoro's Mishnah commentary; Joseph Albo's *Sefer ha'iqqarim*; David Kimhi's *Sefer hashorashim*; the Zohar—and the rabbinic emissary from the Holy Land who comes to Yemen laden with books for sale. There is also a paean to Tiberias and its scholars that bears affinities with the Arabic *faḍā'il al-buldān*, a long-standing literary genre praising the virtues of a certain city or region.[243] But even though this poem of Yemenite provenance is politically deferential in its affirmation of the Tiberian sages' religious authority, there is no evidence in *Sefer hamusar* of a panegyric dedicated to an actual patron or maecenas. The closest we get to such an impulse is a metapoetic meditation that closes with an oblique reference to an unnamed sage "whose words have kept my buckling feet firm, / who has braced my tottering knees." There is no suggestion, however, that the work was composed with the support of a wealthy benefactor in mind; certainly there is nothing approaching Alḥarizi's brazen provision of the *Taḥkemoni* with multiple dedicatees. (Alḥarizi's Arabic biographer notes that he was known for lavishing praise and then unceremoniously retracting it when support was no longer forthcoming.)[244] In fact, in the 25th *maqāma*, there is a subtle lampoon of the genre and its one-size-fits-all platitudes. Mordecai pre-

---

242 See, e.g., "Asher 'oleh 'alei qirot levavi," *Sefer hamusar*, pp. 234–236, addressed to Ṣaddiq ben 'Ovadiah in the city of Diqla (Ṣa'adah) and "Ke-mitokh ha-ḥalom er'eh temunah," ibid., 236–238, addressed to Avraham ben Yeshu'a, also of Diqla.

243 See, e.g., Elinson, *Looking Back at al-Andalus*, 117–150; Enderwitz, "Faḍā'il"; Livne-Kafri, "The Muslim Traditions 'in Praise of Jerusalem' (*Faḍā'il al-Quds*): Diversity and Complexity"; Mourad, "Jerusalem in Early Islam: The Making of the Muslims' Holy City"; and idem, "The *Faḍā'il* of Jerusalem Books as Anthologies." In *Taḥkemoni* #38 (= Toporowski #47), major Levantine cities take turns singing their own praises; see Alḥarizi, *Taḥkemoni*, ed. Yahalom-Katsumata, pp. 425–431.

244 Sadan reasons that his biographer learned of this reputation from a Jewish informant; Alḥarizi would not have dared to lampoon a Muslim patron, lest he endanger the Jewish community hosting him. See Sadan, "Judah Alḥarizi as a Cultural Junction," 38. On the complicated process of dedicating the *Taḥkemoni*, see Rand, *Evolution*, 24–41.

vails upon Abner to come to his hometown of Sidon to be honored with a public feast, and when Abner's "heart is merry with wine" (cf. Esther 1:10), he winks at Mordecai to draw near and recites a panegyric that ostensibly praises his dear friend as a munificent benefactor. But the tropes are so conventional that the poem is not in any way tailored to Mordecai and is really an encomium to the ideal, selfless patron. It is as though Abner has whipped "Ha-yippale be'ein kol nediv ha-lev" out of his arsenal and deployed it on the spur of the moment, for the occasion. Though Abner uses the poem as currency to repay Mordecai for his kindness and generosity, it highlights just how suffused with exaggeration, conventional and impersonal the genre can be.[245]

Complaints about the capriciousness of Time with a capital T (*ha-zeman*; *al-dahr*)—a malign force that causes sudden misfortune—were familiar from Arabic and Andalusian Hebrew poetry. Abraham Ibn Ezra was known for cultivating this genre and often treated the theme in short, quasi-sermonic poems advocating resignation to one's lot. Alḍāhirī, by contrast, seems uncomfortable with the notion that blind fate determines human fortunes, and his poems on the topic tend to introduce an element of doctrinal orthodoxy, with recourse to the notions of divine decree and providence. His reluctance to accept the impious implications of such determinism aligns with what appears to be his avoidance of the more sensual or morally lax genres of erotic and bacchic poetry.[246] On the other hand, there is no animus against enjoying wine in the rhymed prose narratives of *Sefer hamusar*, and Alḍāhirī does not hesitate to include suggestive elements in some of the tales embedded in his picaresque *maqāma*.[247] Several of the folktales whose provenance he labels as "Arab" are conduits for salacious material, suggesting that he is not entirely puritanical, although he prefers to introduce these themes through the back door.[248] That said, in at least one of his poems that draws on *Maḥberot Immanuel*, there are a few

---

245 *Sefer hamusar*, p. 291. On varying models of patronage, see Alfonso and Decter eds., *Patronage, Production, and Transmission of Texts in Medieval and Early Modern Jewish Cultures*, 1–9. On the panegyric, see Decter, *Dominion Built of Praise*.

246 Cf. Itzhaki, "Abraham Ibn Ezra as a Harbinger of Changes in Secular Hebrew Poetry," 150–151. See also Tobi, *Abraham Ben Halfon*, 218–220.

247 For a chaste depiction of wine drinking in a garden with music and poetry, see *Sefer hamusar*, #16, 190–200.

248 See, e.g., *Sefer hamusar* #10, pp. 151–155, published by Schirmann as "Ha-betulah haṣenu'ah ve-sheloshet ha-ḥoshqim" in "Two Maqamas of Zecharia Aldahiri's Sepher Hamussar." In the Stith Thompson index, it appears as international tale type 1730, the Entrapped Suitors. Ratzaby identifies a parallel in al-Jāḥiẓ, *al-Maḥāsin wa'l-aḍdād*. See also *Sefer hamusar* #25, pp. 293–296, published by Schirmann in *Ha'aretz* June 16, 1939 as "Neqamat ha-shifḥah."

erotic turns of phrase and possible double entendres, though compared with Immanuel's precedent Alḍāhirī's piece is fairly sedate.[249] But in several other adaptations of Immanuel, who relishes the insolent and the prurient, Alḍāhirī neutralizes his predecessor's licentiousness considerably; presumably in deference to Yemenite Jewish cultural norms and sensibilities, including his own. This sanitizing tendency is particularly noticeable in his poem on the month of Tishrei in #27, which draws on Immanuel's corresponding poem in his ninth *maḥberet* ("In Tishrei I will rejoice, for the appointed times of the Lord will rouse me to sing a song of erotic desire"), which in turn responds to Alḥarizi's in his chapter on the months of the year.[250] In Alḥarizi's brief tercet, Tishrei is an occasion for imbibing, with no mention of the sacramental.[251] Considering that Tishrei is a penitential month of utmost solemnity, Immanuel's poem is even more deliberately provocative, invoking wine, women, and song—the stock motifs of Andalusian courtly poetry.

6.3 *Contrafaction and Counter-Writing*

Alḍāhirī's re-writing of his predecessors' Tishrei poems is an instance of what is known as *muʿāraḍa*, the emulation of another's poem, achieved by deliberately matching the existing poem's rhyme scheme, meter, and opening words with the intent of critiquing or surpassing it, or presenting an opposing point of view.[252] Such emulation paid homage to the original, but there was also an element of reflected glory in the desire to appropriate the prosodic framework and respond to the themes of an often well-known and highly esteemed poem. Literally, the term *muʿāraḍa* signified opposition or confrontation, and the technique entailed "writing against" or counterfeiting the original by transforming its genre or form or by subverting its meaning. The new poem might borrow specific images or a series of rhyme words or individual rare words from its model in order to turn it "upside down in order to celebrate an opposite set

249 See *Sefer hamusar* #8, p. 136, "Shimʿu shiri ha-qadmonim."

250 See: "Be-tishrei esmeḥa liqrat penei el/ ve-hinneni ashorer shir ʿagavim," *Sefer hamusar*, p. 319, lines 87–96 and "Be-tishrei esmeḥa ki moʿadei el/yeʿiruni le-shorer shirei ʿagavim," *Maḥberot immanuel ha-romi*, ed. Jarden, 1:167, lines 10–16. In Alḍāhirī's case, Ratzaby glosses *shir ʿagavim* as an epithalamium, as Abner recites the poem at a wedding celebration.

251 For the text see Alḥarizi, *Taḥkemoni*, ed. Yahalom-Katsumata, p. 170, lines 237–242. See also Segal's analysis, *The Book of Taḥkemoni*, pp. 449–453.

252 See: Heinrichs, "Allusion and Intertextuality"; Gruendler, "Originality in Imitation," 440; Fakhreddin, *Metapoesis in the Arabic Tradition*, 162–200; Schippers, "Muʿāraḍa"; van Gelder, "Muʿāraḍa."

of values."[253] The oppositional sense of the term also highlighted the artistic rivalry inherent in the bid to improve upon or outdo the earlier poem. Within the patronage system of the Arabo-Persian world, some poetic emulations were undertaken for the sake of professional success and could eclipse the fame of the original.[254] Perhaps the closest Western European analogue was contrafaction, the medieval and Renaissance vocal music practice of setting new poems to older melodies. By re-using the older melody, the new song affiliated itself with its earlier model, but the act of "re-texting" also displaced the words with which the music was previously paired and associated.[255] In the Latin West, the composition resulting from this emulative process was known as a *contrafactum*, from the verb *contrafacere*, meaning "to imitate, counterfeit, or forge." Like a *muʿāraḍa*, the contrafactum not only appropriated the rhymes and meter of its model but also responded to or adapted its meaning.[256]

The technique of contrafaction was discussed by Arabic literary critics, and Moses Ibn Ezra following them, in connection with plagiarism or *sarīqa* (lit. "theft"), the appropriation of a line or entire poem from another poet.[257] Between the eleventh and the fourteenth centuries, Arabic critics generated an unsystematic typology of acceptable and unacceptable literary borrowings. The idea of *muʿāraḍa* presupposed a binary conception that distinguished sharply between the matter and form of a poem. Drawing on Aristotelian poetics, medieval Arabic and Hebrew literary theorists viewed poetry as verbal expression ornamented with figurative language. They worked with a limited inventory of conventional themes and motifs (*maʿnā*, pl. *maʿānī*), which were considered common property and could therefore be borrowed from an existing composition with relative impunity. What differentiated one poem from another, and testified to a poet's skill and creativity, was the wording (*lafẓ*, pl. *alfāẓ*) used to clothe these motifs.[258] Joseph Sadan has surveyed collections

253 Gruendler, "Originality in Imitation," 453.

254 Cf. Gruendler, ibid., p. 440: "This act of direct dialogue with earlier works was performed variously as an act of homage or bravura, an unconscious reflex, a patron's commission, or a test or demonstration of an aspiring poet in a court *majlis*."

255 See Falck, "Contrafactum," and Alexander, "On the Reuse of Poetic Form."

256 See Falck, "Parody and Contrafactum: A Terminological Clarification" and Alexander, "The Elizabethan Lyric as Contrafactum: Robert Sidney's 'French Tune' Identified."

257 See Moses Ibn Ezra, *Kitāb al-muḥāḍara wa'l-mudhākara*, 92b (pp. 174–175); Pagis, "ʿAl mussag ha-meqoriyut ba-shirah haʿivrit mi-tequfat sefarad"; idem, *Secular Poetry and Poetic Theory*, 101–115; Habermann, "ʿAl gonvei ha-shir"; and Levin, "The Concept of Plagiarism in Mediaeval Hebrew Poetry in Spain."

258 See Kilito, *The Author and His Doubles*, 17–23; Heinrichs, "Literary Theory: the Problem and Its Efficiency"; idem, "Sariḳa"; Bonebakker, "Ancient Arabic Poetry and Plagiarism: A Terminological Labyrinth"; von Grunebaum, "The Concept of Plagiarism in Arabic The-

of such motifs, charting the progression from early anthologies included in books of classical Arabic poetic theory (*balāgha*) to practical manuals of *maʿānī* intended as handbooks for poets. He notes that in describing the *maʿnā* "as raw material that is moulded and reshaped by the poet into a relatively new *lafẓ*," the literary theorists invoked metaphors of craftsmanship to convey the poet's skill: carpentry, woodcarving, metal-casting, weaving.[259] There was thus a fine line between legitimate borrowing and plagiarism. Because the artistic and moral guidelines were so elastic, accusations of poetic theft recur throughout the corpus of medieval Hebrew poetry.[260]

Nevertheless, the Andalusian Hebrew poets had employed emulation since the tenth century, imitating, translating, or borrowing from Arabic as well as Hebrew poems. In epistolary exchanges, they replied cleverly to their correspondents in the same meter and rhyme scheme.[261] The products of emulation were not exclusively literary; they fulfilled a social function and had a performative aspect as well. At literary soirées, a rising poet might be challenged to improvise a poem that imitated the formal features of a piece by a senior colleague of great renown. The imitation served both as a means of establishing his literary credentials and as a token of admiration for the original poem. The young Judah Halevi is said to have gained his entrée into Andalusian literary society by successfully imitating a difficult strophic poem by Joseph Ibn Ṣaddiq, which was itself modeled on an Arabic poem.[262] It was not uncommon to find chains of emulations, especially in the realm of the strophic *muwashshaḥāt*, whose complex metrics and rhyme schemes were typically constructed

ory"; Peled, "On the Concept of Literary Influence in Classical Arabic Criticism"; al-Ḥarīrī, *Assemblies*, 1:481–483; and Cooperson, *Impostures*, 200–215.

259 Sadan, "Maidens' Hair and Starry Skies: Imagery System and *Maʿānī* Guides," esp. 64–66, and idem, "Kings and Craftsmen—a Pattern of Contrasts: On the History of a Medieval Arabic Humoristic Form," esp. 26–28. Note that the Hebrew equivalent used for *maʿnā* is the cognate *ʿinyan*; see, e.g., *Sefer hamusar*, p. 227, lines 131–132.

260 See, e.g. Solomon Ibn Gabirol, "Haganavta ve-khiḥashta amaray" in Schirmann, *HPSP*, 1:227, no. 86a. The text is also found, with slight variations, in Brody and Schirmann eds., *Solomon Ibn Gabirol, Secular Poems*, p. 124, no. 199, where the Judeo-Arabic superscription reads, *wa-lahu fī shakhṣ iddaʿā fī baʿḍ qawlihi* ("a poem of his about an individual who arrogated to himself some of his [the poet's] words"). See also ibid., p. 49, no. 86 and p. 102, no. 167; and Moses Ibn Ezra, "ʿAd an be-galut," in Brody and Pagis eds., *Moses Ibn Ezra, Secular Poems*, 1:66–67, vv. 19–24.

261 See Pagis, *Secular Poetry and Poetic Theory*, 103 and 286 and idem, *Change and Tradition*, 48–49, where Pagis notes that poems sent to a poet were often included in his *dīwān* to help the reader make sense of his responses.

262 Halevi alludes to his contrafactual technique in the rhymed prose epistle to Moses Ibn Ezra to which he appended the poem. See Rand, "*Shalom rav veyesha yiqrav*—Yehuda ha-Levi's Epistle to Moshe ibn Ezra: A New Edition and Commentary."

around the pattern established by their concluding verse, or *kharja*, which was often a quote from an Arabic poem or a Romance lyric.[263] There are indications, for example, that Abraham Ibn Ezra's liturgical *muwashshaḥāt* were sung to melodies of non-liturgical, or even Arabic *muwashshaḥāt*. The copyist of his *dīwān* recorded in his Judeo-Arabic superscriptions the opening of the Arabic poem in whose meter a given *piyyut* was written.[264] "Imrat yeḥidah le-yaḥid ya'atah," a poem about the soul and God, is headed: *wa-lahu aiḍan wazn "ward al-khudud wa-siḥr al-muqal …"* ("another poem of his in the meter of 'The rosy cheek and beguiling eyes' …"). Joachim Yeshaya has listed 80 such *wazn* indications in Moses Darʿī's (13th-century) corpus of liturgical poetry, at least one third of which are modeled on poems by Judah Halevi.[265] Many poems in relatively late *dīwāns* from North Africa bear the Judeo-Arabic heading, *bi-laḥn*, "to the tune of," followed by the opening line of a (once) well-known song, not necessarily of Jewish provenance, such as the intriguing snippet, "*Yā muslimūn galbi*" ("O Muslims, my heart!"). This phenomenon, which reminds us that the *dīwān* was not simply read but chanted in unison, and which bears comparison with the emulative musical technique of *contrafactio*, reached its peak with Yisrael Najara (1555–1625), who set his sacred love poems to popular Ottoman songs of the eastern Mediterranean.[266]

Among Yemenite Jewish poets, the mimetic practice came to the fore in the 16th century with Alḍāhirī. Rather than *muʿāraḍa*, they used the term *jawāb*, or "response," to designate a contrafaction. But the approach was essentially the same: a *jawāb* responded not only to the formal features of another's poem but also to its content. Like Alḍāhirī's counter-poem on the month of Tishrei, a *jawāb* was typically a free-standing piece that signaled its intertextual relationship to a particular poem by intentionally matching its rhyme, meter, and opening words and reworking its themes. A closely related technique, which Alḍāhirī deployed with great relish, consisted of "enhancing" an existing poem by braiding into it verses of one's own invention and claiming the

263 See Stern, "Imitations of Arabic Muwaššaḥāt in Spanish-Hebrew Poetry"; Einbinder, "*Muʿāraḍa* as a Key to the Literary Unity of the *Muwashshaḥ*"; and Schoeler, "Muwashshaḥ."

264 Levin, *Abraham Ibn Ezra: His Life and His Poetry*, 314–317.

265 See Yeshaya, *Poetry and Memory in Karaite Prayer*, 44–54. Yeshaya notes that the term *wazn* is usually reserved for the metrical patterns of strophic poetry, as distinct from *ʿarūḍ*, which refers to classical poetic quantitative meters.

266 Ratzaby writes that Yemenite *dīwāns*, by contrast, do not include headers designating a poem's melody because the melody is strictly a matter of oral tradition handed down from one generation to the next; see Ratzaby, "Ṣura ve-laḥan be-shirat teiman le-sugeha," 18. On Najara see Chapter Six.

resulting composite as one's own. The entire piece—effectively a new poem that preserved the *disjecta membra* of the original within it—was referred to as a *ziyāda*, or augmentation. These Judeo-Arabic terms are employed in manuscript superscriptions to Alḍāhirī's *dīwān*: in the 98-poem *dīwān* in ms. Guenzburg 1306 there are countless headers beginning *wa-lahu jawāb* ... or *wa-lahu aiḍan ziyādah ʿala* .... Sometimes the Judeo-Arabic technical terms are preferred over their Hebrew equivalents, even when the rest of the header is in Hebrew. In the Oxford ms. of *Sefer hamusar*, a marginal note reads: *jawāb "az baʿalot mequṭeret mor" le-ha-ravʿa* [*r. avraham ibn ʿezra*], *siman avner*.[267] But most of the time Hebrew analogues, such as *shir meishiv/mushav ʿal* [*ploni*] for *jawāb*, and *tosefet* for *ziyāda*, are used in *Sefer ha-musar*, which eschews the use of Arabic.[268] The act of interpolating one's own verses into another's poem is designated in Hebrew by the verb מלא: *shir le-rabbi shelomoh ben gabirol* ***u-mille' oto*** *mori yiḥye alḍāhirī*. The phrase *mille' oto* suggests a deficiency in the original; by "filling" or fleshing it out, the later poet completed it and filled in its alleged gaps. The mechanism of the *ziyāda* is dialectical: it preserves the lines of the original while inevitably altering their sense. Another Hebrew header reads: *tokheḥah le-rabbi yehuda halevi ... teḥilatah "Hashem negdekha kol ta'avati"* ***u-mille' otah*** *mori yiḥye alḍāhirī ... be-gimmel* [3] *ḥaruzim be-khol bayyit*. ("A *tokheḥah* by Rabbi Judah Halevi opening with *"Hashem negdekha kol ta'avati"* which my teacher, Yiḥye Alḍāhirī, fleshed out by adding three verses to each line.").[269] Although the technical term is not used, this last example is a clear instance of *takhmīs*, a technique prevalent in Arabic poetry from the 13th century on. Wolfhart Heinrichs dubbed *takhmīs* the "fiver gloss," reflecting its commentarial function as well as its expansion of another's poem into a strophic poem of five-line stanzas. This was achieved by prefacing three new hemistichs to each two-stich line of the original which was divided for this purpose into two separate lines. In each stanza, the end rhyme of the additions is determined by the first hemistich of each successive line of the original, while the final line of each stanza retains the rhyme of the original poem. The resulting rhyme scheme is *aaa*aa, *bbb*ba, *ccc*ca, etc., where the italics represent the later poet's additions and aa, ba, ca are the lines of the original poem.[270] Not every

---

267 Oxford Bodleian ms. Opp. Add. 8° 31, fol. 115ʳ.

268 For *shir meishiv/mushav ʿal* [*ploni*] see, e.g., the summaries of Chapters 17, 25, and 31 in the Hebrew rhymed prose Table of Contents; for *tosefet* see the summary for Chapter 19 and the discussion below of Chapter 34.

269 Alḍāhirī's poem is preserved in the ms. of a 17th-c. *tiklāl* in Leiden (= IMHM 13928, 72a–73a); for the text and superscription see Tobi, "Ha-shem negdekha kol ta'avati le-alḍāhirī."

270 See Heinrichs, "Allusion and Intertextuality," and Kennedy, "Takhmīs."

ziyāda was a *takhmīs*: Alḍāhirī's expansion of Ibn Gabirol's "Shaḥar avakeshkha" inserts only two lines before each two hemistichs of the original, but, like the *takhmīs*, it converts a monorhymed poem with no stanzaic breaks into a strophic poem with multiple rhymes.[271] Depending on the length of the poem being expanded, the *takhmīs* had the potential to become quite unwieldy: Alḍāhirī's "fiver gloss" on the well-wrought "Adonai negdekha kol ta'avati" swells Halevi's 22 lines to 110. There is no question that some of his contrafactions dilute the force of the original; the verses he splices into Solomon Ibn Gabirol's exquisitely taut "Sheḥi la'el yeḥidah ha-ḥakhamah" ("Bow to God, my singular, wise soul") riddle the text with non sequiturs and break the flow of its direct address to the soul and its sequence of midrashic analogies between the soul and God.[272] On the other hand, there are instances where Alḍāhirī's augmentation preserves an otherwise unknown poem, allowing us to reconstruct and repatriate poems that have no other surviving witnesses. "Ha-sho'alim bosem be-mirqaḥat," which is headed *wa-lahu aiḍan ziyādah ʿala qawl le-rabbi avraham ibn ʿezra … fi madḥ al-torah*, expands a five-line poem in praise of the Torah, which is ascribed to Abraham Ibn Ezra but is not known from any other source.[273]

Precedents for interpolating one's own verses into another's poem are attested in Hebrew at least as far back as the 12th century. Troubled by the inclusion of a tenth cosmic sphere in Moses Ibn Ezra's "Be-shem el asher amar," Samuel Ibn Jāmiʿ (a contemporary of Abraham Ibn Ezra) composed a kind of palinode for the earlier poet, making him recant his unorthodox cosmology and furnishing him with a petition for divine pardon, all the while matching the formal features of Ibn Ezra's poem.[274] We have two 13th-century interlinear contrafactions of Judah Halevi's above-mentioned "Adonai negdekha kol ta'avati" by Samuel ben Nissim of Aleppo—one of the multiple dedicatees of the *Taḥkemoni*—and Moses Darʿī, a Karaite poet and physician active in Egypt.[275] In a kind of dizzying mimetic web, Halevi's original was modeled

271 See "Aqum ḥaṣot layl/ ashqif be'eshnabi," in Tobi, "Shnei piyyuṭim ḥadashim le-rabbi zekharya alḍāhirī."

272 Alḍāhirī's *ziyāda*, "Le-matai tishni nafshi," appears twice in ms. Guenzburg 1306; see Amir, "Shirim ḥadashim mi-dīwān rabbi zekharyah Alḍāhirī," 145.

273 The incipit is "Even yeqar bi-yqar ve-zoraḥat"; see the appendix to Amir, "The Life of Rabbi Zecharia Al-ḍaheri," 463–466 and ms. Guenzburg 1306, fols. 151ᵛ and 154ʳ. Amir speculates that Alḍāhirī must have had his own collections of Andalusian poems that he was able to draw on for his contrafactions.

274 See Tanenbaum, "Nine Spheres or Ten? A Medieval Gloss on Moses Ibn Ezra's 'Be-shem el asher amar.'"

275 See: Yeshaya, *Medieval Hebrew Poetry in Muslim Egypt*, 70; Yahalom, *Yehuda Halevi: Poetry*

on a frequently imitated 10th-century penitential poem, Isaac Ibn Mar Shaul's "Elohai, al tedineni ke-maʿali" ("O God, do not judge me according to my sin"), which in turn was closely related to an earlier Arabic penitential poem of Islamic provenance.[276]

Both the stand-alone *jawāb* and the more invasive interlinear interpolations of the *ziyāda* often "corrected" a perceived misapprehension in the original or substituted a more orthodox content for that of the earlier poem or modified its intellectual propensities. Secular expressions of longing for a distant friend might be recast as pious yearnings for collective redemption while another poem's open-ended soteriological questions might be resolved in the later poet's response. There was a transformative, exegetical element to these practices since the contrafactum altered the content or tone of the original poem, providing it with an alternative outcome. Alḍāhirī's corpus includes quite a few instances of "counter-writing," but he also wrote non-oppositional contrafactions that do not attempt to rectify unacceptable opinions or unsettling wording. These are variously inspired by the musicality, ideas, lexicon, or imagery of a preexisting poem, without necessarily quoting from it verbatim. Some of his recognizable echoes of earlier poems may not even be conscious; several of the contrafacta in *Sefer hamusar* are identified as such only in the rhymed Table of Contents, but not in the text itself. The poets he chose to contrafact range in temperament, era, and cultural milieu from Alḥarizi to Immanuel of Rome to the 13th/14th-century Adanī poet Abraham ben Ḥalfon, to the 16th-century kabbalist Simon Ibn Lavi (d. 1580, North Africa), but the preponderance of his responses address members of the Andalusian school of the 11th and 12th centuries, especially Solomon Ibn Gabirol, Judah Halevi, and Abraham Ibn Ezra. And, of course, the prototype for his *Sefer haʿanaq* is the similarly titled work by Moses Ibn Ezra, who set the standard for all subsequent collections of homonymic poems, including those of Judah Alḥarizi, Elʿazar ben Yaʿaqov Ha-bavli (1195–1250) of Baghdad, and Joseph ben Tanḥum Ha-yerushalmi (c. 1262–after 1330) of Egypt.[277]

---

and Pilgrimage, 176–177; Scheindlin, "On the Poem *Adonai, Negdekha Kol Ta'avati* by Judah ha-Levi"; Abramson, *Bilshon qodemim*, 13–14; and Kahana, "ʿAl ha-meshorer ha-qara'i mosheh darʿi."

276 See Scheindlin, "Ibn Gabirol's Religious Poetry and Sufi Poetry," esp. 139–141.

277 On the competitive aspect of these emulations, see Kfir, *A Matter of Geography*, 102–122 and *passim*. See also Schirmann, *HPMS*, 387–391; Dishon, "The Maqama of Homonyms by Joseph Ben Tanhum Hayerushalmi" and idem, "The Use of Homonyms in the *Maḥberet ha-Ẓimmudim* by Yosef ben Tanhum Ha-Yerushalmi." As Kfir notes with regard to Ha-bavli's *Sefer haʿanaq*, Alḍāhirī's is divided into alphabetic sections based on the first letter of the rhyming word. In this respect, it is closer to Alḥarizi's model than to Ibn Ezra's, which is divided into ten thematic sections, each arranged in internal alphabetical order.

The Yemenite Jewish affinity for Andalusian Hebrew poetry is legend; the Andalusians' *piyyutim* had long been a fixture of the *tiklāl* while their non-liturgical poems had circulated in Yemenite *dīwāns*. The Andalusian exceptionalist claim to poetic superiority propagated four centuries earlier had been widely internalized, such that Alḍāhirī's dialectical impulses to emulate these poets and to best them at their own game can perhaps also be read as an effort to validate his own literary abilities. His penchant for contrafacting selections from this corpus indicates that the Andalusian texts had achieved canonic status for him personally as well as for his community of readers.[278] The exegetical impulse driving Alḍāhirī's counter-poems presupposes a canon that required re-interpretation through the lens of the time. Philip Kennedy has written that *takhmīs* "feeds off a tendency towards explication (*sharḥ*) in the reception and diffusion of the [Arabic] poetic tradition" in the post-classical period.[279] The exegetical inclination was pronounced in all areas of literary production among Yemenite Jews, be it scripture, midrash, halakhah, or liturgy. But apart from contrafactions, the closest one gets to commentary on earlier poetry is in the context of glosses in the *tiklāl*, particularly those of the 17th-century kabbalist Isaac Wanneh and the 18th-century legal scholar, Yiḥye Ṣāliḥ.[280]

In Arabic *adab* writings, the use of the term *jawāb* (pl. *ajwibah* or *jawābāt*) for a literary genre of retorts had a long history. Joseph Sadan notes that the tenth-century author Ibrahīm Ibn Abi ʿAwn devoted an entire anthology to "Responses Which Reduce the Interlocutor to Silence," *al-Ajwibah al-muskitah*, which features a chapter on the Bedouin, who were considered to have excelled at cutting retorts.[281] Chronologically and conceptually much closer to Alḍāhirī's *jawābāt*, an emulative technique known as *javāb-gūʾī*, or "speaking in reply" was employed by Persian poets of the Safavid-Moghul period (16th–17th c.). Paul Losensky explains that the term *javāb-gūʾī*—an

278 This did not preclude Yemenite Jewish contrafaction of other Yemenite poets; see Yellin, "Ginze teiman"; Tobi, "Shirim ʿal ha-nefesh be-shirat teiman"; and idem, "Shir maʿaneh ʿal ʿyigdal elohim ḥay' le-rabbi david ben shelomoh ha-levi." But note that Alḍāhirī does not seem to be attracted in the same way to the contrafaction of pieces by North African or Iraqi Jewish poets.

279 Kennedy, "Takhmīs."

280 See, e.g., Gavra, "Le-foʿalo shel rabbi yiṣḥaq wannah be-sidduro 'paʿamon zahav'"; idem, *Meḥqarim be-siddurei teiman*; Halamish, "Rabbi yiḥye ṣāliḥ veha-qabbalah"; idem, "Ha-qabbalah be-sidduro shel rabbi yiṣḥaq wannah"; Ratzaby, "ʿIyyunim be-hitpatḥut maḥzor teiman," and idem, *Bemʿagloth Temān*, 74–81.

281 See: Sadan, "An Admirable and Ridiculous Hero," 481 and Appendix 2 for an extensive bibliography of "Witty Answers in Arabic Belles Lettres"; Yūsuf ed., Ibn Abi ʿAwn, *al-Ajwibah al-muskitah*, and idem, *Das Buch der schlagfertigen Antworten*.

Arabo-Persian compound parallel to *jawāb*—"introduces ideas of debate and inquiry" into the concept of poetic imitation. The term suggests that the object of poetic contrafaction has become "a question that calls for an answer or a problem that demands a solution," such that the emulation is not only a reply, but also "an interpretive response to the problem presented by the original." The poet thus "intends ... his response to be read in dialogue with its model and expects the reader or listener to evaluate it in these terms."[282] Both the Yemenite *jawāb* and *ziyāda* are similarly intertextual insofar as their meaning is dependent upon their models, and full appreciation of these contrafactions also requires familiarity with the original texts with which they are in dialogue.

Alḍāhirī produced a striking interpretive response to difficulties he perceived in a liturgical poem by Abraham Ibn Ezra, "Az baʿalot mequṭeret mor." Ibn Ezra's *piyyut* belongs to the *ahavah* genre and is written in strophic form with an opening couplet, or *madrikh*:

אז בעלות מקטרת מור / ריחה למעלה
התרפקה במיטב טעם / על דוד כיעלה.

Then, when the beloved perfumed with myrrh ascended [from the desert],
she embraced her lover like a graceful gazelle.

The *ahavah* genre was linked to the blessing before the *Shemaʿ* praising God for choosing His people Israel in love (*beʾahavah*). This blessing concludes a long benediction describing the gift of the Torah as a supreme expression of that everlasting bond. The *ahavah* drew on these liturgical themes as well as on the rabbinic reading of Canticles as an allegory of the love between God and Israel.[283] Rabbinic exegesis used the harmonies and strains of this amatory relationship—the lovers' union, separation, and reunion—as metaphors for the twin axes of exile and redemption around which Israel's sacred history revolved. If Israel strayed, her beloved spurned her, leaving her to suffer the afflictions of exile. But God's eternal love and covenantal bond ensured that Israel would ultimately be redeemed. To this traditional symbolism, the

282 Losensky, "'The Allusive Field of Drunkenness': Three Safavid-Moghul Responses to a Lyric by Bābā Fighānī," 231–234. See also idem, *Welcoming Fighānī: Imitation and Poetic Individuality in the Safavid-Mughal Ghazal*, 100–133 *passim*.

283 From rabbinic times, the eroticism of the book had precluded a literal interpretation; see Cohen, "The Song of Songs and the Jewish Religious Mentality."

Andalusian *ahavah* added yet another layer of tropes and resonances. Ibn Ezra's *piyyut* very noticeably blends the language and imagery of the Song of Songs with the frankly erotic, sensual language and imagery of medieval Arabic and Hebrew love poetry.[284] Since it was intended for recitation in a liturgical context, it would have been clear that these erotic motifs were being used allegorically. And yet, the poem allows simultaneously for a literal reading. In the absence of explicit historical references until the final stanza, the intimacy and intimations of sexual arousal are so pronounced that most of the *piyyut* reads like a secular love poem (despite the echoes of Exodus 24:7 in v. 6):

> v. 3: Gently, the stag drew her to him in the days of youth; she hurried
> v. 4: to him as the thirsty run to a river to drink, and he aroused her love;
> v. 5: In her heart the waves of desire raged like tall mountains and she said:
> v. 6: "Let my beloved declare what he wants—I will accept whatever he says."

Sadly, the perfect bond of the lovers' halcyon "days of youth" gives way to the gazelle's spurning and separation from her "stag." Wandering sleeplessly in the desert, she anxiously shepherds the stars, stopping to ask for him. These verses, which blend the desert setting of the classical Arabic *qaṣīda* and the stock motifs of its amatory prelude centering on loss and nostalgia for times past (the abandoned campsite; the lovers' tragic separation; the suffering sleepless lover who watches the stars) with the desert imagery of their underlying biblical allusions (to Canticles 3:6, Jeremiah 2:2, etc.), are marked by a degree of ambiguity which is resolved only with the unequivocal promises of divine redemption and exclusive devotion to Israel in the closing lines:

> v. 13: "Why are you frightened, why is your heart fearful, my Beloved?
> v. 14: I will sanctify My name and bring back the sanctuary which my foe has seized;
> v. 15: I will redeem you, and take you as My portion; and the enemy
> v. 16: who defamed us both—[her] doom is coming, and she will [be compelled] to say:

284 For the text see Abraham Ibn Ezra, *The Religious Poems*, ed. Levin, 1: 258–260; *Reime und Gedichte des Abraham Ibn Esra*, ed. Rosin, 2:36; and Schirmann, *HPSP* 1:622. See also Levin "'Al ha-naqam ve'al ha-ge'ulah be-shirei ha-qodesh shel avraham ibn ezra." For similarly sensual imagery and language, cf. Ibn Ezra's "'Ayelet ḥen," *The Religious Poems*, ed. Levin, 2: 600, vv. 3–12 and "Ayumati 'aden shamamt," ibid. 1:200.

> v. 17: 'This is the true God, and happy is the people whom He has chosen for His inheritance.' "

Alḍāhirī's *jawāb* to Ibn Ezra's *ahavah* meticulously matches its formal features and closely mirrors its themes but, apart from the echoes in its initial line, does not incorporate its actual wording.[285] Opening with the words, "Az ba-ḥalom le-rosh har ha-mor," ("Then in a dream, she saw Mt. Moriah's peak …"), it skillfully replicates the earlier poem's auditory pattern by reproducing its strophic form, meter, and complicated rhyme scheme.[286] In a departure from the conventionally end-stopped lines of Andalusian Hebrew poetry, Ibn Ezra's *piyyut* is marked by an unusual number of enjambments, and Alḍāhirī adroitly works this feature into his contrafaction. Particularly ingenious is Alḍāhirī's mimicking of Ibn Ezra's acrostic, which allows him not only to echo the earlier poem's opening words, but also to preserve its precise number of strophes. Where Ibn Ezra signs his poem AVRaM, Alḍāhirī playfully inscribes his with AVNeR, adopting his hero's name as his nom-de-plume; a device that he deploys elsewhere as well. Like its model, the *jawāb* evokes Israel's longing for restoration to her ideal state, but it steers clear of the arresting sensuality of Ibn Ezra's imagery. There are no raging waves of desire or passionate embraces; no terms of endearment; no stags or gazelles; no hint of physicality at all between the two principals. Instead, an unnamed feminine subject has a dream vision of the Temple on Mt. Moriah but awakens to find that she is still mired in the wretchedness of her *galut*.[287] The poem's much more conventional tone is set by the *madrikh*, which employs the language of Lamentations and other pertinent biblical passages to evoke Israel's affliction:

> Then in a dream, she saw Mt. Moriah's[288] peak and pondered
> Her own former glory. How was her gold now dulled?[289] Why was she bowed? Degraded, abased and brought low?

Daily, she prays to be safely reinstalled in her "tent" with an untroubled spirit. In the penultimate stanza, she turns to address God directly with a plea that

---

285 Ibn Ezra's poem is identified as the model for Alḍāhirī's *jawāb* in a marginal note to Oxford Bodleian ms. Opp. Add. 8° 31, f. 115ʳ.

286 *Sefer hamusar*, pp. 302–303 (end # 25).

287 Cf. the later strictures of R. Yehuda Jizfān (1765–1837) and R. Saʿadya Manṣura (d. c. 1880), cited in Ratzaby, "Ṣura ve-laḥan be-shirat teiman," 18–19.

288 There are ample midrashic precedents for identifying *har ha-mor* of Cant. 4:6 with Mt. Moriah, Jerusalem, and the Temple.

289 Cf. Lam. 4:1.

He again show his favor and draw near to Him the one who is "trapped in her house" and has become desolate. She begs him to "cut off the foes who spread nets out for her" and asks that her good deeds be rewarded. Transforming Balaam's words in Numbers 23 to confront God, she asks, "How can You condemn one who should not be blamed; one who is bereft and withers in exile?"[290] As in the final stanza of Ibn Ezra's original, God responds by addressing Israel with a message of consolation and promises of redemption:

> The First Commandment's promises I will not forsake;[291]
> When you trample the wolf and the lion,[292] Jerusalem will
> Expand round about;[293] with iniquity and sin all forgiven.
> There you shall sing songs of praise, and I shall extol My name.
> I will be sanctified with pleasant words, in joy and rejoicing.[294]
> (lines 341–345)

As a counter-poem that intentionally empties its model of its eroticism, Alḍāhirī's *jawāb* radically inverts Ibn Ezra's poem. While it preserves the gist of Ibn Ezra's original and is remarkably faithful to its structure, his response is devoid of its tender tone and evocative imagery. Somewhat paradoxically, Alḍāhirī's biblically allusive diction is both much more sedate, and rather more opaque than Ibn Ezra's. Even more enigmatic is the placement of this seemingly hyper-conservative counter-*piyyut* in a narrative setting that is blatantly non-liturgical and not a little risqué. Even if they may originally have been composed as independent paraliturgical pieces, and even when they hew quite closely to the themes of the Andalusian *piyyutim* on which they are modeled, once they are integrated into *Sefer hamusar*, such *jawābāt* acquire an altered function by virtue of their context. Abner's recitation of "Az ba-ḥalom" is preceded by his regaling his audience with several sidesplitting tales, including one of the most salacious in the book, which Hayyim Schirmann dubbed "The Handmaid's Revenge" (*Neqamat ha-shifḥah*).[295] But no sooner has he sent his audience into paroxysms of laughter than he does an about-face into a renun-

290 Cf. Num. 23:8, "How can I curse whom God has not cursed? How can I denounce whom the Lord has not denounced?" (RSV).

291 I.e., the promise of redemption from Egypt.

292 An evocation of the messianic age; cf. Ps. 91:13. Medieval piyyutim often depict Israel's rival religions as wild animals.

293 Cf. Avot 5:5—"Ten wonders were wrought for our ancestors in the Temple ... and [#10] no man said to his fellow: the place is too congested for me to lodge overnight in Jerusalem."

294 Cf. Is. 12:6, צַהֲלִי וָרֹנִּי יוֹשֶׁבֶת צִיּוֹן כִּי־גָדוֹל בְּקִרְבֵּךְ קְדוֹשׁ יִשְׂרָאֵל׃

295 *Sefer ha-musar*, pp. 293, l. 156–pp. 296, l. 227; see Schirmann, "Neqamat ha-shifḥah."

ciatory mode and declares, "I will be pained if I do not recall the humiliation and impoverishment of the *galut* (*ha-galut, ha-shiflut, ve-ha-dalut*), and the destruction of the Temple on account of our sins." Straightaway he recites a poetic lament over the exile which is a *jawāb* to another poem by Abraham Ibn Ezra.[296] Hearing it, his listeners fall on their faces and, visibly shaken, repent of their appalling frivolity. Abner reassures them that Elijah will appear heralding the Messiah and then recites "Az ba-ḥalom le-rosh har ha-mor" to console them.

If the placement of "Az ba-ḥalom" is a deliberately apologetic gesture for having included a few ribald tales in the work, are readers expected to be conscious of its revisionist subtext? Or is the chapter simply a collage whose artificial transitions between its disparate components are of no real consequence? Does the poem's placement genuinely signal the author's ambivalence and unease regarding the more irreverent features of the picaresque *maqāma*? Perhaps it reflects back on Ibn Ezra's *piyyut*, whose eroticism, unlike that of "The Handmaid's Revenge," was intended allegorically. Does it subtly, perhaps unintentionally, align Ibn Ezra's spiritualized love imagery with the highly concrete carnality of the tale? By clothing Ibn Ezra's themes in a garb that is less overtly sensual, Alḍāhirī deliberately tones it down. Possibly he does so out of deference to the sensibilities of a particular intended (or imagined) audience. Though he is expurgating a religious poem, his rewriting calls to mind the phenomenon of Ibn ʿAbd Rabbīhī's (d. 940) expiatory poems (*mumaḥḥiṣāt*; "cancelers of sin"), each of which offset one of the erotic poems composed in his youth by imitating its form while emptying it of its transgressive content.[297] But is Alḍāhirī's bowdlerizing instinct (if such it is) counteracted by the *jawāb*'s proximity to the racy folk tale? Or is the contrafaction in the end intended to atone for the salaciousness of the tale? The larger narrative context obliges us to consider Alḍāhirī's *jawāb* as a conscious metapoetic undertaking that implicitly comments on certain conventions of Andalusian *piyyut* and of the *maqāma* while also expressing a degree of ambivalence about Alḍāhirī's own relationship to those usages.

6.4 *Contrafaction as Anti-Parody*

Although it does not announce itself as such, another *jawāb* embedded in the narratives of *Sefer hamusar* responds to a provocative exhortation to the soul. In Chapter 6, Mordecai journeys to the Galilean town of Safed, the center of

296 "Eḥeru moʿadei menuḥati," a *jawāb* to Ibn Ezra's "Eḥeru paʿamei meshiḥi"; see Ratzaby, "Me'oṣar ha-piyyut ve-ha-shirah," 175–176.

297 See Hámori, "Ibn ʿAbd Rabbih."

the great mystical revival of the sixteenth century. During his visit to Joseph Karo's *yeshivah*, a prized yeshivah student—whom Mordecai later recognizes as Abner—delivers a brilliant philosophical excursus on the faculties of the soul and the internal senses. Following his oration, he recites a poem chastising the soul. Adopting the sermonizing posture and Neoplatonic commonplaces of the Andalusian *tokheḥah*, a poem of reproof addressed to the soul, the monorhymed poem, "Nefesh yeqarah, eikh be-tokh guf tishkeni," ("Precious soul, how can you dwell in a body?") asks how the soul can dwell in a defiling body when she is inherently pure and hewn from the divine splendor. With an abundance of second person feminine endings that mirror the content in aural effect, it exhorts her to withdraw from the corrupting corporeal world, abandon sin, and prepare for Judgment Day, and warns that she cannot rest until she returns to her celestial abode.[298] While its diction and tropes are those of the penitential, introspective *tokheḥah*, informed readers might detect its echoes of "Nefesh yeqarah, eikh be-sikhlekh tivteḥi" ("Precious soul, how can you trust in your intellect?"), a crafty parody of the genre from the "Dispute of the Soul with the Body and the Intellect" in Alḥarizi's *Taḥkemoni*.[299] Alḥarizi's "Dispute" draws on the conventions of solemn contemplative and liturgical poetry, and harks back to a well-known midrash and earlier *piyyutim* that imagined the mutual recriminations of body and soul during their posthumous judgment.[300] It also recalls the dialogue of personified soul and intellect in Baḥya Ibn Paquda's pietistic *Book of Direction to the Duties of the Heart*. But unlike these precedents, Alḥarizi's "Dispute" introduces the evil inclination as an additional participant who addresses the soul with his own sly and cunning exhortation, "Precious soul, how can you trust in your intellect?"[301]

By transposing the penitential paradigm of the *tokheḥah* to the new and entertaining literary context of the *maqāma*, Alḥarizi tests the limits of pro-

298 *Sefer hamusar*, pp. 122–123, lines 120–134. On the *tokheḥah* genre see Tanenbaum, *The Contemplative Soul*, 19–20.

299 For a fuller discussion of the "Dispute," see Tanenbaum ibid., 203–217.

300 See bSan. 91a–b. There are additional versions of the parable of the lame and the blind in Leviticus Rabbah, Midrash Tanḥuma, and the Mekhilta; it also occurs in Christian and Islamic literature: see Urbach, *The Sages: Their Concepts and Beliefs*, p. 786, n. 23; Malter, "Personifications of Soul and Body," 454–457; and Meisami, *The Sea of Precious Virtues*, 319–320.

301 Baḥya also personifies the rabbinic *yeṣer ha-raʿ* or evil inclination in the fifth treatise of his *Duties of the Heart*, where he warns that the temptations and wicked advice of the *yeṣer* (*waswās al-hawā wa-ishāratuhu*) spoil man's sincere devotion to God; see Tanenbaum, *The Contemplative Soul*, 216.

priety.[302] In his three-way "Dispute," the intellect urges the soul to renounce material temptations and cleanse herself of the body's defilements, and warns her not to succumb to the machinations of the evil inclination or *yeṣer ha-raʿ*. Naturally, the machiavellian *yeṣer* insinuates himself into the proceedings to remind the noble soul of the transience of her worldly pleasures and to urge her to enjoy these fleeting delights while she can. Such *carpe diem* motifs are hallmarks of courtly verse, which sang of the sensuous but passing pleasures of wine decanted by beautiful serving boys in lush gardens filled with bird-song and the plash of fountains.[303] But in urging such indulgence, the wily *yeṣer* cleverly inverts the standard pious advice to the soul to look to the next world precisely *because* the material and sensual satisfactions of this world are ephemeral and transitory. Using words that deliberately subvert Maimonides' purely spiritual interpretation of the World to Come, he denies that there is any kind of afterlife.[304] His evil counsel culminates in the insolent "Nefesh yeqarah, eikh be-sikhlekh tivteḥi," whose every admonition contradicts the intellect's sage advice. If the intellect's poem typifies the Andalusian homily to the soul, the evil inclination's is a clever parody which slyly turns the genre's characteristic themes on their head.

It is this provocation to sin that prompted Alḍāhirī's *jawāb*. His "Nefesh yeqarah, eikh be-tokh guf tishkeni" adopts the rhyme scheme, meter, and hortatory opening of the evil inclination's poem. What it does not duplicate, however, is the element of parody in the original. It is just possible that Alḥarizi's mischievous humor eluded Alḍāhirī. Or, within the context of the larger narrative, Alḍāhirī's high-minded reworking of the earlier parody might be seen

302 Devin Stewart has speculated that Alḥarizi's personification of the intellect may have been inspired by Ibn al-Jawzī; see his "Of Rhetoric, Reason, and Revelation."

303 See, e.g., Scheindlin, *Wine, Women, and Death* and Brann, *The Compunctious Poet*, 9–22 *passim*.

304 In his code of law, the *Mishneh Torah*, Maimonides had cited a well-known passage at bBerakhot 17a in support of his view that there are no bodies in the world to come, only the souls of the righteous who have attained knowledge of the divine. Echoes of his "*Ha-ʿolam ha-ba ein bo guf u-gviyyah ... ein bo lo akhilah ve-lo shetiyyah*" can be heard in the phrasing of the evil *yeṣer*'s "*aḥarei ha-mavet ein simḥah ve-ein marge'ah, ve-ein yeshivah ve-ein nesiʿah*." It is even possible that Alḥarizi's choice of "yeshivah" was intended to remind the reader of Maimonides' figurative interpretation, in the same discussion, of the talmudic statement that the righteous "sit" in *ʿolam ha-ba* with their crowns on their heads, enjoying the splendor of the Shekhinah. Since sitting is a physical act, but there are no bodies in the world to come, Maimonides had explained the phrase as a metaphor for the effortless existence of the souls of the righteous after death, just as he had interpreted the "crowns on their heads" as a metaphor for the crowning knowledge of God, through which they merit eternal life (*Mishneh Torah*, Teshuvah 8:2).

as a calculated effort to further Abner's ruses and deceptions. Posing as a learned seminarian, Abner makes an outward show of godliness that earns him vast admiration and material rewards, because his audience—most of all the esteemed Karo himself—is too taken in to recognize the doctrinally subversive poem lurking behind his pietistic verse. Of course, it is one thing for an invented literary character to subtly exploit a poem that runs counter to spiritual ideals; it is quite another for a well-respected poet and scholarly translator of philosophical texts like Judah Alḥarizi to have flirted with such materialist notions. Alḥarizi's spoof may have provoked Alḍāhirī to produce an *anti*-parody; a contrafaction that deliberately aimed to offset or make amends for the unseemly and irreverent content of his predecessor's poem. Alḍāhirī's implicit criticism and doctrinal rectification requires the reader to go back and read his response in dialogue with the earlier poem and perhaps reassess the original. Remedied and sanitized in the new poem, the evil inclination's excesses lose much of their sting. By retaining its form while displacing its words, Alḍāhirī effectively rewrites Alḥarizi's impish and impudent piece, which was itself an inversion of serious poetic sermons to the soul. By reverting to the straight and narrow, Alḍāhirī's counter-poem left its mark, if not on the fictional yeshivah audience in Safed, then certainly on actual readers in his own cultural milieu. His "Nefesh yeqarah" sparked a chain of no fewer than eight Yemenite contrafactions from the 17th to 19th centuries.[305]

6.5 *Metapoetic Reflections*

The deliberate decision to match the rhyme and meter of someone else's poem and to recast the contents of that poem in light of one's own literary or cultural sensibilities lends the contrafaction a metapoetic aspect.[306] Choosing to compose a *jawāb* or *ziyāda* involves defining one's own art and relationship to the earlier poets in a tradition with which one, to some degree, aligns oneself. But in only a few rare and isolated instances in *Sefer hamusar* does Alḍāhirī reflect explicitly and self-consciously on his poetic process.[307] "Leshoni eshteqad hayyetah amuṣah" is for Alḍāhirī an unusually introspective

305 See Tobi, "Shirim ʿal ha-nefesh be-shirat teman." In keeping with the devout inclination of late medieval Yemenite Jewish society, the later contrafactions are all pious admonitions to the soul, though some accommodate kabbalistic ideas and others, a Judeo-Arabic idiom.

306 See Fakhreddin, *Metapoesis in the Arabic Tradition*, 57–92 *passim*.

307 While it is vexing that Alḍāhirī left us so few explicitly theoretical statements on contrafaction in *Sefer ha-musar*, the paucity of such critical discussions was apparently not so uncommon. Beatrice Gruendler notes that the emulation of entire poems "spurred little theoretical attention" among classical Arabic literary critics, even though there was no

poem in which he examines his creative act by means of an imagined dialogue with his muses.[308] Although not previously noted in the secondary literature, it is also a *jawāb* to Samuel Hanagid's "Leshoni esh'alah mimmekh she'elah," one of the nineteen highly personal elegies the Nagid composed to mourn the loss of his elder brother, Isaac. "Leshoni eshteqad" also picks up on apostrophes to the poet's tongue or misgivings about its inarticulacy in poems about panegyrics for patrons or distant friends by Abraham Ibn Ezra and Judah Halevi.[309]

Alḍāhirī's poem (recited by Abner) opens with the speaker's rueful confession that his formerly potent tongue is now shattered and that his previously formidable thoughts are now crushed. The stark contrast between his former abilities and his current state is due to the flight of his inspiration:

> My tongue yesteryear was potent, robust/ Today it is shattered and wordless.
> My thoughts yesterday were strong and well built, / but today they are like a breached city.
> The poem I once grasped so firmly/ has fled me, and I have no strength left to chase it.
> What shall I do now the thoughts of my heart/have left me abandoned, dishonored?

This cri de coeur is immediately followed by a switch to the second person plural:

> Did you not yesterday run to my side when/ I sought you to praise righteous men?
> Or if I sent you to face down my foes/ to wipe out their name with an axe?
> You were my armor and you were my shield,/ always there for me with the apt word.

Only then does he identify these addressees on whom he has relied for verbal inspiration:

---

shortage of practical implementation of the technique by the poets; see "Originality in Imitation," 339–340.

308 *Sefer hamusar* #29, pp. 339–341, lines 14–38.

309 See, e.g., Abraham Ibn Ezra, "Leshoni baḥari mivḥar leshonot" in *The Secular Poems* ed. Levin, 34 and Judah Halevi, "Leshoni kavdah" in *Dīwān yehudah ben shemu'el ha-levi*, ed. Brody, 1:199.

> Muses of mine! Why rebel against me/ when all my soul wants is to greet you?
> To supplicate princes renowned and acclaimed/ on whose lips all wisdom is fluent.

The speaker's anxiety over his loss of poetic inspiration and his reliable source of *mots justes* is particularly acute because he wants to write panegyrics. But it transpires that he is not talking about flattering rulers or wealthy patrons; his "renowned princes" are the sages to whom the Torah laws of marriage, levirate marriage, and *haliṣah* are clear, and all the tractates of the Mishnah are engraved in their hearts, as are the fine points of the Masoretic text. They offer moral instruction and have no tolerance for the idle, whom they would bite like a fox and sting like a scorpion. The "visions of poetry" (*seʿipei shir*; formerly *benot ha-shir*) reply dubiously at first, voicing their reservations about his capacity to placate them and satifsy their needs. Only then do they reassure him of their fealty:

> The visions of poetry replied asking "How/ will you seek us? If only you would appease us!
> Behold, we are your servants as of old/ even if you send us into battle."

But they express concern that he will worry about being parted once more from his verses if the rhymes sent out to pursue his foes are destroyed. In a final, more conciliatory reply the speaker explains that he never really intended to muster his verses for ill purposes:

> I replied with the wherefore and why of it all/ I meant only to send you together
> To joyfully greet brothers and kin in my name/ to inquire after their welfare.
> To the one whose words have kept my buckling feet firm, / who has braced my tottering knees.
> His kindnesses will come in my hour of need/ they will be a support for my soul.[310]

---

310 The kenning *benot ha-shir*, a common usage for poetry, poetesses, or muses, is an Arabism; for the figurative sense of various compounds of *ibn* or *bint* with another noun see, e.g., Biberstein-Kazimirski, *Dictionnaire arabe-français*, 168–169. For *benot ha-shir* see Pagis' glossary in Moses Ibn Ezra, *Secular Poems* 3:341, 356; Even-Shoshan, *Ha-millon he-ḥadash*, 1:290–291 and Ben Yehuda, *Dictionary*, 1:652.

As though to ensure a properly pious close, the poet appends a coda; a two-line prayer that all may be worthy of beholding God's image and being filled with the vision: that all may behold His Temple and that He may gather in the exiles from the four corners of the earth.

The dialogic structure, often used to convey opposing sides of an argument, here enables Alḍāhirī to broach the intimate relationship between the poet and his sources of inspiration and to externalize and reflect critically on his internal poetic processes. It allows him to verbalize with poignancy his frustration with a growing loss of control over a creative act that used to come to him easily. The dialogue with his muses legitimizes an outpouring of anxieties over his seeming inability either to disparage a "foe" with lacerating and scornful verses, or to praise a righteous man. Images of the poet's paralysis contrast starkly with the movement of his fleeing muses. Gradually it emerges that his apprehensions grow from a desire to compose fitting panegyrics for religious scholars (which is what this poem effectively turns into) and to praise a particular unnamed sage who had previously come to his aid. With its reservations and knotty syntax, the three-line reply of his poetic visions embodies the poet's qualms about poetic inspiration and his conflicted attitudes toward the use of verse to vilify an opponent. The surfeit of violent and bellicose images, from which the poet retreats only at the end, reinforces the expressions of disquiet that surface repeatedly as the dialogue progresses. By contrast, the poem's supremely symmetrical lines and skillful monorhymes introduce a calming sense of balance and testify to the poet's mastery of classical Andalusian form. Taken as a whole, the piece constitutes an intriguing mix of formal and thematic convention with an overflow of powerful emotion and introspection, the delineation of the poet's role, and the nature of the creative act. It is a poem that reflects on its own making.

Elsewhere, penetrating remarks on the augmentation of another's poem are prompted by Abner's recitation of a thirty-eight line *ziyāda*. Toward the end of the nineteenth chapter, Alḍāhirī uses his characters to reflect critically on the processes of emulation, appropriation, and modification—pondering their value, legitimacy, and impact—and to appraise a *ziyāda* he has composed vis-à-vis its poetic model. Opening with the words, "Lifnei elohim eʿemod" ("I will stand in prayer before the Lord"), it is laid out graphically as a chain of couplets with a quasi-strophic rhyme scheme and is written in a variant of *rajaz*, a meter often used in medieval Hebrew and Arabic didactic verse.[311] Of a contemplative tenor, the piece warns against excessive metaphysical speculation

311 The *rajaz* poem often took the form of rhymed couplets (*urjūza muzdawija*). Because *rajaz* lines could be shorter than those of other meters, it was ascribed a mnemonic function;

and advocates emotional and material moderation, repentance, and trust in God. Listening attentively, Mordecai reacts with a mixture of admiration and amusement tinged with reproach:

> When I heard Abner's eloquent words, I bowed before him and laughed without restraint, until my voice could be heard from afar. I said to him: "Truly, in poetry you are potent and gifted, so why is your poem partly stolen? Why lifted? I have heard this one before, long ago; it is imprinted in my mind. It was composed by Judah Halevi, who illumined the ends of the earth. He is counted among the pilgrims of rank; a man of superior birth."[312]

Mordecai's accusation of partial plagiarism (*geneivat shir*) not only has a moral dimension but also seems to contain a dig at Abner's slender talent by insinuating that the new poem required little exertion on his part, as half of it is not even his. Not a little indignant, Abner retorts:

> Know, my lord, that this poem of which you speak—and all you have said is right—this poem was like a bird with one wing, that could not sustain it in flight. So I attached its second wing, without which it would have slouched like a sorry thing. And if poetry brings glory to the one who creates it, credit is due to the one who completes it (*ve'im ha-shirah tif'eret le'omrah, ha-miṣvah niqreit 'al shem gomrah*). Now, in your wisdom, weigh and test my themes (ענייני); cast out from before me falsehood and deceit.[313]

The exchange ends with Mordecai's recommendation that Abner atone for his plagiarism: "My lord, I pray, do not besmirch me, for he who confesses and forsakes his sins shall find mercy."[314]

---

see van Gelder, "Didactic Literature"; Stoetzer, "Rajaz"; Khulūṣī, "Didactic Verse"; and von Grunebaum, "On the Origin and Early Development of Arabic *Muzdawij* Poetry."

312 *Sefer hamusar*, p. 227, lines 125–128. Note that *benei 'aliyyah* is a pun, meaning both those who ascend to the Land of Israel on pilgrimage and those who belong to a distinguished class.

313 *Sefer hamusar*, p. 227, lines 128–132. Alḍāhirī playfully appropriates the phrase, "credit is due to the one who completes it" from rabbinic literature; see, e.g., bSotah 13b; Gen. Rab. 85,3; and Dt. Rab. 8,4.

314 It is also possible that Mordecai is apologizing for angering Abner; the ambiguity is due to the difficult fragmentary quotation from Is. 63:3 (*al yez niṣḥam*). For the phrase "he who confesses and gives up his faults will find mercy," see Prov. 28:13.

The "second wing" that Abner affixes to Halevi's reflective "Libbi ʿamod ki mi be-sod tokhen levavot yaʿamod" ("My heart, be still, for who can know the mystery of Him who fathoms hearts?") not only doubles the length of the original poem, but also partners each of its nineteen verses with a new one that matches in meter and elaborates on the rhyme scheme.[315] Where Halevi's poem is monorhymed, Abner "improves" upon Halevi's euphony by rhyming both hemistichs of each of his lines with the first hemistich of the original line that follows. The net effect is a series of couplets, each differentiated by its own internal rhyme, yet all linked by their identical end-rhyme (a/a a/a, b/b b/a, c/c c/a). Much like the interpolations of the *takhmīs*, though fewer in number, the added hemistichs convert a monorhymed poem with no stanzaic breaks into a strophic poem with multiple rhymes. Thematically, "Libbi ʿamod" resembles other poetic meditations in which Halevi voices a certain metaphysical skepticism.[316] Both his major work of religious thought, *Kitāb al-khazarī*, and a series of his contemplative poems reflect disillusionment with the medieval rationalist belief that the exercise of a finely honed intellect was the pinnacle of human perfection. Adopting a sermonic pose, the speaker in "Libbi ʿamod" warns against the presumption that one may know God through detached philosophical reasoning.[317] He asserts that no one can penetrate the mystery of the One who probes men's minds. Halevi here insists that human beings have no leave to speculate on God's inscrutable essence. Rather, in the spirit of the Sufi ideal of *tawakkul* (Heb. *biṭṭaḥon*), he counsels complete trust in God and the abandonment of worldly ways.[318] How does Abner's "enhanced"

315 Halevi's original can be found (with a slightly different ordering of the lines) in *Dīwān yehudah ben shemuʾel ha-levi*, ed. Brody, 2:218, no. 8. Brody's text follows closely that of Samuel David Luzatto, *Diwan Yehudah Halevi*, 4a–b, no. 10.

316 Both Luzatto and Brody preface "Libbi ʿamod" with the header, *ein le-harher aḥar gezeirot haʾel* ("One must not ponder the Lord's decrees") while the text in *Ginzei Oxford* is headed, *ʿal ha-biṭṭaḥon* ("On complete trust in God"); see Edelman and Dukes, *Ginzei Oxford*, Hebrew section pp. 38–39. It would appear that these superscriptions were added by the 19th-century editors; the heading of Halevi's poem in Bodleian Library ms. Pococke 74= Neubauer 1970 is *fīʾl-waʿẓ* ("in an admonitory vein"); see Neubauer, *Catalogue of the Hebrew Manuscripts in the Bodleian Library*, 1:649.

317 Cf. Halevi's "Yah shimekha" and "Yashen al teradam" in Halevi, *The Liturgical Poetry*, ed. Jarden, 1:30–33 and 2:614–616. On both poems see Tanenbaum, *The Contemplative Soul*, 188–193.

318 The ideal of *tawakkul* gained currency among Judeo-Arabic readers through Baḥya Ibn Paquda's *Book of Direction to the Duties of the Heart*; see *Kitāb al-hidāya ilā farāʾiḍ al-qulūb*, 185–242; Vajda, *La Théologie ascétique de Baḥya Ibn Paquda*, 60–85; Scheindlin, *The Song of the Distant Dove*, 21–25; Lobel, *A Sufi-Jewish Dialogue*; and idem, *Between Mysticism and Philosophy*.

version relate to these themes? The opening line of Alḍāhirī's *ziyāda* furnishes a liturgical context absent in the original: the speaker promises to admonish his own heart as he begins to pray.[319] This preface allows Alḍāhirī to preserve the sermonic tone and rhetorical posture of Halevi's poem, where the speaker addresses his heart directly in the second person. Given the formal constraints that Alḍāhirī set himself, it is remarkable that so many of his interlinear additions hew as closely as they do to the thematic contours of the original. Like the poem onto which they are grafted, these lines warn against exceeding the limits of human apprehension (l. 91) and probing the divine mystery (l. 93); they advocate subjecting one's baser instincts to the rule of one's intellect (l. 97); and they caution against placing one's hope in mortal kings (l. 103). Alḍāhirī repeatedly echoes Halevi's exhortations to faith and trust in God (lines 101, 105, 107, 121), repentance, and piety (lines 113, 117, 119). At the same time, the exercise of inserting a new line for every one of Halevi's is bound to affect the economy and unity of the carefully crafted original. Though it adheres to Halevi's key themes and motifs, the new 38-line poem is, arguably, rather more diffuse than the 19-line original. Yet, if these "improvements" on Halevi's composition are aesthetically and morally questionable, Alḍāhirī's very act of appropriation paradoxically pays homage to his eminent Andalusian predecessor.

Still, Mordecai not only accuses Abner of *geneivat shir* but also urges him to confess his transgression. These admonitions imply that, to Mordecai, Abner's appropriation of Halevi's poem is morally unacceptable. Yet, Abner's defense is also grounded in classical poetic criteria: by "completing" and "improving" on the work of a predecessor, he has earned the right to incorporate the earlier poet's lines into his own poem. And by claiming that the net result is "better" than Halevi's original, Alḍāhirī is asserting his own role as a poet vis-à-vis the Andalusians and one of their most illustrious representatives. From Alḍāhirī's time, the *jawāb* and *ziyāda* became regular features of the Yemenite poetic landscape, with little or no stigma attached.[320] Perhaps, then, the conflicting attitudes towards this practice voiced in our *maqāma* should be seen as a reflection of Alḍāhirī's transitional status. The only Yemenite poet to produce a book of Hebrew *maqāmāt* full of secular as well as sacred themes, he was also the last to adhere rigorously to Andalusian Hebrew poetics, and to cultivate an inti-

319 For the poem see *Sefer hamusar*, pp. 224–226.

320 Yemenite Jewish poets carried on cultivating the *jawāb* and *ziyāda* well into the 20th century: the late Raṣon Halevi's *Shirat yisra'el be-teiman* includes his own interlinear responses to poems by all of the major Andalusians and Shalem Shabbazi as well as to the hymns, "Adon 'olam" and "Yigdal elohim ḥay"; see 2:599–619. On his poetry, see Wagner, "The Flying Camel and the Red Heifer: Yemenite Poets in Modern Israel."

mate familiarity with Arabic belletristic literature.[321] The opposing sides of the argument taken by his two fictional characters might then fruitfully be seen not only as the externalization of an internal moral conflict but also as an attempt to weigh received views on the merits of contrafaction against a newer poetic reality. The stridency of Abner's response suggests that he—which is to say, his creator—still could not entirely ignore the moral condemnation accompanying the charge of poetic theft, and felt compelled to justify his action. But he does seem to anticipate the unquestioning acceptance of the *jawāb* as an indigenous Yemenite Jewish art form when he insists that "Credit is due to the one who completes it."

Ironically, Alḍāhirī's *ziyāda* to Halevi's "Libbi ʿamod" is appended to an unattributed adaptation of a tale of quackery from al-Ḥarīrī's thirty-ninth *maqāma*.[322] So in point of fact, the enterprise of *muʿāraḍa* extends to the larger narrative framework in which his poem and metapoetic reflections are embedded. We have seen that in both the Arabic and Hebrew *maqāma* traditions there are many elements of emulation and contrafaction beyond the strictly poetic, whether of the overall structure; number of episodes; rhymed prose medium; imagined geographies; narrative strategies; or the syntactic, auditory patterns or symbolic significance of the protagonists' names. Alḍāhirī freely borrows or transforms narrative elements from al-Ḥarīrī and Alḥarizi as well as Immanuel of Rome without naming his sources. If his critical reflections on the *ziyāda* of Halevi's poem reflect a certain ambivalence about such appropriation, there is no such hesitation regarding the borrowed tale that precedes it.

One of the only other instances of explicit metapoetic reflection occurs in Chapter 34. Here Mordecai enlarges on the technique of contrafaction and the rationale for it when he asks the silver-tongued Abner to compose an interlinear supplement to an epigram on the inconstancy of Fate:

> I would ... like [to request] ... that you *add a supplement* to a poem which I have placed as a frontlet between my eyes and as a miter on my head. The method will be that you compose it *in the same meter as the original, so that the original author will be glorified by means of the addition*. The added verses will sparkle with the radiance of the poem's sun and *will match its opening line*. I have loved this poem, and have engraved it on my heart, for its words are comforting for an anxious one like me. My soul has desired its abundant advantages. *It will be square, with doubled results*.

321 See Ratzaby, *Sefer hamusar*, 9–23.

322 For the original see *al-Ḥarīrī: Maqāmāt Abī Zayd al-Sarūjī*, 211–216 and *Assemblies*, 2:93–101.

> Its opening is like a prancing horse: "Miyaldei yom al tibbahel" ["Do not fear capricious Fate"]. I will recite the rest of it line by line before my dear friend who is the apple of my eye. You must lay the foundations of the house with precious stones, and I must complete the new poem [*benot ha-shir*] with the other rows.[323]

For the interlinear supplement he is requesting, Mordecai uses *tosefet*, the Hebrew equivalent of the Judeo-Arabic *ziyāda* found in *dīwān* superscriptions. He instructs Abner to compose the additional lines in the same meter and to the same high standard as the original so that the new poem will pay tribute to the author of the original and redound to his credit. The meter should match that of the earlier poem's opening line. As a result of prefacing each verse of the original with a new one, the new poem will be doubled in length. It will also be "square," which is to say that each line of the original consists of four metrical feet of four long syllables each, and each couplet produced by the doubling will consist of four hemistichs. As noted, the standard outcome of the interlinear *ziyāda*, regardless of the number of added hemistichs, was to convert a monorhymed poem with no stanzaic breaks into a strophic poem. Mordecai cites the opening of the original poem, "Miyaldei yom al tibbahel" ("Do not fear capricious Fate"), and explains that he is especially attached to the piece because it allays his fears about Fate's unpredictability. Here, though anxious that the new poem be a credit to the author of "Miyaldei yom," he does not voice any aesthetic or moral qualms about the legitimacy of the appropriation and modification he is advocating, and the tone of his request is remarkably buoyant and enthusiastic. He expresses no concern about transgressing the bounds of poetic propriety. Aesthetically, there is no sense of trying to "outshine" the original nor any fear that the additions will be overshadowded by its brilliance. Rather, the added verses "will sparkle with the radiance" of the original poem's sun—an image that suggests a seamlessness of the two components which may be more hoped for than actualized. Perhaps most notably, Mordecai neglects to mention that the author of this luminous poem is Abraham Ibn Ezra or that the original epigram is all of three lines long and inconsequential, although it seems to have had a centuries-long afterlife.[324] But the rich metapoetic reflections accompanying Mordecai's request make this *ziyāda* well worth examining.

---

323 *Sefer hamusar*, pp. 384–385, ll. 101–119.

324 In the header to this *ziyāda* in ms. Guenzburg 1306, the original poem is simply attributed to "one of the poets"; see fol. 132v:

ולהו איצ׳ן זיאדה עלי הדא אלקול והו לבעץ׳ אלמשוררים

If the mechanics of the addition are straightforward, it is their metaphorical garb that is worth noting. The requirement to match the new verses with the opening line of the original is couched in language borrowed from the construction of the Tabernacle in Exodus 26:24 (*ve-yaḥdav yihyu tamim el rosho*; lit. "they will terminate alike at the top") while the phrase "it will be square and doubled" (*ravuʿa yihyeh, kaful*) comes from the instructions for fashioning the High Priest's breastplate with its four rows of three precious stones each in Exodus 28:16 ff.[325] These metaphors of fashioning and building of the sacred are sustained with an allusion to Solomon's construction of the Temple in 1Kings 5:31, "The king ordered huge blocks of choice stone to be quarried, so that the foundations of the house might be laid with hewn stones." Telling Abner, *ʿalekha le-yassed ha-bayyit avanim yeqarot*, ("You must lay the foundations of the house with choice/precious stones"), Mordecai compares the building blocks of the poem—the metrical feet of the verses—to hewn stones of identical form, while playing on *bayyit* as a verse of poetry and on the medieval conceit of the poem as a string of pearls or finely chiseled gems. While Abner is to lay the foundations, Mordecai must supplement them "with the other rows," presumably by reciting the lines of the original in alternation with each of the improvised additional lines.[326] It is telling that the new lines are cast as the structure's foundations despite the fact that they are interpolated into the existing scaffolding of the original poem. Mordecai's designation of the lines he is to recite as *ṭurim* again harks back to the divine directives for fashioning the High Priest's breastplate with four rows (*ṭurim*) of three precious stones each (Exodus 28:17 ff.). Drawn from scriptural blueprints for numinous venues and sacred artifacts, these tropes afford lofty paradigms of construction, perhaps intended to legitimize (if not exactly sacralize) the appropriation and transformation of another poet's verses. The positive valence of the language surrounding the idea of doubling implies that the act of enlarging is not merely formal but also opens the original poem to new aesthetic and substantive vistas. When Mordecai confesses that he has loved this poem and has yearned for its advantages (*yitronotav*), he perhaps also invokes the idea of abundance embodied in the Hebrew root *y.t.r.* From the start, Mordecai anticipates the meta-language

325 The sacred vestments of the High Priest are already invoked in Mordecai's figurative description of his long-standing esteem for the epigram as "a poem which I have placed as a frontlet between my eyes and as a miter (*miṣnefet*—the High Priest's headgear) on my head."

326 The image of alternation in the construction of the poem calls to mind the passage in the Author's Introduction where Alḍāhirī writes, "One man speaks and the other responds, to build verses of lament and song; one builds battlements of poetry, or memorable *epistolae*, their words a crowning glory, for honor and adornment."

of craftsmanship when he turns to Abner to solicit the additional verses "from the work of your hands" (*mi-maʿaseh yadekha*). And following Abner's completion of the *ziyāda*, Mordecai enthuses, "In truth there is none who embroiders a poem like you," projecting the poem as a richly embellished fabric and the poet as its weaver. At the same time, there is a strong suggestion that all poetry not only involves artistry but also artifice—it is constructed but also contrived. By inserting alternating lines of one's own into another poet's composition, the contrivance is taken to a new level as the original poem is *re*-constructed.

After these theoretical considerations, the actual poem is somewhat anticlimactic, given how brief and monothematic it is. The epigram that Mordecai has "engraved on [his] heart" is formally impeccable, and Abner's *ziyāda* preserves its formal features while effecting some notable transformations in its content. Ibn Ezra's short, quasi-sermonic poem is purely about the vicissitudes of Fate:

> *Mi-yaldei yom al tebbahel/ ki yaldei yom lo yirgaʿu;*
> *Al tismaḥ vam im yeitivu/ gam al teḥat im yareiʿu—*
> *Ki ha-tovot gam ha-raʿot/ baʾasher yaḥnu ken yissaʿu.*
>
> Do not fear capricious Fate/ for it will not stop plaguing you.
> Do not rejoice when Fate is kind; / do not fret when it is cruel.
> Not good or bad luck will endure—/ for as they camp, so they move on.

Like the compound, *benot ha-shir* encountered earlier, *yaldei yom* is an Arabism. Arabic dictionaries note that, when joined with another noun, *ibn* yields metonomies and metaphors, and that one sense of *ibn al-ayām* (lit. "son of days") is misfortune or bad luck.[327] The editor of Ibn Ezra's poetry, Yisrael Levin, writes that *yaldei yom* are messengers of *Zeman*—Time with a capital T—which is fate, a malign force that afflicts human beings causing them sudden misfortune.[328] Ibn Ezra's gnomic poem conveys a universal truth. Although couched in resonant biblical language, there is nothing identifiably Jewish about its content. Addressed to no one in particular, this quasi-sermonic epigram is in the spirit of ascetic literature, which teaches equanimity in the face of misfortune.

---

327 Cf. Biberstein-Kazimirski, *Dictionnaire*, 168–169. Pagis glosses *yaldei yom* as *qorot ha-zeman u-fegaʿav*; see Moses Ibn Ezra, *Secular Poems* 3:315.

328 See the annotation in Abraham Ibn Ezra, *The Secular Poems*, p. 205 and Levin, "Zeman ve-tevel be-shirat ha-ḥol ha-ʿivrit bisfarad," 75.

These axioms are consoling in a back-handed way: although Fate is capricious, it is also haphazard, vacillating, and transient, and therefore will not *permanently* trap you in any one state of affairs. The sentiments, while relatively banal, are of a piece with the image Ibn Ezra liked to cultivate of himself as a luckless fellow and consistent with his emphasis on astrology and astral governance of human affairs.[329] Alḍāhirī's *ziyāda* again reinterprets Ibn Ezra's original. With his lines interwoven, the poem now reads as follows:

> ***ʿAl divrati sov hitnahel/yom ki yaḥshikh o khi yahel***
> *Mi-yaldei yom al tebbahel/ki yaldei yom lo yirgaʿu;*
> ***Ḥeshqi ki lo yasur ṣillakh/yishbor haʾel motot ʿullakh***
> *Al tismaḥ vam im yeitivu/gam al teḥat im yareiʿu—*
> ***Al tiraʾ dod mi-massaʿot/ha-nigzarot meʾel deʿot***
> *Ki ha-tovot gam ha-raʿot/baʾasher yaḥnu ken yissaʿu.*
>
> **Turn, and act as I say/ whether the day is bleak or bright:**
> Do not fear capricious Fate/for it will not stop plaguing you.
> **My wish for you is length of days/ and that God may break your yoke.**
> Do not rejoice when Fate is kind; /do not fret when it is cruel.
> **Friend, do not dread the odysseys/decreed by the all-knowing God.**
> Not good or bad luck will endure—/for as they camp, so they move on.

Alḍāhirī preserves the imperative voice, but also inserts the first person (*divrati, ḥeshqi*). Together with the term *dod* (beloved friend) in the final line, these small modifications create a more intimate tone, converting the anonymous address to one with an ostensible addressee. Most notably, however, the *ziyāda* inserts God into every line. In so doing, it introduces doctrinal orthodoxy, suggesting discomfort with the notion that blind fate determines human fortunes. Verse 3b echoes a phrase from Lev. 26:13, whose context is divine redemption from Egypt, and expresses the wish that *God* will redeem the individual from his burdens whereas Ibn Ezra had said that there is no escaping the vicissitudes of fate. Similarly, instead of ineluctable Fate, it is now God who decrees the odysseys of life (*massaʿot/ha-nigzarot meʾel deʿot*; v. 5a). By appropriating and subsuming the original into his new poem, Alḍāhirī effectively inverts the sense of Ibn Ezra's epigram.[330]

---

329 See Langermann, "Some Astrological Themes in the Thought of Abraham ibn Ezra," and idem, "Abraham Ibn Ezra."

330 Shem Tov Falaquera (c. 1225–c. 1295) cites "Mi-yaldei yom" in his work of consolation but does not seem to find it theologically problematic; see *Ṣori ha-yagon*, 23–24.

By infusing Ibn Ezra's original with interlinear additions, Alḍāhirī preserves it, albeit in an augmented state. But in doing so, he is also writing himself or his persona into the earlier poem and introducing the first person where it was not previously explicit. Perhaps somewhat disingenuously, he claims to enhance the original by threading it with his own verses so that the finished product reflects well on its author. At the same time, however, he appropriates Ibn Ezra's poem, absorbing it into his own and neutralizing its meaning, so that it now redounds to his *own* credit and becomes part of *his* creation and corpus. In both passages in which he muses on the enterprise of contrafaction, Alḍāhirī presents the procedure largely in terms of what he is doing to the earlier poem. What remains unsaid, however, is that he is also molding his *own* poetic voice in the process. As Beatrice Gruendler puts it, *muʿāraḍa* is a form of diachronic dialogue.[331]

How, then, should we assess Alḍāhirī's partiality for contrafaction, both in terms of his own poetic creativity and in terms of its broader ramifications? We might be inclined to emphasize the derivative aspect of his *jawāb* and *ziyāda* poems. But that would not convey the intricacies of the dynamic between his contrafactions and the earlier poems that elicited his response. Medieval literary theory acknowledged that contrafaction requires a degree of inventiveness and the ability to reconfigure conventional motifs in novel ways. Viewed from this perspective, Alḍāhirī's *jawābāt* and *ziyādāt* afforded him a means of putting his own stamp on preexisting poems that spoke to him, thereby achieving a degree of distinctive expression alongside that of his original compositions. The emulations he produced served as a token of esteem for the original poem but also allowed him to rectify whatever shortcomings he perceived in the earlier piece and thereby establish his own literary bona fides.

But the relationship is not unidirectional, for the act of contrafaction forges ties of intertextuality and interdependence between the new poem and the old. Particularly where the *jawāb* or *ziyāda* carries an implicit critique or doctrinal correction of the original, the reader or listener is compelled to revisit and reevaluate the earlier poem. The *ziyāda* especially, by adding new lines to a preexisting poem, implies that the original is in some respect deficient and that the additions remedy its shortcomings. This, of course, is precisely Abner's claim with regard to the "second wing" he affixes to Halevi's "Libbi ʿamod." At the same time, however, by incorporating the earlier poem into a new one of his own, the author of the *ziyāda* preserves his model, though not in its original form, nor precisely in its original sense. In this regard, the later poet acts as a

331 Gruendler, "Originality in Imitation," 440.

mediator, allowing the reconfigured prototype to engage a more contemporary audience, accustomed to a different set of cultural tropes. This is presumably what lies behind Mordecai's assertion that "the original author will be glorified by means of the addition."

When he turns to the Andalusians or Immanuel of Rome, Alḍāhirī does not simply appropriate their poems to enhance them, take credit for them, or pay (qualified) homage to their authors. His contrafaction is also an attempt to naturalize the work of precursors from different cultural orbits within his own spiritual and intellectual universe. Hence his introduction of a volitional, omnipotent God where none was present in Abraham Ibn Ezra's epigram on Fate or his invoking the immortality of the soul where Alḥarizi's parody conveys only the inescapable decay of the grave. In this way, the complex relationship extends beyond the immediate confines of two intertextually related poems to the larger literary and cultural systems that inform them. Perhaps then, the impulse behind the *jawāb* and *ziyāda* might be seen in part as an attempt to negotiate a new poetic identity in response to the tenacious hold, despite the passing of many centuries, of Andalusian Jewish claims to cultural, and particularly poetic hegemony.[332]

The Eurocentric *tendenz* of much modern Jewish historiography has cast Yemenite Jews as the conservators *par excellence* of the cultural production of other Jewish subcultures. But here we see Alḍāhirī not only conserving the earlier poetry but also transforming it.[333] The augmented *ziyāda* both embodies and consumes the original, preserving it in its interstices but also obliterating its original integrity to the point that, as part of a new poem, it can be subsumed in the later poet's corpus. These paradoxes highlight the creative tensions and ambivalences in Alḍāhirī's relationship with the poetry of his predecessors, which he venerated, but which he also considered to need modification or completion. In revising artifacts of the hybrid literary traditions of the Andalusians on the one hand and Immanuel on the other, Alḍāhirī maps out his own Yemenite Jewish literary identity. Building on the receptivity of Yemenite Jewry to spiritual and intellectual stimuli from elsewhere in the Jewish world, he effectively produces a hybridity of his own.

332 Cf. Kfir, *A Matter of Geography*.

333 Cf. Gerber, *Ourselves or Our Holy Books?* 28–51 and "Madda'ei ha-yahadut ve-giluyav shel ha'orient ha-yehudi." But note that the characterization of Yemenite Jews as cultural conservators was advanced by Yehuda Ratzaby as well; see e.g., his "Me'oṣar ha-piyyut ve-ha-shirah," 170.

6.6 *Ways of Encountering the Text*

There was a performative aspect to the *maqāma*, both in terms of its fictional story line and its real-life mode of delivery. Immensely popular throughout the medieval Islamic world, al-Ḥarīrī's *Maqāmāt* were typically read aloud to dramatic effect before live audiences assembled for literary gatherings. On the narrative plane, the work's innate theatricality is evident in its portrayal—in crowded markets, mosques, and town squares—of the rogue-hero's storytelling, popular preaching, and other beguiling oratorical acts and entertainments, which mirror on the textual level the performer-audience dynamics of the work's public recitation. The oral delivery of written texts was characteristic of the early medieval period; reading in the early Islamic, Jewish, and European Middle Ages was not a silent affair undertaken by individuals but was rather experienced by audiences as a performance or by groups of auditors listening to a reader. Scholars of pre-modern European reading practices concur that most reading in the early Middle Ages, even in monastic communities, was undertaken orally in a group setting and hence constituted an essentially auditory and social activity rather than a silent, private one as we tend to think of it today.[334] Early medieval rabbinic culture was also characterized by the ritualized reading aloud and oral/aural acquisition of texts in scholarly sessions and study circles.[335] Islamic religious scholarship, too, was initially disseminated through overlapping oral and written modes; "the *aural*" and "the *read*," as Gregor Scholer has styled them.[336] In the secular realm, the *maqāmāt*, like Arabic and Hebrew courtly poetry, were also part of a literary culture that fostered the oral/aural experience of written texts. We have seen that the rhymed prose (*sajʿ*) medium of the *maqāma* had its roots in oral composition and popular oratory, although by the mid-10th century it had evolved into a written

334 See, e.g.: Saenger, "Silent Reading: Its Impact on Late Medieval Script and Society"; Dumonceaux, "La lecture à haute voix des œuvres littéraires au XVIIème siècle"; Chartier, *The Order of Books, Readers, Authors, and Libraries in Europe between the 14th and 18th Centuries*, 1–23; Duncan, *Index*, 58–59; Richards, *Voices and Books in the English Renaissance: A New History of Reading*, Ch. 1; and Dumitrescu, "How to Read Aloud."

335 Daniel Boyarin traces a shift in the Jewish Middle Ages from public, ritualized reading to private, silent reading for pleasure; see his "Placing Reading: Ancient Israel and Medieval Europe." See also Yassif, "Oral Traditions in a Literate Society: The Hebrew Literature of the Middle Ages." On the relationship between orality and textuality and the gradual process of ascribing greater value to the authority of the inscribed word than to oral testimony, see Elman and Gershoni, "Transmitting Tradition: Orality and Textuality in Jewish Cultures," and Fishman, *Becoming the People of the Book: Oral Torah as Written Tradition in Medieval Jewish Cultures*.

336 See Schoeler, *The Genesis of Literature in Islam*, 41–53 and 111–121.

genre used for a wide range of purposes, both popular and élite.[337] Evidence that medieval compilations of Arabic stories "drew on both written sources and the oral performances of professional storytellers" has been adduced by David Pinault in his study of story-telling techniques in the *Arabian Nights*. Pinault notes that the tales comprising the *Arabian Nights* "were originally oral evening-entertainments and were meant to be recited and listened to."[338] Alain George has explored the intimate nexus between orality, aurality, and writing "from the very origins of the [*maqāma*] genre," citing evidence of the continued oral transmission of al-Ḥarīrī's *Maqāmāt* at public readings during the author's lifetime and for 180 years following his demise. Manuscript marginalia confirm that such public performances played a crucial role in the dissemination of the established text as well. When the entire work was read out in the presence of the author, al-Ḥarīrī certified the soundness of the manuscript, which then became an authoritative copy of the text.[339] George has written on al-Ḥarīrī's *Maqāmāt* as one of the most frequently illustrated works of the thirteenth and fourteenth centuries, a period in which the earlier static iconography of illustrated Arabic manuscripts was transformed into much more dynamic imagery. He observes that in public readings before an educated urban élite, the pictorial images of illustrated manuscripts—often inspired by the plots of the Arabic shadow play—brought a visual dimension to an essentially aural experience and linked al-Ḥarīrī's text to a larger culture of orality and performance in medieval Islamic society from Iraq to Spain.[340] According to Konrad Hirschler, the Mamlūk period (mid-13th to early 16th centuries) saw changes in reading practices that threatened Islamic scholars' exclusive control of textual transmission. These included a broadened social base of those attending public

---

337 The pre-Islamic soothsayers and Abbāsid popular preachers and storytellers with whom *sajʿ* was associated came to be viewed with suspicion by orthodox Islam so that the medium acquired a mixed status in certain quarters; see Wacks, *Framing Iberia: Maqāmāt and Frametale Narratives in Medieval Spain*, 41–85 *passim*, and idem, "The Performativity of Ibn Al-Muqaffaʿ's 'Kalīla Wa-Dimna' and 'Al-Maqāmāt Al-Luzūmiyya' of Al-Saraqusṭī." Widely varied views of *sajʿ* in the Qur'ān were enunciated by medieval Arabic literary critics; for a highly nuanced treatment, see Stewart, "*Sajʿ* in the Qur'ān: Prosody and Structure."

338 See Pinault, *Story-Telling Techniques in the Arabian Nights*, 12–16.

339 See George, "Orality, Writing and the Image in the *Maqāmāt*: Arabic Illustrated Books in Context," 13–14.

340 See George, "The Illustrations of the *Maqāmāt* and the Shadow Play," and idem, "Orality, Writing and the Image in the *Maqāmāt*." On the importance of these illustrations for reconstructing the history of reading, see Hirschler, *The Written Word in Medieval Arabic Lands*, 7–10 and Plates 2–7 and 14–16.

readings of the written word as well as the performance and committing to writing of a wider variety of non-scholarly texts, such as the epic.[341]

Presumably, the dramatic potential of the *maqāma* could be brought to life by means of an animated and skillful public reading that included bodily movement and mimicry of different voices. The narrative qualities that lend the genre to such live and lively rendition are not unlike the story-telling technique Pinault calls "dramatic visualization," which he defines as

> the representing of an object or character with an abundance of descriptive detail, or the mimetic rendering of gestures and dialogue in such a way as to make the given scene 'visual' or imaginatively present to an audience.[342]

In addition to this latent aspect of the *maqāma* as spectacle, there is also a great deal of storytelling and performance in the text itself. David Wacks and others have argued that storytelling is central to the genre, by virtue of its narrative structure as well as its content. Even without an overarching story like the ones that frame the *Thousand and One Nights* or Boccaccio's *Decameron*, the consistent presence of a narrator who opens each chapter serves to bind the independent episodes together and provides a much-needed context (or pretext) for their embedded tales. One of only two protagonists, the narrator fulfills a key role in transmitting the tales told to him by the smooth-tongued rogue hero. Given the hero's relish for improvisational role playing, masks and disguise in the presence of an audience, many of these tales evoke theatrical moments in communal spaces. Wacks has observed that the *maqāma* genre calls attention to the relationship between storytelling and story writing by portraying literary characters in precisely such acts of public performance. So the storytelling occurs on multiple levels: the author conveys his fictions by means of a narrator who in turn relates a series of spectacles staged by the raffish protagonist. And the reception is similarly multi-tiered: fictitious audiences crowd around the hero in the tales, much as real-life auditors gather around the public readers of the work.[343]

341 See Hirschler, *The Written Word in Medieval Arabic Lands*, 164–196. As noted above, Maurice Pomerantz has examined the increasingly blurred lines, as well as the tensions, between popular and élite literature in Mamlūk-era *maqāmāt*; see his "A *Maqāmah* on the Book Market of Cairo"; "An Epic Hero in the *Maqāmāt*?"; "The Play of Genre"; "Tales from the Crypt"; and "A Maqāma Collection by a Mamlūk Historian."

342 Pinault, *Story-Telling Techniques in the Arabian Nights*, 25.

343 See Wacks, *Framing Iberia*, 41–85 *passim* and idem, "The Performativity of Ibn Al-Muqaffaʿ's 'Kalīla Wa-Dimna.'"

Much has been made of the parallels and points of contact between the hybrid, frequently humorous *maqāma* and various publicly performed genres in the pre-modern Islamic world such as storytelling (*qiṣṣa*), live theater (*ḥikāya*) and the shadow play (*khayāl al-ẓill*). In particular, scholars have been keen to highlight the affinities between the shadow plays of the principal extant playwright, Ibn Dāniyāl (1248–1310), and the *maqāma*. Like the *maqāma*, the shadow plays of Ibn Dāniyāl are written in a mixture of verse and rhymed prose, and both feature characters from the margins of society: wandering, displaced tricksters who survive by their wits and have an uncanny ability to deceive the gullible. In one of Ibn Dāniyāl's plays, the narrator even compares himself to the narrator of al-Ḥarīrī's *Maqāmāt*.[344] But in a review of Shmuel Moreh's 1992 book on *Live Theatre and Dramatic Literature in the Medieval Arabic World*, Everett Rowson cautions against overreaching in assuming that the literary *maqāma* "can be used as evidence of the repertoire, structure, themes, plots, dialogue and characters" of various types of dramatic performance about which we have rather less concrete information.[345]

We can only speculate about the ways in which the text of *Sefer hamusar* was encountered through the ages by its audience or readership. Collective recitation was a pronounced feature of Yemenite Jewish culture well beyond the medieval period; whether in prayer, study of sacred texts, elementary education, or declaiming the poems of the *dīwān*, texts were recited or chanted simultaneously in a group social setting. Since writing materials were scarce, copying manuscripts was costly, and original Yemenite works were not printed in other lands for several centuries after the invention of the press, there was a long-standing tradition of reading texts in unison and committing them to memory. Ratzaby notes that in the sixteenth century oil for lamps was costly, so most Torah study was undertaken from memory at night, in the dark. Children learned to read a shared text from all four directions.[346] Vocal cues played a unique role in the form of hand gestures representing the different cantil-

344 See: Badawi, "Medieval Arabic Drama: Ibn Dāniyāl," esp. 106–107; Moreh, *Live Theatre and Dramatic Literature in the Medieval Arabic World*, 104–122; Guo, *The Performing Arts in Medieval Islam*, and George, "The Illustrations of the *Maqāmāt* and the Shadow Play."

345 Rowson review of Moreh, *Live Theatre and Dramatic Literature in the Medieval Arab World*.

346 This practice persisted into the modern era. See Ahroni, *Yemenite Jewry*, 21–22; Ratzaby, *Bem'agloth Temân*, 86; Goitein, *Sidrei ḥinukh*, 52–53; Qāfiḥ, *Halikhot teiman*, 49; and *Sefer hamusar*, p. 464, n. 93. On rote memorization and the chanting of texts in unison in elementary education, see Goitein, *A Mediterranean Society* 2:174–175; idem, "Jewish Education in Yemen as an Archetype of Traditional Jewish Education" esp. 261–262 on the weekly program of study; Qāfiḥ, *Halikhot teiman*, 53–54 and 79–91; and Greidi, "Ḥinnukh ha-yeladim be-teiman."

lation marks, which were used to guide the Torah reading in synagogue and in unison Torah chanting in children's classes. The emphasis on oral delivery and aural reception of written texts for both instructive and leisure purposes points to the likelihood that, like the *dīwān*, Alḍāhirī's *maqāmāt* were read aloud in group settings. We do not know whether the entire work was read out all in one go, though it need not have been, since its division into independent chapters would have provided natural stopping points, precluding the need to stop at an arbitrary point in the text. Though his personal reminiscences are quite brief, even Mordechai Yiṣhari's introduction to his 2008 printing of *Sefer hamusar* gives the impression that he both heard and read the text during his childhood in the first half of the twentieth century. The family possessed a manuscript of the work, and his account of its having been read during the leisurely hours of convivial family get-togethers along with his pride in having known two of the episodes virtually by heart are suggestive of both aural acquisition of the text in a group setting and individual reading for pleasure.[347] As far as portraying acts of performance in public places is concerned, there is no shortage of such vignettes in *Sefer hamusar*: storytelling, poetic recitation and improvisation, popular preaching, religious disputation, impersonation, quackery—all are performed by the shape-shifting Abner with great theatricality and aplomb in public squares, open-air markets, inns, palaces, synagogues and study-houses. Abner's entrances and exits are noted, delimiting the scenes. And the onlookers' reactions are also part of the performance: mass acts of penitence in response to his preaching; clamoring for cures triggered by his touted panaceas; the Muslim mob scene provoked by his blasphemies against Islam during a public disputation. Not merely passive, his audiences become participant observers in his improvisational vignettes and role-playing. Inasmuch as *Sefer hamusar* partakes of the dramatic, mimetic, and often farcical flair of its Arabic and Hebrew antecedents, it too reflects a dynamic play among theatricality, oral transmission, and literary culture.

6.7 *Imagined Audience/Community of Readers*

Who was Alḍāhirī's intended audience? The first line of his Author's Introduction projects a readership conversant with philosophical and mystical commonplaces ("After having given thanks to the First Cause and Supernal Thought, the blessed God who creates His world ex nihilo …") even as he goes on to invoke traditional penitential themes from Scripture and the liturgy. Presumably, he expected such abstruse concepts as the First Cause and Supernal

347 Yiṣhari, *Sefer hamusar*, p. 5.

Thought to be intelligible to, or at least part of the vocabulary of, his readers, and, in any case, he glosses them in an idiom that was bound to be familiar ("the blessed God who creates His world ex nihilo …"). This suggests an imagined audience that, like the author, was scrupulous in its religious observance but was not discomfited by speculative themes that had long been naturalized in various literary genres and institutional settings. Alḍāhirī says he wrote his book so that future generations might learn of his people's ordeal and submit humbly to God, but he also casts the work as a source of consolation, both communal and personal. Was he hoping to reach an intellectual élite within his own community; a scholarly readership that typically infused its halakhic, philosophical, and scientific learning into traditional exegetical genres like midrash, or that composed *piyyutim* but seemingly not secular, fictional stories? Or was the work intended for a Yemenite Jewish audience with a broader social and intellectual base? Could he have contemplated a readership outside of Yemen as well, given that he lived in the age when Hebrew printing came into its own across Europe and the Ottoman Empire? While he had access to Hebrew books printed elsewhere and was aware of the growing transregional Hebrew book trade, there was no press in Yemen, and, given the prevailing manuscript culture, it is unlikely that he had expectations (or was even desirous) of his book circulating in print. (It was not printed until the 20th century, and until the late 19th century remained unknown to European Jews.)[348] Who, then, did Alḍāhirī have in mind when addressing the religious, intellectual, political, and social issues of the day through a stylized literary medium? For what imagined constituency did he endorse particular texts or innovations in textual reproduction? His goal of reaching future generations notwithstanding, was *Sefer hamusar* merely a personal exercise in literary creativity? The paucity of internal clues leaves us with only speculative answers to these questions. And without any mention of *Sefer hamusar* by Alḍāhirī's contemporaries, we cannot say who read the work in his lifetime, though we have references to it several centuries later. The best we can do is point to the overwhelmingly Yemenite provenance of its multiple manuscripts, most of which were copied in the centuries following the author's demise, which suggests fairly local circulation but also speaks to a renewed interest in the work and a sense of its enduring value.

348 Cf. Chartier, *The Order of Books*, 15: "a transformation in the forms and the mechanisms through which a text is proposed authorized new appropriations, thus it created new publics and new uses."

6.8 *Reception, Successors*

Two later rhymed prose works from Yemen claim direct descent from Alḍāhirī's *maqāma*, and the secondary literature takes them at face value, though neither text truly resembles *Sefer hamusar* in conception, artistry, panoramic scope, or intellectual breadth. Yiḥye ben Abraham Ḥarāzī's kabbalistic *Netivot ha'emunah* (The Paths of Faith), from the late 17th or the 18th century, and Saʿadya Manṣura's consolatory *Sefer ha-maḥashavah* (The Book of Thought, or perhaps The Book of Reckoning of the End of Days), from the second half of the 19th century, are both valuable cultural artifacts in their own right, but neither attempts Alḍāhirī's imaginative synthesis of pious response to historical crisis and lively, at times impious, picaresque. These works comprise a far smaller number of discrete prosimetrical episodes than *Sefer hamusar*. Ḥarāzī's *Netivot ha'emunah* is a kind of primer that expounds the fundamentals of kabbalah over a series of ten *maḥbarot*.[349] The work features Ṭuvyah ben Zeraḥ ha-Ṣeʿiri and Shemu'el ben La'el ha-Ya'iri, whose names adhere to the general onomastic pattern of Hebrew *maqāma* protagonists. Ḥarāzī seems to have thought that certain elements of Alḍāhirī's Introduction were *de rigueur* for a rhymed prose work, hence his declaration that his protagonists' names have the same alphanumeric value as his own, "For this is how it should be" (*yaʿan be-ḥeshbonam ke-shmi ve-shem avi be-ṣeruf otiyot/ki ken ṣarikh lihiyot*).[350] Manṣura's *Sefer ha-maḥashavah* comprises seven "journeys" in which the narrator flees the anti-Jewish oppressions of contemporary 19th-century Yemen to draw solace from Abraham the Patriarch. While they clearly retain facets of Alḍāhirī's model, these didactic and devout works move the Yemenite Hebrew *maqāma* away from emulating al-Ḥarīrī and Alḥarīzī, much as the "post-classical" Arabic *maqāma*—from Yemen and elsewhere—had enlarged the scope of the genre to include texts that diverged from the picaresque prototype.

Ḥarāzī explicitly and reverentially acknowledges *Sefer hamusar* as his immediate source of inspiration but also admits that much of his work is an anthology of selections from various (unnamed) speculative books.[351] The ninth

349 For his table of contents, which bears no resemblance to Alḍāhirī's either in substance or form, see Baumgarten, "Netivot ha'emunah le-rabbi yiḥye ḥarāzī," 205.

350 Baumgarten, ibid., 204. Ḥarāzī's introduction is also transcribed in Ratzaby, *Toratan shelivnei teiman*, 237–238.

351 See Baumgarten, "Netivot ha'emunah," 203; Ratzaby, *Toratan shelivnei teiman*, 238. Baumgarten is inclined toward a late 17th-century dating, whereas Ratzaby and Tobi tentatively date it to the 18th century, see: Ratzaby, *Shirat teiman ha-ʿivrit*, 32 and Tobi, "Conversion to Islam among Yemenite Jews under Zaydi Rule," 116.

chapter is a retort to Muslim anti-Jewish polemical claims, supposedly based on Alḍāhirī's seventh *maqāma*, but it lacks the strident actors and suspenseful drama of the public disputation scene in *Sefer hamusar*. Where Alḍāhirī depicts a tense polemical confrontation between a defender of the dominant Muslim faith and a representative of the subordinate Jewish minority, Ḥarāzī simply has his narrator summarize some of the most central Muslim anti-Jewish claims and then adduce a litany of biblical prooftexts to discredit these arguments, more along the lines of a manual of disputation. In general, Ḥarāzī's didactic work does not seem to have any story line and opts for a more expository mode.[352]

Sefer ha-maḥashavah is a rhymed prose narrative by the Ṣanaʿā-born scholar and poet Saʿadya ben Shalom Manṣura (d. c. 1880), which emulates the formal style, biblical diction, and syntax of *Sefer ha-musar* but also draws extensively on more popular Yemenite Jewish linguistic forms, legends, parables and beliefs. The work incorporates poems in both Hebrew and Judeo-Arabic, the latter something of a novelty for the Hebrew *maqāma*, as Alḍāhirī did not include any of his Judeo-Arabic or macaronic verse in *Sefer hamusar*.[353] Written during a period of unimaginable political unrest and in the wake of the Imām al-Mutawakkil's repressive measures against his Jewish subjects during the years 1846–1849, *Sefer ha-maḥashavah* laments the crushing cruelties endured by Yemenite Jews during their long exile and offers promises of future redemption, hence its modern retitling as *Sefer ha-galut ve-ha-ge'ulah*, "The Book of Exile and Redemption."[354] The work is preserved in a single autograph manuscript dated 1849 and is divided into seven chapters called "journeys" (*massaʿot*).[355] It features a narrator whose name, Ḥazmaq ha-teimani, indicates that he is the author's alter ego—Ḥazmaq being the equivalent of Saʿīd in the *atbash* alphabetic code—along with a hero whose various sobriquets—Eitan

352 On Alḍāhirī's seventh *maqāma* see below, Chapter Four. For Ḥarāzī's ninth chapter, see Baumgarten, "Netivot ha'emunah," 248–254. Prior to Baumgarten's edition, the ninth chapter of *Netivot ha'emunah* had been published by Naḥum in *Ḥasifat genuzim mi-teiman*, 173–177; see also Hallamish, *An Introduction to the Kabbalah*, 150; and Ratzaby, "ʿInyanei dat ba-pulmus bein muslimim li-yehudim be-teiman."

353 For one of Manṣura's Judeo-Arabic poems of messianic longing, see his *Sefer ha-galut ve-ha-ge'ulah*, 60–64 and 189–192 (Hebrew translation).

354 The editors found Manṣura's original title somewhat opaque; on their rationale for the name change, see their Introduction, p. 34. Conceivably, the original title alluded to *ḥishuv ha-qeṣ*, the Reckoning of the End of Days. For the historical context see ibid., 19–32 and Klorman, "'The Book of Thought' by Rabbi Saʿadyah ben Yehudah Mansurah and Messianic Expectations in the mid-Nineteenth Century."

355 NLI ms. Heb. 4741.

ben ḥen ha-qadmoni, Eitan ha'ezraḥi, Avram ha-qadmoni, or Avram ben teraḥ ha-qadmoni—identify him with Abraham the Patriarch.[356] The central conceit of each journey is a kind of time travel that enables the narrator to flee the wretched reality of contemporary Yemen into the distant past in order to tell Abraham about the tribulations undergone by his community and to draw solace from the patriarch's parables of ultimate redemption. Throughout the narrative, the community's sufferings are called "the birth pangs of the Messiah," in keeping with a traditional trope of consolation that cast affliction as a prelude to messianic redemption and urged forbearance.[357] The final chapter, inspired by the auto-epitaph in Alḍāhirī's closing *maqāma* (#45), eulogizes several Yemenite Jewish luminaries, starting with Zechariah Alḍāhirī and ending with Manṣura himself.[358] At the close of this chapter, the author reframes the repressive measures of his day as a prognostic vision of what will occur in Yemen at the End of Days. In a marginal addendum, the author extends this vision, "predicting" that the Turks will come to Yemen and in their wake will come the Christians (the British), whose kingdom will be the final one prior to the advent of the Messiah. But he refrains from writing anything further about the British, as "they are able to read our [Hebrew] writings/scriptures."[359]

While neither of these works displays Alḍāhirī's inventive spark or linguistic exuberance, each picks up on one of the more grave or theoretical aspects of *Sefer hamusar* and treats it at great length. Ḥarāzī uses a rhymed prose form loosely modeled on *Sefer hamusar* to expound kabbalistic doctrines while Manṣura focuses on the pathos of Yemenite Jewish existence under Muslim rule, integrates poems of messianic yearning, and transforms the characteristic wandering of the *maqāma*'s rogue hero into a metaphor for collective exile.[360] Alḍāhirī had boldly exploited the lighthearted belletristic framework and complex narratives of the *maqāma* to introduce kabbalistic theosophy, literature, and liturgical customs to a largely uninitiated public in Yemen. *Sefer hamusar* also reveals a poignant preoccupation with the torments inflicted by the ruling

356 Eitan ("steadfast") is regularly used as an epithet for Abraham the Patriarch.

357 See: Klorman, "'The Book of Thought'" and Ratzaby, "An Historical Poem by Rabbi Saʿadia Manṣura."

358 In the manuscript (but not included in the printed version), following *Sefer ha-maḥashavah* Manṣura copied out all of Alḍāhirī's forty-fifth *maqāma*; see the editors' Introduction to *Sefer ha-galut ve-ha-ge'ulah*, 5 and NLI ms. Heb. 4741 fols. 43^v ff. On the epitaph see below, Chapter Seven.

359 *Sefer ha-galut ve-ha-ge'ulah*, Editors' Introduction, p. 17; NLI ms. Heb. 4741, fol. 42^r–42^v.

360 In his Introduction, he seems to suggest that the motif of itinerancy is also to be understood as a parable of the soul's descent; see *Sefer ha-galut ve-ha-ge'ulah*, p. 2.

Zaydī *imām* and expresses longings for messianic consolation and redemption, so substantively, Ḥarāzī and Manṣura could certainly claim inspiration from their predecessor. The distinction is, of course, that unlike the authors claiming to be his heirs, Alḍāhirī embedded his kabbalistic interludes and stirring responses to the tribulations of exile in immensely creative, at times comical, and essentially fictional narratives of ruses and intrigues. He quarried a rich lode of ideas and narrative modes to craft episodes that can be profoundly engaging or rhetorically beguiling. While questions of aesthetic and literary merit are obviously subjective, the later works tend to be more unidimensional, confining themselves to one overarching concern conveyed with less elaborate narrative strategies.[361] This is not to suggest that the later authors were obscurantists: the rest of Manṣura's manuscript consists of select passages he copied from various printed Hebrew books, including scientific texts and illustrations from *Maʿaseh ṭuvya*, a work David Ruderman has called "the most influential early modern Hebrew textbook" of medicine and science by the University of Padua's "most distinguished Jewish medical graduate."[362] Although our corpus of extant texts is far too slim to support much generalization, these two instances of the work's reception offer compelling illustrations of the ways in which *Sefer hamusar* was selectively read and understood in Alḍāhirī's native land in the centuries following his death. The turn to mysticism and prognostication in the later rhymed prose works aligns with what Tzvi Langermann has identified as Yemenite Jewry's response to the "period of religious persecution and intellectual decline" ushered in by the deportation in 1679 of the Jews of Ṣanaʿā to Mawzaʿ, "during which many lives and many books perished" in the parched climate of the Red Sea coastal region known as the Tihāma.[363] Manṣura composed his *Sefer ha-maḥashavah* some 170 years after the Mawzaʿ exile; his preoccupation with apocalyptic themes has been correlated with the relentless political anarchy that engulfed Yemen during the second third of the

361 Cf. *Sefer ha-galut ve-ha-geʾulah*, Introduction, pp. 18–19, 36.

362 Ruderman, *Jewish Thought and Scientific Discovery in Early Modern Europe*, 229. Manṣura's recourse to *Maʿaseh ṭuvya* is particularly intriguing since there were no medical schools in Yemen nor any clinics until the British colonization of Aden in 1839 and the Ottoman conquest of Ṣanaʿā in 1872; both Muslims and Jews relied on traditional medicine and amuletic remedies. See, e.g., Tobi, "Sifrei ha-refuʾah shel yehudei teiman."

363 Langermann, "Cultural Contacts of the Jews of Yemen," 285. On the Mawzaʿ exile, see Hathaway, "The Mawzaʿ Exile at the Juncture of Zaydi and Ottoman Messianism." Baumgarten speculates that Ḥarāzī's *Netivot haʾemunah* may have been composed between the 1667 "Headdress Decree" and the Mawzaʿ Exile of 1679. Manṣura's sympathy for the kabbalistic poetry of Shalem Shabbazi is evident in the introduction he wrote to Shabbazi's *dīwān*; see *Sefer ha-galut ve-ha-geʾulah*, Introduction, 9–11.

19th century, causing untold suffering for the Jewish community of Ṣanaʿā and prompting the Ottomans to get involved.[364] Seen in this context, Ḥarāzī and Manṣura's rhymed prose works are powerful indicators of the ways Alḍāhirī's *maqāma* could be—and was—co-opted to fit altered historical circumstances and new spiritual exigencies.

364 The Ottomans, however, did not establish their rule until 1872. See Klorman, "'The Book of Thought,'" and *Sefer ha-galut ve-ha-geʾulah*, Introduction, 19–32.

CHAPTER 2

Travel in Many Guises: Journeys Real and Imagined

Tantalizingly brief travel accounts frame almost every episode of *Sefer hamusar*. Typically, the roaming narrator opens each *maqāma* with a concise rhymed prose itinerary of places he has passed through to reach his current location and closes with a cursory mention of his next destination. Already in the first *maqāma*, his peregrinations are in full swing, with the narrative beginning *in medias res*:

> Said Mordecai the Sidonian: I journeyed from No Amon [Alexandria] to Mount Hermon, with most luscious Damascus as my terminus.
>
> *amar mordekhai ha-ṣidoni: nasaʿti mi-no amon/ el har ḥermon/*
> *u-megamati le-dammeseq ha-medinah/asher le-khol hamedinot ʿadinah.*[1]

When we arrive at the final *maqāma*, Mordecai has wandered extensively and circuitously throughout the Muslim East. Along the way, he describes the urban centers and towns he visits in strikingly minimalist terms, conveying only the bare essentials of place names and, on rare occasions, journey times, modes of transportation, or waterways contiguous to a given city. The few exceptions that elicit more detailed impressions are Damascus, whose wondrous gardens, fruit-laden orchards, and graceful buildings appeal to Mordecai's aesthetic sensibilities; the holy cities of Safed, Tiberias, and Jerusalem in the Land of Israel; and a town of fruit trees and scholars on the Euphrates that he calls Qiryat Sefer. And even in these instances, his stylized portrayals often draw on common knowledge and focus only on the city's essential features; his praise for the physical beauty of Damascus (#5, #10) matches an idealized image of the city as a paradise on earth that recurs throughout classical Arabic literature. But apart from such exceptions, Mordecai provides little sense of physical layout, architectural detail, local color, or the time frame of his visits. Omissions such

1 *Sefer hamusar*, p. 59. The identification of No Amon (Jer. 46:25) with Alexandria goes back to the Targum of Jonathan ben Uziel; it also occurs in Saadya's *tafsīr*. See Bareket, "Shemot miqra'iyyim-ʿivriyyim le-yishuvim, araṣot, u-qevuṣot etniyot bimei ha-beinayim." NB: Haitham M. Sharqawy and Naoya Katsumata's similarly titled "Travel in al-Ḍāhirī's *Sefer hamusar*: Between Reality and Imagination," *MEAH* 73 (2024) reached me after the manuscript of this book was complete.

 | DOI:10.1163/9789004733787_004

as these are common in the *maqāma* literature, which draws on a world that is actual yet does not itself pretend to veracity.[2] Several instances of geographical continuity between the individual *maqāmāt* of *Sefer hamusar* suggest some authorial redaction. But the frequently random progression from one locale to the next is likely due as much to a deliberate disregard for verisimilitude as to the work's piecemeal composition and minimal editing. Apropos of the itineraries in the *Taḥkemoni*, Michael Rand argues that

> The function of the geographical names with which the *maqāmas* open is not to chart a particular route, but rather to create a general sense of motion and restlessness.[3]

Mordecai's wanderlust invariably leads him to Abner, so from a narrative point of view, his travel digests are generally a pretext for launching into the whimsically engaging, darkly funny, or despairing substance of each *maqāma*. In many episodes, the locations are incidental to the stories. Structurally, the narrator's compressed, seemingly factual itineraries enclose the expansive, at times preposterous tales of the roving hero, whose adventures also unfold haphazardly throughout the Muslim East. Like al-Hamadhānī's picaresque hero (and unlike Alḥarizi's, who hails from Iberia), Abner ignores the Maghreb or Muslim West, but traverses the Islamic heartland and on occasion ranges to a further land of the Eastern Islamic empire. His escapades take him with reckless abandon to Yemen, India, Persia, Mesopotamia, Syria, the Land of Israel, Egypt, and as far west as Ottoman Anatolia and the Balkans. To reach him in each *maqāma*—by design or by chance—Mordecai joins overland caravans, sails on ships, and dabbles in trade. En route, he seeks to gain halakhic competence and kabbalistic wisdom on the one hand, and *musar*—acquaintance with a wide range of refined disciplines, folktales, anecdotes, and proverbs—on the other. This pursuit leads to encounters with Jewish communities whom the protagonists admire for their piety and learning or deplore for their ignorance and immorality, often betraying the limitations of their own culturally determined ability to comprehend what they observe. As discussed in Chapter Four, they also record impressions of Muslims of various stripes, which span the gamut from crude stereotypes to more nuanced depictions.

---

2 See Decter, *Iberian Jewish Literature*, 188–206.

3 Rand, *The Evolution of al-Ḥarizi's Taḥkemoni*, 18. This approach provides a welcome corrective to Goitein's insistence on fixing the precise route and dates of "Alḍāhirī's" travels; see "A Yemenite Poet on Egypt of the XVIth Century," 29–30.

Although many details of these descriptions have the ring of truth, they cannot be taken at face value. Like so much in *Sefer hamusar*, the travel accounts inextricably intertwine the realistic with the imaginary and stand to benefit from more recent critical approaches and cross-disciplinary methodologies recognizing this interdependence of narrative modes and cognitive perspectives.[4] Literary and cultural studies, anthropology, history, geography, and postcolonial studies have all revisited medieval and early modern European travel literature, addressing questions of fictionality, subjectivity, authorial perspective and ideology, assumptions brought to bear on encounters with the "Other" and cultural self-definition.[5] Paul Zumthor's pioneering studies of the diverse texts collectively considered travel narratives in the pre-modern Western tradition—pilgrims' recollections, missionary accounts, ambassadors' reports, navigators' ship logs, merchants' travel guidebooks—highlight their "unavoidable kinship with fiction" due to their often fantastic subject matter, which could not be readily verified by their readership.[6] Stephen Greenblatt sees the anecdote, around which late medieval and Renaissance chronicles of exploration are constructed, not only as the most suitable discursive register for representing unanticipated encounters with the unfamiliar but also as far more captivating than any authorial or editorial attempt to superimpose an orderly narrative on the material.[7] Special scrutiny has been given to the role of fantasy in the travel writings of Renaissance/Early Modern authors, whose records of actual excursions were typically embellished with hearsay and information drawn from other sources and who also penned imagined journeys to uncharted lands that held out the promise of radically new realities. In response to skepticism regarding the credibility of their claims, Renaissance travel writers cited a well-known proverb to the effect that "travelers lie by authority."[8] In such works, the blurring of boundaries was facilitated by situating the activity

> within an unknown but discoverable area of the real world, so that the fantasy could just possibly be fact, presented by travellers who might just possibly be real.[9]

4 Cf. Wood, *How Fiction Works*, xiii: "… fiction is both artifice and verisimilitude, and … there is nothing difficult in holding together these two possibilities."

5 For an overview, see Campbell, "Travel Writing and its Theory" and Thompson, *Travel Writing*.

6 See Zumthor, "The Medieval Travel Narrative," 813.

7 Greenblatt, *Marvelous Possessions: The Wonder of the New World*.

8 See Adams, *Travelers and Travel Liars, 1660–1800* and Carey, "Truth, Lies, and Travel Writing." The term "travel liar" has become a commonplace in the secondary literature.

9 Mezciems, "'Tis not to divert the Reader': Moral and Literary Determinants in Some Early Travel Narratives," 1. Cf. Ginzburg, *The Cheese and the Worms*, 44.

Joan-Pau Rubiés has analyzed the influential 14th-century *Book of John Mandeville* as paradigmatic of works whose author constructed a fictional traveler but never actually visited the places he describes. Relying instead on all sorts of available texts, *Mandeville's* author attempted to conceal his work's composite nature by integrating his sources into a coherent travel narrative.[10] Not unrelated are questions provoked by the notion of Utopia, "an ideal state situated in an imaginary place," (*ou topos*, literally, "no place") which cannot be reached by means of a physical journey.[11] Postcolonial theory has probed the cultural assumptions and lenses determining how authors portrayed and generated knowledge about non-European Others in distant lands and the relationship of these largely deprecating depictions to questions of power. Crude and essentializing representations of unfamiliar groups and customs as exotic and enticing but also primitive or savage not only constructed an otherness intelligible to an author's audience but also played into the hands of those who benefited from the colonial system. In the wake of Edward Said's pronouncements, much has been written about patronizing Western Orientalist perceptions and stereotypes of non-Western societies in relation to imperialist exploitation.[12]

1 Reassessing Pre-modern Arabic and Hebrew Travel Narratives

Drawing on recent critical and theoretical developments, scholars of the Arabic and Hebrew traditions have also produced fresh readings of pre-modern travel narratives. Despite their verisimilitude, works long considered to be reli-

10 Rubiés constructs a typology of different forms of travel literature and their contributions to the development of European intellectual culture; see his "Travel Writing as a Genre: Facts, Fictions and the Invention of a Scientific Discourse in Early Modern Europe."

11 See Zumthor, "The Medieval Travel Narrative," 821; Chloë ed., *New Worlds Reflected: Travel and Utopia in the Early Modern Period* and the literature cited in the Introduction; and Ouyang's preface to "Utopias, Dystopias and Heterotopias: The Spatiality of Human Experience and Literary Expression."

12 See, e.g.: Allen, *Eastward Bound: Travel and Travelers, 1050–1550* and Campbell, *The Witness and the Other World: Exotic European Travel Writing, 400–1600*. Martin Jacobs helpfully points out that Said's notion of orientalism as "a discourse from a position of genuine hegemony" is not applicable to medieval Jewish travelers operating in a pre-colonial context; see his "From Lofty Caliphs to Uncivilized 'Orientals'—Images of the Muslim in Medieval Jewish Travel Literature," and the Introduction to his *Reorienting the East: Jewish Travelers to the Medieval Muslim World*, 1–17. See also Suzanne Conklin Akbari's discussion of the casual use of the label "medieval Orientalism" in her *Idols in the East: European Representations of Islam and the Orient, 1100–1450*, 1–19.

able single-author records of actual journeys offering unmediated observations are now being reassessed. In many instances, they are more fruitfully viewed as composites of first-hand impressions drawn not from the personal experience of actual visits but rather from other travel accounts, hearsay, a common inventory of stock images of the exotic, or the author's imagination. Rather than private diaries kept along the way, these works are now seen through the prism of a more complicated notion of authorship and as windows onto writers' and readers' expectations and "imaginative geographies," shaped by their culture's assumptions and fantasies. Travel was a central feature of life throughout the vast Islamic empire from the early Middle Ages, yielding an abundance of travel writing from the 9th century on. Abū Zayd al-Sīrāfī, a seafarer who moved from the port city of Sirāf on the Persian Gulf—which was central to the Indian Ocean trade of the time—to Basra in 915/16, added a supplementary second half to the mid-9th-century *Accounts of China and India*, written by an unknown mariner and merchant fifty years earlier. The work, which relies on multiple accounts of anonymous informants and has two compilers who each attempted to organize the disparate threads of their rich and wide-ranging material, "leaps from India to China and back" as it reports on maritime commerce and goods (including tea and porcelain), sea routes and tides, as well as unfamiliar Chinese and Indian customs.[13] Also challenging assumptions about factual records of actual journeys, Ross Dunn has written of the Moroccan Ibn Baṭṭūta's oft-cited claim to have visited China that

> The riddle of the journey probably defies solution since the *Riḥla* [his travel account], we must remind ourselves, is a work of literature, a survey of the Muslim world of the fourteenth century in narrative form, not a travel diary composed along the road. We have no way of knowing the precise relationship between Ibn Battuta's real life experience and the account of it contained in the fragile manuscripts that have come down to us from his time.[14]

In a similar vein, Martin Jacobs has revised the long-accepted view of Benjamin of Tudela's Hebrew itinerary from the Crusader period, arguing persuasively that

13 See Mackintosh-Smith, Translator's Introduction to Abū Zayd al-Sīrāfī, *Accounts of China and India*, xvii–xxx.

14 Dunn, *The Adventures of Ibn Battuta*, 253; cited by Beckingham, "The *Riḥla*: Fact or Fiction?" p. 87. Cf. Netton, "*Riḥla*": "with the *Riḥla* of Ibn Baṭṭūta we reach the peak in the articulation of a genre which should be perceived much more in terms of a literary art form than a formal geography."

> the common classification of Benjamin's book as a travel account ... deserves further clarification .... [T]he book should not be read primarily as a factual travel account, but may be better appreciated as a popular anthology of faraway places and countries, including passages providing place-specific information, some of which seems to have been culled from earlier traditions. As such, it can offer us a glimpse not so much into the personal experiences of a solitary traveler, but into the cultural perceptions of a larger, medieval Jewish readership, for whom the text was copied, revised, augmented, and reprinted innumerable times.[15]

While *Sefer hamusar* has multiple aims—didactic, edifying, commemorative, and entertaining—it is first and foremost a creative literary work that does not purport to be a coherent, continuous travel diary or a practical guidebook for pilgrims or merchants even though it may be informed by related travel genres. Nevertheless, Jacobs' caveats regarding earlier scholarship on Benjamin's *Massaʿot* are pertinent to Alḍāhirī's *Sefer hamusar* as well. The tendency of nineteenth- and early twentieth-century scholars to treat medieval Jewish travel accounts as "mere repositories of historical data" was fueled by the same positivist impulse that has marked the study of Alḍāhirī's *maqāma* and which merits reconsideration. In *Sefer hamusar*, the travel is related on the authority of a fictitious narrator, and the lines between the actual and the imaginary are artfully blurred. Yet, as we have seen, readers eager for facts have dwelt on the work's verisimilitude, preferring to view the book primarily as a travelogue, while overlooking its highly fanciful literary character. For much of the twentieth century, the few scholars who dipped into *Sefer hamusar* attempted to reconstruct Alḍāhirī's own itineraries, based on the assumption that the journeys described by the internal narrator were those of the author himself. According to this line of thought, Alḍāhirī's affinity for the *maqāma* was only natural, given that a roaming narrator and vagrant rogue-hero are fixtures of the genre.[16] (Georges Vajda dismissed the author as "une personnalité instable," due to what he saw as Alḍāhirī's compulsive need to wander.[17]) While there is

15 Jacobs, "From Lofty Caliphs to Uncivilized 'Orientals,'" 70–72; cf. idem, *Reorienting the East*, 9–11. Jacobs notes that the title *Sefer ha-massaʿot* was conferred later; see p. 70 and Adler ed., *The Itinerary of Benjamin of Tudela*, Hebrew section, p. 1. Adolf Asher noted that the Hebrew "Preface" was added by another hand "some time after the itinerary had been completed"; see Asher ed. and trans., *The Itinerary of Benjamin of Tudela*, 2:1.

16 See, e.g., Ratzaby, "The Influence of al-Ḥariri Upon Alḍāhiri," 56.

17 Vajda, review of Ratzaby ed., *Sefer Hammusar*.

no inherent reason to doubt the author's mobility, the relationship between Alḍāhirī's actual movements and those of his invented characters is impossible to determine. Unlike the wanderings of the Toledan Judah Alḥarizi, whose extended sojourn in Provence as a translator from Arabic to Hebrew is attested by various sources independent of his *Taḥkemoni*, and whose long journey to the East in search of patrons is documented by the thirteenth-century Muslim biographer al-Mubārak ibn Aḥmad al-Mawṣilī (1197–1256), Alḍāhirī's peregrinations lack external corroboration by a contemporary.[18] But even recent scholarship on the *Taḥkemoni* has had to establish a set of criteria to navigate delicately between what it has deemed the autobiographical episodes and those that appear to be more contrived.[19] Refining this approach, Michael Rand has argued that Alḥarizi's own "telic journey" from a starting point to an end point is integrated into the far-flung imaginary landscape of the *maqāma* genre, such that

> the irreconcilability of the real and the fictional geographical frameworks may obtrude in a case where a real, known place figures within both the autobiographical as well as the conventional-literary strands of the *Taḥkemoni*.[20]

By way of illustration, he points to Jerusalem, which figures as a real place in the "autobiographical strand" (#16), but also serves as a fictional setting in the "literary strand" (#12), when the plot that unfolds there is so implausible—"a literary salon … located in a city without literati"—that the author could not possibly have been thinking of the actual Jerusalem of his own day.[21] In the latter case, Jerusalem becomes a city of the imagination; a conceptual space rather than a geographical one.

18 On al-Mawṣilī's biographical entry, see Sadan, "Un intelectuel juif au confluent de deux cultures" and idem, "Judah Alḥarizi as a Cultural Junction." On the additional records of Alḥarizi's journeys, see: Alḥarizi, *Kitāb al-durar* and *The Wanderings of Judah Alharizi*.

19 Cf. the English Introduction to Alḥarizi, *Taḥkemoni*, ed. Yahalom-Katsumata, xiv–xix ("The Personal Sessions"), where the editors outline their criteria for determining that a chapter is autobiographical rather than fictional.

20 See Rand, *The Evolution of al-Ḥarizi's Taḥkemoni*, 17–23.

21 Ibid., 20–21. But Rand also acknowledges the argument of Uriah Kfir that Alḥarizi deliberately set #12 in Jerusalem as part of his agenda of Andalusian Jewish exceptionalism; see Kfir, *A Matter of Geography*, 77–79 and 116–118.

2 Toponyms

As in the *Taḥkemoni* and other Hebrew *maqāmāt*, some of the place names in Alḍāhirī's itineraries must be discounted as mere rhetorical ornamentation. Although their intertextual associations can at times be relevant, biblical toponyms that no longer correspond to a geographic reality are often invoked purely to preserve a rhyming format, but there is no relationship between any ancient historical memories or sacred history evoked by the names of these places and the stories set there. The itinerary at the beginning of #31 is one such instance:

> Said Mordecai the Sidonian, "I journeyed from the land of *Metim* (Job 24:12) to the land of the *Ḥittim* where the Philistines and Arameans were encamped."
>
> *nasaʿti meʾereṣ metim/el ereṣ ha-ḥittim/ve-sham pelishtim vaʾaram neḥitim* (II Kings 6:9).[22]

This engaging episode is not set in any recognizable locale and revolves around Abner's recitation of a contrived tale of deceit in exchange for food from the local Jews who are taken in by his silver tongue. It is worth noting that #31, #33, and #34, none of whose biblical toponyms have geographic significance, are clustered together. As #33 unfolds, pleasing details of place and topography that at first sight seem realistic enough prove to be of consequence for the construction of Alḍāhirī's imaginary landscape and the unfolding of his narrative. This episode's central tale, which weighs the comparative merits of poetry writing and accounting, opens in a paradisiacal setting of fruit trees and lush vegetation inhabited by people of wisdom and *derekh ereṣ* (consideration for others). Its location on the Euphrates turns out to be predetermined by al-Ḥarīrī's twenty-second *maqāma*, "Of the Euphrates," on which the episode is based.[23] Notably, neither al-Ḥarīrī's underlying Arabic text nor its earlier Hebrew translation by Judah Alḥarizi in *Maḥberot Itiʾel* specifies a particular town along the Euphrates. Alḍāhirī calls the town Qiryat Sefer, a place name

22 *Sefer hamusar*, p. 358. For further examples, see *Sefer hamusar*, p. 26, n. 4. Cf. Rand, *Evolution*, pp. 6–7: "… for purposes of rhyme, his actual stations are interspersed with biblical place names that lack real geographical referents …." And see ibid., p. 17, for Rand's taxonomy of the geographical names invoked in the work.

23 See: *The Assemblies of Al Ḥarīri*, trans. Chenery, 1:229–234; *Maqāmāt al-Ḥarīrī*, 172–178; and Alḥarizi, *Maḥberot Itiʾel*, 181–186.

given to a conquered city subsumed within the territory of Judah in the book of Joshua (Josh. 15:15–17). Using it in its purely lexical sense ("Town of the Book") without any pretense to geographical accuracy, Alḍāhirī conjures up a community of scholars and scribes, in keeping with the spirit of al-Ḥarīrī's original.[24] The plot takes an ironic turn when these wise and decorous men shun and belittle Abner, who has appeared in a bedraggled and impoverished state. But he puts them to shame with a brilliant rhetorical display, from which the narrator aptly deduces the moral of the story: "One should not reject a sword buried in its sheath," which is to say, "Don't judge a book by its cover." (A variant on this adage is cited, also as a rebuke for judging an old man by his decrepit appearance, in Shem Tov Falaquera's *Iggeret ha-musar*: "Don't you know that the whetted sword/ is not harmed by a sheath, be it old or new, /neither does a lowly nest harm the eagle.")[25] In another toponymical oddity that derives from a Yemenite Jewish tradition drawing on late versions of Saadya Gaon's *tafsīr*, Alḍāhirī applies biblical Hebrew names to cities in Yemen, e.g., ʿUzal and Diqla of the postdiluvian genealogy or Table of Nations in Genesis 10:27 for Ṣanaʿā and Ṣaʿadah respectively. As mentioned in the previous chapter, Saadya was opposed to translating biblical toponyms with Arabic equivalents and issued an explicit injunction against doing so in his commentary on Job. The substitutions occur only in later versions of the *tafsīr* due to scribal interpolations that were subsequently replicated, but the tradition had certainly taken hold by the early 14th century.[26]

---

24 In Arabic literature from the Mamlūk period, the poetic device of using book titles or proper names not in their technical sense, but for the everyday meaning of their component words, became quite popular. It was known as *tawjīh*, a term that has other technical meanings in different Islamic disciplines; see Bauer, "'Ayna hādhā min al-Mutanabbī!' Toward an Aesthetics of Mamlūk Literature"; Pomerantz, "A *Maqāmah* on the Book Market of Cairo in the 8th/14th Century"; and cf. the definition in Biberstein-Kazimirski, *Dictionnaire arabe-français*, p. 1496, #5: "ambiguïté, caractère équivoque d'un discours susceptible de double entente." *Sefer hamusar* #17 is also notionally set in Qiryat Sefer. While the locale is irrelevant to most of that episode, it does have some semantic bearing insofar as #16, #17, and #18 include poems of praise for the Torah, the Talmud, and several classics of the medieval Hebrew scholarly canon.

25 Rand identifies Falaquera's text as yet another free translation of al-Ḥarīrī, whose #22 includes an Arabic version of the maxim. In *Maḥberot Iti'el*, there are slight variations in the translation from the Arabic; see Rand, *Maḥberot Eitan ha-Ezraḥi*, 58–60. Rand's conclusion that Falaquera worked "directly from the Arabic version, without the intermediary of al-Ḥarizi's translation," seems equally true of Alḍāhirī.

26 For the substitutions, see e.g., *Sefer hamusar*, p. 64, l. 5 (#2) and p. 187, l. 90 (#15) and Netan'el ben Isaiah, *Ma'or ha-afelah*, p. 74.

3 Reading the Travel Accounts in *Sefer hamusar*

Jonathan Decter has written that, just as pre-modern travel literature incorporates something of the imaginative, *maqāma* literature borrows elements of travel writing

> to lend movement, familiarity, and sometimes irony [to its texts, but] usually reflects little interest in relating detailed information about a place … and generally lacks the travel narrative's sequential progression through a series of locations.[27]

Clearly, *Sefer hamusar* is not travel literature in the sense of a diary detailing an ordered progression through faraway places to record their foreign customs and exotica. Alḍāhirī seems far more at home in internal, imaginary landscapes than in the meticulous or systematic representation of external realia. If we therefore depart from the positivist approach to his work as a source for facts and take an agnostic view of the author's own travels, what are the critical stances that we can profitably apply to the wanderings depicted in the book? To begin with, we can view the reported excursions of narrator and hero through a literary lens, posing questions about the matrix out of which they emerged and their role in the larger sweep of a given episode or of the work as a whole. Are the travel accounts that frame almost every individual *maqāma* in *Sefer hamusar* anything more than a literary convention of the genre? Do they provide narrative structure? What effect, if any, do the work's seemingly matter-of-fact itineraries have on our understanding of the extravagant yarns they often envelop? What do the characters' movements tell us about the author's conception of space and the scale of his mental map? We can also probe Alḍāhirī's texts with an eye to authorial perspectives on intellectual and cultural transformation during his lifetime. What are the stimuli to travel in *Sefer hamusar*? Does Alḍāhirī present the characters' peregrinations as a quest for knowledge (*ṭalab al-ʿilm*)? How do his stories link mobility with the diffusion of religious learning and practices? We can also examine the cultural preconceptions that these texts reflect: What is significant about the orbits in which the protagonists move? Do they cross cultural boundaries, and if so, what differences in cultural sensibility do they reveal toward the unfamiliar? If they are prone to misconception, does their stereotyping apply to Jews as well as non-Jews? Do these representations of "others" fulfill the cultural expectations of Alḍāhirī's

27 Decter, *Iberian Jewish Literature*, 189.

imagined audience? How might these pronouncements have helped the author and his readership shape their sense of identity, since constructing the Other invariably leads to constructing the Self? How does the vagrant hero's repeated use of disguise relate to the experience of being a stranger, whose spatial and social dislocation facilitates the adoption of different identities? And finally, is there anything uniquely Yemenite or distinctively 16th-century about Alḍāhirī's travel accounts that sets *Sefer hamusar* apart from its precursors?

4 Arabic and Hebrew Antecedents to the Travel Narratives

A broad array of Arabic and Hebrew travel writings form the backdrop to the narratives of itinerancy in *Sefer hamusar*. Travel—a topos exploited across the eras in manifold cultures—featured in countless guises in the cumulative corpus of literature antecedent to Alḍāhirī, even though we cannot say for certain whether he knew a particular work like Benjamin of Tudela's itinerary or Ibn Baṭṭūṭa's *Riḥla*. In the medieval Islamic world, there were numerous reasons for leaving one's habitual surroundings and traversing vast distances, many of which gave rise to particular genres of writing.[28] Travel was prompted by: (1) Religion, including the obligation of pilgrimage to Mecca (*ḥajj*), visits to shrines (*ziyāra*), to Sufi lodges and to holy men, and the collection of prophetic traditions (*ḥadīth*); (2) Learning (*ṭalab al-ʿilm*), including the search for individual teachers or Sufi masters[29] and travel to institutions of learning, both religious and non-religious; (3) Embassy (*sifāra*), both within and outside of the Islamic world;[30] (4) Trade and commerce (*tijāra*), both overland and maritime; (5) Propaganda, both religious (e.g., Ismāʿīlī) and political; (6) Government posting; (7) Exploration; (8) Warfare; (9) Migration, both voluntary and forced; and (10) Patronage, including travel to and with a patron.[31] Such abundant movement

28 See: Bosworth, "Travel Literature"; Eickelman and Piscatori eds., *Muslim Travellers*; Netton ed., *Golden Roads*; Touati, *Islam et voyage au moyen âge*; van Leeuwen, *The Thousand and One Nights: Space, travel and transformation*, 18–22; idem, "'*Yā raḥīl*!' Reasons for travelling in al-Ghazālī's *Ihyāʾ ʿulūm al-dīn*." Additional motivations for leaving one's home are discussed in the commentary to Crone and Moreh trans., *The Book of Strangers*.

29 Cf. van Leeuwen, "Travel and Spirituality: The Peregrinations of a Moroccan Sufi in the 16th Century."

30 A striking account of a 10th-century diplomatic mission to the king of the Volga Bulghārs can be found in Ibn Faḍlān, *Mission to the Volga*. In the 16th century, Leo Africanus (c. 1492–c. 1550), an envoy for the sultan of Fez, was captured by a Spanish pirate and taken to Rome, where he was baptized by the Pope and produced a number of learned works on Arabic and Islam aimed at a western readership; see Davis, *Trickster Travels*.

31 This list is largely derived from the comprehensive taxonomy in Toorawa, "Travel in the

led to cross-cultural encounters and confrontations and the dissemination of ideas, texts, and inventions. Moreover, in much medieval literature, whether Islamic, Jewish, or Christian, the physical journey mirrored a metaphorical or spiritual journey or quest. Travel from station to station was often an allegory of the gradual progression from ignorance to wisdom, as in Abraham Ibn Ezra's *Ḥayy ben Meqiṣ*, a philosophical allegory of the soul's journey through the cosmic realms in a quest for wisdom which was closely modeled on Ibn Sīnā's *Ḥayy Ibn Yaqẓān*. The Neoplatonic odyssey of the divine soul that descended temporarily to imprisonment in a mortal body, but yearned to be restored to its celestial source, was a well-known medieval trope that cut across confessional lines, affording philosophers and poets alike a crucial vehicle for exploring the human relationship with the Divine. Even accounts of purely physical voyages might entail elements of personal transformation or heightened self-awareness as the result of geographical discovery, pilgrimage, or encounters with members of other cultures.[32]

The written works affected by the experience of mobility in the expansive Islamic empire comprised geographical treatises or dictionaries and navigational texts;[33] travelogues and guidebooks rooted in scholarly journeys or pilgrimage;[34] accounts of exotic customs and mores (*ʿajāʾib* or "mirabilia");[35] a subgenre of the *faḍāʾil* (virtues) literature devoted to the praise of individual cities; poetic elegies for lost cities (*rithāʾ al-mudun*); literary debates (*munāẓara adabiyya*) between pairs of cities;[36] and the *maqāma*. It stands to reason that different types of text might overlap; reports of exotica discovered on journeys

Medieval Islamic World: the importance of patronage." On seeking a livelihood as a reason for scholarly travel see also Bray, "Starting Out in New Worlds: Under Whose Empire? High Tradition and Subaltern Tradition in Ottoman Syria, 16th and 19th/20th centuries."

32 Cf. Ouyang in "Utopias, Dystopias and Heterotopias," 227: "Travel in Arabic writings is no mere genre. It is, among other things, a central trope, a figurative matrix that drives quest for knowledge, geographical discovery, historical narratives, religious accounts of pilgrimage, spiritual journeys of transcendence, official records of diplomatic missions, literary journeys of transformation, and cross-cultural dialogues."

33 See Richter-Bernburg, "Geographical Literature" and Hopkins, "Geographical and Navigational Literature."

34 See Netton, *Seek Knowledge: Thought and Travel in the House of Islam.*

35 See: Dubler, "ʿAdj̲āʾib"; von Hees, "The Astonishing: A Critique and Rereading of ʿAǧāʾib Literature"; and Berlekamp, *Wonder, Image, and Cosmos in Medieval Islam*, 22–25. See also Jacobs, "Flying Camels and Other Remarkable Species: Natural Marvels in Medieval Hebrew Travel Accounts."

36 See Elinson, *Looking Back at al-Andalus*; Grunebaum, "Aspects of Arabic Urban Literature Mostly in Ninth and Tenth Centuries"; and van Gelder, "City Panegyric, in Classical Arabic." For a delightfully different perspective, see Fakhreddine and Orfali, "Against Cities: On *Hijāʾ al-Mudun* in Arabic Poetry."

(real or imagined) figured in travelogues, as did poetic paeans for particular cities. Ibn Baṭṭūṭa's *Riḥla* is more fully entitled *"For the Curious, A Rare Work Concerning Wondrous Things (gharāʾib) in Great Cities, and Marvels (ʿajāʾib) Encountered on Journeys"* and has been described as "part of a specifically Arabic genre of *riḥla* as *belles-lettres, adab*, rather than history or geography."[37] Along with the Andalusian Ibn Jubayr (1145–1217), the Moroccan Ibn Baṭṭūṭa (1304–1368/9 or 1377) is one of the most frequently cited Muslim travelers.[38] But where Ibn Jubayr's travelogue is considered fairly reliable, Ibn Baṭṭūṭa's is not. The prototype of the genre, Ibn Jubayr's *Riḥla* records his visits to many of the great cities of Islam, undertaken during the fairly circumscribed period of 1183–1185 as part of a pilgrimage to Mecca. By contrast, Ibn Baṭṭūṭa's wide-ranging, trans-hemispheric wanderings unfolded over a period of thirty years (1325–1353), and his *Riḥla*, which borrows directly from Ibn Jubayr and other authors, is not the product of on-site record-keeping but rather of much later oral dictations to an editor who gave the work its final, literary form.[39]

Certain analogues to these stimuli motivated medieval and early modern Jewish travelers. Although no longer incumbent upon individuals post-70 C.E. in the same way as the *ḥajj* was in Islam, pilgrimage was still a forceful incentive to journey. In the summer of 1140, Judah Halevi set sail from al-Andalus for Egypt, with the express intention of living out his last days in the Land of Israel. His stirring responses to his sea voyage and spiritual journey are captured in emotionally charged Hebrew poems of rare beauty and poignancy, while his impressions of the cosmopolitan world he encountered in Egypt are recorded in an archive of Judeo-Arabic letters preserved in the Cairo Genizah.[40] Three centuries later, Meshullam of Volterra (in 1481) and Obadiah of Bertinoro (in 1486) traveled to the Land of Israel as part of what Martin Jacobs has termed "a resurgence of Jewish pilgrimages ... which accompanied the proliferation of trade between Europe and the Levant, dominated by Venice and other Italian centers of commerce."[41] Both left travel diaries in epistolary form, though they differ greatly in the degree of condescension (Meshullam) or openness

37 See Netton, "Ibn Baṭṭuṭa in Wanderland: Voyage as Text—Was Ibn Baṭṭuṭa an Orientalist?"

38 Toorawa laments the disproportionate attention paid to only a handful of travelers; see "Travel in the Medieval Islamic World." On Ibn Jubayr's *Riḥla*, see Netton, "Basic Structures and Signs of Alienation in the Rihla of Ibn Jubayr."

39 See Netton, "Ibn Baṭṭuṭa in Wanderland" and Kilito, *Thou Shalt Not Speak My Language*, 46–55. On Ibn Baṭṭūṭa as a "literate frontiersman," see Dunn, "International Migrations of Literate Muslims in the Later Middle Period: The Case of Ibn Battuta." See also Elad, "The Description of the Travels of Ibn Battuta in Palestine: Is It Original?"

40 See Scheindlin, *The Song of the Distant Dove: Judah Halevi's Pilgrimage*.

41 Jacobs, "Lofty Caliphs," p. 82; see also idem, *Reorienting the East*, 50–59 *passim*. For their

(Obadiah) with which they view Eastern manners and customs.[42] The financier and kabbalist Moses Basola embarked from Venice on his pilgrimage of 1521–1523, in the course of which he visited twenty-four sacred burial places in the Land of Israel, which he described in rich detail. For those wishing to prostrate themselves at the tombs of saints or prophets, itineraries of venerated gravesites in the Land of Israel had circulated widely since the thirteenth century. Apart from its attention to sacred graves, Basola's strictly chronological travelogue takes the form of a practical guidebook, complete with geographical data, shipboard advice to travelers, accounts of commerce and prevailing currencies, and descriptions of local Jewish communities.[43] As with Benjamin of Tudela's itinerary, scholars have recently begun to ask for whom such descriptions were written and to pay attention to the cultural judgments implicit in what was, and was not, considered worthy of reporting.[44]

By Alḍāhirī's time, the history of individuals traveling to centers of Jewish learning could be traced back to antiquity. His own century saw a resurgence when, following the Ottoman conquest of Palestine in 1516–1517 with its attendant political and economic transformations, the Galilean city of Safed attracted a remarkable group of intellectuals and rabbis, many of whom were drawn to the study of kabbalah. Moshe Idel has examined the impact of 16th-century scholarly dislocation, peregrination and trans-communal encounters on the development, reshaping, and transmission of kabbalistic ideas, one aspect of which was the novel impetus to preserve, systematize, and synthesize kabbalistic teachings.[45] The fictional characters in *Sefer hamusar* visit the Galilee in search of kabbalistic knowledge precisely when this region is the center of mystical revival, and, through them, Alḍāhirī brings pre-Lurianic kabbalistic theosophy and Zoharic literature, alongside newer Lurianic liturgical

epistolary journals see: Yaari ed., *Massaʿ meshullam me-voltera*, and Artom and David eds., *From Italy to Jerusalem: The Letters of Rabbi Obadiah of Bertinoro from the Land of Israel.*

42 See Jacobs, "Lofty Caliphs," 82–90 for an analysis of the socio-cultural factors contributing to their differing responses.

43 See David, *In Zion and Jerusalem: The Itinerary of Rabbi Moses Basola (1521–1523)*, 28–44 and *passim.*

44 Jacobs argues that Benjamin paints an idealized portrait of Jewish life under Islam "as a foil upon which to project images of Jewish pride and glory" for the benefit of his readers in Christian Spain; see "Lofty Caliphs," 82. See also Weber, "Sharing the Sites: Medieval Jewish Travellers to the Land of Israel," and idem, *Traveling through Text.*

45 See, *inter alia*, Idel, "On Mobility, Individuals, and Groups: Prolegomenon for a Sociological Approach to Sixteenth-Century Kabbalah"; idem, "Italy in Safed, Safed in Italy: A Chapter in the Interactive History of Sixteenth-Century Kabbalah"; and idem, "Encounters Between Spanish and Italian Kabbalists in the Generation of the Expulsion." On these see Ruderman, *Early Modern Jewry*, 42.

customs, to the attention of his reading public in Yemen. The early modern period of Jewish history offers ample evidence of the acquisition and dissemination of all kinds of texts during travel, and this phenomenon is reflected in a variety of fictionalized accounts in *Sefer hamusar*.[46] Incunabula from Italy and Spain, as well as books from 16th- and 17th-century Constantinople, Salonica, and Venice, made their way to Yemen not long after they were printed, often by means of emissaries from the Land of Israel or European Jewish merchants.[47] While their explicit response is confined to just one *maqāma*, Alḍāhirī's protagonists are quite taken by this new technology of textual reproduction and they enthusiastically sing its praises in a few lines of a long poetic panegyric to the city and sages of Tiberias.[48] Mobility for trade and commerce, a time-honored feature of Yemenite Jewish life going back to medieval times, figures as a prominent motif in *Sefer hamusar*.[49] The theme of migration also resonates throughout Alḍāhirī's literary work. Whether voluntary or forced, migration was a hallmark of medieval and early modern Jewish life: entire populations were expelled or forcibly resettled, while individuals chose to migrate in search of improved political, economic, and social conditions.[50] In the coda to the third *maqāma*, Abner claims that he abandoned his family and native land to escape the untenable conditions imposed by the authorities there, and in a gnomic poem he warns against staying in any one place for too long, lest one become a sitting target for malign fate.[51] Travel was not confined to schol-

46 On the acquisition, transport, and circulation of books by Christian travelers, particularly Western European pilgrims to Jerusalem embarking from Venice, see Toffolo, "The Pilgrim, the City and the Book: The Role of the Mobility of Pilgrims in Book Circulation in Renaissance Venice."

47 On the nexus between travel and the dissemination of printed books, see Ruderman, *Early Modern Jewry*, 99–132 *passim*. For evidence of the circulation of texts among medieval Jews, see, e.g., Goitein, *A Mediterranean Society*, 1:64; 2:194, 237–239; 5:418. Most references to the transmission of early printed Hebrew books to Yemen can be traced back to the publications of Abraham Yaari; see "Sheliḥim me'ereṣ yisra'el le-teiman," esp. 392–404; *Sheluḥei 'ereṣ yisra'el*, 77–78, 256–258; *Meḥqerei sefer*, 163–169. Cf. Assaf, "The Selling of Hebrew Books in Yemen Through Envoys from Palestine."

48 See Chapter Three below.

49 On the extensive mobility of medieval Jews engaged in trade and commerce across the Mediterranean and Indian Oceans, see: Goitein, *A Mediterranean Society*, vol. 1; idem, *The Yemenites: History, Communal Organization, Spiritual Life*, 33–52; Goitein and Friedman, *India Traders of the Middle Ages: Documents from the Cairo Geniza*; and Abir, "International Commerce and Yemenite Jewry: 15th to 19th Centuries."

50 See, e.g., Ruderman, *Early Modern Jewry*, 23–55 and the contributions of Avraham Grossman, Reuven Bonfil, and Haim Beinart in Shinan and Ettinger eds., *Emigration and Settlement in Jewish and General History*, 109–128 and 139–197.

51 *Sefer hamusar*, 88–89.

arly or social elites: as Miriam Frenkel's sobering study of Geniza documents from the High Middle Ages has shown, the itinerant poor were made into a permanent fixture of Jewish life in Islamic lands through their exploitation as invaluable vehicles of communication between dispersed Jewish communities around the Mediterranean and beyond.[52] But for some scholars and intellectuals, the offer of or search for patronage afforded an additional impetus to take to the road. Judah Alḥarizi is a case in point: not only wanderlust but an ongoing search for patronage drove his frequent relocation. His dependence on the generosity of wealthy benefactors—which led him to provide the *Taḥkemoni* with four different dedications to patrons in the East—fits the classic profile of the professional Hebrew poet lacking independent means.[53] Projected through a fictionalizing prism, the authorial quest for financial support is transformed into the hapless narrator's search for generosity and the rogue hero's insatiable hunger for material gain, which together propel the tales of travel and trickery in the Hebrew and Arabic *maqāma*. Although Alḍāhirī's work does not allude to the search for a Maecenas—despite his modest or even reduced circumstances—his fictional narrator repeatedly lashes out at Jewish communities he visits when they do not offer him hospitality. Clearly, the innumerable stories of dislocation, wandering, vagabondage, and vagrancy in the *maqāma* literature furnished one of the most potent and immediate models for the travel accounts in *Sefer hamusar*.

5 Links between Framing Itineraries and Embedded Tales

In his thought-provoking analysis of space and travel in the *Thousand and One Nights*, Richard van Leeuwen observes that in structure and intention, the *Nights* resembles well-known story collections such as the Sinbad cycle and *Kalīla wa-dimna* that date from the dawn of Islamic literatures. These works, which aim to provide both instruction and entertainment, juxtapose a framing story with a cycle of inserted tales. The recurring alternation between the frame and the enclosed stories yields a regular pattern of interruption that serves as

52 Frenkel, "Travel and Poverty: The Itinerant Pauper in Medieval Jewish Society in Islamic Countries."

53 On the professional poet's dependence on benefactors, see the classic study by Schirmann, "The Function of the Hebrew Poet in Medieval Spain." On the four dedications of the *Taḥkemoni* see idem, *HPCS*, 186–188; Rand, *The Evolution of Alḥarizi's Taḥkemoni*, 24–41 *passim*; and Habermann, "Ha-haqdashot le-sefer 'taḥkemoni' u-reshimat tokhen maqamotav."

a narrative device, providing rhythm and movement, and signaling that "the narrative is not a homogeneous and continuous whole, but rather consists of a complex unity …."[54] A similar dynamic is at work in the *maqāma* even though it does not boast one continuous frame story, insofar as its series of individual "boxing tales" punctuate the narrative by enclosing the stories embedded within them. Van Leeuwen asserts that, in works like the *Thousand and One Nights*, "the framing story forms a link between reality and the fictional world of the inserted stories," which "contain an allegorical representation of the world" that takes on meaning through association with "a realistic 'metanarrative.'" He contends that such characteristics

> define what was considered legitimate fictional literature in the Persian-Arabic tradition: a combination of entertaining stories and moral admonition; a moral view of the world wrapped in an intellectually and artistically appreciable form.[55]

Despite the absence of a continuous metanarrative, this model of fictional literature arguably informs *Sefer hamusar* as well and hence offers a useful lens through which to view the relationship between the work's introductory itineraries and the tales they envelop.

The reliability with which Alḍāhirī opens individual *maqāmāt* with a travel account is one of the features that distinguishes *Sefer hamusar* from Alḥarizi's *Taḥkemoni*. Although many chapters of the *Taḥkemoni* open by situating their enclosed narratives in a particular place (real or imaginary), these locations are generally dispatched with even less elaboration than in *Sefer hamusar*.[56] Alḥarizi's references to destinations are often geographically non-specific, so when Heman ha-Ezraḥi longs to hear a formidable preacher in distant lands, he travels by ship and arrives at the sage's "district" (*gelilotav*) and "the place where he was encamped" (*el ha-maqom asher hu ḥoneh sham*).[57] For most of the *Taḥkemoni*, when it comes to travel, the emphasis is on intrigue and invention or pure linguistic and stylistic brilliance rather than particularities of

54 Van Leeuwen, *The Thousand and One Nights*, 6.

55 Van Leeuwen, ibid., 7.

56 Rand lists a few more detailed itineraries but notes that, for the most part, Alḥarizi repeats variants of the catchphrase, "from Egypt to Babylon" throughout the work; see *Evolution*, 6–7.

57 See Alḥarizi, *Taḥkemoni*, ed. Yahalom-Katsumata, (#2), p. 93. Elsewhere, in the company of merchants winding their way from unspecified "city to city" with their wares, he espies a crowd that piques his curiosity; see *Taḥkemoni*, #41 (= Yahalom-Katsumata, #34).

place. In one remarkable rhetorical feat, the disguised hero decries the dangers of travel and then reverses himself to extoll the benefits of journeying without once naming an explicit destination.[58] Only those travelogue-like chapters devoted to Jerusalem under Saladin and the merits of Jewish communities East and West diverge from this norm.[59] These *maqāmāt*, which are paralleled by Alḥarizi's Judeo-Arabic travel book, *Kitāb al-durar* (The Book of Pearls), and a separate Hebrew composition he called "The Maqāma of the Patrons," have no real storyline and are marked by a far greater degree of realism than the rest of the *Taḥkemoni*.[60] Even so, Alḥarizi's survey of Jewish communities devotes far less consideration to geography than to prominent leaders and distinguished scholars.

On the other hand, the regular occurrence of an opening itinerary aligns *Sefer hamusar* with the Arabic *Maqāmāt* of al-Hamadhānī and al-Ḥarīrī, many, if not most of whose individual narratives bear place names. But apart from most of the episodes set in Yemen and the Land of Israel, there is not necessarily an obvious correlation between the geographical settings and the tales they enframe—the boxing tales neither impart local color nor determine the course of the story, so that the two narrative components seem randomly yoked together. Even in #35, the frame setting the narrative prominently in Jerusalem seems to have no bearing on what transpires subsequently. As in #22, Mordecai finds Abner with a study group on the Mount of Olives. Here, however, the focus is on an esoteric work Abner has written on *simanei ha'adam*, a genre that apparently correlated a person's physical traits with their moral qualities, such that it read physical defects as confirmation of character deficits. When Mordecai asks Abner whether he has ever witnessed a true case of physiological signs as behavioral indicators, Abner launches into a shaggy dog story about a journey to Ethiopia where he encountered a man full of physical blemishes who nevertheless turned out to be extremely hospitable. This contradiction caused Abner to doubt the work's premise and contemplate jettisoning the book. Ironically, he was therefore overjoyed when the sickly man proved to be mercenary rather than generous and demanded full payment for Abner's food and lodging at the last moment, just as Abner was preparing to depart. The episode

58 *Taḥkemoni*, #26 (= Yahalom-Katsumata, #27).

59 See *Taḥkemoni*, #28, 46, and 18 (= Yahalom-Katsumata, #16, 39, and 12). Even though Alḥarizi's visit to Jerusalem postdated the reign of Saladin, he still presents him as the city's liberator from the Crusaders; see Alḥarizi, *Kitāb al-Durar*, 14–15; English Introduction, 16–17. See also Rand, *Evolution*, 20–21.

60 See Alḥarizi, *Kitāb al-Durar*, Hebrew section, 9–41 and *The Wanderings of Judah Alharizi*, 49–187.

concludes with a long poem praising the book. The connection to Jerusalem, whether geographical or symbolic, seems tenuous at best.[61]

6 Symbolic Links: Damascus

In select *maqāmāt*, however, the opening locale may provide a controlling metaphor or carry a broader symbolic relevance for the narrative it introduces. The first *maqāma* plunges straight into travel mode, with Mordecai setting his sights on Damascus, "the most well-endowed of all cities."[62] Once there, he rents an upper room and delights in the two rivers which he calls by the biblical names Amana and Pharpar (II Kings 5:12) that water the city's legendary gardens. But almost immediately, the skies blacken and release torrential downpours—Mordecai has reached Syria just in time for the wet and frigid winter season, which leaves him housebound and isolated in his dingy lodgings. A soaked Abner appears at his door in the guise of a wanderer seeking overnight shelter from the inclement weather, and recounts a scatological story, adapted from the fifteenth of al-Ḥarīrī's *Maqāmāt*.[63] Having solved a complicated legal riddle for a stranger, Abner had been rewarded with delectable fruits from the market, but his host, fearful of having his bedding soiled, had turned Abner out into the dark and the rain after he had gorged himself on the fruit. Does the location of the frame story have any bearing on the enclosed tale? Unlike most of the other *maqāmāt* in al-Ḥarīrī's collection, the fifteenth ("The Legal") has no specified geographical setting, so Alḍāhirī's choice of locale was not predetermined.

In early medieval Arabic arts and literature from al-Andalus, Syria was idealized as the cradle of Arabic high culture and aesthetic refinement due to the Syrian origin of the Andalusian Umayyad dynasty, whose founder, ʿAbd al-Raḥmān I, had fled Damascus for Cordoba when the Abbāsids overthrew the Umayyad caliphate in 750 CE. Nostalgia for Syria colored diverse branches of Andalusian creativity, among them Arabic poetry, horticulture, and architecture. ʿAbd al-Raḥmān I had Syrian plant species and methods of irrigation imported to his villa al-Ruṣāfa outside of Cordoba in order to recreate the famil-

61 See *Sefer hamusar*, 44. Apparently, this work is based on Platonic, Galenic, and Hippocratic premises and is no longer extant.

62 For a snapshot of the advantages Damascus boasted in the high Middle Ages as one of the wealthiest trading cities of the region, see Chamberlain, *Knowledge and Social Practice in Medieval Damascus, 1190–1350*, 27.

63 See *The Assemblies of Al Ḥarīri*, 1:185–193 and *Maqāmāt al-Ḥarīrī*, 119–128.

iar Syrian landscape in his land of exile. Similarly, the Great Mosque of Cordoba intentionally echoed that of Damascus in its form. Under Umayyad rule, certain Spanish cities even bore Syrian place names.[64] The veneration of Syria as the font of Arabic culture continued in Islamic Spain for centuries and is evident in the writings of the Toledan Judah Alḥarizi who, in his Eastern search for patronage, chose to spend his final years in Aleppo. Although he gave mixed reviews to the city's Jewish community and its poets, Alḥarizi too had celebrated Damascus at great length in several Hebrew and Arabic reworkings of his travel narratives.[65] While Alḍāhirī was not a Westerner like Alḥarizi but rather a native of Yemen who composed his work in the East, he had a marked affinity for the classics of Iberian Hebrew literature and absorbed many of Alḥarizi's cultural attitudes, among them the Andalusian valorization of Syria. Two additional episodes of *Sefer hamusar*, which are set in Damascus (#5 and #10), extol the city's cultivation, both material and metaphorical, in an idealized manner that calls to mind the saying attributed to the Andalusian Muslim traveler Ibn Jubayr (1145–1217), which builds on an even older tradition:

> Wherever you look on its four sides, its ripe fruits hold the gaze. By God, they spoke truth who said, 'If paradise is on earth, then Damascus without a doubt is in it. If it is in heaven, then it vies with it and shares its glory.'[66]

Ibn Jubayr, a slightly older contemporary of Alḥarizi (c. 1165–1225), had urged the youth of the Maghreb to travel to this "Paradise of the East" (*jannat al-mashriq*) in search of knowledge. Before him, al-Ḥarīrī had alluded to traditions regarding the well-watered city's exceptional beauty in his twelfth *maqāma* ("Of Damascus"). When al-Ḥarīrī's narrator crosses from Iraq into the Ghūṭah, the fertile plain of Damascus, he finds it to be "as men had spoken of it," full

64 See: Hillenbrand, "'The Ornament of the World': Medieval Córdoba as a Cultural Center"; Dodds, "The Arts of al-Andalus"; Dickie, "The Hispano-Arab Garden, Notes Towards a Typology"; Ruggles, "The Gardens of the Alhambra and the Concept of the Garden in Islamic Spain"; Sadan, "Judah Alḥarizi as a Cultural Junction," 20–21; Decter, *Iberian Jewish Literature*, 20–23; Tobi, *Proximity and Distance*, 182; and Elinson, *Looking Back at al-Andalus*, 3–8 and *passim*.

65 See: Alḥarizi, *Kitāb al-Durar*, 124–145 (English section, 83–91) and *The Wanderings of Judah Alharizi*, 82–85 (*Maḥberet ha-nedivim*; "The Maqāma of the Patrons") and 116–130 (*al-Rawḍah al-Aniqah*; "The Splendid Garden"). For his critique of the poets see Alḥarizi, *Taḥkemoni*, ed. Yahalom-Katsumata, 225–228 (#12 [18], *Maḥberet ha-meshorerim*) and 453–454 (#39 [46], *Maḥberet moznei ha-dor*).

66 As translated by Jacobs, *Reorienting the East*, 138. For the original see *Riḥlat Ibn Jubayr*, 234. See also Netton, "Basic Structures and Signs of Alienation in the Riḥla of Ibn Jubayr," and Masarwa, *Praising Damascus*.

of "delights to fill the eyes and quench the longings of the heart."[67] Thanks to the irrigated plain of the Ghūṭah, Damascus was surrounded by splendid gardens and bountiful orchards (apricots, almonds, quince, figs, etc.) "as far as the eye can see," according to Ibn Jubayr. Ibn Baṭṭūta wrote that on Saturdays, the inhabitatants of Damascus took their leisure in the Ghūṭah on the banks of rivers and in the shade of grand canopy trees, between flowering gardens and flowing water.[68]

In *Sefer hamusar*, Mordecai celebrates the exquisite splendor of the spacious city's lush gardens and orchards abundant with fruit and marvels at the branch of the Barada river irrigating its luxuriant plant life. He also praises its built environment:

> I took pleasure in that city and its surroundings, its buildings and streets, and its beautiful things and its trade. How lovely are its palaces; an exceedingly great city (*ʿir gedolah lʾelohim*; Jonah 3:3).[69]

Unlike Benjamin of Tudela, whose effusive 12th-century account had devoted a great deal of space to the famous Umayyad Mosque of Damascus, Mordecai's focus is entirely Judeocentric, and may also be informed by a Talmudic tradition that dubbed Damascus "the gateway of the Garden of Eden" (bEruvin 19a).[70] From Mordecai's perspective, Damascus boasts the additional advantages of proximity to the Land of Israel (both now part of the Ottoman Empire) and exceptional rabbis (whether of the Iraqi or Sephardi congregations, he does not say):

> My sojourn there was sweet, for it is close to Ereṣ Yisraʾel. There are none to compare with its sages, who are punctilious in every way. The city is good and spacious; more important than all other places .... a city that did not lack for anything.[71]

67 See Cooperson, *Impostures*, 99 and *The Assemblies of Al Ḥarīri*, 1:168–169 and 368–369.

68 See Eychenne, "Éléments pour une étude de la Ghouta médiévale."

69 *Sefer hamusar*, #5, p. 100, lines 8–10. Eychenne writes that the Barada, which flowed from West to East, nourished the Ghūṭah so that it not only supported a large population and work force but also yielded a significant portion of the local population's alimentary needs in the form of agricultural produce.

70 Cf. Jacobs *Reorienting the East*, p. 138 and p. 275, n. 71.

71 *Sefer hamusar* #10, p. 146, lines 5–10. As noted, Syria, Palestine, and Egypt became part of the Ottoman Empire in 1516–1517, following which immigration of Iberian refugees to Damascus increased. In the 16th century, close ties were maintained with the rabbis of Jerusalem and Safed and scholars from those communities were appointed to rabbinical

A place of extraordinary natural beauty, Damascus is also a well-tended landscape and prosperous urban center whose refined aesthetics signal its discriminating spiritual and intellectual life. While the first *maqāma* alludes to these virtues in a cursory manner, it rivets our attention on darker atmospherics and Abner's clever, if unseemly trickster tale of Ḥarīrīan provenance. Alḍāhirī's decision to begin the work with a recognizable borrowing from al-Ḥarīrī flagged the book's proclivity for artistic prose and poetry, but also for morally questionable tales of imposture and deceit. And if setting this first *maqāma* in "most luscious Damascus" (*le-khol ha-medinot 'adinah*)—a city whose biblical epithet means 'refined' and 'well-endowed,' but also 'seductive' 'pampered' and 'pleasure-seeking'—aligns it with the fertile font of Islamicate high culture, it also tacitly signals the moral tensions embodied by such a narrative choice.[72]

7 Thematic and Lexical Links: Ḥaḍramawt

Subtle thematic links between frame itinerary and enclosed tale are discernible in the 19th *maqāma*, where Mordecai traverses punishing terrain until he arrives at the arid southeastern region of Arabia known as Ḥaḍramawt ("death is present/has come" in Arabic folk etymologies), which runs parallel to the southern coast of the peninsula and is bounded by the sea in the south and the Empty Quarter in the north. He refers to this area in Hebrew as Haṣarmavet ("the court of death"; cf. Genesis 10:26), conjuring up a harsh, inhospitable desert clime.[73] Almost as soon as he arrives, he is desperate to leave but is stranded for two months until caravans begin to appear. (In pre-Islamic times, the Ḥaḍramī city of Shabwa was the principal entrepôt for the incense trade; frankincense produced further to the east was transported from there by caravan up the west coast of Arabia to the markets of the Mediterranean and Mesopotamia.)[74] Mordecai encounters Abner traveling with a caravan laden

---

positions in Damascus; see Astor and Bornstein-Makovetsky, "Damascus" and Arad, "'A Clearly Distinguished Community': The Musta'ribs in Damascus in the Sixteenth Century."

72 Cf. the prophecy of Babylon's fall in Isaiah 47:8, where *'adinah* has the distinctly censorious sense of "pampered" and "pleasure-seeking."

73 Enseng Ho characterizes Ḥaḍramawt as "an improbable place, poised between the desert sands of the Empty Quarter and the copious waters of the Indian Ocean"; see *The Graves of Tarim*, xx. The equivalence Ḥaḍramawt—Ḥaṣarmavet goes back to later Yemenite recensions of Saadya Gaon's *tafsīr* on Genesis 10:26; see, e.g., *Version arabe du pentateuque*, ed. Derenbourg, p. 17.

74 See Beeston, "Ḥaḍramawt." The writings of the 10th-century Yemeni geographer and poet, Ḥasan b. Aḥmad al-Hamdānī (893–945), reflect an intimate familiarity with caravan

with spices and frankincense. To explain how he came by his wealth, Abner recounts a fabulous tale of quackery that is an unattributed adaptation of the inserted tale in al-Ḥarīrī's 39th *maqāma*, "Of ʿOmān."[75] (The contiguous regions of Ḥaḍramawt and ʿOmān were both considered part of Yemen by medieval Arab geographers.) The enclosed story, which closely follows al-Ḥarīrī's original, takes place on an island off of whose coast Abner had been shipwrecked while sailing from Hormuz to India.[76] Abner, who narrowly escapes a storm at sea with his life and has run out of provisions, espies a palace surrounded by thirty deathly silent young men. When quizzed about their extreme reticence and grief, their leader explains that the lady of the palace—the only one of the king's many wives to conceive—is in the midst of a difficult childbirth, which neither she nor the child may survive. Abner confidently reassures them that he has a cure ("from Aristotle") for such ills and, with great ceremoniousness, proceeds to write a series of amulets and to whisper incantations. He inscribes an old gourd with biblical verses commonly used in amulets to lighten childbirth. At his direction, the gourd and magic spells are tied to the woman's body, and after a moment the baby emerges. The lord of the palace, overcome with joy and gratitude, plies Abner with jewels and raiment, and makes him a member of his household. Despite the fortunate outcome (and some comical interludes), the threat of death hovers over the embedded story: Abner has barely survived a storm at sea; mother and child are at risk of dying; and the continuity of the royal dynasty is imperiled. Ester Muchawsky-Schnapper has written that the wild gourd (*ḥanẓal*) was ascribed apotropaic properties on account of its bitter and poisonous fruit, which was thought to ward off evil spirits. In Jewish homes in Ṣanaʿā, it was hung on the walls of a special receiving room decorated for new mothers, whose lives were at such risk during child-

---

routes, camel breeds, and the challenges posed to convoys by Yemen's difficult terrain; see Jazem and Leclercq-Neveu, "L'organisation des caravanes au Yémen selon al-Hamdânî (xe siècle)."

75 For the original see *Maqāmāt Abī Zayd al-Sarūjī*, ed. Cooperson, 211–216 and *The Assemblies of Al Ḥarīri*, 2:93–101. For a detailed comparison of Alḍāhiri's version with al-Ḥarīrī's original, see Ratzaby, "The Influence of al-Ḥarīrī Upon Alḍāhirī," 70–77.

76 In the frame to #9, Mordecai reports having made the reverse trip, from India to Hormuz, where he remained with Abner for six months. Fischel infers from these episodes that there must have been a Jewish community in Hormuz; see his "The Region of the Persian Gulf and its Jewish Settlements in Islamic Times"; "Hormuz"; and "The Jews in Iran during the 16th–18th Centuries." See also Frank, "A Jewish Tombstone from Ra's Al-Khaimah." In the early 16th century, Hormuz was occupied by the Portuguese and served as a mercantile hub until they were expelled in 1622; see Lockhart, "Hurmuz." See also Ho, *Graves of Tarim* and Tuchscherer, "Des épices au café, le Yémen dans le commerce international (XVIe–XVIIe siècle)."

birth that they were still considered to have one foot in the grave postpartum, when they might die of complications attributed to the evil eye.[77] In Alḍāhirī's tale, this thin line between life and death is reinforced on the phonic and the lexical levels by the occurrence in the frame story of several iterations of the word *mavet*, along with a pair of homonyms containing the syllable *-mut* which derives from the same triliteral root.[78] And just as Abner is stranded at sea until he discovers the distant palace, Mordecai is stranded in the Ḥaḍramawt until Abner's caravan arrives. Along with the parallel motifs, the semantic foreshadowing links the frame itinerary with its enclosed tale of the remote fictional isle where Abner might have perished, had he not had his wits about him.

8 Socio-cultural Relevance: Cochin

In the eighth *maqāma*, Mordecai travels from Aden to India. There he seeks out and sojourns with the Jewish community of Cochin, where he stumbles upon the wedding of Abner ben Ḥeleq. His account of Abner's nuptials is a variant on a medieval misogynist set-piece that emerged in the Hebrew *maqāma* literature of the early 13th century and that enjoyed a long afterlife. Abner (the archdeceiver) is lured into a marriage with a supposedly beautiful and rich woman who, from his perspective, turns out to be a toothless old lady, leaving him desperate to annul the union. Abner tells Mordecai that, when arranging the match, the bride's brother had lured him with the promise that his sister would remove her veil prior to the wedding so that Abner could see how attractive she was.[79] The topos of the groom duped by the surreptitious replacement of his promised bride with a less desirable woman goes back, of course, to the biblical account of Jacob's wives (Genesis 29:25). But Alḍāhirī's storyline also draws on a highly stylized, often savagely misogynist model that emerged in Hebrew with Solomon Ibn Ṣaqbel's *Ne'um asher ben yehuda* (Asher in the Harem) and proliferated in 13th-century Hispano-Hebrew works, primarily Judah Ibn Shabbetai's *The Misogynist* (Toledo, 1208) and Alḥarizi's *Taḥkemoni*.[80] Its degrad-

77 Muchawsky-Schnapper, "Symbolic Decorations for a Woman after Childbirth in Sanʿa."

78 Pinault, citing Robert Alter, notes the use of this device that exploits the triliteral root system; see *Story-Telling Techniques in the Arabian Nights*, 18–22.

79 *Sefer hamusar*, pp. 133–134, lines 77–78. Since the trickster figure is here the victim of the ruse, it would seem that he has been defeated at his own game, but he of course wins at the end of the episode in a vulgar display of hardheartedness and complete lack of compunction. I plan to treat this episode at greater length in a separate publication.

80 See Scheindlin's translations, "*Asher in the Harem* by Solomon Ibn Saqbel" and "*The Misogynist* by Judah Ibn Shabbetai"; see also idem, "Fawns of the Palace and Fawns of the Field."

ing themes also reverberate in Immanuel of Rome's *Maḥbarot*, where they are often exploited to brutal effect. Only relatively recently have such hostile representations of women's gender and sexuality occasioned a thoroughgoing feminist critique; previous scholarship has tended to focus largely on the way these stories relate to the medieval ideal of courtly love.[81]

The Indian setting in *Sefer hamusar* is a novelty that has so far escaped consideration from a narrative point of view. Significantly, Alḍāhirī does not abandon the idea of India at the frame level. Rather, he works it into the enclosed yarn in such a way that an otherwise conventionalized conceit is endowed with geographical and cultural specificity. His version is characterized by a certain ambivalence toward India that medieval Jews in the Islamic world as well as in the West had absorbed from their cultural environments; a simultaneous attraction and repulsion that could ultimately be traced back to ancient Hellenistic attitudes. India was viewed as a distant land, abundant in natural wonders, ancient wisdom, spirituality, and wealth, but at the same time as a place of paganism and superstition located at the margins of the civilized world. Medieval European texts in particular characterized India as a remote place of monstrous races and wise men; seductive yet dangerous, embodying pure and impure wisdom.[82] In the Judeo-Islamic realm, the *barāhima* (Indian sages or sectarians; purportedly derived from 'Brahmin') figure in Muslim and Jewish heresiographies of the ninth and tenth centuries, including those of Dāwūd al-Muqammaṣ, Saadya Gaon, and Yaʿaqūb al-Qirqisānī,[83] while the multifaceted and enigmatic myth of India is reflected in works by Saadya, Moses Ibn Ezra, Judah Halevi, and Maimonides.[84] In medieval texts and maps produced by all three monotheistic cultures, India and Ethiopia were often conflated, due to

81 See Rosen, *Unveiling Eve*, 103–123 and Huss, "Misogyny in the Hebrew Andalusian School of Poetry." For a somewhat different perspective see Fishman, "A Medieval Parody of Misogyny: Judah ibn Shabbetai's 'Minḥat Yehudah sone hanashim.'" Jim Robinson reads Ibn Shabbetai's *The Misogynist* as an allegory of the soul, built on the Maimonidean binaries of "body and soul, matter and form, intellect and imagination, the active life and the contemplative life." My thanks to Professor Robinson for sharing a typescript of his "Interactions between Jewish Philosophy and Hebrew Literature during the Middle Ages," forthcoming in *The Oxford Handbook of Jewish Philosophy*.

82 See, e.g., Campbell, *The Witness and the Other World*, 47–86 *passim* and O'Doherty, *The Indies and the Medieval West*, 53–95.

83 See, e.g., Stroumsa, "The *Barāhima* in Early Kalam."

84 See Melamed, "The Image of India in Medieval Jewish Culture: Between Adoration and Rejection" and Marks, "Hindus and Hinduism in Medieval Jewish Literature." For Jacob Sapir's detailed and complicated 19th-century impressions of India, Indians, and Hinduism see Marks, "Hinduism, Torah, and Travel: Jacob Sapir in India."

what was considered their proximity to the sun, which in turn explained the dark complexion of their inhabitants.[85] "As though by osmosis," writes Abraham Melamed, the negative image of the Black "came to be extended to Indian culture and wisdom, too."[86]

By Alḍāhirī's time, Yemenite Jewry had played an active role in the flourishing Indian Ocean trade for centuries, and there were Yemenite Jewish merchant communities in India, whose members were often in partnership with Hindu as well as Muslim traders.[87] The strategically located, bustling port of Aden was an entrepôt for goods from the Far East or India—pepper, spices, ivory—headed for the Mediterranean via the Red Sea or overland caravans to Egypt.[88] Mercantile traffic and trans-oceanic connectivity between Yemen and India stimulated intellectual exchange, and Yemenite Jewish authors had access to mathematical, philosophical, scientific, cosmological, and mystical ideas and texts of Indian provenance, usually mediated via Arabic translations.[89] Popular anthologies of Indian fables—*The Tales of Sendebar* (of Buddhist origin and featuring an Indian sage), *The Prince and the Ascetic* (based on a Hindu original modeled after the life of Buddha), *Kalīla wa-Dimna* (a book of counsel for kings derived from the *Panchatantra*, an Indian collection of animal fables)—passed into the fund of international folklore and circulated among medieval Eastern Jewish communities in Hebrew adaptations mediated by Persian and Arabic renderings.[90] Yet, despite these intellectual contacts and, presumably, a degree of familiarity with Hinduism communicated by Yemenite Jewish merchants sojourning in India, Alḍāhirī's eighth *maqāma* is oblivious to the unimaginably rich trove of Indian art, architecture, and learning, and articulates only a vague sense of alienation from the subcontinent's strange pagan beliefs and practices. Mordecai recounts that, prior to visiting Cochin,

---

85 See Akbari, *Idols in the East*, 67–111.

86 Melamed, "The Image of India," 310–311.

87 See the following by Goitein: *India Traders of the Middle Ages*, 58–59 and 283–550 *passim*; "Portrait of a Medieval India Trader"; "From Aden to India"; *Letters of Medieval Jewish Traders*, 175–229; and "From the Mediterranean to India." See also Margariti, "*Aṣḥābunā' al-tujjār*: Our Associates, the Merchants," and Goldberg, "Choosing and Enforcing Business Relationships in the Eleventh-Century Mediterranean: Reassessing the 'Maghribi Traders.'"

88 See Margariti, *Aden & The Indian Ocean Trade: 150 Years in the Life of a Medieval Arabian Port* and Chakravarti, "Indian Trade Through Jewish *Geniza* Letters (1000–1300)."

89 See Langermann, "Indian Thought among the Jews of Yemen: *Mir'āt al-ma'ānī*"; *Yemenite Midrash*, xxv–xxix; and "Cultural Contacts of the Jews of Yemen."

90 Yassif, *The Hebrew Folktale: History, Genre, Meaning*, 245–370 *passim* and idem, "Ha-sipporet ha'ivrit be'arṣot ha-mizraḥ."

> I came to the city of Calicut, but when I entered it I was stricken by bitterness and lashings; for the people of that city are all uncircumcised pagans.
>
> *va'avo 'ad medinat qāliqūt/ qibbalti 'alay bikhnisatah merorot 'im malqut/ ki anshei ha-medinah ha-hi kullam 'arelim/ 'ovdei elilim.*[91]

But it is not just this expression of insularity and unease with the idea of the non-monotheistic religions of India that sets Alḍāhirī's eighth *maqāma* apart from its Iberian models. What makes it truly distinctive is its internalization of Indian Jewish socio-religious hierarchies. From Calicut, Mordecai proceeds to Cochin, where he is reassured by the presence of a congregation of Sephardim, "from the seed of the Jews." Indeed, in the wake of the expulsions from Spain (1492) and Portugal (1497), groups of Iberian Jewish exiles had made their way to Cochin via Turkey, Syria, and the Land of Israel.

Cochin was a port city on the Malabar coast of India (now part of the state of Kerala), a region that saw a great deal of cross-cultural maritime traffic in the Middle Ages.[92] Documented evidence of Jewish settlement in Cochin goes back to the 14th century, although local traditions trace the community's origins back to antiquity.[93] Accounts of the community's history mention a charter inscribed on copper plates that was issued in the 10th or 11th century by a Malabar coast Raja to Joseph Rabban, the head of the Jewish guild, granting the local Jewish merchants privileges otherwise reserved for the aristocracy in recognition of their economic contributions to the state.[94] The inauguration of Portuguese colonial rule (1498–1663) and maritime dominance with the landing of Vasco da Gama's second expedition on the Malabar coast subsequently brought with it the import of missionaries, the 1560 establishment of the Inquisition in Goa (where the Portuguese presence had attracted a sizeable number

---

91 At the time of the arrival of the Portuguese, Calicut was one of the principal pepper ports of Kerala, along with Cochin and Quilon; see Malekandathil, *Maritime India: Trade, Religion and Polity in the Indian Ocean*, 68–70.

92 See Malekandathil, *Maritime Malabar: Trade, Culture, and Power*, 168–200 ("The Jews of Kerala and the Indian Ocean Commerce").

93 By exploiting earlier literary sources and historical documents in non-Western languages, Ophira Gamliel attempts to rectify the imbalance in the historiography of Kerala Jewry, which has mainly relied on sources in European languages from the colonial period onward and has failed to account adequately for the premodern history of those communities, privileging the origin myths of the elite. See "Back from Shingly: Revisiting the Premodern History of Jews in Kerala."

94 See Katz, "Kochi," and Mandelbaum, "Social Stratification Among the Jews of Cochin in India and in Israel."

of New Christians now suspected of Judaizing[95]), and anti-Jewish violence. In response, the Hindu Raja of Cochin granted the Jews shelter, refusing to accede to Portuguese demands to persecute his Jewish subjects.[96] In Cochin, as in the Ottoman Empire, Iberian Jewish exiles imposed their Sephardi halakhic norms and liturgical rites on the older, indigenous communities among whom they settled. Cochini Jews already adhered to normative rabbinic observance but had also adapted certain local Indian customs and symbolic cultural patterns into their religious life. Without compromising their halakhic observances, this was a means of cultural adaptation and a way of forging an Indian identity recognizable to the surrounding society.[97]

In addition to the Sephardim, Mordecai notes with some ambivalence the presence of other Jewish communities in Cochin who are "not from the seed of the Jews," for

> They are proselytes/ who converted in ancient times from the Cushites and Canaanites.
>
> *aval hem gerim/ nitgayyeru mi-yamim qadmonim/ min ha-kushim ve-ha-kenaʿanim.*

At the same time, he concedes that

95 See: Tavim, "From Setúbal to the Sublime Porte: The Wanderings of Jacome de Olivares, New Christian and Merchant of Cochin, 1540–1571"; Fischel, "Garcia de Orta: A Militant Marrano in Portuguese-India in the 16th Century"; and idem, "Goa." On the complex religious, political, and mercantile relations between the Jews of Cochin, the New Christians, and the Portuguese authorities, see Tavim, "*Palli Paradesi*: Cochinese Jews, the Portuguese and Identity Reconstructions" and idem, "Purim in Cochin in the Middle of the Sixteenth Century According to Lisbon's Inquisition Trials."

96 See Serjeant, *The Portuguese Off the South Arabian Coast* and Katz, "Kochi." In the succession of European mercantilist nations desirous of controlling international commerce, the Portuguese were routed by the Dutch, who imposed colonial rule from 1663–1795. They, in turn, were displaced by British imperial rule from 1797–1947. On the ramifications for Cochini Jews, see Fischel's dated but still valuable "Cochin in Jewish History."

97 On the imposition of Sephardi *minhag*, see Tavim, "Galut and Empire: On the Way to Final Redemption." On the adaptation of Hindu symbols and rituals, see Katz and Goldberg, "Asceticism and Caste in the Passover Observances of the Cochin Jew"; Katz, *Who Are the Jews of India?*, 59–88; idem, "Kochi"; idem, "The Judaisms of Kaifeng and Cochin"; and idem, *The Last Jews of Cochin*, p. 63: "there were also accretions of indigenous traditions into a new, synthetic *minhag*."

they are versed in law and judgment/and acknowledge the laws of Torah

yodeʿei dat va-din/u-le-dinei ha-torah modin.[98]

Cush and Canaan are descendants of Noah's son Ham (Gen. 10:6) who, according to midrashic tradition, was the progenitor of Black peoples.[99] And Canaan's curse is to be "the lowest of slaves" to his brothers (Gen. 9:25). Although Mordecai only alludes to the notion of color obliquely, Ratzaby—perhaps back-projecting—read this as a reference to the "black" Jews of Cochin, who were scorned by "white" Jews as descendants of converts and manumitted slaves. From roughly the beginning of the sixteenth century—the period that saw the influx of Jews and New Christians from the Iberian peninsula and the growing importance of Malabar in the emerging Portuguese global trade network—the Jews of Cochin underwent a rigid division into sub-castes, reflecting Indian patterns of heritable social stratification as well as the need of the Iberian émigrés to assert their superior lineage and, ultimately, their European "Whiteness" as markers of difference, at a time when Portuguese colonial rule was exporting its notions of purity of blood (*limpieza de sangre*, which had been used against Iberian Jews) and caste (*sistema de castas*).[100] Those who could prove their Jewish lineage called themselves *meyuḥasim* (of distinguished pedigree) while those who could not were considered by the self-styled superior group to be *meshuḥrarim* (literally, those freed from bondage), descendants of domestic slaves freed by their Jewish masters and converted to Judaism, or the offspring of unions between Jewish masters and indigenous women who, once freed on giving birth to the master's child, became proselytes.[101] Newly arrived Sephardim, along with the original Indian *meyuḥasim*, considered themselves and were classified by Europeans as "white" and thus as part of the social and religious elite, while those referred to contemptuously as socially "black" became the numerical majority.[102] In a discussion of social stratification among

98 This appears to be a trope that goes back several centuries; see the similar citation from Benjamin of Tudela's *Massaʿot* in Jacobs, *Reorienting the East*, p. 199. See also below regarding the appeal sent on behalf of the *meshuḥrarim* to Rabbi David Ibn Abi Zimra in the early 16th century.

99 See Melamed, *The Image of the Black in Jewish Culture*, 22, 24, 29, and 53–59.

100 See Schorsch, *Jews and Blacks in the Early Modern World*, 204–213; idem, "Mosseh Pereyra de Paiva: An Amsterdam Portuguese Jewish Merchant Abroad in the Seventeenth Century." See also Xavier, "Languages of Difference in the Portuguese Empire: The Spread of 'Caste' in the Indian World."

101 See Katz, *Who Are the Jews of India?*, 59–88 *passim*; Johnson, "Cochin Jews and Kaifeng Jews: Reflections on Caste, Surname, 'Community' and Conversion"; and Lesley, "Shingly in Cochin Jewish Memory," esp. 14–16.

102 See Tavim, "Galut and Empire," esp. 136–140 and Bar Giora, "Meqorot le-toledot ha–

Cochini Jews in India, David Mandelbaum speculated that the newcomers' sense of alienation from their Malabari coreligionists overrode any potential feelings of shared Jewish identity:

> Those described as *meyuḥasim* in the early 16th century may have been mainly recent arrivals in India … they would have found in Malabar a community of fellow Jews so different in dress, language, diet, and many other cultural traits that they could not readily associate with them despite the undisputed religious affinity. Social barriers … may have been kept strong by the environing influence of caste in Kerala society.[103]

The first documented evidence of caste division is found in an appeal submitted to Rabbi David Ibn Abi Zimra of Cairo in the early 16th century regarding the refusal of the *meyuḥasim* to intermarry with the *meshuḥrarim*, who are described as the far more numerous and prosperous group. On intimate terms with the local princes, they are also learned and devout. The *meyuḥasim*, on the other hand, are described as an impoverished minority who disdain the *meshuḥrarim*. Radbaz ruled (as did his disciple and successor, Rabbi Jacob de Castro of Cairo, when asked again) "that there was no religious bar against marriage between *meyuḥasim* and non-*meyuḥasim*; the latter should, however, first undergo *ṭebilah* [ritual immersion as prescribed for conversion]," in order to eliminate further doubt about their Jewish ancestry. Nevertheless, the *meyuḥasim* ignored the ruling.[104] Nathan Katz has remarked that of all the features Cochini Jews adapted as acculturation strategies from the surrounding Hindu society—"ritual enactments of purity, a show of royal status, and generation of an appropriate historical legend"—the only ones that directly contravened *halakhah* were the refusal of the *meyuḥasim* to intermarry with *meshuḥrarim* and their denial of religious equality to the inferior caste within synagogue life.[105]

---

yaḥasim bein ha-yehudim ha-levanim ve-ha-sheḥorim be-kochin." At some later point, a third distinction was added to the taxonomy so that the *meshuḥrarim* were referred to as "brown" due to their mixed origin and became an intermediate (albeit by then numerically diminished) caste between the contentious "white" and "black" communities; see Mandelbaum, "The Jewish Way of Life in Cochin," 440–441, 447 and Schorsch, "Mosseh Pereyra de Paiva."

103 Mandelbaum, "Social Stratification Among the Jews of Cochin," 173.

104 See Segal, "White and Black Jews at Cochin, the Story of a Controversy," 230–232 and Mandelbaum, "Social Stratification Among the Jews of Cochin," 166, 170–171.

105 Katz, *Who Are the Jews of India?*, 60 and Katz and Goldberg, "Asceticism and Caste in the Passover Observances of the Cochin Jew."

Historians have adduced Alḍāhirī's 8th *maqāma* as early evidence for the existence of two socially stratified Jewish sub-castes in Cochin. With their emphasis on lineage, it seems clear that the protagonists are aware of the internal distinction between *meyuḥasim* and *meshuḥrarim* even though they do not use these precise terms.[106] And though the hereditary and racial terminology often overlapped, they stop short of explicitly identifying the two different congregations by their color.[107] At the same time, there is a recurrence of black/white opposition in the language and imagery of the episode which accentuates some of the other nuances of Blackness and Whiteness. Alḍāhirī's medieval precursors—in Hebrew, Arabic, and Latin literature—regularly identify the "ugly," undesirable woman as Black, and equate her Blackness with evil, corrupt moral qualities and sexual insatiability.[108] These tropes are evident in Abner's litany of his bride's defects. When Mordecai goes to greet the newlyweds the morning after their nuptials, Abner, whose gloomy face is growing darker by the moment (Heb.: "turning white and black"), bursts into tears. Mordecai sends away everyone else present on the pretext that Abner may be under a spell. Abner then reveals his desperation to annul the union and his revulsion at the thought of consummating the marriage:

> Fate has given me this woman with her black face. I had thought to renew my youth in her like the eagle's, but her locks are … white with age. She lazes idly on her palanquin, and has no upper teeth. She longs to have me relieve her of her virginity, but I cannot … lie with an old woman … Advise me—what should I do? I cannot be frank with her relatives … because they are intimates of the local ruler (*qerovei malkhut*).[109] If they knew my intention, my shame would only increase in their eyes; they would not leave me any remnant. For they are proselytes; they are not members of the covenant (*ki hem gerim einam benei berit*).[110]

---

106 Mandelbaum, "The Jewish Way of Life in Cochin," p. 430: "The division [into castes] may have prevailed long before [Alḍāhirī's] time, but there is no certain documentary evidence of it."

107 Katz contends that "our view of Cochin Jewish social stratification becomes confused when we conflate these two distinct systems of separation and prejudice [viz., ancestry and skin color]. Keeping them separate gives us a clearer picture, even if Cochin Jews today often blend them"; see Katz, *Who Are the Jews of India?*, p. 64.

108 See: Melamed, *The Image of the Black in Jewish Culture*, 47–50 and 166–168 and Schirmann, "Der Neger und die Negerin: zur Bildersprache und Stoffwahl der spanisch-hebräischen Dichtung."

109 *Qerovei malkhut*: cf. the query sent to Radbaz, in Segal, "White and Black Jews at Cochin," 231.

110 *Sefer hamusar*, p. 131, lines 27–34. One possible etymology for *apiryon* (palanquin; Cant.

The Black woman is decrepit and repulsive, and there is something vile in her yearning to be relieved of her virginity at her advanced age. (She readily admits to being fifty years old.) Moreover, her Jewish pedigree is defective. There is a striking dissonance—part of a larger debate in medieval Jewish thought—between Mordecai's assertion that the *meshuḥrarim* are "versed in law and judgment/and acknowledge the laws of Torah" and Abner's stark claim that they are not legitimately Jewish because they are proselytes, and proselytes are not truly members of the covenant.[111] Trying to weasel out of the union, Abner explains how he came to be married to this woman, tellingly rhyming *va-yaʿasu lanu ḥuppah* with *li ve-la-shifḥah ha-ḥarufah*. By calling her a *shifḥah ḥarufah* (a betrothed maidservant), he invokes her stained origins as a descendant not just of slaves but of gentiles as well. The term occurs in Leviticus 19:20 regarding the consequences of an Israelite man violating a non-Israelite female slave whose owner has betrothed her to his man-servant.[112] These insinuations certainly set Alḍāhirī's version apart from his Iberian models. By adopting the exclusionary perspective of the elite *meyuḥasim* and calling into question the authenticity of the woman's Judaism, Alḍāhirī marginalizes even further the stock character who is already so contemptible in earlier versions of this contrived plot. Here the bride is spurned not only because she is allegedly old, Black, and an unattractive shrew but also because she is a descendant of converts, tainted by the gentile origin of her forebears.[113] In the Indian context of the tale, she occupies a liminal state; she belongs neither to the unsettling pagans of Calicut nor to the elite Sephardim of Cochin, whose Jewish bona fides are never called into question. Alḍāhirī's embrace of the Cochini caste division adds a socio-religious dimension to the unwanted bride's manifold markers of inferiority. Thus, the Indian setting of the frame has a direct bearing on the way the protagonists picture the Jewish "others" they encounter in the inserted tale. With its social stratification derived from the Hindu caste system and from the racial hierarchy introduced by European colonialism, the Indian context lends

---

3:9) is from the Sanskrit *paryanka*, litter-bed. Whether or not Alḍāhirī could have known that, the term adds local color. See *BDB*, 68.

111 See, e.g., Lasker, "Proselyte Judaism, Christianity, and Islam in the Thought of Judah Halevi," and Diamond, *Converts, Heretics, and Lepers: Maimonides and the Outsider*, 11–31 and 159–189.

112 *Sefer hamusar*, p. 135, line 99. There are many post-biblical discussions of this legal crux; see, e.g., Mishnah Zevaḥim 5 and bGittin 43a.

113 Line 73; cf. Joel 2:20. Tova Rosen notes that Alḥarizi's grotesque depiction of the bride elaborates on the analogous description in Judah Ibn Shabbetai's *Misogynist*; see *Unveiling Eve*, 12–13.

distinctiveness to what otherwise might have been a culturally non-specific reprise of the Hispano-Hebrew prototype.

9 Stasis and Movement: Writing from Prison

Though it might seem counterintuitive, the central, defining role of mobility in *Sefer hamusar* is intimately bound up with stasis. As noted in the previous chapter, Alḍāhirī tells us that he conceived and wrote the work while imprisoned by the ruling Zaydīs following their short-lived 1567 overthrow of the Ottomans. He and his fellow Jews were banished to the *imām's* towers where they were manacled in iron chains, forced to perform backbreaking labor "in hunger and thirst, naked and utterly bereft," and made to pay an extortionate tax.[114] Moved to chronicle the intolerable affliction of his people, Alḍāhirī composed *Sefer hamusar* "so that future generations might know" and so that all who read it would "learn a lesson from the hardships that befell us on account of our sins and transgressions." The desire to document these communal tribulations and frame them as a cautionary tale were not, however, his only motivations for writing. Like other prison authors, he wanted to record his personal experience of incarceration; to do so, he enlists his fictional characters. Though by nature laconic and austere, he nevertheless inscribes some of his own emotions into his preface, telling us that he also wrote the work to find respite from his misery. But whether by temperament or out of regard for cultural norms, he is not terribly indulgent of his own needs; his sparse self-referential remarks pale in comparison with his compassion for his people. His concern is to offer his community of readers a way to overcome their despair by beguiling them with tales of trickery and travel.

Pre-modern prisons and prison writing have attracted growing multidisciplinary attention in recent decades despite the far greater preoccupation with their modern iterations.[115] Social historians have charted the emergence and evolution of the pre-modern prison as an institution, analyzing the effects of its changing topography (remote hinterlands vs. more visible urban

114 *Sefer hamusar*, pp. 51–53. Alḍāhirī's account of the prison ordeal is reprised in greater detail in a lengthy poem of lament in the second *maqāma*. There Abner grieves that the women and children were left without providers. He mourns community members who died in prison of starvation while the deplorable oppressors did nothing. Their corpses were thrown into the valleys without proper burial.

115 Much of the theoretical work on modern incarceration has responded to Michel Foucault's *Discipline and Punish: The Birth of the Prison*.

locations) and purpose (coercive, penal, disciplinary) while taking account of the distinctions between ecclesiastical and secular authority and the widely varying conditions of incarceration over time and in different regions, albeit mainly in Christian Europe.[116] From late antiquity onwards there were writers, thinkers, and political figures—some quite influential—who composed literary, scientific or philosophical works while behind bars. Historians of the medieval Christian literature of incarceration have argued that, in the process of inscribing their own experiences of confinement into their writings, these authors deliberately constructed self-promotional identities. By invoking the conventions and tropes of well-known prison writing or religious genres, incarcerated authors were able to signal their intended readers that they too were members of the intellectual or social elite or virtuous Christians whose reputations had been tarnished by unjust confinement. Intertextual allusions to Boethius' renowned *Consolation of Philosophy* (c. 524) implicitly identified the medieval prisoner with a past exemplar of righteousness and stoicism in the face of unjust incarceration. Framing one's own experience of adversity in terms of hagiography or martyrologies forged an association with the innocent suffering of universally revered saints and martyrs. Particularly in post-Reformation England, where an increasing number of political prisoners were highly literate public figures concerned with rehabilitating their reputations, the unspoken goal of self-promotional writing was to seek the support of a highly positioned patron by appealing to a wider tribunal.[117]

Although the lion's share of secondary literature pertains to Christian prison writing, the phenomenon was by no means unknown among medieval Jewish authors. Abraham Yaari's 1958 *Meḥqerei Sefer* (Studies in Jewish Booklore) includes a descriptive survey of writers who composed works of prose or verse while incarcerated.[118] More recently, Susan Einbinder has elucidated the expe-

116 The coercive detention of debtors was one of the common functions of prisons across the medieval world; see: Dunbabin, *Captivity and Imprisonment in Medieval Europe, 1000–1300*, 76–97 and Peters, "Prison Before the Prison: the Ancient and Medieval Worlds." On the imprisonment of Jews in Islamic lands for nonpayment of the onerous poll tax, see Cohen, *Poverty and Charity in the Jewish Community of Medieval Egypt*, 130–138.

117 See: Ahnert, *The Rise of Prison Literature in the Sixteenth Century*; Carnochan, "The Literature of Confinement"; Dunbabin, *Captivity and Imprisonment in Medieval Europe*; Frances, *Memory and Identity in the Late Medieval Prison*; Freeman, "The Rise of Prison Literature"; Geltner, *The Medieval Prison: A Social History*; Reichardt, "The Constitution of Narrative Identity in Seventeenth-Century Prison Writing"; Summers, *Late-Medieval Prison Writing and the Politics of Autobiography*; and Zim, "Writing Behind Bars: Literary Contexts and the Authority of Carceral Experience."

118 Yaari, *Meḥqerei sefer*, 62–84. See also Riegler, "Kitvei yad ʿivriyyim mi-yemei ha-beinayyim she-hoʿatqu be-vatei kele."

rience and writing of late 13th- to early 15th-century Jewish prisoners from southern Europe and the ways their works relate to the larger phenomenon of Christian prison literature from the same regions. She has shown that each of these highly literate Jewish men (prison literature is almost exclusively male) deliberately chose to cultivate rigorous disciplines (science, philosophy, law), to which they prefaced autobiographical prologues asserting their identities as part of the intellectual elite, and that late medieval Jewish prison authors were aware of the contemporary Christian engagement with Boethius.[119] With few exceptions, scholarship on Jewish prison writing has focused on the Ashkenazi cultural orbit, particularly the well-known case of Me'ir of Rothenburg, (taken captive in the late 13th-century), although Magdaléna Jánošíková highlights cross-cultural elements in her case study of Eliezer Eilburg, a Central European Jew who, against the backdrop of the 16th-century Ashkenazic intellectual revival, was profoundly engaged with late medieval Sephardi and Italian texts while imprisoned in Silesia.[120]

In studies of prisons and carceral institutions under Islam, social and legal historians have adduced poetry and works of *adab*, chronicles, biographical dictionaries, and legal literature in order to reconstruct the origins and emergence of the early Islamic prison; to shed light on the material privations endured by prisoners of various social classes during their confinements; and to trace developments in the theory and practice of Islamic penal law.[121] Literary historians have plumbed the substantial corpus of Arabic prison poetry and epistolary writing, much of it produced by prominent court littérateurs who

119 See Einbinder, "Prison Prologues: Jewish Prison Writing from Late Medieval Aragon and Provence," and idem, *Beautiful Death: Jewish Poetry and Martyrdom in Medieval France*, 70–99 *passim*.

120 See Kanarfogel, "Preservation, Creativity, and Courage: The Life and Works of R. Meir of Rothenburg"; on Eilburg see Jánošíková, "Studying Ibn Sīnā, Performing Abulafia in a Mid-Sixteenth-Century Prison: Emotional, Medical, and Mystical Bodies between Italy and Silesia" and Davis, *Eliezer Eilburg: The Ten Questions and Memoir of a Renaissance Jewish Skeptic*. Abraham Yagel, imprisoned in Mantua c. 1578, cast his incarceration and deliverance through the prism of the soul's heavenly journey and release from bodily captivity; see Ruderman, ed. and tr., *A Valley of Vision: The Heavenly Journey of Abraham ben Hananiah Yagel*.

121 See Anthony, "The Domestic Origins of Imprisonment: An Inquiry into an Early Islamic Institution"; idem, "The Meccan Prison of ʿAbdallāh b. al-Zubayr and the Imprisonment of Muḥammad b. al-Ḥanafiyya"; Hentati, "La Prison en Occident Musulman Médiéval"; Lange, *Justice, Punishment and the Medieval Muslim Imagination*; Rosenthal, "The Muslim Concept of Freedom Prior to the Nineteenth Century"; Schneider, "Imprisonment in Pre-Classical and Classical Islamic Law"; Tillier, "Prisons et autorités urbaines sous les Abbassides"; idem, "Vivre en prison à l'époque abbasside"; and idem, "Les prisonniers dans la société musulmane (IIe/VIIIe–IVe/Xe siècle)."

had fallen out of favor. Not unlike their Christian counterparts, these figures framed their prison plights in an idiom calculated to appeal to their intended courtly audiences. The distinguished ʿAbbāsid poet Abū Firās al-Hamdānī (b. 932/933), a kinsman and protégé of the patronly amir Sayf al-Dawlah, produced a collection of *qaṣīdas* known as the *Rūmīyyāt* while he was held captive in Byzantium from 962–966. Al-Hamdānī's investment in panegyrical *qaṣīdas* was driven by his urgently felt need to attract patrons at court who might intercede on his behalf. The multipartite, polythematic genre also allowed the poet to inscribe his own experience of confinement into his verse.[122] Al-Hamdānī's prison poetry is cited in *Yatīmat al-dahr fī maḥāsin ahl al-ʿaṣr*, the anthology of tenth-century poetry compiled by Abū Manṣūr al-Thaʿālibī (d. 1038).[123] Another prison author included in *Yatīmat al-dahr* is Abū Isḥāq Ibrāhīm b. Hilāl al-Ṣābī (d. 994), a chancellery secretary and littérateur renowned for his eloquence, who served a series of powerful rulers in Baghdad. Considered one of the preeminent writers of his age, Abū Isḥāq was a Sabian who resisted repeated calls to convert to Islam, and was placed under house arrest from 978 to 981 by the Shīʿī Būyid ruler ʿAḍud al-Dawla (d. 983). He is best known for his ornate letters (*rasāʾil*), both personal and commissioned, which he continued to compose during his incarceration. Al-Thaʿālibī anthologized both his prose writings and poetry; the latter, thematically arranged, includes selections "on complaints and imprisonment" (*fī l-shakwā wa-l-ḥabs*).[124] Alexandre M. Roberts has argued that Abū Isḥāq's wide acceptance among elite Muslim circles was due in large measure to the pious self-image he constructed for himself in his letters and poems. By deploying Muslim religious tropes throughout these writings, Abū Isḥāq was able to present his Sabian religiosity in such a way that he was perceived to be just like the influential Muslim courtiers with whom he associated. This deliberate construction of identity was especially marked in his prison writings "when he sought favor or assistance."[125] Matthieu Tillier, who has done extensive work on prisons and imprisonment in the ʿAbbāsid period, writes that al-Jāḥiẓ (d. 868) and Ibn Qutayba (d. 889) both compiled brief anthologies of prison poems in which chains and iron collars feature as

---

122 See: El Tayib, "ʿAbū Firās al-Hamdānī"; Brockelmann, "Abū Firās"; and Sharma, *Persian Poetry at the Indian Frontier: Masʿud Saʿd Salman of Lahore*, 72.

123 Al-Thaʿālibī included accounts of imprisonment in the biographical introductions to his entries on those poets who had been incarcerated; see Orfali, *The Anthologist's Art: Abū Manṣūr al-Thaʿālibī and His Yatīmat al-dahr*, esp. 184–186 and Roberts, "Being a Sabian at Court in Tenth-Century Baghdad." See also Rowson, "al-Thaʿālibī."

124 Roberts, "Being a Sabian at Court in Tenth-Century Baghdad," 255. On al-Ṣābī see also Madelung, "Abū Isḥāq al-Ṣābī on the Alids of Ṭabaristān and Gīlān."

125 Roberts, ibid., 258.

the main leitmotifs.[126] Persian prison poems, which emerged in the second half of the 11th century in the work of the court panegyrist, Masʿūd Saʿd Salman of Lahore (d. 1121/22), became a genre in their own right. Masʿūd, whose formative years coincided with the Ghaznavid expansion into India, was over the course of his career subjected to two lengthy periods of exile and a total of 18 years' imprisonment, owing to court intrigues. His prison poetry—laments, entreaties, *qaṣīdas*—was greatly admired and emulated by subsequent poets and gave rise, in the mid-12th century, to the designation *ḥabsiyyāt*, which became the standard term for the genre.[127]

Alḍāhirī's only element of commonality with these elite Arabic and Persian prison poets was the experience of incarceration in an Islamic orbit. Otherwise, a veritable gulf of chronological, religious, social, and political dimensions lay between them. Even on a literary level, *Sefer hamusar* answers more directly to the poetics and conventions of the medieval Arabic and Hebrew *maqāma* than to those of the Arabic and Persian literature of incarceration with its tacit appeals for patronly succor. But Alḍāhirī's evocations of prison privations firmly situate the work within an Islamic carceral context.[128] A surface reading of his description of the community's prison ordeal aligns with other evidence of the conditions of confinement under the Zaydīs in pre-modern Yemen. Quṭb al-Dīn Muḥammad al-Nahrawālī's chronicle of the 1569–1571 Ottoman campaign and Zaydī resistance, *al-Barq al-yamānī fī ʾl-fatḥ al-ʿuthmānī*—more or less exactly contemporaneous with Alḍāhirī's imprisonment—confirms that hostages, political prisoners and others were regularly incarcerated in hilltop fortresses and citadels that fulfilled multiple functions, rather than in purpose-built prisons.[129] These elevated structures were fortified and strate-

126 Tillier, "Vivre en prison à l'époque abbasside," 646.

127 See: Clinton, "Masʿūd-i Saʿd-i Salmān"; de Bruijn, "Ḥabsiyya"; Sharma, "Masʿūd-i Saʿd-i Salmān"; idem, *Persian Poetry at the Indian Frontier*; and Gould, *The Persian Prison Poem*.

128 In Yemen under the Zaydīs, many of these carceral practices, including the use of massively heavy shackles, carried over into the 20th century; see Wagner, *Jews and Islamic Law in Early 20th-Century Yemen*, 26–28 and Qāfiḥ, *Halikhot teiman*, 370–374. Yemen was carved up into regional centers of power, and rural territories outside of Zaydī authority were controlled by tribal sheikhs, who had their own carceral methods (including banditry). For some 19th-century examples see Verskin, *A Vision of Yemen*, 94–95 and 133–134. In 1757–1758, a descendant of the Qāsimī dynasty vividly evoked Ṣanaʿā as a paradise on earth while writing from prison; see Ibn al-Qāsim, *City of Divine and Earthly Joys: The Description of Ṣanʿā'*.

129 al-Nahrawālī, *Lightning Over Yemen*. Al-Nahrawālī (1511/12–1582) was commissioned to write this account by Sinān Pasha who headed the Ottoman expedition. On the multiple functions of hilltop fortresses and citadels see, e.g., p. 139: "At the edge of Sanʿa' there was a mighty castle where, because of its strength and impregnability, the governor-general

gically situated in order to fend off enemies attempting to trespass.[130] But they were also symbols of power that resonated with warnings of inviolable boundaries between inside and out, not only for external adversaries but also for inmates suffering the sensory and psychological deprivation of being cut off from all contact with the outside world.[131] Imprisonment was the Yemeni authorities' standard administrative mechanism for maintaining order and extorting funds.[132] Forced labor was largely imposed as a means of extracting revenue and perhaps only secondarily as a disciplinary measure, though that hardly made it less grueling for shackled prisoners deprived of their most basic physical needs.[133] Indeed, the collective punishment of the Jewish community was undertaken not solely as a punitive measure but also as a means of asserting the Zaydī *imām's* authority in the face of competition from rival Zaydī factions. Imprisonment was imposed at the discretion of the *imām* and served to secure his self-interest, which often meant that it was implemented for political expediency rather than for the sake of the social good. While Alḍāhirī does not spell out the allegations leveled against the Sanʿānī Jews, nor are they mentioned in any extant external documentation, the community was apparently accused of collaborating with the invading Ottomans. (Despite his meticulous attention to detail, al-Nahrawālī does not appear to take any notice of *imām* al-Muṭahhar's dealings with the Jews.)[134]

---

used to live. Inside, for his protection, there was an arsenal and gunpowder magazine, and beside it a large prison where criminals were confined."

130 See Farah, "Yemeni Fortification and the Second Ottoman Conquest."

131 Cf. van Leeuwen, "Challenging Symbols of Power: Palaces and Castles in the *Thousand and One Nights*."

132 See, e.g., Serjeant and Lockwood eds., *Ṣanʿā: An Arabian Islamic City*, p. 23a: "In true Yemeni administrative tradition, be the ruler sultan or imām, al-Mahdī, 'the Imam, the Caliph of God Exalted, seized from him his house and horses, committed him to prison, and exacted from him the handing over of his property/money which he specified as an obligation on him.'" Cf. ibid., 395: "Imprisonment of its leaders was the normal action rulers took against an offending group to bring it back to order or to punish it for any sort of misdemeanour—this can be observed for instance in Qānūn Ṣanʿā'."

133 On the use of shackles and the bare subsistence provision of food and clothes in early Islamic prisons, see Tillier, "Vivre en prison à l'époque abbasside," 644–651. Goitein notes that in Fāṭimid and Ayyubid Egypt (969–1250), prisoners were obliged to provide themselves with food and to pay for their imprisonment; see *A Mediterranean Society* 2: 372–373. Qāfiḥ describes a remarkably similar situation; see *Halikhot teiman*, 373–374.

134 For the assumption that the Jews were suspected of being a fifth column, see *Sefer hamusar*, 33–35; Ahroni, *Yemenite Jewry: Origins, Culture, and Literature*, 82–86 and Tobi, *The Jews of Yemen*, p. 6: "The Jews suffered at the hands of both, accused by the Zaydis of collaborating with the foreign tyrant and persecuted by the Ottomans seeking to display their spurious sympathy with the Muslim population."

While Alḍāhirī evokes his concrete personal experience of incarceration only in his Author's Introduction, he projects it onto his imaginary characters in multiple episodes.[135] Over the course of the work, he also deploys the trope of imprisonment in more figurative ways. Embodied within his rogue hero's constant striving to excel rhetorically is the challenge of overcoming linguistic and artistic constraints and limitations. By carrying on the tradition of the Andalusian *tokheḥah* or poem of reproof, he adopts the Neoplatonic myth of the captive soul who yearns to be freed from its bodily prison. And the odyssey completed in the final *maqāma* with his protagonists' return to their native land subjects them along the way to involuntary detention: they are trapped in storm-tossed sea vessels; marooned on an island, stranded in Ḥaḍramawt. For Alḍāhirī, the preoccupation with incarceration extends beyond the desire to commemorate or console; the idea of imprisonment and the interplay of constraint and freedom become part of the warp and weft of his storytelling. The tension between confinement and unfettered mobility underpins the narrative of *Sefer hamusar*.

At first blush, the idea of composing animated travel narratives while shackled in prison seems incongruous, as is the thought of regaling cruelly confined readers with tantalizing tales of journey and adventure. But the gestation of *Sefer hamusar* must also have been a process of catharsis in the face of restriction. While incarcerated, Alḍāhirī resiliently defied imposed confinement to conceive a narrative shaped by unconstrained mobility. Not only do the travel accounts delineate the narrative contours of the work but, with their flights of fancy and alluring geographical reach, they take readers on an extraordinary journey, offering them a sense of unbounded movement as well as vicarious enjoyment of encounters with enticing places and people. With settings in markets and town squares, the stories provide an escape from the stagnant world of prison to the teeming world of flux outside. Whether traversing spaces that existed only in his imagination or retracing actual travel, Alḍāhirī could, through his *maqāma*, recover his accustomed freedom of movement and allow his fellow detainees to transcend their physical deprivation and social isolation.[136] *Sefer hamusar* conveys its readers and auditors into a world that is constantly in motion, taking them on a journey where passage from one locale to the next engenders extravagant tales. The unpredictability of the protagonists' geographical and cultural border-crossings and their frequenting of spatial and cultural thresholds parallels the shape-shifting of Abner's disguises

135 See #2, 11, 12, 15, 17, 20.

136 Ophir Münz-Manor makes a similar point in his "Imagined Journeys: Travel Narratives in Judah Alharizi's *Tahkemoni* and Zachariah Aldahiri's *Sefer Hamusar*."

and impromptu verbal showmanship. Enabling the mind to roam freely while physically constrained, *Sefer hamusar* attests to the transformational power of travelers' tales. Once drawn into the narrative, Alḍāhirī's audience could perhaps allow themselves to be transported to other realms before returning to their harsh daily realities. By defying the imposition of stasis by means of his writing and by carrying on his literary vocation under unspeakable conditions, Alḍāhirī could symbolically assert his agency and resist being sealed off and silenced. "Stone Walls do not a Prison make, / Nor Iron bars a Cage …."[137]

10 Alḍāhirī's Conception of Space

Sefer hamusar expands the geographic range of the Hebrew picaresque *maqāma* in unprecedented directions: Alḍāhirī's protagonists are the first in the centuries-old tradition of the Hebrew *maqāma* to traverse a mental landscape extending from Greece and Anatolia in the West to northwestern Iran (specifically Tabriz) and the Eastern lands bordering the Arabian Sea: Yemen, India, Omān, and Hormuz.[138] The itinerary he visualizes foregrounds familiar realms and relegates the unfamiliar to the margins. Alḍāhirī's sense of the contours of the eastern Mediterranean littoral, the Levant, and the Muslim East orients his notional geography while his mental map of Greek, Balkan, and Western Anatolian Jewish communities is less sharply defined. That the latter are for him outlying regions of the Jewish world implies that his geographical perspective is centered in a way that destabilizes contemporary Eurocentric frames of reference, both Jewish and non-Jewish. But, in any case, his narrative conception of space is unfettered by such realistic concerns as geo-

137 Richard Lovelace, "To Althea from Prison" (1642); composed while the author was imprisoned in Gatehouse Prison, Westminster. See, e.g., Anselment, "'Stone Walls' and 'Ironbars': Richard Lovelace and the Conventions of Seventeenth-Century Prison Literature."

138 Although one of Alḥarizi's four dedicatees was the Nagid Shemarya ben David of Yemen, to whom he sent a copy of the *Taḥkemoni*, Yemen was, in Rand's words, "far beyond al-Ḥarizi's geographical horizon"; see Rand, *Evolution*, p. 34. And of the 15th- and 16th-century philosophical or allegorical rhymed prose works from Byzantine and Ottoman lands loosely referred to as *maqamāt*, none is set in Greece, the Balkans, or Anatolia, or includes any travel narratives on the Ḥarizian model. See Schirmann, *Die Hebräische übersetzung der Maqamen des Hariri*, 126–127; Neḥemiah Kalomiti, *The War of Truth* [Crete, 1418]; Cassutto, "Neḥemiah ben Menaḥem Kalomiti u-maḥberotav"; Caleb Afendopolo, *Aviner ben Ner: Shirim u-meliṣot ba-ḥaruzim be-signon ben ha-melekh veha-nazir* [1488]; Danon, "Mishpeḥot sofrim"; and Malachi, "'Toledot yedutun' le-nissim ibn sanchi, ḥibbur allegori mehame'ah ha-16." According to Malachi, Ibn Sanchi's work [Istanbul, 16th c.] was preserved in two recensions, one in prose and the other in verse.

graphical contiguity or scale, and his characters move freely throughout his imagined world, crisscrossing from city to city in seemingly random progression. Space is not viewed as a continuum: an episode set in Ṣanaʿā is directly followed by a journey from Baghdad to Irbīl so that there appears to be little order or forethought to the protagonists' movements from one *maqāma* to the next.[139] The ease with which Mordecai and Abner pass from land to land and ply various bodies of water suggests broad authorial horizons and an unconfined conception of space. At the same time, Alḍāhirī manages to compress the distances between locales in his mind's eye so that his narrator and hero whimsically appear in disparate places in rapid succession. As Michael Rand aptly puts it with regard to the "spatially unbounded vitality" of Alḥarizi's *Taḥkemoni*,

> coming from a particular place and having a specific place to go would constrain Heman and Ḥever to the point that they could no longer play out their game of unexpected meetings and surprise-recognitions as they roam over a far-flung landscape that is tantalizingly real and familiar and at the same time elusive and fantastic.[140]

If the facility with which Alḍāhirī's characters cross boundaries both actual and fanciful is a literary conceit of the *maqāma* literature, it is also true that contemporary geopolitical realities enabled Alḍāhirī to reimagine the layout of his world. The gradual 16th-century consolidation of the Middle East and Mediterranean lands under Ottoman rule allowed for relative freedom of movement within one overarching administrative framework. Following the expulsions from the Iberian peninsula at the end of the 15th century, increasing numbers of Sephardim settled in the southern Balkans and western Anatolia. The Ottoman conquest of Syria, Palestine, and Egypt (1516–1517) prompted a sizable Jewish migration to these areas where Jews could settle, engage in a wide array of occupations, and travel. This is not to suggest, as does 19th-century Jewish historiography, that the Sublime Porte offered Jews an utterly unconstrained haven from persecution, a view that is no longer tenable. Ottoman policy could be heavy-handed, as in the case of the *sürgün*, the forcible re-settlement in Istanbul of Jews and others from various parts of the empire, following the

139 Within individual *maqāmāt* the itineraries sometimes correspond more closely to routes taken by medieval travelers. To journey from Jerusalem to Cairo the narrator sails from Jaffa to Damietta and then travels up the Nile.

140 See Rand, *Evolution*, pp. 22–23.

establishment of the new Ottoman capital in the mid-15th century.[141] But in general, relatively unrestrained mobility contributed to the emergence of Jewish commercial networks and major Jewish cultural centers like Safed that attracted renowned scholars from elsewhere in the Empire and beyond.[142] Rabbinic emissaries from the Land of Israel visited Yemen in search of financial support for their *yeshivot* and new markets for their books. Ottoman expansion into Aden (1538) and inland Yemen (Ṣanaʿā, 1547) had repercussions for Jewish commercial activities. These invasions responded to Portuguese incursions in the Red Sea, the Indian Ocean, and India. In 1514, the Portuguese seized the mercantile hub of Hormuz at the entrance to the Persian Gulf and built a small fortress on the strategically placed island. They interrupted the flow of trade between the Red Sea ports and the Indian Coast, where they also had established fortresses and taken control of key ports (Goa, Calicut, Cochin), enabling them to capture the Indian Ocean trade in spices and other goods. Once the Ottomans took Yemen in the second half of the century, Muslim control of the Red Sea trade was revived and Ṣanaʿā and the port of Mocha (taken, like Aden, in 1538) became important commercial centers.[143] In *Sefer hamusar*, the emissary Rabbi Abraham Ashkenazi enters through the port of Mocha with his book shipment. But otherwise, Alḍāhirī is curiously silent about these geopolitical developments—the Portuguese are never mentioned, and the Ottomans only fleetingly—even as his capacious mental map runs parallel to expanded Ottoman geographical horizons.[144]

141 See, e.g., Hacker, "Ottoman Policy toward the Jews and Jewish Attitudes toward the Ottomans during the Fifteenth Century."

142 See, e.g.: David, *To Come to the Land: Immigration and Settlement in Sixteenth-Century Eretz-Israel*; Hacker, "The Intellectual Activity of the Jews of the Ottoman Empire During the Sixteenth and Seventeenth Centuries"; idem, "The Sephardim in the Ottoman Empire in the Sixteenth Century"; Lehman, *The* En Yaaqov: *Jacob Ibn Habib's Search for Faith in the Talmudic Corpus*; Levy, *The Sephardim in the Ottoman Empire*, 1–41 *passim*; and Rodrigue ed., *Ottoman and Turkish Jewry: Community and Leadership*.

143 On Portuguese expansion into Asia and Africa see Kleinschmidt, *People on the Move: Attitudes Toward and Perceptions of Migration in Medieval and Modern Europe*, 127–138; Serjeant, *The Portuguese Off the South Arabian Coast*, 14–21; and Hathaway, *A Tale of Two Factions: Myth, Memory, and Identity in Ottoman Egypt and Yemen*, 79–93. On Jewish commercial networks, see Margariti, *Aden & The Indian Ocean Trade*; Abir, "International Commerce and Yemenite Jewry"; and Anzi, "Yemenite Jews in the Red Sea Trade and the Development of a New Diaspora."

144 Apparently, even Muslim Damascene authors who experienced the transition from Mamlūk to Ottoman rule in Syria do not directly mention it or show consciousness of political change; see Bray, "Starting Out in New Worlds," p. 205 who refers to Meier, "Perceptions of a New Era? Historical Writing in Early Ottoman Damascus."

11 Periphery and Center

Just as Alḍāhirī's conception of space draws on, but is not confined to, concrete geography and actual places, the relative weighting of periphery and center in his world cannot be understood in terms of the starkly dichotomous distinction between diaspora and ancestral homeland that has been drawn by modern Jewish historiography. Nor does it necessarily align with any one strand of medieval Jewish thought on Jewish attachment to the sacred geography of the Land of Israel.[145] That said, a systematic mapping of the protagonists' seemingly haphazard itineraries across the 45 chapters of *Sefer hamusar* reveals Yemen and the Land of Israel to be the two foci of their peregrinations. These two lands are visited more frequently than any of the others, prompting questions about the respective roles of homeland and sacred Land (*ereṣ ha-qedoshah*) in the protagonists' minds.[146] To what degree do these depictions of Yemen and the Land of Israel reflect or refract pre-modern Jewish notions of diaspora and spiritual center? Are they wholly reliant on tropes and conventions and mythologizing (e.g., The Promised Land), or do they also integrate certain contemporary realia? While Abner's attachment to his native land is evident (he is, after all, Abner ben Ḥeleq "ha-Teimani"), most of the *maqāmāt* situated in Yemen dwell on persecution, privations, and yearning for messianic consolation. Abner and Mordecai repeatedly bewail the anguished sufferings of Yemenite Jewry in the face of grinding oppression and humiliation. In the second *maqāma*, no less than ninety-eight lines of doleful verse are devoted to this bleak state of being, which is termed "our *galut*." Time and again, the protagonists evoke the degrading religious, social, economic, and political hardships of Yemenite Jewish life under the sectarian Zaydī *imāms*, whom they disparage polemically as *zeidim* ("wicked ones") in a play on an epithet from the prophecies of Obadiah and Malachi that was applied through the ages to a succes-

145 For a comparison of the views of Maimonides and Judah Halevi, see Rosenberg, "The Link to the Land of Israel in Jewish Thought: A Clash of Perspectives." Rosenberg distinguishes between Maimonides' view of the Land as instrumental and necessary for the complete observance of the commandments, and Halevi's belief that the Land has intrinsic value in and of itself, and is fundamentally linked to the Jewish people and their potential to receive revelation. The dilemmas for medieval Jews raised by rabbinic dicta on the obligation to live in the Land are discussed in Saperstein, "The Land of Israel in Pre-Modern Jewish Thought: A History of Two Rabbinic Statements."

146 On Yemenite Jewish contacts with the Land of Israel through the ages see Tobi, "Teiman ve-yerushalayim: qishrei yahadut teiman ʿim ereṣ yisrael ba-me'ot ha-7—ha-19," and Qāfiḥ, "The Ties of Yemenite Jewry with the Jewish Centers."

sion of oppressive regimes (but none so felicitously named as the *Zaydīya*).[147] Yemeni Muslim society is viewed as so threatening and inhospitable that the land itself merits a derogatory anagram, *me'on tannim*, or "jackals' lair."[148] In more than half of the *maqāmāt* devoted to Yemen, Abner is in prison; in one of these Mordecai finds Ṣanaʿā in ruins and its residents destitute following a violent flood.[149] In yet another episode, Abner returns to his native land only to find his mother and siblings in dire straits.[150] Taken together, these evocations of subjugation and relentless calamity are the very embodiment of *galut* not just as exile but as "the oppression of exile," an expanded sense which the term *galut* had acquired by the Middle Ages, and which also came to connote exclusion from the majority society.[151] In the modern era, the oppressiveness of Jewish existence outside of the Land of Israel has been an axiom of old-school Zionist historiographers subscribing to the lachrymose conception of diaspora Jewish history, while the phrase *galut teiman*—perhaps on analogy with *galut yerushalayim* in Obadiah 20—has come to be used by Yemenite-Israeli writers of a certain generation to denote the collectivity of Jews in Yemen as well as the dire circumstances of their existence there.[152]

By contrast, for the protagonists of *Sefer hamusar*, the Land of Israel holds the promise of profound religious learning, heightened spirituality, and opportunities for penitence and pilgrimage, all of which are recognizable medieval spurs to travel. (Needless to say, the desirability of life in the Holy Land is not articulated in terms of political autonomy, nor do the protagonists ever mention that the Land is now under Ottoman control.) In Safed Mordecai is overwhelmed by the vast Talmudic knowledge of the community's scholars, and attends a scintillating philosophical discourse on the soul in the yeshivah of the legendary Joseph Karo. In Jerusalem, he joins a group on the Mount of Olives lamenting the destruction of the Temple and reciting penitential

147 See Obad. 3 and Mal. 3:15, 19 where the terms *zadon* and *zeidim* are applied to the arrogant kingdom of Edom, whose downfall they foretell. Jews throughout the ages understood *malkhut zadon* to refer to the contemporary oppressors of Israel; it is fortuitous that Alḍāhirī is able to play on the sound similarity between *zeidim* and *Zaydīya*. On Zaydī attitudes towards the Jews under their control, see Tobi, *The Jews of Yemen*, 142–145.

148 *Sefer hamusar*, #39, p. 418, l. 30; cf. Jeremiah 9:10.

149 *Sefer hamusar*, #30.

150 *Sefer hamusar*, #39.

151 See Cohen, *Under Crescent and Cross*, 192–194. See also the geographical, psychological, and theological components of *galut* in traditional Jewish literature outlined in Saperstein and Berg, "'Arab Chains' and 'The Good Things of Sepharad': Aspects of Jewish Exile."

152 The usage is fairly universal; see, e.g., Yishayahu's preface to *Shevut teiman*; Qāfiḥ, *Halikhot teiman*, 13 and *passim*; and Tidhar, *Encyclopedia of the Founders and Builders of Israel*, 5:2142.

prayers; in Tiberias, he absorbs kabbalistic thought and liturgical customs and spends Rosh Hashanah in uplifting prayer and repentance.[153] Nowhere in these episodes is there a suggestion that access to these sacred sites is denied or hindered in any way by the non-Jewish authorities controlling them.[154] Abner, too, plays a central role in all of these episodes and, notably, declares his imprisonment upon his return to Ṣanaʿā to be a sign of divine displeasure with his having abandoned the Land of Israel.[155] Nevertheless, there are subtle indications that Alḍāhirī's hierarchical ordering of margins and center may be more fluid or complex than one might suppose on the basis of such pronouncements. Throughout Abner's incarceration in Yemen, he continues to compose highly eloquent Hebrew poems and rhetorically ornate epistles, suggesting that his native land nourishes productivity and creativity, notwithstanding the unspeakable hardships its rulers have imposed on the Jews.[156] Several of the other episodes set in Yemen invoke typical *maqāma* topoi to portray Abner not as a dejected victim of persecution but as a wealthy merchant, a free-wheeling littérateur, and the author of a wily swindle.[157] Despite Abner's pious self-reproach for having returned to Yemen, he is not the only one to leave the Land of Israel behind. At the close of several *maqāmāt* set in the Holy Land, Mordecai returns to his home, the city of Sidon. Though he remarks on the proximity of Sidon to the holy city of Tiberias, he clearly considers his hometown to lie outside the sacred precincts of the Land of Israel.[158] In general, his

153 *Sefer hamusar*, #6, #22, and #23. In #22, Mordecai's description is too fleeting to say anything substantive about the mourners on the Mt. of Olives, but it calls to mind the much earlier Jerusalem-based Karaite "Mourners for Zion" (9th–11th c.), a penitential and ascetic movement mourning the destruction of the Temple in order to bring about its rebuilding by hastening the advent of the Messiah. See: Lasker, "Karaite Mourning of Zion as an Ascetic Movement"; Frank, *Search Scripture Well*, 165–203; and Erder, *The Karaite Mourners of Zion and the Qumran Scrolls*. On the eschatological significance of the Mt. of Olives for medieval Jewish pilgrims see Reiner, "Beʿiqvot ʿolei regel yehudim liyerushalayim bimei ha-beinayim." See also: Fleischer, "Pilgrims' Prayer at the Gates of Jerusalem"; Ben-Shammai, "A Unique Lamentation on Jerusalem by the Karaite Author Yeshuʿa ben Judah"; and idem, "Poetic Works and Lamentations of Qaraite 'Mourners of Zion'—Structure and Contents."

154 The freedom of access projected by Alḍāhirī's accounts stands in marked contrast to the realities encountered by Jewish travelers in earlier eras as described by Jacobs; see *Reorienting the East*, p. 14.

155 *Sefer hamusar*, #25, p. 288, lines 48–53. In #12 Abner recounts that, following his release from years of imprisonment, he vowed to make a pilgrimage to the Land of Israel.

156 Mordecai is duly impressed with the high quality of Abner's prison writing; see *Sefer hamusar* #15, p. 187, line 86 and #2, p. 75, lines 232–234.

157 See *Sefer hamusar*, #19, #20, #29, and #44.

158 Some pre-moderns seem to have considered Sidon to be part of the "Greater Land of

expressions of regret have more to do with parting from Abner than with forsaking the Land. At the end of the fourth *maqāma*, which is set in Baghdad, Abner recites an alphabetic acrostic thanking God for restoring his health after a serious illness. At the verse beginning with the letter *nun*, the poem turns to the plight of God's people, dispersed to the ends of the earth (*nefoṣim hem be'afsei ha-qeṣavvot*), and beseeches God to redeem them from the hands of their oppressors. As soon as he is done, Mordecai asks his friend where he is headed next, and Abner replies, "I am going to the sacred Land" (*ani holekh la'areṣ ha-qedoshah*). Mordecai showers him with blessings and says he will follow Abner as soon as he has collected some payments owed him for business he has transacted in Baghdad. After a cryptic, possibly comic rejoinder, Abner boards a boat on the Tigris, but there is no further mention of Mordecai's travels. One cannot help but wonder whether this vignette projects a split conscience, or at the very least a moral tension generated by contending sets of allegiances and priorities—material and spiritual; diasporic and Palestinocentric.

By definition, of course, the protagonists of any *maqāma* are constantly on the move. And yet, Alḍāhirī's narrative choices reveal a world in which—even in adversity—the pull of family and the familiar, the identification with Yemenite Jewish literary and cultural traditions, and the desire to transmit newly acquired knowledge to the community in Yemen, outweigh—or, perhaps, coexist with—the competing impulse toward redemption from exile by means of settling in the Land of Israel, whether collectively or individually.[159] The tension between this simultaneous sense of rootedness in Yemen and awareness of being in exile from Zion corresponds to what Yosef Hayim Yerushalmi, in an elegant and discerning essay, styled the dialectic of Exile and Domicile, a reality of medieval Jewish existence in all the lands of the

Israel"; in a 1495 letter from Jerusalem, an unnamed student of Obadiah of Bertinoro refers to Sidon as "part of Eretz-Israel"; see David, *In Zion and Jerusalem*, pp. 31 and 59, n. 20 and Yaari, *Iggerot ereṣ yisrael*, 149. In the 16th century, Moses Basola counted 20 Jewish households in Sidon out of a total of some 500 when he passed through on his way south to the Galilee, and noted that most of the Jews were Musta'aribs, from the old, established communities of the Levant, and that they maintained a small synagogue. Under the 18th-century Ottoman imperial government, northern Palestine was administratively linked to Sidon; see Lehmann, *Emissaries from the Holy Land: The Sephardic Diaspora and the Practice of Pan-Judaism in the Eighteenth Century*, 6.

159 In #39 Abner, as seen by Mordecai in a dream, fleetingly evokes an unsatisfactory journey to the Galilee, Safed, and Tiberias. The details are quite scanty, but one has to wonder whether this is a revisionist take on #6 (Safed) and #23–24 (Tiberias), or whether it is the germ of a separate travel account that never gets developed; see lines 15–21.

diaspora.[160] While a few of the poems in *Sefer hamusar* incorporate echoes of Judah Halevi's famous Zionide odes, they do not replicate Halevi's intensely personal and idiosyncratic yearnings for deliverance from exile, for revelation, or for dying in the Land in a spirit of submission to God.[161] Alḍāhirī's pieces invoke more conventional, eschatological longings for collective restoration to the Land, which is portrayed as the locus of ultimate redemption.[162] At the same time, his protagonists do not resign themselves to waiting for the eschaton in pious devotion; they intentionally and exuberantly visit the Land, which is presented as a spiritual and scholarly utopia, although they do not settle there. That they return to Yemen at the end of all their journeys, after the uplift of having seen the "sages, the heads of the *yeshivot*, and the graves of the patriarchs" in the Land of Israel, is made abundantly clear by the epitaph Abner composes for Mordecai in the final *maqāma* of the book: *ve-ḥatam be-arṣo, ereṣ ha-teiman* (literally: "he sealed [his travels] in his land, the land of Yemen").[163] Despite Zion's privileged status in Jewish collective memory, there are intimations that *Sefer hamusar* envisions diaspora in localized and culturally specific, rather than monolithic terms, and does not necessarily subscribe to the dialectical notion that, in its very essence, diaspora existence demands a return to the Land of Israel in concrete territorial or geographic terms.[164]

Narrative artifice, too, can implicitly challenge the doctrinal hierarchy that places the Land of Israel above all others. When Abner turns out to be the purveyor of wisdom at the heart of an episode set in the Land, his ruses undermine the customary gravitas associated with that sanctified place. In Safed, the elusive yeshivah student who delivers the eloquent oration on the soul turns out to be Abner; in Jerusalem, the pietist who recites a long penitential litany on the

160 Yerushalmi, "Exile and Expulsion in Jewish History." See also Band, "The New Diasporism and the Old Diaspora."

161 On the role of these themes in Halevi's poetry and thought, see Scheindlin, *The Song of the Distant Dove*.

162 See, e.g., "Yaḥid meromam ʿal kol geviyyah," which laments the destruction of the Temple and Israel's sufferings in exile; *Sefer hamusar*, #22, p. 254. See also Alḍāhirī's poem in praise of Tiberias, "Asher kippat sheḥaqim lo ʿaliyyah"; *Sefer hamusar* #24, 282–283.

163 *Sefer hamusar* #45, p. 463, line 82. Cf. Cooke, "Journeys Real and Imaginary," 151: "without the return, the journey has little meaning."

164 For a range of medieval views of exile, see Alfonso, "The Uses of *Exile* in Poetic Discourse: Some Examples from Medieval Hebrew Literature"; Brann, "Competing Tropes of Eleventh-Century Andalusi Jewish Culture"; and Rosenberg, "Exile and Redemption in Jewish Thought in the Sixteenth Century: Contending Conceptions." See also Lehmann, "Rabbinic Emissaries from Palestine and the Making of a Modern Jewish Diaspora: A Philanthropic Network in the Eighteenth Century," especially 1241–1246. On micro-diasporas, see Ray, "New Approaches to the Jewish Diaspora: The Sephardim as a Sub-Ethnic Group."

Mount of Olives is Abner; and in Tiberias the synagogue precentor with the dulcet voice who composes kabbalistic poems for *Kabbalat Shabbat* is Abner. In large measure, these vignettes conform to the quintessential *maqāma* scenario in which the mercurial hero employs brilliant verbal skills for personal gain. Dazzled by Abner's discourse on the soul, Joseph Karo elevates his rank within the yeshivah and increases his financial support. In Tiberias, the tone and content of Abner's kabbalistic poems are serious and meditative, yet his pose as a pious *ḥazzan* highlights his uncanny ability to fool even the proud and staid Tiberians into accepting him as their representative before God. It seems that the Land of Israel is as ripe for his deceptions as any other. There is also a touch of ironic humor in the fear, expressed by those abstemious souls mourning the destruction of the Temple on the Mount of Olives, that Mordecai will interfere with their eating and drinking. Taken together, these subtle nuances complicate the binary distinction between diaspora and ancestral homeland that we may be tempted to retroject onto pre-modern Jewish texts. Alḍāhirī's narrative reflects a fluid dynamic of coming and going that is characteristic of pre-modern Jewish attitudes toward the interrelationship of periphery and center.[165]

12 Stimuli to Travel in *Sefer hamusar*

Alḍāhirī's characters are galvanized to travel by the prospect of engaging in trade, longings for the Land of Israel, and their quest for knowledge. Plying goods is the ostensible reason for Mordecai's journey from Yemen to India in the eighth *maqāma* (*nasaʿti … el ereṣ hodu ve-khush, le-maʿan heyot li qinyan u-miqneh u-rekhush*) and for his trip to Damascus in the tenth (*nasaʿti … el medinat dameseq—ʿal yedei meʿat ʿeseq*) although both references are so brief that they seem largely intended to set up a rhyme with the destination in question.[166] On the other hand, the 29th *maqāma* suggests that Mordecai does take

165 Setting aside the particular socio-cultural circumstances of each case, the varying responses of 15th- and 16th-century Italian Jewish travelers can be illustrative: Meshullam of Volterra made a pilgrimage to Jerusalem in 1481 and then returned home; Obadiah of Bertinoro left for the Land of Israel in 1486 and remained there for the rest of his life; Moses Basola went on pilgrimage from Venice in 1521 and remained for a year and a half, but ultimately settled in the Land of Israel at the age of eighty in 1560, the year of his death. On the lack of connection felt by 18th-century diaspora Jews to the actual, contemporary Land of Israel, see Lehmann, *Emissaries from the Holy Land*, pp. 4 and 13 and *passim*.

166 See #8, lines 2–3 and #10, line 2; cf. #5, p. 115, line 297: *vaʾelekh le-darki limkor ve-liqnot/u-minei seḥorotai lishmor ve-limnot.*

a serious interest in the sale of merchandise since he is asked by close friends and family members to accompany them throughout Yemen as a commercial advisor. But his persona as a merchant is far from fully developed, and he is in general a somewhat laughable and inept entrepreneur. When he tries his hand at trade, he often bungles or abandons his moneymaking schemes. This is perhaps why Mordecai so admires Abner's unerring instinct for acquiring wealth through an endless array of shrewd stratagems. Mordecai travels with various wares: to Baghdad he brings five hundred wineskins (or perhaps musical instruments; the Hebrew *nevalim* is ambiguous—it also plays subliminally on the word for 'scoundrels'[167]); to Damascus, fifty loads of "merchandise superior and inferior."[168] "Driven to ruin and rack," he journeys to Ḥadrach (Syria), on a tip that cheap wares are to be had there. But, on arrival, Mordecai discovers that the goods on offer are worthless and decides that it would be prudent not to invest in them. Despite this financial caution, Abner still manages to fleece his unsuspecting friend of the cash left in his pocket.[169]

For their overland travel, the protagonists routinely join caravans of Muslim traders. Despite their pronounced antipathy toward the Muslim authorities, Mordecai and Abner are generally accepting of these merchants while the Muslims appear to tolerate their Jewish counterparts, albeit with some bemusement once they discover that Abner is cannier than they are. When Mordecai journeys to the Ḥaḍramawt at the opening of the nineteenth *maqāma*, he is stranded for two months until caravans laden with coveted silks and spices begin to arrive. Inspecting each load of commodities for something suitable to buy, he discovers a shipment labeled with Abner's name. When he inquires of the merchants, "Are there Jews (literally, Hebrews, *ʿivrim*) among you?" he receives a somewhat amused, slightly envious reply:

> A Jewish merchant came with us. He is more robust than are we—he has thirty loads of goods, and he worked his ruses, revealing some of the loads and hiding others, so as not to pay a tariff.

In search of Abner in the 43rd *maqāma*, Mordecai poses the same question of a trader in a Muslim caravan in the region of Aden and is told that there is a Jewish guest merchant among them. It is Abner, who, in response to his friend's all-consuming reverence for Maimonides, tells Mordecai a strange folk-

---

167 *Nevalim*; see II Sam. 13:13.

168 See #4, p. 90, lines 2–3 and #5, line 2.

169 #14, lines 2–5. See Tanenbaum, "Of a Pietist Gone Bad and Des(s)erts Not Had: The Fourteenth Chapter of Zechariah Alḍāhirī's *Sefer hamusar*."

tale about the legendary scholar's birth and recites an impassioned poem fired by indignation at a critique of their cultural hero penned over three centuries earlier. Then, in a complete anticlimax, Abner continues on his way with the caravan. In the 29th *maqāma*, set in Yemen, Mordecai and some companions come to a caravanserai. Each caravan originating in a particular city takes a separate room at the inn, where its members converse and sing before retiring.[170] Mordecai circles the courtyards and hears a man reciting poetry; from his eloquent verse, he knows that it must be Abner.[171] Admittedly, the hero's ubiquity is a convention of the genre, and readers are meant to take these unexpected appearances in stride. But Abner never betrays any sense that he is out of place even though these vignettes suggest that he feels a compulsion to best the Muslim merchants not just at evading tariffs but even at poetry and rhetoric, the pinnacle of their own literary birthright.[172]

For sea travel, the Jewish characters also sail on Muslim vessels. In the 21st *maqāma*, Abner is reported to have departed Prèveza (a port on the western coast of modern Greece) for Egypt on a ship, most of whose passengers are Jewish merchants, but whose crew is Muslim.[173] Certainly, the protagonists are aware of the precariousness of their existence as members of the sole religious minority in Yemen, but even in their fictionalized world, their proximity to and intermingling with Muslim traders appears to be part of their socio-cultural reality.[174] Abner's outfoxing the customs officials is far from the only instance in

---

170 Cf. Saadya's *tafsīr* to Ps. 42:5—"I have translated *adadem* as 'a traveler's song' in the manner of the Arabs who sing on their travels and journeys, particularly at night." Cited in Sokolow, "Saadiah Gaon's Prolegomenon to Psalms," p. 165, n. 154. To parallel the Hebrew, Saadya uses the verbal form of the Arabic root *ḥ.d.w.*, which Wehr glosses as "to urge forward by singing." *Ḥudāʾ* is "animating singsong, chanting of the caravan leader." See Saadya Gaon, *Tehillim ʿim tirgum u-feirush ha-gaʾon rabbeinu seʿadyah ben yosef fayyūmī*, p. 124.

171 On the poem he recites, "Leshoni eshteqad hayyetah amuṣah," see the section headed *Metapoetic Reflections* in Chapter One.

172 Abner's poem (#29 lines 14–38) is in Hebrew while his audience is presumably made up of Muslim traders. One might think this requires some suspension of disbelief, but with travelers of diverse cultural and linguistic backgrounds coming together, caravanserais were traditionally sites of cultural exchange and interaction. See Sims, "Trade and Travel: Markets and Caravanserais"; Hillenbrand: *Islamic Architecture: Form, Function and Meaning*, 331–376; and "Caravanserai," in *The Grove Encyclopedia of Islamic Art and Architecture*.

173 *Sefer hamusar*, p. 241, lines 35–36.

174 The only other non-Muslim population in 16th-century Yemen consisted of Indian merchants known as Bāniyān, who were mostly found in port cities. But unlike the age-old Jewish minority, they were viewed as pagans and therefore did not qualify for *dhimmī* status although they were extended certain protections by Zaydī imāms and tribal chieftans; see Serjeant, "The Hindu Bāniyān Merchants and Traders"; Malkiel, *Strangers in Yemen*, 243; Piamenta, *Dictionary of Post-Classical Yemeni Arabic*, 1:42; and Ibn al-Qāsim, *City of*

which Alḍāhirī imagines his scoundrel of a hero outsmarting Muslim authority figures and thus gaining the grudging admiration of ordinary Muslims. These episodes highlight the permeability between the realities of Alḍāhirī's world and his fantasies of Jewish ingenuity and triumph.

The desire to acquire *musar* or *adab* propels much of Mordecai's travel. In the nineteenth *maqāma*, he prefaces his journey to Ḥaḍramawt with the following remarks:

> Hearing the clever and the wise/ praise those who travel far and wide/ to acquire priceless sayings,/ riddles, parables, ornate phrases,/ I was ready to tramp/ up craggy hills and down steep cliffs, /travel became my custom and habit/ … I sailed on ships and trekked through deserts/ amidst wild beasts and lions' coverts/ (in mortal danger all throughout)/until I came to Ḥaḍramawt.[175]

With their reliance on polish, aphorism, and mental acuity, the sought-after "priceless sayings, riddles, parables, (and) ornate phrases" (*devarim nimraṣot/ u-meshalim ve-ḥidot u-meliṣot*; cf. Prov. 1:6) are the very definition of *adab* which, in its broadest iteration, encompassed social, moral, and educational ideals. Mordecai's quest for *musar* reflects his understanding of the term as the designated Hebrew equivalent of *adab*. Most of the time, he seeks out edifying stories and maxims on his journeys, but at times he equips himself with them before departing on an especially arduous or dangerous expedition. Apprehensive about sailing from Sidon to Egypt, he says that he supplied himself with *musar* "as a provision for the road."[176] A lyrical paean to an almost deified (and certainly reified) *musar* at the opening of the thirteenth *maqāma* identifies Abner ben Ḥeleq as the genre's most gifted adept. Mordecai's craving for instructive material is intertwined with longing for his boon companion, and he is prepared to travel to satisfy these sometimes indistinguishable yearnings. Whether intentionally or not, this elaborate hymn to *musar* anticipates the central theme of the very next *maqāma* (#14):

Divine and Earthly Joys, p. 14, n. 72. Sapir noted the presence of Bāniyān in the Red Sea coastal port city of al-Luḥayya, where the Arabs were pearl fishers and the Bāniyān served as middlemen who sold to the pearls to Bombay where they were pierced and strung; see Sapir, *Even Sapir*, 1:45b.

175 *Sefer hamusar*, p. 220, lines 2–7.

176 See #12, p. 165, line 4. On the dangers of the road and the hazards of sea travel, including the threat of being ambushed by robbers and pirates, see also #12, p. 165, lines 7–8 and #18, p. 212, line 12.

> Said Mordecai the Sidonian, All my days I have loved wayfaring—on New Moons, Sabbaths, and weekdays—to seek out *musar* as has been my custom; in conversation, at rest, in my meditation. I have often asked, Where is its place, that it might be drawn down from the heavens? (*ayyeh meqomo/ le-horidenu mishmei meromo*). Is it acquired from the words of the poor? Or from nobles flush with gold? I sought it with every ounce of my might, with my spirit and soul. If I found just a little of it, I would tread gingerly out of love for it. My soul was greatly attached to it; my feelings and senses delighted in it. Despite all this, I have never found anyone like Abner ben Ḥeleq the Yemenite, in any city I have seen, [no one who could approach] his poems and phrases; his capital creations, his chapters and prologues (*she'arav uftaḥav*); his insight and narration, for God has sent him, endowed with His spirit. I longed to see him, for he is saintly and humble. I would roam crooked paths and sail the deep seas ...[177]

In theory, travel with Muslim caravans holds out the promise of conversation informed by *adab*—which remained "the universal currency of Arabic high culture" even after the Ottoman conquest of the region[178]—although these expectations may be dashed. The 42nd *maqāma* opens with Mordecai undertaking a grueling route from Alexandria to Mt. Hermon through terrain marked by mountains and valleys. He longs for a companion with whom he might converse. But even when he joins several caravans, he finds no one to speak with, since these Muslims seem to him incapable of doing justice to their own rich *adab* heritage. In a withering critique, he accuses them of lacking wisdom and originality, and implies that they are not worthy of their precious literary legacy:

> How can a man mix with beasts? For they are Muslims—there is no delight in their words, only destruction (*ve-eikh yit'arev adam 'im behemah, ki hem yishma'elim/ein be-divreihem no'am ki im ḥovlim*).[179] Some of them declaim a host of elegant Arabic poems and songs. One praises a lover and his beloved, and his desire is for them. Another turns to his eloquent language, to poetics and metrics, but then returns to She'ol, for there lies his home [a pun on "his verse"; *beito*].[180] Yet another recites

177 See #13, p. 171, lines 2–9.

178 See Bray, "Starting Out in New Worlds," p. 202.

179 See #42; p. 439, lines 5–6. *Ḥovlim* occurs as a proper noun in Zech. 11:7; for glosses (it can mean either 'destruction' or 'unity'), see Ben Yehuda, *A Complete Dictionary*, 2:1427b, n. 1.

180 A clever takeoff on 1Sam. 7:17: וּתְשֻׁבָתוֹ הָרָמָתָה כִּי־שָׁם בֵּיתוֹ ("Then he would return to

> parables and animal fables; others praise *adab*. Still others run wild with their flowery language, but when I approached it, I found that it was not a virgin.[181]

Mordecai's gratuitous dismissal seems fuelled by a heady mixture of disappointment, indignation, religious animus, and cultural competition. The rhetorical question with which he opens his words, *Ve-eikh yitʿarev adam ʿim behemah, ki hem yishmaʿelim*, plays on the polyvalent root *ʿa.r.b.* that signifies both "to mingle" and "to become Arabized." Despite his palpable disdain, he had hoped to mingle precisely because he was Arabized and in search of *adab*. That he charges the Muslim travelers with a lack of stylistic originality speaks to his internalization of Arabic aesthetic ideals. But this allegation too is not a little ironic, considering that he and Abner have contrafacted the work of others and have appropriated so many of the Arabic literary genres he names. Perhaps it is not a coincidence that the episode's framing itinerary, *mi-no amon el har ḥermon*, is identical to that of the very first *maqāma* which, in Hebraicizing al-Ḥarīrī's fifteenth *maqāma*, signals the work's propensity for cross-cultural emulation.

The quest for specifically Jewish learning, principally halakhic and kabbalistic, also drives Mordecai's travels. In the sixth *maqāma*, he journeys from Syria via the Upper Galilee to the holy city of Safed, where he is struck by the piety and erudition of the city's impressive scholarly community, especially by the advanced Talmudic learning taking place in its numerous *yeshivot*.[182] Confronted with such mental acuity, he is moved to lament his own intellectual shortcomings. To address his deficiencies, he visits various synagogues and

---

Ramah, for his home was there …"). Note the transformation of Ramah (a high, exalted place) to She'ol (the underworld).

181 I.e., that their flowery language was not pristine and contained nothing that had not previously been used by others; cf. Deut. 22:13–14, "A householder takes a woman [as his wife] and cohabits with her. Then he takes an aversion to her and makes up charges against her and defames her, saying, 'This is the party I took [to wife]; but when I approached her, I found that she was not a virgin.'" Given his overall avoidance of erotically suggestive intertexts, one might not expect Alḍāhirī to make use of an accusation which, in its original scriptural context, is both sexualized and false. But his inspiration likely comes from Immanuel's 8th *maḥberet*, in which the same usage occurs in an epistle denouncing an Italian poet named Joab for a series of linguistic errors; see Immanuel Ha-romi, *Maḥberot Immanuel*, 1:155, l. 352. On the significance of this *maḥberet*, which makes use elsewhere of some remarkably violent sexual imagery, see Brener, "Stealing Wisdom: A Story of Books (and Book-Thieves) from Immanuel of Rome's *Maḥbarot*," and Kfir, *A Matter of Geography*, 130–139.

182 *Sefer hamusar*, p. 116, lines 1–8.

houses of study, in particular, Joseph Karo's yeshivah. There he is treated to a philosophical disquisition on the nature of the soul. Mordecai is aware that Safed is a vital center of both halakhic and kabbalistic studies that boasts the most illustrious names of the day—not only Karo, but also Rabbi Moses di Trani (d. 1580) of the Safed rabbinical court, and Rabbi Moses Cordovero (d. 1570), the renowned kabbalist.[183] While Safed is the historic center of the sixteenth-century mystical revival, Mordecai and Abner join kabbalistic study circles in other venues as well. In the third *maqāma*, Mordecai journeys from Baghdad to Irbīl, an ancient town in upper Mesopotamia, where he is welcomed by a group of Jewish men whose learned discussion turns to theosophical kabbalah. The topics that engage them are fundamentals of classical kabbalah: the *sefirot*, or ten aspects of divinity, their cosmic actions, and the names associated with them. In the twenty-first *maqāma* Mordecai relates that he has always "loved grazing ... in the gardens [of wisdom] ..." and so travels to Ottoman Turkey (*ereṣ togarmah*) "for a purpose both revealed and concealed."[184] The episode unfolds in Bursa, an ancient city in northwestern Anatolia that was the main capital of the Ottoman state in the 14th century and one of the international centers of the silk trade.[185] There he encounters Abner who, after one of his typical ruses, turns pensive and expatiates on kabbalistic questions of man's ultimate reward. In the twenty-third *maqāma* Mordecai journeys to Tiberias in search of that city's renowned sages. Again, he stumbles upon Abner, now in the guise of a *ḥazzan*, who recites two poems incorporating the kabbalistic vision of the Sabbath. Mordecai asks in amazement how it is that his friend has penetrated this esoteric knowledge, and Abner attributes his expertise to assiduous study of two formative works of classical kabbalah.[186] Abner waxes eloquent about the salvific nature of kabbalistic study and recites a poem he has composed in praise of these kabbalistic texts.

13 Mobility and the Diffusion of Religious Knowledge and Practices

As discussed at greater length in Chapter Six, the fictional protagonists' open embrace of kabbalah represents a bold new departure in Yemenite Jewish liter-

183 *Sefer hamusar*, p. 287, lines 40–42.
184 *Sefer hamusar*, p. 239, lines 1–3.
185 See Çizakça, "A Short History of the Bursa Silk Industry (1500–1900)."
186 The anonymous *Sefer ma'arekhet ha-elohut* (The Structure of the Godhead; c. 1300), and one of its classical commentaries, *Minḥat yehudah*, by the Spanish exile, Judah Ḥayyaṭ, from the late 15th century.

ature. Alḍāhirī uses the entertaining framework of *Sefer hamusar* to introduce kabbalistic theosophy, literature, and liturgical customs to a largely uninitiated public in Yemen. On the level of the narrative, the characters' mobility affords them exposure to these new ideas and customs. Their receptivity to kabbalah is related to the regularity with which they travel, constantly leaving the familiar behind to confront new experiences and perspectives. Despite the fact that Mordecai and Abner are in many ways stock characters, the freedom with which they travel from city to city enables them to become conduits for innovations in Jewish learning and practice. That they join or initiate kabbalistic study in Bursa (northwestern Anatolia), Irbīl (northeastern Iraq), and Tiberias (on the western shore of the Sea of Galilee), but not in Yemen suggests that the stimuli for this mode of spirituality originate outside of their native land. In his kabbalistic poem in the twenty-third *maqāma*, Abner endorses a novel liturgical custom introduced into the Friday night *qiddush* by the Lurianic circle of Safed kabbalists, which apparently had not yet penetrated Yemenite practice. Other episodes linking mobility with the diffusion of religious knowledge are the *maqāmāt* (#24, #25, #40) relating the story of the learned emissary from Safed who came to the Red Sea port city of Mocha to sell sacred books while Abner was in prison in Ṣanaʿā. Although the imported books are potential agents of cultural transformation, they are not portrayed as a threat to the indigenous tradition. On the contrary, the protagonists view the envoy's volumes as precious, not only because of their sacred contents and provenance but also because of the scarcity of printed books in Yemen.[187]

14 Journeying and Questions of Identity

Across confessional lines, medieval and early modern travel writing explores multiple dimensions of the journey—physical, intellectual, and spiritual. In fictional as well as more factual texts, voyages are undertaken for purposes of conquest and accruing power, or in search of love or material gain, or as pilgrimage, a quest for knowledge or salvation, or as a means of self-discovery. As with actual voyagers, literary characters who cross spatial boundaries remove themselves from their customary settings to confront the unknown. Their perceptions of unfamiliar places, groups, and mores tend to be misinformed or

---

187 Books brought from the Land of Israel were not necessarily printed there; see Yaari, *Hadefus haʿivri beʾarṣot ha-mizraḥ* 2: 9–14. Bibliophilic rabbinic emissaries eventually operated throughout the Jewish world; see e.g., Teplitsky, "A 'Prince of the Land of Israel' in Prague."

based on stereotypes or myths and are generally refracted through the lens of their culturally and politically determined view of the world. Consequently, rather than embracing difference out of genuine curiosity, the impressions they record are often marked by what we would consider incomprehension or insensitivity and may be distorted by an overriding sense of cultural superiority. Such skewed representations of the others they encounter frequently reveal more about the observers than about those whom they profess to observe. At the same time, the process of uprooting oneself from surroundings in which one is a known quantity helps to obscure one's own identity. Spatial and social dislocation can turn one into an outsider, facilitating the adoption of different masks. As David Malkiel writes,

> The travel experience typically has a destabilizing effect, for travelers tend to reflect upon their identity when and because they find themselves out of context, a situation which often tempts them to experiment with other identities and present these to strangers.[188]

In medieval Arabic literature, strangers (Sufi mendicants, wandering dervishes) were frequently associated with piety and knowledge or wisdom.[189] In *Sefer hamusar*, Abner exercises his uncanny ability to insinuate himself incognito into any number of scenarios. It might be argued that the protean Abner has no fixed or stable identity that could be unsettled by removing himself from a milieu in which he is known. Nevertheless, his constant displacement ensures that he will always be able to conceal his true intentions with some sort of subterfuge. As Robin Ostle has noted with regard to stories of journeying interlopers in the *Thousand and One Nights*,

> It is clear that the process of travelling away from a context in which the traveller is familiar and known helps to blur the identity of the one who will then resort to disguise in order to gain entry to the palace or the castle.[190]

---

188 See Malkiel, *Strangers in Yemen*, 2.

189 See: Fudge, "Strangers in Fiction: Knowledge, Narrative and the 'Friends of God'"; Rosenthal, "The Stranger in Medieval Islam"; and Crone and Moreh trans., *The Book of Strangers*.

190 Ostle, "Introduction: Persons and Passions," in idem, ed. *Sensibilities of the Islamic Mediterranean*. See also van Leeuwen, "Challenging Symbols of Power: Palaces and Castles in the *Thousand and One Nights*"; idem, "Preface: The Journey as Metaphor"; and idem, *The Thousand and One Nights: Space, travel and transformation*, 15–27.

Or, as Richard van Leeuwen puts it, "mechanisms of authority affect [the traveler] only superficially. He remains outside the regular procedures and leaves one domain of power for another."[191] While Abner seldom infiltrates bastions of power such as palaces or castles, his deceptions enable him to subvert authority in subtler ways.

15 The Significance of Place Names

Many of the individual episodes in the *Maqāmāt* of al-Hamadhānī, and most of those in the *Maqāmāt* of al-Ḥarīrī, bear place names. Philip Kennedy has noted that al-Hamadhānī's episodes all unfold within the Islamic world but are "deliberately *not* marked by specific local features in most cases." Nevertheless, particular toponyms do carry symbolic weight. As mentioned in Chapter One, Kennedy notes that the *nisba* al-Iskandarī could refer to more than one Alexandria, so that rather than relating Hamadhānī's protagonist Abū 'l-Fatḥ to a fixed place, it intimates rootlessness. Similarly, the historical associations with the city of Sarūj suggest the liminal status of Ḥarīrī's trickster hero, al-Sarūjī.[192] The biblical toponym Elon Ṣaʿananim, the hometown of Alḥarizi's eloquent rogue, similarly alludes to itinerancy and displacement by virtue of its derivation from the triliteral root *ṣ.ʿ.n.*, which conveys vagabondage or nomadism. By contrast, the narrator's epithet, ha-Ezraḥi, denotes an indigenous person, thereby underscoring Heman's profound rootedness in his native land. As in the *Taḥkemoni*, the *nisbas* of Alḍāhirī's narrator and hero resonate with scriptural significance. While Alḍāhirī somewhat disingenuously states in his introduction that he has randomly chosen his protagonists' names on the basis of their numerical equivalence to his own, it is clear that the toponymical adjectives indicating their places of origin are intended to summon associations with mobility and the cardinal directions. The ancient northern coastal cities of Tyre and Sidon were home to master seamen (often referred to as Phoenicians) who, renowned for shipbuilding, commerce, and seafaring, plied the Mediterranean trading in cedar and delicate artifacts crafted from glass and ivory.[193] The implied link between Mordecai and the ancient maritime traders of Sidon would no doubt

191 Van Leeuwen, *The Thousand and One Nights: Space, travel and transformation*, 15–16.

192 Kennedy, "The *Maqāmāt* as a nexus of interests," 156–157.

193 Recently, Josephine Quinn has argued that the Phoenicians "did not in fact exist as a self-conscious collective or 'people'" above the level of the city or the family. She challenges the claim that all the communities from the Levant to the western Mediterranean long held to be Phoenician defined themselves in terms of one overarching ethnic or cultural

have struck a chord with Alḍāhirī's readers. Scripture associated Sidon with the Canaanites; Genesis 10:15 lists the eponymous Sidon as Canaan's first-born, and the Canaanites are identified as merchants in the Bible.[194] Perhaps, following Kennedy's lead, one might point to the failure of the redoubtable Sidonians and other Canaanites to withstand the test of time as a token of the world's inconstancy and capriciousness, attributes that certainly pertain to the *maqāma* genre and its protagonists. Still, it requires a suspension of disbelief to reconcile the disjunction between Mordecai's putative Sidonian provenance and the fact that he clearly hails from Yemen. Perhaps this is why Shalom Medina, in his 1965 review of Ratzaby's edition, suggested that the gentilic ha-Ṣidoni might actually allude to an origin in Ṣaʿadah, in northern Yemen.[195] Nevertheless, Mordecai unequivocally identifies with Sidon; after parting from Abner and departing Tiberias in the closing line of the twenty-third *maqāma* he says, "I reached my city, which is Sidon" (*va'agiʿa leʿiri, hi ṣidon*).[196]

In relative geographical terms, Mordecai the Sidonian is notionally a northerner while Abner ben Ḥeleq is not only a Yemenite (*ha-teimani*) but also a southerner, since in both Hebrew and Arabic, the root *y.m.n.* signifies the right side or hand, which is to the south when one is facing the sun in the east.[197] (The Arabic words for Yemen [*al-yaman*], right, south [*yamīn*], and good luck or prosperity [*yumn*] all derive from this root, hence Yemen is both "the land of the south" and "Arabia Felix.")[198] This imaginary contrast in provenance comes to the fore at the end of the nineteenth *maqāma*, when Abner parts from Mordecai saying, "Go to your place of rest and repose; I will return to my native land .... You will always be my faithful friend, even if you go via the north and I go via the south (or: by way of Yemen; *derekh teiman*)."[199] Taken together, the aggregate of North and South describes the arc of the two characters' visits to the many corners of their world. Side by side, the two gentilics can be seen as a merism representing the extent of the broader world as conceptualized in *Sefer hamusar*.

---

identity, exposing it as a construction of modern nationalist agendas. See Quinn, *In Search of the Phoenicians*, xiii–xxiv and *passim*.

194 Quinn also discredits the notion that the Phoenicians called themselves Canaanites, exposing this too as a fabrication of modern scholarship.

195 See Medina, "Sefer hamusar, mahadurat ratzaby," 8.

196 *Sefer hamusar*, p. 273; a similar identification occurs in #26, ll. 183–184. On Sidon see Ashtor et al., "Sidon."

197 Accordingly, "E was then 'front' (*qedem*: Gen 2:8); N was 'left' (*śĕmōl*: Gen 4:15); and W was 'behind' (*āḥôr*: Job 23:8)"; see Alexander, "Early Jewish Geography."

198 On *y.m.n.* see: Lane, *Arabic-English Lexicon*, Bk 1, Pt. 8 and Supplement, p. 3064; BDB, 412, s.v. *teiman* (for attestations see 1 Sam 23:24 and Job 39:26); and Schunck, "Benjamin."

199 *Sefer hamusar*, p. 227, lines 134–136.

16 Cultural Orbits of the Travel

Alḍāhirī's peripatetic protagonists roam throughout the heartlands of the Eastern Islamic empire, winding their way across Yemen, Egypt, the Land of Israel, Syria, Mesopotamia, and Persia. They range beyond Ottoman lands as far east as India, and venture—fleetingly—only as far west as Ottoman Anatolia, the Balkans, and Greece, stopping well short of the Maghreb, or Muslim West (which, west of Algeria, never came under Ottoman control). Far from arbitrary, their disinterest in North Africa has sound Arabic literary precedents: al-Hamadhānī's characters do not visit the Maghreb, and even though al-Ḥarīrī expanded al-Hamadhānī's geography, his hero and narrator set foot in North Africa only once, in a highly rhetorical episode that unfolds in a mosque, without much attention to the outside world.[200] That is to say that both the pioneer of the genre in Arabic and the author who gave the *maqāma* its definitive form restricted their characters' movements to the familiar geographic arenas and cultural milieus of the central Islamic lands. Even al-Saraqusṭī (d. 1143), who wrote his *Maqāmāt al-luzūmiyya* in Andalusia, situated most of his episodes in the Middle East, with only a few set further east in India and China or further west in the Maghreb. James Monroe has suggested "that the author was aiming at a readership located in the heartlands of Islam, rather than one narrowly restricted to the Iberian Peninsula, and that his message was pan-Islamic rather than local," while Jonathan Decter has proposed that, out of a sense that some 'golden age' had come to an end in al-Andalus, al-Saraqusṭī "looked to an idyllic place and time outside of the Iberian Peninsula."[201] More generally, the tendency of Arabic *maqāma* authors to limit their characters' adventures to an Islamic cultural orbit (*dār al-islām*) dovetails with the parameters set by certain tenth-century Arab geographers such as al-Muqaddasī, who professed a lack of interest in non-Muslim realms: "We do not bother ourselves with the countries of the unbelievers, because we did not enter them and we see no use whatever in describing them."[202]

---

200 #16 "Of the West"; see *The Assemblies of Al Ḥarīri*, 1:194–199 and *Maqāmāt al-Ḥarīrī*, 129–136. In the time of al-Hamadhānī and al-Ḥarīrī, the Maghreb, of course, included Andalusia. Alḍāhirī had the utmost respect for the cultural creativity and aesthetics of medieval Andalusian Jewry, but in his day the Iberian peninsula had not only been stripped of Jews, but was also under hostile Christian control, presumably making its inclusion inconceivable even in an imaginary itinerary.

201 See: Monroe, *Al-maqāmāt al-Luzūmīyah*, 45–46, and Decter, *Iberian Jewish Literature*, 110.

202 See Kennedy, "The *Maqāmāt* as a nexus of interests," 156–157, citing Kilito, *Les Séances*, 19–20. Kennedy notes that this sort of parochialism "was not shared by all Muslim geographers and travellers in all periods." See also Elinson, *Looking Back at al-Andalus*, 57–59.

It is striking, therefore, that in Alḍāhirī's main Hebrew model, Judah Alḥarizi's *Taḥkemoni*, the protagonists rove from west to east, through the realms of Christendom as well as Islam. But as Joseph Sadan's publication of al-Mawṣili's biographical sketch attests, Alḥarizi was himself a most unusual "cultural junction."[203] A native of Christian Toledo, yet molded by a broad Judeo-Arabic education, Alḥarizi bridges East and West. He excelled not only as a translator and as a master of Hebrew poetry and prose but also—and this is quite rare for a Jewish littérateur—as the author of elegant Arabic poems composed in the East for a receptive Muslim clientele.[204] Disheartened by the decline of Andalusian Jewry in the wake of the Almohad invasion, Alḥarizi traveled to the East in the hopes of finding flourishing Jewish communities and enlightened patrons who could subsidize his creativity. In his introduction to *Kitāb al-durar*, which documents this journey, Alḥarizi writes explicitly of his desire to voyage eastward: "I had long dwelt in the countries of the Maghreb, yearning to sail the seas and wander afar, to visit the Land of Israel and Babylon."[205] But once there, this native son of Christian Spain discovered that, in this rather different environment, Jewish patrons of high culture were not forthcoming, and so, after a good deal of invective, he readjusted his sights, addressing his Arabic poetry to Muslim rulers. In effect, for the final decade of his life (1215–1225), Alḥarizi was *dépaysé*; a displaced westerner in the East.[206] (He stood out not only because of his misguided expectations, but also because of his Maghrebi-Andalusi accent in Arabic, his unusual height, and his thin beard in middle age.)[207] It is therefore not entirely surprising that the *Taḥkemoni*, completed in the East after its author had abandoned his homeland, should encompass a broader geocultural orbit than the *Maqāmāt* of al-Hamadhānī and al-Ḥarīrī on the one hand, and *Sefer hamusar* on the other.

Despite Alḍāhirī's intimate acquaintance with the *Taḥkemoni* and the *Maḥbarot* of Immanuel of Rome, the Jewish communities of western Christendom and other Christian lands are invisible in *Sefer hamusar* (as are the vast numbers of Christian pilgrims visiting Jerusalem during this period). On those isolated occasions when the protagonists journey north and west of the Levant

203 The phrase was aptly coined by Sadan; see his "Judah Alḥarizi as a Cultural Junction" and "Un intelectuel juif au confluent de deux cultures."

204 See Sadan, "Un intelectuel juif," 115; Decter, "The (Inter-religious?) Rededication of an Arabic Panegyric by Judah al-Ḥarīzī," and idem, *Dominion Built of Praise*, 259–264.

205 *K. al-Durar*, English section p. 55, lines 19–20; Judeo-Arabic p. 44, lines 19–20: *fa-la-ṭālamā kuntu fi bilād al-maghrib shadīd al-ishtiyāq/li-rukūb al-biḥār wa-qaṭʿ al-afāq/wa-ziyāra al-shām wa'l-ʿirāq*.

206 See Alḥarizi, *The Wanderings of Judah Alharizi*, English Introduction, esp. vii and xvi.

207 Sadan, "Judah Alḥarizi as a Cultural Junction," 32–40; "Un intelectuel juif," 125–133.

into Asia Minor and the Balkans, they do not exceed the bounds of the Ottoman Empire in its early to mid-16th-century configuration. Twice (#18 and #41) the protagonists locate themselves in "Romah," which renders the Arabic *balad al-rūm*, a term that originally designated the Roman Empire and then Byzantine lands but subsequently came to refer to Ottoman Anatolia as well as the Greco-Balkan region which the Ottomans called Rumeli.[208] When they wander into the latter, they are truly on terra incognita and are unaware that these formerly Byzantine territories in the Balkans were home to native Jewish communities going back to late antiquity. In #41, Mordecai recounts that he traveled from Ottoman Turkey (*ereṣ togarmah*) to a city in the provinces of "Romah," the majority of whose inhabitants were "Ashkenazim." Two additional *maqāmāt* mention travel to or from cities in the Ottoman Greco-Balkans or western Anatolia: In #21 the Jews of Bursa tell Mordecai that Abner has gone to visit the Jews of Greater Constantinople and the passengers on a ship arriving in Bursa from *ereṣ porviṣah* (the port of Prèveza on the western coast of modern Greece) announce that Abner had been in their land. In #36 Mordecai and Abner find themselves in a city they call "Galfer," which is likely Karaferye, located in northern Greece near Salonica.[209] So the westernmost reaches of Alḍāhirī's imagined world extend to the eastern Mediterranean, even though his characters rarely venture in that direction, and are on shakier ground when they do.

17 Crossing Boundaries and Depicting Other Jewish Subcultures

> A journey's point of departure is a place. But it is also, no less importantly, a landscape of the mind. The place which the departing traveller leaves, if it is a place which he or she calls home, has shaped his or her body, habits, and most basic responses. It has also imprinted on the mind an inner map, which the traveller will be likely to project on to any landscapes met with in the future, and to steer by, whether or not it fits with reality.[210]

> … the enduring cultural compass of Islam and Arabdom … orients the traveler to what he sees, how he sees it, and how he reports it, and the reader to how he receives the report …. This constant guiding presence

---

208 See el-Cheikh and Bosworth, "Rūm."

209 In his Introduction, Ratzaby mentions "Galfer" as a city in Turkey but does not attempt to identify it.

210 Bray, "Starting Out in New Worlds: Under Whose Empire?" p. 199. Cf. Shulman, Foreword to Subrahmanyam, *Three Ways to Be Alien*, p. ix.

> not only enables the traveler-traders—merchants in musk and silk and porcelain, but also in knowledge—to make cultural translations for their immediate audience back home. For us, their audience removed in time, it points not just to where those travelers got to but also to where they came from.[211]

For characters who remain almost entirely within an Eastern Islamic cultural orbit, Alḍāhirī's protagonists are remarkably inattentive to their Islamic surroundings.[212] This is not to say that Muslims and Islam do not figure in *Sefer hamusar*, but they are rarely differentiated—according to place of origin, ethnicity, or legal school of thought (*madhhab*), for instance. When the protagonists first arrive in a new place, its Muslim inhabitants often remain invisible. Mordecai and Abner steer by their Judeocentric maps, and in many parts of the Muslim world, their curiosity about unfamiliar surroundings rarely extends beyond the local Jews. As they wend their way through a series of Jewish communities, their touchstones are generally synagogues and houses of study, and though they periodically remark that the tomb of a revered prophet or saint is in the vicinity, they never visit these shrines in the spirit of *ziyāra*.[213] At each new destination, they quickly size up their coreligionists and issue authoritative and judgmental appraisals. While they also make occasional ex cathedra remarks about Muslims, these comments are not specific to a localized cultural milieu. The resulting portrayals of "others," whether Muslim or Jewish, are filtered through the protagonists' lenses and reveal more about their self-understanding than about those whom they are assessing. Inevitably, the characters' culturally determined attitudes preclude more nuanced insights into the unfamiliar communities they encounter so that their comments are rarely, if ever, penetrating and generally take the form of snap judgments. Apart from a few sympathetic appraisals, Mordecai and Abner's impressions of non-Yemenite Jews tend to be marked by suspicion or incomprehension. A sense of Yemenite Jewish cultural superiority seems to lie behind these confident generalizations and categorical dismissals.[214] Such critiques perpetuate a literary

211 Mackintosh-Smith, Translator's Introduction to Abū Zayd al-Sīrāfī, *Accounts of China and India*, p. xxv.

212 Cf. Jacobs, *Reorienting the East*, 12: 'While Jewish travel writings display a certain fascination with the foreign and exotic, they do not systematically focus on the Islamic world. As in much of premodern Jewish literature, references to other religious practices, cultures, and ethnicities are generally made for the purpose of enhancing Jewish self-understanding." The *Taḥkemoni* is similarly Judeocentric.

213 See, e.g., Asatryan, "Ziyāra" and Kosansky, "Holy Shrines-Conceptual."

214 Cf. Shatzmiller, "Travelling in the Mediterranean in 1563," who remarks that Elijah of

topos familiar from the *Taḥkemoni*, which includes a ruthless dismissal of the Hebrew poets and literary culture of the East; the product of Alḥarizi's internalization of Andalusian Jewish cultural exceptionalism. But they also challenge the notion that premodern Jews in disparate parts of the world unreservedly identified with their far-flung coreligionists or were united by belonging to a broader community that transcended regional and cultural boundaries. As Uriah Kfir has remarked, even where there was not a significant regional differentiation in medieval Hebrew poetics,

> geographical concepts were often invoked, rightly or not, by medieval Jews themselves to indicate local affiliations and self-definitions .... [W]ithin the medieval Jewish world ... local groups often strove to distinguish themselves from others, sometimes in confrontational ways.[215]

Even when a particular Jewish community elicits the protagonists' praise, it is often perfunctory. If we were to devise a schematic typology of all the encounters with Jewish Others and the verdicts that ensue, it might look something like this: (1) Eastern Jewish communities outside of Yemen earn either esteem or derision; (2) non-Islamicate Jewish communities west of the Levant are exoticized or met with incomprehension; and (3) the Jews of the Land of Israel are regarded with unquestioning admiration. (Christians and Christianity, though rarely mentioned, are generally reviled, and representations of Muslims and Islam are on the whole ambivalent.)

18 Other Eastern Jews

The protagonists' cultural chauvinism is particularly intriguing when directed at other Eastern Jewish communities with whom they share an Islamicate milieu, but from whom they nevertheless distance themselves. While one might assume a degree of cultural continuity among these groups, Mordecai and Abner's insistence on Yemenite superiority suggests their sense of deci-

---

Pesaro "has only criticism to offer" in his impressions of the Jewish communities he encountered on his Mediterranean travels, and that this censorious tendency was typical of "16th-century Spanish Jews."

215 See Kfir, *A Matter of Geography*, 3–4; see also Rand, *Evolution*, p. 12 and n. 4 and Shatzmiller, "Les limites de la solidarité: antagonismes au sein de la société juive ancienne et moderne." Even in later centuries, "pan-Jewish solidarity" was lacking when it came to fund-raising efforts; see Lehmann, "Rabbinic Emissaries from Palestine," 1239–1240.

sive regional distinctions. Some of their criticisms are so economically phrased and non-specific that it is difficult to deduce much substance from their stylized scriptural wording. Still, it is precisely their protestations of difference that highlight the need felt by these Yemenite Jewish characters to distinguish their own culture, communal norms and traditions from those of other Jewish subcultures in the Islamic world. Mordecai opens the third *maqāma* by relating that he traveled from Baghdad (*Bavel*) to Irbīl (*Arbel*), passing along the way through several communities on the Tigris. One of these featured an unparalleled synagogue and the tombs of Daniel and his companions, sites of saint veneration.[216]

> But the Jews who dwelled there were full of sin, and I sought only upright congregations of exceptional virtue and exemplary conduct before the God of awe-inspiring deeds.
>
> So I departed that place with an embittered soul. To escape the trouble, I went via Arbel … for I had heard there were honorable people there, who trembled at the Lord's command to take the poor wanderer into their homes.

Mordecai's patent search for hospitality suggests that his verdict of sinfulness has more to do with an uncharitable reception at the hands of the Jews living along the Tigris than with any grave moral trespass. This is equally true of his condemnation of the "worthless" Jews of Bursa, who are too preoccupied with their own affairs to pay him the attention he craves.[217] He is often incensed by the lack of compassion the Jewish inhabitants of a given land exhibit for the stranger in their midst, although his moral indignation frequently seems to be fueled by financial considerations. A similar disillusionment motivates his high-handed dismissal of the Jews of Ḥadrach in Syria, whose sin of parsimony is compounded by their tenacious philistinism.[218] In the fourteenth *maqāma*,

216 Ratzaby, citing Sassoon, *Ohel Dawid* 2:1022, notes that there were varying traditions regarding the location of Daniel's burial place. According to Benjamin of Tudela and Petaḥia of Regensburg, it was located in Sūsa (Iran). According to the Jews of Baghdad, it was located in Kirkuk, near Baghdad. The latter, Sassoon notes, agrees with Alḍāhirī. On these shrines, see also Meri, *The Cult of Saints Among Muslims and Jews in Medieval Syria*, 229–232 and 237–240.

217 *Sefer hamusar*, p. 239, lines 4–13.

218 Goitein suggests that Ḥadrach may refer to Damascus, since the two are coupled in Zech. 9:1; see "A Yemenite Poet on Egypt of the XVIth Century," p. 28, n. 1. See also Alḥarizi, *Taḥkemoni*, ed. Yahalom-Katsumata, p. 209, line 2; p. 429, line 104; and p. 559, line 650.

he is accompanied by a ravenous Abner, who accosts a quick-witted local youth and attempts to barter his rhetorical skills and broad expertise in "the sciences and the arts" for food. To the protagonists' dismay, their bid to offer *adab* in exchange for food is unsuccessful: the youth explains that his compatriots do not care at all for *ḥokhmat hamusar*. They guard their worldly goods jealously and bear a provincial, ill-bred hostility to all spiritual and cerebral endeavors. Even if tongue-in-cheek, these disappointments recall those of Alḥarizi, who penned scathing condemnations of the Jewish dignitaries he encountered in the East during an early, frustrating stage of his search for patronage. Initially, the poet measured his eastern coreligionists against the refined standards of the Andalusian Jewish intellectual and cultural tradition to which he was heir, and found them sorely lacking.[219] Alḍāhirī, too, implies through his characters' sardonic critique that the parochial Syrian Jews of Ḥadrach are deficient in precisely those areas in which the Jews of Yemen excel: Hebrew poetry and rhetoric, stylistic elegance and linguistic purity, astronomy, penitential prayers, moral instruction, hospitality, and generosity. Apart from its obvious intention as entertainment, his comical skewering of these Others reveals more about his own cultural perceptions and desire to reinforce his Yemenite readership's sense of identity than about the Jews of Ḥadrach, who are merely a foil.[220]

A sense of cultural disconnection also animates Mordecai's encounter with a particular region of "Babylonia" (*ereṣ meratayyim*) in the thirty-eighth *maqāma*. Mordecai deplores the benighted locals, who are incapable of "understanding proverb and epigram, the words of the wise and their riddles" (Proverbs 1:6). His lament conveys the intellectual and literary bankruptcy of the place, which is, again, devoid of *musar*.[221] But in a striking departure from other complaints of this kind, he tars the local Muslims and Jews with the same brush, accusing them all of arrogance and evil (*kullam yehirim ve-zeidim, ha-yishmaʿelim ve-hayehudim*). The charge that they are all *zeidim* ("wicked") is particularly arresting, given that in virtually every other instance in *Sefer*

219 According to Yahalom and Blau, Alḥarizi reworked and softened these portrayals as he gained a deeper appreciation for the mores and sensibilities of the eastern Jewish communities he visited; on the two distinct versions of "The Appraisal of the People" (#46 =Yahalom-Katsumata #39), see *The Wanderings of Judah Alharizi*, xii–xv.

220 On this episode see Tanenbaum, "Of a Pietist Gone Bad and Des(s)erts Not Had."

221 Compare this with his praise in #37 for the sages of the Jewish community of Patros (Egypt), who understand "proverb and epigram, and riddles." Goitein suggests that *ereṣ meratayyim* ("double bitterness"), "beyond the rivers of Miṣrayim," may refer to a region in Egypt, and that Alḍāhirī uses Patros as another name for Cairo; see "A Yemenite Poet on Egypt of the XVIth Century," 31–32. But in Jer. 50:21 *ereṣ meratayyim* is identified with Babylonia; see "Meratayyim," *Enṣiqlopedia miqraʾit*.

hamusar this term is used exclusively of Muslims as a play on *zaydīya* and alludes to the cruelty of the ruling Zaydī imāms in Yemen. If, with Goitein, we read *meratayyim* as "double bitterness," it is possible to see an intimation of Mordecai's twofold despondency, due to the boorish ignorance of not just the local Muslims but the Jews as well. The idea of doubling is driven home by the aural effect of rhymes in the dual form: *ereṣ meratayyim/me'ever le-naharei miṣrayyim/ve-hayyah levavi bein tannur ve-khirayyim.* (The mishnaic phrase, *bein tannur le-khirayyim,* has the sense here of "between a rock and a hard place" or "between the hammer and the anvil," and reinforces the idea that neither the Muslims nor the Jews of *Meratayyim* offer a suitable option for social interaction.) Mordecai despairs of finding a righteous companion who might guide him "with his refined learning and moral instruction (*be-musaro*), so that I might walk in his light." Only the appearance of the incandescent Abner delivers him from this predicament.

If in *Meratayyim* Mordecai relates to (allegedly) haughty, iniquitous, and uncouth Jews and Muslims in an equally dismissive fashion, elsewhere (#28) he implicates conversion to Islam in the downfall of the local Jews. Finding himself in Tabrīz (northwestern Persia), he deplores the sinful behavior of the Jewish residents, "some of whom burn with lust, and some of whom incline toward sectarianism" (*qeṣatam lohaṭim aḥar ha-zenut/ u-qeṣatam noṭim le-ṣad minut*). There are also some honorable families who keep themselves apart from the rest, and he is curious about the distinction between the two groups. An explanation is proffered for the deviance of the miscreants: these are Jews who had, at some earlier stage, converted to Islam. Their former apostasy became their undoing, for Islam was engraved in their hearts. As a result, when they reverted to Judaism, their return was shaky. They could not distinguish between the true and false faiths, holding fast to one without letting go of the other. Using a Hebrew term that means "to be intermingled" but whose polysemic root also suggests "becoming Arabized," Mordecai declares, "Because of this, they were adulterated/ they became Arabized (*hayu me'oravim*)."[222] But this intriguing aspect of the narrative is not developed any further, and it is difficult to know whether it has any historical basis.[223] Regardless, we come away with the nar-

222 *Sefer hamusar*, p. 327, lines 2–15. Cf. Ps. 106:35, *va-yit'arvu va-goyim va-yilmedu ma'aseihem*; "[They did not destroy the nations as the Lord had commanded them,] but mingled with the nations and learned their ways." A number of medieval Hispano-Jewish authors (Moses Ibn Ezra, Judah Halevi, Judah Alḥarizi, Moses Maimonides) adduce this verse in their often critical reflections on Jewish acculturation in the Islamic world; see Alfonso, *Islamic Culture Through Jewish Eyes*, 18–19 and 28 and Brann, *The Compunctious Poet*, 106–115.

223 Possibly, it is an oblique reference to the latter-day consequences of the upheaval in Tabrīz

rator's palpable disdain for a group of Jews who, in his view, have blurred the boundaries between their Judaism and Islam. We sense his unease with their erosion of the traditional dividing lines between the two faiths through their adherence to a sort of syncretistic, Islamicizing Judaism. He does not seem to entertain the possibility that their conversion might have occurred under duress. Nor does he offer any perspective on the phenomenon of incomplete reversion to Judaism, despite the fact that many contemporary rabbis in the Ottoman Empire were grappling with precisely that problem as it affected congregants forcibly converted to Christianity in the Iberian Peninsula at the end of the fifteenth century.[224]

The protagonists' critiques of the Mesopotamian, Syrian, and Persian Jews they encounter result from the alienation and disappointment they feel once they realize that these Jews do not live up to their expectations. The characters' efforts to situate these subcultures on their mental maps lead them to project cultural significations onto them and to highlight perceived markers of difference that set these Jewish Others apart from Yemenite Jews. But rather than meaningfully exploring these differences, Alḍāhirī uses them as a springboard to focus on the distinctive characteristics of his own community.[225] Within the individual travel narratives, attempts at communal self-differentiation respond to a variety of stimuli: they may be set in motion by the unfamiliar group's exceptionalism, they may be the product of incomprehension, or they may result from an overriding sense of Yemenite cultural superiority. At the same time, on the meta-fictional level, Alḍāhirī is prompted to fashion these images by his perception of his readers' needs. Beyond their immediate role in the unfolding of the narrative, the constructions of identity articulated by the work's fictional characters are an authorial means of fostering a distinctive, collective sense of self.

---

that followed the murder of the Jewish apostate and Grand Vizier Rashīd al-Dīn in the 14th century, although we have no specific information about any accompanying forced conversions or apostasy to Islam. (There is documentation about the persecution of Jews in Tabriz in the 18th and 19th centuries.) On the rise and fall of Rashīd al-Dīn (d. 1318) see Gil, *Jews in Islamic Countries in the Middle Ages*, 484–486. See also Netzer, "The Fate of the Jewish Community of Tabriz," who cites this passage as evidence that Alḍāhirī "had visited Tabriz and had found its Jewish community in a deteriorating state" (412); cf. Fischel, "Azarbaijan in Jewish History," 20.

224 For a thoughtful, highly nuanced discussion of these challenges, see Lehman, *The* En Yaaqov, 17–50.

225 By contrast, Greidi was convinced that Aldahiri embarked on "his" travels precisely in order to familiarize himself with Jewish communities outside of Yemen; see his introduction to Alḍāhirī, *Sefer ṣeidah la-derekh*, repr. in *Peʿilut ve-zikhron ishim 643–646*, pp. 70–74.

19 Ashkenazim

On the rare occasions when Mordecai ventures into the Balkan region of the eastern Mediterranean, he constructs identities for the local Jewish communities out of biblical verse fragments cleverly juxtaposed for their rhymes. The resulting portraits are mainly benevolent but highly compressed and occasionally impenetrable, due to the constraint of using ancient scriptural phrases to characterize latter-day regional Jewish subcultures. In two instances, he locates these groups with a greater than usual degree of geographic imprecision. In #41, Mordecai travels from Anatolia (*ereṣ togarmah*) to a city in the provinces of "Romah" (the Greco-Balkan region) in urgent search of a reliable tradition concerning the end of days. He is consumed with the need to know the date of the Redemption, which suggests that he has intentionally set out to find a Jewish community able to impart the hidden knowledge he so desperately requires. Though now aged, he undertakes to sail the seas and brave drought and wild beasts in its pursuit. Ultimately, he finds himself in an unnamed, "unwalled town," the majority of whose inhabitants he identifies as Ashkenazim: *va-yiqer miqri leʿir meʿarei ha-perazim/ hayyah rubbah ashkenazim.*[226] His impressions, refracted through the evocative language of Scripture, are both colorful and elusive. In his telling, these Ashkenazim have an air of mystery but also distinct markers of kinship about them. Certainly, he recognizes that they are fellow Jews (his next stop is the synagogue, which is filled with the "tumultuous sound" of "praise [that] befits the upright"[227]). But his sense of shared Jewish identity is tempered by their seeming exoticism, conveyed by means of intertexts that conjure up descent from ancient nobility, speech in a foreign tongue, and occult pursuits:

> *me-hem ba-kokhavim ḥozim/ u-mehem yodʿim be-ḥokhmat ha-razim/ u-mehem meḥabberei ḥaruzim// lefanim hayu sarim be-ṣoʿan/ u-leshonotam medabberot sefat kenaʿan.*[228]

226 For *ʿarei ha-perazot* as unwalled towns, see Esther 9:19.

227 Cf. Ezekiel 1:24 and Ps. 33:1.

228 Targum Onkelos and Jonathan ben Uziel translate Ṣoʿan as Tanis; Saadya equates it with Fusṭāṭ. The excoriation of Egypt in Is. 19 disparages *sarei ṣoʿan* as "utter fools" (*evilim*; Is. 19:11, 13), but Alḍāhirī seems to be using the phrase without the opprobrium attached to it in Scripture. For *sefat kenaʿan* see Is. 19:18, "In that day there shall be five cities in the land of Egypt that speak the language of Canaan, and swear to the Lord of hosts; one shall be called the city of destruction." The rhyme *ṣoʿan/ sefat kenaʿan* also occurs in #37 in connection with the Jews of Pathros (Egypt); see Goitein, "A Yemenite Poet on Egypt," p. 31, n. 4, who notes precedents in Judah Halevi and Judah Alḥarizi.

> Among them were stargazers, rhymesters, experts in esoteric lore;
> In days of old, in Egypt, they were noblemen; and they speak the language of Canaan.

Whatever kernels of historicity this quirky, rhyme-driven snapshot may contain, it is the narrator's cross-cultural exposure and consciousness of difference that are fascinating. From a historical point of view, Mordecai could certainly have encountered a local community of Ashkenazim in the Ottoman Balkans, Anatolia, or Greece.[229] Following the Black Death and its attendant massacres, communities of Central European Jews began to emerge around the western and eastern Mediterranean. The presence of Ashkenazi communities in Ottoman Constantinople, Salonica, Adrianople (Edirne), and Sofia is attested from the 15th century, well before the massive influx of Sephardi Jews from Spain and Portugal in 1492–1497. Ashkenazi scholars, economic migrants, refugees, and itinerant poor from Germany and central European lands had settled in the Balkans where they lived side by side with the indigenous Greek-speaking Romaniot communities. The proximity of the two subcultures led the Romaniots, native to the Balkans and Asia Minor since Byzantine times, to adopt certain Ashkenazi liturgical customs and halakhic strictures, and there is evidence of cordial relations between the sages of the two communities.[230] When Sephardim first arrived in certain Ottoman locales, they deferred to particular Ashkenazi practices. But as they grew to outnumber the existing multiethnic Jewish population, they gradually asserted their cultural hegemony, forcing non-Sephardi communities to struggle to protect their distinctive identities.[231]

---

229 See Bornstein, "Ha'ashkenazim ba'imperia ha'uthmanit ba-me'ot ha-16 veha-17"; Shpitzer, "Ha'ashkenazim ba-ḥatzi ha'i ha-balkani ba-me'ot ha-15 ve-16"; Davis, "The Reception of the *Shulḥan 'Arukh* and the Formation of Ashkenazic Jewish Identity"; Reiner, "Bein ashkenaz li-yrushalayim—ḥakhamim ashkenazim be-ereṣ yisra'el le-aḥar ha-mavet ha-shaḥor"; and Levy, *The Sephardim in the Ottoman Empire*, 3–4. Over the course of the 17th century, the Ashkenazic population of the Ottoman Empire grew, principally due to the arrival of Eastern European Jewish refugees and captives; in every medium-sized and large Jewish community there were Ashkenazim organized in independent congregations alongside those of the Iberian and Italian Jews; see Ben-Naeh, "Ve-khi lo aḥeihem anaḥnu?"

230 See Marcus et al., "Bulgaria": "Jewish refugees came to Bulgaria from Bavaria, which had banished them in 1470, and, according to various travelers, Judeo-German was heard for a long time in the streets of Sofia. Despite their adoption of Sephardi customs, language, and names, the Ashkenazi Jews maintained separate synagogues for a long time and followed the medieval German rite. The Ashkenazi prayer book was printed in 1548–1550 in Salonica by R. Benjamin ha-Levi Ashkenazi of Nuremberg who was also the rabbi of the Sofia Ashkenazi community."

231 See Septimus, "Linguistic Ideology and Cultural Hegemony: A Responsum of R. Samuel

The exotic label "Ashkenazim," which occurs nowhere else in *Sefer hamusar*, gives a name to an unfamiliar Jewish subculture from beyond the Islamic orbit, arguably in a type of undifferentiated reverse Orientalism. Mordecai makes no mention of any distinctive halakhic practices, liturgical customs, or scholarship of the Balkan Ashkenazim and does not even invoke the prevailing stereotypical image of medieval Ashkenazi culture as one of rigid piety, Talmudism, and halakhic expertise (in contrast with the scientific and linguistic knowledge, rationalism and literary elegance associated with Sephardim).[232] Nor does he mention any distinctive features of physical appearance (e.g., whether the men wear their *pe'ot* in a way that is similar to or distinct from the Yemenites' *simanim*.) The fictionality of the encounter is driven home by the fact that Mordecai prays with the Ashkenazim in their synagogue and yet says absolutely nothing about any differences between their liturgy and the Yemenite rite to which he is accustomed. This is particularly striking given his careful enumeration of the order of the Friday night service in the Sephardi synagogue he attends in Tiberias. Judging from his deliberate choice of scriptural wording, what captivates him is what he imagines to be the group's patrician lineage going back to antiquity, their astrological pursuits, and their access to esoteric or occult wisdom—ascriptions that seem motivated by his desperate need to know when the Redemption will bring respite from oppression to his own community. (It is just possible that he is also playing on the idea of itinerancy associated with the triliteral root of the biblical toponym *Ṣoʿan* to allude to the displacement of this Ashkenazi community from Germanic lands to the Balkans.) Linguistic exoticism marks the Ashkenazim as well, for they speak *sefat kenaʿan*, the language of Canaan. While Ratzaby has solid exegetical precedents for glossing this as Hebrew (see, e.g., Joseph Kara and Abraham Ibn Ezra on Isaiah 19:18), accepted tradition going back at least to the tenth century identified the Canaanites with Slavs, and *leshon kenaʿan* with Slavic (or Slavonic).[233] The identification occurs in glosses on the genealogy

---

de Medina, Its Sources and Implications" and Shatzmiller, "Les limites de la solidarité," 401–405.

232 A rich trove of information about the communal institutions, economic and spiritual life, liturgical practices, halakhic interpretations, etc. of Ashkenazi communities in the Ottoman Empire is preserved in the responsa literature; see Bornstein, "Ha'ashkenazim ba'imperia haʿuthmanit ba-me'ot ha-16 ve-ha-17." On the stereotypical image of Ashkenazim, see Malkiel, *Reconstructing Ashkenaz*, 1–43 *passim*. On medieval Ashkenazi preoccupation with the supernatural, see Rotman, "At the Limits of Reality: The Marvelous in Medieval Ashkenazi Hebrew Folktales."

233 See, e.g., the (12th-c.?) letter of introduction for a Russian Jew sojourning in Salonica on his way to Palestine, published in Mann, *Jews in Egypt and Palestine Under the Fāṭimid*

in Genesis 10:3, which lists the descendants of Gomer as Ashkenaz, Riphath, and Togarmah. In his *tafsīr* on this verse, Saadya renders Ashkenaz as *saqāliba* or "Slavs," using the medieval Arabic term for Central and Eastern European slaves sold in Muslim slave markets primarily in Spain and North Africa. The application of 'Canaan' to the Slavonic countries found post facto support in an old identification (not just among Jews) of Slavs with slaves, in conjunction with a prooftext from Genesis 9:25–26, "Cursed be Canaan; a servant of servants (*ʿeved ʿavadim*) shall he be unto his brethren."[234] The equation is found in the *Massaʿot* of Benjamin of Tudela in reference to Bohemia: "this is the commencement of the land of Slavonia (*Esclavonia*) and the Jews who dwell there call it Canaan, because the men of that land (the Slavs) sell their sons and daughters to the other nations."[235] Additional biblical verses associated the Canaanites with merchants (e.g., Proverbs 31:24), and in their glosses on Obadiah 20, Rashi, Ibn Ezra, and David Kimhi identify the Canaanites with the Franks or the Alemans.[236] All of this suggests that Mordecai may obliquely, if somewhat uncomprehendingly, have grasped the Balkan linguistic and cultural milieu of the Ashkenazim he encounters while remaining largely under the spell of their colorful otherness.

20 Romaniots?

When, in #36, Mordecai wanders into northern Greece, he comes upon Jews in a town Alḍāhirī represents consonantally as גלפר, which is almost certainly Karaferye, near Salonica. (Qara Ferye was the Ottoman Turkish name for Veroia.)[237] Following the conquest of Constantinople in 1453, Karaferye's large and ancient Romaniot community was among those forcibly resettled in the

Caliphs, 2:192: "*ki eino yodeʿa lo leshon ha-qodesh ve-lo lashon yevani, gam lo ʿaravi ki im sefat kenaʿan medabberim anshei ereṣ moladeto.*" For the identification of *kenaʿan/leshon kenaʿan* with the Slavs/Slavonic, see also Krauss, "The Names Ashkenaz and Sepharad" and Ben Yehuda, *Complete Dictionary*, 5:2451.

234 Saadya renders Riphath as the Franks, i.e., Germanic tribes, and Togarmah as *al-barg(h)ān*. While Baron glossed the latter as "the Burgundians," the annotation to the *Torat ḥayyim* edition of the Pentateuch suggests that the term may be linked to a place in today's Tajikistān; see Baron, *SRHJ*, 3:214–215 and *Torat ḥayyim: ḥamishah ḥumshei torah*, 1:132.

235 See Asher, *The Itinerary … Benjamin of Tudela*, 1:111, 164, and 2:226–229. On 'Canaan' as the name for Slavic countries and 'the language of Canaan' for Slavonic see also Roth ed., *The World History of the Jewish People* 2: 28, 310, 441 n. 5 and 291, 321–322.

236 See Baron, *SRHJ*, ibid., 335–336, n. 53.

237 See Anastasopoulos, "Karaferye," and Marcus, "Romaniots."

new Ottoman capital under Mehmed II's repopulation policy (*sürgün*). There they joined the ranks of the Romaniot community that had been there from Byzantine times, established their own synagogue and maintained the Romaniot *minhag*. Joseph Hacker cites a moving evocation of the exiles' forced passage to Istanbul from the writings of Ephraim ben Gershon, a homilist from Karaferye who fled to Negroponte (under Venetian control) when his community was driven into exile in 1455, but subsequently made his way to Istanbul to be reunited with them.[238] Apparently, some Romaniots managed to remain in Karaferye after 1453; in the 16th century, the population was augmented by Sephardi exiles who settled there and supplanted the Romaniots' Greek vernacular and *minhag romaniya*.[239] No hint of the long-standing Romaniot presence or their communal trauma is conveyed by Mordecai's supremely terse portrait of the local Jews, which, however admiring, lacks all cultural specificity. Through his choice of biblical language, he both idealizes and somewhat diminishes them, even if invoking the innocence and purity of children is intended figuratively. His favorable impression appears to be reinforced by the deferential treatment they accord him:

> … *shammah ra'iti ayyal u-ṣevi va'ofer// mi-qehal 'adat yisrael/asher lo yigre'u siḥah lifnei el* (Job 15:4) *//yeladim asher ein bahem kol mum ve-tovei mar'eh* (Dan. 1:4) */va'ehi le-ḥevratam mishta'eh// va-yesimuni 'aleihem le-rosh ule-qaṣin* (Jud. 11:11) */'ad 'avor 'iddanin ve-qiṣṣin.*[240]

> There I saw ram, stag and gazelle from the community of Israel. They were pious, they did not withhold their prayers; they had the innocence of

238 See Hacker, "Ottoman Policy toward the Jews and Jewish Attitudes toward the Ottomans during the Fifteenth Century," 120. A more detailed account with excerpts from the *derashah* is included in idem, "Shiṭat ha-surgun ve-hashpa'atah 'al ha-ḥevrah ha-yehudit ba'imperiya ha'uthmanit ba-me'ot ha-15–17," 41–45; for an English version see idem, "The Sürgün System and Jewish Society in the Ottoman Empire during the Fifteenth to the Seventeenth Centuries," 12–15. On the Ottoman use of mass deportation for purposes of colonization and repopulation, see also Inalcik, "Ottoman Methods of Conquest," 122–129 and idem, "Istanbul."

239 On the Jews of Veroia and their synagogue, see also R. and B-Z. Dorfman, *Synagogues Without Jews*, 101–108. On the Romaniot immigration and the 15th- and 16th-century Romaniot congregations in Istanbul which, like all the other *kehillot*, were based on their places of origin, see Rozen, *A History of the Jewish Community in Istanbul, The Formative Years*, 45–47 and 64–77. On their liturgical rite see Goldschmidt, "Maḥzor romania." My thanks to Andras Riedlmayer, Antonis Hadjikyriacou, and Robert Dankoff for their generous responses to my query about this community.

240 *Sefer hamusar*, p. 393, lines 4–7.

> children, unblemished and fair. I marveled at their companionship, and they appointed me their commander and captain for many days and seasons.

While there need not be any continuity between the frame and its enclosed tale, it is curious that in both Karaferye and the unnamed location in the provinces of "Romah" in #41, Abner tells folktales about the exemplary behavior of generous and self-sacrificing "Arabs" and Muslims who trust in God even in adversity, and urges his local Jewish audience to adopt the virtues illustrated by these stories in order to hasten the Redemption. Though these exempla have a marked universal dimension with motifs common to the vast fund of international folklore, they are explicitly framed as tales about Arabs (viz., Bedouin) and Muslims. The virtues they epitomize are reminiscent of the Islamic pietistic ideal of *tawakkul* (Hebrew: *biṭṭaḥon*) that had gained currency among Jewish readers through Bahya Ibn Paquda's *Book of Direction to the Duties of the Heart*; Judah Halevi's poetry; and, in Yemen, Nethanel ibn Fayyūmī's *Bustān al-ʿuqūl*.[241] The ironies of the cross-cultural web are striking: without any attempt at cultural translation, Abner uses miraculous tales of Muslims who trust in God and accept their sufferings in love in order to exhort the assembled Balkan Ashkenazim (and possibly Romaniots) to wait patiently for the redemption by cultivating the virtue of *tawakkul* or *biṭṭaḥon*. At the same time, on the metafictional level, Alḍāhirī directs these lessons at his Yemenite Jewish audience, urging them to emulate Muslim forebearance in order to hasten their redemption from Muslim oppression! While commending these tales to his listeners, Abner betrays an ambivalent attitude toward Muslims and subtly responds to Muslim polemical arguments against Judaism. Although in both episodes his fictional audience responds enthusiastically, they are again merely undifferentiated foils. Alḍāhirī's anti-Muslim polemics would have had far greater immediacy for his own Yemenite Jewish audience. Ultimately, the pressing need to reassure his readership and foster a communal sense of self-worth outweighs any curiosity Alḍāhirī might have had regarding the unfamiliar Jewish commu-

241 On *tawakkul* see above, Chapter One. On poetic reflexes of this ideal, see Scheindlin: "Mid-Life Repentance in a Poem by Judah Halevi"; "Ibn Gabirol's Religious Poetry and Sufi Poetry"; "Contrasting Religious Experience in the Liturgical Poems of Ibn Gabirol and Judah Halevi"; "Ibn Gabirol's Religious Poetry and Arabic *Zuhd* Poetry"; and *The Song of the Distant Dove*, 22–25 and *passim*. The fifth chapter of *Bustān al-ʿuqūl* is devoted to reliance upon God, *al-tawaqqul ʿalā allāh*; see Qāfiḥ ed. and trans., *Nethanel ibn Fayyūmī, Bustān al-ʿuqūl* (*Gan ha-sekhalim*) and Levine ed. and trans., *The Bustan al-ukul* (The Garden of Wisdom).

nities he professes to portray. His protagonists' minimal attention to what sets these other Jewish subcultures apart suggests that Alḍāhirī found it difficult to situate such Jews on his mental map in any meaningful way; he really comes into his own when his characters detail the differences between Yemenite Jews and their coreligionists in the Land of Israel.

CHAPTER 3

A Distinctive Sense of Self: Transregional Contacts with Jews in the Land of Israel

1 Introduction

If Alḍāhirī's protagonists are not terribly taken with the unfamiliar Jewish subcultures they encounter from the Balkans to India, their respect for the Jews of the Land of Israel is nothing short of adulatory. Their responses to most Jewish communities outside of their Yemenite purview frequently lack empathy and convey a sense of estrangement, yet they have an almost intuitive appreciation for the religious, spiritual, and intellectual activity of the Jews of the Holy Land. Direct exposure to the rich life of learning and pious devotion they witness in the communities of Safed and Tiberias propels Mordecai and Abner to an unparalleled degree of self-scrutiny. They become self-consciously aware of distinctions, which leads them to identify perceived markers of difference that set their community apart from the Jews in the Land of Israel. This process yields the most explicit and deliberate Yemenite Jewish self-definitions in *Sefer hamusar*. Their consciousness of disparities—curricular, linguistic, liturgical—is heightened by first-hand contact on their visits to Safed (#6) and Tiberias (#23 and #24) and via the testimony of the learned envoy, Rabbi Abraham Ashkenazi, who comes to the Red Sea port city of Mocha with a shipment of sacred books for sale, on a mission to raise funds for the *yeshivah* of Tiberias.

These fictional narratives unfurl against the historical backdrop of the sixteenth-century spiritual revival and intellectual ferment in the Galilee and a far-reaching renaissance in Talmudic and juridical studies among Ottoman Jews in several lands. Following the Ottoman conquest of Mamlūk Palestine in 1516–1517 with its attendant political and economic transformations, the Galilean city of Safed became a center for the manufacture of silk and wool, attracting large numbers of immigrants skilled in textile production.[1] A formidable group of luminaries gravitated to Safed, many of them drawn to the study not only of halakhah but also of kabbalah in a setting known for its ancient

1 See Avitsur, "Safed—Center of the Manufacture of Woven Woolens in the Fifteenth Century." Ottoman administrative registers record that between 1556 and circa 1566, the population of Safed grew at a rate of 25%; see Cohen and Lewis, *Population and Revenue in the Towns of Palestine in the Sixteenth Century*, 21.

 | DOI:10.1163/9789004733787_005

lore and nearby graves of mystics and rabbis of the talmudic period, as well as the cave at Mount Meron where Shimon bar Yoḥai was believed to have composed the *Zohar*. Joseph Karo completed his monumental legal code, the *Shulḥan ʿarukh*, in Safed in 1559. Though Safed's efflorescence lasted less than three quarters of a century, followed by a rapid decline due to economic and political changes as well as natural disasters and plagues, the immense impact of its cultural creativity was felt across the Jewish world.[2] Alḍāhirī's protagonists depict Safed in its heyday, evoking its numinous aura ("for behold, the *Shekhinah* dwelt in its midst") and an idealized spiritual landscape that accords well with the tendency to mythologize the city already in the 16th century.[3] Though they know that Safed boasts the most illustrious names of the day—Rabbi Joseph Karo (d. 1575), Rabbi Moses di Trani (d. 1580), and the renowned kabbalist, Rabbi Moses Cordovero (d. 1570)[4]—they do not mention Karo's formidably influential legal works, the *Beit Yosef* (1551–1559) and *Shulḥan ʿarukh* (1555–1559; 1st printed edition 1565), his rivalry with di Trani for rabbinic leadership of the city, or his visionary mysticism.[5] But, at the same time, they are positively transfixed by Safed's ethos of Talmud study even though they also praise the city's scholars for their kabbalistic knowledge. Their emphasis on Talmudic mastery as the focal point of the city's identity would seem to

2 The scholarship on Safed is extensive. See, e.g.: Schechter, "Safed in the Sixteenth Century"; Wolfson, "Asceticism, Mysticism, and Messianism: A Reappraisal of Schechter's Portrait of Sixteenth-Century Safed"; Weinstein, *Joseph Karo and Shaping* [*sic*] *of Modern Jewish Law*, 121–139; Fine, *Physician of the Soul, Healer of the Cosmos: Isaac Luria and his Kabbalistic Fellowship*; idem, "Pietistic Customs from Safed"; and Werblowsky, "The Safed Revival and its Aftermath." See also Chapter Six below.

3 In point of fact, Eli Yassif includes Alḍāhirī's description among the "ideal depictions which were major factors in establishing the myth of Safed"; see his "Shevarim geluḥei zaqan" and *The Legend of Safed*, 13–15.

4 The three scholars are named in *Sefer hamusar*, #25, p. 287, lines 40–42.

5 This is not to suggest that Alḍāhirī was unfamiliar with Karo's works: a poem praising the *Beit yosef* "upon its arrival in Yemen" is included in his *dīwān* in ms. Guenzburg 1306, and in his comments on Ex. 22 in *Ṣeidah la-derekh*, Alḍāhirī cites "ha-gaon rabbi yosef" on *Tur, Even haʿezer, siman* 66. For the text of the poem, "Hoy nirdamim ʿuru, ʿuru," see Ratzaby, "Rabbi yosef karo vihudei teiman," 86–87. The *Beit yosef* was published during Karo's lifetime; the first two volumes in Venice, 1551 and Sabbioneta, 1553, prior to the forcible closure of the Venetian Hebrew printing industry at the time of the 1553 burning of the Talmud; the last two volumes in Sabbioneta, 1558 and Cremona, 1559. Gaimani speculates that the first editions of the *Beit yosef* and *Shulḥan ʿarukh* reached Yemen via rabbinic emissaries or Jewish merchants not long after they began to circulate in print and that Alḍāhirī himself may have had a hand in their transmission; see Gaimani, "The Penetration of Rabbi Yosef Karo's Literary-Halakhic Work to Yemen." On the dispute between Karo and di Trani, see Dimitrovsky, "Vikuaḥ sheʿavar bein maran yosef karo ve-ha-mabit."

bear out Assaf Tamari's recent revision of received historiography, which had always identified Safed as "the city of kabbalists." In re-evaluating Safed's status as center versus periphery, Tamari argues that the claims made for Safed's preeminence during its period of efflorescence were "primarily an expression (and a project) of the Halakhic élite, and of R. Joseph Karo in particular," rather than of its kabbalists.[6] Still, in broad terms, Alḍāhirī's protagonists express the highest regard for the nascent print culture and imposing halakhic, exegetical, and kabbalistic learning of Palestinian Jewry, both its scholarly élites and general population.[7] This unqualified admiration leads to a harsh self-critique coupled with an apology for Yemenite Jewish deficiencies in precisely those areas in which the Jews of the Holy Land excel. Nevertheless, the protagonists and their interlocutors also identify circumscribed areas of excellence as the unique preserve of Yemenite Jewry. If their dismissal of other Jewish subcultures in the East perpetuates a literary topos familiar from the *Taḥkemoni*, the characters' communal self-critique resulting from their encounter with Palestinian Jewry has no precedent in rhymed prose narratives in the Ḥarizian tradition.

This chapter examines the self-fashioning impulses of Alḍāhirī's identifiably Yemenite characters and the ways in which they define themselves in contradistinction to the Jews of the Land of Israel. Bearing in mind the *maqāma* genre's thin line between fiction and realism and the often enigmatic quality of its rhyming, intertextual prose, the chapter seeks to illuminate how the protagonists perceive themselves as bearers of an ancient and distinctive Jewish subculture and how they are perceived by the non-Yemenite Jews they encounter.[8] It analyzes the ideas they cultivate about themselves and the conventional tropes underlying the collective identity that they construct for their community, suggesting that Mordecai and Abner both respond to and invoke exceptionalist claims. To a striking degree, they appear to internalize the qualities ascribed to them by others. Where they valorize the tremendous talmudic proficiency and kabbalistic creativity of the Jews of the Land of Israel, as well as their embrace of print culture, the protagonists bemoan their own inadequacy in these areas. At the same time, they proudly affirm the superiority of Yemenite Jewry in the realms of rhetorical and poetic virtuosity, a preeminence that

6 See Tamari, "The City of the Kabbalists? Sixteenth Century Safed as Center and as Periphery."

7 On Safed as a hub of these developments, see Shmuelevitz, *The Jews of the Ottoman Empire in the Late Fifteenth and the Sixteenth Centuries*, 11–40 *passim*; Gerber, *Cities of Splendour in the Shaping of Sephardi History*, 99–123; and Levy, *The Sephardim in the Ottoman Empire*, 13–41. Levy notes that during the course of the 16th century, Safed emerged as the third largest Jewish community in the empire and the most important Jewish center in Palestine; see p. 39.

8 Cf. Fishman, "Introduction," *Regional Identities and Cultures of Medieval Jews*.

reflects their peerless mastery of Biblical Hebrew and its grammar and that is readily acknowledged by representatives of the Tiberias community. But even while asserting their linguistic and aesthetic excellence, they are prompted to question the acceptability of their own pronunciation of Hebrew by their encounter with a Jewish subculture known for its patrician airs. Through these vignettes, Alḍāhirī conveys his sense of how others perceived his community. But to what degree are these perceptions informed by Yemenite claims, and to what extent did he subscribe to the self-mythologizing of his personae? The two protagonists do not always agree on these matters, perhaps as a way of externalizing certain authorial ambivalences. Still, highlighting these markers of difference was also a way to address a meta-textual goal. In using points of contact between the two Jewish subcultures as a springboard to define his own community, Alḍāhirī was presumably shaping his stories on the basis of his readers' perceived needs on the assumption that they could recognize themselves in his narratives. Although the Yemenite self-perceptions generated in these contact zones are simultaneously self-deprecating and self-affirming, they are arguably a means of reinforcing a collective sense of identity among the author's community of readers in the face of political instability at home and new developments elsewhere in the Jewish world that presaged potentially unsettling changes in Yemen as well.

2 Encounters with the Emissary from the Holy Land

Three enigmatically interwoven episodes, #24, #25, and #40, piece together the story of Rabbi Abraham Ashkenazi, an emissary or *shadar* (the Aramaic acronym for *sheluḥa de-rabbanan*, "envoy of the rabbis"), who comes to Yemen from the Land of Israel.[9] Heavily fictionalized, these narratives nevertheless depict an early instance of a historical phenomenon that emerged in the early modern era. Well into the 19th century, rabbinic emissaries were sent to diaspora Jewish communities in an international fundraising campaign for the upkeep of languishing institutions and impoverished Jews in Ottoman Palestine.[10] Two versions of the story (#25, #40) relate that the scholarly envoy

---

9 The acronym can also be construed as *sheluḥa de-raḥmanah*, "messenger of the Compassionate One."

10 See Lehmann, *Emissaries from the Holy Land*; Malkiel, "The Shadar-Host Economy"; and idem, *Strangers in Yemen*, 147–188. On the basis of *Sefer hamusar*, Abraham Yaari identified R. Abraham Ashkenazi as the first known rabbinic emissary to Yemen; see his "Sheliḥim me'ereṣ yisra'el le-teiman" and *Massa'ot ereṣ yisra'el*, 196–221.

arrived in Yemen with a consignment of sacred books. In these two recensions, the focus is not so much on his fund-raising mission for the upkeep of the Tiberias *yeshivah* as on the *shadar's* bookselling quest and the Yemenites' overwhelmingly positive response to it and, more broadly, to the emissary as a representative of Palestinian Jewry. The third version (#24) finds Mordecai and Abner in the holy city of Tiberias, where the head of one of the most illustrious congregations recalls the Yemenite Jews' unusually generous response to Rabbi Abraham's appeal for support. Whereas Mordecai's opening frame to #24 relates that a midlife turn to prayer and repentance impelled him to seek Abner in Tiberias just before Rosh Hashanah, and his preface to #40 relates that he traveled to Yemen where he encountered the scholarly Rabbi Abraham Ashkenazi laden with books, #25 has no opening itinerary, is set neither in Yemen or Tiberias, and is told as a flashback. Mordecai recounts that Abner had told him that while he was imprisoned by the Muslim authorities in his native land, he heard that a learned Jew had come to the Red Sea port city of Mocha with a large shipment of sacred books. The envoy, identified only as "our exalted teacher, Rabbi Abraham," arrived by boat and was anxious to sell the volumes at cost so as not to derive any improper benefit "from the honor of the Torah." He sought to disseminate religious knowledge (*le-harbiṣ torah*) and, happily, his books spread throughout Yemen.[11] Those not acquired by Jewish communities across the land made their way to the towers where Abner and the other Ṣanaʿānī Jews were incarcerated. Abner was pleased that his fellow detainees were eager to purchase the texts, and he encouraged them to do so until they had no resources left to acquire the remaining volumes.[12] He then sent an elegant letter of praise to the sage purveyor of texts, whose introductory accolades are followed by a request for help in obtaining specific titles. Abner boasted to Mordecai that the missive was unequaled in its artistic and graceful use of language:

> It speaks in the sacred tongue and conveys words of wisdom. It is fragrant with myrrh and richly embroidered, encrusted with gems of praise for the … scholar whom the Lord has sent and endowed with His spirit …. All who

11 In the final three decades of the 19th century, both the orientalist Joseph Halévy and the forger (and apostate) Moshe Wilhelm Shapira posed as rabbinic emissaries in order to entice Yemenite Jews to part with valuable manuscripts in their possession, but such intentions are never imputed to the *shadar* in *Sefer hamusar*; on the deceptions of Halévy and Shapira see Gerber, *Ourselves Or Our Holy Books?*, 56–58, 139–145 and *passim*.

12 Unconcerned with verisimilitude, the narrator does not attempt to explain how the prisoners could have made such outlays, given the extreme privations of their incarceration as described in several of Abner's poems (and Alḍāhirī's Introduction).

> see it covet it ... for its supreme eloquence and adornment and pearls; there is none that can compare ....

These extravagant vaunts dovetail with the claim of Yemenite superiority in poetry, a recurrent leitmotif throughout these three episodes of cultural contact and contrast. But Abner's crowing also comments metapoetically on his epistle, whose opening is composed in the distinctively ornamental style of medieval Hebrew and Judeo-Arabic epistolary and encomiastic writing, intended to be read out in public.[13] By evoking its fragrance, embroidery, pearls and gems of praise—exquisite qualities that please all the senses—Abner both alludes to the letter's ornate and finely turned poetic language and construes its words as treasures bestowed on its recipient. Weaving a chain of florid honorifics and colored throughout by a highly deferential tone, the missive is set squarely in the tradition of the Hebrew panegyric, a genre that medieval Jewish authors regularly described as an offering or gift to their addressees and that has accordingly been discussed from the perspective of the Maussian theory of cyclical gift exchange.[14] Alongside the transactional exchange of money for books, Abner highlights a parallel economy of immaterial goods by proffering the priceless product of his artistry as reciprocation for the *shadar*'s precious gift of wisdom. Layer upon layer of choice scriptural encomia, in an unbroken chain of rhymes, build to a crescendo before the epistle at last names its addressee, vividly evoked as a life-giving fruit tree:

> To the font of wisdom and the fortress of faith, who does his Maker's will with all his means and most precious possessions; who illuminates our darkness and satisfies us with good things; crown of the saintly and home of kind deeds; glory of the pious; great among the Jews; splendid ornament, who stands among the myrtles (Zech. 1:8), and leads the many—evil and good—to righteousness .... His action has enlightened us ... particularly in the land of Yemen .... He is a tree pleasing to the sight ... planted in the Mocha region; every wise man awaits its fruit; its boughs were sent out through all the districts of Yemen; a delightful sapling in whose shade we may dwell; we shall eat the fruit of his works. How goodly are his tents; his rivers are rivers of honey; a wise man unpar-

---

13 See Worman, "Forms of Address in Genizah Letters," and Goitein, *A Mediterranean Society* 5:230 (openings of letters), 254–272 (rank and honorifics), and 430–431 (honorific epithets for scholars). See also Arazi et al., "Risāla," esp. sec. VII: "The Risāla in Judaeo-Arabic."

14 See Decter, *Dominion Built of Praise*, 67–89 and Malkiel, *Strangers in Yemen*, 20 and *passim*.

> alleled in his generation, happy are they who walk in his light: our exalted, wise teacher, Rabbi Abraham, may God guard him and grant him long life ....[15]

Abner goes on to lament his own incarceration, which prevents him from meeting his esteemed addressee and drawing from the wells of his wisdom. He tells the sage that in his youth, his wanderings took him to India, Iraq, Syria, the Land of Israel (including the four holy cities of Safed, Tiberias, Jerusalem, and Hebron), Egypt, and Ethiopia before he returned to Ṣanaʿā, where he was imprisoned by the Muslims, a fate that he attributes to the sin of having abandoned the Holy Land. He then turns to the crux of his letter. He informs Rabbi Abraham that he sailed home from the Land of Israel with a few precious books, but some of them were lost to storms at sea. He asks the learned envoy to help him restore his lost library by selling him works he has brought to Yemen: the Mishnah with the commentaries of Rabbi Obadiah of Bertinoro or Maimonides; Abudarham's commentary on the prayerbook; "or perhaps you have tractates of the Talmud, even though, for my sins, I am an ignorant boor." Unsettled by his confessed lack of talmudic literacy, Abner then straightaway indicates that Mishnah study would "console my despondent soul" and asks that the *shadar* obtain a copy for him on his travels if he does not have one to hand. He inquires how long the esteemed guest will stay in Yemen, expressing a fervent wish that he may be freed from prison in time to pay his respects in person, and concludes the letter with suitable flourishes.

Throughout the episode, the coveted texts are referred to as *sifrei qodesh*, without any specification of their material form or manner of textual production. The designation *sefer* was used interchangeably for manuscripts and printed books, just as in the Islamic world until the 19th-century advent of Arabic printing, *kitāb* designated a manuscript book.[16] At some point in their dialectal development, Yemenite Jews reserved the term *sefer* for Torah scrolls while other books came to be called *ḥefeṣ* ('[desirable] item,' 'article,' 'object'). In rabbinic and geonic literature, *ḥefṣah* was "a sacred object held in the hand

15 *Sefer hamusar*, p. 286; for the scriptural sources of the intertexts, see Ratzaby's annotation ad loc. There is a suggestion here that the books were too numerous and cumbersome for Rabbi Abraham to transport across Yemen's difficult terrain, so he stationed himself in the port of Mocha and sent out notices to the Jews living in various districts. Once he sold them off, he would have had more mobility for fundraising purposes.

16 In early Islam, the term *kitāb* had a broad range of application; see Schoeler, *The Genesis of Literature in Islam*, p. 21: "The Arabic word *kitāb* denotes all forms of writing, from notes and drafts to contracts, from epigraphic inscriptions to books proper." On the application of the term *al-kitāb* to the Qurʾān, see ibid., 30–39.

at the delivery of an oath."[17] In Yemenite usage, this initially referred to a Torah scroll but subsequently came to designate any sacred book.[18] And in 19th- and 20th-century Yemenite sources, *ḥefeṣ* commonly refers to occult books, so a *baʿal ḥefeṣ* is one who consults such a manual to heal the sick, e.g.[19] But it would seem that, in *Sefer ha-musar*, the emissary's shipment as well as the requested titles are works circulating in print, brought to press by Italian and Ottoman Jewish print houses.

After the expulsion of the Jews from the Iberian Peninsula, Italy became the primary center of Hebrew printing in the Mediterranean world; the printing of Hebrew books had begun in the cities of Italy around 1470, and print houses were established in Spain and Portugal in the 1480's and 1490's. The proliferation of Hebrew printing in the Ottoman Empire was swift, and at the end of 1493, the first Hebrew book was produced in Istanbul, using movable type brought by Iberian refugee printers. Together with Salonica, Istanbul was the center of Hebrew book production in the Ottoman Empire during the 16th century.[20] The works Abner requests were all printed early or mid-century: the commentary of Obadiah of Bertinoro (c. 1450–1509), printed in Venice in 1548–1549, rapidly became the most widely consulted across the Jewish world and was printed in almost all subsequent editions of the Mishnah.[21] A panegyric in Chapter 18 of *Sefer hamusar* calls it the most definitive of all Mishnah commentaries.[22] Composed in Seville in 1340, David ben Joseph Abudarham's liturgical commentary was first printed in Lisbon during the incunable period (1489/90). Demand for the work is evident from its reprinting in

17 See Jastrow, *Dictionary*, 492b, s.v. חפצא.

18 See Gluska, "Dialectal Elements in the Hebrew Language of the Yemenite Jews," 34–35.

19 See: Ratzaby, *Bemʿagloth Temān*, 86; idem, "ʿIyyunim be-hitpatḥut maḥzor-teiman," 99; idem, *Oṣar leshon ha-qodesh she-livnei teiman*, 101b; Fogel, "'They Have Countless Books of This Craft': Folklore and Folkloristics of Yemeni Jewish Amulets"; Qāfiḥ, *Halikhot teiman*, 353–364; and Levi, *Holekh tamim*, 39.

20 See Schrijver, "The Transmission of Jewish Knowledge through MSS and Printed Books"; Hacker, "Authors, Readers, and Printers of Sixteenth-Century Hebrew Books in the Ottoman Empire"; and Offenberg, "The Printing History of the Constantinople Hebrew Incunable of 1493."

21 See Elon, *Jewish Law*, 3:1108; Strack and Stemberger, *Introduction to the Talmud and Midrash*, 147; and Amnon Raz-Krakotzkin, "Persecution and the Art of Printing," 101. Abner's request implies the work was already known in Yemen soon after its initial publication; see *Sefer hamusar*, 213, n. 24. Ratzaby writes that when the printed version began circulating in Yemen, it was accepted alongside Maimonides' Mishnah commentary; see *Bemʿagloth Temān*, 70.

22 *Sefer hamusar*, 214–215.

Istanbul (1513–1514), Fez (1516), and Venice (1546 and 1566).[23] The early publishing history of the Talmud is complicated; it includes twenty-three tractates (some in more than one edition) published by the Soncino family beginning in 1483/84; a few incunable tractates printed in Spain and Portugal prior to the expulsion; some early 16th-century tractates printed in Salonica and Constantinople; and Daniel Bomberg's multiple editions, including his monumental complete Talmud, printed in Venice (1519/20–1523).[24] Abner's request for the print version of the Mishnah with Maimonides' commentary is presumably a sign of his bibliophilia: the Naples 1492 *editio princeps* of the Mishnah published by Joshua Soncino is accompanied by Maimonides' commentary in a composite Hebrew translation rather than the original Judeo-Arabic in which Yemenite Jews had studied it for centuries.[25] The Judeo-Arabic text was not published until 1655 and even then not in full; the Oxford orientalist and bibliophile Edward Pococke included selections from Maimonides' commentary with his Latin translation.[26]

23 See Reif, *Judaism and Hebrew Prayer*, 204; Heller, "A Fleeting Moment, A Short-Lived Press: Hebrew Printing in Sixteenth Century Fez"; and the *Footprints: Jewish Books Through Time and Place* database, s.v. Abudarham. At least 140 Hebrew books were printed in the incunable period by approximately 40 presses in Italy, Spain, and Portugal, and one in Turkey; see Schrijver, "The Transmission of Jewish Knowledge through MSS and Printed Books."

24 See: Piattelli, "New Documents Concerning Bomberg's Printing of the Talmud"; Heller, "Designing the Talmud: The Origins of the Printed Talmudic Page"; idem, *Printing the Talmud: a History of the Earliest Printed Editions of the Talmud*; and Rosenthal, "Daniel Bomberg and His Talmud Editions."

25 For the list of medieval translators Soncino drew upon, see the online British Library catalogue, shelfmark Asia, Pacific & Africa c.50.e.6. Yemenite Jews held Maimonides' Commentary on the Mishnah in the highest regard and typically studied it in the predawn hours, prior to reciting morning prayers. Many of the Yemenite ms. copies of the work in the British Library and the Bodleian date from the 13th–16th centuries. A Judeo-Arabic commentary on Maimonides' Introduction to the work in the Hebrew translation of Alḥarizi is ascribed to Moses al-Balīda (Yemen, early 15th century) in BL ms. Or. 2746. See Margoliouth, *Catalogue of the Hebrew and Samaritan Manuscripts in the British Museum* III:527 and IV:51.

26 See Williams, "Bringing Maimonides to Oxford: Edward Pococke, the Mishnah, and the *Porta Mosis*." See also Kellner, *Dogma in Medieval Jewish Thought*, 218–219. Yosef Qāfiḥ, who published the Judeo-Arabic text from Yemenite mss. with his own Hebrew translation, wrote that from the latter part of the 18th century, there had been no complete copy of all six orders of the Mishnah with Maimonides' Arabic commentary in Yemen. Around 1890, his grandfather began to scour every settlement where Yemenite Jews lived for individual leaves and fragments and copied every bit of the text that he found, until he had assembled four complete orders. He established a weekly study session and encouraged the participants to copy the text for themselves so that mss. proliferated at the end of the 19th century. Following his grandfather's death, Qāfiḥ completed the monumental

Whether intentionally or due to the work's piecemeal composition and imperfect editing, Alḍāhirī returns to Abner's epistolary offerings in the two other accounts of the *shadar*'s visit, each time with a slightly different twist. In the 40th *maqāma*, Abner again addresses the *shadar*; in the 24th he praises the sages of Tiberias at whose behest Rabbi Abraham traveled to Yemen. Though the three versions do not really entertain different perspectives and are hardly Rashomon-like, each adds details not found in the others. The 40th *maqāma* is the only one that identifies the envoy by his full name and refers explicitly to his country of origin. In this version, Rabbi Abraham is also given a voice, and he becomes a conduit for the stereotypical representations of Yemenite and Palestinian Jews that pervade these chapters.[27] Here Mordecai relates that poverty and distress drove him to wander throughout Yemen in search of relief. As luck would have it, he came to a place where he encountered an elderly man of intelligent mien who excelled in all types of learning and came from a distant land. Set out before him were all sorts of religious texts. Intrigued, Mordecai inquired about him of the locals. They told him,

> His name is Rabbi Abraham, son of the esteemed Rabbi Isaac Ashkenazi, who has come from the land of the Amorites and the Perizzites with many books—*gemara* and important commentaries. Friends pay heed to his great learning: he is skilled at intensive Talmud study and subtle dialectics in every instance of legal reasoning (*yode'a 'iyyun u-filpul be-khol sevara/ le-tanna ve'amora*), and he issues decisive responsa to those who consult him (*ve-hu meshiv teshuvah niṣaḥat le-khol sho'alav*) .... All who hear of his wisdom and valiant deeds seek his well-being.

Mordecai sat down in awe opposite the sage who, modest and humble, drew him to his side with pleasant words until they were "nearly friends." In order to lighten his companion's burden, Mordecai perused each of the many letters inquiring after the rabbi's welfare that had arrived from every corner of Yemen. Some sang his praises; others sought to buy books at great expense. But, Mordecai observed, "there was not much eloquent language in them" (*lo' haya va-hem*

undertaking. The study group had found disparities between the printed Hebrew translation and the Arabic original, and, after settling in Israel, Qāfiḥ undertook to produce new Hebrew translations of all Maimonides' Arabic texts and to publish them together with the originals. See Moses b. Maimon, *Mishnah 'im peirush rabbeinu moshe ben maimon*, ed. and trans. Qāfiḥ, 1:5–21.

27 See *Sefer hamusar*, 423–430.

kol kakh ṣaḥut lashon). Puzzled by the pedestrian nature of the notes he has received, the rabbi—whose speech is described as fluent and elegant—asks,

> Have I not heard that the language of the Jews of Yemen is pure and clear, pleasing to the ear, derived entirely from Scripture? And that their accomplishments in the sacred tongue are mighty, so that they say, "By our tongues we shall prevail" (Ps. 12:5)? Why, then, are these notes bereft of wisdom, "shriveled, thin, and scorched by the east wind"? (Gen. 41:23).

Mordecai readily concedes that the criticism is justified but informs the sage that "the blessed Lord has left a remnant for Yemen" in the person of an unusual individual who knows the rules of grammar exceedingly well, is expert in *halakhot* and *aggadot*, and has "ten shares" of excellence in poetry. Unfortunately, he is locked in the Ishmaelites' tower. But were he to hear of the esteemed rabbi's arrival, he would undoubtedly send a fine communication.

After a few days, a highly ornamented letter arrives from Abner ben Ḥeleq the Yemenite. Just as he did in the twenty-fifth *maqāma*, Abner addresses himself to "the font of wisdom and the fortress of faith," but the accolades are otherwise not identically phrased. In this version, as anticipated by Mordecai's frame, the emphasis is on the *shadar*'s incisive textual skills. Abner lavishes praise on the rabbi, who has "built his chambers in the heavenly heights of wisdom"; whose every word is precious; who has exiled himself to the ends of the earth in order to spread knowledge of the Torah; and whose erudition in Scripture, Mishnah, and Talmud is vast due to assiduous study in the *yeshivot* of the Land of Israel. With an intimation of esoteric wisdom, he lauds the emissary's ability to penetrate the secrets of the Torah, and singles out his expertise in plumbing the depths of Gersonides' philosophical *magnum opus*, *Wars of the Lord*.[28] Like Mordecai, he celebrates the rabbi's capacity to "gather pearls of the *gemara*" through intensive study (*ʿiyyun*) and logical inference (*sevara*), and to provide a rationale even for those divine commandments that seem arbitrary.[29]

---

28 Levi ben Gershom (1288–1344) was a prolific Provençal Bible commentator, Talmudist, philosopher, mathematician, and astronomer. Completed in 1329, *The Wars of the Lord* was first printed in Riva di Trento in 1560. See Levi Ben Gershom, *The Wars of the Lord*, 1:3–67.

29 On *sevara*, see Elon, *Jewish Law*, 2:987–1014. On *ʿiyyun* see Boyarin, *A Traveling Homeland: The Babylonian Talmud as Diaspora* and idem, *Haʿiyyun ha-sefaradi*. Medieval Andalusian Jewish thinkers, notably Abraham Ibn Ezra and Moses Maimonides, championed the idea that even seemingly arbitrary commandments are the products of divine wisdom and have a purpose (*ṭaʿamei ha-miṣvot*) and that to suppose otherwise would be blasphemous; see Moses b. Maimon, *Sefer moreh ha-nevukhim* 3:26–50; Pines trans., *The Guide of the Per-*

He extols his addressee for the sacrifice he has made in abandoning his home for Yemen, "the most bitter of all the exiles." He then sends copious greetings to "His Honor, the sage, Rabbi Abraham, son of the esteemed Rabbi Isaac Ashkenazi."

Following this effusive preface, Abner launches into an apology for the downtrodden Jews of Yemen, whose dire circumstances due to Yemeni Muslim mistreatment prevent them from receiving the visitor with the acclaim and respect that befits him, unlike the vibrant Ottoman Jewish communities of "Salonica, Istanbul and Cairo," who unquestionably gave him a proper reception on his fund-raising mission. Tellingly, he highlights the centrality of *yeshivot* to rabbinic learning in the Franco-German and Ottoman realms:

> Wispy hyssop that pokes through cracks in the wall cannot compare with the mighty cedar; those who live in unwalled towns are no match for the dwellers of large, fortified cities. For Yemen and its people are wretched and humiliated, poor and miserable. Their wisdom is meager, their means are dwindling, and an evil kingdom (*malkhut zadon*) rules over them .... Where shall wisdom be found, if not in Ashkenaz, Riphath and Togarmah, whose sons all brandish the sword of Torah; whose every city has a *yeshivah* ... where they come at break of day to hear those who seek the texts' mysteries.[30]

Such textual diligence was particularly evident to Abner in Safed, the scholars of whose *yeshivot* impressed him with their immense Talmudic erudition. He ascribes the Yemenites' scholarly and mannerly shortcomings to the terrible upheaval to which they have been subjected and implores Rabbi Abraham to help rejuvenate them by replacing their illness, ignorance, and impoverishment with the health, wisdom, wealth, and strength of the Safed scholars. Closing with a self-abasing expression of regret for having troubled the saintly rabbi, and for his own lack of learning resulting from the harsh conditions of his existence—oppressive decrees, taxes, and imprisonment—Abner again expresses his wish that they might meet face to face. To the letter he appends

---

plexed 2:506–617; Twersky, *Introduction to the Code of Maimonides*, 373–459 *passim*; *Yesod mora* 6:1–2 and 8:1 in Levin ed., *Abraham Ibn Ezra Reader*, 328, 333. See also Langermann, *Yemenite Midrash*, 85–87.

30 In Alḍāhirī's usage, *malkhut zadon* ("an evil kingdom"; cf. Obad. 3 and Mal. 3:15, 19) is a punning allusion to the Zaydīs. Ashkenaz, Riphath and Togarmah are descendants of Gomer in the genealogy in Gen. 10:3. As noted, in his *tafsīr* on this verse, Saadya renders Ashkenaz as *saqāliba* or "Slavs," and Riphath as the Franks, i.e., Germanic tribes. In the 16th century, Togarmah was the standard term for Ottoman Turkey/Anatolia.

a twenty-five line panegyric poem lionizing the learned visitor who has illumined the Yemenites' spiritual darkness. Even more exuberant in its praise for the *shadar* than the preceding epistle, these verses reprise and richly embroider some of its most salient themes. Its reciprocal gift imagery belies an imbalance in cultural capital: Abner crowns the envoy with his poem of praise while the *shadar* is an ornament for the Yemenites due to the magnificent knowledge he brings them, the succor of his responsa, and the books that he brings them.[31] As the verses of exaltation build to their peak, there are seemingly no limits on hyperbole: "Let us go and kneel before our teacher and king" (cf. Ps. 95:6); "... hero of his generation, he very nearly brings about the advent of our Messiah."[32] Though the poem spotlights the *shadar*, it advances the broader cultural stereotypes informing these three chapters.

Resuming his narration, Mordecai now relates that when the sage heard Abner's words, he longed to see him, for his elegant, clear language (*ṣaḥut leshono*) was extraordinary. The rabbi exclaimed,

> Even though in our land there are discerning sages ... before his poems ... all would be speechless. For they cannot compose a poem in this manner .... Would that the day of his sighting would draw near, so that we might taste the sweetness of his eloquent tongue, the pearls of his speech, his flowery rhetoric and poetry. He is perfection in his majesty. (*Ve-niṭʿam meteq leshono ve-ṣaḥuto, u-feninei siḥav u-meliṣotav ve-shiro, ki khalil hu be-hadaro*).

He then sent a letter of reply to Abner, who, three days later, appeared on the outskirts of town. Mordecai, Abner, and Rabbi Abraham Ashkenazi all rejoice in Abner's miraculous release, and Abner exploits the opportunity to ask the sage all of his textual questions pertaining to Mishnah and Talmud. Rejoicing in the rabbi's great wealth of learning, Abner then recites a four-line panegyric for the peerless scholar, who responds with a shower of blessings, culminating in "May you merit to sing of your songs in Zion."[33]

31 There are several intimations that the *shadar*, regarded as a great authority, is sent halakhic questions along with the book requests he receives and that he issues legal decisions in response to these queries; see *Sefer hamusar* #40, pp. 423, l. 9 and p. 428, line 86. For the phrase *pardes netaʿahu ve-heʾekhilanu*, see ibid., line 87.

32 *Sefer hamusar*, pp. 428–429, lines 91 and 103.

33 Ratzaby notes that, into the modern era, Yemenite Jews customarily saluted a singer who had sung sweetly at a gathering with the wish that he might merit to make his voice heard in Zion; see *Sefer hamusar*, p. 430, n. 128.

∴

The portrait of Yemenite Jewry emerging from these *maqāmāt* is painted with exceptionally broad strokes. Leveling out complexities, it portrays an oppressed minority so plagued by poverty and humiliating maltreatment that it has no capacity for the intellectual and spiritual pursuits so highly valued by other Jewish communities in the Ottoman Empire and beyond. Particularly in Talmud study, Yemenite Jews are said to fall short of their coreligionists in other lands, above all in the Land of Israel. But they excel at Hebrew poetry and rhetoric, and are known for the stylistic elegance of their writing and their linguistic purity. In a kind of literary symmetry, the scholars of the Land of Israel are said to have no flair for poetry.[34] There is a distinctly subcultural element implicit in the comparison drawn by the *shadar*: his fellow Jews in the Land of Israel cannot compete with Abner's virtuosic expression in pure Biblical Hebrew because this gift belongs exclusively to Yemenite Jewry. But this is the only advantage he concedes to the Yemenites; fundamentally, he does not contradict Abner's assessment of their intellectual impoverishment due to their subjugation. There is no mention of how the Jews of Yemen come by their expertise in Biblical Hebrew despite its obvious connection to their immersion in Scripture and the Masoretic tradition and their cultivation of midrashic exegesis, Andalusian Hebrew poetry, and grammar. In truth, the protagonists' self-assessment also relies on a highly selective profile of their community and glosses over regional and class differences. It subsumes a multiplicity of regional traditions and dialects under the umbrella term "Yemenite" while projecting the preoccupations of the Ṣanaʿānī religious and intellectual élite, to which Alḍāhirī belonged, as paradigmatic of the subculture as a whole.[35] The profile of Palestinian Jewry advanced here, while somewhat more ramified, is at base reductive as well, and similarly takes the rabbinic and scholarly élite as representative of the greater whole. Though voiced by members of the two different communities, these views of course ultimately issue from Aldahiri's pen. At base, the question is what motivated him to overlook subtler distinc-

34 See also *Sefer hamusar* #24, p. 278, lines 82–83.

35 On the Ṣanaʿānīs' historical sense of intellectual and genealogical superiority to other Yemenite Jews (despite rifts within the Ṣanaʿā community itself) see, e.g., Anzi, "'Ha'aḥer' ha-yehudi: yehudei ṣanʿāʾ el mul ha-qehillot ha'aḥerot be-teiman"; idem, *The Ṣanʿāʾnīs*, 207–240 *passim*; and Bar-Maoz, "Social Tension Between the Ṣanaʿā Community and Other Communities," 55–61. The historiography of Yemenite Jewry has traditionally been "Ṣanaʿā-centric"; only recently have authors from other communities in Yemen begun to emphasize their distinctiveness and to voice resentment at the way they have been misrepresented by the Ṣanaʿānī hegemony; see Bar-Maoz, ibid., pp. 60–61.

tions and commonalities in favor of oversimplified representations that create the illusion of a binary opposition between the two Jewish subcultures when the reality was much more nuanced.

3 Talmud Study in the Land of Israel

Like their meetings with the emissary in Yemen, the protagonists' first-hand encounters with the *yeshivot* in the Land of Israel elicit unconditional reverence for these institutions and their scholars' diligence, studiousness, and formidable Talmudic knowledge: "How precious are the men of the *yeshivot*," Abner exclaims of Safed in his letter to the *shadar*; "to their palates, the Talmud is sweeter than honey."[36] In the sixth *maqāma*, Mordecai visits the city, which is home to no fewer than eighteen *yeshivot*. He, too, professes hyperbolic, if sincere, admiration for the moral integrity, piety, and profound religious learning of its impressive scholarly community. "There I saw the light of the Torah … they prevailed over all the communities … there was not one ignoramus among them."[37] In the face of so many fine Talmudic minds, he feels woefully incompetent. (Ironically, the lesson he attends in the *yeshivah* of "the great luminary, Rabbi Joseph Karo" is an exposition of the Aristotelian theory of the faculties of the soul, presented by a star student who, of course, turns out to be Abner.) In Tiberias, too, Mordecai laments his inadequacy and ignorance vis-à-vis the men of the *yeshivah* there,

> elders and respected men, the glory of the Jews, masters of Scripture and Mishnah, some of whom were masters of Talmud and legal reasoning, and some of whom were masters of theoretical kabbalah, and some of whom were the seal of perfection [commanded all these disciplines; cf. Ez. 28:12].[38]

Likewise, Abner, in his letter to Tiberias, extols the city's luminaries, "the valiant in Torah, … who excel at explaining enigmatic passages; sages of the Talmud and of *sevara* in Mishnah and *gemara*, as well as kabbalah." It is perhaps no coincidence that of all the communal institutions in Tiberias, it is the *yeshivah*—the hub of such intense intellectual and spiritual activity—that occasions the rabbinic fundraiser's visit to Yemen.

---

36 *Sefer hamusar*, #40, p. 426, lines 51–52.

37 *Sefer hamusar*, #6, p. 116, lines 1–8.

38 *Sefer hamusar*, #23, p. 261, lines 7–12.

While many of the Galilean scholars are steeped in kabbalistic learning as well as rabbinics, the touchstone in all of these encounters is clearly Talmudic expertise. Abner expresses no self-consciousness when asking the *shadar* for copies of the Mishnah with the commentaries of Obadiah of Bertinoro or Maimonides, or for Abudarham's commentary on the prayer book. Only when he requests tractates of the Talmud does he feel compelled to apologize for his inability to navigate the work's complex halakhic argumentation. (Note that he does not request kabbalistic titles from the *shadar* but does acquire them on his own.) Meanwhile, he showers praise on the learned rabbi, whose erudition and skill at intensive talmudic investigation (*'iyyun*), subtle dialectics (*pilpul*), and logical inference (*sevara*) are ascribed to punctilious study in the *yeshivot* of the Land of Israel, whose scholarly community dwarfs all others in its piety and profound learning. In his letter to Rabbi Abraham in the 40th *maqāma*, extensive *yeshivah* study effectively becomes a shorthand for the sharpening of the intellect that leads to mastery of rabbinic culture and the inculcation of *derekh ereṣ*, or decorous behavior and consideration for others. As a generator of "wisdom," the *yeshivah* is portrayed as an institution whose presence in a given land guarantees proper morals and religious etiquette among the Jews of that region. Hence the Yemenites' alleged failure to receive the *shadar* as befits his station is attributed not only to their wretchedness but also to the absence of *yeshivot* from their midst, a deficit that is itself the product of the extreme economic and political privations imposed upon them. Nevertheless, there is a certain delectable irony in the fact that Abner's apology for his own lack of scholarly attainment interweaves several allusions to Talmudic passages.[39] One wonders whether Alḍāhirī is having fun at his hero's expense or whether this is a show of good will on Abner's part; an attempt to communicate with the rabbi in his own scholarly idiom as a way of cementing the bond between them. Or perhaps the author is turning the stereotype on its head, subtly undercutting the claim that Yemenite Jews are devoid of Talmudic learning since Abner's literacy in rabbinics ultimately derives from Alḍāhirī's own agility in summoning up these rhymed intertexts. In the same *maqāma* (#40), Mordecai praises Abner to the *shadar* as an exceptional individual with whom God has graced Yemen, an expert in *halakhot* and *aggadot* who also knows the rules of grammar exceedingly well and has "ten shares of excellence in poetry."[40] While Abner's expertise in *halakhot* may well lie in the practical application of the law, rather than

39 #40, p. 426, lines 57–60. Abner's poem in praise of the Talmud in #18 is hardly the work of someone unpracticed in Talmud study.

40 #40, p. 424, lines 19–21.

in dialectics, his command of poetry, rhetoric, and grammar, liturgy, exegesis, philosophy and kabbalah, together with his knowledge of books in these fields, suggest a broad *paideia* that challenges the more circumscribed picture of Yemenite Jewish learning presented here.

Why is Talmudic expertise, acquired through study in a *yeshivah*, taken as the measure of a community's worth? Was this an age-old assumption among Yemenite Jews, whose ties with the Babylonian center had been quite significant during the talmudic and geonic eras? Or was it an imported notion, emanating from the flourishing Ottoman *yeshivot* in Istanbul, Salonica, and Safed, whose methods and curricular emphases radiated around the eastern Mediterranean basin and beyond? Perhaps, too, it was linked to the dissemination in Yemen, precisely in this period, of Hebrew books reflecting certain assumptions about the cultural function of Talmud study—books brought by a *shadar* who himself came from a cultural milieu that prized the cultivation of close Talmudic reading and intricate interpretation. In these chapters of *Sefer hamusar*, the recurrent rhyming pair *gemara/sevara* is more than a mere stylistic flourish; the aural repetition underscores the idea that dialectical deliberation and logical inference are at the heart of Talmud study. Clearly, the protagonists (and their author) are aware that other Jewish subcultures placed supreme value on immersion in 'the sea of the Talmud' and in subtle halakhic reasoning. In the earlier Middle Ages, the Franco-German Ashkenazi communities had acquired a reputation for Talmudism, halakhic expertise and mastery of rabbinic scholarship to the exclusion of most other disciplines, but Alḍāhirī is evidently concerned with newly invigorated approaches in the Ottoman cultural orbit.[41] Though he does not provide any clues to his precise understanding of the technical terms *'iyyun*, *sevara*, and *pilpul* (lit., peppering; viz. sharp-witted analysis), he may have been aware in a general way that they had taken on new methodological specificity with the revival of Talmudic learning on Spanish soil in the fifteenth century, which was transplanted to the Ottoman centers post-expulsion.[42]

---

41 See Twersky, "Talmudists, Philosophers, Kabbalists: The Quest for Spirituality in the Sixteenth Century."

42 See Boyarin, *A Traveling Homeland*. Boyarin writes that, by infusing its methods with Aristotelian logic, Rabbi Isaac Kanpanton (d. 1463, Castile) revitalized talmudic learning in a way that made it attractive to the Iberian Jewish intelligentsia after nearly a century during which it had not been highly regarded. The term *'iyyun*, ("speculation"), now signified close logical talmudic study. Kanpanton's method of interpreting the Talmud was transplanted by his disciples to the Ottoman Empire, where it became the dominant method of study and interpretation for two centuries. Boyarin demonstrates that *pilpul*, which in other cultural milieus has been denigrated as hairsplitting logic and casuistry, was—as

Given that *Sefer hamusar* straddles the boundaries between realism and fiction, it is worth asking how the Yemenites' self-confessed deficiency in subtle Talmudic argumentation aligns with historical evidence. The prevailing view has long been that, since the Middle Ages, Yemenite Jews favored the cultivation of grammar, mesorah, biblical exegesis, liturgy, mishnah, and midrash over elaborate, minutely detailed halakhic inquiry, and that in matters of halakhah they relied on codes and digests for the practical application of the law, *halakhah le-maʿaseh*. From the mid-19th century, outside observers maintained that Yemenite Jews occupied themselves little, if at all, with Talmud study. On his visit as an emissary of the Jerusalem Ashkenazi community, Jacob Sapir (1822–1885) went so far as to claim that the Talmud was not found in Yemen and that the Yemenites determined their laws and customs solely on the basis of Maimonides' 12th-century legal code. While he encountered learned rabbis who were exceptions to the rule, like Mori Joseph ben Saadya of Jirwāḥ, a mountain village in the Ḥarāz region about halfway from the coast to Ṣanaʿā, the Lithuanian-born Sapir reported that,

> most of the Jews of this land are not devoid of Torah. They are expert in Scripture, and are knowledgeable in *halakhot* and *aggadot*; they recite the Zohar, and occupy themselves with kabbalah and numerology. But of Talmudic study and immersion in the writings of legal decisors (*poseqim*) there is very little. One in a thousand knows the form of the Talmud, because it is not found in this land .... Printed books are dear in this land, because they are only seldom imported, but the scribal art is cheap .... Their principal study is of Maimonides' *Yad* [*Mishneh Torah*], and they determine their laws and customs solely according to Maimonides ....[43]

In the continuation, Sapir relates that "they say that prior to Maimonides, they made their legal rulings solely on the basis of the Talmud and their tradition," suggesting that in the geonic period and early Middle Ages, Yemenite Jews were

---

conceived by its 15th- and 16th-century Sephardi practitioners—grounded in philosophical interpretation and notes that the term was used interchangeably with *ʿiyyun*. See also Boyarin, "'Pilpul': The Logic of Commentary"; idem, *Haʿiyyun ha-sefaradi*; Bentov, "Methods of Study of Talmud in the Yeshivot of Salonica and Turkey After the Expulsion from Spain" (re. *pilpul* see pp. 46–47); Havlin, "On Classifications of *Pilpul*"; Dimitrovsky, "'Al derekh ha-pilpul"; and Yahalom, "The *Pilpul* Method of Talmudic Study: Earliest Evidence." For Western and Eastern European critiques of *pilpul* through the ages, see Rappel, *Ha-vikkuaḥ ʿal ha-pilpul*.

43 See Sapir, *Even Sapir*, 1:53a. See also 50b–51a and Malkiel, *Strangers in Yemen*, 152–153.

conversant with the oral law, and that copies of Talmudic tractates circulated in Yemen.

Yosef Tobi and Noah Gerber trace the claim that very few Jews in Yemen occupied themselves with Talmud study back to Maimonides' epistle to the Sages of Lunel. Sapir, they note, painted a static picture, as though nothing had changed since the twelfth century. This became a stubborn literary topos; the notion was unquestioningly endorsed by late 19th-century Eastern European scholars. Among them was Schneour Sachs (1816–1892), who cited the epistle to the Sages of Lunel in his commendatory preface (*haskamah*) to *Even Sapir*, and commented that, "In the lands of the East, things do not change with the changing of the times."[44] Sachs contended that, had Maimonides not sent them his *Mishneh Torah*, the Yemenites would have lost faith and been cut off from Torah ("God forbid"), seeing as their knowledge of Talmud was so minimal, and what familiarity they had was mostly with the *aggadic* or narrative, non-legal portions. The forger Moses Shapira (c. 1830–1884), in his account of his 1879 visit to Yemen in search of manuscripts, parroted these assertions in his stilted English:

> They do learn only Mishnah and haggadah of all the Talmudical books. I spent a good deal of time in searching if I may not find any thing of a sign if they ever had in the old times M.S.S. of the Talmud but, I could discover no symptom ....[45]

Tobi cites a further instance of this claim in the 1891 monograph of Abraham Epstein (1841–1918) on the late 9th-century traveler and imposter Eldad Hadani (whom he pegged as likely Yemenite, on account of some strange, non-normative *halakhot* that he promoted). Epstein was taken to task by Adolph Neubauer (1831–1907) for asserting that the Jews of Yemen in late antiquity and the early Middle Ages "were completely ignorant of the Talmud and the works of the Geonim."[46] Neubauer reasoned that if rabbinic emissaries had brought the legal and ritual decisions of the Babylonian *yeshivot* to the Jews of Egypt, Asia Minor, Africa and Rome, surely they had also conveyed the oral law to Yemen. He conceded that while

44 Gerber, *Ourselves Or Our Holy Books?*, 80–82. The *haskamot* following Sapir's introduction to *Even Sapir* Part I have no page numbers; Sachs' endorsement is preceded by three shorter ones.

45 See Fenton, "Moses Shapira's Journey to the Yemen," lxxv.

46 Neubauer, review Abraham Epstein, *Eldad ha-Dani*, p. 542. See also Tobi, *'Al ha-talmud be-teiman*, 7–10.

> it may be true that the early Jews of Yemen never saw a copy of the Talmud, … they would not have stood alone in this deficiency. This bulky compilation could not be procured everywhere, and many countries were unacquainted with it until the tenth century; but that does not prove that [they were ignorant of the oral law].

Neubauer also pointed to several 16th-century Yemenite ms. copies of five Talmudic tractates in the Deinard collection whose rich marginal glosses citing geonic opinions, the late 11th-century *ʿArukh* (talmudic dictionary) of Nathan ben Yeḥiel of Rome, and Maimonides' *Mishneh Torah* implied "that Yemen was once well stocked with important works on all branches of learning."[47] Even Goitein, who translated the above-cited passage from *Even Sapir* in his popular 1947 collection of Yemenite folktales, *From the Land of Sheba*, wrote in his preface to the revised edition of 1973 that

> The study of Talmud, so characteristic for the East-European *shtetl*, was not popular in Yemen; it was left (as originally designed) to a few select scholars.

But in a 1962 piece on Yemenites in Jerusalem and Egypt during the period of Maimonides and his son Abraham Maimuni, Goitein remarked that

> it is important to note that Yemenite sages used to cite the *gemara* verbatim in their homilies, *contra* the mistaken impression of some historians who thought that the Yemenite Jews did not engage in Talmud study.[48]

Gerber notes that, as part of his campaign to rehabilitate the rationalist intellectual legacy of Yemenite Jewry which had been eclipsed by kabbalistic study and liturgical customs, Yiḥye Qāfiḥ (1849–1932) sought out mss. preserving the works of Saadya Gaon and portions of the Maimonidean corpus. But he also

---

47 See Neubauer, "The Literature of the Jews of Yemen," 607–613. These tractates, acquired by the Columbia University library in 1890, were copied in Ṣanaʿā in 1547 by David ben Meʿoded b. Seʿadya b. Yosef al-Dashāl; see Neubauer, ibid. 613–614; Tobi, *ʿAl ha-talmud be-teiman*, p. 12 and n. 19; and Ratzaby, *Bemʿagloth Temān*, 107–108. Nathan ben Yeḥiel (d. 1103) "does not merely define and discuss difficult words in his *Sefer ha-ʿarukh*; he also explains the context of the talmudic *sugya* (pericope) in which they appear, including lengthy citations of the passage in question." See Kanarfogel, "Talmudic Studies."

48 See Goitein, *From the Land of Sheba: Tales of the Jews of Yemen*, 40–42; rev. ed, 19, 58–60, and idem, "Teimanim bi-yerushalayim uve-miṣrayim bi-tequfato shel ha-rambam ve-shel beno rabbi avraham," in Ratzaby and Shivtiel eds., *Harʾel*, 136.

located Yemenite textual witnesses to the Babylonian Talmud, perhaps in order to correct the erroneous impression left by Sapir, that the Yemenites had no expertise in Talmud.[49]

One of the earliest Yemenite halakhic works to survive is an anonymous Judeo-Arabic commentary to Isaac Alfasi's 11th-century *Halakhot* on tractate Ḥullin, dated to the beginning of the 12th century.[50] The corpus of extant works includes a number of commentaries and supercommentaries on Maimonides' celebrated code of law.[51] A preponderance of Hebrew and Judeo-Arabic commentaries as well as instructional manuals on the laws of *sheḥitah* has been explained as an outgrowth of the difficulty of travel between the hundreds of scattered Jewish communities, often separated by great distances and treacherous terrain, which required each city or village to have its own *shoḥet*. Alḍāhirī himself composed a commentary on Maimonides' *Hilkhot sheḥitah*, citations of which are preserved in an 18th-century work by Yiḥye Ṣāliḥ; he also issued a collection of relevant legal decisions in conjunction with the Ṣanaʿā *bet din* of his day entitled *Zot torat ha-behemah*, and composed yet another work on *sheḥitah* in verse.[52] Such secondary literature as there is on the practical orientation of Yemenite halakhic works tends to explicate its emergence purely on the basis of circumstances (religious, economic, and geographic) unique to Yemenite Jewry. But well into the high Middle Ages, a preference for rabbinic works of applied law was characteristic of halakhic scholarship in North Africa and al-Andalus. Talya Fishman notes that

> Ashkenazi scholars of northern Europe placed the study of the Talmud at the center of the rabbinic curriculum, while their counterparts in North Africa and al-Andalus studied eleventh-century talmudic commentaries produced in the region by R. Nisim, R. Hananel, and R. Isaac Alfasi, and, later, the *Mishneh torah*, Maimonides' twelfth-century legal code. Unlike the Talmud, each of these works relayed applied legal decisions (*halakhah le-maʿaseh*).[53]

49 See Gerber, *Ourselves Or Our Holy Books?*, 139–140.

50 See Qāfiḥ ed. and trans., *Ha-rif le-masekhet ḥullin*. For a detailed account of the contents, see Sassoon, *Ohel Dawid*, 2:1081–1084, #1062.

51 Ratzaby, *Bemʿagloth Temān*, 71.

52 Ratzaby, ibid., 72–73; idem, *Sefer hamusar*, p. 45; and idem in *KS* 28, 269–270. The use of verse for such purposes was a mnemonic device. Israel Najara, the famed poet of the Safed revival, also composed a versified primer on the laws of *sheḥiṭah* entitled *Shoḥaṭei ha-yeladim* (The Children's Ritual Slaughterers), whose rhymes and short prose passages were designed to be accessible to children, who began their religious studies at a tender age; see Regev, "Najara, Israel ben Moses."

53 See Fishman, "The 'Our Talmud' Tradition and the Predilection for Works of Applied Law

With their practical orientation to Jewish law, these works omitted much of the Talmud's dialectical deliberations (precisely the *pilpul* and *sevara* that Alḍāhirī's characters so admire in the *yeshivah*-trained Jews of the Land of Israel). Given that Yemenite Jewry was also part of the larger Islamicate cultural orbit—even if further to the east than North Africa and al-Andalus—and was in possession of geonic responsa and the halakhic works of Alfasi and Maimonides not long after their composition, it seems reasonable to view its proclivity for applied law in this larger religio-cultural context. Nevertheless, these orientations changed over time: Fishman writes that in the 13th century, a confluence of factors led to a narrowing of the cultural gap between Ashkenaz and Sepharad in this respect. As a result of his encounter with the Talmudic glosses of the northern European Tosafists, the formidable Catalan scholar Naḥmanides (1194–1270) introduced changes into the Iberian approach to halakhic study and had a profound impact on the next generation of students. At the same time, the Talmud burning of the 1240's led the Jews of France to rely on Alfasi's code. Ephraim Kanarfogel characterizes the convergence as "a kind of genre reversal between Ashkenaz and Sepharad," such that Franco-German scholars, who had earlier cultivated extensive Talmudic comments, moved in the 13th century toward halakhic works and codes while Spanish halakhists, who had favored the practical orientation of codes and responsa in the 11th and 12th centuries, now moved toward Talmudic commentaries.[54] Post-expulsion, the 16th century saw an efflorescence of sophisticated Talmudic and juridical studies among Ottoman Sephardim around the eastern Mediterranean basin.[55] Gradual changes of emphasis occurred in Yemenite rabbinic studies as well.

Yehuda Ratzaby's account of rabbinic scholarship in Yemen delineates an early medieval period of active Talmud study up until the arrival of the *Mishneh Torah* followed by several centuries of greater reliance on applied law (a tendency that was reinforced by the subsequent arrival of the *Shulḥan ʿarukh* in the 16th century), and an ensuing resurgence in the 17th, 18th, and 19th cen-

---

in Early Sephardi Rabbinic Culture." See also Kanarfogel, "Talmudic Studies." The references are to Ḥanan'el ben Ḥushi'el (d. 1056) and his contemporary, Nissim b. Jacob, both of Qairowan, North Africa; and Isaac Alfasi (Rif, 1013–1103) who was from Fez and moved to Andalusia toward the end of his career to become the head of the Lucena *yeshivah*.

54 Kanarfogel, "Talmudic Studies," 602–606. See also Grossman, "Relations Between Spanish and Ashkenazi Jewry in the Middle Ages."

55 See, e.g., Bornstein-Makovetsky, "Ottoman Empire: 2. From 1492 to ca. 1650"; Weinstein, *Joseph Karo and Shaping of Modern Jewish Law*, 121–139 *passim*; Ben-Naeh, "City of Torah and Study: Salonica as a Torah Center during the Sixteenth and Seventeenth Centuries"; and Dimitrovsky, "Rabbi Yaakov Beirav's Academy in Safed."

turies of direct engagement with the Talmud and cultivation of original works of rabbinic literature.[56] In his annotation to Alḍāhirī's panegyric to the Talmud in *Sefer hamusar* #18, Ratzaby states that the Bavli was not widespread in Yemen and was studied only by sages and rabbis while the Yerushalmi was virtually not to be found.[57] Yet, he never entertains the notion that the Bavli did not reach Yemen. In an article published just a few years before the appearance of his edition of *Sefer hamusar*, he writes that it is inconceivable that Yemenite Jewry, which was so heavily influenced by Babylonian Jewry in matters of (supralinear) pointing, post-biblical Hebrew, *piyyut*, and liturgy, would not have received the Babylonian Talmud early on. There were Yemenite emissaries who collected funds for the support of the Babylonian *yeshivot* of Sura and Pumbeditha and who conveyed halakhic questions to the Babylonian centers of learning; they would, he asserts, undoubtedly have procured copies of Talmudic tractates for their community.[58] He adduces a genizah letter conveying an 1153 ruling of the Aden rabbinical court on the matter of a wife whose husband drowned at sea that cites tractate *Yevamot* of the Bavli and geonic discussions of the matter at hand; from this he infers that other courts in Yemen must also have based their determinations on the Talmud.[59] But he acknowledges that Yemenite manuscripts of the capacious work are relatively rare due to the costliness of copying it by hand, which was beyond the means of all but the most affluent. (In fact, Emile Schrijver has written that medieval manuscripts, even fragments, of the Talmud are rare, owing not only to its size but also to the Paris book burnings of 1242 and the 1553 Inquisition prohibition against printing the Talmud in Italy.)[60] A fourteenth-century Yemenite copyist produced one complete Talmud manuscript while David ben Meʿoded in 1547 copied out five tractates; his copies contain some variant readings from the printed text. This would seem to indicate that scribes continued to hand-copy the text from manuscripts at the same time that Bomberg was printing the text in Venice since acquiring the printed text would have been quite expen-

56 Ratzaby and Tobi did not see eye to eye on the degree to which Yemenite Jews had engaged directly with the Talmud through the ages; see Tobi, *ʿAl ha-talmud be-teiman*, p. 7, n. 1 and Ratzaby, *Bemʿagloth Temān*, p. 104, n. 3.

57 *Sefer hamusar* #18, p. 213, n. 25.

58 See also Goitein, "The Support of Yemenite Jews of the Academies of Iraq and Palestine and the School of Moses Maimonides."

59 See Strauss, "A Journey to India," 225 and 231; cited in Tobi, *ʿAl ha-talmud be-teiman*, pp. 10–11, n. 16.

60 Schrijver, "Transmission." Schrijver and Ratzaby both note that the only known complete medieval ms. of the Babylonian Talmud, completed in 1343, is now in the Bavarian State Library in Munich (Cod. Hebr. 95).

sive.[61] But Bomberg's volumes did reach Yemen: a 1618 handwritten note from Yemen follows the printed colophon to the final tractate of his Talmud in the collection of the New York Public Library.[62]

Ratzaby reminds us that the status of the Talmud was not monolithic throughout the generations, nor was it necessarily the same in different Jewish communities or subcultures. He observes that in Yemen, the economic model of the *yeshivah* in which young men devoted themselves to full-time study while others provided for their upkeep simply did not exist. Following rabbinic injunctions, there was a sense of obligation to engage in gainful employment while studying sacred texts, which, in accordance with Maimonides' opposition to "an institutionalized and salaried rabbinate," obtained among rabbinic scholars as well.[63] The scarcity of books in a land without a Hebrew press, the costliness both of hand-copying such a voluminous work and of importing printed copies of its manifold tractates, and the young age at which boys were obliged to leave *ḥeder* in order to work all mitigated against full-time immersion in Talmud for all but a select few who carried on studying in the *beit midrash* or in scholarly circles, and for the most part went on to become teachers.[64] Intensive Talmud study was not widespread among ordinary people and was largely replaced by recourse to the more concise halakhic works of the Geonim and Alfasi, which were in turn supplanted by Maimonides' twelfth-century legal

61 See Ratzaby, "Ha-talmud viyhudei teiman." The 1547 mss. were acquired by the Columbia University library in 1890; see Tobi, *ʿAl ha-talmud be-teiman*, 12. Efraim Yaakov, on the other hand, had the sense that the Talmud was never a central book in the Yemenite house of study despite the extant Yemenite copies; see *Eloha mi-teiman yavo*, pp. 87–88 and n. 277.

62 *Seder Kodashim and Massekhtot Ketanot* [The Order of Kodashim and the Minor Tractates]. Venice: Daniel Bomberg, AM 5288 (1528, actually 1547 CE). NYPL, Dorot Jewish Division. On the actual dating see Piattelli, "New Documents Concerning Bomberg's Printing of the Talmud," 193.

63 See Twersky, *Introduction to the Code of Maimonides*, p. 5.

64 In later centuries, there was one *yeshivah* located in Ṣanaʿā, where rabbinical scholars and the members of the *beit din* engaged in Talmud study and issued responsa and halakhic decisions. According to Klorman, it was not an institution of higher learning so much as a judicial association that was the final arbiter of the law and "was responsible for sending inspectors to settlements in central Yemen in order to authorize new slaughterers and to give permission to authorized *moris* to perform marriages and grant divorces." Qāfiḥ, on the other hand, describes it as a venerated institution where the city's Torah scholars gathered daily following the morning prayers for exacting textual study. This model was sustained until the terrible siege and famine of 1905 (*ḥawzat al-nafar*), during which countless lives were lost and most of the city's scholars perished. See Klorman, "Yemen," 400 and Qāfiḥ, "Qehillat ṣanaʿa she-be-teiman," in *Ketavim* 2:869. On the broad authority of the Ṣanaʿā *beit din* see Tobi, *The Jews of Yemen*, 128–141.

code. The *Mishneh Torah* reigned supreme until it was supplemented by the arrival of the *Shulḥan ʿarukh* in the 16th century. Ratzaby acknowledges that reliance on Maimonides' compendium to a great extent obviated the need for Talmud study and prompted the composition of numerous commentaries and, later, supercommentaries. But it did not entirely preclude direct engagement with Talmudic material. In the 20th chapter of *Sefer hamusar*, Mordecai responds to a letter from the sages of Diqla (Ṣaʿadah), the second most important center of Jewish religious learning after Ṣanaʿā, which suggests to him that young disciples studying the laws of ritual slaughter in that northern city are not sufficiently grounded in Scripture, Mishnah, and Talmud prior to embarking on their work as *shoḥetim*.[65] And Alḍāhirī himself apparently authored a collection of novellae called *Ḥiddushim be-ferush arbaʿim baraitot*.[66] Ratzaby also points to Talmudic citations in the rich midrashic texts compiled in Yemen between the fourteenth and early sixteenth centuries: *Nur al-ẓalām, Midrash ha-gadol, Midrash ha-ḥefeṣ, Sirāj alʿuqūl* and others. These works exemplify the most widely cultivated genre of literature among Yemenite Jewish scholars during this period; a genre Y. Tzvi Langermann has done much to illuminate, and which he has called philosophical midrash. Langermann has demonstrated that this prolific literary activity was nourished by productive contact with the writings of many other Jewish communities as well as with texts of Muslim and even Indian provenance. Revealing imposing philosophical and scientific learning, the authors of these works coupled the allegorical interpretation of Scripture with a profound commitment to Jewish law. Alongside the Maimonidean corpus, they quote Talmud and rabbinic sources directly and often at great length although in general do not engage in original halakhic inquiry.[67] Ratzaby notes that the 16th–18th centuries saw fertile literary activity in many fields. There were major developments in the prayer book and a flowering of the responsa literature, supercommentaries on exegesis of the *Mishneh Torah*, and a turn towards esotericism in works of scriptural exegesis and liturgy. In addition, Yosef Tobi, Aharon Gaimani, Yosef Qāfiḥ, and Raṣon ʿArussi have documented the composition of Talmudic novellae, or *ḥiddushim*, as well as a great

65 On the strains between the rabbinates of the two communities, see Bar-Maoz, "Social Tension." He writes that the Jews of Ṣanaʿā typically related to "peripheral" Jewish communities with "haughtiness and a touch of arrogance"; see pp. 58–60.

66 The work is no longer extant; see *Sefer hamusar*, p. 44. In the narrative, it is attributed to Abner; see #27, lines 55–65.

67 Langermann writes that Yemenite Jewish creativity was by no means limited to exegetical literature, although biblical commentary "was probably the most widely read branch of Jewish literature," and therefore "the most important vehicle for conveying values." See *Yemenite Midrash*, xvii–xxx and 85–88.

deal of responsa literature that cites both Talmudim extensively. They have highlighted a particular concern among premodern Yemenite rabbis with the preservation of ancient religious traditions in the face of attempts by visiting sages to change them. When rabbinic emissaries from Palestine questioned the ritual permissibility of Yemenite observances that differed from their own, and were therefore considered to be in violation of rabbinic norms—e.g., the use of the distinctively long Yemenite shofar, or the recitation of eulogies for deceased sages on the second day of a festival, or the baking of matzah according to Yemenite custom—local rabbinic authorities had to produce halakhic justification for maintaining their age-old traditions.[68] Yosef Qāfiḥ, himself a master teacher, has indicated that Talmud teaching in Yemen sought to develop precision in analyzing the language of the *gemara* so that students could appreciate the distinctive methods of the Franco-German scholars versus those of Alfasi and Maimonides in drawing halakhic conclusions. But a penetrating understanding of *pilpul* and the sharp give and take of the *gemara* were not ends in themselves since the main emphasis was on the practical application of the law.[69]

From the narrative perspective of *Sefer hamusar*, however, the real question is not so much the historicity of the shortcomings imputed to Yemenite Jewry. The question is why Alḍāhirī has his Yemenite characters define themselves in a circumscribed and self-deprecatory fashion when they encounter the Jews of the Land of Israel and why they are defined by the latter in a comparably reductive fashion. Why does he have them internalize the qualities ascribed to them by these others, incorporating the traits attributed to them into their own self-image? Put another way, why does Alḍāhirī not portray Yemenite Jews in their full particularity? It is true that passages of praise and fault-finding in medieval Hebrew poetry and rhymed prose narratives tend to work with typologies and formulae rather than fine distinctions. But literary convention alone does not account for the omission of Yemenite accomplishments in the realms of science, philosophy, exegesis, liturgy, and, indeed, halakhah from the communal self-definition constructed in these episodes. The fact that *Sefer hamusar* is a *maqāma* may contribute to Alḍāhirī's emphasis on the Yemenites' elegant

68 See Gaimani, "Rabbinic Emissaries and Their Contacts with Yemenite Jewry"; idem, "Hashadar rabbi david naḥmias u-maṣot teiman"; idem, *Temurot be-moreshet yahadut teiman*, 77–82; Ratzaby, *Bem'agaloth temān*, 67–85; idem, "Shadarim u-minhagei teiman"; Tobi, *'Al ha-talmud be-teiman*; idem, "Caro's *Shulhan Arukh* Versus Maimonides' *Mishne Torah* in Yemen"; Aharon Qāfiḥ, "'Iyyunim be-fisqei ha-rav yiḥye qāfiḥ"; and 'Arussi, "Ha-shulḥan 'arukh ke-gorem she-hisrid et ha-rambam be-teiman."

69 See Qāfiḥ, "Hora'at ha-talmud be-teiman." For an appreciation of Qāfiḥ's scholarship see Langermann, "'Mori Yusuf': Rabbi Yosef Kafah (Qāfiḥ) (1917–2000)."

and fluent expression, as the genre set great store by linguistic virtuosity and poetic mastery. In *Sefer hamusar*, Abner embodies this eloquence, and it is he of the silver tongue whose *nisba, ha-teimani,* signals that he is "the Yemenite" par excellence. These are traits for which Alḍāhirī wanted his community to be known. But why does he feel obliged to restrict their accomplishments to these spheres and to harp on their failings in all others? Why is this their only claim to cultural capital? Even if his narrative of grievous persecution is intended to account for these alleged shortcomings, it does not entirely explain his unidimensional portrayal of Yemenite Jewry. After all, Alḍāhirī's own creative work flourished during this crushing period of political turbulence and communal suffering.

It would seem that the subtext underlying Alḍāhirī's construction of Yemenite Jewish identity is *the need to defer to the Jews of the Land of Israel.* Why would he have felt this so keenly? In no small measure, certainly, because of the aura of sanctity enveloping the Holy Land, its scholars, and its institutions. As a pious ambassador from Eretz Yisrael, the *shadar* embodied that holiness. In the 16th century, Palestine was also one of the most important loci of Jewish religious authority.[70] And inextricably intertwined with these considerations was one additional key detail. Though it is implicit throughout the narrative, it is spelled out only rarely, as though already common knowledge. One of the few occasions in which it is made explicit is the flowery letter of praise sent from Yemen to the Sages of Tiberias (Chapter 24). According to the story, this extraordinary missive accompanied an unusually generous donation from the Ṣanaʿā community in response to a fundraising campaign for the upkeep of the Tiberias *yeshivah*, which had fallen on hard times following the death of the gracious philanthropist, Doña Gracia Mendes (d. 1569) who, together with her nephew, Don Joseph Nasi, had been the moving force behind the revitalization of the city's Jewish settlement.[71] Reprising the by-now familiar encomiastic language of Abner's other two panegyric epistles, this letter adds one crucial element:

70 See Davis, "The Reception of the *Shulḥan ʿArukh* and the Formation of Ashkenazic Jewish Identity," 260 and Weinstein, *Joseph Karo and Shaping of Modern Jewish Law*, 232–235.

71 Most of the secondary accounts of Doña Gracia's support for the Tiberias *yeshivah* rely on these very passages from *Sefer hamusar*; see: Roth, *Doña Gracia of the House of Nasi*, 130–131; idem, *The Duke of Naxos of the House of Nasi*, 120–121; David, *To Come to the Land*, 29–33; Braslavsky, "Jewish Settlement in Tiberias from Don Joseph Nasi to Ibn Yaish"; and Yaari, *Sheluḥei ereṣ yisraʾel*, 256–261. Alḍāhirī does not include the text of the Tiberians' fundraising letter, but a later historical exemplar may give some indication of its gist. A 19th-century letter sent to Yemen from Jerusalem employs a combination of flattery,

> To the valiant in Torah and noblemen imbued with dominion, who defend the Torah and restore its crown to its rightful place ... who occupy themselves with the work of heaven ... who ascend to the highest ranks to explain all that is opaque; sages of Talmud and logical inference (*sevara'*) in Mishnah and Gemara and of the wisdom of kabbalah ... for whom no mystery is impenetrable ... the choicest of communities ... sought by those who seek God's countenance ... who redeem the exiled and heal the sick ... their souls are hewn from the intellect's quarry ... the sages of Tiberias ... its princes and leaders, Levites and priests. At their head are our honored masters and teachers, the perfect scholar (*heḥakham hakolel*), R. Samuel Hacohen, and R. Jacob Halevi, and R. Abraham [Ashkenazi], may his Rock protect him, and R. Moses Gedalya, and R. Abraham Gabriel ... with the rest of their communities ... *They are the sages of Sepharad*, at whose mention every heart leaps and trembles (*hem ḥakhmei sefarad/ kol lev le-zikhram yitar ve-yeḥerad*).[72]

For Alḍāhirī, then, the most compelling reason for the preeminence of contemporary Palestinian Jewry is subcultural: the leading lights of Safed and Tiberias and their disciples are all Sephardim. That Alḍāhirī is aware of Ottoman Sephardi exceptionalism is noteworthy, and that he has accepted and internalized Sephardi claims to cultural superiority is particularly striking.[73]

The work's idealization of Sephardim contributes not only to Yemenite self-deprecation but also to a seeming agnosticism regarding the ordeals of the Iberian expulsion. The Yemenite sense of self as poor, wretched, and intellectually inadequate due to endless cycles of oppression and natural disasters is a leitmotif of *Sefer hamusar*. Through his personae, Alḍāhirī suggests that Yemenite Jewish existence is more politically and religiously precarious than that of Jews living in the thriving cities of Ottoman Palestine, Anatolia and the

pathos, and threat in an effort to extract contributions from its addressees; see Yaari, "Iggeret sheliḥut mi-yerushalayim liyehudei teiman."

72 *Sefer hamusar*, #24, pp. 278–279.

73 Yaari maintained that the scholars singled out here by name were the signators to the begging letter sent to the Yemenite Jews, and that Abner's epistle is actually the response drafted by Alḍāhirī on behalf of the Ṣanaʿā community; see *Masaʿot ereṣ yisraʾel*, 199 and 217 and *Sefer hamusar*, p. 40. Note that R. Abraham Ashkenazi is included among the sages of Sepharad; the surname Ashkenazi was commonly taken by Ashkenazi Jews who moved to a Sephardi milieu and was then borne by their descendants as well. See Heller, "Early Hebrew Printing from Lublin to Safed: The Journeys of Eliezer ben Isaac Ashkenazi," p. 94, n. 12 and Beider, "The Notion of 'Jewish Surnames,'" 190.

Balkans. At a moment when Safed Jewish society is flourishing, he perceives its inhabitants as robust and well-established, possibly due to the mythically salubrious qualities attributed to the Holy Land as much as to the city's commercial and spiritual vitality. But Alḍāhirī was not ignorant of the traumas and upheaval experienced by the generation of the Iberian exiles. Remarking on Israel's subjugation to the wicked kingdom of Esau in his exegesis of Deuteronomy 32 in *Ṣeidah la-derekh*, he makes this telling teleological comment (which seems to be informed by Isaac Abravanel on Isaiah 43:1):

> Those who dwelled securely with the kings of Edom, as it were, forgot their Land. Therefore God planted His advice in [the kings'] hearts so that they rose up and exiled them and burnt some of them and killed some of them and took some of them captive. Just see what Rabbi Judah Ḥayyāṭ recounted in the introduction to his commentary on *Sefer ha-maʿarekhet*. In them was fulfilled "The sword shall deal death without, as shall the terror within …" [Deut. 32:25]. Those who would flee fell into the hands of captors and the inhabitants would kill them, so that they had to flee for their lives until they reached the land of Togarmah [the Ottoman Empire]. Were it not for the mercy of the Lord, and that is what Scripture says, "I might have reduced them to naught …" [Deut. 32:26].

Alḍāhirī was intimately acquainted with Judah Ḥayyāṭ's *Minḥat yehudah*, whose preface chronicles a horrendous ordeal at sea after fleeing Portugal; capture and subjection to cruel conversionary pressures by Catholic clergy in Málaga; and hardships in North Africa before finally reaching Italy.[74] Perhaps it is out of a surfeit of anxiety about his own community's suffering that in *Sefer ha-musar* Alḍāhirī never acknowledges the Iberian refugees' tribulations or sense of deracination. It is anachronistic to expect that Alḍāhirī's fairly flat characters could muster the empathy to draw parallels between their own experiences and those of the exiles or even to see certain analogies with their own yearnings for messianic consolation and redemption. Even Jacob Ibn Ḥabib, who personally experienced the afflictions and displacement of the expulsion does not, in his *En Yaaqov*, directly reflect on these events or their theological significance, unlike contemporaries such as Isaac Abravanel or Solomon Ibn Verga.[75] Still, it is telling that at a moment in history when memories of the expulsion were still fresh, Alḍāhirī's protagonists are com-

74 See *Sefer maʿarekhet haʾelohut* (Zholkva, 1779).

75 See Lehman, *The* En Yaaqov, 5.

pletely consumed with the severe material privations and religious degradation of their own subculture and see only contrasts between themselves and the Sephardim of Ottoman Palestine.

4 Ottoman Sephardi Dominance

Iberian immigrants had settled in Palestine and Egypt even before the 1492 expulsion of the Jews from Spain, the 1497 forced conversion in Portugal (to which many of the Spanish exiles had initially fled), and the 1516–1517 Ottoman conquests of the Levant. Already by the last quarter of the 15th century, leaders of Spanish Jewry had assumed important public posts in the Jerusalem community.[76] Contact between different segments of the Jewish world intensified in the wake of the Spanish expulsion, which coincided with the expansions that transformed the Ottoman state into a world Empire. New waves of exiles arrived in Ottoman lands in the early 16th century, making them agents of cross-cultural fertilization and change. Over time, this massive influx created the religious, cultural, and political realities that inform *Sefer hamusar*. When Abner apologizes for the poor reception given the *shadar* by the downtrodden Jews of Yemen and singles out Salonica, Istanbul, and Cairo as communities that undoubtedly extended him much greater hospitality, the comparison is not random. Salonica and Istanbul were home to exceptionally large and active communities of Iberian Jews who settled there soon after the expulsion. Salonica absorbed the greatest number of Spanish and Portuguese exiles and became a vibrant center of Talmud study as well as of the textile industry on which the Ottoman administration depended.[77] All three cities developed into centers of trade in the 16th century, affording Jewish merchants commercial opportunities and trade networks. After the Ottoman conquest of the Lev-

76 See Hacker, "Links Between Spanish Jewry and Palestine, 1391–1492." Rabbi David ben Solomon Ibn Abi Zimra (b. 1479/80), left Spain during the expulsion, settled in Safed, and not long after, relocated to Jerusalem. By 1514 he was a member of the rabbinic court of the official head of Egyptian Jewry in Cairo; see Morell, "Ibn Abi Zimra, David (Radbaz)" and David, *To Come to the Land*, 142–144.

77 Hacker remarks on the lively response to rabbinic sermons and scholarly publications in the Ottoman Empire during the 16th century; see his "Authors, Readers, and Printers of Sixteenth-Century Hebrew Books in the Ottoman Empire," pp. 33ff. See also Ben-Naeh, "City of Torah and Study: Salonica as a Torah Center during the Sixteenth and Seventeenth Centuries" and Varlik, "Plague, Conflict, and Negotiation: The Jewish Broadcloth Weavers of Salonica and the Ottoman Central Administration in the Late Sixteenth Century."

ant, many Sephardim also moved to cities like Aleppo, Damascus, and Cairo.[78] Iberian Jews who settled in major Ottoman cities founded their own congregations and gradually asserted their nobility and the preeminence of their cultural heritage. Like other Jewish groups who had preceded them, the newcomers initially established many autonomous congregations, or *kehalim*, according to their places of origin and did not from the outset identify themselves as part of a pan-Sephardi entity, an identity which had not existed prior to the expulsion.[79] This more atomistic model of communal organization preserved diverse liturgical traditions, linguistic variations, and independent rabbinical authorities and charitable institutions. In larger towns, the various Iberian congregations came together to form supra-congregational institutions, although regional distinctions persisted well after 1492.[80] But over the course of the 16th century, various factors contributed to the gradual evolution of a trans-regional Sephardi identity and common Judeo-Spanish language.[81] As the Sephardim grew to outnumber existing Jewish communities not only in Palestine and Egypt, but also in many cities of the Ottoman Balkans and Anatolia, they gradually asserted their hegemony, imposing their halakhic norms, liturgical rites, and religious authority on those communities, both immigrant (Ashkenazi, Provençal, Italian, Sicilian—some of whom antedated the 1453 conquest of Constantinople) and indigenous (the Greek-speaking Romaniot Jews whose presence in former Byzantine lands went back to late antiquity).[82] Sephardi

78 Bornstein-Makovetsky, "Ottoman Empire: 2. From 1492 to ca. 1650." See also Gerber, *Cities of Splendour*, 171–213.

79 For example, the Imperial Ottoman register for 16th-century Safed lists the following Jewish communities: Portugal, Cordoba, Castile, Aragon, Seville, as well as "Mustaʿāriba [native Arabic-speaking Jews], Maghāriba [Jews from the Maghreb], Hungarian, Apulia, Calabria, Italian, and German"; see Cohen and Lewis, *Population and Revenue in the Towns of Palestine in the Sixteenth Century*, 158. See also Bornstein-Makovetsky, "Structure, Organisation, and Spiritual Life of the Sephardi Communities in the Ottoman Empire from the Sixteenth to the Eighteenth Centuries," esp. 315–316.

80 See Levy, *The Sephardim in the Ottoman Empire*, 46–53; Rodrigue, "The Sephardim in the Ottoman Empire"; Shmuelevitz, *The Jews of the Ottoman Empire in the Late Fifteenth and the Sixteenth Centuries*, 11–40 *passim*; and Rozen, *A History of the Jewish Community in Istanbul*.

81 Of the period prior to the expulsion Jonathan Ray writes that Spanish Jews "comprised a loosely associated collection of communities with little cohesive identity"; see *After Expulsion*, 8–10 and idem, "Images of the Jewish Community in Medieval Iberia." On the gradual evolution of a shared cultural identity built around the idealization of Iberia as an ancestral homeland, see Ben-Naeh, "Research on Ottoman Jewish History and Culture: The State of the Art," 74 and Ray, *After Expulsion*, 135–155.

82 See, e.g., Rozen, "The Position of the Mustaʿrabs in the Inter-community Relationships in Eretz Israel from the End of the 15th Century to the End of the 17th Century"; Aviv,

intellectual vitality was marked by the establishment of synagogues, houses of learning, and prestigious *yeshivot*. Many of the Hebrew compositions produced by the rabbinic élite circulated in print already from the end of the 15th century. Nor were Sephardi political attainments restricted to internal Jewish affairs: prominent members of Sephardi society achieved positions of influence as bankers, physicians, translators, or counselors to the Imperial Palace.[83] Over the course of the 16th and 17th centuries, the combination of demographic dominance, a vibrant intellectual and religious heritage that continued to evolve, and aristocratic political influence at royal courts facilitated the realization of Sephardi aspirations to cultural hegemony and economic dominance within Ottoman Jewry.

Although the native Greek-speaking Romaniots throughout various parts of the Empire vigorously resisted Sephardi pressure to abandon their ancestral traditions and language, by the mid-17th century they had succumbed to the point of adopting Judeo-Spanish as their spoken language.[84] And a halakhic query posed to Samuel de Medina (1506–1589) of Salonica, one of the greatest Ottoman rabbinic authorities of the 16th century, states that almost all of the diverse immigrant communities in Ottoman lands—including the congregations of Calabria, Provence, Sicily and Apulia—had gradually abandoned their own liturgical traditions for the Sephardi rite "since they [the Sephardim] are the majority in this kingdom and their liturgy is eloquent and sweet."[85] In Salonica, only one Ashkenazi congregation had resisted doing so, but recently the majority of that congregation had also adopted *nusaḥ sefarad*, to the consternation of a minority of the community that was vehemently opposed to the change. The congregation was therefore inquiring whether they should continue to follow the Sephardi order of the prayers. As Bernard Septimus has

"Ottoman Empire: 1. From 1300 to 1492"; and Bornstein-Makovetsky, "Structure, Organisation, and Spiritual Life of the Sephardi Communities in the Ottoman Empire."

83 On the factors contributing to Sephardi ascendancy see Levy, *The Sephardim in the Ottoman Empire*, 59–64; Bornstein-Makovetsky, "Ottoman Empire: 2. From 1492 to ca. 1650"; Hacker, "On the Intellectual Character and Self-Perception of Spanish Jewry in Late Fifteenth Century"; idem, "The Intellectual Activity of the Jews of the Ottoman Empire During the Sixteenth and Seventeenth Centuries"; idem, "The Sephardim in the Ottoman Empire in the Sixteenth Century."

84 Heyd, "The Jewish Communities of Istanbul in the Seventeenth Century," esp. 308 and 313–314 and Bornstein-Makovetsky, "Le-toldot qehillat kushta be'emṣa'itah shel ha-me'ah ha-shva' 'esreh."

85 In what follows, I am indebted to the far more nuanced analysis of Bernard Septimus in "Linguistic Ideology and Cultural Hegemony: A Responsum of R. Samuel de Medina, Its Sources and Implications." The responsum is translated in Goodblatt, *Jewish Life in Turkey in the XVIth Century as Reflected in the Legal Writings of Samuel De Medina*, 139–143.

shown, De Medina chooses to predicate his affirmative response on the distinctions between the liturgical poems recited in the different rites. Invoking the aesthetic ideal of *ṣaḥut* or pure, eloquent Hebrew that was championed by the 11th–12th century Andalusi Hebrew poets, he affirms the superiority of the Sephardi rite on the grounds of its clarity and intelligibility:

> And even the *piyyutim* that we recite [during prayer]—by Judah Halevi, Solomon Ibn Gabirol, and Abraham Ibn Ezra—are all composed in clear Biblical Hebrew which is intelligible to all (*kullam leshon ha-qodesh ṣaḥ muvan la-kol*) .... Not only should we not denigrate those who abandon the order of the other rites [for the Sephardi liturgy], but we should praise them ...[86]

The ideal of clear, elegant expression (*ṣaḥut*) had driven the medieval Spanish poets' insistence upon using only grammatically correct Biblical Hebrew in place of the language of earlier, classical *piyyut* that had developed in Byzantine Palestine and was suffused with rabbinic Hebrew and neologisms. The history of the term *ṣaḥut* (the attested biblical vocalization is *ṣaḥot*; cf. Isaiah 32:4) is bound up with the revival of the Hebrew language in Islamic lands, which was pioneered by Saadya Gaon (882–942) and reached full maturity during the primacy of Iberian Jewry.[87] By adapting classical Arabic prosody and aesthetics, the Andalusians produced a distinctive style of *piyyut* that spread throughout Mediterranean lands but not among Franco-German communities. Their literary virtuosity became a cornerstone of Andalusi exceptionalism. Identifying his community as the latter-day heirs of the medieval Andalusians, De Medina appropriates their claims to exclusivity to support his politically charged ruling that the Ashkenazi rite should be abandoned in favor of the Sephardi liturgy. The argument in favor of a uniform rite is thus justified on both aesthetic and demographic grounds as part of the effort to legitimate Ottoman Sephardi cultural and political hegemony.

In actuality, as Septimus shows, the appeal to *piyyut* may have been largely expedient. Di Medina was at best ambivalent about interrupting the prayers by inserting *piyyutim* into the fixed liturgy, although clear and intelligible poems were preferable to those no worshiper could understand due to their garbled language. In 16th-century Sephardi communities, the status of *piyyut* was

86 See Septimus, "Linguistic Ideology," p. 299 and Goodblatt, p. 142.

87 See Septimus, "Maimonides on Language." For the variant vocalization *ṣaḥut*, see Ben Yehuda, *Complete Dictionary*, 6:5447, n. 1 and Even Shoshan, *Ha-millon he-ḥadash*, 5:2216.

already in decline. At a certain point after Di Medina made his determination in favor of the Sephardi rite, *piyyutim* were forced out of the fixed liturgy. The mounting opposition of halakhists—a process that had already begun in Castile and was accelerated by the *Shulḥan ʿarukh*—together with the increasing influence of Lurianic kabbalah, put paid to the enterprise. Significantly, in response to kabbalistic opposition to the liturgical recitation of *piyyut*, De Medina's older contemporary, Rabbi David ben Solomon Ibn Abi Zimra (Radbaz, b. Spain 1479/80, d. Safed 1573) invoked the legendary erudition of the Andalusian poets. His words betray the totemic image and formidable mystique these medievals had come to embody:

> Were not their authors men of great wisdom like Abraham Ibn Ezra, Solomon Ibn Gabirol, and Judah Halevi? *And they were Andalusians* … And how many brilliant sages who came after them heard their liturgical poems and did not protest against them, for they were true scholars ….[88]

Though marked by more subtle polemical subtexts as well, these responsa illustrate the powerful self-perception of the Ottoman Sephardi élite as the rightful successors to the 11th–12th century Andalusian literati and "courtier-rabbis" whose literary, linguistic, and political exceptionalism they appropriated. The medieval Andalusian poets—aristocratic polymaths and aesthetes who, in addition to their poetry wrote Bible commentaries, ethical tracts, and philosophical treatises—had championed their community's literary and intellectual supremacy over other Jewish subcultures. In the early 11th century, they sought to transfer the authority of the declining Babylonian center to Spain, and in so doing helped to construct a collective cultural identity for Andalusian Jewry. Touting the eloquence of their biblical Hebrew poetry, they ensured that its aesthetic ideals and literary conventions would be the yardstick against which all other Hebrew verse would be measured. These Iberian poets were relentlessly determined to secure Spain's reputation as the preeminent center of Hebrew poetry and Jewish culture, and their efforts succeeded to a remarkable degree in promoting the primacy of the Andalusian Jewish community in the eyes of the Jewish world through the ages.[89]

---

88 Cited in Septimus, "Linguistic Ideology," p. 302, n. 31. On attitudes toward the liturgical recitation of *piyyut* among the rabbinic leaders of the Sephardi diaspora and on the impact of Lurianic kabbalah, see Langer, *To Worship God Properly*, 172–177. On Sephardi claims to superiority see also the classic article of Ben-Sasson, "The Generation of the Spanish Exiles on Its Fate."

89 See Kfir, *A Matter of Geography*.

The mythologizing of Jewish life in al-Andalus was harnessed to a variety of social and political ends in the 19th and early 20th centuries, from Jewish emancipation in Germany to reviving Hebrew and modernizing Jewish culture in the Ottoman Empire. The political and imagined symbolism of Sephardism differed from one context to another. Nineteenth-century *Wissenschaft* scholars, anxious to gain admission into German society, idealized the cultural creativity and cosmopolitanism of the "Golden Age" of Andalusian Jewry with its perceived rationalism and social integration. Concurrent with the Ashkenazi appropriation of Sephardism, Ottoman Jewish intellectuals in the second half of the 19th century embraced the Muslim-Jewish legacy of Andalusia in forging an alternative to the doctrinaire *Wissenschaft* and European Zionist models of political and cultural modernization. The circle of Sephardi Jewish intellectuals in late Ottoman-era Palestine identified with both the Jewish and Arab linguistic and national revivals, responding to the Arabic cultural renaissance known as the *Nahḍa* (revival, rebirth), and they invoked the medieval Judeo-Arabic "symbiosis" of al-Andalus and the Sephardi world in an effort to cultivate a hybrid Arab-Jewish identity and society.[90] Nor has invoking Sephardism been confined to Jewish circles: the fin-de-siècle Arabic *Nahḍa* itself turned to the memory of al-Andalus as a model for reviving a celebrated Arab past.[91] In the postcolonial era, the trope of Sepharad has served as a "politicized literary metaphor" for a wide array of writers, intellectuals, and political activists.[92]

But as evidenced by the rabbinic responsa cited above, already in the 16th century there was an early modern Ottoman Jewish discourse of Sephardism that appropriated medieval Andalusian assertions of cultural superiority for its own political ends. It came to the fore at points of contact and confrontation with other Jewish groups in the Empire. Its proponents claimed real and symbolic continuities of pedigree, aesthetics, and literary and religious sensibility with the medieval Andalusians to legitimate their predominance over other Jewish subcultures. In *Sefer hamusar*, Alḍāhirī's Yemenite protagonists have clearly assimilated the notion of Ottoman Sephardi preeminence, and their uncritical admiration for Sephardi rabbinic leadership and institutions in the Land of Israel seemingly knows no bounds. Yet, even when they are at their most reverent, the resonances of their intertextual language add subtle

90 For a comparative study of the *Haskalah* and the *Nahḍa* and on the role of Arab Jews in bridging the two, see Levy, "The *Nahḍa* and the *Haskala*."

91 Evri, *The Return to al-Andalus* and idem, "Return to al-Andalus beyond German-Jewish Orientalism: Abraham Shalom Yahuda's Critique of Modern Jewish Discourse."

92 See the essays in Halevi-Wise, *Sephardism: Spanish Jewish History and the Modern Literary Imagination.*

nuance to the self-perceptions generated in these intra-Jewish contact zones. It is telling that when Abner bestows his ultimate accolade upon the perfect scholars of Tiberias—"They are the sages of Sepharad, at whose mention every heart leaps and trembles"—he borrows the deferential wording of the young Judah Halevi's letter of praise to the renowned Moses Ibn Ezra, whom he was en route to visit in Granada.[93] In that missive, Halevi valorized the formidable accomplishments of the poets and courtier-rabbis of "Western Sepharad," the intellectually and culturally vibrant al-Andalus, while describing himself as an artless naïf coming from the backwater of Se'ir or Christian Spain:

> From one insignificant and young, / who rouses the heart of friendship / and kindles the fire of love, / as he comes up from Seir // to bask in the light of accomplished men. / *These are the great luminaries* (Gen 1:16), // the sages of Western Sefarad / at whose mention my heart trembles and leaps (Job 37:1).[94]

The writer's expressions of humility are mandated by epistolary etiquette, yet Halevi's self-deprecation belies the outstanding poetic gifts that gained him entrée into Andalusian literary society. Though born in Christian Spain around the time of the Reconquista, Halevi frequently crossed the border into Islamic al-Andalus and partook of its flourishing Judeo-Arabic culture. His youthful letter to Ibn Ezra goes on to describe his attendance at a literary soirée where he was challenged to improvise an imitation of a difficult strophic poem that the more seasoned participants in the contest had been unable to emulate. Though he was successful where his superiors had failed, Halevi again invoked the topos of Christian Spain as a cultural wasteland to politely protest his inadequacy for the task. The absence of eloquence—the *ṣaḥut* so prized by the Andalusians—here serves as a synecdoche for the cumulative cultural deficits of the northern Spanish milieu:

> I will not claim expertise in things I do not know, / lest the hearer reproach me. // … [for] I am *a tongue-tied stammerer* (Exod 4:10) / raised among Dishan and Dishon [i.e., in Christian Spain]—// a fierce and unintelligible folk …[95]

---

93 See Rand, "*Shalom rav veyesha yiqrav*—Yehuda ha-Levi's Epistle to Moshe ibn Ezra." The extracts are quoted in Rand's translation. For Alḍāhirī's borrowing, see *Sefer hamusar*, #24, p. 279, l. 104.

94 *ḥakhmei ma'arav sefarad/ libbi yitar le-zikhram ve-yeḥerad*; see Rand, "*Shalom rav veyesha yiqrav*," pp. 212 and 215, lines 10–12.

95 Rand, ibid., pp. 213 and 215, lines 27–29. Dishan and Dishon are descendants of Seir; see

In appropriating Halevi's language, Abner identifies the 16th-century Tiberian luminaries (now in the "East") with the élite sages of "Western Sepharad" and suggests, perhaps as a requisite expression of modesty, that he by contrast comes from a cultural backwater.[96] But the literary borrowing cuts both ways, insofar as it implicitly associates Abner with Judah Halevi, arguably the greatest of all the Andalusian poets. This bold if tacit self-presentation aligns with the recurrent praise for the pure and clear Scriptural language of the Jews of Yemen and particularly with the tributes to Abner's rhetorical virtuosity and stylistic refinement in rhymed prose as well as metrical poetry. His epistles are lauded as exemplars of polished, elegant expression. In the fortieth *maqāma*, Mordecai trumpets Abner's impressive command of Hebrew grammar and his excellence in poetry, and, after reading his missive and accompanying panegyric verse, Rabbi Abraham Ashkenazi is struck by his extraordinarily eloquent and clear language (*ṣaḥut leshono*), leading him to exclaim,

> Even though in our land there are discerning sages, ... before his poems ... all would be speechless. For they cannot compose a poem in this manner.[97]

The claim that the scholars of the Land of Israel do not excel in poetry is echoed by the head of the Tiberias congregation in the 24th *maqāma*. Recalling the sumptuous letter that had accompanied some gold florins and a precious stone donated by the Ṣanaʿānī Jews for the upkeep of the Tiberias *yeshivah*, the *nasi* recounts that, upon presenting them with these treasures, the fund-raising emissary had announced,

> 'I have one more thing for you that surpasses everything you have seen ....' From his bosom he drew out an epistle ... the likes of whose elegant language we had never seen .... We were astonished by he who uttered it, began and finished it, for at its end was a poem, a delight to the eyes,

Gen. 36:20–21. On the shifting significations of East and West in Halevi's poetry, see Brann, "'How Can My Heart be in the East?' Intertextual Irony in Judah Ha-Levi."

96 In fact, further on in the letter, he alters Halevi's phrase, *tarbut dishan ve-dishon* to *tarbut qedar ve-dishon* in a passage underscoring the unbearable reality of Yemenite Jewish existence under the thumb of unintelligent Muslims; see *Sefer hamusar* #24, p. 281, l. 123. Perhaps it did not escape Alḍāhirī's notice that the transposition of the Tiberian sages of prestigious "Western Sepharad" to the "East" bore a certain ironic parallelism to Halevi's reorientation later in life as an Andalusian pilgrim bound for the East.

97 *Sefer hamusar* #40, p. 429, lines 105–108.

> which made us worthless in our own eyes. For even though we are masters of philosophical speculation and kabbalah, we are not renowned for poetry.[98]

When the *nasi* inquires whether the protagonists can identify the author, whose stupendous display of poetic talent has made such an impression, Abner reveals that it was he who had composed the missive and its appended panegyric on behalf of the Ṣanaʿānī community. Here too, the celebration of Abner's personal virtuosity is framed in a larger context. No matter how much they outshine the Yemenites in Talmud study and kabbalah, the Sephardim of the Land of Israel cannot compete with Abner's outstanding compositional skills and scintillating style because Yemenite Jewry alone has faithfully preserved the aesthetic and poetic ideals of the Andalusian school. Alḍāhirī's insistence on the Sephardi sages' limited poetic abilities is quite gentle in comparison with Alḥarizi's withering denunciations of all the Hebrew poetry composed outside of Iberia—Germany, France, Greece and the East. But the underlying principle may not be dissimilar: Alḥarizi praises the sages of France and Greece for their learning but mercilessly assails their poems for their disregard of grammar, mangled meters, and defective rhymes. Over and over, he hammers home the message that the very existence of this verse constitutes "a violation of the Spanish Hebrew poets' exclusive hold on the art of poetry."[99] Even though the Sephardim encountered by the protagonists in *Sefer hamusar* are first- or second-generation exiles from the Iberian peninsula (some of whom, like Karo, are historical figures), with genetic and cultural lineage descending from the Andalusians, they have forfeited their poetic legacy. Alḍāhirī—whose own verse hewed closely to the prosody and poetics of the medieval Iberians—could therefore reposition Yemenite Jews as the faithful heirs to the Andalusian

98 *Sefer hamusar* #24, p. 278, lines 72–83. In line 77 the *nasi* says that the emissary produced a few *pirḥei zahav*, which Ratzaby glosses as "florins, so-called after the floral motif impressed on the coin." The Florentine gold florin was struck from 1252 to 1533 in one of the most prominent trade centers of the period. The gold ducat, minted in Venice starting in 1284, also circulated internationally as a trade coin; on the ducat's domination of the Eastern Mediterranean money market from the late 14th century, see Bacharach, "The Dinar versus the Ducat." For references to Jewish communal payments in florins subsequent to the 16th-century Ottoman conquest of Egypt and Palestine, see e.g. David, *To Come to the Land*, 45–46, 76–77, and 96. On coins struck in Ṣanaʿā, see "The Mint of Ṣanʿāʾ: A Historical Outline" in Serjeant and Lewcock eds., *Ṣanʿāʾ*, 303–308. See also Bikhazi, "Coins of al-Yaman, 132–569 A.H."

99 Kfir, *A Matter of Geography*, 75. See Alḥarizi, *Taḥkemoni* ed. Yahalom-Katsumata, #12, p. 217 and Segal, *The Book of Taḥkemoni*, #18, pp. 180–181.

poetic mantle. In order to do so, however, he is forced to overlook the creativity of some of the most celebrated poets associated with the kabbalistic revival in Safed and its pious confraternities—Solomon Alqabeṣ (1505–c. 1576), author of "Lekha dodi"; Eleazar Azikri (1533–1600), author of "Yedid nefesh"; and Israel Najara (1555?–1625?), who set his erotically charged sacred verse to Turkish, Greek, and Arabic folk melodies.[100] Judging from his own kabbalistic verse, Alḍāhirī had some familiarity with devotional poems by Alqabeṣ, Azikri, and Isaac Luria, whose work inspired the broader tradition of esoteric verse known as *shirat ha-ḥen*. The Safed poets were schooled in the medieval Iberian tradition, but the discontinuities represented by their mystical content and prosodic innovations suggested that they had not adequately safeguarded the Andalusian heritage. In Alḍāhirī's eyes, that distinction had gone to Yemenite Jewry.

5 Pronunciation as a Marker of Difference

In the twenty-third *maqāma*, Mordecai attends Sabbath eve prayers in the holy city of Tiberias. When the *sheliaḥ ṣibbur* mounts the pulpit, Mordecai is thoroughly taken by the melodiousness of his singing and the kabbalistic content of the Sabbath hymn he recites. (The pulpit is described as "a wooden tower constructed for that purpose" [Neh. 8:4]; presumably the raised *almemar/almemor* [Arabic *minbar*] typical of Sephardi synagogues, but not customary in Yemen.) Upon discovering that the *ḥazzan* with the dulcet tones and inspired liturgical poems is none other than Abner, Mordecai wonders how he could possibly have been chosen to officiate in the synagogue attended by the esteemed sages of Tiberias and the venerable head of its *yeshivah*. Confronting his friend, he voices his disbelief:

> Your poetic imagination is rich and fruitful, I know, but tell me, please, who appointed you *ḥazzan*? After all, you come from a distant land—*how*

100 See: Werblowsky, "A Collection of Prayers and Devotional Compositions by Solomon Alkabeṣ"; Pachter, "The Life and Personality of R. Elazar Azikri According to His Mystical Diary"; Yahalom, "R. Israel Najarah and the Revival of Hebrew Poetry in the East After the Expulsion from Spain"; idem, "Tensions between Sephardic Traditions and Ottoman Influences in Jewish Literary Activity"; Seroussi, "Rabbi yisrael najara meʿaṣev zimrat ha-qodesh aḥarei gerush sefarad"; idem, "From Court and Tarikat to Synagogue: Ottoman Art Music and Hebrew Sacred Songs"; and Beeri, "The Spanish Elements in the Poetry of Rabbi Israel Najara." For legends apparently emanating from the Lurianic school alleging that Najara led a dual existence, one part of which was marked by antinomianism and sexual laxity, see Yassif, *The Legend of Safed*, 28–31.

> *is it that they wanted you when our speech is close to Arabic and is alien from the spirit of the West, the spirit of the Sephardim, the choicest of Jews?* Their tongue is in all matters honed like a sharp sword; their wisdom is beyond measure. We are a people brought low; our faces are covered with thorns. They are expert in Talmud and *gemara*, all of them are masters of *sevara* (logical deduction). I am astounded and astonished like one in a dream: How did you achieve such enormous prestige?[101]

Abner is not in the least bit troubled by the whole affair. He dismisses Mordecai's fears with insouciance, contending that his pleasing voice and poetic prowess earned him the appointment as the congregation's precentor. He does not share Mordecai's concern that his Arabic-inflected Hebrew might offend the aesthetic sensibilities of the patrician Sephardim of Tiberias. But here again, Mordecai's acceptance of Sephardi exceptionalism leads to a trenchant self-critique. Even though Hebrew is their shared liturgical language, the two groups' dissimilar pronunciation is a poignant reminder that they effectively belong to different cultures. If the choicest of Jews, imbued with the spirit of the West, find Hebrew pronunciation that is close to Arabic distasteful and undignified, then by definition, this identity marker brands Yemenite Jews as "Others." It is striking that Alḍāhirī seems to have succumbed to an internal Jewish orientalism *avant la lettre*, whereby the Yemenites' preservation of the purest form of Hebrew is idealized, but, at the same time, their accent—a noticeably "Eastern" trait so intrinsic to his own community—is deemed less desirable than its "Western" counterpart. As in his borrowing from Judah Halevi's letter to Moses Ibn Ezra, the ostensibly binary opposition between East and West here acquires a certain fluidity, such that the meanings of the terms have shifted. No longer purely geographic signifiers, East and West have become cultural constructs. Ratzaby suggests that the phrase *ruaḥ maʿaravit* here reflects the Aramaic epithet *maʿaravaʾei* (Westerners), derived from *maʿarava*, the Babylonian rabbinic term for Palestine, situated to the west of the Babylonian academies.[102] But in Alḍāhirī's usage, "the spirit of the West" conjures the Iberian origin of the Sephardim in the Land of Israel and all it implies about their superior cultural heritage.[103]

---

101 *Sefer hamusar*, #23, p. 272, lines 190–196. See Yaʿakov, "Yemen, Pronunciation Traditions."

102 *Sefer hamusar*, p. 272, n. 192. See, e.g., bBer. 2b, *be-maʿarava*, in the Palestinian colleges.

103 In the medieval tradition, the "West" (*maghrib, gharb, maʿarav*) would technically have included Arabophone North Africa. On the meanings of the phrase "scholars of the West" in the writings of Maimonides, see Davidson, *Moses Maimonides: The Man and His Works*, 22–26.

Abner's pronunciation of Hebrew is a sensitive marker of difference. It betrays not only his geographic origins but also the cultural milieu from which he springs. Accents reveal distinctions in social status both within and across societies; here Mordecai counterposes Yemenite Jewry's humiliation at home with the proud ethnocentricity of the Sephardim. He frets about the deleterious effect that Abner's Arabicized articulation might have on the Tiberian congregation he is leading in prayer. If Abner's Hebrew accent risks assaulting refined Sephardi ears and detracting from their auditory pleasure, then pronunciation has aesthetic as well as social implications.[104] But it can also have halakhic or even theological repercussions and could in theory invalidate the prayers. The unfamiliar pronunciation of a visiting or transplanted *ḥazzan* was the subject of rabbinic responsa as well as the travelogues of *shadarim*, who were often invited to lead public prayers as a mark of respect.[105] The emissary Sapir recounts that he was honored with leading Sabbath prayers in the village of Jirwāḥ, halfway from the coast to Ṣanaʿā, "and even though I was not accustomed to their rite or pronunciation or melody, my prayer was pleasant to them because I came from the holy city of Jerusalem."[106] But Sapir also relates that when his Yemenite hosts heard him utter the phrase "barukh *ḥey* haʿolamim" at the conclusion of the blessing "Boreʾ nefashot," recited after consuming certain foods, they exclaimed that *ḥey* with a *ṣere* was a plural form, which was blasphemous when predicated of God, and that he must vocalize it "*ḥay* haʿolamim" as they did, to affirm God's absolute unity.[107] In conversation, Sapir's hosts laughed at his Ashkenazi Hebrew pronunciation, which was virtually unintelligible to them because it did not distinguish between the phonemes *kaf* and *qof*, for example. Despite Sapir's preconceptions, he was in the end forced to concede that the Yemenites were indeed the keepers of pure and clear Hebrew and that he was the inarticulate one.[108] As in Alḍāhirī's day, there was no trans-regional standardization of Hebrew pronunciation, nor was there any universally "normative" articulation of Hebrew for liturgical purposes. In the 16th-century, Iberian exiles and their descendants in Ottoman Lands presumably had their own distinctive Hebrew pronunciation reflecting

104 Cf. Efron's illuminating discussion of Sephardic Hebrew pronunciation as viewed through the reforming lens of the late 18th-century Berlin Haskalah in *German Jewry and the Allure of the Sephardic*, 21–52.

105 See Zimmels, *Ashkenazim and Sephardim*, 82–90. See also Dotan, "About Pronunciation in Prayer and Torah Reading."

106 See *Even Sapir* 1:51a.

107 *Even Sapir* 1:55b–56a. On the theological implications of the Yemenite vocalization of *teḥiyyat ha-metim*, see ibid., 56a.

108 *Even Sapir* 1:54b.

the influence of Romance elements. Prior to the expulsion, Iberian Jews had developed "a Hebrew letter writing system that included special characters enabling the transcription of Hispanic sounds absent from Hebrew."[109] Later, they developed an extensive vernacular literature, rabbinic and popular.[110] Following the expulsion, the exiles brought to the Ottoman Empire varieties of Ibero-Romance that gradually evolved into Judezmo. At the time that *Sefer hamusar* was composed, the language spoken by the masses of Sephardim in the Land of Israel would presumably have been an early form of this koiné, although Alḍāhirī's fictional characters interact only with members of the rabbinic élite who, like Mordecai and Abner, express themselves exclusively in flawless literary Hebrew. How they pronounced liturgical Hebrew is left to our imagination.[111]

While nothing explicit is said in the text, the rogue hero's proclivity for shape shifting raises the possibility that Abner had consciously altered his accent to suit Sephardi aural ideals in order to attain the coveted position of *ḥazzan*. But the Tiberian congregants have no reservations about Abner's ethnicity or origins and insist that he be appointed *ḥazzan* without further delay. Invited on the eve of Rosh Hashanah to stand before the ark, he recites an original *piyyut* ushering out the old year and welcoming in the new with such aplomb that the congregants exclaim they have not heard such a finely constructed poem for Rosh Hashanah in years. They are anxious to retain Abner and urge the elders to authorize his position at once. Not only is Abner radiant with joy, but the congregants' praise for the poem's eloquent language and superbly pleasing form indicates that they have derived aesthetic pleasure and spiritual uplift from his performance, regardless of his pronunciation.

The protagonists' opposing views on the gravity of these matters is another instance of the author externalizing his own ambivalences. By having Mordecai and Abner each articulate one of his own conflicting stances, Alḍāhirī is able to reflect critically on the relative aesthetic merit of the Yemenite and Sephardi pronunciation of liturgical Hebrew and its consequences for Yemenite Jewish self-perception and self-esteem. On the one hand, Mordecai's sensitivity to the claims of Sephardi preeminence makes him acutely aware of Yemenite Jewish difference. His self-deprecating fears that Abner's accent might disqualify him from leading public prayer is notably at odds with the age-old traditions of precision in Torah reading and liturgical recitation on which his community

109 See Bunis, "Judezmo: The Jewish Language of the Ottoman Sephardim," 24–25.

110 See Borovaya, *The Beginnings of Ladino Literature: Moses Almosnino and His Readers* and Lehmann, *Ladino Rabbinic Literature and Ottoman Sephardic Culture*.

111 On the use of Hebrew in 16th-century Safed, see Yassif, *The Legend of Safed*, 234–235.

prided itself.[112] On the other hand, in Abner's mind, these concerns are outweighed by Yemenite Jewry's acknowledged excellence in *piyyut* and poetry. Ultimately, Alḍāhirī resolves the narrative tension with the Tiberians' unanimous endorsement of Abner as their representative before God. This narrative twist subtly vindicates the Yemenite accent in Hebrew and tacitly responds to Ottoman Sephardi exceptionalism.

Abner's gifts to the Tiberians are manifold: in the synagogue he offers them meaningful prayer and the aesthetic pleasure of his musicality and *piyyutim*. From Ṣanaʿā he sent a munificent contribution toward the upkeep of their *yeshivah* accompanied by a letter lavishing praise on their sages. To this rhymed prose epistle he appended a much remarked-upon poem extolling Tiberias, "the crowning city" (cf. Is. 23:8), which calls to mind Arabic genres devoted to the *faḍā'il* (virtues, excellent qualities) or *maḥāsin* (beauties, merits) of individual cities, as well as the tradition of Hebrew encomiastic verse for communal officials and Jewish communities that was cultivated in Islamic lands.[113] Marked by symmetries and euphony, the twenty-four verse paean is composed in classical Andalusian form featuring quantitative meter and monorhyme. The city's Hebrew name, *Tveryah*, which occurs at the end of the fourth line, sets the final rhyming syllable for the entire poem, and since that monosyllable encapsulates a divine name, its constant repetition foregrounds the city's distinctive relationship with God. The opening glorification of the Creator flows into a celebration of Tiberias as a divinely chosen city, which then modulates into a panegyric for its righteous sages who embody its inherent holiness.

> The heavenly dome is His loft;
> His wonders reach earth's very ends.
> His praises cannot be contained
> by angels, much less mortal men.
> But Israel He chose as His own,
> their souls are since then bound to Him.

112 See Morag, *Mesorot ha-lashon haʿivrit ve-ha-lashon ha'aramit she-be-fi yehudei teiman*. Doron Yaakov notes that the Yemenite reading tradition of Hebrew texts "took shape in the course of the intermediate period of Hebrew, from the time it ceased functioning as a spoken language until its revival in the 20th century"; see his "Yemen, Pronunciation Traditions."

113 See: van Gelder, "City Panegyric, in Classical Arabic"; Enderwitz, "Faḍā'il"; Livne-Kafri, "The Muslim Traditions 'in Praise of Jerusalem' (*Faḍā'il al-Quds*)"; Mourad, "The *Faḍā'il* of Jerusalem Books as Anthologies"; and Masarwa, *Praising Damascus*. See also Decter, *Dominion Built of Praise*, 30–66 and *passim*.

And Zion he chose as His seat, but
Tiberias He did not forsake—
For she stood in, in place of His House
when it was trampled and battered to ruins.
The exiled Sanhedrin moved there,
and thence came a balm for my wound.
In truth, she is healed and is cured
of her illness since being rebuilt
By the saintly and righteous who stood
by the unhappy city in need.
Samuel the priest is their prince
with the Levite and Moses Gedalyah
And Abraham, three-fold in name
whom they sent to good purpose abroad.
Her wastelands they turned into Eden,
her parched soil into a lush park.
If not for their stream, plants would wither
while God's precious vine is far-flung.
Exiled, Israel moans and resembles
a wall askew, a tottering fence.
Her noblemen captive to brutes,
a despised nation rules her élite.
If not for her sages' wise guidance,
she would straggle, as one gone astray;
No insight or prudence would steer her,
nor wisdom nor sense show the way.
But scholars illumine her path
with treatises exquisitely wrought.
They print books of wisdom so that
learning is open to all.
Etched with an iron stylus and lead—
discerning work done with clever tools.
The foolish one says to himself:
'For knowledge I'd sail the vast sea,'
Not seeing that God in His prescience
has with learning consoled Yemen's Jews.[114]

114 "Yemen's Jews" is suggested contextually; the Hebrew actually has *ha-shevuyah*, "the captive one," an epithet evoking Israel in exile. But the two following lines depict the captive

To their oppressors they boast of their lot:
 'We are blessed with Torah and wise works.'[115]
To that taunting handmaid they cry:
 'How is your beloved better than another?
 How esteemed like a lioness was your mother?'
And God will soon say, 'Arise, shine!
 Beloved Israel, your splendor has shone.'[116]

Substantively, this lyrical eulogy combines conventional, timeless motifs with historically specific details that capture a particular moment in time. The inversion of the natural order of things as reflected in the incongruity between God's election of Israel and Israel's cruel subjugation in exile to the descendants of Hagar, "the handmaid," is regularly lamented in Hebrew liturgical complaints from the medieval Islamic world. Christian and Muslim overlords are often portrayed as rivals for God's love, who taunt Israel by claiming that her current degradation is a sign of divine rejection.[117] But Israel remains steadfast in her belief in God's continued affection, and—as here, with God's closing reassurance—these plaintive poems end hopefully, alluding to biblical prophecies of restoration and redemption. These themes, familiar from Andalusian Hebrew verse, are clearly interwoven into Alḍāhirī's poem, yet he is not bound by his conventional models. God's choice of Israel as His people and Zion as His earthly home prefigure His special attachment to Tiberias, which stood in for the Temple after it was destroyed and which became the seat of the exiled Sanhedrin in the middle of the third century C.E.[118] This is the proper beginning of

one engaging in a polemic with Muslim rivals for God's attentions, which Ratzaby took to be an evocation of *galut teiman*.

115 Literally, "Know that my lot is [so rich] that my cup overflows."

116 "Asher kippat sheḥaqim lo ʿaliyyah"; *Sefer hamusar*, 282–283.

117 See, e. g., Scheindlin, *The Gazelle*, 52–57, 76–83.

118 Given its importance, it is curious that Alḍāhirī does not mention Tiberias as home to the Masoretes, but the poem glosses over the earlier Middle Ages, moving from the 3rd century to the 16th. David Stern notes that, already in the 10th century, the Karaites Yaʿaqūb al-Qirqisānī and David al-Fāsī praised the Tiberians for preserving "the purest traditions of native Hebrew pronunciation and Bible reading—a claim … analogous to that made about pre-Islamic Arabic poetry" and, we might add, to that made about Yemenite Jews as well. Swayed by European Romanticism, 19th- and 20th-century Jewish scholars promoted an essentialist myth whereby Yemenite Jewry had escaped any kind of linguistic adulteration by virtue of its centuries-long isolation. This line of thinking merged with bona fide linguistic evidence that the Yemenite reading tradition of Hebrew texts preserved some ancient features to yield repeated assertions that the Yemenite immigrants to Palestine preserved the original, pristine pronunciation of Hebrew. See Stern, *The Jewish*

Abner's tribute to the city throughout the ages, in which he extols the virtues of those who rebuilt her in the mid-sixteenth century and lauds her communal leaders and scholars. The latter are the true heroes of this tale, who have illumined her path with their erudite writings, which they have distributed widely thanks to the technological innovation of printing. Alḍāhirī's thrill is palpable as he extols the mechanical ingenuity that has made learning accessible to all:

> *Be-hadpisam le-sifrei ha-tevunah/ ʿadei shavah leʿein ha-kol geluyah*
> *Beʿeṭ barzel veʿoferet ḥaquqim/ melekhet bin be-taḥbulot ʿasuyah*
> (lines 166–167).

> (They print books of wisdom so that/ learning is open to all.
> Etched with an iron stylus and lead—/ discerning work done with clever tools.)

His paean to the invention of printing "with an iron stylus and lead" (cf. Job 19:23–24) echoes the language of colophons and commendatory poems appended to early printed Hebrew books, suggesting that he was familiar with such paratexts. The phrase occurs in the joint colophon of the editor and proofreader of the Bomberg edition of Maimonides' *Mishneh Torah* (Venice, 1524) (*la-ḥaqoq beʿeṭ barzel veʿoferet ḥibbur mishneh torah*) while Joseph Sarfati's prefatory poem to Bomberg's *Biblia Rabbinica* of 1525 marvels at the "delicate and square type" and the "letters newly cut with an iron pen (*otot beʿeṭ barzel ḥadashim ḥartu*)" used to print the twenty-four books of the Bible together.[119] The notion—so intensely pleasing to Alḍāhirī—that printing invigorates scholarship and enables learning to reach a much broader public was already a recurrent motif in paratexts to incunabula (1450–1500) and early printed books. The afterword to Maimonides' *Commentary on the Mishnah*

Bible: A Material History, 74. For the exoticizing isolation myth see: Idelsohn, "Ha-havarah ha'ivrit"; idem, "Mivṭa ha-teimanim"; and Yishayahu ed., *Shevut teiman*, p. 6. For the linguistic evidence see Morag, *Mesorot ha-lashon haʿivrit ve-ha-lashon ha'aramit she-be-fi yehudei teiman*; Karah, "Reading Traditions Reflected in the Babylonian Talmud's Punctuation According to the Yemenite Tradition"; Dotan, "About Pronunciation in Prayer and Torah Reading"; and Yaʿakov, "Yemen, Pronunciation Traditions."

119 See Brener, "A Poem by Joseph Sarfati in Honor of Daniel Bomberg's *Biblia Rabbinica*, Venice 1525." Brener remarks that the phrase was used for the art of printing already in the period of its infancy (the incunabula period, 1450–1500). See also the citation from the printer's introduction to *Shilṭei ha-gibborim* (Sabbioneta, 1554/55) in Ben Yehuda, *A Complete Dictionary*, 2: 979: … *be-sifreihem ha-mudpasim beʿeṭ barzel veʿoferet*.

(Naples, 1492) praises the enormous effort that went into printing the work "in order to benefit the public": *ki immeṣ koaḥ la'asoto bidfus le-ma'an zekhot bo et ha-rabbim.*[120] And Alḍāhirī's use of the technical term *hidpis* for printing is another indication that he was au courant with such texts; by the 16th-century, the verb forms *hidpis* and *nidpas*, derived from the rabbinic noun *defus*, were in common use.[121]

6 The Impact of Print Culture

Alḍāhirī lived during the first century of Hebrew printing, although no Hebrew press was ever founded in Yemen.[122] Coupled with Yemenite Jewry's centuries-old bibliophilia, the absence of a press ensured the continued longevity of a flourishing manuscript culture.[123] Nor did the import of printed Hebrew books supplant this rich tradition; printed books were expensive and relatively rare, and the work of copying by hand continued for centuries.[124] Copying was a branch of the Yemenite Jewish economy. In Ṣana'ā during the 15th–16th centuries, the multi-generational Benaya family of scribes, known for the accuracy of its transcriptions, had a virtual monopoly on the copying profession.[125] Privately commissioned manuscripts were passed down within families

120 Ben Yehuda, *A Complete Dictionary* 2: 976. See also Schmelzer, "Poems in Praise of Books by David Ben Joseph Ibn Yahya," p. 332, lines 24–27 and p. 334, lines 31–33.

121 The rabbinic *defus* (frame, mold) is etymologically related to the Greek *typos*, a blow, dent, impression, or figure in relief (as well as 'form,' 'character,' or 'type,' yielding the Hebrew *tippus*); see Zilberberg and Breger, "Printing, Hebrew" and Betzer, "Genesis of the Verb *hidpīs* 'Print' and its Cognates."

122 See Yaari, *Hebrew Printing in the East*, 1: 86–91; Ratzaby, "'Iyyunim be-hitpatḥut maḥzor-teiman," p. 99, n. 7; Luqman, "Education and the Press in South Arabia," 264; and cf. Messick, *The Calligraphic State*, 115–119. The 19th century saw the establishment of Arabic-character presses in the Muslim world although Arabic printing with movable type had begun in Italy in the 16th century, initially for the purpose of publishing Christian Arabic texts; see Roper, "The History of the Book in the Muslim World," and idem, "Maṭba'a."

123 A minor press printing in English, Arabic, and Hebrew operated in British-ruled Aden from 1891 to 1935, but in the interior of Yemen, including Ṣana'ā, Jewish manuscript culture continued to thrive until the mass emigration to Israel in 1949/50.

124 Manuscript production often persisted alongside printing; for the case of early modern Venice and the different advantages each medium offered, see Dweck, *The Scandal of Kabbalah*, 32–37 and *passim*.

125 See Tobi, "Benayah." Yaakov Sapir recorded the colophon of a ms. (now lost) copied in a beautiful hand by Miriam, a daughter of the family; see Riegler, "Benayah ha-sofer ve-ṣe'eṣa'av" and Habermann, *Anshei sefer ve'anshei ma'aseh*, 266.

from one generation to another, or donated to synagogues.[126] Particularly valuable manuscripts were given elegant leather bindings with ornamental clasps, requiring the work of skilled artisans and silversmiths. Rabbis and Torah scholars also copied manuscripts to supplement their incomes. But not everyone could afford to engage a professional copyist, and individuals frequently copied works necessary for their own practical use, such as the daily prayer book or the Passover haggadah.[127] Even printed books, costly and scarce, were copied by hand, often in their entirety (including title pages and *haskamot*).[128] In the second half of the 19th century, printed Hebrew books gradually displaced handwritten works as visiting merchants and travelers siphoned off large numbers of valuable manuscripts, offering cheaply produced, superficially attractive books in their place. Yiḥye Qāfiḥ (1849–1932) responded to the willful depletion of Yemenite Jewry's prized possessions with a herculean effort to preserve this patrimony and renew a widespread reverence for manuscripts among ordinary Jews. He collected as many manuscripts as his modest budget would allow and extracted genizah fragments from rotting book bindings, pieced them together, and mobilized his students to undertake a massive copying enterprise so that ancient texts that had fallen into neglect (Maimonides' Arabic commentary on the Mishnah; his *Sefer ha-miṣvot*; Saadya's commentaries; early prayer books; Yemenite poetry) could once again be circulated. His study house developed an assembly line for copying: when a merchant or traveler arrived in town in possession of a rare manuscript or unknown text priced prohibitively, Qāfiḥ recruited his students, borrowed the manuscript for one night, divided it into fascicles, and distributed them among the copyists who worked through the

126 See Tobi, *Yemenite Jewish Manuscripts in the Ben-Zvi Institute*, 8, 12; idem, "Challenges to Tradition"; Riegler, "The Colophon as a Source for the History of Yemenite Books and their Scribes"; Beit-Arié, *Hebrew Codicology*, 105, 147, 174, n. 141; idem, "The Individual Nature of Hebrew Book Production and Consumption," 24; and van der Heide, *Hebrew Manuscripts of Leiden University Library*, 18.

127 This was of course true of Jews in medieval Europe as well; see Schrijver, "The Transmission of Jewish Knowledge through MSS and Printed Books," sec. 3.

128 On the community's bibliophilia and manuscript culture, see Ratzaby, *Bem'agloth Temân*, 86–100. On Yemenite manuscript copies of the *Shulḥan 'arukh* made soon after its appearance, see Ratzaby, "Rabbi yosef karo viyhudei teiman." On the workmanship that went into Arabic manuscript production from the earliest Islamic period, see Sellheim, "Kitāb." To this day it is not uncommon to find manuscript leaves included in printed books of Yemenite Jewish provenance; cf., e.g., Yiḥye Ṣaliḥ, *Tiklāl 'im sefer eṣ ḥayyim*. Reviewing John Boardley's *Typographic Firsts: Adventures in Early Printing*, Gill Partington writes that "Printing initially looked backwards as much as forwards, striving to replicate the conventions of the manuscript book. Gutenberg's first gothic typefaces were designed to look like the handiwork of medieval scribes …"; see Partington, "Noted Incunables."

night. In the morning he had the original manuscript re-stitched and rebound by an expert binder and returned it to its owner.[129]

Its largely fictional content notwithstanding, *Sefer hamusar* reveals an awareness of the growing transregional Hebrew book trade in the 16th century. Its invented characters' encounter with historical titles is yet another instance of the work's whimsical blurring of boundaries. *Sefer hamusar* reflects the attitudes of a book-loving society of limited means at a time when the arrival of printed Hebrew texts was an event of major cultural and religious significance. This sense of wonder also comes across in Alḍāhirī's Torah commentary on *Parashat Ha'azinu*, Deuteronomy 32, where he celebrates the post-Expulsion sages

> who out of their abundance of wisdom established printing for the sacred books—that which had not existed previously—which is a tremendous miracle for those who were not familiar with it, inasmuch as the printer produces a quantity in one day that a man can only produce after an entire year. Would that they would spread Torah throughout Israel!

That many of these treasures were brought by rabbinic emissaries from the Land of Israel endowed them with the sanctity of the Holy Land, so that the texts were esteemed not only in their own right but also as mementos of the interaction with the *shadar*, with perhaps a talismanic value.[130] Reverence for these artifacts is evident in all three versions of the story of Rabbi Abraham Ashkenazi's visit to Yemen. The learned envoy's bookselling is intended to encourage religious study among the broader Yemenite Jewish population. That he is not interested in price gouging earns him unqualified admiration. Almost counterintuitively, even while imprisoned, community members are keen to purchase these edifying tomes despite their reduced means. Abner's request for a variety of classical texts and commentaries is motivated both by a desire to expand his repertoire and a longing to rebuild the personal collection

129 See Yisha'yahu and Zadok eds., *Shevut teiman*, 178–179 and Ratzaby, *Bem'agloth Temân*, 88. Langermann notes that Yosef Qāfiḥ, although only six years old at the time, took part in his grandfather's effort; see "Rabbi Yosef Qafih's Modern Medieval Translation of the *Guide*," 259.

130 Cf. Yaari, *Sheluḥei 'ereṣ yisra'el*, 73. Compare also the admiration and warm reception accorded *shadarim* to North Africa in the 19th century, as documented in Hazan, "The Emissaries of Eretz Israel in the Poetry of the Jews of North Africa." Sapir condescendingly alleges that "because valuable books were not formerly widespread here, they think that anything printed is sacred, true, and correct and should not be criticized"; see *Even Sapir*, 1:61a.

he had assembled while visiting the Land of Israel, part of which had been lost at sea. (On a narrative level, his quest to build a library of physical, scholarly texts imparting religious wisdom complements Mordecai's ongoing search for orally acquired *adab*, a generous selection of which Abner provides at the end of Chapter 25.) In the 40th *maqāma*, the wise emissary is described as a sort of marvelous apparition who has come from the biblical land "of the Amorites and Perizzites" laden with books of all sorts. Many of the letters that he receives from all over Yemen are book orders, and as Abner remarks in his accompanying poem of praise, "over his abundance of books all hearts rejoiced."[131] Together with his readiness to share his own erudition—which is the product of a nimble mind as well as diligent study in the *yeshivot* of the Land of Israel—Rabbi Abraham's commitment to circulating sacred works is portrayed in the most noble (and unmercenary) of terms.[132]

Alḍāhirī's preoccupation with books is evident in several additional episodes of *Sefer hamusar*. There are challenges to compose panegyrics for works and their authors, from Maimonides' *Mishneh torah* and *Guide* to Joseph Albo's *Sefer ha'iqqarim*, David Kimhi's *Sefer ha-shorashim*, the 14th-century halakhist Jeroḥam b. Meshullam, author of *Sefer meisharim* and *Toldot adam ve-ḥavvah*,[133] and the *Zohar*, as well as a poem in praise of Isaac Abravanel's commentary *Naḥalat avot* on *Pirqei avot*—an Iberian and Provençal repertoire that spans halakhah, philosophy, grammar, exegesis, and kabbalah. There are tales of books and righteous sons, and a precious volume entrusted to an unworthy son who allowed it to be stolen.[134] It is noteworthy that Abner's attainment of mystical, esoteric knowledge is predicated not on initiation in a small circle of adepts but on his autodidactic study of some of the most formative works of Spanish kabbalah, the first editions of which appeared during Alḍāhirī's lifetime.[135] The characters' focus tends to be on books primarily as repositories of

131 *Sefer hamusar*, p. 428, line 88.

132 On Yaari's identification of Rabbi Abraham ben Isaac Ashkenazi as a historical figure based in Safed, see Chapter Six.

133 See Galinsky and Robinson, "Rabbi Jeruham b. Meshullam, Michael Scot, and the Development of Jewish Law in Fourteenth-Century Spain." The authors note that Jeroḥam's work was studied in the Ottoman Empire in the 16th century; see p. 495.

134 Ratzaby notes that when a man died, his books were considered the most important items in his estate and were divided among his sons according to his will, by lot, or by mutual agreement; see *Bem'agloth Temân*, p. 98.

135 Among others, Abner mentions the *Zohar* (first editions: Mantua, 1558–1560 and Cremona, 1559–1560) and Judah Ḥayyaṭ's commentary, *Minḥat yehudah*, on *Sefer ma'arekhet ha-elohut* (first edition: Mantua, 1558); see Chapter Six and Idel, "Printing Kabbalah in Sixteenth-Century Italy."

knowledge rather than on their material form (paper quality, elegance/legibility of typeface, aesthetics of bindings, presence of readers' annotations, etc.) or ritual function qua objects (although one of Abner's kabbalistic poems alludes to the purely ritual function of publicly reciting the Zohar, and Abner is aware of the apotropaic value of text when he inscribes sacred verses on a gourd, transforming it into a childbirth amulet). Judging from the story of the *shadar*, they are interested in the dissemination of books and have a sense of their commercial value. When a kabbalistic volume purchased at great expense is looted from Abner's home while he is incarcerated, he sends an emissary to redeem the captive volume. Although the effort comes to naught, the story demonstrates that a book is a valuable enough commodity to command a ransom.[136]

The receptivity of Alḍāhirī's protagonists not just to the idea of printed books but to the transfer of these material objects from differing Jewish cultural spheres implies a degree of dynamism in 16th-century Yemenite Jewish society rather than an unyielding resistance to change.[137] Foundational texts like the Mishnah would have been part of the universal Jewish textual heritage and would not have required comment, but the characters also do not reflect consciously on the cultural specificity of works originating in other Jewish diasporas. (It is worth noting, however, that precisely in the mid-16th century, due to a confluence of cultural developments, the reception of the Mishnah as an independent composition increased dramatically across much of the Jewish world, with the Mishnah attaining "a new and revolutionary status …, playing a crucial role in the cultural revival that took place in Safed," where rituals of reciting mishnaic passages were introduced.)[138] Though in other contexts they are quick to identify markers of difference, their enthusiasm for imported texts suggests a lack of concern that Hebrew prayer books, liturgical commentaries, or legal codes addressing the needs of other Jewish subcultures might be

136 On Yemeni Muslims taking Jewish books for ransom in the 19th century, see Fenton, "Moses Shapira's Journey to the Yemen," p. lxxiii and n. 16.

137 This does not necessarily imply an awareness of innovations in Hebrew printing that were linked to increased Catholic surveillance (censorship, burning) of Hebrew books in mid-16th century Italy; see Raz-Krakotzkin, "Persecution and the Art of Printing," and idem, "The Censor as a Mediator: Printing, Censorship, and the Shaping of Hebrew Literature." Raz-Krakotzkin points out that "during the very years surrounding the burning of the Talmud, nearly the entire Hebrew canon (in form and content) was printed," including the Mishnah, the *Zohar*, and Karo's *Beit yosef*; Idel also points to the dearth of important Hebrew books in the aftermath of the 1553 Talmud burning as a contributing factor in the accelerated printing of kabbalistic books in Italy; see "Printing Kabbalah in Sixteenth-Century Italy," 93.

138 Raz-Krakotzkin, "Persecution and the Art of Printing," 98, 102 *passim*. See also: Idel, "Some Concepts of Mishnah among Sixteenth-Century Safedian Kabbalists."

ill-suited for practical use in Yemen or that the books' contents, textual standardization, accessibility, or affordability might undermine age-old Yemenite Jewish customs or practices. Their equanimity intimates that in Alḍāhirī's time incipient innovations in these realms were gradual and incremental—though they clearly affected patterns of thought and scholarly priorities—and that they coexisted with continuities in religious sensibility, liturgical practice, and traditional modes of production and diffusion of learned literature. While the protagonists are captivated and delighted by the new technology of printing and admire Palestinian Jewry's wide propagation of knowledge via the medium (regardless of where the printing took place), they never suggest that their own time-honored manuscript tradition in any way marks them as less progressive than those Jewish communities with active presses or a vigorous trade in printed books. The meteoric rise of the Safed center and the emergence of Hebrew printing together would have a formative and formidable impact on Yemenite Jewry over the course of the sixteenth and seventeenth centuries.[139] In subsequent centuries, bitter controversies would erupt over the displacement of the "authentic" Yemenite (*baladī*) rite with the advent of printed prayer books containing the Sephardi (*shāmī*) rite of the Holy Land and the arrival from the Land of Israel of Joseph Karo's monumentally influential *Shulḥan ʿarukh*. Together with a shift to kabbalistic study, these developments threatened to supplant the earlier Yemenite tradition informed by the rationalist philosophy, exegesis, halakhic and liturgical guidelines of Maimonides and Saʿadya Gaon, whose writings had been virtually canonical.[140] But with their unconditional esteem for the learned Jews of the Holy Land, Alḍāhirī's Yemenite protagonists seem unperturbed that they may be abetting these latter-day Sephardi cultural influences to make their first inroads into Yemen.

---

139 For the effect of these developments on Jewish communities in the Ottoman Empire (outside of the Land of Israel), see Hacker, "The Intellectual Activity of the Jews of the Ottoman Empire During the Sixteenth and Seventeenth Centuries."

140 See: Gavra, *Ha-tiklāl ha-maddaʿi ha-mehudar*; idem, *Meḥqarim be-siddurei teiman ʿim nusaḥ tiklāl es ḥayyim*; idem, "Le-foʿalo shel rabbi yiṣḥaq wannah be-sidduro 'paʿamon zahav'"; Tobi, "Challenges to Tradition"; idem, "Rabbi yiṣḥaq wannah ve-hitḥazzqut ha-ʿissuq ba-qabbalah"; idem, "Shulḥan ʿarukh le-rabbi yosef karo leʿumat mishneh torah le-ha-rambam be-teiman"; Hallamish, "Ha-qabbalah be-sidduro shel rabbi yiṣhaq wannah"; Ratzaby, "ʿIyyunim be-hitpatḥut maḥzor teiman"; and idem, "Rabbi yosef karo viyhudei teiman." See also Gaimani, *Temurot be-moreshet yahadut teiman be-hashpaʿat ha-shulḥan ʿarukh ve-qabbalat ha-ari*; and Qāfiḥ ed., "*Qorot yisrael be-teiman* le-rabbi ḥayyim ḥabshush," 267–271 on the role of the influential 18th-century figure, Shalom Ha-Cohen ʿIraqi, in distributing printed prayer books containing the Sephardi (*shāmī*) rite.

CHAPTER 4

Representations of Muslims: Perspectives on the Dominant Faith

Quite unusually for a Hebrew *maqāma*, Alḍāhirī's lively cast of characters includes not only an array of Jews but also Muslims of various stripes. Textual representation of Muslims is rare in medieval Hebrew belletristic works, even those composed in an Islamic cultural milieu. Despite Judah Alḥarizi's move from the Iberian Peninsula to the Islamic East, very few of the Hebrew *maqāmāt* in his *Taḥkemoni* betray any awareness of the dominant Muslim society in whose midst he spent much of his productive career.[1] Ross Brann has pointed to the *Taḥkemoni*'s Judeocentric focus and its author's "protonational sensibility" as factors contributing to the work's seeming indifference toward Muslims. Jewish authors in Islamic lands were also wary of portraying Muslims for fear of giving offense, even in Hebrew and Judeo-Arabic texts not readily accessible to non-Jewish readers. In his *Power in the Portrayal*, Brann reads such reluctance among the acculturated Jewish élite in eleventh- and twelfth-century Islamic Spain as "a sign of the Jews' sensitivity to and ambivalence about their status as a subcultural minority in Andalusi society."[2] Rather than attempt to establish the "facts" of Jewish existence under Andalusian Islam, Brann undertakes a fresh reading of literary sources to reveal the nuanced and varied ways in which Jewish intellectuals envisaged their Muslim counterparts and viewed their own place in Muslim society.[3] With an eye to the construction of social meaning in their works, he demonstrates that textual portrayals of Muslims reflect concerns internal to the Jewish community, just as Andalusian Muslim representations of prominent Jews such as Samuel Hanagid do not record historically accurate details but rather project the majority society's own political and military anxieties. Brann argues that, during the peak period of Jewish intellectual creativity and political prominence in Andalusia, Jewish depictions of Muslims—imagined and historical—contributed to the process of communal self-definition and self-legitimation by constructing cultural and religious "otherness."

1 Active in three hubs of medieval Jewish creativity, Alḥarizi wrote mainly Hebrew poetry in Spain, translated Arabic prose into Hebrew in Provence, and composed the *Taḥkemoni* in the East. See Alḥarizi, *Taḥkemoni*, ed. Yahalom-Katsumata, p. v.

2 Brann, *Power in the Portrayal*, 8 and 119–159 *passim*.

3 Brann's project also explores Andalusian Muslim representations of Jews; see ibid., 1–23.

 | DOI:10.1163/9789004733787_006

The type of ambivalence that Brann has detected in the *Taḥkemoni* is, *mutatis mutandis*, also evident in *Sefer hamusar*. Even though Alḍāhirī's *maqāma* collection emerged from an entirely different era and socio-political milieu, it is also the product of a Jewish minority culture attempting to come to terms with the instability of its existence in a Muslim society. Unlike the *Taḥkemoni, Sefer hamusar* is set almost entirely in the Islamic East, yet characters recognizable as Muslims are conspicuously absent from large segments of the work. Its peripatetic protagonists venture from Yemen to India, Persia, Mesopotamia, Syria, the Land of Israel, Egypt, and Ottoman Turkey, but their inquisitiveness about their surroundings rarely extends beyond the local Jewish community. When portrayals of Muslims do occur, therefore, they are worthy of serious scrutiny. Alḍāhirī's representations are not restricted to a Muslim élite but rather extend to all walks of life, from *qāḍīs* to con men, merchants to mobs. That most of the Muslims depicted are imaginary does not detract from the value of the enterprise; it is the cultural assumptions and self-definitions underlying such representations that are significant. Inspired as it is by Alḥarizi's *Taḥkemoni* and Andalusian Hebrew poetry, *Sefer hamusar* looks back to the Iberian belletristic, exegetical, and theological literature that had earlier articulated Jewish attitudes toward Muslims, Islam, and Arabic cultural creativity.[4] At the same time, as the product of sixteenth-century Yemen, the work reflects certain historically and culturally conditioned sensibilities, even if its Muslim characters are largely types, refracted through a fanciful literary lens. Despite the Judeocentrism of *Sefer hamusar*, Alḍāhirī's renderings of the dominant faith and culture are more varied and extensive than those found in earlier Hebrew *maqāmāt*. And though his evocations lack nuance and complexity, they reveal the very real anxieties, aspirations, and self-perceptions of a community that effectively constituted the sole religious minority in pre-Ottoman Yemen.[5]

4 On earlier ambivalences, see Alfonso, *Islamic Culture Through Jewish Eyes*, who pays special attention to the role of language in the formation of Andalusi Jewish communal identity and self-definition and the intertwining of Jewish attitudes toward Arabic with those toward Muslims.

5 Tobi writes that from the 11th century, there were no Christians in Yemen, such that in practical terms the epithets *al-kuffār* ("the unbelievers") and *dhimmayūn* referred exclusively to Jews, even though from a theoretical legal standpoint they applied to other non-Muslims as well; see "Ha-ḥeqer ha-hashva'ati shel ha-sifrut ha'amamit ha-yehudit ve-ha-muslimit be-teiman," p. 430, n. 70. During the first Ottoman occupation, the presence of Turks of Christian origin and Christian captives gave rise to a more complicated spectrum of identities; see Malkiel, *Strangers in Yemen*, 6. Alḍāhirī shows no awareness of these developments.

On the surface, Alḍāhirī's *maqāma* collection is marked by alienation from and contempt for the rival religion at whose hands his people had suffered grinding oppression and humiliation. By all accounts, the socio-political situation of the Jews in sixteenth-century Yemen could not have differed more from that of the upper crust of Andalusian Jewry during its so-called "Golden Age." There was no counterpart to the worldly Andalusian Jewish political and intellectual aristocracy, nor was there a polite courtly culture in Yemeni Muslim society that a Jewish élite might desire to emulate. Unlike the privileged sector of medieval Andalusian Jewish society, Yemenite Jewry in Alḍāhirī's telling did not prosper materially under Muslim rule or benefit particularly from coexistence. Rather, during this politically tumultuous time of internecine violence and tribal disputes among the ruling Muslims, the Jews of Ṣanaʿā were subjected to collective punishment and incarcerated at the discretion of the Imām al-Muṭahhar, possibly on the pretext that they harbored pro-Ottoman sympathies, and as a means of extorting funds, extracting forced labor, and asserting the *imām's* authority in the face of contending Zaydī factions. According to Alḍāhirī, they were shackled and deprived of their most basic physical needs. His account of the ordeal betrays little regard for the Muslim overlords who perpetrated these cruelties. Throughout, his sparse references to historical Muslims are almost entirely confined to the sectarian Zaydī *imām* and his henchmen, whom he disparages as *zeidim* ("wicked/arrogant") in a fortuitous play on the sound similarity between *zaydiyya* and *malkhut zadon*, the arrogant kingdom of Edom whose downfall is foretold in the prophecies of Obadiah (ch. 3) and Malachi (3:15, 19) and which became code for the oppressors of Israel in every age.[6] Accordingly, a salient strand of his story highlights communal adversity and tenuous existence under Yemeni Islam. Despite its omissions and periodic imprecisions, a great deal of weight has been attached to this account since *Sefer hamusar* is the only extant witness to these incidents. In the absence of evidence from Muslim chronicles or other works of Jewish provenance, little else about these events of the 16th-century Yemeni Jewish-Muslim encounter can be reconstructed. (The main Muslim account of the first Ottoman conquest, Quṭb al-Dīn al-Nahrawālī's pro-Turkish and anti-Zaydī *Barq al-yamānī*, does not take any notice of *imām* al-Muṭahhar's dealings with the Jews.[7]) And precisely because *Sefer hamusar* is a unique witness to these historical incidents, scholars have latched on to Alḍāhirī's lachrymose narrative of

6 From late antiquity on, the epithets *zeidim* and *malkhut zadon* were applied to Rome, Christendom, and Islam respectively. See Cohen, "Esau as Symbol in Early Medieval Thought" and Langer, *Cursing the Christians?*

7 See al-Nahrawālī, *Lightning Over Yemen*.

unmitigated Jewish suffering under Zaydī rule without attending to his more fanciful evocations of Muslims from other walks of life that complicate his picture of interfaith dynamics.[8]

And yet, if one digs a little more deeply, it is possible to find imaginary Muslims who do not entirely conform to the expectations established by Alḍāhirī's doleful narrative. By threading his tale of woe through the more colorful fabric of these portraits, Alḍāhirī conveys a certain ambivalence toward the dominant faith and its treatment of the Jewish minority in its midst. The degree of nuance in his representations of Muslims can correspond to his chosen medium of expression. When he employs metrical poetry, Alḍāhirī often feels constrained to work with longstanding generic conventions, such as the inventory of stock epithets used to evoke Muslims and Islam. By contrast, rhymed prose affords him greater freedom to conjure up a variety of types, even if none of his identifiably Muslim characters is truly well-rounded (in keeping with the genre's propensity for flat characters). The sorry condition of *galut teiman* is a recurrent motif of the poems interlaced throughout the book's weave of fanciful escapades. From the second *maqāma* on, the work is punctuated by verses lamenting the cruelty of Yemeni Muslim oppression. Several of these poems reprise the details of the community's incarceration, but, with few exceptions, when they evoke the perpetrators, they rely on familiar biblical tropes whose generic nature has the effect of dehistoricizing the particularities of the 16th-century events.[9] Under the weight of literary tradition, and perhaps out of an abundance of caution, actual encounters with Islam are read as echoes of earlier paradigms, with all Muslims collapsed into one prototype, such as Ishmael, Qedar, or *benei amah*, "the sons of the maidservant." Implicit in this last epithet is a complaint about the inversion of the natural order of things, in which the offspring of the maidservant (Hagar) should be subservient to the descendants of the true "mistress" (Sarah), and not their overlords: *ve-gavar ben amah/ be-qeṣef uvḥemah/ ʿalei yonah tammah/ ke-ḥayyot unmerim* ("The maidservant's son prevailed/ in fury and wrath/ over the innocent, pure dove/ like brutes and wild beasts.")[10]

8 For a welcome corrective to the unremittingly "lachrymose" narrative of Yemenite Jewish existence (persecution, drought, famine, poverty) constructed by the first generation of scholars on the subject, see Schroeter, review of Nini, *The Jews of Yemen, 1800–1914*. For an example of the tendency, see Ahroni, "Tribulations and Aspirations in Yemenite Hebrew Literature."

9 See, e.g., *Sefer hamusar*, 64–76 (#2) and 183–189 (#15).

10 *Sefer hamusar*, p. 69, l. 107. Note that the 9th-century Shuʿūbiyya movement, a backlash of non-Arabs against Arab claims to cultural superiority, "made the issue of lineal descent from Sarah, the free-woman (*Sarah al-ḥūrrah*) and Hagar (*Hājar*), the slave, the mothers

Poignant and long-lived, this kind of symbolism—familiar from Hebrew liturgical poetry—nevertheless does not permit any differentiation that might yield a more nuanced reading or recollection of the power relations between Muslims and Jews in different places and eras. The only exceptions are one reference to Imām al-Muṭahhar by name (which, ironically, means "pure") and a few select uses of his unmistakable epithet, *ha-ḥigger* (translating the Arabic *al-arʿaj*), "the lame one."[11] Even in these instances, when Alḍāhirī celebrates al-Muṭahhar's demise, unleashing his wrath against "that lame one [who] imprisoned us [and] devoured ... us," he relies on scriptural prophecies predicting the downfall of the wicked. By contrast, Alḍāhirī's rhymed prose depictions of Muslims yield a greater array of occupations, personalities, and interactions with Jews, even though these invented characters are still largely caricatures. In their dealings with Jews, his imagined Muslims can be vicious, humiliating, or arbitrary, but they can also be impartial or even fawning or benevolent. What is more, his fictional Jews, although socially subordinate and politically vulnerable, often overstep the accepted *dhimmī* bounds of propriety and discretion to prevail over their Muslim interlocutors. By indulging his literary imagination, Alḍāhirī could summon up fictional alternatives to the inferior social and political status of his people to construct a Jewish literary identity that is audacious, clever, and even invincible.[12]

Despite the hardships Alḍāhirī depicts, the fourteenth to early sixteenth centuries were a culturally fruitful time for the Jewish community in Yemen. Yemenite Jewry absorbed the work of the towering Jewish philosopher Moses Maimonides and produced a richly variegated corpus of philosophical midrash that drew on Jewish, Islamic, and Neoplatonic traditions.[13] Hebrew poetry flourished as well, initially hewing closely to Andalusian models but coming into its own with Alḍāhirī's exuberant creativity. Alḍāhirī's acknowledged debt to Alḥarizi's *Taḥkemoni* and the Arabic *Maqāmāt* of al-Ḥarīrī suggests that the representations of Muslims in *Sefer hamusar* are also mediated by the author's intimate familiarity with these antecedent works and, more broadly, with clas-

of Isaac and Ishmael respectively, a major topic of dispute and a formidable argument in their attempt to denigrate the Arabs"; see Norris, "Shuʿūbiyya in Arabic Literature," 42–43.

11 See Blackburn, "The Era of Imām Sharaf al-Dīn Yaḥyā and his Son al-Muṭahhar," and al-Nahrawālī, *Lightning Over Yemen*. The reference to al-Muṭahhar by name is not particularly informative; Mordecai marvels at Abner's eloquence, given that he suffered the indignities of prison "under the thumb of King Meṭahar"; see *Sefer hamusar*, p. 75, l. 233.

12 Alfonso has argued persuasively that the earlier Andalusian poets evoke the Other in generic, biblical terms while also taking their contemporary historical context into account; see *Islamic Culture Through Jewish Eyes*, 52–82.

13 Langermann, *Yemenite Midrash*, xvii, xxv–xxix.

sical Islamic culture, Arabic lore, and literature. Of his learned circle, he was the only one to draw directly on the vast and colorful corpus of Arabic belles-lettres and folklore in order to produce a work of imaginative prose. Alḍāhirī's *maqāma* collection abounds with cross-cultural borrowings even as he seeks to distance his Jewish characters from, and define them in opposition to, their Muslim interlocutors and antagonists. The complexity of his attitudes toward Islam and Islamicate culture is underscored by his enthusiastic appropriation of Arabic literary forms and themes despite his profound misgivings regarding the indignities to which Yemeni Islam repeatedly subjected his community.[14] If, as Ratzaby maintains, the work's poor reception was due to its perception as a foreign import from the world of Muslim Arabic literature, its limited circulation among Alḍāhirī's immediate audience was then due to the cross-cultural tendencies that make it so intriguing to modern readers.[15]

1 Techniques of Representation

The fictional Muslims who appear in *Sefer hamusar* belong to several political, social, or religious types: oppressive rulers, a hostile mob, a provocative polemicist, ecumenical thieves, and religious judges (*qāḍīs*) who, although credulous, tend to be fair. There are also noble, generous, and God-fearing "Arabs" who serve as foils for some of the less appealing Muslims. Urban and rustic, these characters figure in a variety of literary sub-genres, predominantly prose narratives and folktales, across the work's forty-five self-contained *maqāmāt*. Alḍāhirī conveys mixed feelings about Muslim society through descriptions that range from positive to indifferent to negative. Some of his portrayals are quite minimalist while others are more detailed. Some rely on stereotypes or topoi familiar from classical Arabic literature, such as the generous Bedouin or the gullible *qāḍī*, while others draw directly on the Jewish encounter with Islam. But Alḍāhirī also suggests his ambivalences about Muslims and Islam by means of more subtle techniques that include literary juxtapositions, layered narrative structures that embed one story within another, and manipulations of the expected outcomes of interactions between Muslims and Jews. As we have seen, *Sefer hamusar* opens with a buoyant and unapologetic adaptation of a *maqāma* by al-Ḥarīrī. Yet, at the episode's close, the author steps in to promise that the second *maqāma* will be devoted entirely to the tribulations

14 Cf. Jacobs, "An Ex-Sabbatean's Remorse?"

15 See Ratzaby, "The Influence of al-Ḥarīrī Upon Alḍāhiri," 55–56 and *Sefer hamusar*, 21–23.

of Yemenite Jewry (*galut teiman*). The placement of these terse remarks seems poised to repudiate his appropriation of Arabic literary forms and themes even though he continues to make use of such material throughout the work.[16] Elsewhere, the tale of a munificent Arab is framed by a story in which Muslims are contemptible dupes. Tales of Arabs who trust in God and accept their sufferings in love are presented as object lessons for Jewish "true believers." A fictionalized account of a Muslim-Jewish religious disputation unrealistically allows the Jewish participant to triumph while highlighting the defenselessness of Jews in Muslim society. Alḍāhirī brazenly critiques Muḥammad and the Qur'ān yet concedes Islam's historic function in paving the way for the acceptance of true monotheism. Each of these instances reflects a complex weave of attraction to and repulsion from a powerful rival religion, its cultural traditions, and its literary canon.

These multifaceted narratives defy neat categorization: any one story reveals multiple aspects—distinct subgenres and literary techniques as well as attitudes expressed toward historical and imaginary Muslims, Islam, or the Arabic language. The tale of the munificent Arab in the thirty-sixth *maqāma* shares many features of the exemplum while the *maqāma* in which it occurs illustrates the use of embedded narratives, a device that indirectly reveals conflicted attitudes toward Muslims and Arabic. The following discussion treats the material thematically while also taking note of generic features or stylistic and rhetorical techniques that add complexity to Alḍāhirī's portrayals of Muslims and Islam. It is organized around three main rubrics: (1) Muslim-Jewish polemics; (2) lawsuits before *qāḍīs*; and (3) exempla featuring Arabs as role models.

1.1 *Muslim-Jewish Polemics*

> In every generation Yemenite Jews were subjected to religious disputations which did not please them, for they knew the bitter fate that awaited them. They would always be at a disadvantage, whether they emerged as victors or vanquished. They were drawn into these disputations against their will. As political subjects, they were not free to speak their minds or to voice all of their arguments for fear of offending the Muslims or blaspheming against Islam, as a result of which they and their communities would suffer grievous harm. The Jews' strategy was one of self-defense, while the approach of their Muslim antagonists was one of aggression and provocation. The Jews of Yemen, who wrote little, did not commit

16 Ratzaby, "The Influence of al-Ḥarīrī Upon Alḍāhiri," 62.

> these Muslim-Jewish disputations and polemics to writing. Nevertheless, traces [of these confrontations] may be found in their theoretical and literary works.[17]

Several topoi of Yehuda Ratzaby's somber and sobering (if historically undifferentiated) evocation of Muslim-Jewish relations in Yemen through the ages will be familiar to students of medieval interfaith polemics: forced disputations, self-censorship for fear of reprisal, and a reluctance to commit to writing refutations of the dominant religion.[18] The consensus is that the Jews of Islam produced few books devoted in their entirety to anti-Muslim attacks. Instead, they tended to incorporate their refutations of Muslim doctrinal claims into less obviously polemical contexts, such as exegetical, homiletical, legal, philosophical, or literary works.[19] Scholars have remarked on the relative circumspection of these critiques, which were often implicit or veiled rather than brazenly direct.[20] The rationales offered for this reticence are generally twofold. On a pragmatic level, there was a fear of offending the ruling Muslims who might then exact collective retribution. On a theological level, the restraint was due to the lack of a shared scripture. Whereas medieval Christians felt compelled to combat the erroneous Jewish exegesis of Scripture that willfully denied the Christological reading, Muslims were rather less concerned with biblical interpretation. As a result, the Jewish polemical response to Christianity was far more acrimonious and extensive.[21]

---

17 Ratzaby, "ʿInyyanei dat ba-pulmus bein muslimim lihudim be-teiman," 12.

18 For an overview, see Adang and Schmidtke, "Muslim-Jewish Polemics."

19 See Steinschneider, *Polemische und apologetische Literatur in arabischer Sprache zwischen Muslimen, Christen und Juden*, 244–388 *passim*; Perlmann, "The Medieval Polemics between Judaism and Islam"; Lazarus-Yafeh, *Intertwined Worlds*, 6–10; Stroumsa, "Jewish Polemics Against Islam and Christianity in the Light of Judaeo-Arabic Texts"; Sklare, "Responses to Islamic Polemics by Jewish Mutakallimūn in the Tenth Century" and Schlossberg, "Anti-Muslim Polemics in Medieval Yemenite Midrashim."

20 A small corpus of Judeo-Arabic manuals for participants in polemical debates was produced by Jews in 10th-century Baghdad; see Sklare, "Responses to Islamic Polemics." Early Karaites were less inhibited about committing anti-Muslim remarks to writing despite their frequent use of Arabic characters; see Ben-Shammai, "The Attitude of Some Early Karaites Towards Islam." Jews in Islamic lands also wrote critiques of Eastern Christianity in Arabic; on the relatively small extant corpus, see Lasker, "The Jewish Critique of Christianity under Islam in the Middle Ages."

21 See Lazarus-Yafeh, *Intertwined Worlds*; Stroumsa, "Jewish Polemics Against Islam and Christianity," 242–246; and Cohen, *Under Crescent and Cross*, 139–161. The first Jewish books of anti-Christian polemics appear in Christian Europe in the late 12th century in response to increased missionary pressure; see Lasker, *Jewish Philosophical Polemics Against Christianity in the Middle Ages* and Berger, *The Jewish-Christian Debate in the High*

The transition from purely literary polemics to compulsory, staged disputations is generally associated with the Christian-Jewish debate of the High and Late Middle Ages rather than the Muslim-Jewish encounter.[22] Still, circumstances varied according to time and place. In tenth-century Baghdad under the Buyids, intellectuals from the three monotheistic faiths (and various sects) met for polemical debates (*mujādalāt, munāẓarāt*) about theological matters. These scholarly sessions (*majālis*), sponsored by a ruler or dignitary, were conducted in a spirit of relative tolerance and according to set rules of etiquette. While the outcome could be quite demoralizing, the Jewish participants were given complete freedom to argue their positions.[23] On the other hand, there is evidence that in Fāṭimid Egypt (late 10th century), Jews were forced to attend sessions in which Judaism was aggressively attacked.[24] Assuming that Ratzaby's generalizations are accurate, forced disputations were also the rule in Yemen, with the Jewish participants exercising extreme self-censorship.

The grim state of affairs evoked by Ratzaby bears comparison with the imaginary polemical exchange depicted in *Sefer hamusar*. In the seventh *maqāma*, Mordecai journeys from Jerusalem to Cairo.[25] Meandering through the teeming markets, he chances on a crowd gathered around a Muslim and a Jew engaged in a religious disputation. Far from a genteel *majlis* overseen by a presiding dignitary at a court or literary salon, this is a seemingly spontaneous street disputation between two nameless principals in the rough-and-tumble setting of an open-air market. The Muslim, referred to only as *ha-yishmaʿeli*, opens with a politico-theological argument drawn from the standard medieval arsenal of Muslim anti-Jewish polemics: the Jews' dispersion, humiliation, political subjugation, and lack of a sovereign are all proof of their divine rejection while the worldly success of Islam (and even Christianity) is a sign of divine favor. Growing strident, he asserts the enduring veracity of Muḥammad's prophecy and its superiority to the prophecy of Moses. The Jew counters with a Maimonidean

Middle Ages. But Lasker also notes that the first two works drew upon the earlier Jewish critique of Christianity from Islamic lands; see "The Jewish-Christian Debate in Transition: From the Lands of Ishmael to the Lands of Edom."

22 See Cohen, *The Friars and the Jews*; idem, *Living Letters of the Law*, 317–363; Chazan, *Daggers of Faith*; and idem, *Barcelona and Beyond*.

23 See Sklare, "Responses to Islamic Polemics"; Stroumsa, "Ibn al-Rāwandī's *sūʾ adab al-mujādala*: the Role of Bad Manners in Medieval Disputations"; and Kraemer, *Humanism in the Renaissance of Islam*, 55–60.

24 See Sklare, "Responses to Islamic Polemics," 143; Cohen, "Interreligious *Majālis* in Early Fatimid Egypt"; Cohen and Somekh, "In the Court of Yaʿqūb Ibn Killis: A Fragment from the Cairo Geniza."

25 *Sefer hamusar*, 124–129.

argument: Christianity and Islam are merely transitional phases, ordained by God to wean mankind from idolatry in its progression toward true monotheism. Divine sanction for these highly imperfect dispensations was intended to prepare the world for the advent of the true messiah. The ultimate sign of divine favor will be the restoration of Zion, not the temporal power of the Muslims.

In delivering this salvo, the Jew does not shy away from censuring Muḥammad. When he is done, the Muslim cries out in "desolation, devastation, and destruction (cf. Nahum 2:11), for the Jew had deprived him of his faith." A Muslim mob menaces the blaspheming Jew, but he manages to blend in with the crowd and escape their wrath.[26] The narrator pursues him, and when the disputant sheds his cloak in an alleyway, Mordecai recognizes him as Abner ben Ḥeleq, "the father of all ruses, who speaks lofty words against the Gentiles." Mordecai warns Abner that he has placed himself in mortal danger, alluding to the fact that blaspheming against Islam carried the death penalty. Undaunted, Abner dismisses his friend's fears, insisting that one ought to know how to respond to an unbeliever. In any case, "those engaged in a religious mission cannot be harmed."[27] Abner then joins Mordecai for a celebratory meal in the narrator's rented room. When Abner has been plied with food and drink, Mordecai successfully requests a poem recounting the disputation and thanking God for Abner's deliverance from the irate mob. He urges his impetuous friend to flee, and at daybreak accompanies Abner to the Nile, where they say their farewells and Abner dutifully boards a boat.

1.1.1 The Polemical Arguments

In Alḍāhirī's tale, the dispute hinges on several central cruxes of the medieval Muslim-Jewish debate: Jewish political powerlessness and abasement (*dhull*) as proof of divine rejection; the abrogation (*naskh*) of the Torah by the subsequent revelation of the Qur'ān; and the superiority of Muḥammad's prophecy to that of Moses. The charge that "wretchedness and baseness" (*dhilla wa-maskana*) were stamped upon the Jews for their rejection of Islam appears in the second *sūra* (Q 2:61); this notion of abasement figures in the subtitle to Judah Halevi's *Kuzarī*: *Kitāb al-radd wa'l-dalīl fī'l-dīn al-dhalīl* (The Book of

26 It is instructive to compare the Jew's fortunate escape in this fictional narrative with the historical account published by Tobi of a 15th-century Yemeni Muslim mob that stoned to death a Jew accused of mocking Muḥammad. See Tobi, "Information on the Jews of Yemen in Arabic Writings from Yemen," *Pe'amim* 65, p. 22.

27 *U-sheluḥei miṣvah einan nizzoqin*; cf. bPesaḥim 8b. Maimonides cites this dictum at the end of his *Epistle to Yemen* when he urges his addressee to circulate the document widely despite its anti-Muslim animus.

Refutation and Proof in Defense of the Despised Faith).[28] To substantiate their claim that the Torah had been abrogated, Muslim polemicists cited qur'ānic verses such as 2:106:

> "Such of Our revelations as We abrogate or cause to be forgotten, we bring [in place] one better or the like thereof. Knowest thou not that Allah is able to do all things?"[29]

Though "taken by early Muslim commentators to refer mainly to inner contradictions between different Qur'ānic verses, or between the Qur'ān and the Sunna tradition of the Prophet," the verse conveyed "that the *later* revelation or saying is legally the valid one …."[30] In the disputation depicted by Alḍāhirī, certain other standard claims are not explicitly made by the Muslim disputant, yet the frank retorts of his Jewish opponent suggest that they did not escape notice. These include the charge that Jewish revealed texts are invalidated by their lack of a reliable chain of transmission (*tawātur*) and the accusation that the Scriptures currently possessed by Jews are a post-exilic forgery or contain falsifications of the text (*taḥrīf*) in order to obscure the verses (*aʿlām*) that presage Muḥammad's prophecy.[31] Ishmael's blessing in Genesis 17:20 ("As for Ishmael, I have heeded you. I hereby bless him. I will make him fertile and exceedingly numerous. He shall be the father of twelve chieftains, and I will make of him a great nation") was commonly adduced as predicting Muḥammad's prophecy since the numerical value of בִּמְאֹד מְאֹד (= 92) is identical to the value of the consonants in the name Muḥammad (MḤMD). Deuteronomy 18:15, "The Lord your God will raise up for you a prophet from among your own people, like myself," was also taken to foretell Muḥammad's advent. In Deuteronomy 33:2, the progression Sinai-Seir-Paran was seen by Muslim polemicists to refer to the three successive monotheistic dispensations.[32]

---

28 See also *Kuzarī* 1:113. On the resentment felt by Jewish authors against the "institutionalized humiliation (*dhull*)" imposed on them by the dominant religion, see Perlmann, "The Medieval Polemics between Judaism and Islam," 127.

29 On the abrogation of the Torah, see Lazarus-Yafeh, *Intertwined Worlds*, 35–41; Adang, *Muslim Writers on Judaism and the Hebrew Bible*, 192–222; and idem, "A Jewish Reply to Ibn Hazm."

30 See Lazarus-Yafeh, *Intertwined Worlds*, 35.

31 On the lack of reliable transmission, see Lazarus-Yafeh, *Intertwined Worlds*, 41–47. On *taḥrīf*, see Adang, *Muslim Writers on Judaism and the Hebrew Bible*, 223–248; Reynolds, "On the Qur'anic Accusation of Scriptural Falsification (*taḥrīf*) and Christian Anti-Jewish Polemic"; and Lazarus-Yafeh, "Taḥrīf."

32 See Frank, *Search Scripture Well*, 228–247; Perlmann, "The Medieval Polemics between

Both of Alḍāhirī's disputants invoke Christianity although no Christian is party to the dispute.[33] The Muslim emphasizes that even "the sect of Jesus the Christian whom you reject" had powerful kings until the Muslims conquered large swaths of Christendom. In a peculiar theological twist, he asserts that Christian acceptance of Moses should have legitimized Christianity in the eyes of Judaism. "But according to your (pl.) words, these two faiths were created in vain." The Jew responds that, with the advent of the messiah, the nations of the world will at last be able to distinguish between truth and falsehood. But in the meantime, God in His wisdom made allowance for Christianity and Islam, however flawed, in order to lead mankind in a gradual progression from its immersion in idolatry to true monotheism. Initially, He put Jesus in place so that when mankind wanted to worship by means of images, they would be enveloped in "a spirit of impurity" and would realize that their worship, which relied on visible icons, was an imperfect means of attaining an incorporeal divinity. This dispensation reigned for more than five hundred years. Then, God in His wisdom decreed the emergence of the "idiot prophet and madman" [viz. Muḥammad; cf. Hosea 9:7] so that there would be no graven images or icons, and in this way He advanced mankind somewhat from benightedness so that they might worship God in their hearts. But in his borrowings from the Torah, Muḥammad muddled some of the precepts and had delusions of grandeur. He invented lies and falsehoods, claiming that he had prophesied. His dispensation has lasted a long time and will only be supplanted with the advent of the messiah.[34]

In support of these arguments, the Jew adduces the parable of a child's gradual nutrition: an infant cannot tolerate heavy food but must begin by taking in its mother's milk until it grows stronger. Then one can accustom the child to meat and bread until it is weaned. After that, once its stomach has grown

---

Judaism and Islam," 114, 118; Lazarus-Yafeh, *Intertwined Worlds*, 75–110; Adang, *Muslim Writers on Judaism and the Hebrew Bible*, 139–191; Mazuz, "Tracing Possible Jewish Influence on a Common Islamic Commentary on Deuteronomy 33:2"; and Schmidtke, "Biblical Predictions of the Prophet Muḥammad among the Zaydīs of Yemen."

33 There was, of course, an extensive Muslim polemical literature against Christianity, although the Muslim disputant does not exploit it here; see, e.g.: Steinschneider, *Polemische und apologetische Literatur in arabischer Sprache*; Cohen, *Under Crescent and Cross*, 151–154; Griffith, "The Monk in the Emir's *Majlis*"; Lazarus-Yafeh, "Étude sur la polémique islamo-chrétienne"; and idem, *Intertwined Worlds*, 130–141.

34 The phrase used here to deny the legitimacy of Muḥammad's prophethood, *u-vadah mi-libbo devarim/kazavim ushqarim/be'omro ki hu nitnabba*, echoes Maimonides' discussion of the false prophet in his history of religion; see *Mishneh Torah*, "'Akum," 1:2 (… *u-modi'a lahem ṣurah she-badah milibbo* …).

stronger, it can drink wine and eat delicacies. In a similar manner, God prepared the world with Judaism's two daughter religions to pave the way for the acceptance of true monotheism during the messianic era. Do not think, he warns his opponent, that your religion is perfect! Temporal success is no proof. The true reward lies in the rebuilding of Jerusalem and the Temple, when the *Shekhinah* will dwell in Zion. Prophecy shall go forth out of Zion. Anyone who says otherwise speaks falsely, for prophecy only ever arose in the Land of Israel; it is not found in Seir or Ishmael. Among the preconditions for prophecy are that a man be intellectually superior, not like the mad prophet who every day possesses another maiden.[35] To be a true prophet, one must be sanctified, with a new heart; only then will the *Shekhinah* envelop him. Following these barbs, the Jew sets forth one final rather recondite "proof" that uses ancient Jewish scribal tradition as a peg for the polemical exegesis of several biblical verses.[36]

Alḍāhirī's comments on the purely historical function of Christianity and Islam in preparing mankind for true monotheism can be traced back to the concluding portion of Maimonides' Code of Law, the *Mishneh Torah* (c. 1178). In a discussion of messianism in *Melakhim* (Kings and Wars) 11:4, a passage regularly deleted by censors, Maimonides writes that "all these matters relating to Jesus of Nazareth and the Ishmaelite [Muḥammad] who came after him only served to clear the way for King Messiah, to prepare the whole world to worship God with one accord ...." Maimonides brands Jesus and Muḥammad false messiahs, for the true Messiah will "redeem Israel, save them, gather their dispersed, and confirm the commandments," but these two have done precisely the opposite. Nevertheless, God's ways are inscrutable, and the success of Christianity and Islam in the world, while not a confirmation of their truth, has facilitated the spread of monotheism. This, according to Maimonides, allows for the ultimate emergence of the true Messiah, a mortal king who will restore Israel to sovereignty and strength.[37] In *Kuzarī* 4:23, Judah Halevi also suggests that Christianity and Islam serve as a preparation for the "messiah that is

35 On Jewish responses to Muḥammad's "Haremsverhältnisse," see Steinschneider, *Polemische und apologetische Literatur*, 303–305.

36 Three of the verses cited (Dt. 6:4, Ps. 80:14, Job 38:15) have an oversized letter *'ayin*; see the discussion below.

37 See: Twersky, *Introduction to the Code of Maimonides*, 452–453; Halkin and Hartman, *Crisis and Leadership*, 186–190; and Shamir, "Allusions to Muḥammad in Maimonides' Theory of Prophecy in his *Guide of the Perplexed*." In a responsum to Obadiah the Proselyte, Maimonides replies that contemporary Muslims are not idolators, even though earlier stages of their religion involved idolatrous practices; see *R. Moses b. Maimon, Responsa*, ed. Blau, 2:725–727, #448. Cf. Maimonides, *Guide* 3:29–30.

expected."[38] Echoes of Halevi and Maimonides can also be heard in Alḍāhirī's brief discussion of prophecy. His assertion that true prophecy arose only in the Land of Israel harks back to Halevi's *Kuzarī* (2:14, 5:22) while the requirement that the prophet be intellectually superior recalls Maimonides' discussions of intellectual perfection as a prerequisite for prophecy.[39] In his *Guide of the Perplexed* 2:35–40, Maimonides sets forth the criteria for true prophecy and establishes the special status of Moses vis-à-vis later prophets, both Hebrew and gentile.[40]

Antecedents to some of the anti-Muslim critiques leveled in Alḍāhirī's tale can also be found in Maimonides' *Epistle to Yemen*. Composed in Judeo-Arabic in 1172, the *Epistle to Yemen* was intended to offer reassurance to a community in crisis. Twelfth-century Yemenite Jews were subjected to conversionary pressures instigated by a Jewish apostate to Islam as well as to the claims of a messianic pretender from within their ranks. Protracted suffering bred despair, and the turmoil was undermining confidence in promises of divine redemption. Given this context, Maimonides' refutation of Christian and Muslim arguments for the abrogation of the Torah is overtly polemical and departs from his more dispassionate treatment of the other monotheistic faiths in his legal works:

> … Jesus the Nazarene, may his bones be ground to dust … impelled people to believe that he was a prophet sent by God to clarify perplexities in the Torah, and that he was the Messiah that was predicted by each and every seer. He interpreted the Torah and its precepts in such a fashion as to lead to their total annulment, to the abolition of all its commandments and to the violation of its prohibitions ….

---

38 See Pines, "Shīʿite Terms and Conceptions in Judah Halevi's *Kuzari*," 250–251. Hartman notes, however, that in *Melakhim* 11:4, Maimonides does not imply that the emergence of Judaism's two daughter religions was inevitable or divinely ordained. In this, Alḍāhirī's argument diverges from that of Maimonides.

39 See, e.g., Maimonides, *Mishneh Torah, Yesodei ha-torah* (Foundations of the Torah), 7:1 and *Guide* 3:51.

40 Sarah Stroumsa writes that theological and dogmatic discourse about prophets was central to medieval Islamic thought, and its polemical aspect revived the Jewish preoccupation with prophecy in the Islamic milieu; see Stroumsa: "The Signs of Prophecy: The Emergence and Early Development of a Theme in Arabic Theological Literature; idem, *Freethinkers of Medieval Islam*, 21–36; and idem, "Prophecy *versus* Civil Religion in Medieval Jewish Philosophy." See also Shamir, "Allusions to Muḥammad," 216–224 and Kaplan, "'I Sleep but My Heart Waketh': Maimonides' Conception of Human Perfection."

> ... After him rose the Madman who emulated his precursor since he paved the way for him. But he added the further objective of procuring rule and submission, and he invented his well known religion. All of these men purposed to place their teachings on the same level with our divine religion. But only a simpleton who lacks knowledge of both would liken divine institutions to human practices.[41]

As part of his effort to discredit the Yemenite apostate's allegations, Maimonides rebuts the interpretation of biblical verses—rehearsed *ad nauseum*, he says—which were alleged to foretell Muḥammad's prophecy (Genesis 17:20; Deuteronomy 18:15, 18:18 and 33:2).[42] The disparaging Hebrew epithets he applies to Muḥammad became standard in medieval Jewish anti-Muslim polemics. *Meshuggaʿ* ("Madman") was likely inspired by the Arabic epithet *majnūn* ("possessed," "insane," "madman"), used in the Qurʾān by the enemies of Muḥammad. Jewish authors found scriptural support for the usage in Hosea 9:7 (*evil ha-naviʾ meshuggaʿ ish ha-ruaḥ*; "the prophet was distraught, the inspired man was driven mad").[43] The Hebrew *pasul* ("unfit," "disqualified"), which was used to dismiss Muḥammad as a false prophet, played on the Arabic *rasūl allāh*, meaning the messenger or apostle of God.[44] Despite the personal risk involved in circulating such an incendiary document in Arabic, Maimonides urges his addressee, Jacob b. Nethanel al-Fayyūmī, to send a copy to every community "in order to strengthen the people in their faith" while taking adequate precautions not to divulge its contents to the Muslim authorities.

---

41 Halkin and Cohen, *Moses Maimonides' Epistle to Yemen*, iii–iv. See also Halkin and Hartman, *Crisis and Leadership*, 150–207. Alḍāhirī is fairly eclectic in his use of Maimonidean sources and does not distinguish between the openly polemical and the more dispassionate treatments of Judaism's rival religions.

42 See Halkin and Cohen, *Moses Maimonides' Epistle to Yemen*, 42–59 and English translation, viii–xii; and Halkin and Hartman, *Crisis and Leadership*, 107–114.

43 See: Avishur, "Kinnuyei genai"; Steinschneider, *Polemische und apologetische Literatur*, 302–303; Halkin and Hartman, *Crisis and Leadership*, p. 134, n. 48; Halkin and Cohen, *Moses Maimonides' Epistle to Yemen*, pp. 14–15 and n. 16; Ratzaby, *Oṣar leshon ha-qodesh she-livnei teiman*, 172–173; and Ahroni, "Some Yemenite Jewish Attitudes Towards Muḥammad's Prophethood." In his polemical *Maʾamar ʿal yishmaʿel*, the 13th-century Solomon ibn Adret uses *meshuggaʿ* to refer to the Muslim author of the anti-Jewish tract he refutes; see Adang, "A Jewish Reply to Ibn Hazm," p. 183 and n. 20.

44 The earliest attestations are apparently in Karaite texts; see Ben-Shammai, "The Attitude of Some Early Karaites Towards Islam," p. 14, n. 47 and p. 21; Frank, *Search Scripture Well*, 204–247 *passim*; Avishur, "Kinnuyei genai," 103–105; and Steinschneider, *Polemische und apologetische Literatur*, 302, 349, 356, 366, 383.

1.1.2 Alḍāhirī's Account

One of the most arresting features of Alḍāhirī's tale is its forthright criticism of Islam and unrestrained use of invective against Muḥammad. Particularly stinging attacks characterize its closing poem, "Asher ḥanan le-vanim haʿamusim," which—recited in the safety of Mordecai's room—condemns Christians and Muslims (*benei seʾir u-faran*; cf. Deut. 33:2) for likening their muddled laws and beliefs to the Torah, whose truth is more precious than gold. The allusion to Deuteronomy 33:2 ("the Lord came from Sinai, and shone upon them from Seir, and appeared from Mount Paran …") in this context implicitly responds to Muslim polemical exegesis of the verse, whereby the initial revelation at Sinai was superseded by the Christian scriptures and both were supplanted by the Qurʾān.[45] Abner's poem invokes a series of paired metaphors, some of them drawn from Yemeni realia, to convey the audacity of asserting any resemblance between these inferior scriptures and the Torah:

> How can they liken the crooked to my straight paths?
> The sunken valley to majestic mountains?
> Fools! they compare locust meat to fattened swan.

Continuing in this vein, the poem lashes out at Muḥammad, who is dismissed as a raging fool for supposing that the Qurʾān, in all its deficiency, could compare with the Torah, whose profound truth he has mistaken for its surface meaning:

> The distraught prophet is a madman, and flawed,
> Yet they compare him to an angel of the Lord!
> Against the Most High he spread vile slander
> —A moaning fool whose thoughts are in ruins.
> He contends that his copper is like pure gold;
> that his metallic flecks shine like the sun;
> He compares his bridle to fine mantles;
> His asses' reins to ornaments.
> He could not fathom that God in His wisdom
> Had prefaced the veiled sense to the plain;

45 Various rabbinic and midrashic citations of Deut. 33:2 associate Seir with Esau and Paran with Ishmael; see, e.g., *bAvodah Zarah* 2b. Building on these identifications, the verse was seen by Muslim polemicists to refer to the three successive monotheistic dispensations. Muslims identified Paran with Mecca; see Perlmann, "The Medieval Polemics between Judaism and Islam."

Deep meanings divulged to the wise alone;
  to the precious few, concealed in their hearts.
When our Messiah comes—may it be soon—
  They will see miracles and wonders;
Then kings will heed His word
  And the tribes of Jeshurun shall rejoice.
As God said through His prophet's voice:
  The land shall be filled with devotion to the Lord
as water covers the sea.[46]

Alḍāhirī's indignation at what he views as the illegitimate comparison of not just the two Scriptures but also their subsequent legal elaboration was clearly all-consuming. The wrong-headedness of Muslim supersessionist claims and interpretation of scriptural laws is articulated in *Ṣeidah la-derekh* in a lengthy comment on Deuteronomy 32, the Torah portion known as *Ha'azinu*, in which Moses delivers his valedictory song to the Children of Israel. Broadly following Moses' paradigm, Alḍāhirī reviews Israel's past, present, and future in largely typological terms, reiterating Moses' prophecy that Israel will go astray and that God will punish them but ultimately will reaffirm His covenant and redeem them. After treating their subjugation to Edom, he turns to their tribulations under Ishmael and gives vent to his polemical grievances, adducing as proof-texts verse fragments from the chapter on which he is commenting. His remarks reveal a degree of familiarity with Islamic law as well as outrage at political indignities:

> And God delivered them into the hands of Ishmael, who so abuse us, saying that our Rock is not like theirs (cf. Deuteronomy 32:31). As opposed to our sacred Torah, they established a falsified law, about which it is said, "their vine is from the vine of Sodom" (Deuteronomy 32:32), which is to say that their laws are like those of Sodom and Gomorrah, for a thief's hand will be cut off whether he steals a little or a lot, and they have forbidden [marriage with] a niece (whether the daughter of a brother or a sister), but have permitted a brother's wife. A divorced woman who, according to their law, has had an irrevocable divorce cannot be remarried except following intercourse, whether in the context of harlotry or marriage. In general, when you examine their deeds, you will find them to be contrary to the truth … And regarding those fictions that they invent

46 *Sefer hamusar*, 128–129.

> about us on account of our many sins, Moses said, "their grapes are poison" (Deuteronomy 32:32). [So are] their taxes and *arnonot* [Ottoman-era property taxes], as in the land of Yemen, where they imprisoned us in the towers, each man and his household. And this is what is meant by "a bitter growth their clusters":[47] anyone who dares to contradict them is subjected to rage … all the moreso their chiefs and *qāḍis*—you will not find in them any respect for the honor of Israel …[48]

In much the same spirit as "Asher ḥanan le-vanim haʿamusim," a long double acrostic poem in the twelfth *maqāma*, "Elohai pataḥ pi," celebrates the downfall and death of Imām al-Muṭahhar while villifying Muslims, Islam, Muḥammad, and the Qurʾān in an intimate tangle of the historically specific with polemical motifs of remarkable longevity. It brazenly charges that the core of the Qurʾān is an abomination, full of endless falsehood, and that the descendants of Ishmael defile themselves with their book.[49] Though Alḍāhirī does not explicitly address specific verses or theological cruxes, it is intriguing that he confines his most vitriolic critiques of Muslim scripture to poetry, which suggests that he views that medium as even less accessible to Muslims than prose. Remarkably, these bold texts have gone almost unnoticed in the secondary literature. A handful of scholars of Yemenite Jewish literature have adduced the prose sections of Alḍāhirī's seventh *maqāma* in surveys of anti-Muslim religious polemics, citing them alongside Judeo-Arabic texts from Yemen that vary in their degree of antipathy to Islam: the sixth chapter of Nethanel ibn al-Fayyūmī's theological compendium, *Bustan al-ʿuqūl* (The Garden of Wisdom, 12th c.); selected comments in Nethanel ben Yeshaʿ's philosophical midrash, *Nur al-ẓalām* (Illumination of the Darkness, 1329); the eighth of Peraḥia b. Meshullam's lesser-known *Philosophical Responsa* (date unknown); and the ninth *maqāma* of Yiḥye ben Abraham Ḥarāzī's kabbalistic *Netivot haʾemunah* (Paths of Faith, 19th c.).[50] Despite the acknowledgment that these polemical responses to Islam appear in diverse genres of writing, no real consideration has been given to the belletristic context or literary dimensions of Alḍāhirī's

47 The continuation of Dt. 32:32.

48 *Tāj ʿim perushim ḥamishah ḥumshei torah.*

49 *Sefer hamusar*, #12, pp. 165–170.

50 See Qāfiḥ ed. and trans., Nathanel ibn Fayyūmī, *Bustān al-ʿuqūl*; Levine ed. and trans., *The Bustan al-ukul*; Qāfiḥ ed. and trans., Nathanel ben Yeshaʿ, *Nur al-ẓalām* (*Maʾor haʾafelah*); English excerpts in Langermann, *Yemenite Midrash*, esp. 160–177; Qāfiḥ, "Arbaʿim sheʾelot u-teshuvot ba-filosofiah le-rav peraḥia b. meshullam"; and Baumgarten, "Netivot haʾemunah le-Rabbi Yiḥye al-Ḥarazi."

account.[51] Close examination of the text's narrative structure, rhetorical techniques, and literary antecedents reveals an authorial fantasy of Jewish triumph prompted by the reality of Jewish vulnerability in Muslim society. Despite the realism of their arguments, which invoke actual polemical cruxes, the Muslim's scathing attack and the Jew's extravagant retort are highly contrived. The belletristic format frees the author to manipulate the debate in such a way that he can undermine the Muslim's claims and allow the Jew to come out on top. Abner's bravura and triumphalist tone are entirely at odds with the humiliating social and political realities of Jewish life under Yemeni Islam. But as a consolation for dejected Jewish readers, this fanciful Jewish victory is extremely effective.[52]

1.1.3 Narrative Structure

The tale told in the seventh *maqāma* can be divided into a series of component parts: (i) the brief frame story outlining the narrator's journey and arrival in the city; (ii) the disputation witnessed by the narrator; (iii) the mob's enraged reaction and the Jewish participant's narrow escape; (iv) the narrator's recognition (anagnorisis) of the protagonist's true identity; (v) the narrator's reproach and subsequent reward of the protagonist, from whom he elicits an additional verbal display (the poem); and (vi) the parting of narrator and protagonist. Within this framework, the disputation takes center stage, occupying more than half of the story. Clearly, the polemical encounter and the interconfessional barbs exchanged are the most substantive and fascinating portions of the *maqāma*. And yet, readers in Alḍāhirī's day would have recognized that this drama is governed by literary convention and that the organization and progression of the story conform to a typical *maqāma* pattern. In other words, the very structure of the narrative would have signaled the contrived nature of its content. As outlined by Abdelfattah Kilito and James Monroe, the standard *maqāma* scenario opens with (i) the narrator's arrival in the city, which is followed by (ii) his encounter with the disguised rogue hero and the latter's (iii) brilliant rhetorical display, used to (iv) extract material gifts from gullible onlookers. These are followed by (v) the narrator's reproaches, (vi) the rogue's justification, and (vii)

51 See Ahroni, "From *Bustān al-ʿUqūl* to *Qissat al-Batūl*: Some Aspects of Jewish-Muslim Religious Polemics in Yemen"; Ratzaby, "ʿInyyanei dat ba-pulmus bein muslimim lihudim be-teiman"; Regev, "The Attitude to Islam in Yemeni Jewish Philosophical Literature"; and Mazuz, "Aspects of Polemics with Islam in the Seventh Maqāma of R. Zachariah al-Ḍāhirī's Sefer ha-Mūsar." On polemical content in texts from the 13th–15th centuries, see Schlossberg, "Anti-Muslim Polemics in Medieval Yemenite Midrashim."

52 See Tanenbaum, "Sefer ha-musar le-zekhariah al-dahiri: tekhniqot sifrutiyot ve-tokhen."

their parting.[53] The correspondence between the polemical section of our story and Kilito's sections ii–iv suggests that the Muslim's degrading contentions and the Jewish disputant's defiant riposte are in large measure a literary showpiece. In this way, the narrative structure of Alḍāhirī's tale helps us identify the text as a fictional debate rather than as the transcript of an authentic disputation, even though the *mise en scène* and argumentation owe a great deal to the reality of such confrontations.

A further sign of artifice can be found in the structure of the disputation itself. The Muslim begins his offensive with a rhetorical and loaded question: "What do you [pl.] think of the penitent Muslims (*ha-yishmaʿelim ha-shovavim*) who sanctify and purify themselves (*ha-mitqaddeshim ve-ha-miṭṭaharim*), and who pray morning and evening?"[54] He continues with his lengthy sally before providing the Jew with an opening to respond. For the most part, the Jewish arguments address the specific charges leveled by the Muslim. In this regard, they conform to realistic expectations, as the parameters of such public exchanges would have been set by members of the Muslim majority.[55] Unusually, however, Alḍāhirī's Jewish disputant has the final word in this verbal confrontation, giving him the upper hand.[56] The Muslim becomes distraught over his opponent's invidious refutations, effectively admitting defeat with his anguished cri de coeur. The counterattack undermines not only Islamic doctrines but also the Muslim's self-image, such that he cries out in "desolation, devastation, and destruction, for the Jew had deprived him of his faith." The Jew—a member of the oppressed minority who should have been on the defensive—is, by contrast, self-confident to the point of impertinence. While

53 See Monroe, *The Art of Badīʿ az-Zamān al-Hamadhānī*, 21–24, who cites Kilito, "Le Genre Séance: une introduction." See also Holmberg, "The Public Debate as a Literary Genre in Arabic Literature." The texts adduced by Holmberg are discussed in considerably greater detail in Griffith, "The Monk in the Emir's *Majlis*."

54 The phrase, "who sanctify and purify themselves" (Is. 66:17), had been interpreted polemically by some Jewish exegetes as a reference to the Muslim ablutions before prayer which nevertheless did not render their practitioners holy; see Steinschneider, *Polemische und apologetische Literatur*, 329–331.

55 See Stroumsa, "Ibn al-Rāwandī's *sūʾ adab al-mujādala*" and Griffith, "The Monk in the Emir's *Majlis*."

56 This unlikely outcome calls to mind the discrepancies between the Jewish and Christian accounts of the Barcelona Disputation (1263). In his Hebrew account, Nahmanides is daring, sarcastic, and largely victorious while, according to the Christian account, he was roundly defeated. See Maccoby, *Judaism on Trial: Jewish-Christian Disputations in the Middle Ages*, 55–75; 102–150. See also Lasker, *Jewish Philosophical Polemics*, xiii–xiv, nn. 1 and 5.

the text reflects a genuine Jewish animus toward Islam, its arguments are so inflammatory and its narrative structure so unlikely that it could not possibly be the record of an actual confrontation or even a literary polemic intended for Muslim eyes or ears. It is, rather, an imagined disputation whose brave gambits and contrived outcome could offer solace to dejected Jewish readers, crushed by the indignities of their *dhimmī* existence.

1.1.4 Rhetorical Techniques

True to *maqāma* form, the Muslim disputant is not a terribly well-developed character.[57] But a close reading does reveal some telling oddities in his manner of expression. Most remarkable—and disjunctive—is the fact that he delivers his anti-Jewish attacks, which highlight the downtrodden political status of the Jews and questions of prophetic veracity, in allusive, scriptural Hebrew. As noted, this is a regular narrative feature of the *maqāma*, which allows non-Jewish figures to be identified as such even while speaking "perfectly elegant medieval Hebrew."[58] There is a wonderful irony in the fact that the anti-Jewish diatribe in our tale relies on a dense pastiche of biblical phrases even if some of the verse fragments are cited purely for rhyming effect:

> For years they [the Muslims] have had support from heaven: Truthful speech endures forever (Proverbs 12:19). But you are like morning clouds (Hosea 6:4, 13:3), your decline cannot be fathomed. Let lying lips be stilled! (Psalm 31:19). It is nine hundred and seventy-seven years since [the advent of] our Prophet, who satisfies us with good things in the prime of life (Psalm 103:5). To our advantage, he continues to grow in stature, while you are like grass on the roof that withers in a moment (Psalm 129:6). Your Temples stood eight hundred and thirty years; from the day they were destroyed you have been silenced.[59] Every day you decline further, while the merit of the Prophet is a testament to our [superiority]. Where is your king, who goes out at your head to fight your battles? (1 Samuel 8:20). If you cry out, no one will pay heed. In our presence, you are like sheep that have no shepherd (Numbers 27:17).[60]

57 Brann notes the absence of clear conventions for representing Muslims, who remain stock characters in Hebrew rhymed prose narratives; see *Power in the Portrayal*, 140–159.

58 See Brann, *Power in the Portrayal*, p. 147 and n. 35.

59 Note that the Muslim employs the standard rabbinic chronology of the two Temples, found in *Seder ʿolam rabbah*: the first Temple stood for 410 years and the second for 420.

60 *Sefer hamusar*, pp. 124–125.

The passage luxuriates in biblical language to such a degree that it transposes the standard Muslim arguments into an idiom familiar to an internal Jewish audience. Verses which in their original scriptural contexts rebuke Israel for disregarding God's will (Hosea 6:4, 13:3), contrast human evanescence with divine eternity, or plead for the destruction of "all who hate Zion" (Psalm 129:6) or for a king "to go out at our head and fight our battles" so that "we may be like all the other nations" (1 Samuel 8:20) are here used to contrast Jewish political powerlessness with Muslim superiority. Only readers steeped in the Hebrew Scriptures could fully appreciate such teasing twists of meaning. And by couching the entire polemical exchange in Hebrew rhymed prose, Alḍāhirī not only adheres to literary convention but also, in theory, restricts his inflammatory anti-Muslim remarks to an internal Jewish readership, thereby safeguarding them from Muslim scrutiny. (Although, in point of fact, the incendiary content could have been conveyed orally to non-Hebrew readers, even with dialectal differences, given the close interactions between Jews and Muslims in Yemen and the role that oral recitation played in both societies. This is precisely why Shalom Medina argued that *Sefer hamusar* had been internally suppressed: had word of its critiques of Islam gotten out, it would have brought disaster upon all the Jews of Yemen.[61])

Additional subtle ironies are achieved with individual lexical items. The term that the Muslim uses to evoke his coreligionists' piety may actually be read as a double entendre: *ha-yishmaʿelim ha-shovavim* is both "the penitent Muslims" and "the wild, unruly Muslims."[62] The latter meaning picks up on the standard anti-Muslim polemical epithet, *pereʾ adam*, "a wild ass of a man," derived from the prophecy of Ishmael's birth in Genesis 16:12 and used freely in poetic complaints about Muslim oppression.[63] In a text intended for an internal Jewish readership, such clever wordplay could be used to great effect

61 See Medina, "Sefer hamusar, mahadurat ratzaby," 11.

62 For *shovavim* as 'rebellious,' see: Jeremiah 3:14, 8:5, 31:22; Micah 2:4. *Shovavim* as 'penitents' derives from an acronym designating the eight successive Torah portions in the book of Exodus. In a medieval Germano-Polish custom that spread to 16th-century kabbalistic circles in Turkey and Safed, pious Jews fasted in leap years on the Mondays and Thursdays before the Sabbaths when these portions were read, hence *ṣomot shovavim* are the fasts of the penitent. Certain customs of the Safed circle reached Yemen during Alḍāhirī's lifetime, and while it is not clear that this one did, Alḍāhirī may have had some knowledge of it through literary or other channels. See Cohen, *Sources and History*, 107–129; Werblowsky, *Joseph Karo, Lawyer and Mystic*, 184; Sperber, *Minhagei yisrael, meqorot ve-toledot*, 3:216–217; and Eisenstein, *Ozar Dinim u-Minhagim*, 403–404.

63 On the use of *pereʾ adam* as a derogatory epithet for Islam see, e.g., Steinschneider, *Polemische und apologetische Literatur*, 300. See also Schlossberg, "Anti-Muslim Polemics in Medieval Yemenite Midrashim," 208–209. The continuation of Gen. 16:12, "his hand will

without increasing the risk of religious confrontation or punitive measures. Similarly, self-critical concessions seem out of place in a polemical argument, where they could serve the opponent as ammunition. But such admissions would be perfectly reasonable if they were never intended for a Muslim readership. Thus, the Jew begins his rejoinder as follows:

> If you want to distinguish between truth and falsehood, heed my words … Know that God gave his Torah to his people through his trusted servant, Moses. He called them his treasured possession, but they sinned against Him and his Torah. He looked down from His dwelling place and chastised them as a father disciplines his son. He will take them back in everlasting repentance and bear them, as He once did, on eagles' wings by means of His anointed prophet.

At the conclusion of his extensive refutation, the Jew sets forth one final "proof" that requires familiarity with a particular interpretation of several biblical verses in order to be intelligible. Grouped together on the basis of ancient Jewish scribal tradition, each of these verses has an oversized letter *ʿayin* that serves as the peg for polemical exegesis. Once more, it seems highly unlikely that any Muslim, apart from a learned apostate from Judaism, could make any sense of such arcane material. The verses are Deuteronomy 6:4 (*shemaʿ yisrael*; the word *shemaʿ* ends with an enlarged *ʿayin*); Psalm 80:14 (*yekharsemennah ḥazir mi-yaʿar* ["wild boars gnaw at it"]; the *ʿayin* in *mi-yaʿar* is suspended); and Job 38:15 (*va-yimmanaʿ me-reshaʿim oram* ["their light is withheld from the wicked"]; the *ʿayin* in *reshaʿim* is suspended, leaving the word *rashim*, "poor," or "destitute."[64]) Alḍāhirī's polemical exegesis—really a little homily—runs as follows:

> "The first *ʿayin* is ordered in line with the letters … while the two others are suspended. The first alludes to the religion of Israel, and the two suspended ones allude to Esau and Ishmael [Christianity and Islam]. For they are now insolent and proud [they, like the letters above the line, are currently superior to Israel], lording it over the pleasant nation, but in the end they will fall and their carcasses will be burnt in flames, may it be speedily and soon! To this the knowing prophet [King David] alluded, 'All the horns of the wicked I will cut' (Psalm 75:11). The end of the verse refers to Israel, 'but the horns of the righteous shall be lifted up.' About them it is

be against every man …" was taken by Muslim authors as a blessing, referring to Muḥammad and the early conquests of Islam; see Lazarus-Yafeh, *Intertwined Worlds*, 92–93.

64 See, e.g., bSanhedrin 103b.

said from the hidden heavens, 'For every eye shall behold the Lord's return to Zion' (Isaiah 52:8; *'ayin be-'ayin yir'u be-shuv ha-shem ṣiyyon* [the word for eye is taken as an allusion to the letter *'ayin*.])"[65]

1.1.5 Authorial Voice

Another rhetorical strategy typical of the *maqāma* is the deliberate masking of the author's own views. Scholarly readers of the seventh *maqāma* have assumed that the Jewish disputant is Alḍāhirī's mouthpiece.[66] Yet, from a literary vantage point, Abner, "the father of all ruses," is an unreliable figure whose truth claims are suspect, and whose views are therefore not *a priori* those of the author. Throughout the work, Alḍāhirī obscures his real opinion on a variety of topics by dividing his own voice between the narrator and the protagonist, neither one of whom should be wholly identified with him.[67] It is reasonable to assume that Alḍāhirī's reaction to Muslim oppression was one of despair and resentment. Yet, the contrast between Abner's intrepid, reckless response to his opponent and Mordecai's extreme caution suggests a certain authorial ambivalence about openly maligning Islam in writing, even in a Hebrew text not readily accessible to Muslim readers. As noted previously, compared to their brethren in the Christian West, Jews in medieval Islamic lands were generally reluctant to respond in writing to anti-Jewish polemics, and tended to exercise self-censorship, even though their Hebrew-character texts (whether Hebrew or Judeo-Arabic) were unlikely to attract Muslim attention. Thus, the divergent reactions of Abner and Mordecai reflect two historically recognizable responses to polemical provocation but also two conflicting projections of authorial voice. Alḍāhirī externalizes his ambivalences by having Mordecai and Abner each advocate one of the two conflicting sides in his inner struggle over whether to vilify Islam overtly, even though Abner's impulse ultimately wins out.

---

65 Tzvi Langermann kindly informs me that the unpublished speculative work from Yemen entitled *Ḥafiṣah* included a long chapter on the forms of the Hebrew letters, but the section devoted to the symbolism of the letter *'ayin* is not extant. See Langermann, "The Yemeni Treatise Known as *Ḥafiṣah*."

66 See, e.g., Ahroni, "From *Bustān al-'Uqūl* to *Qissat al-Batūl*," 317–323 and Regev, "The Attitude to Islam in Yemeni Jewish Philosophical Literature," p. 26. Such an assumption is problematic not only vis-à-vis belletristic works but also with regard to polemical compositions; see Lasker, *Jewish Philosophical Polemics*, xx: "If one wants to know a particular author's true view on a subject, a polemical treatise is the last place one would look to determine it. ... Drawing historical, theological, social, or intellectual conclusions from polemical literature should be attempted only in a restrained manner."

67 See Decter, *Iberian Jewish Literature*, pp. 135–136 and 157–163.

1.1.6 Internal Tensions and Ambiguities

The tensions between the text's realism and patently fictional elements are evident on a number of levels. The confrontation as presented could plausibly be an accurate report of a theological disputation. Alḍāhirī even puts the current *hijrī* date (977), corresponding to the year 1569, into the mouth of the Muslim antagonist. Yet there are too many coincidences for the account to be entirely believable: the Jew prevails despite his outspokenness and lowly status, and—uncannily—turns out to be Abner. There is also a certain ambiguity surrounding the genre of the text: the story embedded in the frame purports to record a public confrontation, yet its improbability and conventional structure point to a purely literary invention. While the author would have us believe that Abner's speech is adroitly improvised, it seems carefully scripted.

Even the nature of Abner's deception is not quite straightforward. Although incognito, he is not heavily disguised and is identifiably Jewish. Only a cloak prevents his recognition, allowing him to pose as an earnest polemicist. On the narrative plane, Abner's convincing posture deceives the Muslim, Mordecai, and the reader (who relies on Mordecai for his version of the story). While the Muslim remains a victim of the ruse, the narrator and reader are seemingly enlightened once Abner's true identity is revealed although even the point of anagnorisis is marked by an internally contradictory statement. When Mordecai exclaims, "*va'akkir oto … ve-hinneh hu' avner avi ha-taḥbulot*," he claims to have penetrated to Abner's true core and yet must concede that Abner is a perennial source of dissimulation and subterfuge. There is also something unusual about Abner's trickery in this instance. In most other episodes of the work, the quick-witted Abner is sly and scheming, but once his mask has been exposed, he is not so much interested in the substance of his hoax as in the tangible rewards that ensue. Yet here he appears to be morally, theologically, and intellectually invested in the polemical arguments he has put forward. Although outwardly affecting a pose, Abner is inwardly serious, defying the reader's expectation of a humorous dénouement. And yet, Abner is strangely detached from "reality," for only Mordecai recognizes the risks his friend courts by openly flouting social, religious, and political convention.

The discrepancy between Mordecai's concern and Abner's disregard for danger calls our attention to an additional layer of textual deception: though initially made to think that Abner's polemics are intended for Muslim consumption, we come to see that their universe of discourse render them intelligible only to an internal Jewish audience. Some of the most incendiary attacks on the Qur'ān are reserved for the poem Abner recites toward the end of the *maqāma*. According to convention, poems inserted into Hebrew rhymed prose narratives generally recapitulate or otherwise comment on the preceding text.[68] Here, however, the poem treads ground not covered in the prose section, proclaiming the inferiority of the Qurʾān to the Torah, and indignantly dismissing Muḥammad's misguided comparison of the two. The poem's relationship to the preceding text thus diverges from the expected literary norm and, in so doing, calls attention to its imprudently provocative content.

1.1.7 Literary Antecedents

Philosophical dialogues and theological debates are depicted in a number of earlier rhymed prose works from Spain and Provence, such as Shem Tov Falaquera's 13th-century *Iggeret ha-vikuaḥ* (Epistle of the Debate) or Isaac Polleqar's 14th-century *Ezer ha-dat* (Support of the Faith). Few of these medieval Hebrew texts are purely belletristic, however; most are didactic compositions that exploit the highly readable medium of rhymed prose to popularize technical, speculative ideas.[69] Alḍāhirī's polemical *maqāma* is much closer to an episode in Alḥarizi's *Taḥkemoni,* a work he acknowledges as one of his literary models. Like Alḥarizi's "Tale of the Astrologer" (*Taḥkemoni,* Ch. 22), Alḍāhirī's imagined disputation includes rare portrayals of identifiably Muslim characters; both touch on the power relations between the dominant Muslim majority and members of the Jewish minority; and there are certain parallels between the two plots, even though the narratives are distinct.

The unsettling Muslim-Jewish dynamics depicted in Alḥarizi's "Tale of the Astrologer" have been subjected to penetrating and insightful analyses by Ross Brann and Raymond Scheindlin.[70] In this uncommonly vivid *maqāma,* a group of Jewish boys comes upon a Muslim street astrologer who tells fortunes for members of the crowd gathered around him. The skeptical youths decide to test him by agreeing on a single, collective question that they conceal from him and ask him to guess: When will the Jews be redeemed, and when will Jewish sovereignty be restored? The astrologer identifies them as Jews and, furious, tells them that they deserve to die for having asked such a politically explosive question. Incensed by the boys' alleged seditiousness, the Muslim mob drags them to the local *qāḍī* for judgment. The judge, described as reasonable and benevolent, keeps the youths in prison until the fanatical throng has dispersed

68 See Pagis, *Change and Tradition in the Secular Poetry,* 211–212.

69 See Hughes, *The Art of Dialogue in Jewish Philosophy,* 50–106.

70 See Brann, *Power in the Portrayal,* 140–159 and Scheindlin, "Al-Ḥarizi's Astrologer." For the Hebrew text of the *maqāma,* see Alḥarizi, *Taḥkemoni,* ed. Yahalom-Katsumata, 327–332 and *Taḥkemoni,* ed. Toporowsky, 213–217. For English translations, see Reichert, *The Tahkemoni,* 2:95–102 and Segal, *The Book of Taḥkemoni,* 205–209 and 526–528.

and then lets them go. This story is told to the narrator by the protagonist, who participated in the escapade and who therefore ends his tale by thanking God for his deliverance from danger.

As Brann notes, this is the only *maqāma* in Alḥarizi's collection in which two of the main characters are identified as Muslims. Through careful examination of his representation of Muslims and the way they are made to interact with the Jewish characters in the "Tale of the Astrologer," Brann finds evidence of ambivalence toward the sociopolitical experience of Jews under Islam. On the one hand, the unscrupulous street astrologer foments popular hostility toward the Jews; on the other hand, the noble judge offers them sanctuary. The precarious existence of minority outsiders in Muslim society is also reflected in the text's transformation of the normally smooth-talking and roguish protagonist into a passive and mute victim; "a Jew who has overstepped his bounds." Scheindlin too highlights the perilous crossing of boundaries that is so central to the text: boundaries between the secular and the religious; between different social classes; and, most significantly, between religious communities. The skeptical boys' mistake was not only to pull a prank on the credulous Muslim masses and not only to call attention to their religious identity but also to publicize their community's centuries-old yearning for an end to Jewish subjugation.

It is instructive to compare Alḍāhirī's polemical *maqāma* with Alḥarizi's "Tale of the Astrologer." Both stories involve a public Muslim-Jewish confrontation that centers on diametrically opposed perceptions of Jewish subjugation, *dhimmī* status, and messianism. Both encounters unfold in the presence of inhospitable Muslim masses who are roused to threaten the physical well-being of the Jewish protagonists. Yet in other respects the similarities are only superficial. In Alḍāhirī's *maqāma*, there is no indication of the main Muslim character's occupation or socioeconomic background. We cannot tell whether he is supposed to conjure up a *qāḍī*, an *imām* or an otherwise learned individual, a populist demagogue, or simply a man in the street. Even allowing for his omission of certain types of arguments, one wonders whether an ordinary person would have been quite so well-versed in anti-Jewish polemics. Scheindlin notes that Alḥarizi's astrologer is a sincere Muslim, whether or not he is an authentic fortuneteller. By contrast, it is hard to assess whether Alḍāhirī's disputant is a convincing, believable Muslim, particularly as his capitulation is so swift, unexpected, and counterintuitive. There is even an intriguing if vague suggestion that he is an apostate from Judaism, for Abner defends his actions by citing the famous mishnah in *Avot* 2,14: "Know what to reply to the *apikorus*," a term more commonly applied to skeptics or heretics from within the fold.[71] And while the

71 The phenomenon of anti-Jewish polemical tracts composed by Jewish apostates to Islam

menacing mobs in both stories highlight the vulnerability and defenselessness of Jews in Muslim society, it cannot be said that Abner is transformed from victimizer to victim. Rather, he is characteristically defiant and persuasive and, despite his brush with danger, comes off looking strong. His resilient refusal to be cowed is reflected in his unrepentant closing poem, "Asher ḥanan le-vanim haʿamusim" which, within a few lines, turns from a prayer of thanksgiving into a highly polemical piece. By contrast, Ḥever ha-Keni, the Jewish protagonist of Alḥarizi's *maqāma* is, as Brann observes, uncharacteristically silent. Breaching literary convention, he does not recite a single line of poetry at the end of the tale. It is almost as though Alḍāhirī wishes to "correct" the disheartening outcome of the Jewish-Muslim encounter in Alḥarizi's tale—as well as in his own actuality. Abner's triumph is entirely at odds with the discriminatory measures recounted throughout *Sefer hamusar*, and indeed with being "imprisoned and devoured" at the whim of the *imām*. Clearly, this belletristic *maqāma* derives its potency from an unresolved tension between insurmountable realities and liberating fictions; between (self-)imposed silence and the yearning to speak freely; between enforced submission and fantasies of ascendancy. Perhaps, then, Abner's chimerical, preposterous victory is best viewed as a consolation for an internal Jewish readership whose sociopolitical status under Yemeni Islam was far more precarious than this tale's conclusion would lead us to believe.

1.2 *Lawsuits before Qāḍīs*

1.2.1 The Ninth *Maqāma*: A Tale of Three Swindlers

In the ninth *maqāma*, Alḍāhirī crafts a highly comical response to Muslim accusations of Jewish weakness. The yarn he spins is an outlandish story of one-upmanship between confidence men of three different faiths (which Hayyim Schirmann dubbed *Maʿaseh bisheloshah ganavim*, "A Tale of Three Thieves").[72] In its perverse ecumenicism, it projects the fantasy of a Jewish author desperate to rectify the imbalance of power between his downtrodden coreligionists and their contemptuous overlords. But even though the Jewish triumph in this story is completely implausible, Alḍāhirī's portrayal of Muslim (and Christian) char-

was certainly attested in the early Ottoman period; see Adang, "Guided to Islam by the Torah" and Schmidtke, "Epistle forcing the Jews [to admit their error] with regard to what they contend about the Torah."

72 For earlier publications of the 9th and 10th *maqāmāt*, see Schirmann, "Two Maqamas of Zecharia Aldahiri's Sepher Hamussar" and Ratzaby, *Yalqut ha-maqāma haʿivrit*, 149–154. Haim Schwarzbaum noted affinities between this story and the international folklore motif of "the master thief"; see his review of Ratzaby ed. *Sefer hamusar*, p. 35.

acters is telling. In the frame story, Mordecai sails for seventy days from India to Hormuz on the Persian coast. With language and imagery redolent of the book of Jonah, he describes a storm at sea, during which the terrified sailors cast the ship's cargo overboard in a desperate attempt to keep it afloat. As a result, he arrives in Hormuz bereft of all his belongings. In search for some means of subsistence, he seeks out the silk merchants' market on the theory that he might be able to secure a loan. There, to his astonishment, he finds Abner ben Ḥeleq leading the life of a successful textile merchant. Without revealing his identity, he beseeches Abner for a loan, as mandated under such circumstances by the Torah. Recognizing the petitioner as his old friend, Abner extends his hospitality to Mordecai, and while they "drink wine and swill liquor," Mordecai begs to know the secret of his friend's extraordinary prosperity. Abner replies with a hilarious tale that is as unbelievable as it is riveting, in which he is cast as the quintessential trickster who makes capital out of his rhetorical gifts.

Abner relates that, earlier in his career, in the city of Mosul, he was befriended by two thieves, a Christian and a Muslim. Deriding the Jews for their general impotence and lack of daring, they claimed that a Jew could not even carry out a respectable theft. Abner promises to prove them wrong, but only after they have first done their swindling. Arriving at the market (a regular venue for charlatans and mountebanks), the Christian distracts a butter merchant with a feigned toothache and a pair of tongs. While the Christian implores the man to extract his throbbing tooth, the Muslim steals his wares. (When the Muslim is mistakenly about to grab the smaller of two vessels filled with butter, the Christian mischievously cries out to the merchant groping his teeth, "Take the larger one! For I've said of my teeth, 'I will reduce them to naught.' "[73] The Muslim understands the hint, takes the larger skin, and flees.)[74] Here the narrator interjects, "That was the deception of the wicked, despicable, and abhorrent Christian." The next day, the Muslim dupes an elderly moneychanger, locking him inside his shop under the guise of showing him how would-be robbers could hide his crate of precious gems under their cloaks. Though the man cries out for help, the other merchants in the market abandon him to his fate. They reason that he must have lost his mind to have succumbed to a robbery in broad daylight. All the passersby laugh, and the narrator comments, "That was the ruse of the dastardly Muslim, who dealt cruelly

73 Cf. Dt. 32:26.

74 Cf. the exposé of quack dentistry in al-Jawbarī (13th-century Syria), *The Book of Charlatans*, Ch. 15. Theft by distracting attention is one of the subdivisions of the international folk motif of "The Master Thief"; see Aarne-Thompson, *The Types of the Folktale*, 1525D. On thieving, see also Bosworth, *The Mediaeval Islamic Underworld*, 1:103–106.

with his coreligionist." (That the victim is a coreligionist can also be seen from the Muslim thief's initial greeting, "Shalom ʿaleykha, baʿal haʾemunah," a direct translation of the Arabic salutation, *as-salām ʿalayka, yā ayuhā ʾl-muʾmin*. The concentration of Arabisms in the thief's speech is perhaps also intended to simulate the way a Muslim would converse.)[75] Finally, Abner proves his mettle by breaking into the home of a wealthy merchant under cover of darkness. In the chest containing the man's valuables, he plants an inventory signed in his own name and writes a duplicate, which he keeps. In the morning, he compels the merchant to appear before the local *qāḍī* and charges him with having unlawfully kept a deposit that Abner had entrusted him with a dozen years earlier. The merchant swears that no such deposit was made, but when they open the chest in the presence of the judge, they find the inventory. Abner produces the second copy, thereby disgracing the merchant and convincing the *qāḍī* that the valuables are his. He then takes the chest to the Christian and Muslim thieves who react with amazement and adulation, saying: "Truly you are a man of valor who performs great deeds. We praise you and it is fitting that we prostrate ourselves before you. From now on you will be our master."

The gentile thieves' fawning approbation of Abner's elaborate hoax runs counter to the narrator's moral judgments of all three thefts. Mordecai roundly censures the deceit of the "wicked, despicable, and abhorrent Christian" and "the dastardly Muslim who dealt cruelly with his coreligionist." But he also rebukes Abner for having transgressed a moral prohibition as well as for having endangered himself. That all three hoaxes were played against Muslims does not mitigate the impropriety or pronounced element of risk in Abner's deception. Alluding to a biblical discussion of one who willfully veers from a judicial verdict, Mordecai states, "The truth is that this matter is forbidden according to Scripture which says, 'You must not deviate.'"[76] Abner replies that he would not have done the deed had he not been bated:

> Had not the Muslim and the Christian forced me, I would not have done this thing, but they would not leave me alone. In their eyes, they were above the clouds while we were like grasshoppers in our own eyes.

---

75 See *Sefer hamusar*, pp. 140–141, nn. 60–63. Ratzaby, ibid., p. 20, notes that there is an anecdote about a Muslim who stole a cask of jewels from a vendor and managed to flee in an 11th-century *adab* anthology; see al-Iṣfahāni, *Muḥāḍarāt al-udabāʾ*, 2:189–194 (*Wa-mimmā jāʾa fī ʾl-talaṣṣuṣ wa-mā yajrīʾ majrāhu*; "And From What Was Said About Thievery and What Is Analogous to It"); and Malti-Douglas, "Classical Arabic Crime Narratives: Thieves and Thievery in Adab Literature."

76 Cf. Deut. 17:11.

Abner is so consumed by the charge of Jewish inferiority that he does not stop to imagine—as Mordecai does with horror—what might have happened to a Jew who not only victimized an innocent Muslim but did so by lying to a Muslim judge. Nor is he troubled by the inherent immorality of his act, which is, ironically, underscored when his innocent victim meekly accepts the unfounded charges against him, proclaiming "Heaven forbid that faithful merchants should lie, for that would make them false and deceitful."[77]

Nevertheless, Alḍāhirī seems keen to suggest that his Jewish rogue-hero is savvier and more literate than his non-Jewish counterparts, as his ability to forge a legal document sets him apart from the Christian and Muslim thieves. Ultimately, the admiring narrator once again acclaims Abner as "the father of all ruses … [from whom] no secret is hidden."[78] In this respect, Abner conforms to the stock *maqāma* figure of the slippery, silver-tongued hero who exploits his stylistic gifts to defraud credulous strangers and line his own pockets. At the same time, his trick recalls a recognizable motif from Arabic folk traditions, namely that of the thief who marks another's property and then claims it as his own.[79] In its valorization of crafty stratagems, Alḍāhirī's anecdote is very much in line with the emphasis on *dhakā'* or cleverness in Arab *adab* treatments of thieves and thievery, which was an entire literary subgenre unto itself.[80] But with its additional element of interconfessional competition, the story is also a commentary on power relations and Jewish perceptions of Muslim magistrates.

1.2.2 Portrayal of the *Qāḍī*

The *qāḍī*, or religious judge, is frequently subject to ridicule in Arabic folklore and literary works despite—or perhaps because of—the respect that his office demanded. A glance at an index of folk motifs reveals that judges were routinely depicted as corrupt, complacent, nepotistic, gullible, or otherwise disreputable.[81] In al-Ḥarīrī's *Maqāmāt*, judges are miserly, lecherous, or the credulous victims of scams, most often in the form of staged disputes between

77 Cf. Ps. 119:118: "You reject all who stray from Your laws, for they are false and deceitful."

78 Note that the two final phrases praising Abner are in Aramaic and that the second of the two appropriates the language of Dan. 4:6 describing Belteshazzar, Nebuchadnezzar's chief magician.

79 See, e.g., El-Shamy, *Folk Traditions of the Arab World* 1: 232, motif K405, and idem, *Types of the Folktale in the Arab World*, p. 890, tale-type 1642B, False proof of ownership: thief marks other's property and then claims it as his own.

80 See Malti-Douglas, "Classical Arabic Crime Narratives."

81 See: El-Shamy, *Guide to Motif Classification*, 2:267–268; Marzolph, *Arabia Ridens*, 2:367, s.v. Richter; idem and van Leeuwen, *The Arabian Nights Encyclopedia*, Index, s.v. *qāḍī*. See also

the rogue hero and accomplices who pose as his son or wife.[82] Alḍāhirī picks up on several strands of this satirical tradition but exploits the familiar topoi from his own vantage point. Along with his rhetorical strategies, his manipulation of the plot of the ninth *maqāma* suggests an anti-Muslim subtext. The intertextual allusions in the *qāḍī's* speech are particularly intriguing. Upon the "discovery" of his inventory in the accused merchant's chest, Abner asks what the judicial procedure will be if he can provide proof of his deposit. By way of response, the Muslim judge quotes a rabbinic principle of tort law: "The burden of proof lies on him who would exact restitution from his fellow" (*ha-moṣi me-ḥavero ʿalav ha-raʾayah*).[83] And when the aggrieved merchant protests that he is the most faithful of Muslims, the judge again replies with biblical and rabbinic phrases and classical Jewish treatments of judgment.[84]

Upon first consideration, one could attribute such striking incongruities to the literary convention of Judaizing Islamic material in Hebrew *maqāmāt*.[85] But there would seem to be something more at stake in having the *qāḍī* rattle off an axiom of rabbinic jurisprudence. For one thing, the discrepancy is deliberately humorous: A *qāḍī* has recourse to Jewish law in order to uphold a principle of fairness in a Muslim religious court. On a more serious note, it is as though Muslim religious law is inadequate to the task. Ironically, it is his very adherence to this rabbinic guideline that leaves the *qāḍī* open to deception since Abner trumps the argument by producing his forged inventories. It is also ironic that the *qāḍī* subsequently warns the innocent victim against perverting justice since that is precisely what Abner intends to do, using the gullible judge as his instrument. While the *qāḍī* initially seems honest, Abner's trickery makes him look terribly naïve. Abner flatters the *qāḍī*, saying, "God appointed you over the Muslims to arbitrate among them and to assist the needy." While

Goldziher, "Mélanges Judéo-Arabes," 7–8 and Hamori, "Rising to Greet You: Some Comedies of Manners."

82 Staged disputes between the rogue hero and his "son" or "wife" occur in front of a judge in #8, 9, 10, 23, 34, 37, 40, 45; see Cooperson trans., *al-Ḥarīrī, Impostures*; for the Arabic see al-Ḥarīrī, *Maqāmāt Abī Zayd al-Sarūjī*. This scenario became a convention of Arabic and Hebrew *maqāmāt* composed in the Ḥarīrian/ Ḥarizian tradition. For unflattering portrayals of judges, see also al-Ibshīhī (1388–c. 1446), *Al-Mustaṭraf fī kull fann mustaẓraf*, 1:309–317 and 2:648–655. I am grateful to the late Professor Joseph Sadan for having called al-Ibshīhī to my attention.

83 See mBaba Qamma 3,11; cf. mBaba Bathra 9,6.

84 See *Sefer hamusar*, p. 143, lines 109–111; cf. Prov. 4:27; Mekhilta *Mishpatim* on Ex. 23:8; Dt. 1:17.

85 Cf. Lavi, "The Rationale of al-Ḥarīzī in Biblicizing the Maqāmāt of al-Ḥarīrī" and Decter, "The Rendering of Qurʾānic Quotations in Hebrew Translations of Islamic Texts."

he may have been appointed by God, as a judge of human character he is hopelessly obtuse, and as an arbitrator he is woefully incompetent.

On the surface, this encounter is not cast as an interconfessional lawsuit.[86] After summoning his unfortunate victim to appear before the *qāḍī*, Abner lets slip that he himself was dressed in the garb of a merchant from Muslim lands.[87] If we take this to mean that Abner is outwardly indistinguishable from the Muslim defendant, the *qāḍī* presumably believes he is judging between coreligionists, hence his sincere efforts to be impartial and to base his decision on empirical evidence. But the reader knows that Abner the Jew has duped the Muslim judge with his smooth talk. In so doing, he wins the eternal admiration of the non-Jewish thieves who had taunted him at the outset precisely because he was Jewish. And instead of bringing succor to a fellow Muslim, the *qāḍī*'s misguided ruling deprives him of his life savings. At the end of the tale, the accused merchant retreats in shame, and the judge is not even permitted to speak. Alḍāhirī has clearly conjured up a fictional alternative to his bleak reality: this is a world in which the Jewish author controls how much voice Muslims have and in which Jews do not take gentile taunts lying down.

Although it originates in the underworld, the non-Jewish thieves' charge that Jews are ineffectual aligns with the more mainstream anti-Jewish arguments from political powerlessness voiced by the Muslim polemicist in the seventh *maqāma*. While Alḍāhirī's tale of three swindlers is farcical in the extreme, there is a certain pathos in the fact that even common thieves deride the Jews for their impotence and cowardice. Here is a Jewish author imagining the contempt in which gentile crooks hold the Jews. ("Had not the Muslim and the Christian forced me, I would not have done this thing, but they would not leave me alone. In their eyes, they were above the clouds while we looked like grasshoppers to ourselves.") These episodes therefore reveal not only historically attested anti-Jewish arguments but also imaginary critiques that reflect

86 There are a few instances of lawsuits between Muslims and Jews included in Tobi, "Information on the Jews of Yemen in Arabic Writings from Yemen"; see esp. vol. 65, p. 19. On the powers of the Muslim judiciary as reflected in Geniza documents, see Goitein, *A Mediterranean Society*, 2:363–368; on Jews making use of Muslim courts see ibid, 398–402; Ratzaby, "ʿInyanei yehudim be-teiman beʿarkha'ot shel goyim"; Wagner, "Jewish Mysticism on Trial in a Muslim Court" and idem, *Jews and Islamic Law in Early 20th-Century Yemen*, 83–90.

87 *Sefer hamusar*, p. 142, lines 99–100: *Va'omar lo: yesh li mishpaṭ ʿimmakh eṣel ha-qaṣin lo te'aḥer. Va'ani lavush levush ha-soḥarim ha-ba'im me'ereṣ ha-hagrim. Va-yaqom ha-soḥer va-yelekh ʿimmi eṣel ha-qaṣin* .... The phrasing is ambiguous, so it is not entirely clear whether Abner is disguised as a Muslim or simply dressed as a merchant from Muslim lands but identifiable as a *dhimmi*.

Jewish sensitivities about the inferior status and vulnerability of Jews in Muslim society. To counter this humiliating sense of inadequacy, Abner contrasts the superior sophistication of his elusive, untraceable methods with the arrogantly blatant trespasses of the other two thieves, invoking "our Torah" to set himself apart from these religious "others":

> I do not do things as you do, for it says in our Scripture, 'If you have been scandalously arrogant ... [Then clap your hand to your mouth]' (cf. Proverbs 30:32). You, if you are found out, they will hang you from the treetops. Or if any of the stolen goods are found to be in your possession, see what evil you will face. Come, let us walk through the city's markets. Choose a successful merchant for me and show me his courtyard and where his money is kept. Then be on your way and I will show you how I will put an end to his splendor.

By making his Jewish conman more cunning and resourceful (not to mention literate) than his non-Jewish counterparts, Alḍāhirī addresses these anxieties, indulging his fantasy of Jewish bravura, resilience, and control.[88]

1.2.3 The Seventeenth *Maqāma*: The *Qāḍī* and the Mule

Alḍāhirī's one other portrayal of a *qāḍī* occurs in the frame story to the seventeenth *maqāma*. There Mordecai recounts an incident he witnessed together with Abner. A Muslim (*yishmaʿeli*) from the caravan with which Mordecai's group is traveling covets a Jew's mule. He consults with two scoundrels, and together they haul the Jew and his beast before a judge.[89] The Muslim baldly claims that the mule had been stolen from him. The judge demands that he bring a witness, so he summons his cronies who testify in support of his false claim to ownership. On the basis of their testimony, the judge rules in favor of the Muslim and deals a blow (whether figurative or literal is not clear) to the innocent Jew (*va-yakh et ha-yehudi va-sheli*).[90] Abner is outraged and declares,

88 Hence Ratzaby dubbed the episode "The Wisdom of the Jew" in his *Yalqut ha-maqāma haʿivrit*, even though the rhymed table of contents in *Sefer hamusar* calls it "The ninth *maḥberet*, which includes the admirable schemes of three partners, Jewish, Christian, and Muslim"; see *Sefer hamusar*, p. 55. This is also how it appears in BL Or. 11337 and Oxford Bodleian ms. Opp. Add. 8° 31. The rhymed table of contents in NLI Ms. Heb. 8° 6748 and the former Sassoon 995 erroneously label it the eighth *maqāma*.

89 The judge is repeatedly referred to as *qaṣin* (lines 15, 21, 22, 31), the Hebrew cognate for *qāḍī*, but also once as *dayyan* (line 13) and once as *shofeṭ* (line 19).

90 It is perhaps not coincidental that the language here is borrowed from the story of the biblical Abner ben Ner; see II Sam. 3:27.

"It is time to act for the Lord [for they have violated Your teaching]."[91] He proceeds to cover the mule's head with a blanket and angrily challenges the witnesses, saying, "Know that this mule has a growth in its eye; if you are honest, tell me whether it is in its left or its right." The men tremble in the knowledge that they are about to give themselves away. The judge admonishes them not to speak deceitfully, and they agree that the growth is in the right eye. The judge records their testimony in writing and seals it so that it cannot be altered. Then Abner uncovers the mule's eyes and reveals that the animal is free of all blemish. Once Abner has called their bluff, the judge strikes the false witnesses, and his servants send the Muslim claimant on his way, "lest his disgrace be revealed." The judge orders the Jew to go home, ride his mule and enjoy success. In so saying, he echoes Psalm 45:5, a verse whose continuation ("ride on the cause of truth and meekness and right ...") suggests that the Jewish defendant occupies the moral high ground.

Like the *qāḍī* in Alḥarizi's "Tale of the Astrologer," the judge in the seventeenth *maqāma* is an ethical figure who attempts to uphold the law to the best of his ability. His initial portrayal is fairly sympathetic: seeing the Jew standing before him with tears streaming down his cheeks, the judge is described with language evoking God's compassion for the Israelites in Egypt ("he saw our plight, our misery, and our oppression"; cf. Deuteronomy 26:7). His reverence for the law is underscored by his trembling when calling for a witness. Nevertheless, his initial hasty ruling in favor of the Muslim suggests that he is blinded by an instinctive sense of religious solidarity with the claimant, whose actions betray deeply ingrained assumptions of *dhimmī* inferiority. (And thus the allusion to Deuteronomy 26:7 also implicitly identifies Muslim and Pharaonic oppression of the Jews.) To the *qāḍī*'s credit, however, he reverses that decision once he is made aware that it was based on inadmissible testimony. Although he allows himself to be taken in by deceitful fellow Muslims, he is not above reprimanding those Muslims in the presence of Jews despite their socially subordinate status. Still, the reader is left wondering whether the Muslim claimant has been let off lightly because his suit is with a Jew.

Alḍāhirī's two tales of *qāḍīs* imagine encounters between Jews and Muslims in the quasi-institutional setting of a makeshift courtroom. Together, the two texts portray an assemblage of contemptible, laughable Muslim characters: shady con artists, bumbling thieves, credulous merchants, and deceitful witnesses not clever enough to extract themselves from a trap. In contrast

91 Cf. Ps. 119:126. While Alḍāhirī's use of the verse is somewhat comical, Maimonides uses it to justify committing the esoteric doctrines of his *Guide of the Perplexed* to writing; see Pines trans., *Guide*, Introduction to Part I, 1:16; cf. bBer. 63a.

with these lowlifes and naïve souls, there are two essentially benevolent judges intent on upholding the law but lacking in perspicacity. One remains unaware that he has been duped by a Jew dressed as a Muslim. The other allows himself to be swayed by underhanded fellow Muslims but ultimately restores his credibility with a show of impartiality toward an innocent Jewish defendant. Without a doubt, these characters are fictional and stereotypical, and their behavior is largely predetermined by familiar plots drawn from folk traditions, the *maqāma* literature, or *adab* narratives of thievery and judicial corruption or ineptitude. Nevertheless, their portraits are also shaped in accordance with Jewish perceptions of Muslims from various walks of life and sensitivities about the precariousness of Jewish existence in Muslim society. While Abner's cunning victories in both tales adhere to stylized *maqāma* plots, they are also the products of a Jewish literary imagination anxious to see Jews prevail over Muslim rivals.

1.3 *Exempla Featuring Arabs and Muslims as Role Models*

Toward the end of *Sefer hamusar*, a cluster of didactic folktales reflects the rich, if complicated, interplay between Jewish and Muslim folklore. Alḍāhirī's enthusiastic use of these tales marks the absorption and naturalization (oicotypification) of Arabic folk elements within the culturally distinct context of a Hebrew *maqāma* at the same time that it betrays the complexity and ambivalence of his attitudes towards Arabs, Muslims, and Islamic culture.[92] Through his protagonists, he explicitly urges his Jewish readers to learn from the praiseworthy conduct of a beneficent "Arab" and to emulate Muslims who trust in God despite all odds while not hesitating to voice his antipathy to Islam. (The term 'Arab' denotes a villager, tribesman, or Bedouin.) In the thirty-sixth *maqāma*, a self-sacrificing Arab serves as a foil for the ignoble Muslims who appear in the frame story. The rhymed table of contents presents the tale as an exemplum: "The thirty-sixth *maqāma* tells of a munificent Arab who caused all the benefactors' spirits to languish. His recorded name is Taḥkam; observe his deeds so that you may acquire wisdom."[93] A few episodes later, in the forty-first *maqāma*, Abner relates two anecdotes of Arabs who endure extreme hardship but are ultimately recompensed for accepting their sufferings in love and remaining steadfast in their trust in God. He urges his Jewish audience of "true believers" to view these tales as object lessons, and, even though his exhortation

92 See Hasan-Rokem, "Ecotypes: Theory of the Lived and Narrated Experience" and Rotman, "Folktales/Folk Literature."

93 *Ha-maḥberet ha-sheloshim va-shesh kolelet le-dabber 'inyan ish 'aravi nadiv. Nafshot kol ha-nedivim he'ediv. U-shemo ha-rashum Taḥkam. Ve-shur ma'asehu le-ma'an teḥkam.*

has an anti-Muslim edge, he counsels them, without irony, to adopt the type of patience and piety illustrated in the stories in order to hasten the redemption that will free them from Muslim oppression.

Chapter 41 opens with Mordecai desperate to know when the redemption will come so that his people will no longer be like "dung on the face of the earth" (cf. Jeremiah 8:2). He travels to a city in the provinces of "Romah" (the Greco-Balkan region) in urgent search of a reliable tradition concerning the end of days. There he discovers an aged Abner in splendid headgear and robe officiating as the much respected precentor in a local synagogue. At the home of a local host, community members divine Mordecai's fixation with the length of the exile. Mordecai conveys his preoccupation to Abner, who advises all those present that "The end of days and its mysteries are sealed/ for heavenly reasons that are concealed." Nevertheless, he indicates that there are ways to grant respite to those anxiously in need of knowing, and—seemingly abandoning the prudence he just urged—proceeds to prognosticate. Abner predicts highly specific Hebrew dates for the ingathering of the exiles which correspond roughly to the end of the 16th century, a time of widespread millenarian expectations.[94] But, he cautions, there are conditions that must be met in order to hasten the redemption: complete trust in God and acceptance of suffering in great love. To illustrate these supreme virtues, he tells two tales, of an Arab (*ish ʿaravi*) who clung to his faith in God and another who submitted to hardship and affliction with grace.

> A believer (*maʾamin*), whose occupation was to sell soil for plastering roofs and houses, and who earned just enough for a day's food at a time, was troubled that he had no inheritance or field to leave his family after his death. One day he went out as usual to collect soil and found a lizard sitting at the opening of his hole, healthy, but blind. He marveled at the lizard's health and wondered how he stayed alive. So he sat down to see how he sustained himself. He watched joyfully as a grasshopper popped into the mouth of the lizard. Then he said, "God feeds every creature to its heart's content (Psalm 145:16)," and concluded that "Heaven decrees both for those who sit idly at home and those who go out to toil." So he went

94 16th-century millenarian expectations among Christians, Muslims, and Jews were fueled by the upheavals of imperial struggles for global rule. See, e.g., Yerushalmi, "Messianic Impulses in Joseph ha-Kohen"; Jacobs, "Joseph ha-Kohen, Paolo Giovio, and Sixteenth-Century Historiography"; idem, *Reorienting the East*, 96; and Verskin, *Diary of a Black Jewish Messiah*, 1–29 *passim*. On messianism in 16th-century Safed, see Yassif, *The Legend of Safed*, 231–239.

> home empty-handed and told his family that God would provide. As a result, his wife and sons did not eat their daily bread and were oppressed by hunger. They thought he was a fool for speaking so rashly; they did not understand his great faith, that he had "put his trust in the Lord ..." (Genesis 15:6). His wife had to sell everything in the house in order to feed and clothe the family until she had nothing left.
>
> After some time, a merchant came to buy soil for plastering his house. The wife told him that her husband had gone out of his mind and had abandoned her and the family. The merchant, who agreed to get the soil himself, asked to borrow the man's donkeys, to load them with the amount that he needed. When he went to the source of the soil, he found ancient buried treasures. Rejoicing, he loaded his trove onto the donkeys and concealed it beneath piles of soil. But to his great misfortune, he forgot his spade underneath the mound, and when he went to retrieve it, an avalanche of soil and rocks fell on him and killed him.
>
> The donkeys returned to their owner's house and threw off their sacks. The family discovered the treasure, gold, and silver. They said to the husband, "the faith of the blind lizard stood you in good stead." To which he replied, "God's mysteries are profound, who can discover them. He who trusts in the Lord shall be surrounded by favor (Psalm 32:10)." He turned to gather up the treasure and thanked God for his good luck. And from that day on, he gave generous gifts to his wife and sons, he had fields and vineyards, and gave copious charity to the poor. This was the reward for his trust (*sekhar havṭaḥato*) and remaining steadfast in his faith (*ve'omdo 'al emunato*).

Abner admonishes his Jewish audience of "true believers" to take this tale as an example and to adopt the type of forbearance and pietism it illustrates in order to hasten the redemption. But while he extols the virtues epitomized by the story, he betrays a profound ambivalence toward their agent:

> And if this was the recompense of an Arab from the sons of Kedar, who had no fine traits or beauty, how many times over would the wise reward be for us, the true believers (*kat ha-ma'aminim*), and for a righteous man from among our treasured people who keeps the faith.[95]

95 The ambivalence is completely elided in the rhymed prose table of contents: "The forty-first *maḥberet* addresses the issue of the End of Days with eloquent proofs taken from

He then tells the next tale, about

> an Arab who had many sheep and cattle and worked the land. He had a wife and an only son, about whom he worried, lest some terrible misfortune befall him. On the day of their gentile festival, the Arab and his son went up on their roof while the townspeople celebrated below with drums and dances and all kinds of levity.[96] The father was concerned about his son: there was a venomous viper sharpening his tongue like a sword opposite him, and there was no escaping it. The father sensed that the end was near and said to the serpent: do whatever your heart desires. So it jumped on the son, bit him and killed him. The father, overcome, acknowledged his guilt for the boy's death, confessed his sin, and chastised himself, believing this to be a punishment for his own sins. He went and told his wife, who wept bitterly. He said to her:
>
>> God has uncovered our sin. But it is a festive occasion, it is not fitting that we should diminish our neighbors' joy. If they knew that our son had died, their joy would turn to mourning. So it is best for us to endure the pain. Let us bury him and praise God who has taken his soul. If only God would replace our grief or accept his death as atonement for our sins.
>
> She heeded his words, and they quietly buried their son without anyone finding out until three days had passed. Then the townspeople understood that the couple had endured a tragedy (lit.: "had been burnt with hot coals") and spoke words of consolation to them .... The man was com-

---

two Muslims. All those who see them will trust in our redemption and the advent of our messiah." For Arabic tales about the lizard's ability to endure being without water, see van Gelder, "In the Time of *al-Fiṭaḥl* When Stones Were Still Moist and All Things Spoke: Very Short Arabic Animal Fables and Just-So Stories."

96 See *Sefer hamusar*, p. 435, line 79. Literally, the text says, "On the day of their disaster [their gentile holiday; cf. Chp. 36], he and his son went up on the roof .... The townspeople gashed themselves with knives until the blood streamed. There were drums and dances, young and old, youths and maidens and all kinds of levity. They parted their jaws in a measureless gape and their voices could be heard from afar." The cumulative effect of the biblical allusions is quite derogatory, with intimations of paganism and doomed debauchery. 1 Kings 18:28 describes the self-laceration of the prophets of Baal in their confrontation with Elijah on Mt. Carmel—"So they shouted louder, and gashed themselves with knives and spears, according to their practice, until the blood streamed over them." And Is. 5:14 reads, "Assuredly, Sheol has opened wide its gullet/ And parted its jaws in a measureless gape/ And down into it shall go/ That splendor and tumult,/ That din and revelry."

> forted over his son and returned to his previous routine, gathering grass for his cattle, tending his sycamore figs, plowing the earth, and tending his cattle, sheep and donkeys .... He gave bread to the hungry, as well as figs and grapes. He gladdened the disconsolate with songs of love and loved all human beings in his heart.
>
> After some time, his wife became pregnant with a difficulty pregnancy, the likes of which there had never been. She vowed she would give cakes to the poor upon giving birth. When she was due, her husband said,
>
>> No-one must know; for who knows what is in this full belly? Lest we become shameful by means of this creature, to the utter ruin of everything.
>
> She gave birth to an amniotic sac (*shilyah*) as large as a water-skin, with no arms, legs or eyes. The man hurried to bury it before the neighbors would come to see it. With a burning heart, he dug a grave outside of the city. He said to himself, "Before I bury this amniotic sac, I will see the great and mighty God's deed." So he tore it open, and there were seven sons inside. His mouth filled with laughter and his lips with shouts of joy. Then he carried them home in his bosom and brought them to his wife. And all the members of his household rejoiced. He said to her,
>
>> God has rewarded us according to our deeds and has turned our mourning into joy. We must thank Him according to our ability. And you must nurse these children and hide them from scoffers.
>
> His seven sons grew up to become wise and intelligent men. And this was his reward for accepting his sufferings in love.

Once again, Abner frames this tale as one of exemplary conduct yet feels prompted to refute Muslim anti-Jewish polemics:

> And if such a thing was done for this Muslim (*le-zeh ha-yishmaʿeli*), how can we, who are discerning, not believe that our Torah surely does not speak in vain? All the more so that it is from Sinai and is very ancient. And we understand God's prophecy of redemption, "Even if your outcasts are at the end of the world, [from there the Lord your God will gather you, from there He will fetch you"; Deuteronomy 30:4] ... And now, my brothers, wait for God, and purify yourselves; remove your impurities in the waters of repentance; doff your filthy clothes, and don clothes of upright conduct. Our Messiah will come soon, at a time chosen by God. If he tar-

ries, wait for him still, for he will surely come, without delay (cf. Habakuk 2:3).

1.3.1 Cross-Cultural Elements

While they are framed as tales about Arabs and Muslims, these exempla also have a marked universal dimension, suggesting an origin in the vast fund of international folklore. Alḍāhirī may well have encountered the tales orally, in Arabic, before transposing them into his elegant written Hebrew. These narratives feature common motifs: elements of the animal fable, pious deceptions, restored honor as a reward for almsgiving, serendipitously discovered treasure that comes to the deserving, monstrous births, reversals of fortune, and miracles.[97] While folktales often mirror recognizable details of a culture, here some specific characteristics are blurred. These tales lack precise geographic settings; they refer generically to faraway lands, unspecified agricultural locations, and towns. In certain respects, their protagonists, too, are typological, symbolic, and archetypal; they do not engage in identifiably Muslim rituals (despite oblique and derisory references to unnamed religious festivals and sacrifices) and do not have Arabic names—or names of any sort, for that matter.

And yet, these exempla clearly reflect religious and moral values shared by Muslims and Jews living in a common cultural milieu, where Yemenite Jews might hear folktales from itinerant Muslim preachers and storytellers. They are lessons in generosity, forbearance in the face of adversity, and complete trust in and reliance on God, the pietistic ideal known in Arabic as *tawakkul* and translated into Hebrew as *biṭṭaḥon*.[98] Even so, the cross-cultural ironies are striking: Alḍāhirī marshals miraculous tales of long-suffering Arabs in order to exhort his Jewish audience—in Hebrew resonant with particularistic scriptural associations—to wait patiently for the redemption by cultivating the virtue of *tawakkul* that these uncomplaining Arabs embody. By stringing together biblical verse fragments, particularly from the book of Proverbs, and by having his "Arabs" cite Genesis and Psalms on the virtue of trusting in the Lord, Alḍāhirī Judaizes the stories, but also—whether consciously or not—forges a link with Arabic gnomic poetry and the larger body of ancient Near Eastern wisdom literature. Yet, in validating attitudes, beliefs, and mores, his transposed folktales highlight not only commonality but also difference. By confronting the cultural and religious "otherness" of the actors in these narratives, he reinforces

---

97 See Aarne-Thompson, *The Types of the Folktale* and El-Shamy, *Folk Traditions of the Arab World*.

98 For *tawakkul*, see the sources cited in Chapter One. There is also a chapter on *tawakkul* in the 12th- century Yemenite theological compendium *Bustān al-ʿuqūl*; see Qāfiḥ ed. and trans. Nethanel ibn Fayyūmī, *Bustān al-ʿuqūl* and Levine ed. and trans., *The Bustan al-ukul* (The Garden of Wisdom).

the self-definition of his own subcultural group and community. Stories such as these, framed exclusively for an internal audience, permit minority groups to articulate dangerous views that could not otherwise be expressed openly.[99] While Abner commends the meritorious conduct of Arabs and Muslims to his Jewish audience, he betrays an overt animus toward Islamic triumphalism and supersessionism. The moral drawn from his second tale both reaffirms God's promises of redemption and refutes well-known Muslim polemical arguments against Judaism. In his rhetorical question, "how can we … not believe that our Torah surely does not speak in vain—all the more so that it is from Sinai and is very ancient?" there is an implied denial of the claim that the revelation of the Qurʾān superseded or abrogated the Torah, an allegation he also refutes—along with the notion that Muhammad's prophecy was superior to that of Moses—in his street disputation in the seventh *maqāma*. And in his citation of Deuteronomy 30:4, there is a calculated response to the Muslim contention that the Jews' dispersion, humiliation, and political subjugation are all proof of their rejection by God. Though the Muslim characters in these tales are fictional, archetypal, and largely instrumental, Alḍāhirī's appropriation of their stories reveals very real sensitivities to Muslim anti-Jewish animadversions. His use of folktales about exemplary Arabs, therefore, embodies an inherent tension between bridging boundaries and constructing barriers.[100]

1.3.2 *Maqāma* Thirty-Six: The Tale of the Generous Arab

The central tale of the thirty-sixth *maqāma*, as told by Abner, portrays a surpassingly generous Arab named Taḥkam who gave in abundance to anyone who approached him with a request for help. One day, a group of Muslims who knew of Taḥkam's reputation came to seek relief from the famine that had engulfed their faraway land. They found him in a field, standing over his harvest. When they asked the way to the famous benefactor's house, Taḥkam posed as one of his own servants and went to search his treasure house and his flocks for something to give them. Ashamed that he had to emerge empty-handed, he told his petitioners that his master could not find anything to satisfy their hunger, so he was giving them Taḥkam to sell or to use as they saw fit. Falling for this noble ruse, they took Taḥkam with them and went on their way. After a grueling month-long march, they reached their land. They sent Taḥkam to

---

99 See, e.g., Alexander and Harari, "Jewish Folklore—Ethnic Identity, Collection and Research"; Yassif, *The Hebrew Folktale: History, Genre, Meaning*, 265–282 ("Tales from International Folklore") and 283–297 ("The Exemplum"); and Simon, "The Muslim in the Folk Literature of the Jews of Libya."

100 See, *inter alia*, Stillman, "Judaism and Islam: Fourteen Hundred Years of Intertwined Destiny?"

guard their parched and distant vineyards during the hot summer. When the harvest season arrived, the vineyards yielded abundant fruit under his watchful eye. Taḥkam made sure to satisfy all who asked for food. He sat in his guard's booth singing bittersweet songs, which led the passersby to recognize his true identity. Out of remorse for the way they had exploited such a charitable individual, the people of the city sent for the Muslims of all the provinces "to see this tremendous wonder." They came by the thousands, every prince and his clients, family by family. Their judges scrutinized their legal codes but could find no indication of a fitting reward for one who was so selfless as to offer himself to his supplicants. So each man brought a donation until they had gathered great quantities of gold and silver. They gave Taḥkam everything they collected but, even so, repaid only the smallest portion of their debt. With great fanfare, they carried him back to his homeland on their shoulders, accompanying him with song and dance. He rewarded all who helped him, and everyone who saw him sang his praises.

A few remarks about the tale itself are in order before commenting on the larger context in which it occurs. The ideal of generosity, held in high esteem already in pre-Islamic times, was a favorite subject of Arabic *adab* literature, folktales, and proverbs. Copious anecdotes were devoted to individuals so renowned for their munificence that they were seen as the very embodiment of this virtue.[101] The traits of generosity and hospitality were particularly associated with the Bedouin (*badawī, aʿrābī*), the figure of whom was preserved in medieval Arabic *adab* literature as the instantiation of authentic pre-Islamic virtues and traditions. But as Joseph Sadan has shown, Arabic belles-lettres also ridicule the Bedouin, to whom the refinements of civilized life are alien, such that the Bedouin came to represent the naïve, albeit faithful and unselfish, rustic antithesis of urbane city-dwellers.[102] Alḍāhirī's account of the unstinting, openhanded Arab clearly makes use of these tropes. The distinction he draws between Taḥkam, whom he calls *ʿaravi,* and his petitioners, who are *anashim mi-mishmaʿ ve-dumah u-massa* (i.e, sons of Ishmael; cf. Genesis 25:14), suggests that Alḍāhirī envisions Taḥkam as a Bedouin or tribesman who embodies

101 See Marzolph and van Leeuwen eds., *The Arabian Nights Encyclopedia*, s.v. "Generosity," and "Ḥātim of the Tribe of Tayy." On Ḥātim see also van Arendonk, "Ḥātim al-Ṭāʾī" and Chauvin, *Bibliographie des ouvrages Arabes*, 6:49.

102 Sadan notes that in classical Arabic literature, the Bedouin is a stand-in for the "fool" or the "farmer" in other cultures but is both admired and despised, clever and foolish; see "An Admirable and Ridiculous Hero." See also Marzolph and van Leeuwen eds., *The Arabian Nights Encyclopedia* s.v. "Bedouin"; *al-Hamadhānī, Maqāmāt*, 138–141 (#27, "The Maqāma of al-Aswad"); *The Maqāmāt of Badiʿ al-Zamān al-Hamādhāni*, 110–113; and al-Ibshīhī, *Al-Mostaṭraf*, 2: 640–648 ch. 76, sec. 1: Des Traits Plaisants des Arabes.

pre-Islamic mores and the genuine traditions of the ancient Arabs.[103] By contrast, a negative valence is associated with the names of the sons of Ishmael. Playing on the meanings of their triliteral roots, a traditional Yemenite Jewish homily read the names *Mishma, Dumah, and Massa* as an admonition to "listen, be silent, and endure" in the face of Muslim persecution.[104] While there are instances when Taḥkam is judged to be excessively generous—so that he becomes a caricature rather than an exemplary figure[105]—the derivation of his name from the Arabic root denoting wisdom (it is an anagram of Ḥikmat) links him to universal wisdom motifs and signals authorial approval of his deeds, as does his description as *tov la-shamayim ve-la-beriyyot* ("he was good to Heaven and good to man"), a phrase derived from a Talmudic definition of a righteous man.[106] Arguably, the contrast between Taḥkam's selflessness and the exploitative behavior of the Muslims who indenture him may be read as a veiled critique of Muslim mores. The fact that the Muslims' law codes offer no precedent for rewarding him implies that his largesse is of a degree somehow unknown to Islam.[107]

1.3.3 Narrative Structure: The Larger Context

The tale of Taḥkam is framed by an opening story told by Mordecai. As elsewhere, the *maqāma* technique of embedding one story within another allows Alḍāhirī to produce a layered narrative structure that adds nuance to the enclosed tale. Here the frame story confronts blameless Jews with ignoble Muslims who, by implication, also stand in sharp moral contrast to the unimpeach-

---

103 Robert Irwin writes that a "belated cult of the Bedouin, his chivalry, courage and generosity, was formed by back-projection" as part of the "narrative about the Arabness of the pre-Islamic and early inhabitants of Arabia and Syria [that] was forged" by urban scholars during the centuries following the advent of Islam; see his review of Peter Webb, *Imagining the Arabs*.

104 See Ḥabshush, *Massa'ot Ḥabshush*, p. 3, n. 8 and Verskin, *A Vision of Yemen*, p. 83.

105 See lines 29–30 (*noten be-shefa' limvaqshav … 'ad hiflig be-ma'asehu; zar ma'asehu*; "he gave abundantly to those who asked … to the point where he outdid himself; his deed was strange") and line 100 (*be-shuram ish kefi sikhlo yehullal/kemo gever asher yayin 'avro*; "when they saw a man commended for his intelligence/become like one overcome by wine").

106 bQid 40a.

107 The motif of selling oneself into slavery for a charitable purpose occurs in Nissim Ibn Shāhīn's Judeo-Arabic collection of tales, *Kitāb al-faraj ba'da al-shidda*. See *An Elegant Composition Concerning Relief after Adversity*, 48–52 and 99–102; *The Arabic Original of Ibn Shāhīn's Book of Comfort*, 44–48 and 100–104; and Obermann, "Two Elijah Stories in Judeo-Arabic Transmission." Brinner notes that although Ibn Shāhīn's choice of genre was inspired by the Arabic *faraj* literature, he relied primarily, though not exclusively, on Jewish sources for his tales; see *An Elegant Composition*, p. xxxi.

able Taḥkam. Mordecai relates that when he tired of dwelling among inhospitable gentiles, he hastened to travel to the Land of Israel (*meqom simḥat libbi*; "the place of my joy") to attain relief from sorrow and trouble and to establish a dwelling there.[108] He undertook a strenuous journey until he came to the city of "Galfer" which, as noted, is likely Karaferye in northern Greece, where he found an unblemished Jewish community:

> *… shammah ra'iti ayyal u-ṣevi va'ofer/ mi-qehal 'adat yisrael/ asher lo yigre'u siḥah lifnei el*[109]*/ yeladim asher ein bahem kol mum ve-tovei mar'eh*[110]*/ va'ehi le-ḥevratam mishta'eh/ va-yesimuni 'aleihem le-rosh ule-qaṣin*[111]*/ 'ad 'avor 'iddanin ve-qiṣṣin.*[112]

> There I saw ram, stag, and gazelle from the community of Israel. Their piety was such that they did not withhold their prayers; they had the innocence of children, unblemished and fair. I marveled at their companionship, and they appointed me their commander and chief until many seasons had slipped by.

While he was there, the local Jews heard that Muslims (*ha-yishma'elim*) from every outlying region had gathered on the border, so a group of men went with Mordecai to see the Muslims "fall into a trap." The Muslim women and men, "debauched and depraved" (*nashim va'anashim ve-ḥayyatam baqdeshim*; cf. Job 36:14), were indiscriminately scattered across a field enveloped in a great commotion. At the center of the chaos was a fortuneteller responding to the crowd's barrage of requests for divination. To some he replied in scorn, so that they covered their faces in shame. To others he foretold the entire arc of their lives, from birth to death. Mordecai scrutinized his aged face and recognized him as Abner ben Ḥeleq the Yemenite. He said to his companions,

> This is Abner, the wise and the cunning. Without him, no one lifts up hand or foot in the art of poetry and its melodies, or in words aptly spoken.[113] He has made himself a name in all the sciences, exoteric and esoteric. And

108 Mordecai never reaches his final destination, the Land of Israel, in this episode.

109 Job 15:4.

110 Dan. 1:4.

111 Jud. 11:11.

112 *Sefer hamusar*, p. 393, lines 4–7.

113 "Without him, no one lifts up hand or foot": cf. Gen. 41:44. In its original context, this phrase is uttered by Pharaoh regarding Joseph, whom he has put "in charge of all the land of Egypt."

> what he does to the Muslims, as a brave soldier who performs great deeds, is to take from them whatever they have at hand (Genesis 32:14), because the time of their disaster [viz., their religious holiday] is drawing near and because they hurry to do evil and to spill blood [i.e., to slaughter sacrificial animals].[114]

> Let us go and appear before him with a friendly demeanor .... Do not contradict what he says; simply inquire after his welfare.

Mordecai's comrades defer to him, and they visit Abner after nightfall. Mordecai asks after Abner's health and notes that he seems imbued with a different spirit than previously. Abner takes them to his dwelling—a cave in the cleft in the rocks—and sets out whatever he has: a table and lights, and many strange servings of food. After they have eaten, Mordecai asks Abner to explain the appearance of the motley crowd (doubtless drawn by Abner's own arrival), and one of the other guests asks for an explanation of Proverbs 18:16, "A man's gift eases his way/ And gives him access to the great." Abner replies, "If you are willing to listen, I will tell you something that answers both queries: Each man in this crowd, who causes shame and disgrace, seeks someone who will tell them of the fiercely generous Arab." He proceeds to tell the story of Taḥkam.

The juxtaposition of this peculiar frame with the story of the saintly Taḥkam yields not only moral contrasts but also subtle and surprising correspondences between the roguish Abner and the noble Bedouin. While the tale of Taḥkam is presumably of non-Jewish provenance, Alḍāhirī's Hebrew reworking is colored by imagery and language evocative of the biblical Joseph saga. Conceivably, the story could have been part of an oral repertoire in Yemenite Judeo-Arabic that made its way into a corpus of tales about Bedouin. Or, it may have been an Arabic folktale that already refracted elements of the Qur'ānic version of the Joseph story (Sūra 12, Yūsuf) that Alḍāhirī Judaized in his Hebrew retelling by substituting biblically resonant language.[115] The mutually fructifying relationship between oral and written *adab* is explored by Joseph Sadan in "An Admirable and Ridiculous Hero: Some Notes on the Bedouin in Medieval Arabic Belles-Lettres." Focusing on a chapter in an 11th-century *adab* anthology, *Muḥāḍarāt al'udabā'* by al-Rāghib al-Iṣfahāni, Sadan explains how the written anthology grew out of gatherings of intellectuals and literati who all con-

114 See *Sefer hamusar*, pp. 393, l. 13–pp. 394, l. 17.

115 For echoes of the Qur'ānic Joseph story in the literature of the *tafsīr*, *sīrah*, and *ḥadīth*, as well as in various genres of the subsequent Arabic narrative tradition, see Kennedy, *Recognition in the Arabic Narrative Tradition*, 16–186.

tributed to the creation of an oral corpus of materials, such that the written anthology drew on oral *adab* but in turn also furnished the *ʾudabāʾ* with anecdotes for their oral *adab* conversations. He notes that this effort yielded "a special kind of correlation between oral and written forms" that did not involve the usual oppositions between popular and literary, canonical and noncanonical, since both oral and written materials were in this case produced by intellectuals. But he does concede that "the anecdotal parts in their books often reflect relatively more popular material."[116] Yosef Tobi emphasizes that the Hebrew folk tales told in *Sefer hamusar* are exceptional, insofar as they are drawn from the fund of international folktales but are written in the elevated, ornate Hebrew of the *maqāma*. He notes that Yemenite Jews distinguished between written stories (*maʿaseh, pl. maʿasayot* [in Yemenite pronunciation]) and oral (*ḥizwiya*, pl. *ḥazāwī*), where the written tales were almost always Hebrew or Aramaic exempla—wondrous stories about the sages of Israel—drawn from Jewish sources. By contrast, the oral tales were conveyed in dialect and not committed to writing. They were not associated with the canonical literature, nor did they occupy an honored place in the repertoire of Yemenite Jewish preachers. The folk tales in *Sefer hamusar* are therefore unusual for several reasons: they can be construed as exempla, but the model figures in the tales are not Jews, and certainly not Jewish sages, and they diverge from the pattern of orally transmitted tales that were not generally transposed from dialect into Hebrew and were not committed to writing.[117]

Also noteworthy is the use of the Taḥkam narrative to illustrate a verse from the biblical book of Proverbs. This is yet another instance of cross-pollination in a work composed in a land where Jews had for centuries been deeply embedded in the local culture and which mines a rich vein of Jewish and Muslim folklore. The prefacing of a scriptural verse to a folktale was not unknown in medieval Hebrew literature. Eli Yassif points to the phenomenon in *Midrash ʿaseret ha-dibberot*, a collection of Hebrew tales of Eastern provenance from the 8th/9th centuries, although he notes that the connection between the opening biblical citation and the tales that follow "is often tenuous and forced."[118] There are also strings of proverbs, aphorisms, and short anecdotes drawn from Ara-

116 Sadan, "An Admirable and Ridiculous Hero," 471–472.

117 See Tobi, "Ha-ḥeqer ha-hashvaʾati." For collections of Yemenite Jewish folktales and legends transcribed from oral informants in the 20th century, see, e.g., Gamlieli, *Ḥadrei teiman* and Goitein, *From the Land of Sheba*. On Muslim stories that entered the Jewish repertoire and vice versa in the modern period, see Noy, "The Folk Tale." For additional bibliography, see Klorman, "The Jews of Yemen" (Oxford Bibliographies).

118 Yassif, "The Hebrew Narrative Anthology in the Middle Ages."

bic *adab* literature in Joseph Ibn Zabara's *Sefer sha'ashu'im* and Judah Alḥarizi's *Taḥkemoni*. But no attempt is made in these earlier rhymed prose narratives to relate the *adab* materials to specific biblical verses or sayings.[119] Perhaps a closer parallel to Alḍāhirī's narrative device might be found in Nissim Ibn Shāhīn's Judeo-Arabic *Kitāb al-faraj ba'da al-shidda* (Relief after Adversity), where a moral lesson conveyed by a story about Elijah the prophet is borne out by a popular proverb, which in turn is substantiated by a statement from the apocryphal or extrabiblical book of Ben Sira (also known as "Sirach" or "Ecclesiasticus").[120] While the prefacing of biblical citations to particular tales in *Sefer hamusar* can also feel a bit arbitrary, it is instructive to read the story of Taḥkam in light of exegetical comments on Proverbs 18:16, "A man's gift eases his way/ And gives him access to the great." Medieval biblical exegetes glossed "a man's gift" mainly in monetary or material terms. Reflecting a certain precariousness of medieval Jewish existence, Saadya Gaon took the phrase to refer to a voluntary payment or gift to kings and courtiers as a means of ensuring honorable treatment in this world. But he also understood it to refer to charitable donations that win the approval of the righteous and secure one's place in the world to come. Abraham Ibn Ezra rather cynically remarks that the "gift" refers to the bribery required to extract oneself from a tight situation while "the great" are those who are urged to accept monetary inducement so that the donor does not fail in legal matters.[121] Although Abner never explicitly spells out how he understands the verse, it would appear that he is reading "a man's gift" in its altruistic rather than politically expedient vein. In his opening gloss on *Ve-zot ha-berakhah* (Deuteronomy 33) in *Ṣeidah la-derekh*, Alḍāhirī adduces Proverbs 18:16, saying that, by means of this maxim, King Solomon taught us the power of generosity, "on account of which a person is elevated from one height to the

119 See Joseph Ibn Zabara, *Sefer sha'ashu'im*, ed. Davidson, 65–80 and *The Book of Delight*, 101–110 ("Parables and Saws"). Yehuda Ratzaby has noted that the sayings in Chapters 44 and 45 of the *Taḥkemoni* are cited anonymously, randomly grouped, and provided with an artificial narrative framework; see his "On the sources of *sefer taḥkemoni*" and idem, "Adab Maxims in Medieval Literature."

120 See Obermann, "Two Elijah Stories in Judeo-Arabic Transmission," 390–394.

121 For Saadya's comments see *Mishlei 'im tirgum u-feirush ha-ga'on rabbeinu se'adyah ben yosef fayyūmī*, p. 135. For Ibn Ezra's, see the standard rabbinic Bible. Rashi's comments are quite similar to Saadya's. Although not part of the geonic-Andalusian exegetical tradition, Rashi may well have been known to Alḍāhirī through printed Hebrew books from Italy and elsewhere. Certainly, in the mid-17th century, Rabbi Isaac Wanneh relied heavily on Rashi in his commentary on Andalusian liturgical poems in the Yemenite prayer book; see Giat, "The Linguistic Stratum in Rabbi Isaac Wanneh's Commentary on the *Seliḥot*." For the association of Proverbs 18:16 with charity, see also Ex. Rab. 31:2; Lev. Rab. 5;4; Num. Rab. 13:17; Deut. Rab. 4:8.

next, and increases his honor to the point where he is destined to serve those greater than he." By way of illustration, he points to Abraham's hospitality to the angels and comparable examples from the narratives of Isaac, Jacob, Joseph and Moses in which self-sacrifice and forbearance ultimately garner recognition and reward. Abner cites the verse again at the end of the story of Taḥkam, suggesting that through his extraordinary acts of charity and self-abnegation Taḥkam ultimately earns the admiration and material recompense that "ease his way."

The figure of Taḥkam functions as a foil against which Alḍāhirī can develop an unflattering picture of Muslims which, in turn, is crucial to the Jewish self-definition implicit in, and fostered by the text. Although the frame story is laconic in the extreme regarding the Muslim "others" it evokes, there is a suggestion of sexual libertinism: the Muslims who have assembled to have their fortunes told are "debauched and depraved," with no separation between the sexes. In addition, they are gullible, allowing themselves to be taken in by Abner's imposture; their religious festivals are denigrated as "the time of their disaster" (Deuteronomy 32:35), and their animal sacrifices are maligned ("they hurry to do evil and to spill blood"; cf. Proverbs 1:16). By contrast, the Jews of "Galfer" (Karaferye) are celebrated as "handsome youths without blemish" (cf. Daniel 1:4) who do not withhold their prayers to God (cf. Job 15:4). The original contexts of the biblical allusions deployed in representing these two confessional groups reinforce the identification of the Muslims as sinful enemies doomed to destruction, and the Jews as noble, wise, and pious. By means of these intertexts, Alḍāhirī conveys to the Jewish reader the idea of a moral and religious chasm between "self" and "other" in an effort to shape a sense of communal self-definition. Despite—or perhaps because of—his deception of the Muslim fortune seekers, Abner is described as a *segullah*, a highly charged ethnocentric term used in Scripture to refer to Israel as God's treasured possession, although it likely also alludes to Abner's recourse to amulets and incantations in the course of his divination.[122] Abner's knavery is cast in a positive light precisely because his victims are Muslims who are about to sacrifice in honor of their festival. (And anticipation of their entrapment motivates Mordecai's very desire to observe them.) Here, too, we see an inversion of the expected power relations between the two groups, with Abner depicted as "a brave soldier who performs great deeds, in taking from them whatever they have at hand (Genesis 32:14)." Yet there is more than a little moral uncertainty in the delineation

122 In medieval texts, *segullah* takes on the additional meaning of an (occult) remedy or an apotropaic quality. See Tobi, "Ha-ḥeqer ha-hashva'ati," p. 425 regarding the writing of amulets and whispering of spells in Yemenite Jewish folk medicine.

of Abner's fictional persona ("the wise and the cunning"). This is, of course, entirely in keeping with the literary conventions of the *maqāma*, and Abner is generally happy to fleece gulls of any religious persuasion.[123] From a structural point of view, it is interesting that his shortcomings are highlighted by parallels between the frame story and its embedded tale. As Philip Kennedy has noted regarding the *Arabian Nights*, "a story will often mirror, whether inversely or otherwise, the cognitive structure and thematic development of the story that contains it."[124] Both Abner and Taḥkam dissemble, but for diametrically opposed reasons. When Muslims come to Abner, he poses as a fortune teller and swindles them; when Muslims come to Taḥkam, he poses as a servant and indentures himself to them for their benefit. Like Abner in the frame story, the Muslims who enslave Taḥkam are morally suspect whereas the Bedouin Taḥkam is entirely honorable.

Taḥkam fits the profile of what Philip Kennedy calls an 'avatar of Joseph.'[125] He is separated from his family and taken as a slave by a group of wandering Muslims and deported to their distant lands; in his guise as a servant, he wisely tends their crops during a time of famine. Like Joseph's, Taḥkam's dedication and watchfulness produce abundant fruit where there had been none, such that he is able to satisfy the hunger of his petitioners. With patience and forbearance, he overcomes all obstacles and rises to prominence, his servile state is reversed, and his virtue is rewarded.[126] Echoes of the Joseph narrative are especially pronounced in the language and imagery of the poem that reprises his tale at the end of the *maqāma*. Taḥkam tells his supplicants:

> My master has given me to you/even though I am his favorite and the most senior in his household.[127]
> Go, sell me to provide for your hunger (*le-shever ra'avonkhem*)[128] …
> …
> So they took him and placed him in custody (*netanuhu be-mishmar*)/ until they came to their land ….[129]

123 Cf. # 11, #32, and *Taḥkemoni* #22.
124 Cf. Kennedy, "Islamic Recognitions: An Overview," 33.
125 See Kennedy, *Recognition in the Arabic Narrative Tradition*, 146–186.
126 See Gen. 37–50; for biblical and post-biblical interpretations, see Kugel, *In Potiphar's House*, 13–155.
127 Cf. Gen. 39:4–6.
128 Cf. Gen. 42:19.
129 *Sefer hamusar*, p. 397, ll. 87–91. Cf., e.g., Gen. 40:3. While many salient details of the biblical narrative are reflected in the tale of Taḥkam, the element of sexual temptation does not enter into it.

It is striking that some of the language and tropes of the Joseph narrative spill over onto Abner, linking the two characters with further points of correspondence.[130] Abner, who has been profoundly affected by his own experience of captivity, is also a wanderer. When importuned, he tells fortunes and interprets dreams, although we are led to suspect that however convincing he is to his petitioners, his prognostication is pure charlatanism. In general, Abner's wisdom is of the wily variety while Taḥkam's is much closer to a sagely virtue. And, like the dénouement of the Joseph story, both the frame and the embedded tale in the 36th *maqāma* entail a recognition scene or anagnorisis. However, where Joseph at a certain point is no longer able to conceal his true identity from his brothers, neither Abner nor Taḥkam divulges his identity of his own accord. Rather, both are given away by their artistry and improvisational skills. It is these gifts that, implausibly, lead to their paths converging. At the end of the *maqāma*, the narrative takes a curiously riveting turn when Abner instigates a visit to Taḥkam prompted by his supreme confidence in his own poetic and linguistic prowess.

1.3.4 Translations: From Hebrew to Arabic; from Frame to Embedded Tale

Following his story of Taḥkam's exemplary generosity, Abner recites a long monorhymed poem that faithfully retells the prose narrative and casts Taḥkam in an exceedingly positive light.[131] The wording of the final hemistich is identical to that of the opening one, and this stylistic nicety serves as a closure device that also reinforces the semantic sense of the final phrase, which conveys that, after his long enslavement in a distant land, "the generous Arab returned to his sanctuary." Predictably, Mordecai and the rest of the audience are duly impressed with Abner's eloquence and supreme craftsmanship. Then, without any warning, Abner declares,

> I must fulfill your (pl.) desire before you return to your land. Let us go to this benefactor! You will see him with your own eyes and discern the munificent from the miserly. In his presence I will render my poem of praise for him into Arabic (*ve'aʿtiq shiro lefanav be-lashon ʿaravi*). Then you will see how great is my ability.[132]

---

130 See the echo of Gen. 41:44 in line 14. In line 124, Mordecai says of Abner, *va-yimalle amtaḥti maḥamadim* ("he filled my sack with desirable things"). The term *amtaḥat* occurs only in the Joseph cycle, Gen. 42–44.

131 It is conceivable that the poem was written first; cf. Pagis, *Change and Tradition in the Secular Poetry*, 204–212.

132 *Sefer hamusar*, p. 398, ll. 111–114. "The munificent from the miserly"; lit. "the sleek from the lean."

No sooner is the plan hatched than it is realized, Abner having "girded his loins, and put his thoughts in order." Instantaneously, they stand before Taḥkam (*va-naʿamod lifnei Taḥkam/ veʾavner nitḥakam*), and Abner extemporaneously converts his praise "from the Hebrew tongue into the language of Hagar (*va-yahafokh qilluso milshon ʿivri el leshon hagri*)." His brilliant feat of translation yields immediate fruit—Taḥkam bestows extravagant gifts on his visitors and an especially lavish reward on Abner (described with wording drawn from the provisions Joseph gives Benjamin after revealing himself to his brothers).[133] Although we might expect Taḥkam to accompany his magnanimity with a verbal response, no conversation between the Arab maecenas and his Jewish beneficiaries is recorded. The party joyfully departs, and nothing further is heard of Taḥkam.

The report of this tantalizing encounter unfolds over a mere seven lines of text and is frustratingly laconic. Does the noble Arab regard Abner's Jewish identity with equanimity, does he choose to overlook it, or is he unaware of it? Does he know that the Arabic poem—which may or may not exist—has ostensibly been translated from Hebrew? Why does Alḍāhirī imply that Taḥkam would not understand the panegyric in its original when his non-Jewish characters regularly speak Hebrew? What does Abner's bilingualism say about the author's attitudes toward language as a vehicle of cross-cultural contact and as a means of communal self-definition? As presented here, Arabic is not particularly freighted with religious associations despite the fact that the claims made for the language by Muslims traditionally had a theological as well as an aesthetic dimension.[134] And where Judah Alḥarizi had personified the Arabic language as both a cruel oppressor and a dangerous seductress, Alḍāhirī—writing three centuries later in a wholly Islamic environment—voices no qualms about Jewish proficiency in Arabic, even though in his Introduction he pays lip service to Alḥarizi's concern about the abandonment of Hebrew. Alḍāhirī's references to Arabic have none of the adversarial edge of 13th-century Jewish authors active in Christian lands. Rather, his hero's mastery of literary Arabic, a given for someone of his linguistic abilities, is both admirable and useful.[135] Given that

133 "Five hundred pieces of silver and five changes of clothing"; cf. Gen 45:22. The same phrase is used in #42, l. 51 to describe the royal reward Abner receives in a tale about his provision of the hawthorns that restore a beautiful but languishing queen to her former health.

134 On the inimitability of Qurʾānic Arabic or *iʿjāz al-qurʾān*, see Chapter One.

135 On the medieval Jewish preoccupation with the status of Hebrew vis-à-vis Arabic, see Sadan, "Identity and Inimitability—Contexts of Inter-Religious Polemics" and Alfonso, *Islamic Culture Through Jewish Eyes*, 9–33.

the poetry produced by the true Bedouin Arabs of pre-Islamic times became the authoritative yardstick for correct Arabic usage, Abner's move is particularly bold.[136]

Abner's impulsive decision to visit a fictional character from a tale he has just told is delightful, particularly since he himself is an imaginary creation. The crossover from frame story to embedded tale is highly contrived and reminds the reader that the entire *maqāma* is a literary fabrication. It also embodies a kind of structural fluidity that corresponds to Abner's seamless switch from Hebrew to Arabic, and it points to the sense of translation (*translatio*) as transference or 'carrying across,' a movement from one place or condition to another. In the Latin tradition, saints who are transferred directly to heaven without dying are said to be translated. Abner uses the Hebrew root *ʿa.t.q.*, whose biblical sense is 'to move, proceed, or advance.' The *hiphʿil*, "to cause to move," also comes to mean 'to transcribe' and, in medieval usage, 'to copy' or 'to translate' (to put into the words of another language; the German *übersetzen* likewise suggests moving from one place to another). So Abner not only translates his poem from one language to another and across cultures but is himself translated as he effortlessly traverses narrative boundaries and enters the folktale that he has just told.[137] The setting of these proceedings in "Galfer" may not be entirely coincidental since Karaferye represents a liminal space: a formerly Byzantine Christian realm, it is now Ottoman, though outside of the traditional Islamic heartlands. To the Yemenite protagonists, this territory in "Roma" or *balad al-rūm* is an outlying region of the Jewish world, and the "crossing of borders" to get there mirrors the traversing of linguistic and narrative boundaries within the tale. Moreover, the story's unexpected ending furnishes several new twists to the stock motif of the cunning scoundrel who employs dazzling verbal skills for personal gain. Here, the sleight of hand that elicits a material reward involves transposing a Hebrew poem of praise into Arabic. Since this induces Taḥkam to part with his money, it suggests that even this generous, noble Arab is somehow Abner's dupe.[138] Abner has the upper hand because he is equally at home in the two languages and literary traditions while Taḥkam is not. For Abner's translation to be as effective as it is and to redound to his credit, his Arabic must be exceedingly eloquent since the pure Arabic of the Bedouin was considered the benchmark for correct Arabic usage. (Since the Arabic text of

136 See Heinrichs, "Prosimetrical Genres in Classical Arabic," 250.

137 Cf. Hassan, "Translator's Introduction" in Kilito, *Thou Shalt Not Speak My Language*, ix–xi.

138 As noted, Sadan observes that *adab* literature mocks and admires the Bedouin at one and the same time, reflecting a degree of ambivalence; see "An Admirable and Ridiculous Hero."

his poem is not included, much is left to the reader's imagination.) Yet his mastery of the language is portrayed primarily as an expedient tool; as a means to reaping material benefit or, as Mordecai fawningly puts it, for capturing hearts and seducing noblemen. Ultimately, it is Abner's feat of translation that truly illustrates Proverbs 18:16: "A man's gift eases his way/And gives him access to the great." His gift is his way with words in Hebrew and Arabic, his familiarity with both poetic traditions, and his facility with cross-cultural frames of reference. It is Abner's eloquence and cunning that "ease his way" and give him access to Taḥkam and his rewards.[139]

2 Conclusion: Historical and Imaginary Muslims

As he represents them, Alḍāhirī's historical and imaginary Muslims could not be more different. While the ruling Zaydīs and their *imām* are nondescript—apart from their cruelty—his panoply of imaginary Muslims and Arabs spans the gamut of character types, and they are types, albeit flamboyant, endearing, or malevolent. While his anguished complaints of Zaydī oppression are voiced by invented characters, these are some of his only depictions of Muslim-Jewish relations that resist fictionalizing. To be sure, his laments rely on familiar biblical tropes and standard, nonspecific topoi to conjure up Muslim persecution, such that the Yemeni Zaydīs are depicted through the lens of scriptural paradigms and prototypes.[140] But alongside these dehistoricizing, generic references, Alḍāhirī invokes local realia, precise dates, and Imām al-Muṭahhar's unmistakable epithet, *ḥigger* ("the lame one"), in order to record for posterity his community's tribulations. By contrast, his fictional Muslims far outstrip the monochromatic Zaydīs in their vividness and variety despite their lack of nuance. As the products of his literary imagination, the gullible merchants, conmen, inept thieves, well-meaning *qāḍīs*, righteous Arabs, and even the humorless polemicist are all more immediately engaging even if the contours of their largely stereotypical characters are drawn from folk traditions or the *maqāma* literature.

When Alḍāhirī refers to the historical Zaydīs who crushed his people, he is as unequivocal in his loathing as he is in casting his fellow Jews as helpless

139 Proverbs 18:16 is also used in connection with the kingly reward bestowed on Abner in #42, line 88.

140 See, e.g., *Sefer hamusar* #2, p. 68, l. 83 and #12, p. 167, l. 51 ("Like doves of the valley, they are sold for no price to Kedar and Nebaiot"; "Hide but a little moment from the madman's offspring, for his … defeat shall be severe").

victims. But when he conjures up his fictional Muslims, he allows himself to reimagine the power dynamics between the dominant religion and society and the Jewish minority in its midst. In the case of the Zaydīs, he falls back on the familiar quietistic trope of communal suffering as divine punishment for sin. But in the case of his imaginary Muslims, he devises fictional encounters in which Jews, however vulnerable, do not resign themselves to their condition of political powerlessness or social marginalization. Despite the dangers inherent in openly polemicizing against Islam or even anecdotally tricking a Muslim religious judge, Alḍāhirī engineers the outcome of these confrontations so that his Jewish characters triumph. Deftly manipulating narrative structure and rhetorical technique, he invents Jewish victories that offer his readers a means of transcending their demoralizing reality. The vehemence of his responses to the unfathomable callousness of the Zaydīs and to Muslim polemical arguments against Judaism points to a scenario in which the boundaries between Jews and Muslims are clearly delineated. But those lines of difference can still be fruitfully crossed when it comes to appropriating outstanding Arabic literary models and naturalizing them in the Sacred Tongue. On occasion, Alḍāhirī even claims to outdo the Muslims at their own literary tradition, surpassing them with his eloquent, keenly formal poetry and edifying fables. As we saw in Chapter Two, Mordecai's profound disappointment with a group of Muslims reciting Arabic poetry and animal fables in a caravan he joins (#42) leads to a withering critique of their lack of intellectual rigor and originality. To his mind, their boorishness disqualifies them from any claim to excel at their own literary heritage while his mastery of Arabic and linguistic refinement entitle him to make precisely such claims despite his *dhimmī* status.[141] In an odd way, his outburst, "How can a man mix with beasts, for they are Muslims; there is no favor in their words; only destruction," concretizes Abdelfattah Kilito's assertion that "When two languages live side by side, one or the other will always appear bestial."[142] Alḍāhirī's conflicted attitudes toward Muslims, Islam, and Arabic reflect the extent to which he valorized the Islamicate cultural heritage of the majority and internalized its aesthetic ideals while remaining acutely aware of what separated Yemeni Muslims and Jews.

141 *Sefer hamusar*, p. 439, lines 1–14, esp. lines 5–6.
142 Kilito, *The Author and His Doubles*, 108.

CHAPTER 5

Didacticism or Literary Legerdemain? Philosophy, Ethics, and the Picaresque

When he chose a title for his picaresque *maqāma*, Alḍāhirī did not reach for something distinctive or overtly provocative. Early *maqāma* collections in Arabic and Hebrew did not necessarily have a single dedicated title; those that did often bore names that offered only the most general sense of what lay in store for the reader: *Maqāmāt al-Ḥarīrī*; the ten *Maqāmāt* of Ibn Nāqiyā; *Ne'um Asher ben Yehudah*; *Sefer Sha'ashu'im* (the latter at least provided a glimmer of what was to come). In opting for the generic *Sefer hamusar*, Alḍāhirī echoed Alḥarizi's description of his own *maqāma* as *maḥberot musar ḥamishim* ("fifty *maqāmāt* of moral instruction").[1] At the same time, he deliberately invoked associations with a long line of medieval Hebrew prose works belonging to the genre of *sifrut ha-musar* or ethical literature, many of which bore the nondescript titles *Sefer hamusar, Iggeret musar* (Epistle of Moral Instruction), *Tokheḥot musar* (Ethical Exhortations), *or Sheveṭ musar* (Rod of Chastisement).[2] These texts, by respected Iberian and Provençal Jewish scholars of the 12th–15th centuries and their North African and Eastern Mediterranean heirs, were variously homiletical, contemplative, philosophically informed ethical treatises, or collections of wisdom literature that offered moral instruction and models for exemplary conduct. The unsuspecting reader might therefore have assumed that Alḍāhirī's work was entirely devoted to moral guidance without any inkling that it was interlaced with highly irreverent and diverting episodes. Devin Stewart observes that, although medieval authors "were certainly aware that the genre was inherently ironic, it was difficult, if not impossible, for later readers to draw a neat line between its ironic and earnest elements."[3]

1 See Alḥarizi, *Taḥkemoni*, ed. Yahalom-Katsumata, p. 63, l. 7.

2 As noted, these include Abraham Bar Ḥiyya's *Sefer hegyon ha-nefesh o sefer ha-musar*; Joseph Ibn Caspi's *Sefer ha-musar ha-niqra yoreh de'ah*; Joseph Ibn Aqnīn's *Sepher musar*; Shem Tov Falaquera's *Iggeret ha-musar*; Samuel Benveniste's *Sefer ha-musar*; Solomon Alami's *Iggeret musar*; Ephraim ben Joab ben Moses of Modena's *Sefer ha-musar*; and Judah Khalaṣ' *Sefer ha-musar*. The extremely popular homiletic work *Sheveṭ musar* (Constantinople, 1712) of Elijah b. Solomon ha-Kohen of Izmir (d. 1729) postdates Alḍāhirī.

3 See Stewart, "The Maqāma," 154–157. See also Keegan, "Commentarial Acts and Hermeneutical Dramas: The Ethics of Reading al-Ḥarīrī's *Maqāmāt*."

 | DOI:10.1163/9789004733787_007

As both a "Book of Moral Instruction" and a "Book of *Adab*," Alḍāhirī's *Sefer hamusar* aimed to educate while amusing, embedding didactic passages in entertaining tales of clever and deceitful behavior. Although seemingly uncontroversial, its multivalent title subtly encapsulated the unresolved tension between the author's stated goal of providing uplift and his structuring of the work around a hero given to immoderate, ethically indefensible behavior. Ostensibly solemn while imparting speculative wisdom or spiritual advice, Abner nevertheless remains a wandering bard, adventurer, and impostor who largely supports himself through guile and cunning, exploiting the generosity of trusting strangers who unfailingly succumb to his rhetorically brilliant trickery. While his identity is notoriously fluid, an overriding sense of Abner's cynical disregard for ethical niceties provides *Sefer hamusar* with a certain continuity that transcends its episodic structure. The sensitive reader is mindful of Abner's many masks, his mendacity fueled by greed, and his general lack of moral substance, so that even when he transmits philosophical or ethical material, our awareness of his unreliability leads us to question the integrity of his teachings. Despite Abner's gift of gab and convincing performances, his theoretical philosophy does not always stand up to rigorous scrutiny, just as the sincerity of his sermonizing is often suspect.

1 Philosophical and Medical Conceptions of the Soul: The "Internal Senses"

The proverbial travel in search of knowledge (*ṭalab al-ʿilm*) frames the sixth *maqāma*, where the narrator journeys from Syria, via the upper Galilee, to Safed.[4] Mordecai is duly impressed by the local *yeshivah* ethos, which fosters not only textual brilliance but also *derekh ereṣ*—proper morals and seemly behavior. Already in the 16th century, popular lore painted Safed as a place where "Torah scholars and simple Jews devoted their days and nights to Torah and good deeds and led pure and honest lives."[5] To remedy his pervasive sense of intellectual inadequacy when confronted with so many erudite sages and scholars, Mordecai visits synagogues and houses of study where preachers skilled in esoteric exegesis explicate their texts in different ways (*lishmoʿa*

4 On *ṭalab al-ʿilm*, see Rosenthal, *Knowledge Triumphant*, p. 89, n. 33; Gellens, "The Search for Knowledge in Medieval Muslim Societies"; as well as the previously cited Goldziher, *Muslim Studies*, 2:164–180 *passim*, and Kraemer, *Humanism in the Renaissance of Islam*, 24–25.

5 Yassif, *The Legend of Safed*, 232.

ha-darshanim ha-dorshim ʿal kammah ofanim ki hem yodʿim kol sod).[6] One Shabbat, he attends the *yeshivah* of "the great luminary, Rabbi Joseph Karo," whose halakhic mastery is legendary and whose commitment to kabbalah is widely known.[7] Mordecai seats himself at the entrance and is enraptured as the estimable Karo expounds on Psalm 19:8 ("The teaching of the Lord is perfect, restoring the soul") "according to the plain sense of the verse as well as its kabbalistic significance" (*ʿal derekh ha-peshaṭ ve-ha-qabbalah*) before an audience of some two hundred disciples. At the conclusion of his homily, and prompted by the word *nefesh* in his chosen verse, Karo signals to a student sitting across from him to discourse on the soul, its faculties, and its ultimate purpose (*ledabber ba-nefesh ve-khoḥotehah ve-takhlitah ve-odotehah*).[8] Rising, the student declares, "Our Rabbis have taught us … that the soul has ten faculties, five internal and five external" (*ki la-nefesh ʿasarah koḥot nafshiyyim; ḥamishah tokhiyyim va-ḥamishah penimiyyim*).[9] Though he attributes his information to the Rabbis, he proceeds to enumerate—in rhymed prose—the special properties of the internal and external senses (*segulat ha-ḥushim ha-ḥiṣoniyyim ve-ha-penimiyyim*) as conceived by the medieval medical and philosophical traditions.[10]

As Harry Wolfson has shown in his magisterial studies, the term "internal senses" applies in medieval Arabic, Hebrew, and Latin texts to those faculties

6 *Sefer hamusar*, p. 116, lines 8–11.

7 See Werblowsky, *Joseph Karo, Lawyer and Mystic*; Davis, "The Reception of the *Shulḥan ʿArukh* and the Formation of Ashkenazic Jewish Identity"; Raz-Krakotzkin, "Ḥaqiqah, meshiḥiyut ve-ṣenzura: hadpasat ha-shulḥan ʿarukh ke-reshit ha-moderniut"; Kelman, "Ketuvot beʾot barzel veʿoferet bidfus"; Weinstein, *Joseph Karo and Shaping* [*sic*] *of Modern Jewish Law*; and Hallamish, "Joseph Karo—Kabbalah and Halakhic Decisions."

8 Yaʿari was convinced that Alḍāhirī heard Karo expounding in a speculative vein but that this discussion of the soul's faculties would not have been heard in Karo's *yeshivah* and must have been inserted by the author; see *Masaʿot ereṣ yisraʿel*, 198. On the other hand, David writes that the vignette in *Sefer hamusar* "implies that in Caro's yeshivah halakhic studies were supplemented by philosophical and kabbalistic inquiries"; see *To Come to the Land*, 126–128.

9 Literally, "the soul has ten *psychic* faculties …." This is an odd formulation, presumably dictated by the exigencies of the rhyme (*nafshiyyim … tokhiyyim … penimiyyim*). Various medieval thinkers use the term "spiritual" for the internal senses, in contradistinction to the five "corporeal" or external senses that require physical organs, but not for all ten; see Wolfson: "The Internal Senses in Latin, Arabic, and Hebrew Philosophic Texts," 250–251; idem, "Isaac Israeli on the Internal Senses"; idem, "Notes on Isaac Israeli's Internal Senses," 331–343; and idem, "Maimonides on the Internal Senses."

10 *Sefer hamusar*, p. 117, line 20–p. 122, line 119. On Rabbinic theories of the soul, see Hirsch, *Rabbinic Psychology*, 150–280 *passim*; Urbach, *The Sages*, 214–254; and Rubin, "From Monism to Dualism: Relationship Between the Body and Soul in Talmudic Thought."

of the soul that reside within the brain and, as opposed to the five external senses, operate without bodily organs.[11] The distinction between these faculties and the five senses goes back to Aristotle, though he does not use the designation "internal senses."[12] Insofar as they process information supplied by the external senses for use by the intellect, the internal senses serve as a bridge between the corporeal and the spiritual in human beings. Alḍāhirī's *yeshivah* student lists three of the "post-sensationary" faculties that are standard in virtually every medieval classification scheme: imagination (*koaḥ ha-medammeh*), cogitation (*koaḥ ha-meḥashshev*), and memory (*koaḥ ha-zokher*), which reside respectively in the anterior, middle, and posterior ventricles of the brain.[13] Despite the constraints of rhymed prose, he describes their functions in a manner that would have been intelligible to anyone familiar with philosophical accounts of perception, apprehension, and abstraction, even though there is a certain eclecticism to his scheme. The imagination receives sensory data and supplies images to the intellect via the faculty of sight.[14] Cogitation comprises four branches that work in concert to receive, preserve, and assemble sensory impressions as well as to distinguish between matters of greater and lesser importance and to know the true from the false.[15] Memory preserves these judgments of the cogitative faculty.[16]

Ratzaby notes that there is a precedent for dividing the faculty of cogitation into these four branches in Saadya Gaon's discussion of the complete acquisition of knowledge in the introduction to his *tafsīr* on Proverbs.[17] Some of

11 Wolfson, "The Internal Senses in Latin, Arabic, and Hebrew," 251.

12 This group of faculties is discussed in *De Anima*, Book Three and *De Memoria et Reminiscentia*; see Wolfson, ibid., 250–254 and *passim*.

13 Wolfson, ibid., 252–254.

14 Literally, the imagination "grasps all the forms, even if they are in the hidden heavens, and establishes them for the intellect by means of the faculty of sight, and in this fashion man understands wondrous things." This implies that the imagination also processes data of an abstract nature, for which the faculty of sight is the conduit. Employing images that have been seen and stored in memory, the imagination produces visual images of the heavens and their workings by representing these abstract ideas in sensory form and then channels them to the intellect. On this process see, e.g., Stern, "Maimonides' Epistemology," esp. 107–108.

15 *Sefer hamusar*, p. 117, lines 30–36.

16 Cf. Wolfson, "The Internal Senses in Latin, Arabic, and Hebrew," 258–259 and Harvey, *The Inward Wits*, 52–53 (on Ibn Sīnā). There is an earlier (13th-century) Hebrew rhymed prose presentation of the internal senses in Ibn Sahula's *Meshal ha-qadmoni*; see Loewe's edition and translation, 1:94–95 and 2:506–513.

17 See Ratzaby's notes to p. 117, lines 30 and 36 and Saadya Gaon, *Mishlei ʿim tirgum u-feirush ha-gaʾon rabbeinu seʿadyah ben yosef fayyūmī*, 16–19. Note that Saadya does not use the term "internal senses" or any of its equivalents.

the functions Alḍāhirī ascribes to the *koaḥ ha-meḥashshev* can be traced back to Aristotle: Wolfson writes that the Stagirite describes the cogitative soul "as the faculty which judges what is good and what is evil, what is to be pursued and what is to be avoided" and attributes to *dianoia* "the functions of combination and separation, that is to say, of the cognition of what is true and false."[18] In large measure, Alḍāhirī's treatment of the soul also draws on the psychological theory set forth in Part Five, Section 12 of Judah Halevi's *Kuzari*, which in turn derives from a treatise on the soul by Ibn Sīnā (*Risāla fi'l-nafs*), whose classifications of the internal senses in both his medical and philosophical writings were highly influential for subsequent thinkers in the Arabic, Hebrew, and Latin traditions.[19] The discussion in *Kuzari* 5:12 opens with the assertion that, in animate beings, the existence of the soul is proven by motion and sensation (Arabic: *yatabayyan wujūd al-nafs bi'l-ḥarakāt wa'l-iḥsās li'l-ḥayawān*; Ibn Tibbon: *yitba'er meṣi'ut ha-nefesh bitnu'ot ve-hargashot la-ḥayyim*). As the form, or perfection (entelechy), of a natural, organic body, endowed with life *in potentia*, the soul is the cause of motion and sensation in living beings.[20] Halevi then sets forth the commonplace three-fold division of the faculties of the soul—vegetative, animal, and rational—and outlines the component faculties or powers of the vegetative soul.[21] He declares that the external senses are well-known and passes immediately on to the internal senses, consisting of the common sense (*al-ḥāssa al-mushtaraka*), which brings together the impressions perceived by all five senses; the imagination

18 See Wolfson, "The Internal Senses in Latin, Arabic, and Hebrew," p. 259 and n. 44 and p. 261.

19 For Ibn Sīnā's *Risāla fi'l-nafs* see Landauer, "Die Psychologie des Ibn Sīnā." For his treatment of the internal senses see also Rahman, *Avicenna's De Anima*, index s.v. *ḥass*; idem, *Avicenna's Psychology*, 30–31, 38–40, and Rahman's commentary, pp. 77–83. On the impact of Ibn Sīnā's discussions of the internal senses see, e.g.: Wolfson, "The Internal Senses in Latin, Arabic, and Hebrew," 276–294; idem, "Maimonides on the Internal Senses," 346–347 and *passim*; and Harvey, *The Inward Wits*, 21–30, 39–53.

20 See Halevi, *Kitāb al-radd wa'l-dalīl fi'l-dīn al-dhalīl* (*al-kitāb al-khazarī*), 200–208; *Sefer ha-kuzari* ed. Zifroni, 292–302; *Sefer ha-kuzari*, ed. and trans. Qāfiḥ, 201–209. On the section's derivation from Ibn Sīnā's *Risāla fi'l-nafs*, see Pines, "Shī'ite Terms and Conceptions in Judah Halevi's *Kuzari*," 210–217. The notion that voluntary movement distinguishes the animal soul from the vegetative soul goes back to Aristotle; see *De Anima* III, 9–10, 432a–434a.

21 Langermann draws the following helpful distinction: in the Arabic Aristotelian tradition, the rational soul (*al-nafs al-nāṭiqa*) is "perhaps the noblest part of the soul, but nonetheless, it remains just one component within a complex of faculties, each of them defined by its functions and all of them essentially biological, that together constitute the soul." By contrast, "in the eastern Islamic tradition, most notably the philosophical allegories of Ibn Sīnā, the rational soul is … an independent unit, whose origin and destiny is external to the human it inhabits temporarily." See "Saving the Soul by Knowing the Soul," 156.

(*al-quwwa al-mutakhayyila*), which combines or separates the sensory data brought together in the common sense, whether plausibly or implausibly; estimation (*al-quwwa al-mutawahhima*), which discerns the truth or falsity of that which the imagination devises; and retentive memory (*al-quwwa al-mutadhakkira al-ḥāfiẓa*), which preserves that which estimation has affirmed as true.[22] Halevi then returns to the notion that all the powers of a living being are either motive (*muḥarrika*) or perceptive (*mudrika*), with the latter comprising the external and internal senses. Perhaps this juxtaposition led to some confusion in Alḍāhirī's *maqāma*, for he lists motion and sensation as two of the five internal senses, though he distinguishes cursorily between them and the other three, which reside in the brain.[23]

2 The Soul's Moral Qualities

Alḍāhirī's *yeshivah* student then briefly lists the five external senses and moves on to the appetitive faculty (*koaḥ ha-mit'avveh*) and its seven "branches," which in *Kuzari* 5:12 as well as the first of Maimonides' *Eight Chapters* (*Shemonah Peraqim*) are given as the vegetative powers of the soul (attraction, retention, digestion, repulsion, propagation, growth, and nutrition) and are generally enumerated prior to any discussion of the internal senses, which are associated with the sensitive or animal soul, the next rung up in the psy-

---

22 On the history of the philosophers' addition of "common sense" and "estimation" to the older, threefold medical classification of the internal senses, see Wolfson, "The Internal Senses in Latin, Arabic, and Hebrew," 267–294. On Halevi's classifications in *Kuzari* 3:5 and 5:12, see ibid., 285–286. Wolfson notes that, following the *Risāla fi'l-nafs*, Halevi counts as two distinct faculties the "compositive animal imagination," which results from the combination of estimation and imagination in animals, and the "compositive human imagination," which results from the combination of reason and imagination in human beings. Halevi calls the latter the cogitative faculty (*mufakkira*). On the functions of these two faculties, which differ from imagination proper, see Wolfson, ibid., 273–274. For a 15th-century Yemenite list of the internal senses that conforms closely to Halevi's (and Ibn Sīnā's), see the extract from Sa'adya ben David's *Midrash ha-be'ur* in Langermann, *Yemenite Midrash*, p. 75, sec. 4.13 and Qāfiḥ ed. and trans., *Midrash ha-be'ur*, 1:449–450.

23 *Sefer hamusar*, p. 117, lines 22–25. Wolfson notes that in the works of Aristotle and his followers, "those faculties which later became known as internal senses are all considered as belonging to what is called cognitive faculties ..., in contradistinction to those which are known as motive faculties ...." Only the appetitive faculty is somewhat intermediate between the cognitive and the motive: "While cognition creates desire in the appetitive faculty, the appetitive faculty excites action in the motive faculty." See "Maimonides on the Internal Senses," 364–366.

chological hierarchy.[24] Finally, he turns to the moral qualities of the soul, whose refinement is essential to the acquisition of virtues and of the knowledge of God, man's highest goal. Initially, he follows Maimonides in defining virtue as the mean between the extremes of excess and deficiency (*ve-ha-ḥesron ve-ha-tosefet qilqul / ve'emṣa'i metuqqan ve-shaqul*), but manages to inject a slyly mischievous, decidedly un-Maimonidean, element into the proceedings by asserting that an excess of thought is not good for the intellect (although, conversely, the complete absence of thought wreaks damage and destruction).[25] Subsequently he turns to the soul's ten pairs of contrasting moral qualities—pride/humility, shame/audacity, love/hate, compassion/cruelty, anger/appeasement, valor/weakness, miserliness/generosity, jealousy/remorse, fear/trust [in God: *biṭṭaḥon*], joy/grief—and specifies their praiseworthy and blameworthy aspects.[26] Pride can be useful if it enables the soul to be wholehearted in devotion to God and attain eternal reward, but if improperly exercised, it causes a man to depart this world empty-handed. Shame is beneficial in that it keeps the soul from sinning. Hatred is productive if it is directed towards falsehood and those who pursue it. Were it not for envy, the idle man would never get out of bed. In commending the moderate exercise of character traits that, on the surface, appear to be entirely blameworthy, Alḍāhirī harks back to the *Book of Improvement of the Moral Qualities* (*Kitāb iṣlāḥ al-akhlāq*) by Solomon Ibn Gabirol, whose list of twenty moral dispositions seems to have served as a model for our author.[27] (That Alḍāhirī does not cite his sources is

24 In Chapter One of *Shemonah Peraqim*, Maimonides dismisses "the detailed discussion of these seven faculties … [which] belongs to the science of medicine, and need not be taken up here"; see Gorfinkle, *The Eight Chapters of Maimonides On Ethics*, 40. Informed by Galenic medicine, Alḍāhirī's text gives the particular combination of hotness, coldness, dryness, and wetness characterizing each of the first four of these faculties.

25 *Sefer hamusar*, p. 119, lines 55–60. On virtue as the mean between the extremes of moral excess and deficiency, see Maimonides, *Shemonah Peraqim*, Ch. 4 in *Haqdamot le-feirush ha-mishnah*. In *Shemonah Peraqim*, "deviation from the mean is purely therapeutic or else prudential, i.e., in order to preserve the mean one moves a bit to either side"; see Twersky, *Introduction to the Code of Maimonides*, 459–468.

26 As noted, Alḍāhirī's *biṭṭaḥon* reflects the Islamic pietistic ideal of *tawakkul*—complete trust in God and the abandonment of worldly ways—which gained currency among Judaeo-Arabic readers through Muslim Sufi sources and through Baḥya Ibn Paquda's *Book of Direction to the Duties of the Heart*. The fifth chapter of Nethanel ibn Fayyūmī's theological compendium *Bustān al-ʿuqūl* (12th- c. Yemen) is also devoted to *tawakkul*.

27 *Sefer hamusar*, p. 119, line 66–p. 122, line 119. Cf. Ibn Gabirol, *The Improvement of the Moral Qualities*, p. 44: "… we would say here that the sum of the human qualities which we can enumerate is twenty, of which some are praiseworthy *per se*, and others blameworthy *per se*"; p. 84: "There is no quality so reprehensible, but that it at times serves a use, even as no quality is so praiseworthy, but that it frequently becomes detrimental."

not unusual; with regard to medieval Arabic literature, Franz Rosenthal has written that the more scholarly a work was, the greater the care taken by scholars to cite their sources. *Adab* literature encompassed such a wide variety of works, from the purely entertaining to the highly technical, that its attribution of sources varied greatly. Rosenthal notes that, unlike the sciences of tradition and jurisprudence, "little exact documentation was required in systematic philosophy" or medicine, which dealt with what were considered to be scientifically established facts.)[28] By way of summation, the student encapsulates the medieval synthesis of philosophical psychology, which construed ultimate happiness as the soul's attainment of metaphysical knowledge, with more traditional eschatological beliefs: "These are the faculties and moral traits of the soul/ the immortal soul/ who will merit eternal bliss/ if she observes God's precepts to the fullest."

3 A Poetic Coda

Following this highly technical disquisition couched in rhymed prose, the as-yet-unnamed student recites a hortatory poem of his own devising. Studded with second person feminine endings, "Nefesh yeqarah, eikh be-tokh guf tishkeni" ("Precious soul, how can you dwell in a body?") is a Neoplatonically informed sermon to the soul, seemingly in the tradition of the Andalusian Hebrew *tokheḥah*.[29] It asks rhetorically how the soul can dwell in an impure material body when she is inherently pure, having emanated from the divine splendor. It urges her to extract herself from the moral contamination and decay of the corporeal world, forsake sin, and prepare for Judgment Day; and it cautions her that she cannot rest until she returns to her celestial home. Together with the preceding rhymed prose discourse on the internal senses, this poetic exhortation to the soul constitutes an innovative exegetical approach to Psalm 19:8 in both form (prosimetrum) and content (Neoplatonic and Aristotelian psychology), seeing as they pick up where Karo's kabbalistic exegesis leaves off. Mordecai recounts that, when Karo heard this discourse, he was so taken by its eloquence that he elevated the student's rank above that of

---

28 See Rosenthal, *The Technique and Approach of Muslim Scholarship*, 41–45. See also Stroumsa, "Citation Tradition: On Explicit and Hidden Citations in Judaeo-Arabic Philosophical Literature."

29 For further discussion of "Nefesh yeqarah," see the section headed *Contrafaction as Anti-Parody* in Chapter One.

all his fellow disciples and increased his financial support. At this crucial juncture, the narrator scrutinizes the elusive seminarian-cum-philosopher/ poet, and recognizes him as his old resourceful and cunning friend, Abner ben Ḥeleq the Yemenite.[30]

At first glance, we might be inclined to think that the embedded "Nefesh yeqarah" is intended as a lyrical reprise of Abner's rhymed prose exposition of the internal senses and moral qualities of the soul. While the poem is certainly topical and shares many of the ethical concerns introduced earlier, it invokes the Neoplatonic myth of the soul rather than the largely Aristotelian psychology found in the preceding section. Additional piquancy is afforded by the fact that this seemingly innocuous poem is modeled on a cheeky parodic inversion of the *tokheḥah* genre found in the "Dispute of the Soul with the Body and the Intellect" in the *Taḥkemoni*. As mentioned in Chapter One, Alḥarizi's "Nefesh yeqarah, eikh be-sikhlekh tivteḥi" ("Precious soul, how can you trust in your intellect?") is delivered by the evil inclination with the insolent intention of provoking the soul to sin. Even though Abner's poem serves as a doctrinal corrective to Alḥarizi's lampoon, the fact that he does not mention his predecessor's provocative piece suggests that he might have something to hide. On the authorial level, Abner's *jawāb* is a deliberate anti-parody that attempts to rectify Alḥarizi's subversion of the pious advice proffered in conventional *tokheḥot*.[31] On the narrative level, however, it deflates Abner's learned and virtuous pose, ridiculing him for his sanctimony and literary and scholarly pretentiousness. Surely, the revelation of the student's identity sets the entire chapter in a new light: Abner's unmasking calls the reader's attention to moral discrepancies between his assumed pious persona and his roguish character. Like the anti-heroes of the Arabic *maqāmāt* of al-Hamadhānī and al-Ḥarīrī, Abner is so often a charlatan who poses as a preacher or a holy man that his high-minded reworking of Alḥarizi's burlesque strikes one as part of his stratagem and imposture.[32] If his outward show of godliness is convincing to his fictional *yeshivah* audience in Safed, the savvy reader knows that underlying Abner's orthodox verse is a doctrinally subversive poem that he may genuinely have enjoyed.

30 *Sefer hamusar*, pp. 122–123, lines 120–134.

31 For the "Dispute of the Soul with the Body and the Intellect," see Alḥarizi, *Taḥkemoni* #13 (#5 in Yahalom-Katsumata). Stewart has speculated that Alḥarīzī's personification of the intellect may have been inspired by Ibn al-Jawzī; see "Of Rhetoric, Reason, and Revelation."

32 See Monroe, *The Art of Badīʿ az-Zamān al-Hamadhānī*, 21–24. See also Stewart, "Professional Literary Mendicancy in the *Letters* and *Maqāmāt* of Badīʿ al-Zamān al-Hamadhānī."

4 Reliable Transmission?

In the recognition scene that comes on the heels of Abner's poetic recitation, Mordecai waits until Karo and his disciples leave before expressing his deep affection for his old friend, whose sincerity he never doubts. Thus reunited, the two proceed to Abner's impoverished home, where he spreads out a tattered cloth, sententiously paraphrasing the *Ethics of the Fathers*, "Such is the way befitting the study of Torah: a morsel of bread with salt thou must eat, thou must sleep upon the ground while thou toilest in the Torah."[33] Then, rather incongruously, he treats Mordecai to a feast of meat and wine, served on a fine tablecloth. This rich fare may have been reserved for a Sabbath meal, but the indulgence suggests that Abner's dedication to a devout life of abstemiousness may not be as genuine as he would like his credulous friend to think. Certainly, the largesse bestowed on him in recognition of his elegant discourse on the soul reminds the reader of any number of instances in which the disguised and mendacious Abner uses polished rhetoric (*ḥaliqut amarav*) to dupe his unsuspecting audience into enriching him. It is intriguing that, in rewarding his student, the esteemed Joseph Karo has seemingly fallen for Abner's ruse (and contravened at least the spirit of the Sabbath by making a monetary promise). By intertwining historical and fictitious characters in this *maqāma*, Alḍāhirī calls attention to the artifice of the episode, notwithstanding its realistic Safed setting and extensive philosophical content. By resetting the terms of the intellectual competition from *yeshivah* learning to philosophy, Alḍāhirī ensures that Abner will best all the other students and elicit Karo's supreme admiration.

As James Monroe has written in his monograph on the art of al-Hamadhānī, the *maqāma* genre makes questionable claims to moral authority, alerting the reader to ethical and doctrinal irregularities through a variety of subtle hints. The unscrupulous anti-hero of the *maqāma* exploits the charitable inclinations of his listeners to trick them into giving alms under false pretenses, and only the inconsistencies between what the protagonist says and does clue the more perceptive reader in to his moral bankruptcy. In the frame story to our *maqāma*, the narrator's emphasis on the rectitude, learnedness, and even saintliness of the Safed Jewish community provides an ironic contrast with Abner's tendency throughout the work to avarice, cynicism, and subterfuge for selfish purposes. Moreover, even though Mordecai takes Abner's claims at face value, he indi-

33 *Avot* 6,4, after the translation of Hertz, *Sayings of the Fathers*. See *Sefer hamusar*, p. 123, lines 135–145.

rectly casts doubt on his friend's erudition two lines from the end by alluding to Proverbs 17:28: "Even a fool, if he keeps silent, is deemed wise; Intelligent, if he seals his lips."[34] While Abner's bluff is not explicitly called in this particular episode of *Sefer hamusar*, the reader's awareness of his deceitful comportment elsewhere casts doubt on his learned discussion of ethical virtues and provokes the suspicion that he may not be philosophically reliable either. Inevitably, Abner's unpredictable personal ethics call into question the educative integrity of his oration.

On the surface, Abner's pronouncements suggest more than a glancing acquaintance with philosophical theories of the soul, but a closer look reveals a somewhat unsystematic pastiche. Motion and sensation are presented as two of the five internal senses (which they are not in any of the classification schemes outlined by Wolfson[35]), and the Maimonidean definition of virtue as the mean between the extremes of excess and deficiency is adopted but then seemingly jettisoned in favor of Ibn Gabirol's approach. Nevertheless, the propensity for philosophical eclecticism is by no means unique to Alḍāhirī. Langermann has highlighted the blend of Maimonidean and Neoplatonic ideas evident in the allegorical commentary on Canticles by Zechariah ha-Rofé, one of Alḍāhirī's illustrious 15th-century predecessors, which revolves around the philosophical imperative to know one's own soul (the "Delphic maxim") and ultimately breaks with the Maimonidean interpretation of the Song of Songs under the impact of the psychological theory of eastern Islamic thinkers.[36] Regarding Zechariah's commentary on Maimonides' *Guide*, *Sharḥ al-Dalāla*, Langermann writes:

> Like most of the Yemeni-Jewish intellectuals of his period, his philosophical posture and his approach to texts fit into the current known today as Islamic neoplatonism. Yemeni Jews seem to have become acquainted—and enamored—with this stream of thought chiefly by way of treatises written or promulgated by the Ismāʿīlīs.[37]

34 *Sefer hamusar*, p. 123, line 143.

35 Rather, as noted, in *Kuzari* 5:12 motion and sensation are identified as proof of the existence of the soul in animate beings.

36 See Langermann, "Saving the Soul by Knowing the Soul." On other extant works of Zechariah ha-Rofé, see Langermann, *Yemenite Midrash*, 269–270; idem, "*Sharḥ al-Dalāla*"; Tobi, "Ketav-yad ḥadash"; and Havatselet ed. and trans., *Midrash ha-ḥefeṣ*. See also Ivry, "Neoplatonic Currents in Maimonides' Thought" and idem, "Maimonides and Neoplatonism: Challenge and Response."

37 Langermann, "*Sharḥ al-Dalāla*," 165. See also Tobi, *The Jews of Yemen*, 207–208.

In numerous instances, Langermann has demonstrated that Yemenite Jewish intellectuals took Maimonides' injunction to "accept the truth from whomever speaks it" as a mandate to draw on a wide range of philosophical sources in their quest for Wisdom.[38]

Apart from these substantive precedents for embracing diverse schools of thought, Alḍāhirī could have deliberately inserted inconsistencies into Abner's discourse on the internal senses as an artful means of puncturing his pomposity. Alternatively, the non-conformity of Abner's presentation to any one conventional psychological scheme might be part of the rogue-hero's ruse: capitalizing on an impressionable audience, he is able to mislead his listeners with a patchwork of ideas, delivered with confidence and ease in an exuberant flow of cleverly rhymed phrases. Monroe argues that the ornate, extravagant diction of the rhetorician in the *maqāma* literature is a means of misrepresenting reality as well as an authorial device for calling attention to the ironic contrast between what the characters say and what they do.[39] Mordecai's report that Karo himself was dazzled by Abner's extraordinarily eloquent and clear language (*ṣaḥot leshono*) suggests that even the renowned sage lacked discernment when it came to philosophical theories of the soul. There is, in fact, a striking disjunction between the psychology Abner sets forth here and Karo's own kabbalistic teachings on the soul, which admitted the doctrine of metempsychosis.[40] Furthermore, the historical Karo was known to be rather credulous: he believed that he was the recipient of mystical revelations conveyed by a guiding spirit or *maggid* that spoke through his own mouth, revealing the mysteries of the Torah and the secrets of the transmigration of souls. Karo's *maggid* took the material form of the Mishnah, guiding him in his composition of the *Beit yosef* and *Shulḥan ʿarukh*. For the last forty years of his life (1535–1575), Karo kept a journal of these extraordinary mystical experiences, *Maggid Meisharim*. Yassif writes that Karo "had delusions of grandeur" and that the Safed community knew about his *maggid*.[41] In context, therefore, it is perfectly plausible

38 See Langermann, *Yemenite Midrash*, xvii–xix and 276; idem, "Maḥshevet hodu be-qerev yehudei teiman"; and idem, "Cultural Contacts of the Jews of Yemen." In "*Sharḥ al-Dalāla*," Langermann notes that Zechariah ha-Rofé was also aware of the Ishraqi or Illuminationist school of thought and included extracts from al-Ghazālī's *Maqāṣid al-Falāsifa* in his commentary to the introduction to the *Guide*.

39 See *The Art of Badīʿ az-Zamān al-Hamadhānī*, Ch. 7.

40 See Werblowsky, *Joseph Karo, Lawyer and Mystic*, 234–256. Note that when Abner is in kabbalistic "mode," he too alludes to the doctrine of metempsychosis in one of his poems.

41 See: Werblowsky, *Joseph Karo, Lawyer and Mystic*, 9–23; Jacobs, *Jewish Mystical Testimonies*, 98–122; Wolfson, "Asceticism, Mysticism, and Messianism," 166–167; Yassif, *The Legend of Safed*, 126 and 200–201; Altshuler, "Prophecy and Maggidism in the Life and

that the historical Karo fell for the fictional Abner's subtle deception. There is no small irony in the fact that here and elsewhere in the work, Abner displays some of the very qualities of the soul that are enumerated in his discourse as unacceptable—pride, impudence, greed—and that he is far from exercising them in moderation or adhering to the ethical golden mean whose cultivation he advocates.

5 Pietist Pose

In the fourteenth *maqāma*, Abner appears late at night in the guise of a solitary pietist. After rising to wash his face, hands, and feet as part of his ablutions prior to prayer, he improvises a pre-dawn devotion.[42] However, instead of asking God for forgiveness while his fellow men sleep, he endeavors to purify his soul by praising God's creation using an emanative cosmology framed in language distinctly reminiscent of Ibn Gabirol's *Keter Malkhut*.[43] In a highly condensed version of the Neoplatonic scheme, Abner traces the downward flow of all existence from a transcendent God, who effortlessly created the cosmic Intellect, from which He caused to emanate the Universal Soul.[44] This cosmogony takes

Writings of R. Joseph Karo"; and Elior, "Joseph Karo and Israel Ba'al Shem Tov." Elior (268–269) characterizes *Maggid Meisharim* as "a unique mystical autobiography, attesting to the hidden world of a towering halakhic figure undergoing intense internal struggles and giving free expression to the way in which the mystical experience breaches established boundaries." *Maggid Meisharim* was printed posthumously, Part I (Lublin, 1646), Part II (Venice, 1649).

42 The 15th-century Yemenite Jewish author Ḥoṭer ben Shelomoh writes, "... it is incumbent upon the religious individual ... every morning ... to wash himself in perfect purity, in order to make his soul ready for [reciting] the obligatory blessings ...." Cf. Alḍāhirī, *Ṣeidah la-derekh* on Lev. ch. 6 (*parashat Ṣav*). An earlier precedent, inspired by Muslim practices, can be found in the pietist circle of Abraham Maimonides (1186–1237) in Egypt, who adopted a series of ritual reforms that included purifying the feet before prayer; see Wieder, "Islamic Influences on the Jewish Worship," esp. 664–676.

43 For a philosophical approach to early morning prayer, see the excerpt from *Sirāj al-ʿuqūl* by Ḥoṭer ben Shelomoh in Langermann, *Yemenite Midrash*, 108–114. Ibn Gabirol's younger contemporary, Baḥya Ibn Paquda, recommended the performance of supererogatory nighttime devotions to ensure that prayer would be meaningful. To this end, he composed a poetic exhortation to the soul entitled "Barekhi nafshi," which he appended with a *baqqashah* (confessional meditation) to his *Book of Direction to the Duties of the Heart*, and included instructions for their recitation in the work's final treatise; see Baḥya Ibn Paquda, *Hidāya*, 10:6.

44 In his Hebrew Introduction to the *Taḥkemoni*, Alḥarizi also construes praise for God in terms of Ibn Gabirol's Neoplatonic scheme; see Alḥarizi, *Taḥkemoni* ed. Yahalom-

as a given Ibn Gabirol's innovation of subordinating the emanative process to God's will and thus preserves the theologically traditional view of God as volitional creator. Our pietist praises God for establishing the physical universe, which consists of the rotating spheres, at whose center stands the Earth with its diverse creatures. Of these, man is preeminent, for he alone is endowed with a divine, immortal soul that may—if it is disciplined—attain eternal repose in the world to come.

> Blessed be He who has chosen us over all other nations, and favored us with His sacred obligations .... He who is veiled in highest mystery, exalted above all that is heavenly (*ha-neʿelam be-rum ḥevyon/ha-naʿaleh ʿal kol ʿelyon*), who created the First Intellect without toil or moil—no word was heard—and from it caused to emanate the precious Universal Soul, distinct from angels all (*baraʾ ha-sekhel ha-rishon/beli ʿamal ve-lo raḥshon/ve-heʾeṣil mimmenu nefesh yeqarah kollelet/min ha-malʾakhim nivdelet*). He set the spheres in perpetual motion; they went wherever the spirit impelled them. In wisdom He compounded each sphere of the four elements, so that creatures of all kinds would emerge with their own lineaments. Of them all, He chose man—bone, flesh, and blood; a whole—whom He gave a precious soul, a thing of glory, mined from the divine quarry, and bequeathed it the world to come; a spiritual domain it might attain. If it hews to the good, it will be like a fresh shoot. I am duty-bound to laud His ways and render thanks with songs of praise.[45]

Its biblical diction pregnant with philosophical meaning, Alḍāhirī's language testifies to Ibn Gabirol's remarkable success in translating speculative motifs into a more traditional idiom, naturalizing the highly technical ideas elaborated in *Keter Malkhut* by couching them in a lexicon familiar to the worshiper. Ibn Gabirol's poetic medium had rendered this weighty and daring synthesis accessible and acceptable to traditional audiences in a way that a more discursive form likely could not.[46] Although *Keter Malkhut* transcends the limits

---

Katsumata, pp. 64–69, lines 27–140. For the Hebrew text of *Keter Malkhut* see Schirmann, *HPSP* 1:257–285 and Ibn Gabirol, *The Liturgical Poetry* 1:37–70. For English translations and secondary bibliography see Tanenbaum, *The Contemplative Soul*, p. 58, n. 4. On Neoplatonic influences and the role of the universal soul in Yemenite Jewish cosmology, see Langermann, *Yemenite Midrash*, 21–44, and idem, "Yemenite Philosophical Midrash as a Source for the Intellectual History of the Jews of Yemen."

45 *Sefer hamusar*, pp. 178–179, lines 2–20.

46 Cf. Petuchowski, *Theology and Poetry*, 5: "Statements and arguments which, in prose, would immediately be branded as 'heretical' have become, once they were couched in

of prayer as traditionally conceived, its hymnic framework and closing series of confessions and petitions for aid in purifying the soul likely account for its integration into the penitential liturgy for Yom Kippur in the Yemenite *tiklāl* and *maḥzorim* of other rites.[47]

Nonetheless, in the picaresque continuation of Chapter 14, Abner's pious, philosophically informed devotion devolves into less noble pursuits. Although he initially appears as a virtuous divine who expounds profound theological and cosmological doctrines, he very quickly metamorphoses into a suave rhymester and, ultimately, a swindler. In the central section of the chapter—a sort of comedy of manners—a ravenous Abner attempts to barter his rhetorical skills and expertise in "the sciences and the arts" for food, but the local Syrian Jews, whose sin of parsimony is compounded by their philistinism, will have none of it. Following some clever but fruitless gastronomic repartee with a quick-witted youth who affirms his community's insularity, Abner resorts to a more devilish means of satisfying his hunger. He orders a meal far more lavish than he can afford, and then, on the pretext of going to fetch something sweet for dessert, abandons the hapless Mordecai to face the ire of the unpaid shopkeeper. This ruse closely resembles the plot of the twenty-first *maqāma* of the *Taḥkemoni*, which is in turn a reworking of al-Hamadhānī's "Maqāma of Baghdad" (#12). In Alḥarizi's version, as in al-Hamadhānī's, the shrewdly selected victim of the trick is an unsuspecting Arab peasant: a rustic on an ass, who has the misfortune to cross the famished and scheming protagonist's path. The farcical and slightly lurid tale of his premeditated entrapment fills an entire *maqāma* in both works. By contrast, Alḍāhirī compresses Abner's devious betrayal of Mordecai's trust into the final twelve lines of his *maqāma*. While the earlier versions are recounted by the protagonist (in al-Hamadhānī) or the narrator in the voice of the protagonist (in Alḥarizi), Alḍāhirī adds a measure of poignancy by telling the story through the eyes of the victim. By deliberately juxtaposing this display of gluttony and deceit with Abner's initially virtuous and high-minded devotion, the author severely undercuts his hero's gravitas. The contiguity of the episode's scenes highlights Abner's rapid transformation from austere divine to cunning man of letters to outright fraud,

---

poetic form, ingredients of the liturgy, and continue to be rehearsed—often with more devotion than comprehension—by multitudes of the unsuspecting pious who would be utterly shocked to discover the true intent of their authors." On the diversity of literary genres used to convey philosophical ideas to broader audiences, see also Hughes and Robinson eds., *Medieval Jewish Philosophy and its Literary Forms*.

47 Alḍāhirī's echoes of Ibn Gabirol's *Book of Improvement of the Moral Qualities* is further evidence of his attraction to Gabirolean texts and ideas. He also composed a poem on the ten *sefirot* for insertion into *Keter Malkhut* in the *tiklāl*; see Chapter Six.

signaling that his piousness was at best a temporary pose. Depending on his (and our) degree of cynicism, Abner could have appropriated the lofty ideas of *Keter Malkhut* in order to make his disguise more credible. Though entertaining, his transgression of social conventions also exposes the human weaknesses lurking behind the façade of excessive piety. In its larger narrative context, then, the cosmogony borrowed from Ibn Gabirol is coopted as part of a social satire.[48] Still, it is noteworthy that Alḍāhirī chooses to put Ibn Gabirol's exalted language and emanative scheme in the mouth of his fictional pietist, even if that poseur quickly relapses into his characteristic verbal swagger and caprice.[49]

6 Medical Imposture and Abstract Cures

Abner's masquerade as a paragon of wisdom and purveyor of sage advice is delightfully effective when he pretends to medical knowledge. The thirty-second *maqāma* opens with Mordecai's arrival in the upper Galilean city of Sepphoris, ostensibly to view its magnificent tower. Once there, he notices throngs of people hurrying to one of the squares where they crowd around an elderly man who, head shaded from the fierce sun by an awning, poses as a doctor (*ve-hinneh ish zaqen yoshev ʿal rosho qubbah/ le-hagen ʿalav me-hashemesh/ ke-minhago mitmol u-meʾemesh/ ve-hu maḥaziq ʿaṣmo le-rofe*).[50] As in any number of medieval caricatures ridiculing the physician as a quack, an endless stream of wounded come to him with their injuries, and like any mountebank worth his salt, he proffers medicaments and remedies to each of them, promising a wondrous cure. The initial mise-en-scène is very close to Alḥarizi's lampoon of a mercenary doctor in *Taḥkemoni* #43/30, although there the focus is on Ḥever ha-Keni's rhetorical extravagance as he hawks his fraud-

48 Were Alḍāhirī not so completely immersed in the received medieval world view, we might even construe this as an attempt to poke fun at the perceived arcana of Ibn Gabirol's system.

49 On this episode, see Tanenbaum, "Of a Pietist Gone Bad and Des(s)erts Not Had."

50 *Sefer hamusar*, p. 365, lines 6–8. Ratzaby glosses *qubbah* as *sekhakhah le-haṣel ʿal rosho*. In his entry on *qubbah*, Ben Yehuda cites this passage, glossing the word as *sokhekh ʿal ha-rosh mi-penei ha-shemesh*; see Ben Yehuda, *Complete Dictionary*, 6:5671. It is unclear whether what is intended is some sort of protective thatch, a screen, an awning, or a parasol, either freestanding or mounted on the individual's headgear. In line 40, the narrator suggests that this protective covering had, at least partially, obscured the doctor's face. For the Arabic cognate, *qubba*, meaning tent, cupola, pavillion, palanquin, parasol, or sunshade, see Dozy, *Supplément aux Dictionnaires Arabes*, 2:297; Lane, *Arabic-English Lexicon*, 2:2478; and Steingass, *The Student's Arabic-English Dictionary*, 815.

ulent cures and collects payments for every nostrum he dispenses to the credulous crowd. Alḥarizi's episode ends with the narrator reprimanding Ḥever for his shameless deceptions, to which Ḥever responds in angry self-justification.[51] In chapter 32 of *Sefer hamusar*, however, Alḍāhirī charts his own course, portraying the spurious doctor as something of a philosopher or moralist as well.[52] Mordecai greets the physician and inquires whether, among his many restoratives and medicinal compounds, he has a cure for sins and transgressions. The doctor replies that he does and, provided that no detail of his instructions is altered, no harm will befall his interlocutor. He then issues the following prescription:

> Go and stand by the well of withdrawal after you have anointed your heart with the oil of weakness and frailty. Then doff your cloak of desire in its entirety, your frocks of faithlessness and trousers of lust, which sicken the soul all day long. Immerse yourself in that spring for seven consecutive days, until you are rid of your sullenness. After this, don trousers of restraint, a turban of courage, and the garb of salvation, and wrap yourself in a robe of righteousness. From the straight path do not stray; turn towards the garden of faith, to pluck the roots of meditative devotion (*kavvanah*), the seeds of contrition, ... the leaves of upright conduct, ...the magnificent and splendid lily of humility, the fruit of wisdom that distinguishes man from beast, the grasses of prudence and patience, ... the branches of charity dispensed in love to all men, the husks of righteousness, ... the unripe fruit of honesty, which cools inflamed passions. Take these medicaments with a firm heart, intelligence, and your esteemed and precious soul ... from the garden beds ... and pound them in the mortar of repentance, which causes man to be remembered for good. Sift it all ... and pour over it the waters of spiritual communion (*devequt*), drawn from piety, and decant [the potion] into the kettle of hope, to be spared from

51 See Alḥarizi, *Taḥkemoni*, ed. Yahalom-Katsumata, pp. 485–489. For a general overview of satirical treatments of physicians in medieval Hispano-Jewish literature, see Dishon, "Harofe be-re'i ha-satirah ba-sifrut ha'ivrit bisfarad bimei ha-beinayim." On al-Ḥarīrī's 47th *maqāma*, in which his protagonist poses as a cupper in order to defraud the onlookers crowded around him, see Pormann, "The Physician and the Other: Images of the Charlatan in Medieval Islam," 222–225.

52 Medieval Arabic medical writings distinguished between a true or academic physician (*ṭabīb*) who studied medicine theoretically alongside philosophy and other sciences, and a lesser medical practitioner (*mutaṭabbib*), concerned with practical applications; see e.g., Pormann, "The Physician and the Other," 216 and Gadelrab, "Medical Healers in Ottoman Egypt, 1517–1805," 369–370.

> scalding. Kindle beneath it the flames of awe, using the timber of competition and envy, until its aroma wafts with the effervescence of faith, and the elixir is seasoned with a fiery law (*esh dat*). Finally, let it be poured into the bowl of favor, which is not used for cow's butter or sheep's milk. Wave over it the sieve of confession, in truth and free of falsehood, and sprinkle tears over it in the dark hours of the night. Thus will you find a cure for your transgressions: drink it all and sit alone. After that your sins will no longer have force; they will sink into the depths of the sea; "as they encamped, so shall they march (Numbers 2:17)."[53]

Mordecai responds with extreme gratitude to the physician for having saved him from miring himself in sin. As the heat of the day subsides, the doctor removes the protective covering from his head, and Mordecai discovers that he is none other than Abner ben Ḥeleq. Mordecai quickly jots a note of thanks, in which he identifies himself and encloses two florins in payment for services rendered; the long-lost friends embrace to the astonishment of the onlookers, who are so impressed by Mordecai's rapid recovery that they prepare a sumptuous celebratory meal for the two protagonists.

Like the quack medicines that Abner administers to his other petitioners, the antidote that he prescribes for Mordecai's sins is a product of his fertile and nimble imagination. Unlike his remedies for physical ailments, however, this fanciful elixir is entirely metaphorical. While it uses the language of compounding a drug—crushing, diluting, decanting, simmering—the remedy relies on abstract ethical qualities and spiritual states for its ingredients. Each of its many construct phrases consists of a concrete noun (cloak, trousers, leaves, etc.) bound by an abstract noun (withdrawal, faithlessness, contrition, etc.). At the same time, the piece draws on recognizable themes and motifs from medieval Jewish penitential and ethical literature, lending it an aura of authenticity and moral weight. Abner's opening injunction that Mordecai doff his clothes of ignobility and immerse himself in the well of withdrawal, or spring of asceticism, recalls Abraham Ibn Ezra's *Ḥayy ben Meqiṣ*, a rhymed prose philosophical allegory of the soul's quest for metaphysical wisdom that is closely modeled on Ibn Sīnā's *Ḥayy ibn Yaqẓān*.[54] In preparation for his journey through the cosmic realms, Ibn Ezra's narrator (the soul) is disrobed and

53 *Sefer hamusar*, pp. 365–366.

54 On Ibn Ezra's allegory and its relationship to Ibn Sīnā's philosophical tale, see Hughes, *The Texture of the Divine*, 13–47; Greive, *Studien zum jüdischen Neuplatonismus*, 104–175 *passim*. See also Tanenbaum, "Nine Spheres or Ten?" and Stroumsa, "The Makeover of *Ḥayy*."

purified in the healing waters of the spring of life.[55] The twin metaphorical motifs of doffing and donning recur throughout medieval Jewish philosophical and ethical literature, as well as an entire class of Hebrew penitential poems where, drawing on biblical precedents such as Zechariah 3:3–5 and themes from Islamic speculative and pietistic works, they symbolize the repudiation of odious, excessively worldly character traits and the cultivation of virtuous qualities that are prerequisite to the perfection of the soul.[56]

The remedy for sin is, naturally, repentance, and Alḍāhirī's prescription is tinctured with concepts regularly found in philosophically informed discussions of penitence from the Judeo-Islamic cultural orbit, such as Ibn Gabirol's *Book of Improvement of the Moral Qualities* (*Kitāb iṣlāḥ al-akhlāq*); Baḥya Ibn Paquda's *Book of Direction to the Duties of the Heart* (*Al-hidāya ilā farāʾiḍ al-qulūb*); and Maimonides' *Laws of Repentance* (*Hilkhot Teshuvah*) in his *Mishneh Torah*. Though hardly intended to be systematic, Alḍāhirī's flowery, inventive cure for sins touches on some of the essential conditions of repentance as outlined in these sober works: withdrawal from noisome worldly habits, the recognition and confession of sin, contrition, contemplative and prayerful nighttime vigils, and knowledge of one's God-given soul, as a means to drawing closer to the Divine.[57]

Precedents for the conceit of a fanciful, abstract cure are found in medieval belletristic and ethical works in both Hebrew and Arabic. Ratzaby has written that the idea of a remedy with imaginary ingredients appealed to littérateurs and moral philosophers alike; the former exploited it in a farcical vein while the latter saw it as a vehicle for serious ethical discussions.[58] Bilal Orfali and Maurice Pomerantz have edited a previously unknown *maqāma* of al-Hamadhānī that "describes a fraudulent doctor's sale of medicinal compounds allegedly composed of rare *materia medica*."[59] While serious and comical treatments of technical medical material appear in Hebrew belletristic texts already in the 12th century with *Sefer shaʿashuʿim* by Joseph Ibn Zabara (himself a physician),

55 See Levin ed., *Ḥay ben mekiṣ leʾavraham ibn ʿezra*, p. 60, lines 70 ff. and Hughes, *The Texture of the Divine*, 119–121.

56 See Tanenbaum, *The Contemplative Soul*, 132–145 ("The Adornment of the Soul: A Philosophical Motif").

57 See Tanenbaum, "The Andalusian *Seliḥah* and Its Individualistic Conception of Penitence," esp. 383–384.

58 See Ratzaby, "Terufah hitulit u-musarit."

59 Accordingly, they have called it "al-Ṭibbiyya"; see Orfali and Pomerantz, "A Lost *Maqāma* of Badīʿ al-Zamān al-Hamaḏānī?" See also Kennedy and Farrell ed. and trans., Ibn Buṭlān, *The Doctors' Dinner Party*, and Pormann, "The Physician and the Other." According to Dishon, Ibn Buṭlān's *Daʿwat al-atibbāʾ* was known to Ibn Zabara; see *The Physician and the Demon*, 62–65.

Judah Alḥarizi appears to have introduced the figurative, immaterial prescription into the Hebrew rhymed prose narrative.[60] In the forty-eighth *maqāma* of his *Taḥkemoni*, a distraught lovesick patient describes his malady to an elderly, regally attired doctor who specializes in healing the brokenhearted. The physician prescribes two medicinal compounds whose ingredients are entirely whimsical and are drawn either from the catalogue of amatory emotions and physical descriptions of the beloved—the spices of fellowship, the powder of pure love, the lilies of the lips, the apples of the breasts, the ivory of the teeth—or states of mind associated with unrequited love—the grasses of hope, the fruit of separation, the leaves of wrath and trembling, the thorns of worry. The comical chapter has decidedly erotic overtones, and the two proposed cures are couched in a largely metaphorical idiom.[61] Immanuel of Rome (c. 1265–1335) calls the chimerical cure in the eleventh of his *Maḥbarot* "facetious," which it certainly is. Posing as a court physician, his protagonist and namesake is called to minister to a strikingly beautiful noblewoman suffering from severe labor pains. When he wishes to "grope for" her pulse, she covers her face with a blanket and insists that he examine her through her garment. Offended by her excessive and, in his view, affected modesty, the doctor has his revenge by taking her pulse through a brick and prescribing an utterly ludicrous confection of wolves' horns, hens' milk, marble juice, and the splendor of the moon, and by enjoining one of her retinue to hasten and pluck a frog's tail to bandage the woman's belly. Upon his return to court, the doctor recites a flippant poem about the affair, which amuses his patron no end and earns him a promise of reward.[62] (The physician in Shem Tov Falaquera's thirteenth-century *Sefer ha-mevaqqesh* also gropes his young "virginal" patient in order to take her pulse.[63]) Kalonymus ben Kalonymus (1286-after 1328) included biting satires of various professions from fourteenth-century Jewish society in his rhymed prose work, *Even Boḥan*.[64] His doctor is a fraudulent, ignorant money-grubber who drives

60 On medical themes in *Sefer sha'ashu'im* see Dishon, ibid. and Kozodoy, "The Jewish Physician in Medieval Iberia," 126–128.

61 See Alḥarizi, *Taḥkemoni*, ed. Yahalom-Katsumata, #48, pp. 515–519. For a translation and discussion of the *maqāma*, see Segal, *The Book of Taḥkemoni*, 362–365 and 622–626. See also Rand, *Studies in the Medieval Hebrew Tradition of the Ḥarīrīan and Ḥarizian Maqama*, 18–20. Most of *Taḥkemoni* #43/#30 is devoted to the extravagant healing claims of a quack who then dispenses his "cures" to large crowds of credulous petitioners in exchange for payment.

62 See Immanuel Ha-romi, *Maḥbarot*, pp. 195–215.

63 See Schirmann, *HPSP*, 2:332–333.

64 For the text, see Kalonymus ben Kalonymus, *Even Boḥan*, 44–48 and Schirmann, *HPSP*, 2:510–514. On *Even Boḥan*, see Schirmann, *HPCS*, 529–541.

his patients and their families to financial ruin and hastens the demise of the sick with his improbable potions and compounds, whose ingredient lists are endless ("Take ... a shoelace, the tooth of a fox, tentpins, ... marble juice, a lion's claws, etc.").[65]

Two of the more circumspect uses of the immaterial, abstract cure cited by Ratzaby are found in less well-known quarters: the preface to a work called *Sefer ha-nimṣa*, which is ascribed to Maimonides, and an appendix to the glossary of difficult terms in the *Mishneh Torah* by the late fifteenth-century Yemenite savant, Alu'el (David) ben Yeshaʿ ha-Levi al-ʿAdani. A work of Maimonidean pseudepigrapha, *Sefer ha-nimṣa* is a miscellany of philosophical, ethical, and medical material that opens with a metaphorical remedy for despair: "Take ... the roots of praise and thanks, joy and trust in God, remove from them the seeds of sorrow and anxiety, take the pomegranate blossoms of knowledge and understanding and the roots of patience and contentment, and crush it all in the mortar of humility ... and mix the whole with the waters of grace and lovingkindness ...."[66] A potion for sins (*sharbat al-dhunūb*), Alu'el's rhymed, Judeo-Arabic prescription calls for crushing the roots of poverty and the leaves of patience in the mortar of repentance and sifting the whole in the sieve of reflection and recovery.[67] According to Ratzaby's typology, Alḍāhirī's remedy fits squarely with these earnest ethical recommendations more than with the hilarious travesties of Alḥarizi and Immanuel.

Taken on its own, Alḍāhirī's imaginary cure would seem to be a serious, if figurative, treatment of a genuine ethical topic. Certainly, it does not deliciously affront our sense of propriety in the manner of the droll and bawdy remedies of Alḥarizi and Immanuel, nor does it explicitly ridicule the medical profession in the withering way that Shem Tov Falaquera or Kalonymus do. Nevertheless, when read in context, the piece acquires a subtly suspect coloring. In the thirty-second *maqāma*, Abner is clearly a quack, although Mordecai is the one who

---

65 The longevity of these satires was impressive. When asked whether his questioner should consult a *baʿal ḥefeṣ* [one who relies on occult books to heal the sick], the rationalist Yiḥye Qāfiḥ (1849–1932) responded, "Yes, he will recommend a cure of flea's milk and the creaking of a door"; see Levi, *Holekh tamim*, 39.

66 See Ha-Kohen Maimon, "Sefer ha-nimṣa la-rambam"; the cure is on p. 202. For other works in which such cures appear, see Steinschneider, *Die hebraeischen Übersetzungen des Mittelalters*, Pt. 2, p. 771, n. 87. Ratzaby also cites two Arabic works of Muslim provenance in which the fictitious cure occurs; see "Terufah hitulit u-musarit."

67 See the citation in Steinschneider, *Verzeichnis der hebräischen Handschriften der königlichen Bibliothek zu berlin*, 2:11. Steinschneider, *Die arabische Literatur der Juden*, p. 255, theorized that Alu'el's rhymed Judeo-Arabic version was based on a Hebrew model.

provides the occasion for his foray into the realm of the ethical by requesting a cure for transgressions. Mordecai's inquiry borders on the specious, as medical practitioners do not usually traffic in recipes for repentance, and sins are not reversed with potions. While his demand might be seen as a challenge—medical and rhetorical—in much the same way that Alḥarizi's patient challenges the doctor to cure his lovesickness, it is almost as though Alḍāhirī's two protagonists are in collusion. Well before each has identified himself to the other, Mordecai greets the physician with "Peace unto you, O greatest of doctors," and Abner replies, "Peace unto you, O craftiest of schemers" (*shalom ʿalekha, abir ha-rofʾim … shalom ʿalekha, abir ha-mezimah*), suggesting that he recognizes from the outset that Mordecai is no ordinary supplicant but a kindred spirit and willing conspirator. Mordecai does not expose Abner's ruse but rather connives with him, and both profit handsomely from the doctor's show of eloquence. Yet, we are given sufficient hints of Abner's imposture to make us wary of taking anything he says too seriously. When the narrator first espies the elderly man at the center of the teeming town square, his chosen phrase, *ve-huʾ maḥaziq ʿaṣmo le-rofeʾ* ("he posed as a doctor") should already give us pause.[68] (The same locution, with its suggestion of inauthenticity, is used by Immanuel of his persona's stint as a court physician in his chapter headed, "The Facetious Remedy."[69]) If this is not enough to arouse our suspicions, Mordecai adds the rhyming phrase, *ve-laʿatidot ṣofeh*: Abner is also a soothsayer, as becomes apparent in the latter half of our *maqāma*, where he answers a query about the end of days.

Impostures employing a combination of scientific and occult medicine are a hallmark of the Hebrew and Arabic rhymed prose narrative. Such "medical pluralism" reflects the use of popular talismanic and amuletic remedies alongside more learned approaches to medicine in medieval Islamic and Jewish societies.[70] Abner's facility with amulets and spells comes to the fore in Chapter Nineteen where, as noted, Alḍāhirī produces a Judaized version of the tale of quackery in al-Ḥarīrī's 39th *maqāma*, "Of ʿOmān."[71] Following a shipwreck while sailing from Hormuz to India, Abner washes up on an island where, to

68 *Sefer hamusar*, p. 365, lines 7–8.

69 See Immanuel Ha-romi, *Maḥbarot*, p. 195, line 1.

70 See Pormann and Savage-Smith, *Medieval Islamic Medicine*, 144–161 ("Popular Medicine"); Dori, *Traditional Medicine among the Yemenite Jews*, vol. 1; Madar and Raiany, *Nutrition and Popular Remedy*; Muchawsky-Schnapper, "Healing through Medicinal Plants"; Lev, "Eastern Mediterranean Pharmacology and India Trade as a Background for Yemeni Medieval Medicinal Plants"; and Qāfiḥ, *Halikhot teiman*, 349–353.

71 See Ratzaby, "The Influence of al-Ḥariri Upon Alḍāhiri", esp. 70–77.

meet his dire need for provisions, he presents himself as an expert in invocations. With great fanfare and claiming to be armed with a remedy "from Aristotle," he writes amulets and whispers incantations over an elixir compounded from myrrh, saffron, and frankincense in order to ease the lady of the palace through a difficult delivery. He inscribes an old gourd with Exodus 11:8, a verse commonly used in amulets to lighten childbirth. Taken from the story of Moses and Pharaoh in Egypt, the verse includes the phrase, "Depart [from Egypt], you and all the people who follow you." In the original Hebrew, "the people who follow you" literally reads "and the people at your feet," which was understood as an incantation for safe delivery, (i.e., to get out safely from between the legs of the woman giving birth).[72] Abner also cleverly plays with the plain sense of Psalm 58:4 ("The wicked are estranged from the womb"). His exaggerated ministrations and magical remedies are efficacious, and the baby is safely delivered. Triumphantly he declares, "On that day I resembled Samuel and Isaiah, Elisha and Eliyah." Abner's resounding success earns him extravagant rewards of jewels and finery from the grateful lord of the palace while members of the royal retinue surround him and kiss his hands.[73]

In the thirty-second *maqāma*, too, Abner's remedies, which culminate in the nostrum he prescribes for Mordecai, earn him a lavish reward from his credulous onlookers. Insofar as it adheres to the standard pattern of employing brilliant verbal skills for personal gain, Abner's ethical cure for sins is ever so slightly tainted, even if it is Mordecai who provides him with the pretext for issuing it. There is a sublime irony in the fact that advocating abstemiousness and self-restraint earns him a material, gustatorily satisfying reward, not to mention admiration and acclaim. Even Abner's seemingly serious use of clothing metaphors is freighted with irony: while he recommends that Mordecai replace the garb of faithlessness and desire with that of righteousness and moderation, he himself masks reality by wearing the disguise of one who occupies the moral high ground. At first blush, then, Abner simply appears to dispense sound ethical advice in an elevated, somewhat oblique fashion, in conformity with an established literary tradition. Nevertheless, a closer look suggests that

72 See Sabar, "Childbirth and Magic: Jewish Folklore and Material Culture," 670 and 673 and Schrire, *Hebrew Magic Amulets*, p. 132, no. 52. On amulets and whispered spells, see also Qāfiḥ, *Halikhot teiman*, 353–364. For an insightful analysis of the blurred religious boundaries that characterize these occult traditions, see Fogel, "'They Have Countless Books of This Craft.'"

73 *Sefer hamusar*, pp. 223–224. Al-Ḥarīrī's original winks at the sham by having Abū Zayd inscribe his efficacious amulet not with Qur'anic verses but with a poem warning the unborn child of the evils awaiting it in the world.

the therapy he recommends, with its florid, figurative turns of phrase and calculated outcome, results in part from ulterior motives of a worldly nature.[74]

As always, there is a sense that Abner's rhetorical mastery lends weight to what otherwise might be a less compelling performance. When he cautions Mordecai not to alter one word of his prescription, he is presumably keen to preserve the force and integrity of his choice locutions as much as the potency of his potion. Mordecai replies that he will do everything he is told, provided that the healer not try him or conceal anything from him. Of course, Abner obscures his identity and in the end is only given away by his incantatory prowess: *va-avin ba'areshet sefatav ve-laḥasho/ ki hu avner ben ḥeleq be-ṣurato ve-tavnito*.[75] Moreover, the use of riddling metaphor serves as a link between the ethical cure Abner proposes and his veiled messianic prognostications in the latter half of the chapter, where he is hesitant to accede to an urgent request to predict the duration of the exile, and, ironically, Mordecai counsels him to speak in enigmatic terms. Here, too, we are told that Abner's scintillating poems and parables earn him the boundless esteem of his listeners, who beg him to accept their gifts.

7 Sham Preachers and Moral Ambiguities

If *musar* as both felicitous expression and moral instruction animates Abner's pretense to medical knowledge, the combination of persuasive rhetoric and castigation is even more pronounced in his appearance as a preacher who delivers a moralistic admonition to renounce worldly desires in preparation for the world to come. Mendicant preachers who sermonized to impromptu popular audiences became a fixture of the *maqāma* genre already with al-Hamadhānī. On the surface, their exhortations invoked recognizable Scriptural and theological motifs, but a closer look could reveal questionable doctrine, the effect of which was often satirical.[76] In the frame story to Alḍāhirī's eleventh *maqāma*, which is strikingly similar to that of Chapter 32, Mordecai reports flatly, though perhaps not without a touch of self-mockery, that he longed to hear words of rebuke so that he might be saved from the pit and become a man

74 Medieval Jewish ethical literature often warns against adopting a pious or abstemious lifestyle in order to win acclaim rather than out of genuine devotion; see, e.g., Baḥya Ibn Paquda, *Hidāya*, 1:10, p. 91, and 5:5, p. 261.

75 *Sefer hamusar*, p. 365, lines 14–16; p. 367, line 40.

76 See Young, "Preachers and Poets: The Popular Sermon in the Andalusī *Maqāma*" and Kilito, *Les Séances*, 57–59.

of honorable character. His soul would “walk in the paths of *musar*” until he became habituated to comporting himself uprightly. One day, while dwelling in his city of Sidon, preoccupied with keeping his distance from evil men, Mordecai noticed groups of penitents rushing to hear a fire-and-brimstone preacher from the land of Yemen whose spellbinding oratory had earned him great repute. Galvanized by the opportunity to purge his soul of dross, the eager narrator elbows his way into the innermost circle of spectators where he discerns an elderly man in tattered clothes delivering a rousing exhortation to repentance in prose and verse. This scenario, right down to the narrator’s determination to secure the best seat in the house, is typical *maqāma* fare; al-Ḥarīrī’s 50th *maqāma* opens with the narrator al-Ḥārith ibn Hammām hastening to the main mosque of Basra, where he espies a man in tattered clothes perched on an elevated stone, around whom throngs were crowded. “Therefore I hasted in his direction and sought access to him, hoping to find with him the cure of my disease, and I ceased not shifting places, heedless of knocks and blows, until I was seated opposite to him ....”[77] The Yemeni preacher’s themes are familiar; he draws upon the common repertoire of Jewish and Islamic pietistic and wisdom literature, particularly the *zuhd* motif of *dhamm al-dunyā*—the censure of the mundane world and its vanities. He denounces the compulsion to amass worldly goods that have no value in the grave, rebukes his listeners for thinking they can escape death and ultimate reckoning, and reminds them—alluding to Avot 2:1—that God sees, hears, and records their deeds:[78]

> Son of man, why do you yearn for what is harmful, but keep away from what is useful? ... You do not heed rebuke, you do not shed a tear from fear of punishment; you frequent sinners while scorning modest, wise men; all your days you have drowned in the sea of foolishness and folly ... you labor to amass belongings old and new that in the end will only go to your heirs ... perhaps you think that death can be bribed and that you will escape his sharp sword ... I swear by the beloved Lord that death wants neither silver nor gold .... Happy is he who heeds my words and takes to heart my proverbs and epigrams, and knows that [there is above you] an eye that sees and an ear that hears, whether deed or speech or thought.[79]

77 See al-Ḥarīrī, *The Assemblies*, 2:176.

78 Avot 2:1: “Apply your mind to three things and you will not come into the clutches of sin: Know what there is above you: an eye that sees, an ear that hears, and all your deeds are written in a book.”

79 Awakening “from the sleep of negligence and the slumber of foolishness” is a recurrent metaphor in medieval evocations of the purification and illumination of the soul; see the

These chidings are followed by a confession that he himself has suffered affliction as punishment for sin, but even so there is a vestige of venality in his words:

> Accept these words without charge from him who has acquired them with his heart's blood. For how many troubles have afflicted me because I did not act properly. I have become an example for the many … take me as a sign, it should suffice you that I have sunk appallingly. Take reproof from me now (*ve-attah kaḥ musar mimenni*), before you seek me and find I am gone.[80]

Taking these warnings to heart, the audience resolves to repent and banish backsliding from their midst; feverishly they rebuke one another and confess their sins. But when the preacher rises and returns home with his companions, his façade of humility crumbles as he boasts about the success of his sermon (*va-yitga'eh lifnei ḥaverav/ eikh ho'ilu devarav*). The narrator, having pursued him, now discovers that he is none other than Abner ben Ḥeleq who, although prematurely aged due to his imprisonment by the Muslim authorities, elicits identification with no less a prophet than Moses: "His eyes were undimmed and his vigor unabated" (cf. Deuteronomy 34:7). At the same time, the intertext suggests that Abner is essentially unchanged and therefore unrepentant. The allusion is so misplaced that it has an ironic effect. The narrator's closing remark to his friend indulges in a similarly over-the-top comparison with biblical prophets known for their censure of the ungodly: "Blessed is He who sent you to sustain us; we shall have no further need for Isaiah and Jeremiah."[81]

Apart from his preacherly pretense, Abner does not engage in any discernible ruse in the eleventh *maqāma*, much like Alḥarizi's sermonizer in the Second Gate of the *Taḥkemoni*. He also receives no reward for his performance, yet al-Ḥarīrī's paradigm of the preacher unmasked as a hypocrite is so pervasive that it hovers in the background of all such scenarios.[82] In *Sefer hamusar*, there are subtle ironies that undercut the force of Abner's jeremiad. While he

---

famous passage from Epistle Twenty-Seven of the Ikhwān al-Ṣafā' cited by Isaac Israeli in Altmann and Stern, *Isaac Israeli*, 186. In his Judeo-Arabic commentary on Canticles, Joseph Ibn Aqnin writes that "excellent moral qualities protect the soul from drowning in her desires and from neglecting to acquire wisdom"; see Ibn Aqnin, *Hitgalut ha-sodot ve-hofa'at ha-me'orot*, 364–365. There are numerous similarities between this admonition and that delivered by Abū Zayd in al-Ḥarīrī's first *maqāma*, "Of Ṣana'ā"; see *The Assemblies* 1:108–112.

80 *Sefer hamusar*, p. 158–159, lines 15–29.

81 *Sefer hamusar*, p. 163, l. 109.

82 See Segal, *The Book of Taḥkemoni*, p. 434.

admonishes his listeners for their worldly preoccupations, warns against self-indulgence, and offers his wisdom freely, the fact that he presses them to accept his counsel without charge suggests that he would have preferred to be compensated. He urges his addressees to be conscious of their mortality and to repent while there is still time, yet he himself is an inveterate scoundrel who has only confronted his own misdeeds now that he has grown old and has been beset by cruel forces beyond his control. Abner's complaint of oppression at the hands of wicked men, or *zeidim*—another oblique reference to the Zaydis—adds pathos to his plight but does not alter the fact that his repentance is too little too late.[83] That the frame of this chapter is virtually interchangeable with that of Chapter 32—crowds rush to see an elderly stranger with a reputation for honeyed speech and the ability to cure the body or the soul—implies that the penitent persona Abner adopts here is no more authentic than his pose as a physician, or indeed any of the other identities that he assumes and sheds throughout *Sefer hamusar*. The ambiguity surrounding his contrition immediately calls to mind the questions raised by Abū Zayd's ostensibly genuine repentance in al-Ḥarīrī's fiftieth and final episode. Before crowds of worshipers in the Grand Mosque of Basra, Abū Zayd confesses his transgressions and hopes for divine forgiveness. As Monroe points out, Abū Zayd says he does not want the Basrans' money, just their intercessory prayers. Nevertheless, in the end he accepts their gifts and returns to his hometown where he retires from public life and becomes an *imām* at public expense. Though the narrator suspects that the performance in the mosque is yet one more instance of the hero's sham religiosity, he is won over when he discovers that Abū Zayd has returned to his native city of Sarūj and has taken on a life of devotion and asceticism. Though Abū Zayd is not unmasked in this culminating episode, modern scholars have questioned the sincerity of his conversion, noting the profound irony of a final scriptural allusion, and the incongruity—given all that has come before—of his renunciation of everything that he once held dear.[84]

The tensions between Abner's preaching, which demands (and prompts in his audience) an ethical response, and his frequent duplicity heighten the sense of moral conflict that was considered to inhere in the *maqāma* genre as a

83 On the allusion to the Zaydīs, see *Sefer hamusar*, p. 163, n. 103.

84 See: Kilito, "Foreword" to *al-Ḥarīrī, Impostures*, xiv; Cooperson, *Impostures*, 481–482; Kennedy, *Recognition in the Arabic Narrative Tradition*, 303–306; and Monroe, *The Art of Badīʿ az-Zamān al-Hamadhānī*, 77–85. By contrast, Raymond Scheindlin argues in "Ḥever the Pious" that Ḥever's religiosity is sincere; on the Second Gate of the *Taḥkemoni* see pp. 285–287 and Segal, *The Book of Taḥkemoni*, 433–437.

whole.[85] Abdelfattah Kilito has explored the dissimulation and fiction that figure in al-Ḥarīrī's *Maqāmāt* not just as elements of the plot but also in the rogue-hero's enigmatic narrative techniques and deliberately obscure style.[86] He calls attention to al-Ḥarīrī's anticipatory apology, which attempts to neutralize the accusation that his *Maqāmāt* contravene the Law. In their defense, al-Ḥarīrī asserts that his tales are intended to be didactic, in the manner of exempla or fables. Kilito, however, points out that, throughout his peregrinations, al-Ḥarīrī's protagonist passes for what he is not and dazzles his audiences with untrue stories.[87] At the same time, he delivers edifying discourses and periodically conducts himself as a man of integrity, and, in any case, his unacceptable comportment is counterbalanced by that of the narrator, who for the most part behaves irreproachably.[88] According to Kilito, al-Ḥarīrī's analogy between the *maqāma* and fables or exempla does not take account of the function of each type of narrative or of the educational nature of the two genres. A fable does not require interpretation; one is explicit in the form of the tale's moral. On the other hand, narrative literature demands interpretation in order to ferret out some universal truth from a series of events that otherwise seem unique. By accentuating the didacticism of his work, al-Ḥarīrī obscures its inherent ambiguity and imposture, which result not only from the protagonist's morally suspect behavior but also from the author's "dissimulating his voice by transferring it to his characters who acquire, through this trickery, an autonomy and a presence that are not different from those of real beings." By not speaking in his own name, and attributing his speech to someone else, the author engages in a kind of imposture, which speaks to the very nature of fiction.[89]

In a similar vein, Alḍāhirī's decision to set philosophical theories and ethical ideals—regarding the soul, sin, repentance, and ultimate reward—in the mouth of a character of dubious moral standing also creates a kind of dissonance. While a modern reader might puzzle over the inclination to insert such subject matter into a mostly fictional framework, one need only recall that philosophical and ethical materials are embedded in the Hebrew *maqāmāt* that served Alḍāhirī as models, and that his stated intent in composing *Sefer hamusar* was to offer moral guidance and spiritual edification, which he achieved by means of a narrative accessible to a broad readership.[90] Alḍāhirī

85 See *Sefer hamusar*, 9 and Beaumont, "The Trickster and Rhetoric in the *Maqāmāt*."
86 Kilito, *Les Séances*, 248–259 ("Le menteur professionel").
87 Ibid., 259.
88 Ibid., 249.
89 Ibid., 251.
90 This is not meant to imply that Alḍāhirī held a view of the *maqāma* comparable in its util-

was clearly preoccupied with the ultimate purpose and soteriology of the soul, regardless of who delivered the message. Repudiation of the material world in order to purify the soul, observance of the commandments, and immersion in philosophical or kabbalistic study are repeatedly emphasized as the only paths to eternal reward, which is in turn the only true consolation for sufferings at the hands of cruel oppressors. Long naturalized within Yemenite Jewish learned culture, and part of Alḍāhirī's own universe of discourse, philosophical and ethical topics would have spoken to the different sectors of his audience according to their capacity to make sense of the material. Intellectually sophisticated readers could see the value in the perfection of one's soul, whose refinement is essential to the acquisition of virtues and the knowledge of God, man's highest goal, according to the philosophers. Nevertheless, even without complete command of the technical literature, one could be moved by the theatricality of these vignettes—by a compelling sermon accompanied by suitable gestures or a hortatory poem whose resounding recitation urged one to repent of one's sins in order to attain the world to come. At the same time, readers from varied walks of life and degrees of urbanity could appreciate the humor in Abner's convincing impostures and comical missteps. Although Alḍāhirī's didacticism was genuine enough, his impulse to refract the ethical and spiritual notions that he valued through the lens of a morally compromised character was a function of using an inviting narrative form to popularize weighty ideas. Additionally, Abner's reorientation of the curricular focus in Karo's *yeshivah* from halakhic learning to philosophical exposition has ramifications for Yemenite Jewish self-definition. By embedding Abner's philosophical oration in the Safed Sephardi institution that had elicited from the Yemenite characters such self-doubt and feelings of intellectual inferiority, Alḍāhirī allows his protagonist to play to his strong suit. We should not underestimate the authorial sleight of hand and picaresque setting that enabled Alḍāhirī—much like medieval poems of argument and counter-argument—to instruct and perhaps reassure his readers, and at the very same time to destabilize his didactic material, transforming it into a source of sheer enjoyment.

---

itarianism to that of Shem Tov Falaquera (13th c.), who favored rhymed prose primarily for its readability and mnemonic value and utility in popularizing technical and speculative ideas. For a remark to this effect, see the preface to his didactic poem on the proper maintenance of a healthy body, *Battei hanhagat guf ha-bari'*, 3.

CHAPTER 6

A Conduit for Kabbalah: Belles-Lettres as a Medium for Mysticism

Sefer hamusar offers a fascinating window onto the transmission of kabbalistic thought to Yemen some 300 years after the emergence of early kabbalah in Europe. Firmly belletristic in nature, Alḍāhirī's *maqāma* is nonetheless, as the previous chapter illustrated, a rich repository of intellectual history. Through its vignettes and poems, the work provides evidence of intellectual trends that resonated in 16th-century Yemenite Jewish scholarship. If Alḍāhirī's literary tastes tend toward the classicizing, favoring medieval Hebrew prosodic forms and the picaresque *maqāma* as conceived in the eleventh century, his integration of kabbalistic ideas represents a bold new departure. It is the contention of this chapter that he used the lighthearted belletristic framework of *Sefer hamusar* to bring kabbalistic theosophy, literature, and liturgical customs to the attention of a largely uninitiated public in Yemen. In much the same way that he integrated highly technical philosophical ideas, he could make arcane mystical material seem less formidable to the reader unschooled in kabbalistic thought by embedding it in entertaining, fictionalized frame stories. Just as he did with the cosmology and psychology of the philosophical tradition, Alḍāhirī puts his mystical teachings into the mouths of his two fictional characters whose sometimes fraught relationship with the truth yields a complicated dynamic of doctrinal transmission. Their advocacy of theosophical ideas is woven into such an intricate narrative mesh that, on occasion, Alḍāhirī seems to question the very enterprise of communicating rarified teachings to a less restricted, more inclusive audience. In one of his tales, his narrator and hero convert erstwhile proponents of discretion in matters of kabbalah into enthusiasts of openly recited kabbalistic verse by plying them with sumptuous foods and dazzling them with feats of poetic virtuosity, for which Abner is handsomely rewarded. By highlighting the protagonists' ulterior motives and poking fun at their unsuspecting victims' ready change of heart, Alḍāhirī conveys a subtle authorial ambivalence towards the project of popularizing kabbalistic ideas through poetry and belles-lettres. This uncertainty, which has gone undetected in the secondary literature, finds a metapoetic corollary in Alḍāhirī's critique of his poetic medium, which surfaces in those episodes devoted to kabbalah.

This chapter is divided into six sections: (I) a synopsis of the kabbalistically informed *maqāmat* in *Sefer hamusar*; (II) an examination of Alḍāhirī's role as a

 | DOI:10.1163/9789004733787_008

conduit for kabbalistic learning and its reception in Yemen; (III) an assessment of his relationship to Lurianic kabbalah and the poetry of the Safed mystics; (IV) a discussion of the salient kabbalistic themes in *Sefer hamusar* and the concomitant critique of poetry; (V) an exploration of the effect of, and possible motivations for, integrating such mystical material into a decidedly belletristic context; and (VI) conclusions.

1 The Kabbalistic Chapters

The places in which Alḍāhirī's protagonists join or initiate kabbalistic study are ancient cities that form something of a geographic triangle: Bursa in northwestern Anatolia, Irbīl in northeastern Iraq (Kurdistan), and Tiberias in the Galilee. Bursa, the main capital of the Ottoman state in the 14th century, became one of the international centers of the silk trade and was an important emporium of Eastern goods for Istanbul and the Balkans until the 17th century. It had a small Romaniot community from Byzantine times and absorbed an influx of Sephardi exiles in the first half of the 16th century.[1] Irbīl was home to a Jewish community from late Second Temple times and a central junction on the trade route from the Far East to Turkey and thence to Europe. Tiberias, on the western shore of the Sea of Galilee, loomed large in Jewish sacred history from antiquity. In close proximity to Safed with its silk and wool industry and vibrant halakhic and mystical circles, Tiberias was briefly revitalized as a Jewish city in the 1560's.[2] Though the stories told in the kabbalistic chapters are clearly fictional, their settings are not randomly chosen. Trade routes were conduits for the dissemination of books, the transmission of knowledge, and the channeling of religious learning and practices. During the Ottoman period, Bursa's Jews were entrenched in the local and regional economy as shopkeepers, textile workers, guild members and merchants, many of whom imported Persian silk. Evidence for the transmission of kabbalistic knowledge to 16th-century Bursa can be found in *Agudat ezov*, a little-known commentary on the liturgy compiled by Isaac ha-Ezobi, who dates himself to the reign of Suleiman

1 See: Bornstein-Makovetsky, "Bursa (Prousa)" and "Textile Manufacture and Trade"; Çizakça, "A Short History of the Bursa Silk Industry (1500–1900)"; Inalcik, "Bursa"; idem, "Bursa and the Commerce of the Levant"; and Gerber, *Crossing Borders: Jews and Muslims in Ottoman Law, Economy, and Society*, 65–92.

2 See: Sabar, "Arbil" and Avitsur, "Safed—Center of the Manufacture of Woven Woolens in the Fifteenth Century." On Jewish settlement in Tiberias during the 1560's, see *Sefer hamusar*, 31–32; David, *To Come to the Land*, 29–33; Braslavsky, "Jewish Settlement in Tiberias from Don Joseph Nasi to Ibn Yaish"; and Yaari, *Sheluḥei ereṣ yisra'el*, 256–261.

the Magnificent and recounts that he moved to Bursa from Constantinople. Quite a few of his acknowledged kabbalistic sources are the same pre-Lurianic works available to Alḍāhirī: the *Zohar, Maʿarekhet ha-elohut*, Gikatilla's *Shaʿarei orah*, and Ibn Gabbai's *Tolaʿat yaʿaqov*. Preserved primarily in manuscripts of Yemenite provenance, *Agudat ezov* circulated widely in Yemen, providing an additional impetus for the penetration of kabbalah into the liturgy, which was generally one of the areas of Jewish life most resistant to change.[3] Kurdistan, too, was a site of kabbalistic activity. Eliezer Baumgarten has documented the transfer to Kurdistan of visual kabbalistic knowledge in the form of arboreal diagrams from Italy in the late 16th and early 17th centuries. The Jewish communities of Kurdistan had extensive ties with those of Safed and Damascus, and in the late 16th and early 17th centuries benefited from the educational efforts of Rabbi Samuel Barzani, a rabbinic scholar and kabbalist who founded a yeshiva in Mosul where he trained a cohort of scholars (including his learned daughter and successor, Asenath) who went on to teach elsewhere in the region.[4]

In the fanciful account of Alḍāhirī's third *maqāma*, Mordecai journeys from Baghdad to Irbīl in the hopes of a hospitable reception from the local Jewish community following some unpleasant encounters with coreligionists living along the Tigris River. Having recuperated sufficiently from the strains of the road in a pleasantly furnished rented room, he ventures into the marketplace where he comes upon a group of Jewish men of all ages engaged in sacred study. Mordecai approaches them and is received with warmth and deference. Their conversation ranges over a variety of disciplines, exoteric and esoteric, and culminates in an expansive discussion of theosophical kabbalah that encompasses the *sefirot*, or ten aspects of divinity; their cosmic actions; the names associated with them; and the "limbs"—presumably of the primordial man or *adam qadmon*—to which the various divine hypostases correspond.[5] Suddenly, one of the company rises and everyone grows silent. Wearing an absurdly

3 See Hallamish, "Ha-qabbalah be-sidduro shel rabbi yiṣḥaq wanneh." *Agudat ezov* is cited by Wanneh in his liturgical commentary *Ḥiddushin*, and by Yiḥye Ṣāliḥ in his *Tiklāl eṣ ḥayyim*; see Ratzaby, "Agudat ezov: ḥibbur bilti nodaʿ," and Ben-Shalom ed., *Sefer agudat ezov*.

4 See Baumgarten et al., "'See the Entire World Resembling a Ladder': Rabbi Yehoshua ben Rabbi David of Kurdistan's Kabbalistic Tree" and Baumgarten, "From Kurdistan to Baghdad: The Transfer of Visual Knowledge during the Early Modern Period." On Samuel Barzani and his daughter, see Melammed and Melammed, "Rabbi Asnat: A Female Yeshiva Director in Kurdistan" and Benayahu, "Rabbi Samuel Barzani, Leader of Kurdistan Jewry." On the Jewish communities of Kurdistan see Mann, *Texts and Studies* 1:477–549; Brauer, *The Jews of Kurdistan*; and Sabar, *The Folk Literature of Kurdistani Jews*.

5 See *Sefer hamusar*, 77–78. On the notion that the emanation of the *sefirot* assumes the form of *adam qadmon* or primordial man see Scholem, *Major Trends in Jewish Mysticism*, 265–267; Idel, *Kabbalah: New Perspectives*, 119; idem, "Kabbalah," 628, 642, and 645; Ginsburg, *The*

bloated turban, he challenges anyone from the group to compose a poem about this kabbalistic wisdom that would incorporate the names and order of the ten *sefirot* "up to *Ein sof*, the Cause of all Causes."[6] He promises to host a lavish repast in honor of the successful candidate—an offer that appeals greatly to his audience. But the group expresses grave reservations about openly celebrating such esoteric matters when they have traditionally been transmitted orally and cautiously and only by the elders of the community. The man calling for the composition is visibly impatient with their inhibition and so Mordecai steps in, dismissing their concerns with a laugh and offering with bravado to recite the requisite poem. His opening line, "Yedidi im tivḥar le-havin sod zohar/ʿamod na va-shaḥar le-shaʿar haʾorah" ("Friend, if the *Zohar*'s mystery you choose to master/rise at dawn to seek the gate of light"), states that the mysteries of the *Zohar* (Book of Splendor, 1280–1286; in actuality an anthology or composite text that only later became a "book") can best be comprehended through study of Joseph Gikatilla's *Shaʿarei orah* (Gates of Light, c. 1290), an influential commentary on the ten *sefirot* and their symbolism.[7] Mordecai's piece names the *sefirot* from lowest to highest as they appear in *Shaʿarei orah* and intersperses divine names and limbs associated with them.[8] When he is done, the others rejoice and retire to the home of the man who issued the challenge. There, at the promised banquet, Mordecai and the host are assigned the task of entertainment, and the other guests, having undergone a rapid conversion, now request a poem in praise of the *Zohar*. The host accedes with an alphabetic acrostic, whose opening line may be read as an appeal to village-dwelling Jews across Yemen's craggy highland terrain: "Ishim eqra me-har el har/ boʾu limdu sefer zohar" ("O men, from mountain to mountain I call to you: Come and study the *Zohar*!"). Sermonic in tone, the poem urges its addressees to seek out the

---

Sabbath in the Classical Kabbalah, 28–30; and Wolfson, *Language, Eros, Being*, 35, 154, and 508–509, n. 244.

6 *Ein sof* is the ineffable aspect of the godhead. The epithet *ʿillat ha-ʿillot* ("The Cause of Causes") derives from the medieval philosophical tradition, on which the thirteenth-century kabbalists freely drew. See, e.g., Wolfson, *Through a Speculum That Shines*, 288–306.

7 On the composite nature and multiple authorship of the *Zohar*, see Liebes, "How the Zohar Was Written." On the development of Gikatilla's thought see, e.g., Yadin, "Theosophy and Kabbalistic Writing" and Huss, "R. Joseph Gikatilla's Definition of Symbolism and Its Versions in Kabbalistic Literature." See also Chajes, "The Kabbalistic Tree."

8 Ratzaby notes that "Yedidi im tivḥar le-havin sod zohar" is to this day sung by Jews of Yemenite descent as a *nashid*, a genre of poem performed at social gatherings on the Sabbath. On the *nashid*, see Ratzaby, *Shirat Temān Haʿivrit*, 25–26. The poem is listed without attribution in Davidson, *Thesaurus*, 2:280, #481. A strophic poem on the ten *sefirot* ascribed to Alḍāhirī ("Yedidi veneh bamah ramah") is found in ms. Guenzburg 1306 and is printed in Idelsohn and Torczyner *Shirei teiman*, pp. 28–30, no. 16.

mysteries of the *Zohar*, called the True Path, for through such study the initiate grows wise and avoids sin. It commends an esoteric method of explaining the rationale for the commandments of the Torah (*ṭaʿamei miṣvot ha-neʿelamot*) and affirms that metempsychosis affects male souls only, a view propounded by Isaac Luria's principal apostle, Hayyim Vital, in his *Sefer ha-gilgulim*.[9]

On the strength of this performance, Mordecai recognizes the host as his old crony, the generally roguish Abner ben Ḥeleq the Yemenite. Since the anagnorisis occurs relatively early in the episode, the two protagonists conceal their identities from the others, who are astonished by Abner's display of rhetorical brilliance and theosophical profundity. Several of the guests request additional poetic feats of Abner, who complies and is showered with generous rewards, in conformity with the typical *maqāma* pattern. Then, without warning, Abner turns pensive and reveals that the Sages considered the art of poetry to be insignificant. The great sciences, he insists, entail the cognition of the intelligibles, and it is the kabbalists who occupy the first rank in the kingdom of knowledge and understanding, and who attain eternal reward. He goes on to describe the kabbalists' Paradise and lament his own sufferings in one exile after another. After reiterating these thoughts in verse, the chapter veers away from anything to do with mysticism and soon concludes.

Kabbalistic themes only resurface in earnest in the twenty-first chapter of *Sefer hamusar* even though the sixth chapter is set in the Safed *yeshivah* of the renowned mystic and legal scholar, Joseph Karo.[10] Chapter 21 unfolds in Bursa, which was no stranger to Islamic or Jewish mysticism or esotericist discourses, quite apart from the presence of Isaac ha-Ezobi. In the 15th century, the city was home to a ramified network of Sufi mystics and Islamic scholars of the occult sciences who shared an interest in millenarian speculation. As noted, it attracted Isaac ha-Ezobi in the 16th century and, following Safed's economic decline at the start of the 17th century, it was one of the places Isaac Luria's disciples chose to resettle in order to carry on his kabbalistic teachings.[11] It is

9 For Vital's position, which was not unanimously endorsed, see Hallamish, *An Introduction to the Kabbalah*, 283. There is, of course, no way of ascertaining Alḍāhirī's immediate source for this notion. The idea that metempsychosis is exclusive to male souls should be considered vis-à-vis Elliot Wolfson's argument that "ostensibly female images are valenced as masculine in the androcentric culture of the Kabbalists." See *Language, Eros, Being*; "Occultation of the Feminine and the Body of Secrecy in Medieval Kabbalah"; and "Coronation of the Sabbath Bride." On kabbalistic approaches to the significance of the commandments, see Wolfson, *Abraham Abulafia—Kabbalist and Prophet*, 186–228.

10 As we have seen, the episode set in Karo's *yeshivah* skews heavily toward the philosophical.

11 See Gardiner, "Forbidden Knowledge? Notes on the Production, Transmission, and Reception of the Major Works of Aḥmad al-Būnī," 117; idem, "Esotericist Reading Communities

probably no coincidence that in Bursa Abner appears as a prognosticator who, unbidden, concludes an otherwise unobjectionable poem in praise of the 14th-century Spanish halakhist, Jeroham ben Meshullam, with a prediction of the Messiah's imminent arrival in 1579 or, "if he tarries," 1585.[12] Both chronograms are configured as millenarian anticipations of Jewish sovereignty: השל״ט (1579) encapsulates the Hebrew root signifying rulership, and שיל״ה (1585) alludes to Genesis 49:10, "the scepter shall not depart from Judah ... until Shiloh come," a crux of interreligious polemic that had long been read messianically.[13] Ratzaby sees the Yemenite Jewish predilection for messianic prognostication as a response to persecution and observes that Alḍāhirī gives no fewer than six different dates for the end of days. But his messianism should also be viewed in its broader historical, geopolitical, and religious contexts.[14] Sixteenth-century millenarian expectations among Christians, Muslims, and Jews were fueled by the upheavals of imperial struggles for global rule; the battles between Ottoman Muslims and European Christians were viewed in apocalyptic terms.[15] In this context, the sudden appearance on the scene of the charismatic poseur David Reuveni, making claims of Jewish royalty and descent from the ten lost tribes, fed Jewish messianic fervor; Reuveni visited Safed in the 1520's, predicting that the Redemption would occur in 1540. Jews in Italy—for whom the 1550's burning of the Talmud and burning at the stake of conversos heightened the sense of apocalypticism—identified 1575 (של״ה—Shilo spelled defectively without the *yod*) as the year of Redemption.[16]

Having sufficiently alarmed his (Jewish) audience by venturing into such religiously delicate and potentially explosive territory, Abner—now viewed as something of a clairvoyant—is inundated with requests for dream interpretation, medical cures, and solutions to intractable problems. His responses

---

and the Early Circulation of the Sufi Occultist Aḥmad al-Būnī's Works"; and Hacker, "Jews in the Ottoman Empire (1580–1839)," 856.

12 On R. Jeroham see Galinsky and Robinson, "Rabbi Jeruham b. Meshullam, Michael Scot, and the Development of Jewish Law in Fourteenth-Century Spain."

13 For polemical use of this verse by Muslim authors, see Schmidtke, "Biblical Predictions of the Prophet Muḥammad among the Zaydīs of Yemen."

14 Ratzaby, *Sefer hamusar*, 36–37. On 17th-century Yemeni Jewish messianism in its Zaydī context, see Hathaway, "The Mawzaʿ Exile at the Juncture of Zaydi and Ottoman Messianism," 111. On the 19th century, see Klorman, "Jewish and Muslim Messianism in Yemen," and idem, "Muslim Supporters of Jewish Messiahs in Yemen."

15 See, e.g., Yerushalmi, "Messianic Impulses in Joseph ha-Kohen" and Jacobs, "Joseph ha-Kohen, Paolo Giovio, and Sixteenth-Century Historiography."

16 See Verskin, *Diary of a Black Jewish Messiah*, 1–29 *passim*; Yassif, *The Legend of Safed*, 231–239; Paz, "Holy Inhabitants of a Holy City"; Tamar, "The Messianic Expectations in Italy for the year 1575"; and idem, "Isaac Luria and Ḥayim Vital as the Messiah Son of Joseph."

duly impress his unsuspecting, charitable questioners who, again, in typical *maqāma* fashion, are so taken in by his seemingly unlimited knowledge and smooth speech that they reward him with endless praises and a sumptuous feast. One guest who has fallen under his spell—"The hapless fall prey to his might" (Psalm 10:10)—asks him to decode seven riddle poems, three of which are apparently translations from Arabic originals. Abner proceeds to transpose all seven into pure biblical Hebrew, after which he reveals their solutions. Once again, he is honored and remunerated for his keen intelligence. It is worth noting that, in the episode's opening frame story, when the group wants to commission a panegyric for Rabbenu Jeroham, Mordecai promotes Abner's outstanding talent and urges them to seek him out to fulfill the task. This simple referral earns Mordecai bounteous compensation. After traveling for several months, during which he is said to have gone to Greater Constantinople and is sighted in Prèveza, Abner makes his grand entrance to Bursa and instructs Mordecai to announce that all requests for poems must be accompanied by offerings. His imperiousness suggests that he is planning to give the locals a good run for their money. But after he has improvised the panegyric and dispatched the riddle poems, he does a volte-face:

> When Abner considered their fine recompense, and saw that his thoughts were like a well-watered garden, he said to them, "My lords, if you will heed my voice, and respect my words, know that all that was just said in these previous poems is a vain waste of effort and time …"

He urges abandoning such trivial fare—which serves only to sharpen the intellect and hone a shrewd ingenuity—in order to probe that which is truly worthy of investigation: the nature of the *summum bonum*. Using rabbinic terms, he identifies this weighty and enigmatic matter as man's reward in the world to come. Abner cautions, however, that one must speak of such eschatological truths only in veiled and esoteric fashion, lest they be exposed to the intellectually unsophisticated. Those whose intellects are refined can make do with Maimonidean "chapter headings" (*ve'im yitbonen bo gibbor ba'anaqim, yaspiqu lo rashei feraqim*); they will understand of their own accord.[17] But for the benefit of the masses, he will employ a parable comparing these ethereal truths to tangible things. He tells them that by this they shall be put to the test; if they grasp his intentions, they will be considered wise and will be freed of the bonds of this world. "For that is the ultimate goal of the human intellect." He

17 Cf. Pines trans., *Moses Maimonides: The Guide of the Perplexed*, Introduction, p. 7.

then recites a riddling poem comparing this world to grapes and the world to come to wine. When pressed by Mordecai to interpret his mysterious verses, Abner demurs that this is not the place to expand upon such arcana, but for a fuller exposition he should consult Abner's work entitled *Ṣeidah la-derekh* (Provision for the Road), on the verse beginning *va-yekhullu ha-shamayim* (Genesis 2:1). "Then you will don the cloak of humility ... on whose hem are a golden bell and a pomegranate [i.e., marginalia that will unlock] the secret of the primeval light."[18] *Sefer ṣeidah la-derekh* is, of course, Alḍāhirī's own esoteric Torah commentary, which, in a somewhat rambling excursus on Genesis 2:1–3 (the verses prefaced to the blessing over the wine on Sabbath eve) develops the parable further. There the analogy hinges on man's inability to imagine the rewards of the world to come while still in this life. Alḍāhirī suggests that this is like someone who does not recognize the vine plant when he sees it denuded in winter and therefore, when given grapes, cannot believe that they are the fruit of this plant until summer arrives and he actually sees the laden vine.[19] In light of Abner's textual cross-reference, Mordecai requests a poem in praise of *Ṣeidah la-derekh* and Abner readily complies. Mordecai relates that upon hearing Abner's verses, the audience marveled at his brilliance, saying, "Surely this is a man of God." Some of them were frightened and astounded by his eloquence. Some bestowed him with festive garments while others donated small decorative purses filled with pearls. Then he took his leave.[20]

Alḍāhirī's interest in kabbalah manifests itself again two chapters later even though the two independent episodes are otherwise unconnected as far as setting, plot line, or narrative are concerned. In the 23rd *maqāma*, Mordecai journeys to Tiberias in search of that city's renowned sages. When he reaches the town center, he asks a lad where he can find the seven "good men" of the community and is directed to the *yeshivah*, which is in the city's eastern sector, on the outer side of the city wall on the shore of the Sea of Galilee.[21] There he beholds a group of venerable elders, "the glory of the Jews," who are masters of

18 Cf. the description of the High Priest's garments in Ex. 28:34. The metaphor was also used by the kabbalist Isaac Wanneh in naming his marginal commentary on the prayer book he compiled; see below.

19 See Alḍāhirī, *Sefer ṣeidah la-derekh* on Gen. 2:1. See also Mansur, *Shiṭato ha-parshanit shel rabbi yiḥye al-ḍāhirī*.

20 See *Sefer hamusar*, pp. 239–252. Note that there is no evident kabbalistic symbolism in the poem praising *Ṣeidah la-derekh* and only the most general allusions to esoteric wisdom.

21 "Seven good men": *shiv'ah tovei ha'ir*; a rabbinic locution for seven men who acted as representatives of the town in communal matters. Cf. bMeg 26a–27a and Maimonides, MT *Hilkhot Tefillah* 11:17.

Scripture and Mishnah.[22] Some of these esteemed scholars are authorities in Talmud and legal reasoning while others are steeped in theoretical kabbalah, and some are impressively accomplished in all these disciplines. Mordecai is assailed by terror, for by comparison he is "a dolt without knowledge." As in Safed, he seats himself self-effacingly at the edge of the famed *yeshivah* in the hopes of absorbing some fraction of its collective wisdom.

Following the *minḥah* prayer, all those present hasten to immerse themselves in the hot springs of Tiberias, as it is the eve of the Sabbath.[23] Mordecai returns from his ablutions to find the house of worship suitably prepared to usher in the Sabbath, illuminated by candles and oil lamps. The head of the *yeshivah* arrives and sits in his place of honor. When he recites *Ba-meh madliqin* (Mishnah Shabbat chapter 2), even though he is already aged, the congregation trembles at the sound of his voice. Then the *sheliaḥ ṣibbur*, or precentor, mounts the pulpit "like a mighty lion upon a wooden tower constructed for that purpose" and recites the *Shemaʿ* and its accompanying benedictions, glorifying the Sabbath with his melodious singing. Having completed his mellifluous chanting of Psalm 23, he recites "Liqrat penei shabbat asis veʾagilah" ("I greet the Sabbath with joy and delight"), a strophic poem of his own devising that betrays an esoteric view of the Sabbath and bears resemblance to Solomon Alqabeṣ' kabbalistic hymn "Lekhah dodi" and similar poems that were known to have circulated in Safed and its environs in the 16th century.[24] On the basis of the composition's rich store of ideas and dulcet rendering, Mordecai realizes that the *ḥazzan* is none other than his old friend and kindred soul, Abner ben Ḥeleq

22 During the Safed revival of the mid-16th century, kabbalistic rituals of reciting mishnaic passages were introduced; see Idel, "Some Concepts of Mishnah among Sixteenth-Century Safedian Kabbalists" and Fine, "Recitation of Mishnah as a Vehicle for Mystical Inspiration."

23 Ritual immersion on Friday afternoon was favored by the kabbalists of nearby Safed. According to Hayyim Vital, as practiced by his teacher, Isaac Luria, immersion served to remove the weekday "husks" (*qelipot*), which are the mundane garments of the human soul; see his *Shaʿar ha-kavvanot, ʿinyan leyl shishi*. See also Ginsburg, *The Sabbath in the Classical Kabbalah*, 227–231 and the sources cited in Hallamish, *Kabbalah: In Liturgy, Halakhah and Customs*, p. 316, n. 189. Ratzaby writes that most members of the Tiberias *yeshivah* had relocated there from Safed, which suggests that their traditions were informed by the innovative customs and rituals of the Safed kabbalists; see *Sefer hamusar*, 31–32.

24 For "Liqrat penei shabbat," see Davidson, *Thesaurus*, 3:63, #1369 (no attribution) and supplements 4:326, #1369 (attributed to Alḍāhirī). Alqabeṣ' "Lekhah dodi" was incorporated into the *tiklāl* by R. Isaac Wanneh in the 17th century; see Ratzaby, *Bemʿagloth Temān*, 75. On similar poems see Kimelman, *The Mystical Meaning of Lekhah Dodi and Kabbalat Shabbat*, 23–25; Kaunfer, "The History and Meaning of the 'Other' 'Lekha Dodi' Poem(s)"; and Ratzaby, "Lekha dodi shel ha-mequbbal rabbi shelomo alqabeṣ u-meqorotav."

the Yemenite, who appears to be guided by the spirit of God. After an emotional reunion, the two repair to Abner's well-appointed home for a generous meal during which the elated host recites a poem that, like "Liqrat penei shabbat," reflects the multifaceted kabbalistic vision of the Sabbath as a marriage ceremony within the divine realms, the central point of the week, and a day of spiritual regeneration on which the individual is blessed with an additional Sabbath-soul.[25] Opening with the words, "Matoq le-miṣuf u-fannag/ mul ṣur ve-libbo khe-donag" ("His poem is sweeter than honeycomb/ but fear of God melts his heart") and closing with a Judeo-Arabic *envoi*, the poem advocates study of the *Zohar* and meditation on the ten *sefirot*.

When Abner is done declaiming his poem, Mordecai asks in amazement how his friend has penetrated this mystical, esoteric wisdom. Abner attributes his expertise to assiduous study of two formative works: (1) the anonymous *Sefer ma'arekhet ha-elohut* (The Structure of the Godhead), an influential treatise most likely composed in Barcelona (c. 1300) that attempted to systematize the theory of the *sefirot* and was one of the most widely read kabbalistic works until the mid-16th century, and (2) one of its classical commentaries from the late 15th century, *Minḥat yehudah*, by the prominent kabbalist and Spanish exile Judah Ḥayyāṭ,who migrated via North Africa to Italy.[26] Then he adds,

> had I not held fast to this knowledge, I would have descended in grief to my grave. [Kabbalah] is what raises man from death to eternal life; without it, man would not be distinct from beast.[27] It is the reason for the soul's immortality; in its company the soul finds rest and repose.

He reveals that he has composed a poem in praise of *Sefer ha-ma'arekhet* (as he styles it), and proceeds to recite twelve monorhymed lines that exploit the kabbalistic conceit of the ten *sefirot* as a cosmic tree. The piece urges the reader

---

25 See Ginsburg, *The Sabbath in the Classical Kabbalah*, 59 and Scholem, *On the Kabbalah and Its Symbolism*, 139. For the view that the coronation of the Sabbath queen is not a sacred marriage, but rather a gender transformation of the *Shekhinah*, see Wolfson, "Coronation of the Sabbath Bride."

26 On these works, see Idel, "*Sefer Ma'arekhet ha-'Elohut* and its Reverberations" and idem, *Kabbalah in Italy, 1280–1510*. Idel notes that several of the Spanish kabbalists in Italy shared "a deep interest in the nature of the *Sefirot* ... whether they are the essence of the divine or only the instruments or vessels for divine activity" and that Ḥayyaṭ rejected the philosophical interpretation of kabbalah fashionable in Italy at that time in both Jewish and Christian circles; see "Spanish Kabbalah after the Expulsion," 169 and 173–174 and "Encounters Between Spanish and Italian Kabbalists in the Generation of the Expulsion," 199–206.

27 Man would not be distinct from beast: lit., "wildcats shall meet hyenas"; cf. Is. 34:14.

to probe *Sefer ha-maʿarekhet* well and to eat and drink deeply of Judah Ḥayyāṭ's "choice offering blended with its wine."[28] Mordecai then inquires about Abraham Saba's kabbalistically informed commentary on the Pentateuch, *Ṣeror ha-mor* (A Bundle of Myrrh), whose study Judah Ḥayyaṭ had advocated.[29] This elicits a pained reminiscence of how in his youth, Abner had purchased a copy of Saba's work at great expense but was then imprisoned, along with his coreligionists in Yemen, by the Muslim authorities. Base men commandeered his home and confiscated the precious book. While incarcerated, he several times sent an emissary to redeem the captive volume but to no avail.[30] He then recites a poem composed during his internment that praises *Ṣeror ha-mor*. The chapter ends with the sad story of his eldest son's lack of filial piety and Abner's defiant account of how, with his Arabic-inflected Hebrew, he came to be appointed *ḥazzan* in the synagogue of the patrician Sephardim of Tiberias.

2 Alḍāhirī as a Conduit for Kabbalistic Learning and Its Reception in Yemen

Kabbalistic thought, which first emerged in Provence and Catalonia in the late 12th and early 13th centuries, soon spread to Castile and then to the Land of Israel in the second half of the 13th century, to the Byzantine Empire in the 14th century and to Italy, North Africa, and the Holy Land following the Expulsion from Spain and the arrival of large numbers of exiles in the lands of the Ottoman Empire, which conquered Mamlūk Palestine in 1516–1517. Each of these centers had its own history and trajectory of development, in large measure due to culturally specific factors that affected its reception and interpreta-

28 "Asher shat malkhuto ʿalei khol mamlekhet" ("He whose kingship is above all kingdoms"), see *Sefer hamusar*, 267. On the *sefirot* as a cosmic tree, see Ginsburg, *The Sabbath in the Classical Kabbalah*, 28–30 and Scholem, *Major Trends*, 214–215. Arboreal diagrams of the ten *sefirot* were included in kabbalistic mss. from the late 13th century on. The metaphor and schematic representation were gradually conflated; see Chajes, "The Kabbalistic Tree as Material Text"; idem, "The Kabbalistic Tree"; idem, "Spheres, *Sefirot*, and the Imaginal Astronomical Discourse of Classical Kabbalah"; and idem, "Imaginative Thinking with a Lurianic Diagram."

29 Saba was also an exile from Spain who then spent five years in Portugal before being expelled to North Africa. See Gross, *Iberian Jewry from Twilight to Dawn: The World of Rabbi Abraham Saba*. On *Ṣeror ha-mor* see especially pp. 40–93.

30 The forger Moses Shapira (c. 1830–1884), in his account of his 1879 visit to Yemen in search of manuscripts, recounts that in the early 19th century Yemeni "nomade tribes" [*sic*] plundered Jewish books, knowing that Jews would pay ransom; see Fenton, "Moses Shapira's Journey to the Yemen," p. lxxiii and n. 16.

tion of kabbalistic materials.[31] The Galilean city of Safed began to flower in the 1530's and 1540's, attracting a redoubtable group of kabbalists and halakhists. Joseph Karo (1488–1575), Solomon Alqabeṣ (1505–c. 1576), Moses Cordovero (1522–1570), Eleazar Azikri (1533–1600), Moses Alsheikh (c. 1508–1594), and the charismatic master Isaac Luria (1534–1572) founded or joined pious confraternities given over to mystical speculation, repentance, and prayer. Central to the kabbalistic doctrine that assumed its most influential form in its Lurianic version was the idea that human deeds have cosmic repercussions. A life of piety, therefore, could help to restore the original unity of the divine realm, which had been ruptured through human sin. To this end, the Safed circles of masters and disciples produced a series of mystically informed ethical treatises and religious manuals (*hanhagot*) that mandated new rituals, such as midnight vigils (*tiqqunei ḥaṣot*) dedicated to study, prayer, repentance, lamenting the destruction of the Temple, and mourning the exile of the *Shekhinah*, which in turn created a need for new devotional texts and poems. The kabbalists also introduced mystical meditations to ensure the proper intention during prayer (*kavvanot*), and the ceremony of going out to greet the Sabbath bride. These practices and additions to the prayerbook were rapidly disseminated throughout the wider Jewish community of Safed and beyond, inaugurating a potent popular spirituality.[32]

Kabbalah began taking root in Yemen only during the late 16th and early 17th centuries, largely spurred by the appearance in print of the *Zohar* and other kabbalistic works.[33] The kabbalistic books brought to Yemen by emissaries

31 See the methodological considerations outlined by Idel for studying the emergence and development of these distinct centers of Kabbalah in his "Jewish Mysticism Among the Jews of Arab/Moslem Lands." There was differentiation among the Sephardi kabbalists who settled in Safed following the Ottoman Conquest, coming as they did "from Turkey, Salonica and Adrianople, where they had formed groups of their own and had developed their own ways of devotion"; see Benayahu, "Devotion Practices of the Kabbalists of Safed in Meron."

32 See, e.g., Fine, "Pietistic Customs from Safed"; idem trans., *Safed Spirituality: Rules of Mystical Piety, The Beginning of Wisdom*, 1–80 *passim*; Werblowsky, "A Collection of Prayers and Devotional Compositions by Solomon Alkabets"; Pachter, "Kabbalistic Ethical Literature in Sixteenth-Century Safed"; Meroz, "Spiritual Life in 16th Century Safed"; and Shalem, *Rabbi Moshe Alsheikh*, 22–23, and 73–84. For precursors to the Safed kabbalists' midnight rituals see Wolfson, *Through a Speculum That Shines*, 373–392 and idem, "Forms of Visionary Ascent as Ecstatic Experience in the Zoharic Literature."

33 See Bar-Maoz, "Hishtarshut ha-qabbalah be-teiman"; Baumgarten, "Kabbalah and Printing"; Yaakov, *Eloha mi-teiman yavo*; and Ratzaby, *Bem'agloth Temān*, 77. The first editions printed in Mantua (1558–1560) and Cremona (1559–1560) solidified perceptions of the *Zohar*'s composite text as a "book" and contributed to its canonization; see Huss, *The*

from the Land of Israel and by European Jewish merchants were primarily printed in Italy, a center of kabbalistic activity and Hebrew printing for domestic use as well as export.[34] They comprised classics of Spanish kabbalah like those mentioned in *Sefer hamusar*. Though Alḍāhirī does not mention by name texts of Safedian kabbalah, it seems that at least some of the 16th-century innovations of the Safed kabbalists were transmitted to Yemen during this period. Moshe Hallamish argues that openness to the imported kabbalistic treatises would likely not have been as great without the enthusiastic endorsement of Alḍāhirī, who was a living conduit for kabbalistic learning and whose personal efforts to secure a foothold for kabbalah in Yemen left a lasting impression.[35] Although scholarship on the early stages of kabbalistic activity and modes of reception in Yemen is scanty due to a lack of documentation, the consensus is that Alḍāhirī greatly facilitated the transmission of kabbalistic ideas and texts to his native land. Identifying Alḍāhirī with the fictional characters at the heart of *Sefer hamusar*, modern scholars have assumed that the author visited Safed in the second half of the 16th century, precisely when it was the center of the great mystical revival. Alḍāhirī is said to have met illustrious kabbalists and celebrated poets associated with their circles, although there is no concrete evidence to this effect.

In particular, Alḍāhirī's engagement with the Safed kabbalists and their works has been inferred from the story of the *shadar* Rabbi Abraham ben Isaac Ashkenazi who came to Yemen with a consignment of sacred books. Based on the composite of Chapters 24, 25, and 40 of *Sefer hamusar*, Abraham Yaari identified Rabbi Abraham as a historical figure based in Safed. In *Hebrew Printing in the East*, Yaari says that Abraham Ashkenazi provided the funding and venue for the itinerant printer Eliezer ben Isaac Ashkenazi (no relation), who came to Safed from Lublin in the last quarter of the 16th century and established the first Hebrew press in the region.[36] In his article on emissaries to Yemen from the Land of Israel, he calls Rabbi Abraham Ashkenazi the "printer" in whose home Eliezer Ashkenazi's press was established.[37] An eight year hiatus in the operations of the press is attributed not only to Eliezer Ashkenazi's

Zohar: Reception and Impact; Abrams, "The Invention of the Zohar as a Book"; and Tishby, *The Wisdom of the Zohar*, 1:97–99.

34 See Baruchson-Arbib, "On the Trade in Hebrew Books Between Italy and the Ottoman Empire during the 16th Century."

35 See Hallamish ed., *The Kabbalah in Yemen at the Beginning of the Seventeenth Century*, 9–10.

36 Yaari, *Ha-defus ha'ivri be'arṣot ha-mizraḥ*, 1:10–11.

37 Yaari, "Sheliḥim me'ereṣ yisra'el le-teiman," 403–404.

sojourn in Constantinople, but also—based exclusively on the testimony of *Sefer hamusar*—to R. Abraham's book-selling/fund-raising mission to Yemen. The reconstructed identity and chronology are rehearsed in additional works by Yaari on booklore and emissaries from the Holy Land.[38] Yaari speculated that on his charitable mission, R. Abraham sold the titles printed in Safed in the first years of the press there: three works of biblical exegesis by the Safed scholars Yom Tov Ṣahalon, Moses Galante, and Samuel Aripul, together with other Hebrew books printed outside of the Land of Israel as a supplementary source of income.[39] (According to Yaari, Ashkenazi's press closed after printing the second set of three books in 1587, including two collections of poems by Israel Najara, after which there was no Hebrew press in the Land of Israel until the mid-19th century.) Yaari's claim, perpetuated still in recent scholarship, that Alḍāhirī met key members of the Safed kabbalistic elite and that he returned from the Galilee with kabbalistic texts is derived via inference from a series of juxtapositions in the elegant letter of praise that Abner sends to R. Abraham in the 25th *maqāma*. There Abner relates that his own wanderings had taken him

> to Safed and Tiberias where the members of a distinguished class were to be found .... Chief among them were the sages Rabbi Joseph Karo, Rabbi Moses di Trani and Rabbi Moses Cordovero the kabbalist.[40]

That Alḍāhirī knew of these eminences is clear, but the mere mention of these historical figures has been deemed sufficient to suggest a personal encounter. When, several lines further on, Abner mentions that he had sailed home from the Land of Israel with a few precious books, some of which were lamentably lost to storms at sea, the conjecture is that his haul included kabbalistic texts, even though not one of the replacement titles he requests from the learned envoy is a kabbalistic work. In the absence of any autobiographical testimonies or other corroborating evidence, the reader is left to steer a course between the competing claims of fictionality and the author's delicate insinuation of his own personal narrative into the story. Where the details are relatively spare, there is a danger of reading too much into the text. Speculations regarding

---

38 See Yaari, *Meḥqerei sefer*, 163–164 and idem, *Sheluḥei ʾereṣ yisraʾel*, 77–78, 256–258. See also Assaf, "The Selling of Hebrew Books in Yemen Through Envoys from Palestine."

39 On these works, see also Habermann, *Toldot ha-defus bi-ṣfat*. For brief biographies of Galante and Ṣahalon, see David, *To Come to the Land*, 166 and 171–172. On Aripul, see Berenbaum and Skolnik eds., "Aripul, Samuel ben Isaac." On the literary exchanges between Ṣahalon and the poet Israel Najara, see Mirsky, "New Poems of R. Israel Nagara," 261–262.

40 See *Sefer hamusar*, 287, lines 40–42.

Alḍāhirī's encounters with leading Safed kabbalists recur throughout the scholarly literature, and with repetition they have tended to lose any tentative formulations to become certainties.[41]

These reservations aside, there is no denying Alḍāhirī's obvious receptivity to kabbalah or his patent desire to bring its mystical spirituality, distinctive literature, and innovative ritual practices to the attention of a wider audience in Yemen. Nor is *Sefer hamusar* the only evidence for his preoccupation with kabbalah: moved by *Keter Malkhut* with its sublime praise for God and exposition of Neoplatonic cosmology, he composed a short poem on the ten *sefirot*, whose incipit signals its intertextual relationship to Ibn Gabirol's monumental hymn by reworking the beginning of its 30th canto.[42] Alḍāhirī's poem was inserted *en bloc* into the text of *Keter Malkhut* in Yemenite prayer books (*takālil*) from the 18th and possibly even the 17th century, and in Yemenite liturgical practice the two were (and are) recited together on Yom Kippur.[43] The opening line underscores the limits of human apprehension: "*Adonai mi yagiʿa ʿad takhlit ḥokhmatekha/ meʾod ʿamqu maḥshevotekha*" ("My Lord, who can attain the limits of Your wisdom? How profound are Your thoughts.")[44] Alḍāhirī praises God as the source of the ten *sefirot* as elaborated in classical kabbalah and delineates the descending *sefirot* from highest to lowest, tracing God's "flowering

41 See, e.g., Ratzaby, *Sefer hamusar*, 43: *hu zakhah le-vaqqer biṣfat … ve-la-daʿat et isheha: kordovero, alqabeṣ ve-najara*; ibid., p. 210, n. 166; Hallamish, *The Kabbalah in Yemen*, 10; Bar-Maoz, "Hishtarshut ha-qabbalah be-teiman," 90; Tobi, "Nusaḥ ha-tefillah shel yehudei teiman," 29; idem, "Rabbi yiṣḥaq wannah ve-hitḥazzqut ha-ʿissuq ba-qabbalah," 18; idem, "Seder ba-ashmoret ha-boqer le-rabbi yiḥye al-ḍāhirī"; Yaari, *Massaʿot ereṣ yisrael*, 198; and Gaimani, *Temurot be-moreshet yahadut teiman*, 69. See also Baumgarten, "Kabbalah and Printing in Yemen"; idem, "From Kurdistan to Baghdad," 82; and Baumgarten, Safrai and Chajes, "'See the Entire World Resembling a Ladder,'" 846–847.

42 30th canto: *Adonai mi yagiʿa le-ḥokhmatekha, be-titekha la-nefesh koaḥ ha-deʿah, asher bah tequʿah?* ("My Lord, who can reach Your wisdom, in giving the soul the faculty of knowledge, which is fixed in her, so that knowledge is her glory, and decay has no rule over her … the wise soul is not subject to death.") It seems that the choice was not random: in the 30th Canto, Ibn Gabirol sets out a philosophical conception of purgatory that complements his spiritualized interpretation of ultimate reward in the 27th Canto. He specifies that his remarks pertain to the rational soul, whose capacity for reason renders her immortal. If tainted by sin at the conclusion of her earthly sojourn, this highest of souls must undergo an ordeal "more bitter than death." Only so will she be purged of her impurities and made fit to "approach the sanctuary," that is, to take her place in the world to come.

43 Ms. Jerusalem Krupp 5076.19, a fragment of a *tiklāl* dated to the 17th or 18th century, includes instructions for the *sheliaḥ ṣibbur* to recite Alḍāhirī's piyyut when he reaches the insertion point and then to continue with the rest of *Keter Malkhut*.

44 *Meʾod ʿamqu maḥshevotekha*: cf. Ps. 92:6. For the text with commentary by Yiḥye Ṣāliḥ, see *Tiklāl eṣ ḥayyim*, Part II, 3:109–110.

into the cosmos" and thereby reversing *Keter Malkhut*'s upward progression.[45] It is clear that he saw an affinity between the Neoplatonic emanationist scheme of *Keter Malkhut* and the kabbalistic doctrine he was attempting to convey to his Yemenite audience. By interweaving his kabbalistic verses into Ibn Gabirol's capacious poem, Alḍāhirī suggests that his is an analogous, albeit far more modest, attempt to evoke a cosmogony that mediates between the metaphysical and the acutely physical. In his "Bereishit qedumat yomayyim," a *piyyut* on the ten *sefirot* intended to embellish the Friday night *qiddush*, Alḍāhirī identifies the process of emanation with the six days of creation.[46] His esoteric commentary on the Pentateuch, *Sefer ṣeidah la-derekh*, is suffused with theosophical notions drawn from classical kabbalah. In his introduction to that work, Alḍāhirī acknowledges as his principal sources "the words of the divine *Zohar* of Rabbi Simeon ben Yoḥai …, and of the author[s] of the *Maʿarekhet*, and of *Shaʿarei orah*."[47] This bibliography dovetails closely with the titles that Alḍāhirī's invented characters single out as influential in the 3rd and 23rd chapters of *Sefer hamusar*. Ratzaby confirms that, alongside the *Zohar*, the kabbalistic books that had the greatest impact in Yemen were those squarely within the medieval Spanish tradition, which indeed represented the majority of kabbalistic books printed in the 16th century: *Maʿarekhet ha-elohut*, Gikatilla's *Shaʿarei orah*, and *Tolaʿat yaʿaqov* of Meir Ibn Gabbai (1480/81-after 1543), a Spanish kabbalist and synthesizer of classical kabbalah who settled in the Ottoman Empire after the Expulsion.[48] The effect of these works can be gauged from their frequent citation in kabbalistic writings of Yemenite provenance, as well as the many extant Yemenite manuscript copies made from printed editions of these texts.[49]

45 See Ginsburg, *The Sabbath in the Classical Kabbalah*, 24.

46 See Tobi, "Seder qiddush leilei shabbat le-rabbi zechariah al-ḍāhirī." Tobi transcribed the poem from a privately held ms.; it also appears in ms. Guenzburg 1306.

47 See *Tāj ʿim perushim ḥamishah ḥumshei torah*, vol. 1, Author's Introduction, p. 10. He also cites *Sefer yeṣirah*, Saba's *Ṣeror ha-mor*, and Ḥayyaṭ's *Minḥat yehuda*, alongside works from the geonic-Andalusian philosophical tradition, particularly Maimonides' rationalistic *magnum opus*, *The Guide of the Perplexed*.

48 See also Idel, "Printing Kabbalah in Sixteenth-Century Italy." It is useful to compare this bibliography with the list of recommended books in the index compiled by Judah Ḥayyaṭ in the introduction to his *Minḥat yehuda*; see Idel, ibid., 88–89 and *Kabbalah in Italy*, 219–220. On Ibn Gabbai's life and works, see Goetschel, *Meir Ibn Gabbay: le Discours de la Kabbale Espagnole*. Ibn Gabbai's *Tolaʿat yaʿaqov* (1507) is a handbook for mystical meditation in prayer; for a translation of the portion devoted to the Sabbath see Ginsburg, *Sod ha-Shabbat*.

49 See Ratzaby, *Bemʿagloth Temān*, 77 and Yaakov, *Eloha mi-teiman yavo*, 86.

Hebrew printing certainly played a role in the reception of kabbalah in Yemen and elsewhere, even though the number of kabbalistic books in print in the 16th century was quite small relative to other branches of Jewish literature. First editions of many of these works appeared during the 16th century.[50] Alongside formative kabbalistic texts from the 13th through 15th centuries, new works became available to a broader reading public relatively soon after their composition. Moshe Idel has remarked that the increased use of the printing press contributed directly to the surge in kabbalistic creativity among Spanish Jewish exiles anxious to preserve and systematize their inherited mystical traditions following the Expulsion.[51] While oral teachings were already committed to writing in some form, printing made manuscripts of kabbalistic texts more accessible.[52] And although Yemenite Jewish manuscript culture persisted long after the rest of Jewish world had switched to printed books, the 16th-century proliferation of Hebrew printing and dissemination of Hebrew books helped in no small measure to shape Alḍāhirī's intellectual development and foster his fascination with kabbalah.[53]

As one of the first scholars to introduce kabbalistic teachings and texts to his native land, Alḍāhirī was implicated by 20th-century anti-kabbalists in the erosion of Yemenite Jewry's earlier rationalist tradition. During the bitter 20th-century controversy in Ṣanaʿā over the legitimacy of kabbalah, Rabbi Yiḥye Qāfiḥ, a leading anti-kabbalist and founder of the reformist *Dor Deʿah* movement, wrote in his *Milḥamot hashem* (The Wars of the Lord) that

> the faith in this new, alien kabbalah was first introduced to Yemen by means of the books that arrived during Rabbi Yiḥye Ḍāhirī's day. Prior to this there had never even been a kabbalist engaged in oral transmission of esoteric traditions in Yemen (*u-meʿolam lo nimṣa be-teiman ish mequbbal mi-peh el peh*), and the books of our ancient sages attest to this.[54]

50 See Ratzaby, *Sefer hamusar*, p. 266, n. 94 and Idel, "Spanish Kabbalah After the Expulsion," p. 169, n. 8.

51 Idel, ibid., 168–169. On the impact of printing on the conception and reception of kabbalistic ideas, see also Idel, "Printing Kabbalah in Sixteenth-Century Italy"; Baumgarten, "God as a Printer"; and idem, "Kabbalah and Printing in Yemen."

52 On the nature of the esoteric in kabbalah and the relationship between the oral and the written, see Wolfson, "Beyond the Spoken Word."

53 No works of Yemenite Jewish authors were printed anywhere until the middle of the 19th century, when a series of works were printed in Calcutta and Jerusalem.; see Yaari, *Hebrew Printing in the East*, 1: 86–87.

54 I.e., there had never even been a kabbalist handing down secret traditions orally, much less

Despite the categorical nature of Qāfiḥ's accusation, however, Alḍāhirī's efforts were not wholly unprecedented. A handful of late 15th- to early 17th-century Yemenite works informed by kabbalah have come to light, although the corpus of extant printed and manuscript texts is still too modest to permit a comprehensive account. These writings are by no means uniform in genre: in addition to Alḍāhirī's picaresque *maqāma* and commentary on the Pentateuch, the assemblage includes rhymed prose exempla, theoretical handbooks, and liturgical texts. Taken together, they testify to the existence of a small core of authors committed to presenting the rudiments of classical kabbalah to a largely uninformed reading public even when, in the late 16th century, Lurianic kabbalah was already leaving its singular stamp on piety and spirituality elsewhere in the Jewish world.[55] Yosef Tobi has detected the kabbalistic belief in metempsychosis in a rhymed prose cautionary tale for ritual slaughterers entitled *Mashal ʿal ha-tarnegol* (Parable of the Rooster), which he has ascribed to the late 15th-century poet and exegete David ben Yeshaʿ ʿAdani Halevi.[56] Moshe Hallamish counts five kabbalists active in Yemen at the beginning of the 17th century who are known to us by name. His edition of *Sefer segulloth* by Shalom ben Joseph Haqorḥi and *Sefer leḥem shelomo* by Solomon ben David Hakohen reveals a preliminary stage of kabbalistic awareness in which Yemenite authors produced didactic, anthologizing works with the express purpose of consolidating and distilling "precious kabbalistic secrets" found in the sources at their disposal, so

by means of printed books. See Qāfiḥ, *Milḥamot hashem*, 114 (cited in Tobi, "Rabbi Yitzhaq Wanneh," 17). See also Ratzaby, "Le-toldot ha-maḥloket ʿal ha-qabbalah bikhillat ṣanaʿa"; idem, "*Dardeʿim: minhagim u-massorot*"; Sharʿaby, "Peraqim mi-parashat ʿdor deʿahʾ be-teiman"; Wagner, "Jewish Mysticism on Trial in a Muslim Court"; and idem, *Jews and Islamic Law in Early 20th-Century Yemen*, 83–90. Qāfiḥ's antipathy to kabbalah and desire to reinstate the primacy of the medieval rationalist tradition and liturgical guidelines of Saadya Gaon and Maimonides were reinforced by his exposure to the orientalist Joseph Halévy's (1827–1917) fierce animus toward mysticism and the occult, and subsequent encounters with Eduard Glaser (1855–1908), a European Jewish explorer and Arabist who encouraged Qāfiḥ's interest in science. See Verskin, *A Vision of Yemen*, 53–54 and Klorman, *Traditional Society in Transition*, 30–31.

55 See Hallamish, *The Kabbalah in Yemen*, 9 and Tobi, "Rabbi Yiṣḥaq Wanneh," p. 21 and n. 21.

56 See Tobi, "Iggeret haman u-mashal ʿal ha-tarnegol" and idem, "Rabbi David ben Yeshaʿ ha-Levi." See also Tanenbaum, "Hidden Gems: The Hebrew *Maqāma* from Yemen." Elsewhere, Tobi notes that the earliest citations of the *Zohar* in Yemenite manuscripts are found in the commentary of Abraham ben Solomon on the books of the Prophets, which dates from the end of the 14th or beginning of the 15th century, but he also concedes that the Yemenite provenance of this work has been called into question. See Tobi, "Rabbi Yitzhaq Wanneh," 18.

that even readers with minimal background or no access to kabbalistic books would have access to the rarefied world of the *sefirot*, angelology, and the transmigration of souls.[57]

By the mid-seventeenth century, there were two circles of kabbalists in Yemen, one in the southern Sharʿab region and the other in the central Ṣanaʿā region.[58] Shalom ben Joseph Haqorḥi and Solomon ben David Hakohen were prominent in the Ṣanaʿā circle, as was Hakohen's disciple, Isaac ben Abraham Wanneh. Wanneh, whose precise dates are not known but who is thought to have died after the Mawzaʿ exile of 1679, played a decisive role in the dissemination of kabbalah. He was a professional scribe who produced different versions of his prayer book, *Paʿamon zahav ve-rimmon*, and the first Yemenite sage to compose a commentary encompassing the entire *tiklāl*.[59] Wanneh's audaciousness is evident in his replacement of time-honored liturgical formulae and practices with variants derived from the *Zohar* and works of Spanish kabbalah and his recourse to the legal determinations of Karo's *Shulḥan ʿarukh*, which effectively supplanted earlier Yemenite tradition based on Maimonides' laws of prayer. A century later, such ruptures provoked a controversy of considerable asperity over the authority of the *Shulḥan ʿarukh* that was particularly acute in Ṣanaʿā.[60] While Alḍāhirī helped to prepare the ground for such consequential departures and was clearly conversant with the Sephardi rite—in *Ṣeidah la-derekh* he outlines the morning blessings and prayers "as they are in the *siddur* of the Sephardim"—these critical changes only acquired authoritative status with Wanneh's *tiklāl*, particularly in its later recensions.[61]

Most of the scholarly literature suggests that all the communities in Yemen adhered to the original *baladī* (i.e., local) rite of their ancestors until the 17th century, when the increased availability and relative affordability of printed

57 See Hallamish, *The Kabbalah in Yemen*, 9–36, 42–55 and idem, "Rabbi shalom ha-qorḥi ve-rabbi shelomo hakohen." See also Bar-Maoz, "Hishtarshut ha-qabbalah be-teiman."

58 See Tobi, *The Jews of Yemen*, 54 and Wagner, "Arabic Influence on Shabazian Poetry in Yemen."

59 The later recensions are more heavily kabbalistic than the earlier ones, although Wanneh's manuscripts were also copied by other scribes who saw fit to make their own emendations in keeping with local custom. See Hallamish, "Ha-qabbalah be-sidduro shel rabbi yiṣhaq wanneh" and Giat, "The Linguistic Stratum in Rabbi Isaac Wanneh's Commentary on the *Seliḥot*." See also Ratzaby, "ʿIyyunim be-hitpatḥut maḥzor teiman"; idem, *Bemʿagloth Temān*, 74–81; Gavra, "Le-foʿalo shel rabbi yiṣhaq wanneh be-sidduro ʿpaʿamon zahavʾ"; and Tobi, "Rabbi Yitzhaq Wanneh."

60 See Hallamish, "Ha-qabbalah be-sidduro shel rabbi yiṣhaq wanneh," 68–70.

61 See Gaimani, *Temurot be-moreshet yahadut teiman*, 71; Hallamish, "Ha-qabbalah be-sidduro shel rabbi yiṣhaq wanneh," 66–67; Ratzaby, "ʿIyyunim be-hitpatḥut maḥzor teiman"; and Gavra, "Le-toldot nusaḥ ha-baladi ve-ha shāmi."

prayer books (in a society that relied on costly manuscripts), the advent of the *Shulḥan ʿarukh*, and the innovations of Wanneh's *tiklāl* led to the widespread adoption of the Sephardi (*shāmī*) rite of the Palestinian kabbalists. However, Moshe Gavra has detailed a much more complicated reception history of the Sephardi rites and customs disseminated via the printed Palestinian prayer books, which varied according to a given community's proximity to or distance from Ṣanaʿā.[62] Efraim Yaakov argues for the centrality of oral tradition in any reconstruction of the life of Jewish communities in the East, and postulates that there were other, now-forgotten Yemenite kabbalists who were influential in ensuring that kabbalah took root in their local communities, but who have disappeared because they taught orally and did not leave any written works. Lamenting our inability to identify not only these unnamed kabbalists but also the regions in which they were active, as well as the kabbalistically inflected religious customs they may have observed, Yaakov notes that all of these lacunae complicate the narrative of the spread of kabbalah in Yemen.[63] In addition, he remarks that the printed books that flooded Yemen included all sorts of texts, which were not uniformly disseminated, giving rise to cultural disparities not only on the regional level but even between one village and the next, such that no two synagogues followed identical liturgies.[64]

3 Alḍāhirī's Relationship to Lurianic Kabbalah and the Poetry of the Safed Mystics

There is no consensus in the scholarly literature about the variety of kabbalah that informs Alḍāhirī's writings. Most 19th- and 20th-century studies describe the author of *Sefer hamusar* as the first to import "the kabbalah of Safed" to Yemen without specifying whether what is meant is Lurianic or pre-Lurianic

62 He also argues that the use of the terms *baladī* and *shāmī* to distinguish between different strains in Yemenite liturgical usage is of relatively recent vintage, emerging only in Yemenite prayer books printed in Israel following the massive *ʿaliyah* of the Yemenite Jews in 1949–1950, and that a principal source for this terminological distinction was R. Amram Qoraḥ, the last chief rabbi of Ṣanaʿā prior to the *ʿaliyah*. Even Yiḥye Ṣāliḥ, considered the "founder" of the *baladī* rite, did not use that term in his *tiklāl* in the second half of the 18th century. See Gavra, "Le-toldot nusaḥ ha-baladi ve-ha shāmi."

63 Yaakov, *Eloha mi-teiman yavo*, 23–35 and 58–59.

64 Yaakov notes that shrewd merchants, once they discovered the Jewish population's enthusiasm for printed books, directed all sorts of volumes toward them, whether requested or not, so that Yemen effectively became a repository for Jewish texts. For his perspective on the impact of printed books, see *Eloha mi-teiman yavo*, 85–99.

mysticism or some amalgam of different systems. Much of the discussion hangs on the precise dates of Alḍāhirī's presumptive stay in Safed, which cannot be definitively determined. Even allowing for the possibility that the author visited Safed (and not just his protagonists), his fictionalized account makes it difficult to ascertain which circles of mystics Alḍāhirī might have encountered. Not only is *Sefer hamusar* largely fanciful, but its piecemeal composition seems to have precluded any authorial attempts at reconciling the conflicting dates given for various peregrinations. Ratzaby valiantly tackles the vexing chronology of what he assumes is Alḍāhirī's journey (or journeys) to the Land of Israel, but the outcome of his deliberations is of necessity inconclusive.[65] Most scholars maintain that the author visited Safed prior to Isaac Luria's arrival in 1570 and therefore had no firsthand exposure to Lurianic kabbalah.[66] In large measure, the theosophical content of the kabbalistic chapters in *Sefer hamusar* and of Alḍāhirī's Torah commentary seem to bear out this assumption. There does not appear to be any evidence of the hallmark myths of Luria's dramatic cosmogony: no *ṣimṣum* (the divine contraction that allows the universe to come into being) with its attendant notions of *shevirat ha-kelim* (the breaking of the vessels unable to contain the divine light that flows into primordial space following *ṣimṣum*) and the *kelipot* (the "shells" or cosmic forces of evil that cause the vessels to fracture).[67] And, as noted, the mystical works explicitly acknowledged as sources in *Sefer hamusar* and *Ṣeidah la-derekh* all antedate Luria's monumental reworking of classical Spanish kabbalah. Additional support for this argument, though admittedly *ex silencio* and less compelling, is the fact that Alḍāhirī mentions Karo and Cordovero with great admiration but makes no reference to Luria or his disciples in *Sefer hamusar*.[68] Karo and Cordovero—Spanish exiles who had spent time in Greece before settling in the Land of Israel—were major figures in the pre-Lurianic circle of kabbalists active in Safed from the 1530's. Their coterie also included Karo's disciple (and Cordovero's brother-in-law) Alqabeṣ. But even if one assumes that Alḍāhirī visited Safed, there is no way

65 See *Sefer hamusar*, 30–32.

66 For this view, see Tobi, "Seder qiddush leilei shabbat"; idem, *The Jews of Yemen*, 54–55; idem, "Rabbi yiṣḥaq wannah ve-hitḥazzqut ha-ʿissuq ba-qabbalah," p. 21, n. 21; *Sefer hamusar*, 30–32 and 43–44; Ahroni, *Yemenite Jewry*, 86, and Wagner, "Arabic Influence on Shabazian Poetry in Yemen."

67 See Scholem, *Major Trends*, 244–286 and more recently, Magid, *From Metaphysics to Midrash*, 16–33.

68 Shimon Greidi is virtually alone in saying explicitly that Alḍāhirī wrote his *Ṣeidah la-derekh* in his final years, after having absorbed the kabbalistic teachings of the Safed circle of Cordovero and Karo; see his introduction to the work in *Taj ḥamishah ḥumshei torah*.

of knowing whether he made the acquaintance of these luminaries or whether he was simply aware of their striking innovations and galvanized by his stay to adopt a kabbalistic approach to spirituality and kabbalistic explanations for various observances (though not necessarily Cordovero's theosophy, which differed considerably from the earlier kabbalah).[69] Consequently, it would be difficult to say which doctrines and customs he embraced due to possible first-hand exposure, which he acquired from written sources, and which he adopted from popular usages that grew out of the devotional practices of the Safed confraternities.

As far as Lurianic influence is concerned, we do know that Alḍāhirī eagerly subscribed to a liturgical innovation associated with the Lurianic circle which, over time, gained universal acceptance. His Torah commentary and two of his kabbalistic Sabbath hymns, "Liqrat penei shabbat" and "Bereishit qedumat yomayyim," endorse the custom of prefacing the words *yom ha-shishi* ("the sixth day"; Genesis 1:31) to the Friday night *qiddush* in order to spell out the Tetragrammaton. Some scholars have also seen an embrace of Lurianic practice in Alḍāhirī's two-stanza addition to Simon Ibn Lavi's "Bar yoḥai," a kabbalistic hymn that was widely appropriated by Luria's disciples, although its author (d. 1580, North Africa) was not himself an adherent of that school.[70] However, the kabbalistic ideas in Alḍāhirī's addition derive from Ibn Lavi's original poem, which evokes Bar Yoḥai's ascent through the ten *sefirot*, and is not noticeably Lurianic in its symbolism.[71] There are also some *baqqashah* poems for the Lurianic midnight and pre-dawn prayer vigils (*tiqqun haṣot* and *ashmoret ha-boqer*) that are attributed to Alḍāhirī, which, if they are indeed his, again suggest an enthusiasm for Lurianic practices that gained widespread popularity.[72] Perhaps, therefore, it is safest to say that Alḍāhirī's understanding of kabbalistic

---

69 In *Ṣeidah la-derekh* on Lev. 23, Alḍāhirī's explanation of the reasons for blowing the shofar is headed, "Commentary on the shofar blasts and their esoteric meaning according to the kabbalah of Moses Cordovero, one of the inhabitants of Safed"; see Gaimani, *Temurot be-moreshet yahadut teiman*, p. 70 and n. 41.

70 Scholem remarks that Ibn Lavi's *Ketem Paz* is "the only commentary on the Zohar that was not written under the influence of the new Kabbalah of Safed"; see Scholem, *Kabbalah*, 70. On Ibn Lavi's kabbalistic sources, see also Huss, *Sockets of Fine Gold*, 27–42.

71 See Liebes, "Bar yoḥai be-shiro shel shim'on lavi." For the text, see Ben Menahem, *Zemirot shel shabbat*, pp. 42 and 152–157. For Alḍāhirī's addition, see Tobi, "Piyyut ḥadash le-rabbi yiḥye al-ḍāhirī." On the reception and ritual use of "Bar yoḥai," see Hallamish, "Ha-shir bar yoḥai." Hallamish notes that Alḍāhirī's contrafaction is one of the earliest in a series of emulations.

72 See Tobi, "Seder ba'ashmoret ha-boqer"; idem, "Piyyuṭ ḥadash"; and Wagner, "Arabic Influence on Shabazian Poetry in Yemen," 129.

doctrines and theosophy is largely pre-Lurianic but that this did not preclude his receptivity to new liturgical customs originating in the Safed circles of Cordovero and Luria.

The question of Alḍāhirī's familiarity with the poetry of the Safed mystics also remains largely unresolved.[73] In his discussion of the poetry of Shalem Shabbazi, one of the central figures in the 17th-century group of Lower Yemeni mystics, Mark Wagner highlights the extent to which Alḍāhirī is considered the link between the kabbalistic poets of Safed and Shabbazi's Mashta school.[74] Wagner revises the critical consensus, arguing persuasively that Shabbazi's verse should not be seen as a direct outgrowth of the esoteric poetry associated with the Safed revival but rather as a complex cultural artifact that at least in part reflects the influence of Arabic Sufi poetry from Lower Yemen. In doing so, he disputes the claim of earlier scholars that Alḍāhirī was intimately acquainted with the esoteric poetry of Safed luminaries such as Alqabeṣ, Azikri, and Luria and the broader tradition of *shirat ha-ḥen* ("the poetry of *ḥokhmah nistarah*," i.e., esoteric wisdom) inspired by their verse. Such caution is a welcome corrective to certain generalizing tendencies. Yet it would seem that Alḍāhirī was alive to the thematic innovations of his kabbalist contemporaries in Safed and elsewhere and might well have commanded the modest combined corpus of Ibn Lavi, Alqabeṣ, Azikri, and Luria.[75] From his addition to the poem, it is clear that he knew Ibn Lavi's "Bar yoḥai" as well as "Lekhah dodi" and similar hymns. As noted below, echoes of the exorcism of demons that features in each of Luria's three Aramaic Sabbath hymns may be heard in "Liqrat penei shabbat," where the speaker sets the kabbalistic Sabbath observance before him as a kind of amulet to ward off his mythical enemies. Some of Alḍāhirī's several poems interweaving the names of the ten *sefirot* are not unlike "Adon ha-kol ve-ḥayy ʿolam," a short piece by the Italian kabbalist Mordecai Dato (1525–1591/1601), who visited Safed during its heyday and studied with Moses Cordovero between 1560 and 1565. Dato's kabbalistic poem, "Boʾi kallah, boʾi kallah, kellilat yofi kellulah," bears resemblance to "Lekhah dodi" and was similarly intended for recitation when greeting the Sabbath.[76] While there is no

73 On the poetry of the Safed mystics, see Tanenbaum, *The Contemplative Soul*, 232–239.

74 Wagner, "Arabic Influence on Shabazian Poetry," 127–130 and idem, *Like Joseph in Beauty*, 160–166.

75 For the texts see Ben Menahem, *Zemirot shel shabbat*. On Luria's small corpus see Liebes, "*Zemirot liseʿudot shabbat she-yasad haʾari ha-qadosh*" and Beeri, "Two Unpublished Poems by R. Isaac Luria Ashkenazi."

76 For "Adon ha-kol ve-ḥayy ʿolam," see Schirmann ed., *Mivḥar ha-shirah haʿivrit beʾitalya*,

a priori reason to posit direct literary influence in any of these instances, it certainly seems that the points of convergence between Alḍāhirī's compositions and these poems are more than coincidental. By contrast, Alḍāhirī's kabbalistic poems bear little resemblance to those of the enormously prolific Israel Najara (c. 1550–c. 1628; likely a younger contemporary), whose vast poetic corpus outstripped all the others associated with the Safed revival.[77] In his wanderings throughout the Near East and the eastern Mediterranean, Najara acquired an ear for Turkish, Greek, and Arabic folk songs as well as for the Judeo-Spanish romances of the Sephardi diaspora. Though in many respects a latter-day adherent of the Andalusian poetic tradition—to which his corpus is replete with intertextual allusions—Najara was also an immensely creative innovator who set his devotional poems to these popular melodies and drew on kabbalistic lore. In crafting each poem to fit a specific foreign tune, many of them Turkish, he adapted the Hebrew to the syllabic structure of the borrowed song.[78] Najara's musical poetry was rapidly incorporated into the new para-liturgical rites like the *tiqqun haṣot* and *ashmoret ha-boqer* introduced by the Safed kabbalists. His devotional songs became extraordinarily popular among the Jews of Mediterranean lands, yet they do not appear to have left their impress on Alḍāhirī's poetry. Much of Najara's sacred verse is erotically charged to such a degree that it drew severe criticism for its fusion of evocative phrases from the Song of Songs with kabbalistic symbolism and the sensual imagery of secular love songs to depict the relationship between God and Israel. In an exceedingly suggestive poem, he uses both female and male metaphors for God:

> If I were an infant and you were my nurse,
> I would suckle your beautiful breasts, and quench my thirst.

246. For "Bo'i kallah, bo'i kallah, kellilat yofi kellulah," see Greenup ed., *Shemen ʿarev*. On the "memoir" of his visit to Safed, *Iggeret halevanon*, see Tishby, "Demuto shel rabbi moshe kordovero be-ḥibbur shel rabbi mordekhai dato."

77 On Najara's verse see the references listed in Chapter 3, p. 277, n. 100. See also: the Introductory essays by Beeri and Seroussi in Najara, *She'erit Yisrael*, vol. 1; Beeri, "*ʿOlat ḥodesh* le-rabbi yisrael najara"; and idem, "Israel Najara: A Beloved and Popular Poet."

78 On Najara's innovative appropriation of the Ottoman *makam* system and other Mediterranean musical models, see: Najara, *She'erit Yisrael*, 1:94–198; Tietze and Yahalom, *Ottoman Melodies Hebrew Hymns*; Beeri, "Music and poetic structure in XVI–XVII c. oriental piyyut"; Seroussi, "From the Court and Tarikat to the Synagogue"; and idem, "Rabbi yisrael najara meʿaṣev zimrat ha-qodesh aḥarei gerush sefarad."

If I were a tent and you dwelt in me,
we would delight ourselves with love and clothe ourselves with joy.[79]

Certainly, Alḍāhirī's "Liqrat penei shabbat" takes inspiration from the kabbalistic myth of Sacred Marriage (*hieros gamos*), in which the masculine and feminine aspects of the Godhead unite on the Sabbath, producing a state of divine harmony that overflows into the created world on the seventh day. But most of Alḍāhirī's kabbalistic poems are far less sexualized. Formally, they bear no similarity to Najara's verse, and Najara's frank eroticism, however figurative the intent, goes far beyond the more muted sensuality of Alḍāhirī's pieces.[80]

4 Recurrent Kabbalistic Themes

Several salient themes recur throughout the kabbalistic material in *Sefer hamusar*: the desirability of contemplating the ten *sefirot*, the ultimate reward awaiting those engaged in kabbalistic study, the centrality of the kabbalistic Sabbath, praise for foundational kabbalistic works, and the need for prudence when discussing profoundly mystical matters openly. Some of these motifs are theosophical in nature while others touch on matters of eschatology, and still others explore the tension between a tradition of concealment and esotericism and the impulse to popularize and disseminate kabbalistic teachings. Frequently, these ideas are presented in formal poetry, whose mannered diction, elaborate style, and allusive language add expressive constraints to those already imposed by the discretion required in esoteric teaching.

4.1 *The Sefirot*

Medieval kabbalists speak in intricate symbolism and mythical language of the emanation of ten *sefirot* from *Ein sof*—the infinite, concealed, and unknowable aspect of the divinity—to convey the unfolding self-revelation of the divine in the cosmos. While God in Himself is inscrutable, the *sefirot* emanating in

79 "Tiddad shnat ʿeini," quoted in Carmi's translation, *The Penguin Book of Hebrew Verse*, 477; on this poem see Yahalom, "Tensions," 212–213. There is some scholarly disagreement regarding the degree to which Najara's poetry is truly kabbalistic rather than simply the product of an environment suffused with mysticism; see, e.g., Beeri, "Israel Najara: A Beloved and Popular Poet," p. 66 and the references cited in n. 29.

80 In his *Shetei Yadot*, the kabbalist Menaḥem de Lonzano (1550–before 1624) assailed Najara's use of erotic language and borrowings from non-Jewish models in his sacred verse as "abominations"; see Yahalom, "Tensions," 210–211.

successive stages from *Ein sof* correspond to more immanent aspects of the Godhead that can be known through contemplation. The reverse order of emanation, though less frequently discussed, signifies the ascent of the mystic into the numinous realm through reflection on the *sefirot*. Two of the poems in *Sefer hamusar* suggest this ascending path. In "Yedidi im tivḥar le-havin sod zohar/ʿamod na va-shaḥar le-shaʿar haʾorah" ("Friend, if the *Zohar*'s mystery you choose to master/ rise at dawn to seek the gate of light"), the reversal is inspired by Joseph Gikatilla's *Gates of Light* (*Shaʿarei orah*). The poem praises *Shaʿarei orah* and mentions the work's ten chapters, each of which is devoted to one of the *sefirot* and its symbols, starting with the lowest, and culminating in the highest. Like *Shaʿarei orah*, "Yedidi im tivḥar le-havin sod zohar" invokes the divine names that correspond to each of the *sefirot* and alludes to the vocalization of the ineffable Tetragrammaton. The order of emanation is also reversed in "Asher shat malkhuto ʿalei khol mamlekhet" ("He whose kingship is above all kingdoms"), Alḍāhirī's panegyric to *Sefer maʿarekhet ha-elohut* and the commentary of Judah Ḥayyāṭ. While the poem itself does not expand on the idea of mystical ascent, it is prefaced by a rhymed prose passage that links the study of kabbalah to the soul's perfection and ultimate reward.[81]

4.2 *Kabbalistic Study and the Summum Bonum*

Alḍāhirī's preoccupation with the ultimate purpose and soteriology of the soul is evident in both philosophical and kabbalistic contexts in *Sefer hamusar*. In the chapters under consideration, immersion in kabbalistic learning is repeatedly championed as the path to the soul's eternal reward. In Chapter 3, the theme of kabbalistic study as the true key to man's ultimate felicity features in rhymed prose as well as verse. Following his handsomely compensated improvisation of two rhetorically ingenious poems—one reading forward and backward, the other horizontally and vertically—Abner suddenly interrupts the arc of the story to repudiate the pursuit of poetry in favor of kabbalah. Just as in Chapter 21, he urges abandoning such trivial affairs in order to probe the far weightier question of the *summum bonum*:

---

81 On Gikatilla's ordering of the *sefirot* and emphasis on their divine names, see Idel's Historical Introduction to Gikatilla, *Gates of Light*, xxvii–xxix. On the divine names corresponding to the *sefirot*, see also Scholem, *Kabbalah*, 107–108. The recitation of divine names and recombination of their component letters was a mystical technique employed by adherents of ecstatic kabbalah, among them Gikatilla's teacher, Abraham Abulafia; see Idel, *Kabbalah: New Perspectives*, 96–103 and idem, *The Mystical Experience in Abraham Abulafia*, 13–52.

> My friends …, know that the Sages considered this [art of poetry] utterly insignificant. The great sciences are those that entail the attainment of the intelligibles. And the manifold good lies in store for those wise in kabbalah. They have pride of place in the kingdom of knowledge and understanding. Theirs is the eternal reward …. Their souls partake of the supernal light under several canopies, each with a palace and a candlelabrum and every type of precious stone.[82]

This disavowal calls to mind the topos of the "compunctious poet": figures such as Moses Ibn Ezra, Judah Halevi, or Shem Tov Falaquera, who towards middle age claimed to have renounced their youthful literary indiscretions for the pursuit of philosophy or pious living.[83] The implicit analogy is apt (apart from the fact that Abner's reversals occur over the space of a very few lines), for just as those historical predecessors never entirely discarded poetry, the fictional Abner does not single-mindedly abandon versifying to devote himself to kabbalah, nor does he abjure his more frivolous ways in subsequent chapters. But here he sustains his grave stance, reworking the preceding passage into a poetic vision of the celestial Eden and the illumination awaiting the purified soul:

> In Eden, the Lord's garden, sapphire stones bedeck each gem.
> Heavenly palaces (*heikhalot*) and canopies, with a candlelabrum set out like cornerstones trimmed.[84]
> Wisdom crowns the heads of saints; silver and gold overlay their thrones.
> He of clean hands and a pure heart, teacher of the true faith shall be blessed.
> At the gate: angels of grace; a pond drawn from the river of fire
> For immersing souls that become pure, for cleansing the sullied soul,
> To make it fit to greet the living God, in radiance, and not dulled.[85]
> Happy is the man who purifies his soul and graciously saves it from ruin.

82 *Sefer hamusar*, p. 85, lines 161–167.

83 See Brann, *The Compunctious Poet*, 59–137. The motif as presented by Ibn Ezra, Halevi, and Falaquera is perhaps more biographically oriented than it is in *Sefer hamusar*.

84 Cf. Ps. 144:12.

85 Cf. Tishby, *The Wisdom of the Zohar*, p. 1457, n. 158, citing Rabbi Moses de Leon's *Sefer ha-nefesh ha-ḥakhamah* to the effect that "the spirit of the perfectly righteous man" on its way to the Garden of Eden "passes likewise through the fire on its journey to the world above, and it is washed and cleansed, so that it might be bound up in the bond of life." See also Scholem, *Kabbalah*, 159.

> The path is straight for those who seek, but hard and long for those who spurn.
> If fate would grant me respite from its sharp arrows and drawn bow,
> I would meditate in solitude in the houses of learning (*ve'etboded be-vattei ha-tevunah*) to soothe and cure my pain ....
> Out of the depths I would raise my prayer to the Master of the kingdom
> That He deem me worthy to delight in His Eden and in Zion the blessed ...

If much of its language and imagery lend themselves to more than one interpretation and its kabbalistic symbolism is less than fully integrated, the poem as a whole conveys a spiritualized conception of individual salvation and ultimate reward and invokes several terms with decidedly mystical associations. The opening phrase, "Be'eden gan elohim kol yeqarah," is adapted from Ezekiel 28:13, a prophecy conjuring up a magnificent Eden full of precious stones and gold. Possibly, Alḍāhirī was aware of Joseph Gikatilla's gloss of the verse in *Sha'arei orah* in accordance with his view that *'eden* and *gan elohim* are not synonymous, but rather, as Idel explains, Eden stands for the first *sefirah* and the Garden for the last, and together they symbolize the entire sefirotic realm.[86] So too, whether intentionally or not on Alḍāhirī's part, the term '*heikhalot*' (l. 2) resonates with associations, immediately calling to mind the Jewish mystical literature of late antiquity and the early Middle Ages with its visions of ascent through seven heavenly palaces to the Chariot-Throne of God, the Merkavah. Appropriating facets of these ancient mystical texts, the 13th-century Zoharic corpus adopted the idea of palaces, although there are important distinctions between "the bodily forms of ascent dominant in late antiqu[e] Jewish mysticism" and the ascent of the soul "as mediated by ... philosophical writings" in medieval kabbalah.[87] Zoharic literature comprises a section known as *Heikhalot*, "a description of the seven palaces in the celestial Garden of Eden, where souls luxuriate during their ascent, which follows their devotion in prayer or their departure from the world."[88] The poem aligns these *heikhalot* with celestial canopies, which have paradisiacal associations, recalling midrashic passages in which God erects canopies for the righteous

86 See Gikatilla, *Sha'arei orah*, Ninth Gate, Second Sefirah, 77 as cited on Sefaria.org. For the sefirotic symbolism of Eden and the Garden see Idel, *Ascensions on High in Jewish Mysticism*, 207–208 and idem, "On Paradise in Jewish Mysticism."

87 Idel, *Ascensions on High*, p. 57.

88 Tishby, *The Wisdom of the Zohar*, General Introduction, p. 4.

in the Garden of Eden.[89] In the third line, the phrase *ve'atarot bin be-rashei ha-ḥasidim* recalls the well-known Maimonidean interpretation of a Talmudic passage (bBerakhot 17a), which portrays the righteous in the next world enjoying purely spiritual deserts:

> In the world to come there is no eating (or) drinking ... rather, the righteous sit with their crowns on their heads, delighting in the splendor of the Shekhinah.

In his Commentary on the Mishnah and his *Mishneh Torah*, Maimonides interprets these crowns as a metaphor for the knowledge of the divine, which is attained by the souls of the righteous and on account of which those souls merit eternal life.[90] But where Maimonides advocates philosophical speculation as the means to achieving knowledge of the divine, Abner's "true faith" is here attained by means of theosophical contemplation and *hitbodedut*, the mental concentration or solitude associated with the praxis of Gikatilla's teacher, Abraham Abulafia and other kabbalists as a means to elevate one's soul.[91] And while the speaker's closing request "That He deem me worthy to delight in His Eden and in Zion the blessed" can be read in traditional terms, there is perhaps an allusion here to what Idel has termed the eschatological pillar of the souls and the two paradises in Zoharic literature. Idel writes that in portions of the *Zohar*, a pillar "serves as a conduit for the ascent of the souls of the deceased righteous" from a terrestrial paradise to a celestial one. This pillar, called "the foundation of the mount of Zion" (Isaiah 4:5), is an axis "that penetrates the entire world, beginning with the lower paradise and reaching the sphere of the supernal palaces found immediately beneath the divine realm." In later Zoharic strata, the terms 'Eden,' 'the Garden,' and 'the pillar' are each identified with specific *sefirot*.[92]

---

89 See, e.g., Ecc. Rab. 8, 2 and Yalqut Shim'oni Gen. 20 (on Gen. 2:9).

90 See his Commentary on Mishnah Sanhedrin, Introduction to Chapter 10 ("Ḥeleq") in *Mishnah 'im peirush rabbenu moshe ben maimon*, 4:204–205 and *Mishneh Torah*, *Teshuvah* 8:2.

91 See, e.g., the passage from Hayyim Vital's *Sha'arei qedushah* cited in Idel, *Ascensions on High*, p. 45 and Idel, "Hitbodedut as Concentration in Jewish Philosophy."

92 See Idel, *Ascensions on High*, 101–133 *passim* and Bar Asher, "The Ontology, Arrangement, and Appearance of Paradise in Castilian Kabbalah." Alḍāhirī's phrase *yezakeni le-hit'adden be'edno* is also reminiscent of several passages in *Zohar, Va-yeḥi*, Chapter 21 that evoke the soul worthy of ascending to the point of attaining "the glory of the King, reveling in supernal delight above the place called Heaven ...," where "above the place called Heaven" is understood to mean even higher than the *sefirah Tif'eret*; see Matt, *The Zohar* Pritzker Edition, vol. 3, and (in Hebrew translation) *Zohar, Va-yeḥi*, 21:175 וְאִם זָכָה לַעֲלוֹת יוֹתֵר—צַדִּיק

The soteriological value of immersion in kabbalah is also emphasized in Chapter 23 when Abner affirms that the study of kabbalah

> is what raises man from death to eternal life; without it, man would not be distinct from beast. It is the reason for the soul's immortality; in its company the soul finds rest and repose.[93]

In all these instances, Alḍāhirī takes his cue from the medieval Jewish speculative traditions that had spiritualized the view of the world to come (*'olam ha-ba*) prevailing in earlier rabbinic literature. Rather than "the historical period ushered in by resurrection in which the righteous receive their ultimate reward and the wicked their ultimate punishment," the future world is portrayed as the timeless existence of the disembodied souls of the righteous who, having returned to their supernal abode, enjoy the rewards of illumination and eternal repose.[94] This bold reinterpretation of traditional eschatological ideas was familiar to Alḍāhirī not only from Maimonides but also from Solomon Ibn Gabirol's magisterial *Keter Malkhut,* to which he clearly alludes in his evocation of the world to come in Chapter 21 of *Sefer hamusar*.[95] While Alḍāhirī is fairly harmonistic in his approach, medieval kabbalists and philosophers differed on the actual source and, therefore, eternal abode of the soul. In claiming that the soul derived from the celestial sphere of the Intellect, Neoplatonic thinkers such as Ibn Gabirol implied that it was a product of the created realm. But kabbalists such as Moses Naḥmanides placed the soul's true origins and ultimate home far higher, in the world of the divine *sefirot,* within the Godhead itself.[96]

4.3 *The Sabbath*

The Sabbath too is associated with the afterlife in a number of classical Jewish texts. The rabbis characterize the world to come as *menuḥah* (rest), or a form of Sabbath for which one toils in this world and of whose joys one partakes in

---

הוּא, שֶׁזּוֹכֶה לַכָּבוֹד שֶׁל הַמֶּלֶךְ וּלְהִתְעַדֵּן בְּעִדּוּן עֶלְיוֹן שֶׁלְּמַעְלָה מִמָּקוֹם שֶׁנִּקְרָא שָׁמַיִם, שֶׁכָּתוּב אָז תִּתְעַנַּג עַל ה׳.

93 *Sefer hamusar*, p. 266, line 96–p. 267, line 98.

94 Septimus, *Hispano-Jewish Culture in Transition*, 40–41.

95 See *Sefer hamusar,* p. 248, line 154. On the reinterpretation of eschatological ideas in *Keter Malkhut,* see Tanenbaum, *The Contemplative Soul,* 73–79. In the wake of the early 13th-century controversy sparked by Maimonides' purely spiritual view of *'olam ha-ba,* Naḥmanides noted that Maimonides' controversial stance was anticipated by Ibn Gabirol in *Keter Malkhut;* see Septimus, "'Open Rebuke and Concealed Love'" and idem, *Hispano-Jewish Culture in Transition*, 39–60.

96 See Septimus, "'Open Rebuke and Concealed Love'" and Scholem, *Kabbalah*, 152–165.

the next.[97] Medieval kabbalah also linked Sabbath observance with a foretaste of otherworldly bliss, emphasizing the nexus between the seventh day and the devotee's ability to penetrate the mysteries of the divine world. The kabbalists imbued the rabbinic Sabbath with mythic significance, transforming it into

> a day on which the divine lovers reunite; ... a cosmic Axis, around which Time is organized and through whose channels the week is ennobled and blessed; and ... a festival of spiritual restoration, whereby the Jew is graced with an additional *pneuma*, the Sabbath-soul ....[98]

In his guise as *ḥazzan* of the Sephardi synagogue in Tiberias (Chapter 23), Abner recites two poems that showcase these themes, "Liqrat penei shabbat" and "Matoq le-miṣuf u-fannag":

4.4 "Liqrat penei shabbat"

"Liqrat penei shabbat" is a strophic poem of five stanzas inscribed with the acrostic Zechariah.[99] Its alternating rhyme scheme is that of a *muwashshaḥ*, or "girdle poem," in which each strophe has its own rhyme as well as a rhyme set by the opening couplet, which remains constant throughout (aa bbbbaa ccccaa, etc.).[100] Despite some difficult syntax resulting from Alḍāhirī's rigorous insistence on internal as well as end rhymes, the poem clearly reflects a kabbalistic view of the Sabbath and the notion that proper observance of the Sabbath has theurgic effects. As portrayed here, the Sabbath is the fulcrum of the week, a day of spiritual regeneration, and the occasion of a mystical marriage within the divine world. On the formal plane, this last idea is reinforced by the rhymes that echo the word *kallah* ("bride"; v. 2) at the end of each stanza.

---

97 See, e.g., the wonderfully alliterative phrase in bBer. 57b: "Three things are a taste of the world to come: Sabbath, sunshine and conjugal relations (*shabbat, shemesh, vetashmish*)"; and ibid.: "Sabbath is one-sixtieth part of the world to come." See also bRH 31a: "On the seventh day (the Levites) said, 'A psalm, a song for the Sabbath day' (Ps. 92), that is, for the day which will be all Sabbath." In addition, see the sources cited in Wolfson, "Coronation of the Sabbath Bride," p. 307, n. 19.

98 Ginsburg, *The Sabbath in the Classical Kabbalah*, 59.

99 For the Hebrew text, see *Sefer hamusar*, pp. 262–264.

100 On this type of strophic poem, see Rosen, "The Muwashshaḥ" and Rosen-Moked, *The Hebrew Girdle Poem (Muwashshaḥ) in the Middle Ages*; for a brief discussion of Hebrew *muwashshaḥāt* from Yemen, see ibid., pp. 60–61 and 127–131. On the origins of the form, see Einbinder, "The Current Debate on the Muwashshaḥ." See also Jones and Hitchcock eds., *Studies on the Muwaššaḥ and the Kharja* and Corriente and Sáenz-Badillos eds., *Poesía Estrófica*.

I greet the Sabbath with joy and delight
like a groom taking pleasure in his bride.
The radiance of my face on the six weekdays is dimmed;[101]
likewise my thoughts grow dark, and my soul abhors fine things.
A snare, a throng of foes, rises up to terrify me.
So I set before me the true faith, my inheritance, for protection,
And contemplate the cause of the wonders of the Lord.
I guard that secret in my heart, for its future fame and praise.

My grief comes to an end when my day of rest arrives:
How marvelous the gift of the double share of food![102]
I will open wide my purse to provide a festive meal
and sing my Sabbath hymns to the sweetest melodies.
Goblets red as flames flash like sparkling jewels.[103]
A fine table is spread; I sleep in a canopied bridal bed.

The chariot of the living God is made of myriad angels
Who, when they hear my prayers, bear them, soaring to His throne.
They are watching as I murmur, in a chorus of my brothers,
The mystic mysteries of Ben Yoḥai, sweet as honeycomb.
In every word I find the closeness of the Lord;
I adorn myself with them, and hope for His redemption.

Mounted on a swift cloud, his mind in a state of rest,
He joins the mysterious half sheqel with its other half,
and clears the soul's path of stones, mire, mud, and crookedness
until she finds rest (from mundane impediments).
She rebuffs the nations' slanderers and humbles their spirits;
she crushes their pride for all eternity.

101 The phrase *ziv hod* would seem to have kabbalistic overtones, as *hod* (Majesty) is one of the four lowest *sefirot*.

102 For Zoharic exegesis of *leḥem mishneh*, see, e.g., *Zohar, Vayeḥi* 72:754–755.

103 The syntax in v. 37 is not that graceful. The poet seems to be comparing winecups to a flame and a treasure. For a possibly comparable usage of *segullah* as the jewels in a treasure, see the citation from Moses Darʿi, "*Ṣeriaḥ shir mesuggar ha-sheʿarim*," in Ben Yehudah, *A Complete Dictionary*, 5:3953a. For the text, see Yeshaya, *Medieval Hebrew Poetry in Muslim Egypt*, 247–248; Pinsker, *Lickute Kadmoniot*, 1:89–90 and Weinberger, *Jewish Poet in Muslim Egypt*, p. 461. The line reads, "*u-va-ḥadarav segullot ʿinyenei khol/ ne'um ḥazaq kekhokhavim me'irim.*"

Behold, two words I preface to "*va-yekhullu ha-shamayim*"—
Accept my offerings of praise; O Lord, let them not cease.
I will abstain from the mundane, even in my thoughts.
Remember the Patriarchs' merit, their prayers in days of old;
Console the exiled nation: all things have their limit.
Sustain us from day to day; Your mercy do not withhold.

The opening couplet speaks of welcoming the Sabbath with the rapture and delectation of a groom delighting in his bride. There are decidedly erotic resonances to the *hitpaʿel* verb, *etʿalesah* ("I take pleasure"), whose only biblical attestation in this form occurs in Proverbs 7:18, "Let us drink our fill of love till morning; let us delight (*nitʿalesah*) in amorous embrace."[104] At the same time, the continuation of the poet's line, *kimsos ḥatan ʿalei khallah* ("as a bridegroom rejoices over his bride"), has its source in Isaiah 62:5, a prophecy of national restoration that uses the language of betrothal to describe God's enduring love for the Land and people of Israel. Thus, the marital imagery and sensual overtones of Alḍāhirī's words most clearly evoke the individual's love for the Sabbath Bride but may also be read with reference to the covenantal bond between God and Israel, with its lasting promise of ultimate redemption. Isaiah 62:5 is also cited at the close of the seventh stanza of "Lekhah dodi," which may have served Alḍāhirī as an inspiration. There it parallels earlier verses evoking the messianic redemption of Jerusalem and the People of Israel but also, according to Reuven Kimelman, sustains a kabbalistic reading that celebrates the union of the *sefirot Tifʾeret* and *Shekhinah*.[105]

Alḍāhirī's amatory tropes are in keeping with the kabbalistic myth of Sacred Marriage (*hieros gamos*), in which the masculine and feminine aspects of the Godhead unite on the Sabbath, producing a state of divine harmony that overflows into the created world on the seventh day. The richly layered, associative symbolism of the kabbalah enabled its proponents to forge multifaceted connections between the drama unfolding on the theosophical plane and earthly Sabbath observance, both communal and individual. Imagery of bride and groom was applied to the dynamics within the sefirotic realm; to the relationship between God and His beloved people, Israel; and to Israel's love for the Sabbath. While the Sabbath is portrayed as a bride in some earlier Jewish sources, including a few passages in Talmud and midrash, the motif underwent

104 The erotic charge is evident in quite a few of Ben Yehudah's medieval citations; see *A Complete Dictionary*, 9:4529a.

105 See Kimelman, *The Mystical Meaning of Lekhah Dodi and Kabbalat Shabbat*, 178–180.

its fullest elaboration in the *Zohar*. The *Zohar* also infused Sabbath ritual with nuptial symbolism, paving the way for the liturgical innovations of the Safed kabbalists.[106]

The first stanza of "Liqrat penei shabbat" quickly immerses us in a web of dualistic contrasts: the luminous aura enjoyed by the speaker on the Sabbath is dulled on the profane weekdays; a throng of foes rises up against him; terrified, he upholds the true faith in the face of that which threatens it and carefully guards an esoteric teaching, thereby leading to its public recognition. Several of these binary oppositions are eloquently elucidated in the following brief extract from Gershom Scholem's *On the Kabbalah and Its Symbolism*:

> It would be no exaggeration to call the Sabbath *the* day of the Kabbalah. On the Sabbath the light of the upper world bursts into the profane world in which man lives during the six days of the week. The light of the Sabbath endures into the ensuing week, growing gradually dimmer, to be relieved in the middle of the week by the rising light of the next Sabbath. It is the day on which a special *pneuma*, the 'Sabbath-soul,' enters into the believer, enabling him to participate in the right way in this day which shares more than any other day in the secrets of the pneumatic world. Consequently it was also regarded as a day specially consecrated to the study of the Kabbalah.[107]

For Alḍāhirī's speaker, the six weekdays entail a lamentable descent into obscurity and gloom from the blessed radiance, intellectual stimulation, and spiritual elevation of the Sabbath. What is more, these mundane days are aligned with the realm of the demonic, such that a throng of mythical enemies is roused against him, filling his heart with fear. To overcome his terror and ward off the ominous threat of weekday captivity to these diabolical forces, he sets the true, kabbalistic Sabbath observance before him as a kind of amulet or apotropaic protection, not unlike the exorcism of demons evoked in each of Isaac Luria's three Sabbath table hymns. In "Benei heikhala," Luria's song for the third Sabbath meal, the forces of the "other side" are "insolent dogs [who] must

106 The foregoing discussion of the Sabbath as Sacred Marriage is indebted to Ginsburg, *The Sabbath in the Classical Kabbalah*, esp. pp. 101–121. For a different perspective, see Wolfson, "Coronation of the Sabbath Bride." On earlier sources that apply marital imagery to the Sabbath, see also Kimelman, *The Mystical Meaning of Lekhah Dodi*, 1–9. On the feminine in kabbalistic theosophies, see Idel, *Kabbalah & Eros*, esp. 104–152. On the androcentrism of Zoharic kabbalah, see Wolfson, *Language, Eros, Being*, 46–110.

107 Scholem, *On the Kabbalah and Its Symbolism*, 139.

remain outside and cannot come in," and are hurled "back into their abysses" on Shabbat.[108] To honor the Sabbath, the speaker in Alḍāhirī's poem engages in theosophical speculation (literally, "I contemplate the cause of the supernal Lord's wonders"), guarding the esoteric meaning of the seventh day in his heart. Paradoxically, concealing this mystery yields renown, although the seeming contradiction may be resolved by examining the original biblical context of the phrase *le-shem ve-li-tehillah*. Zephaniah 3:20 promises the restoration of Israel's reputation among all the peoples on earth but also suggests a confrontation between Israel and the nations of the world. Refracted through a mythical lens, this motif fits with the preceding lines of the poem, in which the kabbalistic understanding of Shabbat protects the speaker from the demonic enemies who threaten him. As Elliot Ginsburg notes,

> Some kabbalists, whom we might call the dualists, … tended to see good and evil as absolutely distinct and opposing forces, and highlighted the ontological gap between the profane week and the holy Shabbat. In this schema, the entrance of Shabbat marks a kind of Changing of the Cosmic Guard, as the harsh Profane realm that holds sway during the week gives way to the blessed rule of divinity.[109]

In the second stanza, the speaker catalogues the special customs and aesthetically pleasing rituals that he observes in honor of the Sabbath. As Ginsburg has demonstrated, the classical kabbalists endowed existing rabbinic praxis with new, mythical meaning, transporting the devotee "from one cosmic order to another."[110] Of particular note in this regard is the speaker's assertion that he sleeps in a canopied bridal bed (*alun be-tokh kilah*; v. 38). Presumably, this is an allusion to the special status the kabbalists accorded marital union on Friday

108 See Scholem, *On the Kabbalah and Its Symbolism*, 142–145; Ben Menahem, *Zemirot shel shabbat*, 71 and 180–181; and Liebes, "*Zemirot lise'udot shabbat she-yasad ha-ari ha-qadosh*," esp. 553–555. On the apotropaic significance of Sabbath observance in Meir Ibn Gabbai's *Sod ha-shabbat*, see Ginsburg, *Sod ha-Shabbat: The Mystery of the Sabbath*, p. 54, sec. 15 and pp. 165–167. On the ontological status of evil and the realm of the demonic in the *Zohar* as opposed to the conception in *Ma'arekhet ha'elohut*, see Scholem, *Kabbalah*, 122–128. Alḍāhirī's exorcism is in keeping with the Zoharic notion that proper observance of the commandments and their attendant rituals is necessary to defeat the forces of evil and subdue the power of the *sitra aḥra*.

109 Ginsburg, *The Sabbath in the Classical Kabbalah*, 93. Ginsburg indicates that "The authors of the TZ/RM (*Tiqqunei ha-zohar/Ra'aya meheimna*) and the *Qanah/Peli'ah*, e.g., tended towards such a position."

110 Ginsburg, ibid., 186–276.

night as a symbolic means of emulating and aligning oneself with the supernal drama of Sacred Marriage.[111] The theme of ritual also figures in the next stanza, which evokes the divine chariot, made up of myriad angels who carry the speaker's prayers upward to the throne of God.[112] At the same time, the angels watch as, down below, the speaker participates in the public recitation of the *Zohar* ("the mystic mysteries of Ben Yoḥai") as part of the Sabbath liturgy. This custom is mentioned in Yiḥye Ṣaliḥ's 18th-century *Tiklāl eṣ ḥayyim*, where his remark is particularly revealing:

> The pious men of old used to first [before *minḥah* on Shabbat] read a little from the books of the kabbalah, such as the *Zohar*, or the *tiqqunim*, or [Judah] Ḥayyaṭ, and even if one didn't understand, there is a precious, apotropaic quality (*segullah*) in doing so, which cannot be achieved with thousands of non-literal or contextual readings of Scripture (*derushim/peshaṭim*).[113]

Knotty syntax and several enjambments make the fourth stanza of "Liqrat penei shabbat" difficult to parse, although it almost certainly refers to mystical union. Based on a passage in the *Zohar*, a symbolic identification is made in v. 46 between the biblical *maḥaṣit ha-sheqel* (the half sheqel paid as a ransom by each Israelite counted in the census; cf. Exodus 30:12–13) and the *sefirah Tif'eret*, which is also symbolically aligned with the letter *vav* joining the two halves of the Tetragrammaton.[114] Ratzaby understands the line to say that on Shabbat, *Tif'eret* ("sod maḥaṣit ha-sheqel") joins *Shekhinah* ("nefesh") with

111 See Wolfson, "Coronation of the Sabbath Bride," 308–310.

112 The line literally says that the angels fly with the prayers to the cherub. On the identification of the cherubim with the throne, an ancient motif that goes back to Scripture, see Wolfson, *Along the Path*, p. 157, n. 227.

113 See *Tiklāl eṣ ḥayyim* 1:144a. On 19th- and 20th-century Jews of Middle Eastern and North African origin who regularly gathered to read portions of the *Zohar* ritually without necessarily understanding the texts, see Shtal, "Qeri'ah pulḥanit shel sefer ha-zohar." See also Goldberg, "The Zohar in Southern Morocco: A Study in the Ethnography of Texts"; Deshen, "Ritualization of Literacy: the Works of Tunisian Scholars in Israel"; and Huss, "*Sefer ha-Zohar* as a Canonical, Sacred and Holy Text," esp. his discussion of the *Zohar* as a holy book and object of veneration used for non-semantic purposes, pp. 295–300. Ratzaby notes that in Yemen it was customary to read the *Zohar* in unison on the eve of the Sabbath before the recitation of the Song of Songs; on Friday night; and on Saturday afternoon before the *minḥah* prayer. On the role of Simeon Bar Yoḥai in the *Zohar*, see Ginsburg, *The Sabbath in the Classical Kabbalah*, 17–18. For a detailed study of his messianic image, see Liebes, "Ha-mashiaḥ shel ha-zohar: lidmuto ha-meshiḥit shel rabbi shim'on bar yoḥai."

114 See *Zohar* 2:187b.

Yesod ("kol"), thereby effecting a union in the sefirotic realms. An alternative reading would be that for every individual or soul (*le-khol nefesh*), God connects the mystery of the half sheqel with its other half, which is to say that He joins the two halves of the Tetragrammaton.[115] The enjambment in vv. 47–48 would then refer to clearing the path either of the individual soul or of *Shekhinah* (whose code name is *nefesh*) of "stones, mire, mud, and crookedness until she finds rest," which suggests liberation from a workaday and exilic existence. Once this redemptive Sabbath union has been realized, the soul/ *Shekhinah* has the power to ward off the evil emanating from her foes, here referred to as "the nations."

The final stanza invokes the custom of prefacing the two words *yom ha-shishi* ("the sixth day"; Genesis 1:31) to the paragraph beginning *va-yekhullu ha-shamayim* ("The heaven and the earth were finished"; Genesis 2:1–3), which opens the sanctification over the wine for Sabbath eve. The purpose of this liturgical innovation, apparently of Lurianic origin, was to encode the Tetragrammaton in the *qiddush*, as the resulting four-letter acrostic spells out the Divine Name (YHWH).[116] The way in which Alḍāhirī calls attention to this practice here as well as at the end of his kabbalistic poem for the Friday night *qiddush*, "Bereishit qedumat yomayyim," suggests that it was still not entirely familiar to, or customary among, his intended readership. This surmise is reinforced by his prescriptive comments on Genesis 2:1 in *Sefer ṣeidah la-derekh*: "One must say *yom ha-shishi va-yekhullu ha-shamayim* to include that Name from which all the other [divine] names are derived." In closing "Liqrat penei shabbat," the speaker moves from the realm of individual spirituality to the col-

115 Part of the difficulty lies in identifying the agent of the verb *ḥibbar*, who is presumably described in v. 45. The phrase *yoshev ʿalei ʿav qal* in the first half of v. 45 comes from Is. 19:1, where it refers to God. But the second half of the verse speaks of someone whose mind is in a state of rest, which doesn't seem suited to God. It is also unclear whether we are to construe *sod maḥaṣit sheqel* as the direct object of *ḥibbar* and how *ḥeṣyah* fits in syntactically. On the esoteric meaning of half a shekel as half of one's soul, see the citation from Isaac of Acre in Idel, "Metamorphoses of a Platonic Theme in Jewish Mysticism," 72. Alphanumerically, *sheqel* and *nefesh* (soul) are equivalent (= 430).

116 See Vital, *Shaʿar ha-kavvanot*, 2:79, *Derush qiddush leyl shabbat, derush #1*. See also the sources cited in Hallamish, *Hanhagot qabbaliot be-shabbat*, 307–308. Hallamish notes that the practice is already taken for granted in the glosses of Moses Isserles (1525/30–1572) on the *Shulḥan ʿarukh*; see *Oraḥ ḥayyim, Hilkhot shabbat*, 271:15. But the custom was not yet universal among Luria's immediate successors; see Ibn Makhir, *Seder ha-yom*, s.v. *seder qiddush leyl shabbat ve-yom tov: ve-yesh matḥilin yom ha-shishi va-yekhullu ha-shamayim kedei le-hashlim shem ben arbaʿ otiyot yitbarakh ve-yitʿalleh shemo ... ve-khen minhagenu*. On Ibn Makhir's late 16th-century mystical circle in ʿEin Zeitun, near Safed, see Meroz, "Ḥavurat rabbi mosheh ben makhir ve-taqqanotehah."

lective fate of the nation. Concluding with a supplication, he asks that God accept the offerings of his lips, that He remember the merits of the Patriarchs and reveal that the exile will end, and that He sustain His exiled people throughout their ordeal.[117] In intertwining these motifs, he again underscores the redemptive power of kabbalistic Sabbath observance.

There are several points of contact between "Liqrat penei shabbat" and "Lekhah dodi." The resemblances are most noticeable in the poems' opening couplets, the final rhyme of each of their stanzas (*-lah*), and their use of kabbalistic symbolism to celebrate the Sabbath. Nevertheless, in *Sefer hamusar*, the liturgical function of the poem is not identical to that of "Lekhah dodi" as we know it today: Abner recites "Liqrat penei shabbat" in the Tiberias synagogue following the evening service rather than as a preliminary to *maʿariv*. Ratzaby deduces from this *maqāma* that, at the time of "Alḍāhirī's" visit, the recitation of "Lekhah dodi" and *Qabbalat shabbat* was not yet part of the rite followed in Tiberias.[118] But Reuven Kimelman notes that in 16th-century Safed, *Qabbalat shabbat* customs were still very much in flux.[119] Nevertheless, the association of "Liqrat penei shabbat" with the Sabbath eve liturgy suggests that Alḍāhirī may have been aware of Alqabeṣ' poem or others like it. Poems composed in the mid-16th century by the kabbalists Mordecai Dato ("Boʾi kallah, boʾi kallah") and Simon Ibn Lavi ("Bar yoḥai") parallel "Lekhah dodi" in their language, symbolism, and liturgical function, prompting scholars to theorize that Alqabeṣ' Sabbath hymn was already known at that time to a limited circle, if not yet a

---

117 As pointed in Ratzaby's edition, v. 55 is somewhat tangled. My translation reflects the reading *gelot leʾom rabbat* instead of *galut leʾom rabbat* (where *gelot* is the infinitive absolute used as an imperative). The speaker's request would then be: "Reveal to the multitudinous nation that there is an end to every thing, (i.e., to the exile), but in the meantime, sustain us, do not withhold Your mercy."

118 See Ratzaby, "Lekhah dodi shel ha-mequbbal rabbi shelomoh alqabeṣ u-meqorotav," esp. p. 164 and idem, *Sefer hamusar*, p. 32, n. 44. Ratzaby notes that there is no mention of "Lekhah dodi" in either of Joseph Karo's works, the *Beit yosef* or the *Shulḥan ʿarukh*. As delineated in the 23rd *maqāma*, the Friday evening service consists of *Ba-meh madliqin*, the *Shemaʿ* and its benedictions, and Psalm 23, followed by the recitation of "Liqrat penei shabbat." There is no sign of the series of preliminary Psalms as outlined, e.g., by Ibn Makhir in his *Seder ha-yom* s.v. *seder qabbalat shabbat* (pp. 71–72). Hallamish notes that even in one of the mss. of Wanneh's *tiklāl* which is otherwise full of kabbalistic references, the Sabbath eve service appears in two recensions: initially, as it used to be in the older Yemenite prayerbooks and, further on, in its Lurianic incarnation as *Qabbalat shabbat*. See "Ha-qabbalah be-sidduro shel rabbi yiṣhaq wanneh," 72–73. According to Ratzaby, the older Yemenite prayerbooks prefaced only Ps. 92 to the Friday evening service, and even that was not universal; see "ʿIyyunim be-hitpatḥut maḥzor teiman," 102.

119 See Kimelman, *The Mystical Meaning of Lekhah Dodi and Kabbalat Shabbat*, 1–32.

wider public. At the very least, Alḍāhirī knew Ibn Lavi's "Bar yoḥai," judging from the supplemental verses he devised.[120] But even if "Lekhah dodi" was not the prototype, it is clear that these poems drew on a common pool of sources.[121]

4.5 "Matoq le-miṣuf u-fannag"

Abner's impressive performance in the Tiberias synagogue leads Mordecai to recognize him. Once reunited, Abner hosts his long-lost friend at a plentiful Sabbath meal, at the conclusion of which he is moved to recite another kabbalistic poem. "Matoq le-miṣuf u-fannag" touches on some of the same themes as "Liqrat penei shabbat" and has recourse to equally intricate webs of symbolism. Constructed of thirteen couplets, with the rhyme scheme *aaab cccb dddb*, etc., the poem is inscribed with the acrostic *Mi-zekharyah ben seʿadyah* in double letters and—somewhat unusually for *Sefer hamusar*—concludes with a Judeo-Arabic *envoi*. The tone is sermonic and hortatory, enjoining study of the *Zohar*, meditation on the *sefirot*, and proper appreciation of the extra soul that accompanies the devotee on the Sabbath. Repeated reference is made to rituals and customs that the kabbalists invested with mythic significance: the *qiddush*, the Sabbath meals, and the donning of finery in honor of the Sabbath bride:

> His poem is sweeter than honeycomb/ but fear of the Lord melts his heart.
> The Sages' command is: delight in/ the Sabbath, its secrets unlock!
>
> If you study the *Zohar* completely/the dead you will soon revive.
> "Remember," "Observe"—both are binding, /Sanctify the Sabbath with wine.
>
> ...
>
> Elevate your thoughts to the Patriarchs, /and afterwards to the Three Crowns.
> Finery in place of mourning clothes/you must don to honor the bride.

---

120 Kimelman, ibid., 23–25 and n. 153, includes "Liqrat penei shabbat" among the contemporary poems that resemble or parallel "Lekhah dodi" in their content and or function. Hallamish, in "Ha-shir bar yoḥai," notes that the earliest sources to mention "Bar yoḥai"—including the 1637 ms. of Wanneh's *tiklāl* containing Alḍāhirī's contrafaction—all link Ibn Lavi's piyyut with the Sabbath eve liturgy. Ratzaby attests that "Bar yoḥai" is to this day recited as part of *Qabbalat shabbat* by many Yemenite congregations; see "ʿIyyunim be-hitpatḥut maḥzor teiman," 102.

121 See Kaunfer, "The History and Meaning of the 'Other' 'Lekha Dodi' Poem(s)."

It is dear to the Lord of the universe/who dwells in celestial realms
That you join *yod-heh* to *vav-heh*/and perfect your soul while alive.
...
You are graced with the gift of a Sabbath-soul; /she brings rest, but you rule over her.

At day's end[122] she returns to her source on high; /her branch reaches as far as the sea;
The mysterious seventh is her fountainhead; /the tenth is also her seat.

He who dons a fine cloak[123] out of love/for God, and nobly prepares
Sabbath delights ...
...
... will come to his Garden in utter bliss /and feast on its succulent fruits.[124]
God will restore the soul of His pious one/to her source on account of his deeds.
...
Two or three times He redeems her/until she repents and returns.

Oh, Creator of all, be there for me!/ For if You are not there for me, who will be for me? (*Yā khāliq al-kul, kun li/wa-in lam takun li fa-man li?*)

In a kabbalistic context, the injunction to fulfill "remember" and "observe," the two versions of the biblical commandment to keep the Sabbath (Exodus 20:8, Deuteronomy 5:12), intimates the union of the feminine and masculine aspects of the divine. The *qiddush* serves as the marriage ceremony between *Shekhinah* and the Holy One.[125] Elevating one's thought to the Patriarchs refers to reflection on the fourth through sixth *sefirot, Gedullah* (*Ḥesed*), *Gevurah, and Tif'eret*, while "the Three Crowns" correspond to the three highest *sefirot, Keter, Ḥokhmah*, and *Binah*. The apparent paradox of locating the source of the extra Sabbath-soul in both the seventh and tenth *sefirot* is resolved once it is clear

122 I.e., at the end of Shabbat.
123 *Me'il hod*, "a majestic cloak," has kabbalistic overtones, *hod* (Majesty) being one of the four lowest *sefirot*.
124 Cant. 4:16, understood here as a reference to ultimate reward.
125 See Kimelman, *The Mystical Meaning of Lekhah Dodi*, English summary, p. ix: "*Shamor ve-zakhor* of the first strophe [of *Lekhah Dodi*] represent the feminine and masculine respectively." See also Ginsburg, *The Sabbath in the Classical Kabbalah*, pp. 107 and 169, n. 196.

that the reference is to *Malkhut*, the seventh *sefirah* in descending order when the enumeration is from *Gedullah* (*Ḥesed*), but the tenth when the count begins from *Keter*.[126] The poet's closing affirmation that God redeems the soul "two or three times" alludes to Job 33:29–30: "Truly, God does all these things two or three times to a man, To bring him back from the Pit, that he may bask in the light of life." Alḍāhirī's verse reflects the kabbalistic belief in transmigration, according to which the sinning soul is condemned to several expiatory *gilgulim* before it can return to its celestial source.[127] Kabbalist exegetes from Naḥmanides (13th century) on addressed the question of theodicy raised by the book of Job with reference to the transmigration of souls, explaining the righteous Job's sufferings as punishment for his sins in a previous existence.[128] Scholem notes that in 16th-century kabbalah, transmigration became a symbol for the exile of the soul and thus

> explained, transfigured and glorified the deepest and most tragic experience of the Jew in the *Galuth*, in a manner which appealed most strongly and directly to the imagination.[129]

Seen in this light, the poet's use of redemptive language (*hu go'alah*) is not incongruous.

4.6 *Discretion vs. Openness*

The openness with which Alḍāhirī treats certain key aspects of kabbalistic theosophy, literature, and liturgical custom bespeaks a keen desire to bring this richly variegated body of mystical belief, writing, and practice to the attention of a broader audience in Yemen. At the same time, several passages in *Sefer hamusar* and *Ṣeidah la-derekh* express a palpable reticence, urging discretion

126 See *Sefer hamusar*, p. 266, n. 82.

127 On the doctrine of transmigration, see Hallamish, *An Introduction to the Kabbalah*, 281–309; Fine, *Physician of the Soul, Healer of the Cosmos*, 300–358; Scholem, *Devils, Demons and Souls*, 186–214; idem, *Major Trends*, 242 and 281–284; idem, *Kabbalah*, 344–350; Verman, "Reincarnation (*gilgul*) and Sephardic Societies," and idem, "Reincarnation and Theodicy." See also Margaliot ed., *Tiqqunei ha-zohar*, sec. 69:112a (cited by Ratzaby, *Sefer hamusar*, p. 266, n. 90).

128 See, e.g., Chavel's notes to Naḥmanides' cryptic comments at the end of his gloss on Job 33:30 in *Kitvei ramban*, 1:101. Scholem notes that Naḥmanides does not use *gilgul* as a technical term for transmigration and that this usage only begins to appear in the second half of the 13th century. Several 13th-century kabbalists had reinterpreted resurrection in terms of transmigration; see Septimus, *Hispano-Jewish Culture in Transition*, pp. 112 and 171, n. 68.

129 Scholem, *Major Trends*, 283–284.

and prudence when discussing matters of kabbalah. The tension between the two impulses seems to confirm Alḍāhirī's status as an early agent of transmission: his enthusiasm for introducing this material to a largely uninitiated public is tempered by the residue of a deeply rooted kabbalistic culture of oral transmission and a time-honored hesitancy to expose the intellectually unsophisticated to such potent ideas and vice versa. In *Ṣeidah la-derekh* he writes:

> When read kabbalistically, these matters have marvelous mysteries, but right now I have only come to make them intelligible to the common man, by means of the plain meaning.[130]

In a number of instances, his ambivalence is evident. Following unambiguous allusions to the metempsychosis of the messianic essence, he immediately expresses regret: "We have already revealed a little of that which it is not seemly to reveal, may God forgive us, Amen."[131] In the third chapter of *Sefer hamusar*, Abner's call for a poem that would incorporate the names of the ten *sefirot* in ascending order is met with extreme reluctance. His audience expresses serious qualms about openly articulating arcane and potentially subversive ideas that have traditionally been the exclusive preserve of the elders of the community. "Bind up the message, seal the instruction with my disciples," they warn, quoting Isaiah 8:16. In the twenty-third chapter, Abner's poem of praise for Abraham Saba's *Ṣeror ha-mor* also betrays an ambivalence about making kabbalistic mysteries accessible to a wider public:

> The man who opens *Ṣeror ha-mor* finds pure myrrh bound up inside;
> It decodes veiled treasures for the wise, turns darkness into light.
> A book that always speaks the truth; guard its mysteries!
> They were gathered by diligent hands, but you may harvest them freely.
> Profound secrets inspire awe, but if you probe, they are sweet.
> …
> Eden's trees were planted for you by the lion cub, who is firstborn.[132]
> …
> You may gather his lilies, but to anyone else do not unlock his door![133]
> …

130 Alḍāhirī, *Sefer ṣeidah la-derekh* on Lev. Ch. 6.

131 Alḍāhirī, *Sefer ṣeidah la-derekh* on Ex. Ch. 25.

132 An allusion to Judah Ḥayyāṭ's commentary on *Ma'arekhet ha-elohut*; see *Sefer hamusar*, p. 269, n. 137.

133 *Sefer hamusar*, pp. 268–269.

The notion that only certain types of readers are deserving of admittance into the inner sanctum is developed at some length in the twenty-first chapter. Here Abner invites his audience to delve into the nature of the *summum bonum* but cautions that such lofty truths may only be discussed in an oblique and cryptic mode. Subtle hints at the truth will be enough for the discerning reader already conversant with the complexities of kabbalistic thought and symbolism:

> For this [question of reward and punishment in the world to come] will not occur to every God-fearing man, but only to the select few .... If an intellectual giant reflects on it, chapter headings will be sufficient for him. Concealing this matter is a wise course of action, while revealing it is a crime. Therefore I will speak in parables .... To the adept, wisdom is openly accessible, while the heart of the fool will surely tremble .... The wise man understands of his own accord.[134]

In adopting a two-tiered approach to disclosing non-literal interpretations of traditional eschatology, Alḍāhirī is following in the footsteps of medieval Andalusian thinkers such as Solomon Ibn Gabirol and Abraham Ibn Ezra, who addressed themselves simultaneously to a philosophically informed intelligentsia and an intellectually less sophisticated audience by couching their bold metaphysical insights in the familiar idiom of the liturgy and classical Jewish sources. And while Alḍāhirī is concerned here with a kabbalistic interpretation of reward and punishment, there is a sense that philosophy and mysticism are both concerned with the all-important quest for spirituality, albeit in different modes. His dismissal of naïve believers and preference for esotericism in such matters calls to mind certain well-known Maimonidean passages.[135]

---

134 *Sefer hamusar*, p. 248, lines 155–160.

135 See: Maimonides, Guide, Introduction to Part I and I:35 in Moses ben Maimon, *Rabbeinu mosheh ben maimon, moreh ha-nevukhim*, ed. and trans. Qāfiḥ, pp. 3–5 and 82–84 and Pines trans., *Moses Maimonides: The Guide of the Perplexed*, pp. 5–6 and 80–81. For Maimonides' discussion of different degrees of sophistication with regard to eschatology, see his Commentary on Mishnah Sanhedrin, Introduction to Chapter 10 ("Ḥeleq") in *Haqdamot le-feirush ha-mishnah*, 109–113 and Twersky, *A Maimonides Reader*, 402–404. On Maimonides' justifications for esotericism and definition of its boundaries, see Halbertal, *Concealment and Revelation*, 49–68. For an instructive discussion of esotericism in early and pre-Expulsion kabbalah see ibid., 69–104. Elliot Wolfson distinguishes between philosophical esotericism as exemplified by the Maimonidean corpus, which "involves the withholding of a profound idea ... that may be communicated," and kabbalistic esotericism in which the truth that must be kept secret is inherently ineffable. See Wolfson, *Abraham Abulafia—Kabbalist and Prophet*, 9–93. On gender symbolism in kabbalistic esotericism see idem, "Occultation of the Feminine and the Body of Secrecy in Medieval Kabbalah."

Both philosophy and kabbalah endeavored to shield knowledge intended for the select few from misinterpretation. The echoes here of the Introduction to Part One of the *Guide of the Perplexed* and *Pereq ḥeleq* are not surprising since Alḍāhirī says explicitly that he drew on the *Guide* alongside the *Zohar* in *Ṣeidah la-derekh*. The conviction of an underlying unity of purpose among his metaphysical sources meant that he was not opposed to integrating philosophy and kabbalah, and saw no contradiction in using Maimonides' rationalistic *magnum opus* or other philosophical works in conjunction with kabbalistic texts.[136] Presumably, due to the particular cultural circumstances shaping their reception and interpretation of kabbalistic materials, early modern Yemenite Jews did not see a rigid dichotomy between rationalism and mysticism—a binary opposition that, although it has pre-modern antecedents, is largely the legacy of 19th-century Western European Jewish scholarship.[137]

5 The Interplay between Kabbalistic and Narrative Elements

Sefer hamusar affords intriguing glimpses of the transmission of kabbalistic thought to Yemen in the 16th century, yet those scholars who have mined the work for such factual information have invariably ignored the belletristic settings in which it is embedded. It hardly needs saying that, with its contrived plots and panoply of stock characters, *Sefer hamusar* bears little resemblance to purely theoretical kabbalistic treatises, such as those mostly Spanish works Alḍāhirī names as his sources, or the didactic, anthologizing texts of 17th-century Yemenite authors. Even Alḍāhirī's own esoteric Torah commentary, *Ṣeidah la-derekh*, is governed by such a distinct set of generic conventions that

136 See, e.g., Alḍāhirī's statements to this effect in *Ṣeidah la-derekh* on Gen. Ch. 2, as quoted in Gaimani, *Temurot be-moreshet yahadut teiman*, 72. On Maimonides and classical kabbalah, see Wolfson, "Beneath the Wings of the Great Eagle: Maimonides and Thirteenth-Century Kabbalah."

137 Hava Tirosh-Samuelson writes of the emergence of kabbalah that it "became a self-conscious program for the interpretation of Judaism at the end of the twelfth century, to counter Maimonidean intellectualism. Nonetheless, kabbalists addressed the theoretical issues of concern to the rationalist philosophers and theorized within the conceptual framework of contemporary philosophy .... In Jewish intellectual history, kabbalah and philosophy were closely intertwined." She notes that the difference between philosophy and kabbalah "concerned the precise content of the esoteric meaning of the revealed tradition and the proper way of transmitting it." See her "Philosophy and Kabbalah: 1200–1600." See also Schwartz, "Contacts Between Jewish Philosophy and Mysticism at the Beginning of the Fifteenth Century."

it is often difficult to recognize that the two works are by the same author. Where the tone of his Torah commentary is grave, prescriptive, and often lackluster, despite its mystical content, the kabbalistic ideas in *Sefer hamusar* are refracted through layers of narrative invention, disguise, and buoyant creativity. Even though the work's individual *maqāmas* can at first blush seem disjointed, they are self-contained literary units that, on closer reading, may reveal subtle links between their component parts. With this in mind, it is worth considering the kabbalistic sections in the larger context of the chapters in which they appear and not simply in isolation. The kabbalistic poems and prose passages are consistently serious, meditative, and didactic, in keeping with their teachings whose mastery requires initiation into an arcane realm of cosmic symbols and associations. But the frame stories surrounding these pieces are often ironic or downright comical, firmly anchored in the here and now. These entertaining settings may well have been intended to draw the audience in and make the frequently opaque mystical material more palatable to readers encountering it for the first time. But the incongruity can work in the opposite direction as well, to undermine the gravity of the protagonists' metaphysical or theosophical excursuses. In this reading, Alḍāhirī deliberately deflates the pious postures of the fictitious characters who present the work's mystical ideas, and in so doing betrays a certain ambivalence about the very ideal of disseminating kabbalah through poetry and belles-lettres.

The narrative in the third *maqāma* is full of humorous elements that color the chapter's kabbalistic interludes. The initial challenge to compose a kabbalistic poem is issued by Abner masquerading as an individual of commanding presence ("one of the men rose and we all grew silent") but whose attire suggests pomposity, or perhaps excessive religiosity ("on his head was a turban [of cloth] more than fifty cubits long"). This depiction recalls Judah Alḥarizi's satirical evocation of a feckless cantor in the city of Mosul, whose beard not only reaches down to his navel but whose head is crowned with "a turban of wondrous size, a cloud of linen some two hundred cubits round."[138] Inasmuch as Alḍāhirī explicitly names the *Taḥkemoni* as one of his literary models and sets this chapter in Irbīl (roughly one hundred kilometers east of Mosul, and a city that figures in Alḥarizi's critique of Hebrew poets in the East), he may well have had his predecessor's lampoon of the incompetent precentor in mind

138 See: Alḥarizi, *Taḥkemoni*, ed. Yahalom-Katsumata, #30/24; Reichert trans., *The Tahkemoni of Judah Al-harizi*, 2:110–121; Segal, *The Book of Taḥkemoni*, 215–223 and 534–540 (the quote is from p. 216); and Tanenbaum, "Arrogance, Bad Form, and Curricular Narrowness," esp. 63–66. There is also a poem mocking an empty-headed scoundrel with an oversized turban in the 50th *maqāma*; see Yahalom-Katsumata p. 545, #48.

when portraying Abner in a mildly ridiculous light which, arguably, detracts from his credibility as a connoisseur of kabbalistic ideas. Alḍāhirī's chapter opens with negative remarks about the moral turpitude of a Jewish community he encountered on his way to Irbīl, harking back to Alḥarizi's Mosul spoof, which reflects a refined Andalusian's disdain for the philistinism of his ill-bred eastern coreligionists. Even though Yemenite Jews also hailed from an Eastern Islamicate milieu, Alḍāhirī's protagonists consider themselves culturally distinct from their Iraqi brethren. Yet, in the integration of kabbalah, Alḥarizi's work could not serve as a direct model. There is no kabbalistic content in the *Taḥkemoni*, which antedates the *Zohar* by more than six decades and takes no notice of the early, closed kabbalistic circles of Provence or of the arrival of kabbalah in Spain.[139]

Abner's promise to fête the individual who successfully improvises a poem on the ten *sefirot* sets up a variation on the standard *maqāma* scenario in which brilliant rhetorical displays are used to extract material gifts from credulous onlookers. If it is generally the roguish hero who employs verbal skills for personal gain, here it is initially Mordecai, the narrator, who produces the winning verses while Abner furnishes the reward. Paradoxically, the blandishments appear ill-suited to the composition of a poem with transcendent theosophical content. There would seem to be an intentional irony in the promise of a lavish feast and material profit for drawing on one's knowledge of otherworldly doctrines, particularly when such insights are acquired through intensive study predicated on abstemiousness. The disjunction suggests that the narrator recites his poem in order to obtain a sumptuous reward and is motivated by self-interest rather than an altruistic desire to share his kabbalistic expertise. Or perhaps, anticipating a theme that later becomes explicit, Alḍāhirī intimates that, in its susceptibility to such remuneration, the composition of poetry—even kabbalistic poetry—is inherently trivial and therefore of far less consequence than immersion in "the great sciences ... that entail the attainment of the intelligibles." When Abner's audience is leery of crafting such a poem, for fear of disclosing heretofore guarded knowledge, there is a sense that they are either naïve or overly cautious. This impression is compounded when Mordecai scoffs at their reservations and brashly offers to recite the verses he has penned. He makes sure to impress us with his savoir-faire, which contrasts starkly with their timid response to Abner's challenge:

139 On the rapid diffusion of kabbalah in Spain during the lifetime of Rabbi Meir Halevi Abulafia (c. 1165–1244), a Talmudist and exact contemporary of Alḥarizi based in Toledo, see Septimus, *Hispano-Jewish Culture in Transition*, 104–115.

> When I heard their words, I … laughed in front of them, then I sat enthroned like a god. I quickly rose and said in my heart, "In a place where there are no men, strive to be a man."[140]

The circus-like preparations for the celebratory meal that ensues are marked by an almost manic quality as the guests perform tasks normally delegated to a wealthy man's scullery staff:

> at the beginning of the evening, while our minds were still clear, the host paired off the guests and they cast lots—to the accompaniment of timbrel and dance—for the preparation and arrangement of the feast. Some of them slaughtered and some skinned the beasts; some supervised and judged; some prowled in search of spices and gathered various greens; some were cooks and some were bakers …

It is even possible that the phrase used in line 73, *le-taqqen hase'udah* (to arrange the feast), is an ironic play on the kabbalistic *tiqqun haṣot*, the midnight vigils dedicated to study, prayer, repentance, lamenting the destruction of the Temple, and mourning the exile of the *Shekhinah*. At this "*tiqqun*," it falls to the narrator and the host to compose and recite poems "and to open unseeing eyes with pointed epigrams, parables and mysteries." The previously diffident guests are now won over to the idea of kabbalistic verse and explicitly request a paean to the *Zohar*:

> Seeing as today we heard awe-inspiring mysteries and wonders that resemble prophecies, take counsel … and compose a poem that sings the praises of the *Zohar* … and of the great luminary, Rabbi Simeon ben Yoḥai.

This swift about-face suggests that the initial, desperate objections to any such enterprise ("because of our sins we shall be bowed down in humility, for these matters are ancient … and their transmitters have already been decided upon") were either baseless or not as principled as they seemed. In Alḍāhirī's hands, the guests' conversion is thus either a didactic device, intended to reassure his readers that open discussion of mystical ideas is acceptable, or a moral critique of those who oppose such candor. Alternately, the reversal underscores their gullibility: the guests are dupes who have been taken in by the pleasures of a feast; unawares, they fall prey to the machinations of the scheming protago-

---

140 *Sefer hamusar*, p. 78, lines 30–32; cf. *Avot* 2:6.

nist who intended all along to exploit their generosity. Read in such a light, the *maqāma* becomes a cautionary tale concerning the vulnerability of the common folk, who are so easily swayed by smooth-tongued strangers. That kabbalistic poetry is the proximate cause of their corruption suggests some authorial misgiving or uncertainty regarding the project of popularizing esoteric teachings through that medium.

There is a curious dynamic between the revelation and concealment of the main characters' identities and the disclosure and suppression of kabbalistic ideas. Narrator and host are less than completely honest and far from transparent in their dealings with their eager disciples: although sympathetic to their request, Mordecai now claims to have exhausted his fund of kabbalistic poems and deferentially urges the host to recite one instead. The man laughs, unnerving Mordecai with a reaction that seems out of character, but then proceeds to rise to the challenge. Following his delivery of "Ishim eqra me-har el har" ("O men, from mountain to mountain I call to you: Come and study the *Zohar*!"), the assembled look at one another in astonishment. The allusion to Genesis 43:33 (*va-yitmehu ha'anashim ish el re'ehu*) is particularly apt—like Joseph's brothers, Abner's audience is manipulated by a knowing agent who has deliberately concealed his identity. The narrator, who is also struck by the poet's eloquence, inspects the man more closely and confesses:

> When I saw his majesty and splendor, I hid his secret in my heart, and he whispered in my ear, "Are you Mordecai the Sidonian?" I answered him meaningfully, "Are you Abner ben Ḥeleq the Yemenite?" So he embraced and kissed me, but I was unable to query him about the profundity of his words, for I knew that he was cunning and that we would conceal our intention from the people facing us. These men exclaimed unanimously, "How good and how pleasant it is that brothers dwell together. Blessed be God, the Lord of Israel, who has not withheld a redeemer for each type of wisdom (*asher lo hishbit le-khol ḥokhmah go'el*)."

In most chapters of *Sefer hamusar*, Mordecai unmasks Abner towards the end of the episode, but here the two recognize each other simultaneously. Out of innate sympathy, Mordecai knows instinctively that his old chum will want to conceal their identities from their audience. Thus they have a private anagnorisis from which the ancillary characters are excluded but to which the reader is privy. There seems to be an ironic symmetry, or perhaps an inverse proportion between the willingness of narrator and hero to reveal the hidden mysteries of kabbalistic doctrine and their reluctance to disclose who they are. But where the opacity of kabbalistic tradition belongs to a world of heightened spirituality, the disguises of the work's protagonists are fuelled by ulterior motives of a worldly nature. By conspiring to remain nameless, Mordecai and Abner augment their mystique to manipulate the emotions and purse strings of their uncritical admirers, who never demand to know their names. Even Mordecai is a bit bemused when, at chapter's end, Abner asserts with a certain pathos that the oppressive yoke of the non-Jewish authorities in Yemen led him to abandon his wife, family, and native land entirely and reveals that he has taken a new wife in Irbīl and has utterly forgotten his home and former life.

Despite the sober patina, the persona Abner has adopted here is no more authentic or less capricious than any of the others he assumes and sheds throughout *Sefer hamusar*. In the present chapter, Abner's way with words rubs off on Mordecai, and they both accede to requests for additional literary creations. In one of these there is, again, an intimation that things are not quite what they seem. A member of the audience asks for a Hebrew riddle that may be read from beginning to end or the other way round, like the precious one he has found in Arabic. He specifies that it should vilify a man he had considered a loyal friend but who had insulted him outrageously. Abner trembles and sheds tears at the enormity of this request. Mordecai consoles him, saying, "Since we are both here there is no reason to fear, 'but woe betide him who is alone and falls with no companion to raise him!'"[141] Mordecai then produces an enigmatic, reversible passage that functions as a sort of automatic palinode: read forward, it praises the former friend, but read backward it curses him. As noted, this rhetorical feat is modeled on a reversible letter of praise in Chapter 8 of the *Taḥkemoni* (#7 in Yahalom-Katsumata), which was in turn inspired by al-Ḥarīrī's 17th *maqāma* ("The Reversed"). David Simha Segal's insight that Alḥarizi "plays (seriously) with the phenomenon of things being the reverse of what they seem" is particularly apt here as well.[142] Alḍāhirī's juxtaposition of mystical passages with subtle caricatures of human foibles, tales of mendacity, concealed identities, and ironic reversals of opinions and texts helps to make his esoteric doctrines more accessible to a broad readership. But it also highlights the mutability of this world, suggesting that the key to understanding the universe and its relationship to the divine lies elsewhere, in the inner workings of the sefirotic system. If there is any thread of continuity between the chapter's seemingly disparate vignettes, it is that they all involve skilled poetic improvisation. Seen in this light, the composition of kabbalistic poems might become

141 *Sefer hamusar*, p. 83, lines 126–128. The quotation is from Ecc. 4:10.

142 See Segal, *The Book of Taḥkemoni*, 469. Alḍāhirī's poem is discussed in greater detail in the section on constrained writing in Chapter One above.

simply one more rhetorical feat, intended to amuse as well as edify. As products of the honeyed speech that serves the work's protagonists so well, these poems become part of the entertainment as much as of Alḍāhirī's educational mission. This strategy is not unlike that deployed to transform the work's philosophical and ethical teachings into a source of enjoyment.

The narrative in Chapter 21 also exploits the *maqāma* conceit of employing dazzling rhetorical gifts for personal gain. As noted above, even before Abner makes an appearance, Mordecai advises the sages of Bursa to send for him in order to satisfy their yearnings for a paean to Rabbenu Jeroham. Out of gratitude for this recommendation, the sages tell Mordecai to remain with them, promising to extend their generosity to him until Abner arrives. After three months, Abner's ship docks and he instructs Mordecai to spread the news of his arrival and warn those who have a request not to come empty-handed. The services he renders to each petitioner are received to great acclaim, and a feast is made "with much killing of cattle and slaughtering of sheep," and with "royal wine ... served in abundance."[143] Following his elegant translation and solution of the riddle poems that are brought to him by one of the guests, Abner is again lionized and richly rewarded. And even when Abner insists that he and his audience abandon these frivolous amusements in favor of sober, eschatological matters, alluding to his own kabbalistically informed comments on Genesis 2:1 in *Sefer ṣeidah la-derekh*, and producing a poem in praise of that work, his listeners acknowledge his astounding eloquence with precious gifts. The donations could be framed in terms of reciprocal, agonistic gift exchange: feeling profoundly indebted to the wise stranger for the priceless secret wisdom he imparts, the onlookers are unable to match his benefaction but show their gratitude with material gifts. But, as always, the *maqāma* blueprint superimposes itself on the proceedings: Abner takes his leave and disappears, implying that even his deepest kabbalistic musings are grist for his mill.

The kabbalistic poems in Chapter 23—dense with demanding allusions to cosmic myths and symbols that require associative unraveling—are embedded in and refracted through the narrative of Mordecai's visit to the synagogue in Tiberias. With the wonder and enthusiasm of an amateur ethnographer, he remarks on the fast pace of the worship and the unfamiliarity of the precentor's towering wooden platform (the raised *almemar/almemor* of Sephardi synagogues) as well as on the synagogue décor and the content of the Friday night prayers. The ostensibly fortuitous meeting between narrator and protagonist

143 Cf. Esther 1:7, "Royal wine was served in abundance, as befits a king, in golden beakers, beakers of varied design." It is just possible that the allusion is intended to introduce an element of the carnivalesque atmosphere of Purim.

introduces a familiar note of artificiality into the plot. The recognition scene provokes a self-abasing portrait of Yemenite Jewry, with Mordecai wondering how Abner could possibly have been installed as *ḥazzan* in the synagogue attended by the Sephardi élite, given his inferior, Arabic-inflected Hebrew. Abner replies that his pleasing voice, fluency, and poetic prowess earned him the appointment, ignoring Mordecai's fear that his pronunciation might offend the aesthetic sensibilities of the culturally refined Sephardim. Abner's defiant retort not only flows from his given role as a seductive speaker but also exploits the cultural stereotype of Yemenite Jews as uncommonly gifted poets and unparalleled stylists. Strikingly, Abner has overcome the cultural divide delineated by Mordecai's typology by composing kabbalistic Sabbath hymns and immersing himself in kabbalistic study at a time when such endeavors were still rare in his native land. Despite hints of authorial reticence, this too may be a didactic touch, intended to suggest that such intellectual and spiritual achievements are within the grasp of Yemenite Jewry. (The landscape would change radically with the advent of Shalem Shabbazi.[144])

On the other hand, Abner's pose as pious precentor enables Alḍāhirī to showcase his hero in yet another shape-shifting guise: with an uncanny ability to mimic diverse styles, the clever Yemeni fools even the proud Tiberians into accepting him as their representative before God. The admiration with which Mordecai relates Abner's impressive performance is a function of the narrator's inability to view his crafty friend critically. Since the wily Abner is the conduit for the serious kabbalistic verse in this chapter, the reader has to wonder whether his questionable claim to moral authority detracts from the sincerity or effectiveness of his kabbalistic teachings.[145] In other words, how veracious are profound spiritual truths spoken by a mendacious protagonist? And without looking outside the text, how do we know whether the author wholeheartedly endorses the mystical study his fictitious characters present while he remains discreetly in the background? Does this chapter advocate kabbalistic study and mystical Sabbath practices as a means to spiritual regeneration and ultimate reward? Does the inscription of "Liqrat penei shabbat" with the acrostic "Zechariah" imply the author's imprimatur on the poem's mystical content? If so, we can read the *maqāma* as an attempt to make a broader Yemenite Jewish readership aware of kabbalistic spirituality. The work's belletristic medium then becomes an important vehicle for popularizing kabbalah. But using an unreliable scoundrel like Abner as a mouthpiece for weighty ideas blurs the

144 See Tobi, "Shabazi, Shalom" and idem, "Politics and Poetry in the Works of Shalom Shabazī."

145 Cf. Monroe's arguments in *The Art of Badīʿ az-Zamān al-Hamadhānī*.

lines between trustworthy and suspect sources of wisdom, again suggesting an authorial reticence regarding the propriety of disseminating kabbalah through poetry and belles-lettres.

In point of fact, Alḍāhirī's esoteric Torah commentary, *Ṣeidah la-derekh*, explores many of the same kabbalistic motifs but in an exegetical mode, without the elaborate storytelling and side shows. The tone of the work is entirely unsuitable for drawing in diffident readers, there is nothing playful or humorous about it. Its kabbalistic content still has an introductory, midrashic feel and is not densely symbolic or mythical; Alḍāhirī has frequent recourse to numerology/*gemaṭria* (determining the alphanumeric value of words), *notarikon* (treating each word of the Bible as an acronym), and homilies based on the identification of biblical figures such as the Patriarchs with particular *sefirot*. Periodically, he is too reticent to explicate a difficult crux kabbalistically, and at other times he avails himself of parables to convey esoteric matters obliquely. Yet, qua exegete he may have assumed he was writing for a more homogeneous audience that would not have required (or even sanctioned) embedding his theoretical material in drollery.

6 Conclusions

Along with its levity, aesthetic emphases, and moral instruction, there are a number of indications that Alḍāhirī envisioned *Sefer hamusar* as a means of introducing kabbalistic traditions to a broader audience than might be inclined to consult his solemn exegetical work, *Ṣeidah la-derekh*. He introduces kabbalistic themes close to the beginning of *Sefer hamusar*; praises classical works of Spanish kabbalah, among them the *Zohar*, *Shaʿarei orah*, *Sefer maʿarekhet ha-elohut*, *Ṣeror ha-mor*, and *Tolaʿat yaʿaqov*; invokes the basic doctrine of the ten *sefirot*; embraces an esoteric reading of the Sabbath and endorses Safedian Sabbath rituals; composes a poem resembling "Lekhah dodi" and similar kabbalistic hymns that touch on the mythical and the demonic; and advocates kabbalistic study as the true key to man's ultimate reward. By setting highly symbolic theosophical representations of the godhead and man's relation with the divine in an engaging, fictionalized setting, Alḍāhirī could appeal to a Yemenite Jewish public unfamiliar with kabbalistic thought. By reversing the reluctance of fictional sages to engage in the composition of kabbalistic poems, he could reassure his readers that open discussion of mystical ideas was acceptable. And by having his protagonists contradict a cultural stereotype that proclaimed kabbalistic wisdom beyond the ken of Yemenite Jewry, he could suggest that such intellectual and spiritual achievements were within their grasp. The tales of deception and human fallibility that were hallmarks of the *maqāma* genre could help to valorize the ethereal kabbalistic speculations embedded within them. The anti-hero's moral shortcomings could serve as useful foils for nobler character traits, underscoring the need for the heightened spirituality that might be attained through immersion in kabbalah. While Alḍāhirī does not gloss the more abstruse doctrines alluded to in his verse, his poems in praise of kabbalistic books do steer the reader towards expositions of the sefirotic system and commentaries on those theoretical works.

At the same time, Alḍāhirī intimates some hesitation about the use of poetry to popularize kabbalah. By exploiting the layered narrative structure of the *maqāma* genre, he pokes gentle fun at his self-appointed educational task. His ambivalence may be ascribed in part to his status as an early agent of transmission, but it also grows out of the very nature of the *maqāma*. Unlike more theoretical genres of Hebrew writing, the belletristic *maqāma* derives its potency from a creative and unresolved tension between truth and falsehood. By placing his kabbalistic material in the mouth of an ignoble character posing as a pious individual, or by weaving it into complex narratives entailing reversals of opinion, Alḍāhirī not only perpetuates that moral ambiguity, but also diffuses and masks his authorial voice, obscuring his true view of his own intellectual enterprise. In an ironic twist, Alḍāhirī's apparently profound regard for kabbalistic myth and its recherché symbolism prompts him to question the worth of his poetic medium despite the potent and fertile imagination they both require and the power of both media to invest language with a magical aura. His protagonist twice repudiates poetry as frivolous and ultimately futile when compared with the pursuit of mystical knowledge and its attendant spiritual rewards. His critique hinges not so much on the tenacious medieval view that falsehood is integral to poetry ("the best part of poetry is the most false"; *meitav ha-shir kezavo*)—though it may well be hovering in the background—as on the related assumption that the type of skills required to produce poetry are inferior to those necessary for the attainment of kabbalistic insights. While it avoids technical terminology, this appraisal recalls Shem Tov Falaquera's condemnation of poetry, whose metaphorical language not only lies but is the product of the imaginative faculty. Aristotelian epistemology, to which Falaquera (c. 1225–1295) subscribed, ranked the imagination below the rational faculty which is responsible for the attainment of philosophical truths. To an extent, then, Alḍāhirī's seeming disenchantment with poetry when confronted with kabbalah parallels Falaquera's reorientation of curricular priorities in his 13th-century *Book of the Seeker*, although Falaquera renounces the cultivation of poetry and belles-lettres for the pursuit of true philosophical wisdom rather than kabbalistic illumination.[146] In both cases, the disillusionment is particularly acute vis-à-vis rhetorically clever occasional, non-devotional poetry, which Abner dismisses with the zeal of the convert as "a vain waste of effort and time."

It is curious that Alḍāhirī's reservations vis-à-vis poetry surface particularly in those chapters with kabbalistic content where Abner's reversals occur as unpredictably as his quicksilver transformations from one imposture to another. Perhaps, in attempting to introduce mystical thought to his coreligionists, Alḍāhirī was aware here more than elsewhere of the limitations of language to express the ineffable, despite the obvious pleasure he derived from the jewelled stylistics of poetic composition and the emulative challenges of contrafaction. Unlike many authors before and after him (Falaquera, Ḥarāzī, Manṣura) who valued the prosimetric medium primarily for its instructive potential, Alḍāhirī genuinely relished cultivating the picaresque *maqāma* in all of its narrative abundance, savoring its mélange of humble and sublime and its literary potpourri of pre-existing genres. And yet, despite the text's obvious delight in its own complexity, and despite Alḍāhirī's voracious intellectual curiosity, *Sefer hamusar* was completely eclipsed by the celebrated verse of Shalem Shabbazi and his circle and by the broader turn to kabbalah in 17th-century Yemen. There is perhaps a cruel irony in the fact that the mystical content of Shabbazi's poetry made it so much more appealing and acceptable than Alḍāhirī's lone exemplar of the *maqāma* genre, with its sincere if sometimes uneven attempts at kabbalistic verse. Nevertheless, Alḍāhirī was destined to be remembered as the one who facilitated the transmission of "this new, alien kabbalah" to his native land.

---

146 For the complete Hebrew text (not a critical edition) see Falaquera, *Sefer ha-mevaqqesh*, ed. M. Tamah; for selections see Schirmann, *HPSP* 2:331–342. Ayelet Oettinger is preparing a critical edition that will bring to fruition the late Michael Rand's planned edition and commentary. See also Levine trans., *Falaquera's Book of the Seeker*. On Falaquera's arguments for and against poetry see: Brann, *The Compunctious Poet*, 129–137; Ossorio, "Shem Tov Ibn Falaquera: From Logic to Ethics; a Redefinition of Poetry in the Thirteenth Century"; and Harvey ed. and trans., *Falaquera's Epistle of the Debate*, esp. Appendix III, pp. 128–132, "Why the Philosopher Stopped Writing Poetry: Some Notes on the Role of Poetry for Falaquera."

CHAPTER 7

The Urge to Be Immortalized: Auto-Epitaphs, Eulogies, and the Afterlife of *Sefer hamusar*

In the forty-fifth and final chapter of *Sefer hamusar*, the much-traveled and long-suffering narrator, Mordecai the Sidonian, is overcome with an unappeasable sense of despair at the realization that his days are numbered and that there is no one to lament him after he is gone.[1] Terrifying thoughts of Judgment Day cause his heart to melt and his bones to quake, while the numbing dread of being forgotten nearly paralyzes him. Adapting a line from Shem Tov Ardutiel's 14th-century *viddui* (a poetic confession for the Day of Atonement), he bemoans his hopeless predicament: "If I speak, my guilt will be revealed, but if I keep silent, my bones will waste away."[2] In other words, touting his own accomplishments smacks of hubris and may expose his worst defects, but if there is no one else to celebrate his achievements, excessive modesty will almost certainly ensure his irreversible descent into oblivion.

Mordecai retreats to the outskirts of the city to find some relief from his inner turmoil. Sitting under a bush, he espies a man roaming aimlessly in the distance.[3] The man is bowed with age and leans on a staff. While walking, he peruses a missive that he shields with his cloak and then wearily sits down on the path. Mordecai runs to him, driven by his self-proclaimed love for his fellow man, and upon reaching him discovers that he is none other than Abner ben Ḥeleq. The narrator asks his beloved friend, "how it [is] that Time [has] so altered him" (*eikh shinnah zeman et ta'amo*; cf. Ps. 34:1) and inquires "where he [has] come from, and where he [is] going" (cf. II Sam. 3:25).[4] By way of response, Abner gives a brief and curious account of an epistolary exchange with a young man of noble lineage named Abraham ben Zechariah Halevi from the southern

1 *Sefer hamusar*, 459–470.

2 Alḍāhirī cites this line again on p. 418, ll. 23–24 (#39). Payyeṭan, author, and translator, Shem Tov Ardutiel (c. 1290–c. 1369) commanded Hebrew, Arabic, and Castilian. He is best known for his *Proverbios Morales*, but his *viddui* for Yom Kippur, "Ribbono shel 'olam, bir'oti baḥurotai," is preserved in numerous *maḥzorim* of Sephardi and eastern rites; see Davidson, *Thesaurus*, 3:375, no. 479. For the text with English translation, see Loewe, *Hebrew Poems and Translations*, 276–290. See also Nini and Fruchtman eds., *Rabbi Shem Tov Ben Izḥak Ardutiel*, 17–18.

3 The allusion to Hagar and Ishmael (Gen. 21:15) reinforces the outcast status of narrator and hero, who exist on the margins of society.

4 In Ps. 34:1, the phrase *be-shannoto et ta'amo* means to feign madness.

 | DOI:10.1163/9789004733787_009

Yemeni city of Jibla, who had sent him "wise questions and puzzling problems" to which Abner has replied with "myriad instructive responses."

There is a subtle suggestion of something disquieting in the letter of inquiry from Abraham ben Zechariah Halevi. Abner says that, rather than avoid his correspondent, he has written him a solicitous response in which he sings his praises and will send it via a Muslim caravan whose arrival he is now awaiting. Mordecai begs to see the clear and elegant language (*ṣaḥut leshono*) of Abner's epistle even though he does not know the sage in whose honor it is written, and his friend complies, conceding that its "language is eloquent, even though I am a broken man." The letter is lavish in its accolades, interweaving fragments of biblical verses into an extended metaphor of an intellectual vineyard that Halevi has cultivated with care to produce a choice vintage. But several of its scriptural phrases are drawn from prophetic allegories of chastisement, notably Isaiah chapters 5 and 63 and Ezekiel chapter 31, intimating, perhaps, subtle disapproval of the young scholar's brazen self-assuredness. The ambivalence may relate to Halevi's kabbalistic pursuits: in the 34th *maqāma*, Mordecai finds a letter praising Abraham ben Zechariah Halevi of Jibla for his profound knowledge of kabbalah despite his relative youth.[5]

The account of this correspondence is then abruptly dropped, not to be resumed. The story seems to serve mainly as evidence of Abner's ability to praise a contemporary with supreme elegance and fluency. Convinced of his companion's generous capacity to eulogize, Mordecai conveys his preoccupation with his own posthumous reputation and entreats Abner to compose his epitaph, not in the strict sense of a tombstone inscription so much as a literary monument, a final homage to his eventful life and fruitful intellectual efforts. Mordecai is so unsettled that he does not use a conventional technical term for the memorial he has requested; instead, he frets that "there is no one to sing my praises after I am gone" and tells Abner that he fled the city because his "heart was inflamed" with worry. Abner is the one who introduces the vocabulary of lamentation, freely interchanging the biblical terms *qinah* (lament), *misped* (eulogy), and *evel* (mourning), largely on the basis of Micah 1:8, even though by Alḍāhirī's time these had evolved into distinct literary genres.[6] However, Abner is visibly shaken by Mordecai's request and protests that it is inappropriate to lament his cherished friend while he is still alive. Mordecai counters that it would be an even greater disgrace to allow him to pass away unremarked, "like

5 See *Sefer hamusar*, pp. 45, 379–382, and 460–461, and Ratzaby, *Toratan shelivnei teiman*, 234.

6 See, e.g., *Sefer hamusar* p. 462, lines 55, 60, and 62, and p. 464, lines 99–100. The biblical model of the elegy exercised a powerful hold over later poets; see e.g., Salah, "A Contextual Analysis of the Jewish Italian Elegy." For rabbinic prototypes, see Feldman, "The Rabbinic Lament."

a useless vessel." If Abner does not memorialize him, "who will save my soul from Sheol?" (*mi hu asher ya'amod le-haṣil nafshi mi-yad she'ol?*). He bolsters his argument with a rhyming intertext from Ruth 4:4 whose original scriptural context confirms Abner's unique qualification to perpetuate Mordecai's name for posterity: *ve'ede'ah ki ein zulatekha lig'ol* ("for there is no one to redeem but you"). Mordecai begs Abner to write an elegy or *qinah* that would speak in the name of his sons, "so that through it they might be honored and befriended by my people and so that 'all who see them shall recognize them.'"[7] Despite his misgivings, Abner consents, reciting a heartfelt rhymed prose lament whose rueful introduction teems with biblical images of woe and whose main portion traces the departed's life journey, specifying the rich array of disciplines in which he excelled, and naming the enduring works he composed in these fields. Abner's elegiac style is well suited to memorializing his boon companion, combining a highly personalized appreciation with more conventional language and tropes drawn from venerable biblical models.

The opening apostrophe, "O hills of Yemen, let there be no dew or rain on you," draws on David's dirge for Saul and Jonathan (II Samuel 1:21) and leads into metaphors of cosmic mourning ("the lights of our heavens have darkened") and universal grief at "the passing of our father, our chariot and horseman, Mordecai the Sidonian, before his friend, Abner ben Ḥeleq the Yemenite."[8] The details of Mordecai's extensive travels to distant lands and his distinctive intellectual contributions are then reviewed:

> He made the circuit of all the provinces of India, Hormuz, and Basra … he passed through the lands of Babylonia, Aleppo, Damascus, and on his way his learning did not cease. He reached upper Galilee, the cities of Safed and Tiberias, all of the Land of Israel, the city of Zion, and Jerusalem rebuilt. He saw her sages, the heads of the *yeshivot* and the graves of the patriarchs. He did not cease trying to learn each one's wisdom. He went to sea; crossed wildernesses; moved about among wild animals, all in order to restore righteousness, uprightness, and purity ….[9] He reached Egypt and Ethiopia with acquisitions and wealth, and concluded [his journey]

7 Cf. Is. 61:9.

8 Cf. II Kings 2:12, where Elisha witnesses Elijah's ascent to heaven and cries out, "Oh, father, father! Israel's chariot and horsemen!" The allusion suggests an implicit comparison between Mordecai and the biblical prophet who does not die an ordinary mortal's death.

9 There are echoes here of phrases in the *Taḥkemoni*; see Alḥarizi, *Taḥkemoni*, ed. Yahalom and Katsumata #23 (= #35), p. 317, lines 14–15. On the import of these phrases in the specific context of Alḥarizi's narrative, see Kfir, *A Matter of Geography*, 70–71 and Rand, *The Evolution of al-Ḥarizi's Taḥkemoni*, 11–12, 19.

in his land, the land of Yemen, as a worker and an artisan.[10] He settled among a people not bereft [of their God] and disseminated Torah according to his ability .... He gave others to drink of his spiced wine: with words of kabbalah his way was paved. He dwelled there many years with friends who listened, full of sap and freshness, until the day they were banished to the towers by the decree of the one by Whom actions are measured. Close to forty years he dwelled there, gathering various kinds of wisdom, a little here, a little there, and several delightful treasures from the lairs of leopards and the dens of lions. He clearly explained several opaque aggadot; he was renowned in scriptural study; he understood every instance of legal reasoning; he diligently bent his knee [a scribal pose].[11] He wrote *Sefer ṣeidah la-derekh* on the Torah; in poetry he was prodigious and wise, composing splendid verse in myriad forms; everyone recited his poems .... How many eulogies did he compose for every perfect and upright man according to what his honor dictated![12] His attainments were vast. His *Sefer haʿanaq*, full of homonymic rhymes, is sweeter than honeycomb. He is the author of *Sefer ha-musar ve-ha-ḥokhmah* which offers the young knowledge and foresight.[13] He made time for regular Torah study by night as well as by day, and comported himself correctly; not a night passed without study; he went wherever the spirit of Torah impelled him.[14] He was raised on the fear of God; humility was his constant companion; he was crowned with piety.[15]

10 *Ve-ḥatam be-arṣo ereṣ ha-teiman/ke-foʿel veʾumman* [*sic*]. Scholars have inferred that Alḍāhirī was an artisan in Yemen, particularly as he seems to have been familiar with the properties of precious metals; for evidence, see *Sefer hamusar* #15, l. 41 (p. 185) and #32, lines 117–129 (pp. 371–372) and his gloss on the Golden Calf (Ex. 32:3–4) in *Ṣeidah la-derekh*.

11 There is no extant work of aggadic exegesis by Alḍāhirī; see *Sefer hamusar*, p. 464, n. 88. "He diligently bent his knee": scribes copied books while seated on one knee on the ground with the other knee tucked underneath them; see *Sefer hamusar*, p. 464, n. 88. For an image see https://www.loc.gov/item/2019710061/.

12 It is difficult to assess Abner's praise for the many eulogies Mordecai composed since none are extant; see *Sefer hamusar*, p. 464, n. 90. Almost all the poems in ms. Ginsburg 1306 (folios 119^{b}–176^{b}) have Judeo-Arabic superscriptions, but none are labeled *marthiya* or *rithāʾ*, the standard headers for laments over the passing of a beloved individual.

13 Cf. Prov. 1:2–4. The allusion draws an implicit parallel between Alḍāhirī's *Sefer hamusar* and the book of Proverbs, perhaps with the intention of legitimizing what is actually a rather unorthodox book of moral instruction.

14 The phrase "by night as well as by day" could also be understood as "in the dark as well as the light." Ratzaby notes that in the 16th century, oil for lamps was costly, so most Torah study was undertaken from memory at night, in the dark. See *Sefer hamusar*, p. 464, n. 93.

15 *Sefer hamusar*, pp. 463, l. 76–pp. 464, l. 95.

Having extolled Mordecai for his impressive achievements in the realms of kabbalah, biblical and aggadic exegesis, oral law, poetry, and belles-lettres, Abner accedes to his friend's request for a threnody that his sons might recite (there is no mention of a wife or wives), and concludes with brave words of consolation:

> He bequeathed a blessing in connection with his work: ten sons who lament him bitterly, saying, Woe is us, for the ark of the covenant has been taken from us without leaving us a remnant; he dwells in tranquil repose, but has left us to suffer; he sits among the myrtles while we are in flames; he went to his rest but left us to grieve. Woe is us on his departure. Who will feed us from the fruit of his pen? Over him we will growl like bears morning and evening; we will recite lament after lament as sadly as the jackals and mourn like the ostrich. And now, all you who knew him, eulogize him! You who fear the Lord, praise him![16] All descendants of Jacob, honor him! ... Summon the dirge singers, let them come; send for the skilled women, let them come[17] .... Would that he would pour out on us a spirit from on high to console us. As a mother comforts her son, so will we be comforted if you deal kindly with us .... Just as he dealt kindly with every man, so shall it be done to him. He treated every man as though he were a scholar .... Let him be rewarded with your praise and prayer; may you have a full recompense from heaven. May his death atone for his iniquities, may his trials and tribulations expiate his sins. Let us bear in mind, with our slumbering hearts, that "this is all of man." The same fate awaits the former and the latter [generations]. In the end it will occur to us, according to our limited knowledge, to leave aside our trouble and sorrow, for who has taken him if not his Creator, who has sheltered him in paradise, and installed him in His courtyard, and has given him an inheritance among the righteous? Why should terrors assail us when a delightful place has fallen to his lot? No eye has seen, O God, but You, who act for those who trust in You;[18] to gaze upon the beauty of the Lord, to frequent His temple.[19]

16 Cf. Ps. 22:24. In its original context, the verse urges praise of God, but Alḍāhirī's allusion playfully demands a new reading in which the author himself is the object of praise.

17 Cf. Jer 9:16. Yemenite Jewish women maintained a central role in oral lamentation of the dead into the 20th century; see Madar, "Women's Oral Laments."

18 Cf. Is. 64:3.

19 Cf. Ps. 27:4. This section corresponds to *Sefer hamusar*, pp. 464, l. 95–pp. 465, l. 112.

After hearing Abner's superlative elegy, Mordecai decides that he can now face his death with equanimity. Full of admiration for his friend's mastery of language and lapidary style, he suggests that Abner compose an epitaph for himself as well, lest he too be forgotten. Abner replies with a Talmudic maxim: "'The pit cannot be filled up with its own earth.'[20] If *you* want to compose a lament for me ... gird your loins like a man ... and recompense me as I have you." Mordecai demurs, arguing that he cannot remotely approach Abner's crystalline and dignified command of language, but Abner persuades him to proceed. The resulting piece, likewise in rhymed prose, strikes a suitably elegiac note, mourning the loss of "the diadem of poets; the crown of friends; the master of the Law, who understood every proverb and epigram and riddle ... [who] was summoned to the heavenly council and left us in the dark hours of the night." The departed's aesthetically pleasing way with words is a recurrent motif: "Sorrow is bound up in every corner, ... and rage reaches to the heart of the heavens because the golden tongue is no more." Adapting a line from "Eleh ezkerah" (a poetic lament over ten sages from the rabbinic period who were martyred by the Romans), Mordecai deplores the irretrievable loss of Abner's gifts: "the tongue that embellished every fine phrase (*le-khol meliṣah yishpor*) now licks the dust."[21] Abner is not solely remembered for his literary and linguistic skills; a series of rhetorical questions celebrates his prowess in the fields of biblical exegesis, oral law, and esoteric study as well:

> Who will illuminate the Torah for us? Who will know how to draw legal conclusions through reasoning? Who will bring us out from darkness to light ...? Who will reveal to us all that is obscure? Who will explain to us all that is impenetrable? Who will resolve every difficult question for us? ... Who will reconcile the scriptural verses for us? ... Who will issue a responsum to everyone who inquires?

The epitaph concludes with words of comfort similar to those at the end of the previous eulogy:

> Our only consolation is the knowledge that he now dwells in a peaceful and secure habitation, flourishing among quiet and tranquil brethren. It will be announced in all the distant provinces and coastlands that his soul

20 bBer. 3b.

21 "Eleh ezkerah" is recited in many rites on Yom Kippur and is included in the Yemenite *tiklāl*; see *Sefer hamusar*, p. 467, n. 146 and Davidson, *Thesaurus*, 1:196, #4273. On the poem's martyrology, see Einbinder, *Beautiful Death*, 167.

> is bound up in the bond of life (1 Samuel 25:29), and every believer will know that he will arise to his destiny at the end of days (Daniel 12:13).

At this point, the author (*ha-kotev*) of *Sefer hamusar* steps in, breaking the narrative framework to address his invented character. Then, in a twinkling, he is gone, having melded imperceptibly with the narrator.[22] Abner is reassured by the eulogy that there will be someone to memorialize him after his death. After a brief consolatory vision of collective redemption ("Perhaps God will be gracious to the remnant of Jacob"), the author/narrator asks Abner to recite a poem as recompense for "my kindness, in view of the work I have ahead of me, and for the sake of the children," seemingly a reference to Mordecai's ten sons, or perhaps to posterity more generally.[23] Abner declaims "Benei ʿelyon, benei ḥokhmah, benei ish" ("Sons of the Most High, Sons of Wisdom, Sons of Man"), a pensive, pious meditation on man's ultimate purpose. Sermonic in tone, these final verses remind the reader that God created us to serve Him and to observe His Law during our lifetimes and that every individual will be called to account for his deeds and will either merit paradise or purgatory. The speaker advises his audience to set times for Torah study, seek truth, be humble and God-fearing. He remarks that the limit of our days is seventy years; a miracle if they reach eighty. In closing, he declares that if the poem's words of moral instruction yield fruit, it will redound to his credit and he will submit it joyfully as an offering to God, who is compassionate and forgives transgression. Following this moralizing coda, whose themes recall the trope of the rogue-hero's final penitential turn (whether genuine or not), the narrator unequivocally reappears (*amar ha-maggid*) for the two concluding lines of the work. After so many encounters with his kindred spirit, Mordecai is visibly distressed by the specter of a perma-

---

22 The identity of the speaker in the sequence, *amar ha-kotev* (l. 163) … *vaʾomar lo* (l. 165) … *vaʾomar lo* (l. 174), followed by the reappearance of the narrator (*amar ha-maggid*; lines 203–204), is shrouded in indeterminacy. In context, the first-person locutions could just as easily be generated by the narrator as by the author, or by some fluid convergence of the two, especially since this speaker then goes on to recall the life experiences he has shared with Abner. By contrast, in the Author's Introduction and first *maqāma*, Alḍāhirī identifies himself explicitly with the phrase, "*amar ha-ṣaʿir zekharya ben seʿadya*." The wording in #45 is attested in four complete mss. (British Lib ms. Or 11337; Jerusalem NLI 8v° 2080; Bodleian ms. Opp. Add. 8° 31; and the former Sassoon 995), suggesting that *amar ha-kotev* is not a scribal substitution (unless all four stem from the same progenitor). For comparably complex blurring of author and narrator in the *Taḥkemoni*, see Rand, *Evolution*, 56–58 and Segal, *The Book of Taḥkemoni*, 428–429; 452–453; and 632.

23 Cf. Gen. 33:13–14. Fragments of this scriptural phrase, which has a different sense here than in its original context, are also interwoven into Abner's epitaph for Mordecai: "he left behind a blessing, in view of [all his] work: ten sons who wail over him bitterly …."

nent separation: "When I heard Abner's words, *I held him fast and would not let him go* (Canticles 3:4)." Exulting in Abner's sublime wisdom, he expresses his love, profound admiration, and a blessing that invokes Psalm 36:10 to praise his dear friend's gift for spiritual illumination: "With you is the fountain of life; by your light do we see light." While Mordecai speaks the final words of the book, Alḍāhirī's inclusio of self-insertion into the first and last *maqāmāt* suggests an authorial effort to frame the entire narrative as his own creation. The gesture recalls the integration of real protagonists—usually the author and his patron—at the close of Hebrew *maqāmāt* such as Ibn Shabbetai's *Minḥat yehudah sone' ha-nashim*. This device offered patrons a chance to be immortalized through narrative and reassured audiences that the sometimes bedevilling episodes that had preceded were a fiction. (In *Minḥat yehudah*, the author interrupts the trial at which the protagonist has just been condemned to death and tells the judge that his characters are entirely invented.) Though Alḍāhirī did not compose *Sefer hamusar* to please a benefactor, his bookending of the work in this manner bespeaks a desire to assert his ownership of a narrative in which he is so often indistinguishable from his personae, the invented characters who seem to merge with him at so many junctures and yet are, crucially, distinct from him by virtue of their fictionality.

1 The Conflation of Author and Protagonists

While providing a sense of finality, the concluding chapter of *Sefer hamusar* goads the reader to reexamine Alḍāhirī's ambiguous relationship with his invented characters and to contemplate the porosity of the boundaries he sets between the fictional and the real. Admittedly, he is adapting well-established conventions of Hebrew rhymed prose works by blurring the actual with the imagined and interposing himself towards the end of the narrative as well as in the very first *maqāma*, where he promises that his next chapter will focus on *galut teiman*, as if to atone for the "foreign" content of his opening borrowing from al-Ḥarīrī. Judah Alḥarizi's intrusion into the first chapter of the *Taḥkemoni* had already complicated the distinction between author, narrator, and hero to such a degree that, in the words of Dan Pagis, "the fiction is disrupted even before it begins."[24] These instances of textual deception and equivocation are specifically aimed at the audience or readership. Ross Brann argues that such literary devices were designed to subject the reader "to the text's

24 Pagis, "Variety in Medieval Rhymed Narratives," 96.

thematic, stylistic, and narrative trickery just as the characters ... fall prey to dissimulation, disguises, substitutions, illusions, and self-deception," and thus to engage the reader in a process of distinguishing illusion from reality.[25] As noted, Abdelfattah Kilito highlights the dissembling and duplicity that figure in al-Ḥarīrī's *Maqāmāt* not only as elements of the plot but also as complex literary devices.[26] Kilito writes that the work's inherent ambiguity and imposture result in part from the author's

> dissimulating his voice by transferring it to his characters who acquire, through this trickery, an autonomy and a presence that are not different from those of real beings.[27]

Regarding the author's self-insertion into the narrative, we recall Rina Drory's assertion that

> Jewish authors understood the idea of the fictional hero as a disguised appearance of themselves in the text, not of some plausibly existing person, as was the case in the Arabic *maqāmāt*.[28]

It is clear that Alḍāhirī is working within these narrative traditions. He conflates his authorial identity with the personae of his characters to an extent that raises questions about his conception of *Sefer hamusar* as a whole and about his self-perception as a Torah scholar who, alone among the members of his learned circle, penned a "Book of Moral Instruction" that is often lighthearted and at times subversive.

Even the most cursory glance at Abner's elegy for Mordecai suggests that it is intended for the author as much as for the character haunted by his mortality. The conflation of narrator and author soon becomes clear since the titles ascribed here to Mordecai are Alḍāhirī's own: *Sefer ṣeidah la-derekh*, his esoteric Bible commentary informed by his knowledge of philosophy and kabbalah; *Sefer haʿanaq*, his book of homonymic rhymes; and *Sefer hamusar*. This catalogue of works recalls the index (*fihrist*) of an individual's writings that was included in medieval Arabic biographical dictionary entries and auto/biographies.[29] By celebrating Mordecai and Abner's literary contributions in their

25 Brann, *The Compunctious Poet*, 138–140. See also Pagis, ibid., 95–98.
26 Kilito, *Les Séances*, 248–259 ("Le menteur professionel").
27 Kilito, ibid., 251.
28 See Drory, "The Maqama," 201.
29 Reynolds ed., *Interpreting the Self*, p. 38 and n. 8.

epitaphs, Alḍāhirī slips in a retrospective summation of his own oeuvre in order to ensure his posthumous reputation or, at least, to familiarize future generations with "the bare titles" of his works.[30] Mordecai's expertise in halakhah and poetic composition dovetails with Alḍāhirī's *curriculum vitae*, and the extensive travels recalled in the epitaph are generally assumed to be the author's own. That Mordecai returns to his native land of Yemen at the end of his travels has also been ascribed an autobiographical impetus. Even more pointedly than the individual *maqāmāt*, the epitaph highlights the catholicity of the narrator's quest for knowledge and desire to master a multiplicity of disciplines despite the risky travel this enterprise entails. It is striking how the epitaph reassembles the scattered puzzle pieces of the map to describe an orderly progression through space with an East-West itinerary more purposeful and geographically sequential than the random crisscrossing of regions from one episode to the next. The premeditated travel suggested by Mordecai's "inbound journey" (India, Hormuz, Basra; Babylonia, Aleppo, Damascus; Safed, Tiberias, Jerusalem; Egypt, Ethiopia, and Yemen) is also hard to square with the scattered, serendipitous encounters of the two characters that lend the work such joie de vivre.[31] Similarly, by telling us that Mordecai dwelled in Yemen teaching and studying for close to forty years following his return to his native land, the epitaph gives the impression of a homecoming marked by continuity and purpose, as opposed to the more intermittent sojourns in Yemen suggested by reading the work sequentially.

If Abner is for much of the time a cunning scoundrel or charlatan who swindles his way through life by means of his dazzling speech, the final *maqāma* portrays him as something of a world-weary penitent, an elderly poet chastened by the ravages of Time who does not revert to any of his more irrepressible personae. His restraint may well be due to an authorial desire to end the work on a pious, propitiatory note. But even so, Alḍāhirī cannot resist inserting a subtle reminder of Abner's perfidy by means of an allusion to his biblical namesake. In inquiring, "where had he come from and where was he going," Mordecai incorporates a fragment of II Samuel 3:25, where Joab chides King David:

> Don't you know that Abner son of Ner came only to deceive you, to learn your comings and goings and to find out all that you are planning?[32]

30 Petrarch, "Letter to Posterity."
31 Hence its appeal to scholars attempting to reconstruct the author's "actual" travels. Compare Rand, *Evolution*, pp. 4–9.
32 *Sefer hamusar*, p. 460, line 23.

Nevertheless, Abner is not excluded from Alḍāhirī's playful fusion of identities: as though in anticipation of the ambiguity of the epitaphs, the elegant letter to Abraham ben Zechariah Halevi bears not Abner's but Alḍāhirī's signature ("Zechariah ben Seʿadya ben Jacob"), a subtly teasing gesture that is reversed in poetic acrostics signed "Abner," perpetuating the illusion that his imaginary character is an accomplished littérateur.[33] In another variation, the two main characters are implicitly conflated when a phrase used in the eulogy to trace Mordecai's travels ("He made the circuit of all the provinces of India, Hormuz, and Basra") is applied verbatim in a different *maqāma* to Abner's journeys.[34] Finally, if the dénouement of almost every chapter involves a recognition scene or anagnorisis, the closing *maqāma* departs from this formula insofar as the narrator discerns early on that he has stumbled on his old crony. Paradoxically, this discovery does not resolve the vexing question of who is who as the boundaries between the author and his protagonists become ever less distinct.

At the same time that Alḍāhirī tells us in his preface, per *maqāma* convention, that his protagonists are invented, he confesses to a certain affinity between his authorial voice and theirs. Forty-five episodes later, in the final chapter, he still maintains the fiction of two characters who are distinct from each other as well as from him, even though he has placed his own epitaph in their mouths, such that his literary creations are eulogizing their flesh and blood creator. Should the two eulogies be read as one composite whole? Or perhaps their differing emphases and degrees of detail are meant to suggest disparities not only in the achievements of their fictitious subjects but also in their respective compositional skills. After all, Mordecai protests that he is not as gifted a stylist as Abner. Possibly, Alḍāhirī has chosen to highlight different aspects of himself in each of the two pieces, viewing his narrator and hero as distinct projections of his personality and abilities. A comparison of the protagonists' elegies reveals that Abner paints a comprehensive portrait of Mordecai's travels, intellectual attainments, and scholarly works while Mordecai focuses on Abner's consummate eloquence and peerless verse and mourns the loss of his "golden tongue," although he also extols his expertise in illuminating Torah, reconciling scriptural verses, drawing legal conclusions, and issuing responsa. Each gives a sense of the other's communal standing: both are devoted to teaching, and Abner is known for his epistolary exchanges with sages who turn to him from all over Yemen, with specialties ranging from kabbalah to astronomy

33 See, e.g., the two poems on pp. 300–303, each of which is a contrafaction of a poem by Abraham Ibn Ezra.

34 See *Sefer hamusar*, #39, p. 417, line 12.

to Maimonides' legal code.[35] Alḍāhirī's auto-epitaphs display a great degree of verisimilitude, yet by putting them into the mouths of his fictional surrogates, he challenges the reader to sort out the real from the imaginary and to make sense of the distance he has intentionally placed between himself and the memorial he has written.

2 The Structural Function of the Epitaphs

From a structural point of view, a final chapter contemplating the death of the work's two protagonists provides closure to an otherwise open-ended and kaleidoscopic narrative. Like most picaresque *maqāmāt*, what lends *Sefer hamusar* unity—apart from some subtle thematic correspondences between select sections of the work—is the consistent presence of its ubiquitous narrator and hero. That Abner takes center stage in almost every adventure and that the events of each encounter are related on Mordecai's authority enables us to go beyond an atomistic view of the book's component tales and consider the work as a larger whole. How fitting, then, to conclude the narrative's succession of changing exploits, locations, and literary subgenres with epitaphs for these two fictional characters. And how striking that neither of the works Alḍāhirī names as his models—the Arabic *Maqāmāt* of al-Ḥarīrī and the Hebrew *Taḥkemoni* of Alḥarizi—ends with such a neat finishing touch. This raises a larger literary question of how, if at all, *maqāma* authors thought about closure in a genre given to narrative open-endedness.[36] Alḥarizi's *Taḥkemoni* concludes with a catchall chapter of poems on a wide range of topics. But even if one discounts this anthology as an appendix, and even if, as Michael Rand argues, the penultimate chapter, *maqāma* #49 ("The Garden"), marks a type of coda, it nowhere mentions the deaths of the protagonists, nor does it fulfill a memorializing function in any way comparable to that of Alḍāhirī's final *maqāma*.[37] Al-Ḥarīrī's *Maqāmāt* close with the work's roguish protagonist Abū

35 *Sefer hamusar* names eight sages who exchanged letters with him. Ratzaby is convinced that these were the author's own scholarly correspondences, indicating that he was sought after as a religious authority; see *Sefer hamusar*, pp. 45–46. On epitaphs as a source of information on social and communal status see, e.g., Malkiel, *Stones Speak*, 249–330 *passim*.

36 See Blankinship, "As Barren as Mother Eve: Why Some Poems End Badly, According to Premodern Arabic Critics."

37 In #49, Heman is invited to join a group of young men reciting poetry in a garden and explains that he is a Spanish pilgrim en route to Jerusalem; see Rand, *Evolution*, 64–65.

Zayd preaching in the Grand Mosque of Basra, having seemingly repented of his sins but actually fleecing his audience before devoting himself to a life of piety. If his "questionable conversion," as James Monroe terms it, is taken seriously, it provides a coda to the work. While Abner's similarly penitential turn at the end of *Sefer hamusar* recalls this trope, al-Ḥarīrī's 50th *maqāma* does not otherwise furnish a close model for Alḍāhirī's final episode, apart from the fact that, in confessing his lifetime of deceit, Abū Zayd also reviews his wanderings and the perils he braved. Kilito paints a melancholy picture of Abū Zayd's final transformation and seeming abandonment of everything he formerly held dear. Although the rogue's renunciations signal closure, there are no epitaphs, nor is his death explicitly invoked:

> Having put to an end his wanderings, his rogue's life, any sort of adventure, he is now leading the life of an ascetic .... He lives alone, and whereas he used to relish good food, he now subsists on bread soaked in oil. Remarkably, he no longer speaks, except when praying. He wears no disguise—unless his asceticism is to be understood as the crowning disguise, one he will not be able to shed .... He renounces literature, he repents of *adab* and of everything this word entails: language, society's rules of conduct, places of gathering, verbal jousts, audiences ...[38]

Al-Ḥarīrī's penultimate *maqāma* also does not fulfill the same function as Alḍāhirī's closing chapter, even though it parodies a father's ethical will to his son (the aging protagonist exhorts his son to make a living from mendicancy).[39]

A closer Arabic literary antecedent to Alḍāhirī's epitaphs, which itself represents a departure from al-Ḥarīrī's model, can be found in *al-Maqāmāt al-luzūmīyah* of the 12th-century Andalusian author, al-Saraqusṭī (d. 1143), whose 50th and final *maqāma* records the protagonist's death, thereby furnishing an ending of sorts. The narrator inscribes on the trickster's tomb some verses of poetry that the protagonist had once entrusted to him. In a kind of literary ventriloquism common to epigraphic literature, the words of the poem are put into the mouth of the deceased, who addresses the passerby stopping to contemplate his tombstone. He speaks from his grave, warning of the universality of death, confessing his sins, and requesting an intercessory prayer. The narrator

38 Kilito, "Foreword: In Praise of Pretense," xiv–xv; Monroe, *The Art of Badīʿ az-Zamān al-Hamadhānī*, 81–83.

39 See Kilito, *Les Séances*, 62.

remains beside the grave for a week and is visited in his dreams by the ghost of the protagonist who urges him to repent, which he does. Nevertheless, through nuanced analysis, Monroe concludes that this story, too, "has the stamp of inauthenticity about it" and that the repentance of both protagonist and narrator seem to be false.[40]

Although al-Saraqusṭī's coda provides closure, a more immediate literary antecedent to Alḍāhirī's final chapter is found in an unacknowledged Hebrew source of inspiration: the *Maḥbarot* of Immanuel of Rome (c. 1261–1335). Immanuel's final chapter (#28) addresses matters of reward and punishment in the Afterlife on a grand scale. A guided journey through the Inferno and Paradise, *Maḥberet ha-tofet ve-ha'eden* ("Hell and Heaven") is in conception, form, and imagery indebted to Dante's *Divine Comedy* and draws on rabbinic eschatology.[41] But even though this literary tour de force opens with a personal reckoning, it is still not the closest model for the auto-epitaphs that conclude Alḍāhirī's work. Indeed, if we can take Immanuel's preface at face value, the placement of *Maḥberet ha-tofet ve-ha'eden* at the end of the *Maḥbarot* may not have been intended as a grand finale since the author claims that his chapters were not conceived as a self-contained book but rather were pieced together from preexisting poems and stories written over an extended period.[42] It has been suggested that this dream vision of heaven and hell was a later addition altogether, given how markedly it differs in conception and execution from the rest of the *Maḥbarot*, despite its philosophical and exegetical affinities with Immanuel's oeuvre as a whole. While there are also signs that *Sefer hamusar* was composed in separate installments, Alḍāhirī envisaged the work as an integral whole and organized it himself, deliberately placing his characters' epitaphs at the very end in order to impart a sense of finality. If Immanuel's final *maḥberet* is not really analogous, there is a closer antecedent to Abner and Mordecai's eulogies earlier in the *Maḥbarot*. Without a doubt, Alḍāhirī drew his inspiration from the poetic tombstone inscriptions and rhymed prose elegy that Immanuel composes for himself in the 21st chapter of the *Maḥbarot*, even if this *maḥberet* does not furnish a comparable closure device, since it comes seven chapters before the end of his spirited and piquant work.[43]

---

40 See Monroe ed. and trans., *Al-maqāmāt al-Luzūmīyah*, 96–100 and 499–500.

41 See: Fishkin, *Bridging Worlds*, 85–154; Kahanov, "Ha-tofet ve-ha'eden le'immanuel ha-romi"; Fishelov, "From Dante's *Inferno* to Immanuel's 'Inferno' "; and Gollancz, *Tophet and Eden*. For the text see Immanuel Ha-romi, *Maḥbarot*, 511–554.

42 See Immanuel Ha-romi, *Maḥbarot*, p. 5, lines 40–45.

43 See *Sefer hamusar*, p. 461, n. 52.

2.1 *Hebrew Literary Antecedents: Parallels, Divergences*

Immanuel's laments for himself consist of two formal tombstone poems and a rhymed prose auto-eulogy.[44] His extravagant self-eulogy is likely the most immediate model for Alḍāhirī's epitaphs, although a close comparison reveals some not insignificant dissimilarities that may be due as much to the distinct cultural contexts of the two works as to differences in the temperaments of the two authors. Immanuel, whose narratives are tinged with irony, relates that he (i.e., his fictitious namesake), together with his patron and partner in crime, visited a church where they discovered gravestone inscriptions so morally edifying and aesthetically pleasing that they momentarily forgot their lust for young women and thought of becoming saints in the afterlife. (His tongue-in-cheek remark plays in reverse order on the names of two consecutive weekly Torah lections that are often read together, "*ve-ḥashavnu lihiyot qedoshim aḥarei mot.*") The prince marvels that the Jewish community could be so remiss in not similarly inscribing laments and moral reproofs in their houses of worship and cemeteries. Immanuel replies that in his far-flung travels he has found splendid and moving eulogies on the gravestones of rabbis and communal officials. Indeed, about twenty years earlier, he had composed two epitaphs for his own tombstone that would, in keeping with the memorializing and hortatory functions of funerary inscriptions, "speak when I became mute; chastise those who take no heed; and ... shame the proud out of their arrogance."[45] The prince is miffed that his boon companion has kept these gems from him and insists that Immanuel recite them. Immanuel acquiesces but defends his former reticence by saying that he did not share them with the prince lest the prospect of death cause him to tremble and spoil his pleasures since readers will see from his verses that no one escapes death—not kings, officials, or magistrates. By means of a play on the root *ḥ.sh.q.*, he touts his first elegy as both the object of desire and the product of the intellect: *ha-rish'onah ha-ḥashuqah/ be-faz ha-sekhel meḥushshaqah* ("the first one, alluring, is bound with the gold of the intellect") and enjoins the prince to "incise it on a stone tablet and inscribe it in a record," as though it were a prophetic utterance (cf. Isaiah 30:8). What follows are two poems, both in strict Andalusian meter (*ha-shalem*; Arb. *al-kāmil*) and monorhyme, whose form signals their thematic continuity with Hispano-Hebrew poetic elegies, epitaphs, and meditations on death. In both pieces, the deceased apostrophizes the living from the grave:

---

44 Immanuel also furnishes a precedent for Alḍāhirī's adaptation of II Samuel 1:21 ("O hills of Yemen, let there be no dew or rain on you") in an elegy in his twenty-fourth *maḥberet* ("O Apennines ... let there be no dew or rain on you"); see *Sefer hamusar*, p. 16, n. 8.

45 Immanuel Ha-romi, *Maḥbarot*, p. 384, lines 20–22.

> *Haʿovrim, hittammhu utmahu*! "Passersby, observe well, and be utterly astounded! ... Pray for a prisoner of death who recounts everything that has befallen him!"
>
> *Roʾay ve-yodʿay lefanim/ʿalay seʾu taḥanunim*! "You who saw me and used to know me, pray for me!"[46]

Stressing the finality of death, the departed urges the living to pray on his behalf now that he has descended from tranquility and comfort to the depths of sepulchral darkness and extinction. Similarly morbid topoi and modes of address can be found in medieval tombstone inscriptions from Latin Christendom, where the dead speaker urges those who pass by his grave to read his epitaph, learn from his death, and intercede on his behalf with their prayers.[47] The poetic convention of the talking epitaph goes back to classical antiquity.[48] (In a much later Italian Hebrew epitaph poem, *ʿOlam hafukh* by Judah Maṣliah Padova of Modena [d. 1728], the exhortation to passersby to remember the vanity of human life is placed in the mouth of the inanimate tombstone.[49]) With graphically macabre imagery reminiscent of Samuel Hanagid's *memento mori* poems, Immanuel conveys an almost voyeuristic obsession with the inescapable decay of the grave. The stages of bodily decline he details are shocking and terrifying. Nettles and thorns grow from his cheeks; he now dwells among hordes of the insensate. His dirge-like anaphora imparts a cumulative sense of loss and obliteration as he exploits conventional motifs of physical decomposition and the universality of death to powerful, Ozymandias-like effect:

> Friends who yesterday desired my company are today alienated and repulsed by me ...
> With me is a host of corpses that yesterday were fresh; today they are your pavement—yesterday they were your lords; they have become fare for delicacy-eating worms.[50]

---

46 Cf. Hab. 1:5. On such forms of address in Andalusian Hebrew elegies, see Ratzaby, "Motivim ʿaraviyyim ba-qinah haʿivrit ha-sefaradit," 741 and 757–763 and Levin, *The Lamentation Over the Dead*, 222–225.

47 See the subsection headed "The Appeal to the Passerby and the Prayer" in Ariès, *The Hour of Our Death*, 218–221.

48 See, e.g., Stallings, review of David Sider ed. and trans., *Simonides: Epigrams and Elegies*.

49 See Malkiel, "Christian Hebraism in a Contemporary Key," 141; for the text see Schirmann ed., *Mivḥar ha-shirah haʿivrit beʾitalya*, 354–356. For the conceit of speaking stones among Jews in early modern Padua and Hamburg respectively, see Malkiel, *Stones Speak*, 69–72 and Wilke, "Dialogues of the Dead: Talking Epitaphs by Sephardi and Ashkenazi Rabbis of Hamburg."

50 See Bregman, "The Realistic and the Macabre in the Poetry of Samuel Ha-Nagid." The use of

The prince is suitably impressed with Immanuel's poignant, admonitory rhetoric and swears they will not return home until his protégé composes a poetic epitaph for him as well. Immanuel fulfills this request, after which the prince chides him for neglecting to compose a lament for himself while assiduously eulogizing every eminence who has passed away. He urges Immanuel to write a tribute to himself while still alive, for after he is gone, there will be no one talented enough to do so. The underlying assumption is that life is transient, but words endure. This exchange and the ensuing rhymed prose elegy were clearly Alḍāhirī's immediate inspiration, although he was no doubt aware that in the Arabic poetic tradition, besides *maqāmāt* such as al-Saraqusṭī's 50th, there were elegies that poets wrote for themselves. In a contemplative auto-eulogy attributed to Abū Nuwās (d. c. 813), the most celebrated and notorious Arabic poet of the ʿAbbāsid period imagines himself after death, invoking penitential and eschatological themes in anticipation of his demise. Known for his mordant wit, Abū Nuwās also composed a dirge (*marthiya*) for his living mentor, the poet and *rāwī* (reciter and transmitter of poetry), Khalaf al-Aḥmar (d. c. 796), to the latter's reported consternation.[51]

Like Alḍāhirī, Immanuel confounds the boundaries between historical reality and fiction. As Matti Huss notes, Immanuel's preface contains deliberately contradictory statements about the authorship of the *Maḥbarot*. In one version of the preface, a seemingly historical prince with no aptitude for poetry advises Immanuel to create an imaginary companion and interlocutor for his own persona, to be modeled on the prince himself. In the alternate version of the preface, Immanuel identifies his anonymous patron as an outstanding poet and the true inspiration for the *Maḥbarot*. Huss cites this contradiction as evidence that Immanuel did not adopt wholesale the Western European literary convention according to which fictional events were depicted as historical realities but rather tempered it with the Hispano-Hebrew view of fiction as embodied in the *maqāma* tradition, which represented possible realities rather than historically valid ones.[52]

---

anaphora to convey anguish and mourning goes back to antiquity; see, e.g., David's visceral expression of grief for Absalom, II Sam. 19:1. On anaphora in Arabic and Hebrew elegies, see Levin, *The Lamentation Over the Dead*, 32–42.

51 See Kennedy, *Abu Nuwas: A Genius of Poetry*, 121–134; idem, "Abu Nuwas (circa 757–814 or 815)"; Hämeen-Anttilla, *Maqama*, p. 17, n. 6; and Ratzaby, "Motivim ʿaraviyyim ba-qinah haʿivrit ha-sefaradit," 764–765.

52 See Huss, "The Status of Fiction in the Hebrew *Maqama*" and Kfir, *A Matter of Geography*, 127–129. The contrast Huss draws between the status of fiction in the Western European and Hispano-Hebrew literary traditions might be profitably juxtaposed with the comparison Rina Drory makes between the Arabic *maqāma* authors' view of fiction as a plausible

How, then, does Alḍāhirī's auto-eulogy compare with Immanuel's? Overall, its self-praise is more subtle, in part because it is put into the mouths of two fictitious characters who do not overtly share the author's name and celebrates their accomplishments. By contrast, the lament composed by Immanuel's eponymous hero is blatantly self-referential even though it is ostensibly written to be recited by someone else after his death and so refers to its subject in the third person or addresses him in the second. In keeping with the insolent tone of his *Maḥbarot*, Immanuel displays little restraint in his self-glorification, happily penning such lines of biblical pastiche as,

> Alas, our prince, Immanuel/ sweet singer of Israel/the breath of our life and our annointed one/frontlet for the holy diadem on our foreheads/the life of our flesh and spirit/ … you were our chief joy, /through you we forgot all our sighing/and said: 'This one will provide us relief from our work and from the toil of our hands.'/ All our honor depended on you ….[53]

While Alḍāhirī's auto-eulogy also opens with larger-than-life expressions of universal grief, it leaves a less patently immodest impression since it is presented as Abner's lament for Mordecai. And where Immanuel's hunger for recognition is thinly veiled, Alḍāhirī's preoccupation with his posthumous reputation is somewhat more delicately disguised as Mordecai's.[54]

Immanuel's self-appreciation dances precariously on the edge of egotism. Not only does he address himself with honorifics (*ha-sar; nesi'einu*), but he enumerates his signal contributions in biblical exegesis, communal affairs, grammar, and even musical study in a way that suggests that he considered himself to be irreplaceable:

> Now, who will console us … when our trembling has become violent, and there is no room for consolation? Were it not for your blessing, O Prince, which you reserved for us, laying bare the books of prophecy

---

representation of reality and the Jewish *maqāma* authors' assertion that their stories are not only false but completely implausible.

53 See Immanuel Ha-romi, *Maḥbarot*, p. 390, lines 167–171. "This one will provide us relief from our work and from the toil of our hands" is pronounced upon the birth of Noah, cf. Gen. 5:29; for the original context of "all our honor depended on you," see Is. 22:24.

54 Alḍāhirī borrows a few phrases directly from Immanuel; compare, e.g., *Sefer hamusar*, p. 465, l. 109 with Immanuel Ha-romi, *Maḥbarot*, p. 394, l. 256 and *Sefer hamusar*, p. 466, l. 136 with Immanuel Ha-romi, *Maḥbarot*, p. 391, l. 184.

> according to the gift of your intellect ... the breath of our life would no longer have been left, and our twilight stars would have remained dark ... Alas, community of Rome! Who will illuminate your twilight stars? Alas, world of the intellect! Who will penetrate the mystery of your angels and seraphim? ... Alas, the scroll of the Lord's Torah! Who will expose the silver filigree-work (*maskiot kesef*; lit.: settings of silver) around your golden apples?[55] ... Alas, science of melody! Who will prepare the work of your sockets and drums?[56] ... Alas, Book of Chronicles! Who will explain your opaque words? Alas, Book of Proverbs! Who will tie together your pleasant verses? Alas, Book of Job! Who will illuminate your sealed mysteries? Alas, Book of Psalms! ... Alas, Daniel! Who will reveal the mystery of the end of days? ... Lament like a maiden, science of grammar, for the man who made you his wife is dead ...[57]

(Distinct echoes of the anaphora, "Alas ... Who will ... Alas ... Who will ...," which Immanuel deploys to great rhetorical effect, can be heard in Mordecai's lamenting the vacuum that will be left by Abner's demise: "Who will illuminate the Torah for us? Who will know how to draw legal conclusions through reasoning? Who will bring us out from darkness to light? ....")[58] Though obviously not

55 Cf. Prov. 25:11. Exposing the silver filigree-work around the Torah's golden apples is a metaphor for uncovering the esoteric meanings of Scripture that goes back to Maimonides; see Pines, trans. *Moses Maimonides: The Guide of the Perplexed*, 1:11–12. See also Talmage, "Apples of Gold: The Inner Meaning of Sacred Texts in Medieval Judaism," esp. p. 315.

56 See Immanuel Ha-romi, *Maḥbarot*, p. 391, lines 193–194, and note the play on the phrase *melekhet tupekha unqavekha* from Ez. 28:13, which occurs in the context of a dirge over the king of Tyre.

57 Immanuel Ha-romi, *Maḥbarot*, pp. 390, l. 179–p. 391, l. 203. Immanuel was a prolific biblical exegete who commented on virtually every book of the Bible. His extant commentaries encompass Genesis, Exodus, Leviticus, Numbers, Deuteronomy, Psalms, Proverbs, Job, Esther, Song of Songs, Ecclesiastes, Ruth, Lamentations, and portions of Prophets. On the mss. and printed editions in which they are preserved see Goldstein, "The Commentary of Immanuel ben Solomon of Rome on Chapters I–X of Genesis," 5–14 and idem, Introduction to *The Book of Proverbs with the Commentary of Immanuel of Rome*, 7–19 (Hebrew) and VII–IX (English Summary). (The commentary on Proverbs was one of the first Hebrew books printed in Naples, c. 1486/87.) See also: Fishkin, *Bridging Worlds*, 5–8; Robinson, "From Digression to Compilation"; idem, "Maimonides, Samuel Ibn Tibbon, and the Construction of a Jewish Tradition of Philosophy"; idem, "We Drink Only from the Master's Water"; idem, "'The 'Secret of the Heavens' and the 'Secret of Number'"; and idem, "Allegorical Readings of Qohelet 7:19 in Medieval Jewish Exegesis." Immanuel's book of Hebrew grammar, *Even boḥan*, is still in ms.

58 *Sefer hamusar*, pp. 467–468, lines 148–157.

troubled by the unseemliness of his vaunts, Immanuel realizes that they might be considered in poor taste and so issues a disclaimer, acknowledging that he has exaggerated his virtues,

> for such is the way of poets of all faiths to inflate praise and derision. Therefore the sage [Aristotle] said … "the best part of the poem is the most false" (*meitav ha-shir kezavo*). I wrote them as though one of my relatives or intimates had recited them about me in an overstated fashion after my death.

In other words, Immanuel claims license to exaggerate by invoking the Aristotelian view that falsehood is integral to poetry since it not only employs figurative language which, taken literally, would not be true, but poets also flatter or deride their subjects undeservedly (calling miserly patrons generous, for example).[59] He also disingenuously suggests that the relatives who would likely recite his lament would want to lavish praises on him. His *qinah* is followed by an amusing concatenation of philosophers, scientists, and biblical figures and the works or qualities that they left behind when they departed this world, which appears to be arranged helter-skelter according to the exigencies of rhyme alone:

> One need not wonder that Immanuel left behind the flock in his care … or the gems of his books and poems, for … Aristotle left behind his philosophy, and Tamar the sister of Absalom—her beauty, and Solomon—the throne of the Lord and Bitya, and Naomi—Ruth the Moabite … Ptolemy left behind the science of astronomy … and the science of optics, and Jacob—the twelve tribes …

Taken together with this comical litany, Immanuel's disavowal of his auto-eulogy seems designed not only to deflect potential criticism but also to undercut the seriousness of his intent. One wonders whether Alḍāhirī read his jocular and cynical predecessor with the requisite sense of humor and skepticism.

---

59 On *meitav ha-shir kezavo* see, e.g., Brann, *The Compunctious Poet*, 72–75 and Pagis, *Secular Poetry and Poetic Theory*, 46–50. Medieval Aristotelians scorned poetry's metaphorical language as the product of man's imaginative faculty, viewed as inferior to the rational faculty; for the inroads these ideas made into various genres of literature see, e.g., Moses Ibn Ezra, *Kitāb al-muḥāḍara wa'l-mudhākara*, 62a, p. 116; Shem Ṭov Falaquera, *Sefer ha-mevaqqesh*, extracts in Schirmann, *HPSP*, 2:334–342; and Meshullam da Piera, "She'eluni ḥakham levav," ibid., 2:303. See also Immanuel Ha-romi, *Maḥbarot*, p. 149, lines 224–229.

Alḍāhirī's borrowings from Immanuel's *Maḥbarot* are noteworthy in light of the cultural synthesis and hybridity that such appropriation theoretically entails. *Maḥberot Immanuel* fuses elements of the medieval Iberian Jewish literary tradition with poetic forms, stylistic conventions, and cultural allusions drawn from the world of Renaissance Italy, as Pagis, Dvora Bregman, and Huss have shown. One instance of Immanuel's cross-cultural appropriation in his second epitaph poem, "Ro'ay ve-yodʿay lefanim," is its use of the Italian convention of *commiàto* (*ha-peridah*), whereby the poet takes leave of the reader by giving his name and genealogy at a poem's end.[60] Immanuel's moorings in the culture of 14th-century Italy are evident from his familiarity with Dante's *Divine Comedy* and his exchanges of sonnets with contemporary Italian poets.[61] By contrast, the Yemenite Hebrew *Sefer hamusar* is more closely modeled on the classical *maqāma*, an Eastern Arabic literary genre. For Hebrew authors in Christian Europe like Immanuel, familiarity with the *maqāma* was largely mediated by Alḥarizi's *Taḥkemoni*, which in many respects Hebraicized the Arabic prototype of the genre, al-Ḥarīrī's *Maqāmāt*.[62] Alḍāhirī, on the other hand, had direct access to al-Ḥarīrī's *Maqāmāt* in the original, as well as to Alḥarizi's Hispano-Hebrew opus and Immanuel's Italianate *Maḥbarot* when he wrote one of the last in a series of medieval Hebrew rhymed prose narratives composed over four centuries.[63] The question is whether by drawing on Immanuel he consciously attempted a cultural translation, indirectly produced a blend of Western European and Eastern forms, motifs, and cultural references, or borrowed selectively only those elements that resonated with him as a Yemenite Jewish author. Clearly, the impetus for self-assessment in his eulogies draws on medieval Arabic traditions of auto/biography and auto-

60 See Jarden's introduction to Immanuel Ha-romi, *Maḥbarot*, xxxvii, and p. 387, lines 108–112.

61 See Pagis, *Change and Tradition*, 257–273; Bregman, "The Metrical System of Immanuel of Rome"; idem, *A Bundle of Gold*, 29–30; and Huss, "The Status of Fiction in the Hebrew *Maqama*."

62 See Lavi, "The Rationale of al-Ḥarīzī in Biblicizing the Maqāmāt of al-Ḥarīrī" and Sadan, "Judah Alḥarizi as a Cultural Junction"; see also Drory, *Models and Contacts*, 215–232. Immanuel explicitly mentions Alḥarizi's *Taḥkemoni* as a valuable if not precise model for his *Maḥbarot*; see his introduction, pp. 4–5, lines 32–45. In addition, he praises Alḥarizi's incomparable poetry and rhymed prose at the beginning of his 9th *maḥberet*; see p. 167, lines 1–8. On his ambivalences toward the Iberian Hebrew poets and their exceptionalism, see Kfir, *A Matter of Geography*, 123–139.

63 For a comprehensive list, see Schirmann, *Die hebräische Übersetzung der Maqamen des Hariri*, 111–132. The rhymed prose narrative was periodically cultivated in ensuing centuries and into the modern period by such eminences as Moses Mendelssohn and Hayim Nahman Bialik; see the excerpts in Ratzaby, *Yalqut ha-maqāma haʿivrit*.

elegies as well as Iberian Jewish models and, via Immanuel, Italian Jewish practices of literary memorialization. Alḍāhirī was far from insular, having—one assumes—traveled throughout the Muslim East to India, and as far west as Ottoman Anatolia and the Balkans. Nevertheless, for all of its geographically diverse settings, *Sefer hamusar* takes an exceedingly Judeocentric point of view and rarely shows appreciation even for other Jewish subcultures. Since Alḍāhirī had no first-hand experience of Jewish life in a western Mediterranean or European cultural orbit, he likely read *Maḥberot Immanuel* at a remove, through the familiar lens of the Hebrew *maqāma* but not necessarily with any sense of its European socio-historical or intellectual contexts.

Immanuel's frame story of wandering among the tombstones in a Christian cemetery in awe of their admonitory epitaphs calls to mind the Renaissance Humanist passion for collecting inscriptions from classical funeral monuments and ruins as both rhetorical models and tangible ties to Roman Antiquity.[64] This fascination with ancient epigraphy, tied to the Humanist cult of antiquity, apparently did not speak to Alḍāhirī, who supplies his own, unrelated pretext for composing his elegies. This is not to imply that burial grounds were unimportant to him; Jews in the Islamic world, like Muslims, ascribed special sanctity to cemeteries and especially to the tombs of saints and holy men as sites endowed with supernatural power, to which they made pilgrimage (*ziyāra*) in search of blessing and intercession with God.[65]

Although neither of our authors intended his rhymed prose auto-eulogy for inscription on his gravestone, Immanuel did compose his two formal poems for this purpose. As literary artifacts, they are forerunners of the Hebrew epitaph poems commissioned by Italian Jews from professional poets in the 16th and 17th centuries. Inspired not only by internal Jewish traditions but also by contemporary funerary practices among Christians, Italian Hebrew verse epitaphs were written both for engraving on tombstones and for incorporation into poetry collections. In the early modern period, Italian Hebrew authors

64 See Guthke, *Epitaph Culture in the West*, 37–55. In early modern Italy, Christian Hebraists collected Hebrew epitaphs; see Andreatta, "Collecting Hebrew Epitaphs in the Early Modern Age" and Malkiel, "Christian Hebraism in a Contemporary Key."

65 For the disagreement between Sapir and the orientalist Joseph Halévy regarding the antiquity of tombstones in Aden, see *Even Sapir*, 2: 9–11 and 162–164 and Halévy, "Voyage au Nedjran," 262. See also Goitein, "The Age of the Hebrew Tombstones from Aden" and Klein-Franke, "Tombstones Bearing Hebrew Inscriptions in Aden." Tobi has documented the opposition of the Zaydī school to the construction of graves above ground, as well as to their ornamentation and inscription; see *'Iyyunim bi-megillat teman*, 56. Gaimani maintains that, apart from the grave of Shalom Shabbazi, Yemenite Jews visited the graves of saints on a very limited basis only; see "Visiting Graves of *Ẓaddiqim* in Yemen."

and literati also composed their own epitaphs, which they included for circulation in their published works, without necessarily intending them for incision in stone. (Lengthy poems were in any case unsuitable for engraving, given the finite physical dimensions of tombstones.) Such "fictionalized epitaphs" often took as their models contemporary Christian analogues in Latin and Italian, which were sometimes dedicated to distinguished individuals during their lifetimes.[66] The composition of verse epitaphs by rabbis and gifted literary figures became a sort of profession during this period: Leon Modena (1571–1648) wrote almost 150 such poems for others, as well as two for himself—the first, as a literary exercise when he was fifteen years old, and the second when he was an adult. The later epitaph was engraved on his tombstone and is still extant.[67]

Immanuel's epitaph poems brood darkly on death and, like many of Samuel Hanagid's meditations on mortality, do not imagine the end as a quietus or welcome release from life but rather as a horrifying dissolution into dust and worms. The speaker in these pieces bemoans life's dreadful end as a putrid carcass in the grave and does not seem consoled by the promise of the soul's return to the celestial realms. Bregman's remarks regarding the realistic and the macabre in the Nagid's poems on death could equally be applied to Immanuel's auto-epitaphs, insofar as they too identify the deceased with his interred body rather than with an immortal soul and portray death less as a divine decree than as the wanton act of an alien, capricious force that the poet is powerless to subdue or appease.[68] His *memento mori* motifs—the vanity of worldly existence, death as the great leveler, the finality of the grave—were common to Andalusian Hebrew sermonic poems informed by Islamic pietism and intended to rouse those who heard or read them to repentance. Despite the conventionality of these themes, Immanuel's irredeemably dark reading conveys an existential anxiety that seems real enough. His pessimism and fatalism may well have been

66 See Malkiel, *Stones Speak*, 9–105; idem, "Poems on Tombstone Inscriptions in Northern Italy in the Sixteenth and Seventeenth Centuries"; and Andreatta, "Collecting Hebrew Epitaphs in the Early Modern Age," 260–263.

67 Andreatta, "Collecting Hebrew Epitaphs in the Early Modern Age," p. 261 and n. 5. See, e.g., Bernstein ed., *The Divan of Leo De Modena*, English Introduction, p. XVIII, and pp. 225–258. Modena's brief auto-epitaph from his mature years, "Arbaʿ amot qarqaʿ," is on p. 231, no. 225. See also Cohen ed. and trans., *The Autobiography of a Seventeenth-Century Rabbi*, 177–180.

68 See Bregman, "The Realistic and the Macabre in the Poetry of Samuel Ha-Nagid." By contrast, the Neoplatonically informed Andalusian poets portrayed death as the soul's release from her bodily prison; see Tanenbaum, *The Contemplative Soul*. Although Judah Alḥarizi also invoked this paradigm, there is an unsparingly graphic description of bodily putrefaction in *Taḥkemoni* #2, where Heber poses as an itinerant preacher who warns his audience to repent before it is too late; see Alḥarizi, *Taḥkemoni*, ed. Yahalom and Katsumata, 93–101.

shaped by the tragedies that befell him: in 1321, his son-in-law was murdered in Rome. Around the same time, he lost his parents, wife, and eldest son.[69] A not dissimilar obsession with death would characterize the European poetry of the Baroque (16th–17th centuries), as attested by the nightmarish images of "the sickbed, the grave and the charnel-house" recurrent in French poetry of the late 16th century. Across much of Europe, the Baroque era was one of religious, political, and societal upheaval and transformation, and its literary "preoccupation extended beyond the death and decay of the body to an equally gloomy prognosis of society."[70] The Italian Hebrew poetry of the Baroque shared this fixation, as evidenced by Moses Zacuto's (17th-century) epitaph poems, which develop the macabre themes adumbrated by Immanuel, albeit shaped by the new poetics of the period.[71] Alḍāhirī, however, was not touched by the European Baroque, and his auto-eulogy does not convey a comparably gruesome, grim picture of death. While he, too, is horrified by the thought of passing into oblivion, his fears center on his posthumous reputation. More than a dread of worms and physical decay, Alḍāhirī's personae live in terror of their attainments going unrecorded for posterity.

Of the other possible literary antecedents to Alḍāhirī's self-lament, none is quite as close in conception and execution as Immanuel's. The composition of elegies and epitaph poems was integral to the Andalusian Hebrew poetic tradition that Alḍāhirī knew well. Laments for illustrious religious scholars include Solomon Ibn Gabirol's elegies for Hai Gaon and Moses Ibn Ezra's tombstone inscription for Isaac Alfasi.[72] Among Judah Halevi's many moving elegies is one mourning the loss of his beloved friend and fellow poet, Moses Ibn Ezra.[73] The most common kind of Andalusian *qinah* is a formal poem of lamentation over the dead with a highly stylized structure and repertoire of motifs. Typically, it

69 See Bregman, *A Bundle of Gold*, 29. Immanuel's 21st *maḥberet* concludes with two brief *qinot* for his son, Moshe; see Immanuel Ha-romi, *Maḥbarot*, pp. 394–395, lines 266–286.

70 See Cohen, *The Baroque Lyric*, especially 30–51 and Maravall, *Culture of the Baroque*, 149–172. In northern Europe, the late Middle Ages also saw the emergence of a cult of the macabre; see, e.g., Binski, *Medieval Death: Ritual and Representation*, 123–163.

71 See Bregman, "Hen ʿatah tihiyeh ʿal biti even" and idem, *The Golden Way*, 93–95. See also Pagis, "Yesodot baroqiyim ba-shirah haʿivrit beʾitalya."

72 See Solomon Ibn Gabirol, "Nigdeʿah qeren ʿadinah" and "Bekhu, ʿammi" in Schirmann, *HPSP* 1:203 and Moses Ibn Ezra, "Kitvu beʿet barzel ʿalei shamir," in *Moses Ibn Ezra, Secular Poems*, ed. Brody and Pagis, 2:212–213. Ibn Ezra's poem is cited in the 17th-century chronicle of Joseph Sambari; see Shtober ed., *Sefer divrei yosef*, 189.

73 See "ʿAli kha-zot tivkenah," in *Judah Halevi, The Liturgical Poetry*, ed. Jarden, 4:1110–1112. Most fittingly, a brief elegy by Halevi ("Ha-yedʿu ha-demaʿot mi shefakham") was read at Ezra Fleischer's funeral; see the obituary by Yehoshua Granat in *Haaretz*, Aug. 4, 2006. For the text, see *The Liturgical Poetry*, ed. Jarden, 4:1119.

consists of an introduction complaining of the malign machinations of fate, a transitional verse linking these plaints to the death of the individual being mourned, and a eulogy in the body of the poem that invokes stock motifs and gnomic dicta about the ineluctable nature of death. It concludes with a brief, often formulaic prayer that the deceased's grave be watered with the dew of resurrection or that the departed's good deeds intercede on his behalf so that he receive his just reward in the world to come. This genre, with its conventional form, themes, and imagery, was modeled on an Arabic prototype that went back to the heroic dirge of the pre-Islamic period. Arabic literary theorists classified the elegy as a type of *qaṣīda*, a long monorhymed ode in quantitative meter typically used for praise, such that panegyrics for rulers and patrons (*al-madīḥ*), poems of self-praise (*al-fakhr*), and elegies for the dead (*al-rithāʾ*) all fell under the *qaṣīda* rubric. The Arabic antecedents to the Andalusian *qinah* are detailed by Israel Levin in his monograph, *ʿAl mavet* (The Lamentation Over the Dead); by Pagis in his study of Moses Ibn Ezra as the foremost exponent of the Arabicizing poetics of the Andalusian school; and by Ratzaby, who points to the poets' Judaizing of pre-Islamic motifs by synthesizing or replacing them with biblical analogues.[74]

Some *qaṣīda*-type elegies were written for the poets' close relatives or friends, but often they were commissioned pieces or official eulogies for public figures like Solomon Ibn Gabirol's patron, Yequtiel Ibn Hassān, who was executed in 1039. Nevertheless, the conventional *qaṣīda* model could prove inadequate for venting heartfelt sorrow or personal reflections on death.[75] Samuel Hanagid, the first to exploit fully the potential of the Arabicizing *qinah*, preferred a more intimate poetic mode to mourn the loss of his elder brother, Isaac, for whom he composed a cycle of nineteen laments.[76] While he wrote aphoristic poems on mortality, he also penned more extensive and less con-

---

74 See: Levin, *The Lamentation Over the Dead*; abridged version in idem, *The Embroidered Coat*, 2:7–145; Pagis, *Secular Poetry and Poetic Theory*, 197–224; and Ratzaby, "Motivim ʿaraviyyim ba-qinah haʿivrit ha-sefaradit." See also Schippers, "Hebrew Andalusian Elegies and the Arabic Literary Tradition," and Pellat, "Marthiya." For an extensive collection of Arabic epitaphs and discussion of their social, material, religious, and literary dimensions, see Diem and Schöller, *The Living and the Dead in Islam*.

75 Levin has argued that impassioned outbursts of deep-seated pain can be detected among the 102 verses of "Bi-mei yequtiel asher nigmaru"; see Levin, *The Lamentation Over the Dead*, 9–10 and 112–114. For the text see Schirmann, *HPSP* 1:196–201. See also Loewe, "Lament for a Lost Leader." Scheindlin contends that Ibn Gabirol's exquisite miniature nature poem, "Re'eh shemesh le-ʿet ʿerev" is far more moving; see his *Wine, Women, and Death*, 152–153.

76 See Samuel Hanagid, *Diwan* 1:236–250 and Levin, *The Lamentation Over the Dead*, 95–106.

ventional meditations on old age and death, some of which are quite ghastly in their realism. In one particularly lyrical complaint, "Ha-nimṣa be-reʿay," the speaker mourns himself, lamenting the passing of his youth and bodily vigor, and imagining his death with horror.[77]

The auto-elegy—in which the deceased speaks as a skeptical or sardonic witness to his own burial and its attendant rituals, describing his grave and its inscription, and musing on the vanity of life—was considered a sub-genre of the lamentation by classical Arabic literary critics. Although rare in Andalusian Hebrew poetry, there are notable auto-elegies by Samuel Hanagid and Moses Ibn Ezra.[78] Abraham Ibn Ezra is alleged by later sources to have recited a brief auto-epitaph on the day of his death.[79] But in terms of both form and content, only Immanuel's extravagant self-appreciation seems to have served as a direct model for Alḍāhirī's rhymed prose eulogy for himself.

3 The Epitaph: Apology or Swan Song?

What attitudes and, perhaps, ambivalences can we glean from the final chapter of *Sefer hamusar*? Can Alḍāhirī's attribution of his own exemplary/ idealized biography to his fictional characters be seen in part as an apology for—if not exactly a disavowal of—the reprobate behavior of his protagonist in most other chapters? If so, does it bespeak his awareness of, or deference to, his coreligionists' uneasiness with the belletristic genre in which he chose to write? Alḍāhirī was a respected religious scholar whose opinions were cited by later generations, notably Yiḥye Ṣāliḥ, one of the most eminent halakhic authorities in 18th-century Ṣanaʿā whose legal decisions held sway in Jewish communities throughout Yemen and as far as India.[80] Ratzaby maintains that contem-

77 See Samuel Hanagid, *Diwan*, 1:121–124 and the discussion in Pagis, *Hebrew Poetry of the Middle Ages and the Renaissance*, 16–18. The aphoristic poems are collected in Samuel Hanagid, *Diwan*, Vol. 3. These pieces draw on the sober themes of the book of Ecclesiastes (hence the title *Ben Qohelet*) but also reflect the pessimism of Arabic gnomic poetry.

78 See Levin, *The Lamentation Over the Dead*, 81–94 and Padva, "The Voice of the Dead in the Elegy."

79 See Shtober ed., *Sefer divrei yosef*, 215–217. For the text, see "Kevodi sas be-ṣur ʿuzzi," in Ibn Ezra, *Reime und Gedichte*, p. 226 and Kahana ed., *Rabbi Avraham Ibn Ezra: Qoveṣ ḥokhmat ha-raʾbaʿ*, #24. I am grateful to the late Raphael Loewe for having called Ibn Ezra's poem and the Sambari account (reproduced in Neubauer's *Mediaeval Jewish Chronicles* [Oxford, 1887]) to my attention.

80 Ṣāliḥ repeatedly cites Alḍāhirī's lost work on Maimonides' *Hilkhot sheḥiṭah* in his *Zevaḥ todah*, a collection of novellae and glosses on the section of the *Shulḥan ʿarukh* dealing

poraries "from Jibla in the South to Ṣa'adah in the North" turned to Alḍāhirī for halakhic guidance, yet *Sefer hamusar* was poorly received due to those aspects that marked it as "secular" and frivolous. Even when interest in the work revived in the 18th and 19th centuries, it was selectively read and understood in Alḍāhirī's native land, judging from the two works that claim direct descent from *Sefer hamusar*, Ḥarāzī's *Netivot ha'emunah* and Manṣura's *Sefer ha-maḥashavah*. Ratzaby argues that the overall paucity of belletristic prose in Yemenite Jewish literature resulted from the community's low regard for such irreligious and lighthearted writing, although there is ample manuscript evidence of the circulation and reception of the *Taḥkemoni* in Yemen, despite his claim to the contrary.[81] Moreover, *Sefer hamusar* has survived in a 17th-century ms. of Yemenite provenance, suggesting that it was not entirely neglected following Alḍāhirī's death. That Alḍāhirī did not openly acknowledge his debt to Immanuel was almost certainly deliberate, for the *Maḥbarot* had been condemned for their eroticism and banned by no less a halakhic authority than Joseph Karo in his *Shulḥan 'arukh*.[82] Alḍāhirī's sensitivity to the conservative religious and social mores of Yemenite Jewish society is also evident in his attempt to frame *Sefer hamusar* as a salutary and morally instructive book, in much the same way that al-Ḥarīrī had issued a prefatory apology for his *Maqāmāt*. In light of the tension between Alḍāhirī's sober stated goals and the sometimes immoderate, impulsive content of the work, it is perhaps not coincidental that the book ends with the author eliciting a pious poem from his protagonist. These solemn reflections on death and ultimate reward are, after all, Alḍāhirī's last words, intended, one would assume, to sit well with a less than favorably disposed readership.

If placing his own epitaph in the final chapter furthered an apologetic end, and if the literary stimulus to write such an auto-*tombeau* came from Immanuel's *Maḥbarot*, it is still reasonable to assume that Alḍāhirī's tribute to himself was also motivated by a very human desire to preserve his memory from oblivion. Evidently, he was able to reconcile his this-worldly yearning for recognition and literary immortality with his belief in the immortality of the disembodied soul as conceived by medieval Jewish philosophers and kabbalists—a coexistence of impulses not unlike the complementarity of

---

with the laws of ritual slaughter, and his collection of responsa, *Pe'ulat ṣadiq*; see Ratzaby's introduction to *Sefer hamusar*, pp. 44–47 and idem, *Toratan shelivnei teiman*, 61–67.

81 See Tanenbaum, "Hidden Gems: The Hebrew *Maqāma* from Yemen," p. 200 n. 25.

82 See *Oraḥ ḥayyim* 307:16.

desires for earthly and eschatological survival observed by Philippe Ariès in late medieval and early modern Christian attitudes toward death.[83]

Each of the corpora informing Alḍāhirī's *maqāmāt* valued the practice of literary memorializing. Early on, Arabic literary critics—among them al-Jāhiẓ (9th c.) and Ibn Qutayba (d. 889)—highlighted the ability of poetry to preserve the glorious deeds of the past, whether tribal or personal.[84] Immanuel, too, turned to poetry and rhymed prose to reassure himself that his magisterial biblical commentaries, poetic works, and command of philosophy, grammar, and melody would keep his name alive. In the first half of the 16th-century, because printing was still relatively new and it was not common to print works by a living writer, authors in Ottoman Constantinople and Salonica anticipated charges of publicity-seeking and felt obliged to apologize for publishing their own works. Rabbi Jacob ben Tam Ibn Yaḥya invoked the age-old metaphor of the book as a lasting literary monument that would perpetuate his name in much the same way as physical buildings preserve the names and memory of those who erected them.[85] Viewed through this prism, the literary memorial was an act of resistance against the perceived threat of permanent extinction and non-being. It embodied the hope that the living would not forget the deceased, who would continue to speak to them through their literary legacies as well as directly, through their funerary inscriptions. There was, of course, a certain irony in such commemorative rituals since the authors of auto-epitaphs are still very much present while imagining and anticipating their absence with dread. Hence the care with which they shaped their legacy and undertook to preserve their presence for posterity through texts they hoped would outlive them. Despite his considerable talents in many fields and the acclaim accorded his scholarship during his lifetime, Alḍāhirī's fear of slipping into obscurity was perhaps not completely unfounded, in light of the lukewarm reception his belletristic opus was to receive until more modern times.[86] The trying circumstances of the work's

83 Ariès, *The Hour of Our Death*, 202–215. The distinction derives from Panofsky, *Tomb Sculpture*.

84 See Heinrichs, "Prosimetrical Genres in Classical Arabic," 251–253.

85 See Hacker, "Authors, Readers and Printers of Sixteenth-Century Hebrew Books in the Ottoman Empire," 33. Horace calls his poem, "Exegi monumentum aere perennius," "a monument more lasting than bronze" that will ensure that he will "not wholly die"; see Horace, *Odes* III.30, 1–8 in Bennett trans. *Horace, Odes and Epodes*.

86 Ratzaby infers from comments put into the mouths of other characters in *Sefer hamusar* that Alḍāhirī's poetry received recognition during his lifetime, though the narrator also reports criticism of Abner's poetry; see *Sefer hamusar*, pp. 46–47 and nn. 1–6. Note that Abner's epitaph for Mordecai includes the phrase "everyone recited his poems."

composition would presumably have made its recognition in perpetuity all the more precious to him. As fate would have it, *Sefer hamusar* was Alḍāhirī's literary swan song.

The urge to be immortalized is universal, and countless individuals throughout history have written their own epitaphs, often in verse.[87] What is so intriguing about Alḍāhirī's attempt to secure his reputation for posterity is that, apart from Immanuel's auto-eulogy, it had no precedents in the long tradition of Hebrew *maqāmāt* and rhymed prose narratives. As one of the few 16th-century Yemenite Jewish intellectuals who likely traveled outside of his native land, Alḍāhirī was alive to the transformative potential of Hebrew printing and the kabbalistic innovations emerging from the Safed center and may have sensed that he represented the end of an era in Yemenite Hebrew literature, even as he encouraged the import of agents of change. Seen in this light, the epitaph he wrote for himself was not just an attempt to preserve his personal reputation, but also a way to confer lasting fame on Yemenite Jewish literary creativity as he had known it. Whether or not he was fully conscious of it, *Sefer hamusar* marked the temporal end and furthermost geographic reach of the 400-year-old tradition of Hebrew rhymed prose narratives. Alḍāhirī's preoccupation with posterity was arguably also a way of celebrating his own contribution to this rich and long-lived mode of literary expression.

Alḍāhirī was recognized posthumously within his community, primarily for his halakhic works but also through the perpetuation of his poems in *takālil* and liturgical anthologies. There is also a curious appreciation of his accomplishments by Saʿadya Manṣura (d. c. 1880) in *Sefer ha-maḥshavah* (*Sefer ha-galut ve-ha-geʾulah*), the consolatory Hebrew rhymed prose work that claimed descent from *Sefer hamusar*. In the final chapter, inspired by the auto-epitaph in Alḍāhirī's closing *maqāma*, Manṣura eulogizes not only himself but also several Yemenite Jewish luminaries, starting with Zechariah Alḍāhirī:[88]

---

87 Western European epitaph practices are particularly well-documented since anthologies of epitaphs have been collected since Antiquity. See, e.g., Petrucci, *Writing the Dead*; Guthke, *Epitaph Culture in the West*, esp. pp. 143–189; Ariès, *The Hour of Our Death*; and Scodel, *The English Poetic Epitaph*.

88 In the uniqum ms. in which the work is preserved, Manṣura also copied out Alḍāhirī's 45th *maqāma* in its entirety; see NLI ms. Heb. 4741 fols. 43^{v} ff. Following Alḍāhirī's model, Manṣura's narrator asks the 'hero' figure to eulogize him while he is still alive. The narrator/author is praised for his diligent study of Mishnah, astronomy, and calendrical calculation, and for his prognostication. The other luminaries memorialized are Yiḥye Bashirī, an esteemed 17th-century scribe, exegete, grammarian, and kabbalist; Shalem Shabbazi, the larger than life and much-beloved 17th-century poet, kabbalist, and exegete; and Yiḥye Ṣāliḥ, the most eminent scholar of halakhah, mesorah, and liturgy of the 18th-century.

> The great rabbi, our revered teacher, Yiḥye Ḍāhirī, whose influential wisdom and commanding reputation were known throughout Yemen, and whose deeds were renowned throughout the land, was a master of Scripture, Mishnah, Talmud, Aggadah, Sifra and Sifre, epigrams and riddles, animal fables, washermen's tales (*mishlot kovsim*), demons' speech (*siḥat shedim*), the speech of palm trees (*siḥat deqalim*), and the speech of the ministering angels (*siḥat mal'akhei ha-sharet*). He was an expert in the sciences of astronomy, mathematics, geometry, and politics (*ḥokhmah medinit*), as well as in natural science, grammar, and music, which is the science of melody (*ḥokhmat ha-musiqa, hi ḥokhmat ha-niggun ba-shirim*), and above all, in metaphysics, which enables one to know the divine stature (*shiʿur qomah*).[89]

This memorial draws on and derives some of its more colorful components from two talmudic passages detailing the studies of the legendary first-century C.E. *tanna*, Rabbi Johanan Ben Zakkai.[90] But with its mélange of classical Jewish disciplines, quadrivium, trivium, mysticism, and occult sciences, Manṣura's biographical note pays a peculiar sort of homage to his illustrious predecessor. Even if much of it is shaped by its talmudic models, there are some intriguing additions and omissions. Particularly glaring is the absence of any explicit mention of Alḍāhirī's accomplishments as a littérateur and poet. Nor is Alḍāhirī's kabbalistic expertise explicitly acknowledged, though it is alluded to with phrases whose mystical overtones presumably would not have gone unremarked (*ve-ʿal kulam ḥokhmah ha-elohit leidaʿ shiʿur qomah*). The obliqueness of the wording is puzzling, given that in his auto-elegy Manṣura acknowledges his own devotion to kabbalah and that, only three decades after Manṣura's death, the anti-kabbalistic *Dor Deʿah* movement would implicate Alḍāhirī in the introduction of this 'pernicious' doctrine to Yemen.[91] In crediting Alḍāhirī with largely uncorroborated expertise in the sciences of astronomy, mathematics, geometry, and politics, as well as in natural science, grammar, and music, Manṣura's eulogy echoes Immanuel's self-lament:

89 Manṣura, *Sefer ha-galut ve-ha-ge'ulah*, 129. See also *Sefer hamusar*, p. 47.

90 See bSukkah 28a and bBB 134a.

91 Manṣura's auto-elegy says, "*Rov ʿosqo ba-qabbalah be-hitbodedo/ sheʿur qomah be-sod yeḥido*"; see *Sefer ha-galut ve-ha-ge'ulah*, p. 135. Manṣura also wrote a preface to Shabbazi's *dīwān* in which he criticizes performers and audiences who misinterpret or make light of Shabbazi's profoundly spiritual kabbalistic poems; see ibid., pp. 9–11 and Wagner, *Like Joseph in Beauty*, 218–219.

> "Alas, community of Rome! Who will illuminate your twilight stars? … Alas, science of melody! Who will prepare the work of your sockets and drums? … Lament like a maiden, science of grammar, for the man who made you his wife is dead."

At the same time, it retrojects elements of Manṣura's own auto-epitaph onto his predecessor, perhaps as a way of signaling the continuities between them, whether real or imagined.[92] Alḍāhirī's forty-fifth *maqāma* gained a kind of afterlife in Manṣura's closing chapter, but if this was to be the final word on his achievements, then the reputation about which he was so concerned would have come to something of a bittersweet end. Laudatory and admiring to the point of hagiography, Manṣura's tribute is, paradoxically, also a misrepresentation by and for posterity. Though Manṣura intended no harm, and undoubtedly regarded the implicit comparison with Johanan Ben Zakkai as a compliment, he might have done better to heed the impassioned plea voiced in Alḍāhirī's valediction: "Lament him with the eulogy he composed for himself!"[93]

---

92 See Immanuel Ha-romi, *Maḥbarot*, pp. 390–391 and *Sefer ha-galut ve-ha-ge'ulah*, p. 135 where Manṣura credits himself with expertise in the science of astronomy as well as in *ḥokhmat ha-niggun, 'im tenu'o ve-yetedo*. The latter phrase suggests that *ḥokhmat ha-niggun* may refer to the chanting of poetry according to its metrical scansion, rather than to the science of music *per se*.

93 *U-teqonenu 'alav me-asher yissad*; see *Sefer hamusar*, p. 465, lines 103–104 and n. 104.

Bibliography

Bibliographic Abbreviations

Alḥarizi, *Taḥkemoni*	References are to Yahalom-Katsumata's edition. Where relevant, their numeration is followed by the numeration in earlier printed editions and the translations by Reichert and Segal. (#43/#30).
AJS Review	*Association for Jewish Studies Review*
b	Babylonian Talmud.
BDB	F. Brown, S.R. Driver, C.A. Briggs, *A Hebrew and English Lexicon of the Old Testament*. Oxford: Clarendon Press, 1939.
BSOAS	*Bulletin of the School of Oriental and African Studies.*
Cant. Rab.	*Midrash Canticles Rabbah*. In *Midrash Rabbah.*
CHALABL	*The Cambridge History of Arabic Literature: ʿAbbasid Belles Lettres*, ed. Julia Ashtiany et al. Cambridge University Press, 1990.
CHALAND	*The Cambridge History of Arabic Literature: The Literature of al-Andalus*, ed. Maria Rosa Menocal et al. Cambridge University Press, 2000.
CHAL-PCP	*The Cambridge History of Arabic Literature: Arabic Literature in the Post-Classical Period*, ed. Roger Allen and D.S. Richards. Cambridge University Press, 2006.
CHALRLS	*The Cambridge History of Arabic Literature: Religion, Learning and Science in the ʿAbbasid Period*, ed. M.J.L. Young, J.D. Latham and R.B. Serjeant. Cambridge University Press, 1990.
Deut. Rab.	*Midrash Deuteronomy Rabbah*. In *Midrash Rabbah.*
EAL	*Encyclopedia of Arabic Literature*. Ed. Julie Scott Meisami and Paul Starkey. London/New York: Routledge, 1998.
Ecc. Rab.	*Midrash Ecclesiastes Rabbah*. In *Midrash Rabbah.*
EI^{1}	*Encyclopaedia of Islam*. 1st ed. Brill Online.
EI^{2}	*Encyclopaedia of Islam*. 2nd ed. Brill Online. P.J. Bearman et al. eds.
EI^{3}	*Encyclopaedia of Islam*. 3rd ed. Brill Online.
EJ^{2}	*Encyclopaedia Judaica*. 2nd ed. Michael Berenbaum and Fred Skolnik eds. Gale EBooks.
EJIW	*Encyclopedia of Jews in the Islamic World*. Executive editor Norman Stillman; editors Phillip Ackerman-Lieberman et al. Brill Online.
Ex. Rab.	*Midrash Exodus Rabbah*. In *Midrash Rabbah.*
Gen. Rab.	*Midrash Bereschit Rabba*. Ed. J. Theodor and C. Albeck.
HAR	*Hebrew Annual Review*
HPCS	Hayyim Schirmann, *The History of Hebrew Poetry in Christian Spain and Southern France.*

HPD	Hayyim Schirmann, *Studies in the History of Hebrew Poetry and Drama*.
HPMS	Hayyim Schirmann, *The History of Hebrew Poetry In Muslim Spain*.
HPSP	Hayyim Schirmann, *Ha-shirah ha-ʿivrit bi-sfarad u-ve-provans*. [Hebrew Poetry in Spain and Provence].
HTR	*Harvard Theological Review*
HUCA	*Hebrew Union College Annual*
IFEAD	Institut Français d'Études Arabes de Damas
IHIW	*Intellectual History of the Islamicate World*
IMHM	*Institute for Microfilmed Hebrew Manuscripts*
IOS	*Israel Oriental Studies*
JAIS	*Journal of Arabic and Islamic Studies*
JAL	*Journal of Arabic Literature*
JAOS	*Journal of the American Oriental Society*
JAS	*Journal of Abbasid Studies*
JE	*The Jewish Encyclopedia*
JESHO	*Journal of the Economic and Social History of the Orient*
JJS	*Journal of Jewish Studies*
JJTP	*Journal of Jewish Thought and Philosophy*
JNES	*Journal of Near Eastern Studies*
JQR	*Jewish Quarterly Review*
JSAI	*Jerusalem Studies in Arabic and Islam*
JSS	*Journal of Semitic Studies*
JSQ	*Jewish Studies Quarterly*
KS	*Kiryat Sefer*
Lev. Rab.	*Midrash Vayyikra Rabbah*. Edited by M. Margulies.
m	Mishnah
Maimonides, MT	Moses b. Maimon, *Mishneh Torah*. References to Treatise, Chapter, and Halakhah.
MEL	*Middle Eastern Literatures*
MES	*Middle Eastern Studies*
NJPS	*New JPS Tanakh*. Philadelphia: Jewish Publication Society, 1985, 1999.
Num. Rab.	*Midrash Numbers Rabbah*. In *Midrash Rabbah*.
PAAJR	*Proceedings of the American Academy for Jewish Research*
REJ	*Revue des Études Juives*
RSV	Revised Standard Version
SI	*Studia Islamica*
SRHJ	Baron, Salo W. *A Social and Religious History of the Jews*. 3 volumes. New York: Columbia University Press, 1937.
ZDMG	*Zeitschrift der Deutschen Morgenländischen Gesellschaft*

Primary Sources

Afendopolo, Caleb ben Eliyahu. *Aviner ben Ner: Shirim u-meliṣot ba-ḥaruzim be-signon ben ha-melekh ve-ha-nazir*. Edited by Yosef Algamil. Ashdod, 2006/7.

Alami, Solomon. *Iggeret musar*. Edited by Adolph Jellinek. Leipzig, 1854.

Alḍāhirī, Zechariah ben Seʿadya ben Yaʿaqov. *Sefer haʿanaq*. Ms. Guenzburg 1306, The Russian State Library, Moscow; IMHM film no. F 48786.

Alḍāhirī, Zechariah ben Seʿadya ben Yaʿaqov. *Sefer hamusar: maḥberot rabbi zekhariah al-ḍāhirī*. Edited by Yehuda Ratzaby. Jerusalem: Ben-Zvi Institute, 1965.

Alḍāhirī, Zechariah ben Seʿadya ben Yaʿaqov. *Sefer hamusar, ha-shirah ve-ha-piyyuṭ le-rabbenu yiḥye (zekhariah) ben seʿadya be-rav yaʿaqov al-ḍāhirī*. Edited by Mordechai Yiṣhari. Rosh Haʿayin, 2008.

Alḍāhirī, Zechariah ben Seʿadya ben Yaʿaqov. *Sefer ṣeidah la-derekh*. In *Tāj ḥamishah ḥumshei torah ʿim peirushim ve-sefer avqat rokhel*. 2 vols. Jerusalem: Y. Hasid, 1964; repr. 1991.

al-Hamadhānī, Badīʿ al-Zamān. *Maqāmāt*. Edited by Muḥammad ʿAbduh. Beirut: al-Maṭbaʿa al-Kāthūlīkiyya, 1889; repr. Beirut: Dār al-Mashriq, 1973.

al-Hamadhānī, Badīʿ al-Zamān. *The Maqāmāt of Badīʿ al-Zamān al-Hamadhānī*. Translated by W.J. Prendergast. London and Madras: Luzac & Co., 1915; repr. London: Curzon Press, 1973.

al-Ḥarīrī, Abū ʾl-Ḥasan. *The Assemblies of Al Ḥarīri*, vol. 1. Translated by Thomas Chenery. London: Williams and Norgate, 1867; repr. Gregg International, 1969.

al-Ḥarīrī, Abū ʾl-Ḥasan. *The Assemblies of Al Ḥarīri*, vol. 2. Translated by Francis Steingass. London, 1898; repr. Gregg International Publishers Limited, 1969.

al-Ḥarīrī, Abū ʾl-Ḥasan. *al-Ḥarīrī: Maqāmāt Abī Zayd al-Sarūjī*. Edited by Michael Cooperson. New York: New York University Press, 2020.

al-Ḥarīrī, Abū ʾl-Ḥasan. *Maqāmāt al-Ḥarīrī*. Beirut: Dār Bayrūt, Dār Ṣādir, 1958.

Alḥarizi, Judah. *Kitāb al-Durar: A Book in Praise of God and the Israelite Communities* [*Kitāb al-Durar: ve-hu sefer peninei ha-musarim ve-shivḥei ha-qehalim*]. Edited and translated by Joshua Blau, Paul Fenton, and Joseph Yahalom. Jerusalem: Ben-Zvi Institute, Yad Izhak Ben-Zvi, and the Hebrew University of Jerusalem, 2009.

Alḥarizi, Judah. *Maḥberot Itiʾel*. Edited by Y. Peretz. Tel Aviv: Maḥbarot le-sifrut, 1950.

Alḥarizi, Judah. *Taḥkemoni*. Edited by I. Toporowsky. Tel Aviv: Maḥbarot le-Sifrut and Mossad Harav Kook, 1952.

Alḥarizi, Judah. *The Tahkemoni of Judah al-Harizi*. Translated by V.E. Reichert. 2 vols. Jerusalem: Raphael Haim Cohen's Ltd., 1965–1973.

Alḥarizi, Judah. *Taḥkemoni or The Tales of Heman the Ezraḥite* (Hebrew). Edited by Joseph Yahalom and Naoya Katsumata. Jerusalem: Ben-Zvi Institute, Yad Izhak Ben-Zvi, and the Hebrew University of Jerusalem, 2010.

Alḥarizi, Judah. *The Wanderings of Judah Alharizi: Five Accounts of His Travels* (Hebrew). Edited by Joseph Yahalom and Joshua Blau. Jerusalem: Ben-Zvi Institute, Yad Izhak Ben-Zvi and the Hebrew University of Jerusalem, 2002.

al-Ḥibshi, ʿAbdallah Muḥammad, ed. *Majmūʿ al-maqāmāt al-yamanīyah*. Ṣanaʿā: Maktabat al-Jil al-Jadid, 1987.

al-Ḥibshi, ʿAbdallah Muḥammad, ed. *Maqāmāt min al-adab al-yamanī*. Ṣanaʿā: Dar al-Yaman al-Kubrā lil-Nashr wa'l-Tawziʿ, 1984.

al-Ibshīhī, Muḥammad ibn Aḥmad. *Al-Mustaṭraf fī kull fann mustaẓraf*. Translated by G. Rat (French; *Al-Mostaṭraf*). Paris: E. Leroux, 1899–1902.

al-Iṣfahāni, al-Rāghib. *Muḥāḍarāt al-udabāʾ wa-muḥāwarāt al-shuʿarāʾ wa ʾl-bulaghāʾ*. 2 vols. Beirut, 1961.

al-Jāhiẓ, Abū ʿUthmān ʿAmr ibn Baḥr. *al-Maḥāsin wa'l-aḍdād*. Cairo, 1978.

al-Jawbarī, Jamāl al-Dīn ʿAbd al-Raḥīm. *The Book of Charlatans*. Edited by Manuela Dengler and translated by Humphrey Davies. New York University Press, 2020.

al-Nahrawālī al-Makkī, Quṭb al-Dīn. *Lightning Over Yemen: A History of the Ottoman Campaign (1569–1571), being a translation from the Arabic of Part III of al-Barq al-yamānī fī ʾl-fatḥ al-ʿuthmānī ... as published by Ḥamad al-Jāsir (Riyadh, 1967)*. Translated by C.K. Smith. London/NY: I.B. Tauris, 2002.

al-Saraqusṭī, Abū l-Ṭāhir. *al-Maqāmāt al-Luzūmīyah by Abū l-Ṭāhir Muḥammad ibn Yūsuf al-Tamīmī al-Saraqusṭī ibn al-Ashtarkūwī (d. 538/1143)*. Edited and translated by James T. Monroe. Leiden/ Boston/ Köln: E.J. Brill, 2002.

Bar Ḥiyya, Abraham. *Sefer hegyon ha-nefesh o sefer ha-musar*. Edited by E. Freimann. Leipzig, 1860; repr. Jerusalem 1967.

Ben Elʿazar, Jacob. *Sippurei ahavah shel yaʿaqov ben elʿazar*. Edited by Yonah David. Tel Aviv: Ramot Publishing/Tel Aviv University Press, 1992–1993.

Benveniste, Samuel. *Sheloshah sefarim niftaḥim: Sefer ha-musar, Sefer orekh yamim*. Jerusalem, 1996.

Ephraim ben Joab ben Moses of Modena. *Sefer ha-musar*. Edited by Jochanan S. Wittkower. Lyck: Mekize Nirdamim, 1871.

Falaquera, Shem Tov. *Battei hanhagat guf ha-bari'*. Edited by S. Muntner. Tel Aviv: Maḥbarot le-sifrut, 1950.

Falaquera, Shem Tov. *Sefer ha-mevaqqesh*. Edited by M. Tamah. The Hague, 1772; repr. in *Kitvei r. shem ṭov falaquera* vol. 3. Jerusalem: Sifriyat Meqorot, 1970.

Falaquera, Shem Tov. *Ṣori ha-yagon* (The Balm for Sorrow). With German translation by David Ottensosser. Fürth, 1854.

Ha'ezovi, Yiṣḥaq b. Shelomoh. *Sefer agudat ezov*. Edited by Yair Ben-Shalom. Netanya, 1994.

Halevi, Judah ben Samuel. *Dīwān yehudah ben shemu'el ha-levi*. Edited by Hayyim Brody. 4 vols. Berlin: Mekize Nirdamim, 1894–1930.

Halevi, Judah ben Samuel. *Diwan Yehudah Halevi*. Edited by Samuel David Luzatto. Lyck: Meqize Nirdamim, 1864.

Halevi, Judah ben Samuel. *Kitāb al-radd wa'l-dalīl fi'l-dīn al-dhalīl* (*al-kitāb al-khazarī*). Edited by D.H. Baneth and H. Ben-Shammai. Jerusalem: Magnes Press, 1977.

Halevi, Judah ben Samuel. *The Liturgical Poetry* (Hebrew). Edited by Dov Jarden. 4 vols. Jerusalem: By the Author, 1979–1986.

Halevi, Judah ben Samuel. *Sefer ha-kuzari*. Translated by Judah Ibn Tibbon. Edited by A. Zifroni. Tel Aviv: Maḥbarot le-Sifrut, 1948.

Halevi, Judah ben Samuel. *Sefer ha-kuzari*. Edited and translated by Yosef Qāfiḥ. Qiryat Ono: Makhon Mosheh, 1997.

Ibn Aqnīn, Joseph b. Judah. *Hitgalut ha-sodot ve-hofa'at ha-me'orot*. Edited and translated by A.S. Halkin. Jerusalem: Mekize Nirdamim, 1964.

Ibn Aqnīn, Joseph b. Judah. *Sepher musar, Kommentar zum Mischnatraktat Aboth*. Edited by W. Bacher. Berlin: Mekize Nirdamim, 1910.

Ibn Caspi, Joseph. *Sefer ha-musar ha-niqra yoreh de'ah*. In Abrahams ed. and trans., *Hebrew Ethical Wills*, 1:127–161.

Ibn Ezra, Abraham ben Meir. *Dīwān des Abraham Ibn Esra mit seiner Allegorie Hai Ben Mekiz*. Edited by Jacob Egers. Berlin, 1886.

Ibn Ezra, Abraham ben Meir. *Reime und Gedichte des Abraham Ibn Esra*. Edited and translated by David Rosin. Breslau, 1885–1894.

Ibn Ezra, Abraham ben Meir. *The Religious Poems of Abraham Ibn Ezra* (Hebrew). Edited by Israel Levin. 2 vols. Jerusalem: Israel Academy of Sciences and Humanities, 1975–1980.

Ibn Ezra, Abraham ben Meir. *The Secular Poems of Abraham Ibn Ezra: Critical edition with introduction and commentary by Israel Levin* (Hebrew). Lod: Makhon Haberman, 2016.

Ibn Ezra, Moses ben Jacob. *Kitāb al-muḥāḍara wa'l-mudhākara* (*sefer ha'iyyunim ve-hadiyyunim*). Edited and translated by A.S. Halkin. Jerusalem: Mekize Nirdamim, 1975.

Ibn Ezra, Moses ben Jacob. *Secular Poems* (Hebrew). Edited by H. Brody and D. Pagis. 3 vols. Jerusalem: Schocken Institute, 1935–1977.

Ibn Faḍlān, Aḥmed. *Mission to the Volga*. Translated by James E. Montgomery, foreword by Tim Severin. New York: New York University Press, 2017.

Ibn Gabirol, Solomon ben Judah. *The Improvement of the Moral Qualities* (*Kitāb iṣlāḥ al-akhlāq*). Edited and translated by Stephen S. Wise. New York: Columbia University Press, 1902; repr. New York: AMS Press Inc., 1966.

Ibn Gabirol, Solomon ben Judah. *The Liturgical Poetry* (Hebrew). Second Edition. Edited by Dov Jarden. 2 vols. Jerusalem: By the Author, 1979.

Ibn Gabirol, Solomon ben Judah. *Secular Poems* (Hebrew). Edited by H. Brody and J. Schirmann. Jerusalem: The Schocken Institute for Jewish Research, 1974.

Ibn Gabirol, Solomon ben Judah. *The Secular Poetry* (Hebrew). Edited by Dov Jarden. 2 vols. Jerusalem: By the Author, 1975–1976.

Ibn Jubayr, Muḥammad ibn Aḥmad. *Riḥlat Ibn Jubayr*. Beirut: Dār Sādir, 1964.

Ibn Makhir, Moses. *Seder ha-yom*. Jerusalem, 1996.

Ibn Naghrila (Hanagid), Samuel b. Joseph Halevi. *Diwan Vol. 1: Ben Tehilim*. Edited by Dov Jarden. Jerusalem: Hebrew Union College Press, 1966.

Ibn Naghrila (Hanagid), Samuel b. Joseph Halevi. *Diwan Vol. 2: Ben Mishle*. Edited by Dov Jarden. Jerusalem: By the Author, 1982.

Ibn Naghrila (Hanagid), Samuel b. Joseph Halevi. *Diwan Vol. 3: Ben Qohelet*. Edited by Dov Jarden. Jerusalem: By the Author, 1992.

Ibn Paquda, Baḥya ben Joseph. *Kitāb al-hidāya ilā farā'iḍ al-qulūb* (*torat ḥovot ha-levavot*). Edited and translated by J. Qāfiḥ. Jerusalem: By the Author, 1973.

Ibn Paquda, Baḥya ben Joseph. *Sefer ḥovot ha-levavot*. Translated by Judah Ibn Tibbon. Edited by A. Zifroni. Tel Aviv: Maḥbarot le-sifrut/Mossad Harav Kook, 1949.

Ibn Sahula, Isaac. *Meshal Haqadmoni: Fables from the Distant Past*. Edited and translated by Raphael Loewe. Oxford & Portland, OR: Littman Library of Jewish Civilization, 2004.

Ibn Shāhīn, Nissim ben Jacob. *The Arabic Original of Ibn Shāhīn's Book of Comfort*. Edited by Julian Obermann. New Haven: Yale University Press, 1933.

Ibn Shāhīn, Nissim ben Jacob. *Kitāb al-faraj ba'da al-shidda: An Elegant Composition Concerning Relief after Adversity*. Translated by William M. Brinner. New Haven: Yale University Press, 1977.

Ibn Zabara, Joseph. *Sefer sha'ashu'im*. Edited by Israel Davidson. Berlin: Eshkol, 1925.

Ibn Zabara, Joseph. *The Book of Delight*. Translated by Moses Hadas. New York, Columbia University Press, 1932.

Ibn Zabara, Joseph. *The Physician and the Demon: A Critical Edition of the Book of Delight by Joseph Ibn Zabara* (Hebrew). Edited by Judith Dishon. Jerusalem: Habermann Institute for Literary Research, 2017.

Idelsohn, A.Z. and H. Torczyner, eds. *Shirei teiman*. Cincinnati: Hebrew Union College Press, 1930.

Immanuel Ha-romi. *Maḥberot Immanuel Ha-romi*. Edited by Dov Jarden, 2d ed. Jerusalem: By the Author, n.d.

Kalomiti, Neḥemiah. *The War of Truth*. Edited and translated by Pinchas Doron. New York: Ktav Publishing House, 1978.

Kalonymus ben Kalonymus. *Even Boḥan*. Edited by A.M. Habermann. Tel Aviv: Maḥbarot le-sifrut and Mossad Harav Kook, 1956.

Khalaṣ, Judah. *Sefer ha-musar, 'esrim peraqim be'inyenei ha-miṣvot ve-ha-tefillot, musar u-middot*. Mantua: Yaqomo Rufinelo, 1560–1561.

Levi ben Gershom. *The Wars of the Lord*. Translated by Seymour Feldman. 3 vols. Philadelphia: The Jewish Publication Society of America, 1984.

Lovelace, Richard. "To Althea from Prison." Accessed at: https://www.poetryfoundation.org/poems/44657/to-althea-from-prison

Margaliot, Reuben, ed. *Tiqqunei ha-zohar*. Jerusalem: Mossad Harav Kook, 1948.

Matt, Daniel C., trans. *The Zohar* Pritzker Edition. Volume Three. Stanford: Stanford University Press, 2005.

Midrash Bereschit Rabba. Edited by J. Theodor and C. Albeck. 3 vols. Berlin, 1912–1936.

Midrash Canticles Rabbah. In *Midrash Rabbah*. Vilna, 1878.

Midrash Deuteronomy Rabbah. In *Midrash Rabbah*. Vilna, 1878.

Midrash Ecclesiastes Rabbah. In *Midrash Rabbah*. Vilna, 1878.

Midrash Exodus Rabbah. In *Midrash Rabbah*. Vilna, 1878.

Midrash Haggadol on the Pentateuch. Edited by M. Margulies et al. Jerusalem: Mossad Harav Kook, 1947–1975.

Midrash Numbers Rabbah. In *Midrash Rabbah*. Vilna, 1878.

Midrash Rabbah. 2 vols. Vilna: Romm, 1878.

Midrash Vayyikra Rabbah. Edited by M. Margulies. 5 vols. Jerusalem: Ministry of Education and Culture/AAJR, 1953–1960.

Modena, Leon. *The Divan of Leo De Modena*. Edited by Simon Bernstein. Philadelphia: The Jewish Publication Society of America, 1932.

Moses b. Maimon (Maimonides). *Haqdamot le-feirush ha-mishnah*. Edited by M.D. Rabinovitz. Jerusalem: Mossad Harav Kook, 1961.

Moses b. Maimon (Maimonides). *Mishnah ʿim peirush rabbeinu moshe ben maimon*. Edited and translated by J. Qāfiḥ. 7 vols. Jerusalem: Mossad Harav Kook, 1963–1968.

Moses b. Maimon (Maimonides). *Mishneh Torah*. Warsaw, 1881.

Moses b. Maimon (Maimonides). *R. Moses b. Maimon, Responsa* (Hebrew). Edited by Jehoshua Blau. Jerusalem: Mekize Nirdamim, 1960.

Moses b. Maimon (Maimonides). *Rabbeinu mosheh ben maimon, moreh ha-nevukhim*. Edited and translated by J. Qāfiḥ. Jerusalem: Mossad Harav Kook, 1972.

Moses b. Maimon (Maimonides). *Sefer moreh ha-nevukhim*. (*Guide of the Perplexed*). Translated by Samuel Ibn Tibbon. Warsaw, 1872.

Moses ben Naḥman (Naḥmanides). *Kitvei Ramban*. Edited by C. Chavel. 2 vols. Jerusalem: Mossad Harav Kook, 1963–1964.

Moses ben Naḥman (Naḥmanides). *Peirushei ha-torah le-rabbeinu moshe ben naḥman* (*ramban*). (Commentaries on the Torah). Second Edition. Edited by C. Chavel. 2 vols. Jerusalem: Mossad Harav Kook, 1980.

Najara, Israel. *She'erit Yisrael*. Edited with Introductory Essays and Commentaries by Tova Beeri and Edwin Seroussi. 2 vols. Jerusalem: The Ben-Zvi Institute & The Rabbi Moses and Amalia Rosen Foundation, 2023.

Najara, Israel. *Zemirot Yisrael*. Edited by Judah Vries-Horeb. Tel Aviv: Maḥbarot le-sifrut and Mossad Harav Kook, 1946.

Saadya b. Joseph al-Fayyūmī Gaon. *Mishlei ʿim tirgum u-feirush ha-ga'on rabbeinu seʿadyah ben yosef fayyūmī*. Edited and translated by J. Qāfiḥ. Jerusalem, 1976.

Saadya b. Joseph al-Fayyūmī Gaon. *Tehillim ʿim tirgum u-feirush ha-ga'on rabbeinu seʿadyah ben yosef fayyūmī*. Edited and translated by J. Qāfiḥ. Jerusalem, 1966.

Saadya b. Joseph al-Fayyūmī Gaon. *Version arabe du pentateuque de R. Saadia ben Iosef al-Fayyoūmī.* Edited by J. Derenbourg. Paris, 1893.

Ṣāliḥ, Yiḥye. *Peʿulat ṣadiq.* Jerusalem 1978/9.

Ṣāliḥ, Yiḥye. *Tiklāl ʿim sefer eṣ ḥayyim.* Jerusalem, 1971.

Ṣāliḥ, Yiḥye. *Zevaḥ todah.* Jerusalem, 1899.

Sefer keter ha-torah, ha-tāj ha-gadol. Jerusalem: Y. Ḥasid, 1982.

Sefer maʿarekhet haʾelohut. Zholkva, 1779. https://hebrewbooks.org/33877

Tāj ʿim perushim ḥamishah ḥumshei torah ve-sefer avqat rokhel. Jerusalem: Yosef Aharon Hasid, 1991.

Toledot yehudei teiman mikhitveihem (*The History of the Jews of Yemen from their Own Chronicles*). With an Introduction by Y. Tobi. Jerusalem: The Zalman Shazar Center and The Dinur Center, 1979. [Series: Qunṭresim, meqorot u-meḥqarim; 53.]

Torat ḥayyim: ḥamishah ḥumshei torah mugahim ʿal-pi ha-nusaḥ veha-masorah shel keter aram ṣovah. Jerusalem: Mossad Harav Kook, 1986.

Vital, Hayyim. *Shaʿar ha-kavvanot.* Tel Aviv, 1961/2.

Secondary Literature

Aarne, Antti. *The Types of the Folktale: A Classification and Bibliography.* Trans. Stith Thompson. Helsinki, 1964.

Abdar, Carmela. "Reflections on Magical Texts on Jewelry and Amulets of Jewish Women and Children from Yemen and Habban" (Hebrew). *Jerusalem Studies in Jewish Folklore* 32 (2019): 89–149.

Abdar, Carmela. "White as the Sun—The Language of Dress of Jewish Brides in Yemen in the First Half of the 20th Century." In *Ascending the Palm Tree*, ed. R. Yedid and D. Bar-Maoz, 170–203. Rehovot: Eʿeleh BeTamar, 2018.

Abir, Mordechai. "International Commerce and Yemenite Jewry: 15th to 19th Centuries" (Hebrew). *Peʿamim* 5 (1980): 4–28.

Abrahams, Israel, ed. and trans. *Hebrew Ethical Wills.* 2 vols. Philadelphia: The Jewish Publication Society of America, 1926.

Abrams, Daniel. "The Invention of the Zohar as a Book: On the Assumptions and the Expectations of the Kabbalists and Modern Scholars." *Kabbalah: Journal for the Study of Jewish Mystical Texts* 19 (2004): 7–142.

Abramson, Shraga. *Bilshon qodemim.* Jerusalem: Schocken Institute, 1965.

Adams, Percy G. *Travelers and Travel Liars, 1660–1800.* Berkeley: University of California Press, 1962.

Adang, Camilla. "Guided to Islam by the Torah: The *Risāla al-hādiya* by ʿAbd al-Salām al-Muhtadī al-Muḥammadī." In *Contacts and Controversies*, ed. Adang and Schmidtke, 57–72.

Adang, Camilla. "A Jewish Reply to Ibn Hazm: Solomon b. Adret's Polemic against Islam." In *Judios y musulmanes en al-Andalus y el Magreb*, ed. M. Fierro, 179–209. Madrid: Casa de Velazquez, 2002.

Adang, Camilla. *Muslim Writers on Judaism and the Hebrew Bible: From Ibn Rabban to Ibn Hazm*. Leiden: E.J. Brill, 1996.

Adang, Camilla and Sabine Schmidtke, eds. *Contacts and Controversies Between Muslims, Jews and Christians in the Ottoman Empire and Pre-Modern Iran*. Würzburg: Ergon-Verlag, 2010.

Adang, Camilla and Sabine Schmidtke. "Muslim-Jewish Polemics." In *Muslim Perceptions and Receptions of the Bible*, ed. Adang and Schmidtke, 39–47.

Adang, Camilla and Sabine Schmidtke, eds. *Muslim Perceptions and Receptions of the Bible: Texts and Studies*. Atlanta: Lockwood Press, 2019.

Adler, E.N. and I. Broydé. "An Ancient Bookseller's Catalogue." *JQR* o. s. 13 (1900): 52–62.

Adler, Marcus N., ed. *The Itinerary of Benjamin of Tudela: Critical Text, Translation and Commentary*. London: Oxford University Press, 1907.

Ahnert, Ruth. *The Rise of Prison Literature in the Sixteenth Century*. Cambridge: Cambridge University Press, 2013.

Ahroni, Reuben. "From *Bustān al-ʿUqūl* to *Qissat al-Batūl*: Some Aspects of Jewish-Muslim Religious Polemics in Yemen." *HUCA* 52 (1981): 311–346.

Ahroni, Reuben. *The Jews of the British Crown Colony of Aden: History, Culture, and Ethnic Relations*. Leiden & New York: E.J. Brill, 1994.

Ahroni, Reuben. "Some Yemenite Jewish Attitudes Towards Muḥammad's Prophethood." *HUCA* 69 (1998): 49–99.

Ahroni, Reuben. "Tribulations and Aspirations in Yemenite Hebrew Literature." *HUCA* 49 (1978): 26–94.

Ahroni, Reuben. *Yemenite Jewry: Origins, Culture, and Literature*. Bloomington: Indiana University Press, 1986.

Akbari, Suzanne Conklin. *Idols in the East: European Representations of Islam and the Orient, 1100–1450*. Ithaca and London: Cornell University Press, 2009.

Alexander, Gavin. "The Elizabethan Lyric as Contrafactum: Robert Sidney's 'French Tune' Identified." *Music and Letters* 84/3 (2003): 378–402.

Alexander, Gavin. "On the Reuse of Poetic Form." In *The Work of Form: Poetics and Materiality in Early Modern Culture*, ed. E. Scott-Baumann and B. Burton, 123–143. Oxford University Press, 2014.

Alexander, P.S. "Early Jewish Geography." *Anchor Bible Dictionary*, II:980–982. New York/London/Toronto: Doubleday, 1992.

Alexander, Tamar and Yuval Harari. "Jewish Folklore—Ethnic Identity, Collection and Research." *European Journal of Jewish Studies* 3/1 (2009): 1–17.

Alfonso, Esperanza. *Islamic Culture Through Jewish Eyes: Al-Andalus from the Tenth to Twelfth Century*. London/New York: Routledge, 2008.

Alfonso, Esperanza. "The Uses of *Exile* in Poetic Discourse: Some Examples from Medieval Hebrew Literature." In *Renewing the Past, Reconfiguring Jewish Culture*, ed. R. Brann and A. Sutcliffe, 31–49. Philadelphia: University of Pennsylvania Press, 2004.

Alfonso, Esperanza and Jonathan Decter, eds. *Patronage, Production, and Transmission of Texts in Medieval and Early Modern Jewish Cultures*. Turnhout: Brepols, 2014.

Allen, Rosamund, ed. *Eastward Bound: Travel and Travelers, 1050–1550*. Manchester: Manchester University Press, 2004.

Almagor, Dan. "Ketav ʿet ʿaṣmaʾi ve-loḥem: holadeto shel ketav haʿet *Afikim*." *Afikim* 136–137 (2011–2012): 58–61, 64.

Almansi, Guido. *The Writer as Liar: Narrative Technique in the Decameron*. London: Routledge & Keegan Paul, 1975; repr. Routledge, 2020.

Almbladh, Karin. "The 'Basmala' in Medieval Letters in Arabic Written by Jews and Christians." *Orientalia Suecana* LIX (2010): 45–60.

Alnadāf, Avraham. *Ḥoveret seridei teiman ... kollelet toldot ha-rav ... shalem al-shabbazi ... toldot ha-rav shalom sharʿabi ... sefer oṣar sifrei teiman ....* Jerusalem, 1927/8.

Altmann, Alexander and S.M. Stern. *Isaac Israeli*. Oxford: Oxford University Press, 1958.

Altshuler, Mor. "Prophecy and Maggidism in the Life and Writings of R. Joseph Karo." *Frankfurter Judaistische Beiträge* 33 (2006): 81–110.

Amir, Yehuda. "The Life of Rabbi Zecharia Al-ḍaheri" (Hebrew). In *Halikhot qedem be-mishkenot teiman*, ed. Seri and Kessar, 459–466.

Amir, Yehuda. "Shirei rabbi zekharyah alḍāhirī (bibliographiyah)." *Tema* 9 (2006/7): 135–148.

Amir, Yehuda. "Shirim ḥadashim mi-dīwān rabbi zekharyah alḍāhirī." In *Mabuʿei afikim, sefer ha-yovel: meḥqarim be-moreshet yahadut teiman ve-tarbutah*, ed. Yosef Dahuḥ-Halevi, 119–148. Tel Aviv: Afikim, 1995.

Anastasopoulos, Antonis. "Karaferye." *EI*³ online.

Andreatta, Michaela. "Collecting Hebrew Epitaphs in the Early Modern Age: The Christian Hebraist as Antiquarian." In *Jewish Books and their Readers: Aspects of the Intellectual Life of Christians and Jews in Early Modern Europe*, ed. Scott Mandelbrote and Joanna Weinberg, 260–286. Leiden/Boston: Brill, 2016.

Anselment, Raymond A. "'Stone Walls' and 'Iron Bars': Richard Lovelace and the Conventions of Seventeenth-Century Prison Literature." *Renaissance and Reformation* 17/1 (1993): 15–34.

Anthony, Sean. "The Domestic Origins of Imprisonment: An Inquiry into an Early Islamic Institution." *JAOS* 129/4 (2009): 571–596.

Anthony, Sean. "The Meccan Prison of ʿAbdallāh b. al-Zubayr and the Imprisonment of Muḥammad b. al-Ḥanafiyya." In *The Heritage of Arabo-Islamic Learning*, ed. Pomerantz and Shahin, 3–27.

Anzi, Menashe. “Ben ish mozeg u-ven ha’orgim: yisra’el yisha‘yahu u-qesharav ‘im bialik,” *Pe‘amim* 119 (2009): 211–220.

Anzi, Menashe. “From Biblical Criticism to Criticism of the Kabbalah.” *Journal of Levantine Studies* 10/1 (2020): 91–109.

Anzi, Menashe. “Cultural Exchange and Religious Guidance along the Shores of the Arabian Sea: Yemenite Jews in India and Indian Jews in Yemen.” In *Jewish Communities in Modern Asia: Their Rise, Demise and Resurgence*, ed. Rotem Kowner, 127–142. Cambridge: Cambridge University Press, 2023.

Anzi, Menashe. “‘Ha’aḥer’ ha-yehudi: yehudei ṣan‘ā’ el mul ha-qehillot ha’aḥerot beteiman.” In *Yahadut teiman: zehut u-moreshet*, ed. Yosef Tobi and Aharon Gaimani, 119–141. Jerusalem: Ben-Zvi Institute/ Dahan Center, Bar-Ilan University, 2019.

Anzi, Menashe. *The Ṣan‘ā’nīs: Jews in Muslim Yemen, 1872–1950* (Heb). Jerusalem: Zalman Shazar Center, 2021.

Anzi, Menashe. “Yemenite Jews in the Red Sea Trade and the Development of a New Diaspora.” *Northeast African Studies* 17/1 (2017): 79–100.

Arad, Dotan. “‘A Clearly Distinguished Community’: The Musta‘ribs in Damascus in the Sixteenth Century” (Hebrew). In *Syrian Jewry: History, Culture and Identity*, ed. Y. Harel, 95–130. Ramat Gan, 2015.

Arazi, Albert. “L’*adab*, les critiques et les genres littéraires dans la culture arabe médiévale.” *IOS* 19 (1999): 221–238.

Arazi, Albert, H. Ben-Shammai, et al., “Risāla.” *EI*² online.

Ar’el, Yarom. “Kenes ḥagigi le-sefer hamusar.” *Afikim* 2/1 (Mar. 30, 1966): 1.

Ariès, Philippe. *The Hour of Our Death*. Trans. Helen Weaver. New York: Alfred A. Knopf, Inc., 1981.

Aristotle. *De Anima*. Trans. R.D. Hicks. Cambridge: Cambridge University Press, 1907.

Artom, Menachem and Abraham David, eds. *From Italy to Jerusalem: The Letters of Rabbi Obadiah of Bertinoro from the Land of Israel* (Hebrew). Ramat Gan: Bar-Ilan University, 1997.

‘Arussi, Raṣon. “Ha-shulḥan ‘arukh ke-gorem she-hisrid et ha-rambam be-teiman.” In *Le-rosh yosef: meḥqarim be-ḥokhmat yisra’el*, ed. Y. Tobi, 387–394. Jerusalem: Hoṣa’at afikim, 1995.

Asatryan, Mushegh. “Ziyāra.” *Encyclopedia of Medieval Pilgrimage*. Brill Online.

Asher, Adolf, ed. and trans. *The Itinerary of Benjamin of Tudela*. 2 vols. New York: Hakesheth, 1840–1841.

Ashtor, Eliyahu et al. “Sidon.” *EJ*² 18:549–551.

Assaf, Simcha. “The Selling of Hebrew Books in Yemen Through Envoys from Palestine” (Hebrew). *KS* 16/4 (1940): 493–495.

Astor, Alexander and Leah Bornstein-Makovetsky. “Damascus: Under Muslim Rule.” *EJ*² 5:392–396.

Avishur, Yitzhak. “Kinnuyei genai ‘ivriyyim la-goyim ve-lihudim ba‘aravit-yehudit bimei ha-beinayim ve-gilguleihem." In *Shai le-hadassah* (= *Eshel be'er sheva*ʿ 5), ed. Y. Bentolila, 97–116. Be'er shevaʿ, 1997.

Avishur, Yitzhak. *In Praise of Maimonides: Folktales in Judaeo-Arabic and Hebrew from the Near East and North Africa* (Hebrew). Jerusalem: Magnes Press/ The Hebrew University, 1998.

Avitsur, Shmuel. "Safed—Center of the Manufacture of Woven Woolens in the Fifteenth Century" (Hebrew). *Sefunot* 6 (1962): 41–79.

Aviv, Efrat E. "Ottoman Empire: 1. From 1300 to 1492." *EJIW*. Brill Online.

Babcock-Abraham, Barbara. "'A Tolerated Margin of Mess': The Trickster and His Tales Reconsidered." *Journal of the Folklore Institute* 11/ 3 (1975): 147–186.

Bacharach, Jere L. "The Dinar versus the Ducat." *IJMES* 4 (1973): 77–96.

Badawi, M.M. "Medieval Arabic Drama: Ibn Dāniyāl." *JAL* 13 (1982): 83–107.

Band, Arnold. "The New Diasporism and the Old Diaspora." *Israel Studies* 1/1 (1996): 323–331.

Bar Asher, Avishai. "The Ontology, Arrangement, and Appearance of Paradise in Castilian Kabbalah in Light of Contemporary Islamic Traditions from al-Andalus." *Religions* 11/11 (2020): 1–12.

Bar Giora, Naftali. "Meqorot le-toledot ha-yaḥasim bein ha-yehudim ha-levanim ve-ha-sheḥorim be-kochin." *Sefunot* 1 (1957): 243–278.

Bareket, Elinoar. "Shemot miqra'iyyim-ʿivriyyim le-yishuvim, araṣot, u-qevuṣot etniyot bimei ha-beinayim." In *Pesher Naḥum: Texts and Studies … Presented to Norman Golb*, ed. Joel L. Kraemer and Michael G. Wechsler, Hebrew Section, 11–16. Chicago: Oriental Institute, 2012.

Bar-Maoz, Daniel. "Hishtarshut ha-qabbalah be-teiman." *Tema* 7 (2001): 85–112.

Bar-Maoz, Daniel. "Social Tension Between the Sanaʿa Community and Other Communities" (Hebrew). In *Halikhot qedem be-mishkenot teiman*, ed. Seri and Kessar, 55–61.

Baron, Salo W. *A Social and Religious History of the Jews*. 3 volumes. New York: Columbia University Press, 1937.

Baruchson-Arbib, Shifra. "On the Trade in Hebrew Books Between Italy and the Ottoman Empire during the 16th Century" (Hebrew). *Mi-mizraḥ umi-maʿarav* 5 (1986): 53–77.

Bauer, Thomas. "'Ayna hādhā min al-Mutanabbī!' Toward an Aesthetics of Mamlūk Literature." *Mamlūk Studies Review* 17 (2013): 5–22.

Bauer, Thomas. "Mamlūk Literature: Misunderstandings and New Approaches." *Mamlūk Studies Review* 9/2 (2005): 105–132.

Bauer, Thomas. "In Search of 'Post-Classical Literature': A Review Article." *Mamlūk Studies Review* 11/2 (2007): 137–167.

Baumgarten, Eliezer. "God as a Printer: On the Theological Status of Printing in the Kabbalistic Tradition of Israel Sarug." *Zutot* 19 (2022): 121–133.

Baumgarten, Eliezer. "Kabbalah and Printing in Yemen: Two 17th century Yemenite

Scholars and Kabbalistic Knowledge from Europe" (Hebrew). *Pe'amim* 157 (2019): 9–37.

Baumgarten, Eliezer. "The Kabbalistic *Ilan* of Rabbi Yitzhak Wanne: Local Kabbalah in a Global World" (Hebrew). *Da'at* 87 (2019): 359–382.

Baumgarten, Eliezer. "From Kurdistan to Baghdad: The Transfer of Visual Knowledge during the Early Modern Period." *Ars Judaica* 14 (2018): 79–92.

Baumgarten, Eliezer. "Netivot ha'emunah le-rabbi yiḥye ḥarāzī: haqdamah ve-he'arot." *Kabbalah* 43 (2019): 185–270.

Baumgarten, Eliezer, Uri Safrai, and J.S. Chajes. "'See the Entire World Resembling a Ladder': Rabbi Yehoshua ben Rabbi David of Kurdistan's Kabbalistic Tree" (Hebrew). In *Meir Benayahu Memorial Volume*, ed. M. Bar-Asher et al., 2: 843–872. Jerusalem: Carmel/ Tel Aviv: Tel Aviv University, 2019.

Beaumont, Daniel. "Hard-Boiled: Narrative Discourse in Early Muslim Traditions." *SI* 83 (1996): 5–31.

Beaumont, Daniel. "A Mighty and Never Ending Affair: Comic Anecdote and Story in Medieval Arabic Literature." *JAL* 24 (1993): 139–159.

Beaumont, Daniel. "The Trickster and Rhetoric in the Maqāmāt." *Edebiyāt* n.s. 5 (1994): 1–14.

Beckingham, C.F. "The *Riḥla*: Fact or Fiction?" In *Golden Roads*, ed. Netton, 86–94.

Beeri, Tova. "Israel Najara: A Beloved and Popular Poet." In *The Poet and the World: Festschrift for Wout van Bekkum on the Occasion of His Sixty-fifth Birthday*, ed. J. Yeshaya, E. Hollender, and N. Katsumata, 59–76. Berlin/ Boston: De Gruyter, 2019.

Beeri, Tova. "Music and poetic structure in XVI–XVII c. oriental piyyut." In *Jewish Studies in a New Europe*, ed. U. Haxen et al., 75–81. Copenhagen: C.A. Reitzel, 1998.

Beeri, Tova. "*'Olat ḥodesh* le-rabbi yisrael najara—nos'im u-tekhanim." *Asufot* 4 (1990): 311–324.

Beeri, Tova. "Reevaluation of Najara's Debt to the Tradition of the Spanish School of Poetry" (Hebrew). *Jerusalem Studies in Hebrew Literature* 32 (2021): 359–377.

Beeri, Tova. "The Spanish Elements in the Poetry of Rabbi Israel Najara" (Hebrew). *Pe'amim* 49 (1991): 54–67.

Beeri, Tova. "Two Unpublished Poems by R. Isaac Luria Ashkenazi ("Ha'ari") and an Examination of the Corpus of Poems Attributed to Him" (Hebrew). *Pe'amim* 128 (2011): 9–34.

Beeston, A.F.L. "The Genesis of the *Maqāmāt* Genre." *JAL* 2 (1971): 1–12.

Beeston, A.F.L. "Ḥaḍramawt." *EI*^{2} online.

Beeston, A.F.L. "Al-Hamadhānī, al-Ḥarīrī, and the *Maqāmāt* Genre." In *CHALABL*, 125–135.

Behmardi, Vahid. "Author Disguised and Disclosed: Uncovering Facts in al-Hamadhānī's Fiction." In *Concepts of Authorship in Pre-Modern Arabic Texts*, ed. Behzadi and Hämeen-Anttila, 129–152.

Behzadi, Lale and Jaakko Hämeen-Anttila, eds. *Concepts of Authorship in Pre-Modern Arabic Texts*. Bamberg: University of Bamberg Press, 2015.

Behzadi, L. and V. Behmardi, eds. *The Weaving of Words: Approaches to Classical Arabic Prose*. Würzburg: Ergon Verlag, 2009.

Beider, Alexander. "The Notion of 'Jewish Surnames.'" *Journal of Jewish Languages* 6 (2018): 182–220.

Beinart, Haim ed. *Moreshet Sepharad: The Sephardi Legacy*. 2 vols. Jerusalem: Magnes Press/ The Hebrew University, 1992.

Beit-Arié, Malachi. "'Emunah yoṣrah eṣlo amanah': shir she-nahagu le-haʿatiqo be-sof kitvei yad shel ha-torah be-teiman." In *Shai le-heman: A.M. Habermann Jubilee Volume*, ed. Zvi Malachi, 37–50. Jerusalem: Rubin Mass, 1977.

Beit-Arié, Malachi. *Hebrew Codicology*. Trans. Ilana Goldberg. Jerusalem/Hamburg: Israel Academy of Sciences and Humanities, 2021.

Beit-Arié, Malachi. "The Individual Nature of Hebrew Book Production and Consumption." In *Manuscrits hébreux et arabes: Mélanges en l'honneur de Colette Sirat*, ed. N. de Lange and J. Olszowy-Schlanger, 17–28. Brepols, 2014.

Beit-Arié, Malachi. "Publication and Reproduction of Literary Texts in Medieval Jewish Civilization: Jewish Scribality and Its Impact on the Texts Transmitted." In *Transmitting Jewish Traditions*, ed. Elman and Gershoni, 225–247.

Bellos, David. *Georges Perec: A Life in Words*. London: Harvill, 1999.

Ben-Ari, Oz. "Ha-makhon le-ḥasifat ginzei teiman." *Afikim* 1/6 (1965): 2.

Benayahu, Meir. "Devotion Practices of the Kabbalists of Safed in Meron" (Hebrew). *Sefunot* 6 (1962): 10–40.

Benayahu, Meir. "Rabbi Samuel Barzani, Leader of Kurdistan Jewry" (Hebrew). *Sefunot* 9 (1964): 21–105.

Ben Menahem, Naftali. *Zemirot shel shabbat*. Jerusalem, 1949.

Ben-Naeh, Yaron. "City of Torah and Study: Salonica as a Torah Center during the Sixteenth and Seventeenth Centuries" (Hebrew). *Peʿamim* 80 (1999): 60–82.

Ben-Naeh, Yaron. "Research on Ottoman Jewish History and Culture: The State of the Art." *Revue Européenne des Études Hébraïques* 18 (2016): 53–89.

Ben-Naeh, Yaron. "Ve-khi lo aḥeihem anaḥnu?: yaḥasei ashkenazim u-sefaradim bi-yerushalayim be-sof ha-meʾah ha-shevaʿ ʿesreh." *Cathedra* 103 (2002): 33–52.

Bennett, C.E., trans. *Horace, Odes and Epodes*. Loeb Classical Library. Cambridge, Mass.: Harvard University Press, 1947.

Ben-Sasson, H.H. "The Generation of the Spanish Exiles on Its Fate" (Hebrew). *Zion* 26/1 (1961): 23–64.

Ben-Shammai, Haggai. "The Attitude of Some Early Karaites Towards Islam." In *Studies in Medieval Jewish History and Literature*, ed. I. Twersky, 2:3–40. Cambridge, Mass.: Harvard University Press, 1984.

Ben-Shammai, Haggai. "Poetic Works and Lamentations of Qaraite 'Mourners of

Zion'—Structure and Contents" (Hebrew). In *Knesset Ezra: Literature and Life in the Synagogue*, ed. S. Elizur et al., 191–234. Jerusalem: Yad Izhak Ben-Zvi and the Ben-Zvi Institute, 1994.

Ben-Shammai, Haggai. "A Unique Lamentation on Jerusalem by the Karaite Author Yeshuʿa ben Judah" (Hebrew). In *Mas'at Moshe*, ed. Fleischer et al., 93–102.

Bentov, Haim. "Methods of Study of Talmud in the Yeshivot of Salonica and Turkey After the Expulsion from Spain" (Hebrew). *Sefunot* 13 (1971): 5–102.

Ben Yehuda, E. *A Complete Dictionary of Ancient and Modern Hebrew*. 16 vols in 8. New York and London: Thomas Yoseloff, 1959.

Berenbaum, Michael and Fred Skolnik. "Aripul, Samuel ben Isaac." *EJ*² 2:455.

Berger, David. *The Jewish-Christian Debate in the High Middle Ages*. Philadelphia: The Jewish Publication Society of America, 1979.

Berger, Shlomo and Irene E. Zwiep, eds. *Epigonism and the Dynamic of Jewish Culture*. *Studia Rosenthaliana* 40 (2007–2008).

Berkey, Jonathan. "Storytelling, Preaching, and Power." *Mamlūk Studies Review* 4 (2000): 53–73.

Berlekamp, Persis. *Wonder, Image, and Cosmos in Medieval Islam*. New Haven: Yale University Press, 2011.

Betzer, Zvi. "Genesis of the Verb *hidpīs* 'Print' and its Cognates." *HAR* 14 (1994): 5–20.

Biale, David, ed. *Cultures of the Jews: A New History*. New York: Schocken Books, 2002.

Biberstein-Kazimirski, Albert de. *Dictionnaire arabe-français*. Paris: Editions G.P. Maisonneuve, 1860.

Bikhazi, Ramzi J. "Coins of al-Yaman, 132–569 A.H." *al-Abḥāth* 23/1–4 (1970): 3–127.

Binski, Paul. *Medieval Death: Ritual and Representation*. Ithaca: Cornell University Press, 1996.

Blachère, Régis. "Étude sémantique sur le nom *maqāma*." *al-Machriq* 47 (1953): 646–652.

Blackburn, Richard. "The Collapse of Ottoman Authority in Yemen, 968/1560–976/1568." *Die Welt des Islams*, n.s., 19/1–4 (1979): 119–176.

Blackburn, Richard. "The Era of Imām Sharaf al-Dīn Yaḥyā and his Son al-Muṭahhar (10th/16th Century)." *Yemen Update* 42 (2000): 4–8.

Blackburn, Richard. "The Ottoman Penetration of Yemen." *Archivum Ottomanicum* 6 (1980): 55–100.

Blankinship, Kevin. "As Barren as Mother Eve: Why Some Poems End Badly, According to Premodern Arabic Critics." *al-Abḥāth* 71/1–2 (2023): 9–37.

Blumenthal, David R. *The Commentary of R. Hoter Ben Shelomo to the Thirteen Principles of Maimonides*. Leiden: Brill, 1974.

Blumenthal, David R. *The Philosophic Questions and Answers of Hoter Ben Shelomo*. Leiden: Brill, 1981.

Boardley, John. *Typographic Firsts: Adventures in Early Printing*. Chicago: University of Chicago Press, 2021.

Bonebakker, S.A. "*Adab* and the Concept of *Belles-Lettres*." In CHALABL, 16–30.

Bonebakker, S.A. "Ancient Arabic Poetry and Plagiarism: A Terminological Labyrinth." *Quaderni di Studi Arabi* 15 (1997): 65–92.

Bonebakker, S.A. "Early Arabic Literature and the term *Adab*." JSAI 5 (1984): 389–421.

Bonebakker, S.A. "Nihil obstat in Storytelling?" In *The Thousand and One Nights in Arabic Literature and Society*, ed. R.C. Hovannisian and G. Sabagh, 56–77. Cambridge/New York: Cambridge University Press, 1997.

Bonebakker, S.A. "Some Medieval Views on Fantastic Stories." *Quaderni di Studi Arabi* 10 (1992): 21–43.

Bonfil, Robert. "A Cultural Profile." In *The Jews of Early Modern Venice*, ed. R.C. Davis and B. Ravid, 169–190. Baltimore: Johns Hopkins University Press, 2001.

Bonfil, Robert. *Rabbis and Jewish Communities in Renaissance Italy*. London/ Washington: The Littman Library of Jewish Civilization, 1993.

Bornstein, Leah. "Ha'ashkenazim ba'imperia ha'uthmanit ba-me'ot ha-16 ve-ha-17." In *Mi-mizraḥ umi-ma'arav*, ed. Hirschberg, 1:81–104.

Bornstein-Makovetsky, Leah. "Bursa (Prousa)." EJIW. Brill Online.

Bornstein-Makovetsky, Leah. "Ottoman Empire: 2. From 1492 to ca. 1650." EJIW. Brill Online.

Bornstein-Makovetsky, Leah. "Structure, Organisation, and Spiritual Life of the Sephardi Communities in the Ottoman Empire from the Sixteenth to the Eighteenth Centuries." In *The Sephardi Heritage*, ed. R. Barnett and W. Schwab, 2:314–348. Grendon, Northants: Gibraltar Books, 1989.

Bornstein-Makovetsky, Leah. "Textile Manufacture and Trade." EJIW. Brill Online.

Bornstein-Makovetsky, Leah. "Le-toldot qehillat kushta be'emṣa'itah shel ha-me'ah ha-shva' 'esreh: qehaleha, isheha, ve-ḥakhameha ha-sefaradim ve-ha-romanioṭim." *Michael* 9 (1985): 27–54.

Borovaya, Olga. *The Beginnings of Ladino Literature: Moses Almosnino and His Readers*. Bloomington: Indiana University Press, 2017.

Bös, Birte and Matti Peikola. "Framing Framing: The Multifaceted Phenomena of Paratext, Metadiscourse and Framing." In *The Dynamics of Text and Framing Phenomena: Historical Approaches to Paratext and Metadiscourse in English*, ed. M. Peikola and B. Bös, 3–31. Amsterdam/Philadelphia: John Benjamins Publishing Company, 2020.

Bosworth, C.E. "A *Maqāma* on Secretaryship: al-Qalqashandī's *al-Kawākib al-durriyya fī'l-manāqib al-badriyya*." BSOAS 27/2 (1964): 291–298.

Bosworth, C.E. *The Mediaeval Islamic Underworld: The Banū Sāsān in Arabic Society and Literature*. 2 vols. Leiden: Brill, 1976.

Bosworth, C.E. "Travel Literature." EAL, 2:778–780.

Boullata, Issa J. "The Rhetorical Interpretation of the Qur'ān: *i'jāz* and Related Topics." In *Approaches to the History of the Interpretation of the Qur'ān*, ed. A. Rippin, 139–157. Oxford: Clarendon Press, 1988.

Boyarin, Daniel. *Haʿiyyun ha-sefaradi*. Jerusalem: Ben-Zvi Institute, Yad Ben-Zvi, and The Hebrew University, 1989.

Boyarin, Daniel. "'Pilpul': The Logic of Commentary." In Daniel Boyarin, *The Talmud—A Personal Take: Selected Essays*, ed. T. Hever-Chybowski, 47–65. Tübingen: Mohr Siebeck, 2017.

Boyarin, Daniel. "Placing Reading: Ancient Israel and Medieval Europe." In *The Ethnography of Reading*, ed. J. Boyarin, 10–37. Berkeley: University of California Press, 1993.

Boyarin, Daniel. *A Traveling Homeland: The Babylonian Talmud as Diaspora*. Philadelphia: University of Pennsylvania Press, 2015.

Brann, Ross. "Competing Tropes of Eleventh-Century Andalusi Jewish Culture." In *Ot Le-Tova: Essays in Honor of Professor Tova Rosen*, ed. E. Yassif et al., English Section, 7–26. Beer-Sheva, 2012.

Brann, Ross. *The Compunctious Poet: Cultural Ambiguity and Hebrew Poetry in Muslim Spain*. Baltimore: Johns Hopkins University Press, 1991.

Brann, Ross. "'How Can My Heart be in the East?' Intertextual Irony in Judah Ha-Levi." In *Essays in Honor of William M. Brinner*, ed. B. Hary et al., 365–379. Leiden/ Boston/ Köln: Brill, 2000.

Brann, Ross. *Power in the Portrayal: Representations of Jews and Muslims in Eleventh- and Twelfth-Century Islamic Spain*. Princeton: Princeton University Press, 2002.

Braslavsky, J. "Jewish Settlement in Tiberias from Don Joseph Nasi to Ibn Yaish" (Hebrew). *Zion* n.s. 5 (1940): 45–72.

Brauer, Erich. *Ethnologie der Jemenitischen Juden*. Heidelberg, 1934.

Brauer, Erich. "Ha-ḥaqla'ut ve-ha-melakhah eṣel yehudei teiman." In *Shevut teiman*, ed. Yishaʿyahu and Zadok, 75–91.

Brauer, Erich. *The Jews of Kurdistan*, ed. Raphael Patai. Detroit: Wayne State University Press, 1993.

Bray, Julia. "Starting Out in New Worlds: Under Whose Empire? High Tradition and Subaltern Tradition in Ottoman Syria, 16th and 19th/20th centuries." In *Tropes du voyage: Départs*, ed. Ghersetti, 199–220.

Bray, Julia, ed. and trans. *al-Muḥassin ibn ʿAlī al-Tanūkhī, Stories of Piety and Prayer: Deliverance Follows Adversity*. New York: New York University Press, 2019.

Bray, Julia Ashtiany. "Isnāds and Models of Heros: Abū Zubayd al-Ṭāʾī, Tanūkhī's sundered lovers and Abū ʾl-Anbas al-Ṣaymarī." *Arabic and Middle Eastern Literatures* 1/1 (1998): 7–30.

Bregman, Dvora. *A Bundle of Gold: Hebrew Sonnets from the Renaissance and the Baroque* (Hebrew). Jerusalem and Beer-Sheva: Ben-Zvi Institute and Ben Gurion University of the Negev Press, 1997.

Bregman, Dvora. *The Golden Way: The Hebrew Sonnet during the Renaissance and the Baroque*. Trans. Ann Brener. Tempe, AZ: ACMRS, 2006.

Bregman, Dvora. "Hen ʿatah tihiyeh ʿal biti even: shirei maṣevah shel Moshe Zacut." In

Studies in Arabic and Hebrew Letters in Honor of Raymond P. Scheindlin, ed. Decter and Rand, Hebrew section, 13–21.

Bregman, Dvora. "The Metrical System of Immanuel of Rome" (Hebrew). *Tarbiẓ* 58 (1989): 413–452.

Bregman, Dvora. "The Realistic and the Macabre in the Poetry of Samuel Ha-Nagid" (Hebrew). *Jerusalem Studies in Hebrew Literature* 15 (1995): 75–82.

Brener, Ann. "A Poem by Joseph Sarfati in Honor of Daniel Bomberg's *Biblia Rabbinica*, Venice 1525." In *Tradition, Heterodoxy and Religious Culture: Judaism and Christianity in the Early Modern Period*, ed. C. Goodblatt and H. Kreisel, 263–285. Beer Sheva: Ben-Gurion University of the Negev, 2006.

Brener, Ann. "Stealing Wisdom: A Story of Books (and Book-Thieves) from Immanuel of Rome's *Maḥbarot*." *Prooftexts* 28 (2008): 1–27.

Brinner, William M., trans. *An Elegant Composition Concerning Relief after Adversity by Nissim Ben Jacob Ibn Shāhīn*. New Haven & London, 1977.

Brockelmann, Carl. "Abū Firās." *EI*[1] online.

Brockelmann, Carl. "Maḳāma." *EI*[2] 6:107.

Brody, Ḥayyim. *Maṭmunei mistarim*. Cracow: Y. Fischer, 1894.

Brookshaw, Dominic P. "Palaces, Pavilions and Pleasure Gardens: The Context and Setting of the Medieval Majlis." *MEL* 6/2 (2003): 199–223.

Brown, F., S.R. Driver, and C.A. Briggs. *A Hebrew and English Lexicon of the Old Testament*. Oxford: Clarendon Press, 1939.

Bunis, David M. "Judezmo: The Jewish Language of the Ottoman Sephardim." *European Judaism* 44/1 (2011): 22–35.

Bursi, Adam et al., eds. *'His Pen and Ink Are a Powerful Mirror': Andalusi, Judaeo-Arabic, and Other Near Eastern Studies in Honor of Ross Brann*. Leiden/Boston: Brill, 2020.

Campbell, Mary Baine. "Travel Writing and its Theory." In *The Cambridge Companion to Travel Writing*, ed. P. Hulme and T. Youngs, 261–278. Cambridge: Cambridge University Press, 2002.

Campbell, Mary Baine. *The Witness and the Other World: Exotic European Travel Writing, 400–1600*. Cornell University Press, 1988.

Carey, Daniel. "Truth, Lies, and Travel Writing." In *The Routledge Companion to Travel Writing*, ed. C. Thompson, 3–14. London/ New York: Routledge, 2016.

Carmi, T. *The Penguin Book of Hebrew Verse*. New York & London: Penguin Books, 1981.

Carnochan, W.B. "The Literature of Confinement." In *The Oxford History of the Prison*, ed. N. Morris and D. Rothman, 427–455. Oxford University Press, 1995.

Cassutto, M.D. "Neḥemiah ben Menaḥem Kalomiti u-maḥberotav." *Sefer ha-yovel le professor shmu'el krauss*, ed. Va'ad ha-yovel birushalayim, 211–216. Jerusalem: Reuven Mass, 1936.

Castaño, Javier, Talya Fishman, and Ephraim Kanarfogel, eds. *Regional Identities and Cultures of Medieval Jews*. London: Littman Library of Jewish Civilization, 2018.

Cave, Terence. *Recognitions: A Study in Poetics*. Oxford: Clarendon Press, 1988.

Chajes, J.H. "Accounting for the Self: Preliminary Generic-Historical Reflections on Early Modern Jewish Egodocuments." *JQR* 95/1 (2005): 1–15.

Chajes, J.H. "Imaginative Thinking with a Lurianic Diagram." *JQR* 110/1 (2020): 30–63.

Chajes, J.H. "The Kabbalistic Tree." In *The Visualization of Knowledge in the Middle Ages and the Early Modern Period*, ed. M. Kupfer et al., 449–473. Turnhout: Brepols, 2019.

Chajes, J.H. "The Kabbalistic Tree as Material Text." *Henoch* 43/1 (2021): 162–196.

Chajes, J.H. "Spheres, *Sefirot*, and the Imaginal Astronomical Discourse of Classical Kabbalah." *HTR* 113/2 (2020): 230–262.

Chakravarti, Ranabir. "Indian Trade Through Jewish *Geniza* Letters (1000–1300)." *Studies in People's History* 2/1 (2015): 27–40.

Chamberlain, Michael. *Knowledge and Social Practice in Medieval Damascus, 1190–1350*. Cambridge: Cambridge University Press, 1994.

Chartier, Roger. *The Order of Books, Readers, Authors, and Libraries in Europe between the 14th and 18th Centuries*. Translated by Lydia G. Cochrane. Stanford: Stanford University Press, 1994.

Chauvin, Victor. *Bibliographie des ouvrages Arabes ou relatifs aux Arabes, publiés dans l'Europe chrétienne de 1810 à 1885*. 12 vols. Liége: H. Vaillant-Carmanne, 1892–1922.

Chazan, Robert. *Barcelona and Beyond: The Disputation of 1263 and Its Aftermath*. Berkeley/ Los Angeles/ Oxford: University of California Press, 1992.

Chazan, Robert. *Daggers of Faith: Thirteenth-Century Christian Missionizing and Jewish Response*. Berkeley/ Los Angeles/ London, 1989.

Chraïbi, Aboubakr, ed. *Tropes du voyages: Les Rencontres*. Paris: L'Harmattan, 2010.

Christie, Manson & Woods. *Important Hebrew Manuscripts from the Salman Schocken Collection*. New York: Christie's, 15 November 2005.

Çizakça, Murat. "A Short History of the Bursa Silk Industry (1500–1900)." *JESHO* 23/1–2 (1980): 142–152.

Clinton, J.W. "Masʿūd-i Saʿd-i Salmān." *EI*^{2} online.

Cohen, Amnon and Bernard Lewis. *Population and Revenue in the Towns of Palestine in the Sixteenth Century*. Princeton: Princeton University Press, 1978.

Cohen, Gerson D. "Esau as Symbol in Early Medieval Thought." In *Jewish Medieval and Renaissance Studies*, ed. A. Altmann, 19–48. Cambridge, Mass.: Harvard University Press, 1967.

Cohen, Gerson D. "The Song of Songs and the Jewish Religious Mentality." In idem, *Studies in the Variety of Rabbinic Cultures*, 3–17. Philadelphia/New York: Jewish Publication Society, 1991.

Cohen, Jeremy. *The Friars and the Jews: The Evolution of Medieval Anti-Judaism*. Ithaca: Cornell University Press, 1982.

Cohen, Jeremy. *Living Letters of the Law: Ideas of the Jew in Medieval Christianity*. Berkeley/ Los Angeles/ London: University of California Press, 1999.

Cohen, J.M. *The Baroque Lyric*. London: Hutchinson & Co., 1963.

Cohen, Mark R., ed. and trans. *The Autobiography of a Seventeenth-Century Rabbi: Leon Modena's Life of Judah*. Princeton: Princeton University Press, 1988.

Cohen, Mark R. "Interreligious *Majālis* in Early Fatimid Egypt." In *The Majlis*, ed. Lazarus-Yafeh et al., 128–136.

Cohen, Mark R. *Poverty and Charity in the Jewish Community of Medieval Egypt*. Princeton: Princeton University Press, 2005.

Cohen, Mark R. *Under Crescent and Cross: The Jews in the Middle Ages*. Princeton: Princeton University Press, 1994.

Cohen, Mark R. and Sasson Somekh. "In the Court of Yaʿqūb Ibn Killis: A Fragment from the Cairo Geniza." *JQR* 80 (1990): 283–314.

Cohen, Mordechai Z. *Three Approaches to Biblical Metaphor: from Abraham Ibn Ezra and Maimonides to David Kimhi*. Leiden/Boston: Brill, 2003.

Cohen, Yitzhak Yosef. *Sources and History* (Hebrew). Jerusalem: Rubin Mass, 1982.

Cooke, Miriam. "Journeys Real and Imaginary." *Edebiyāt* n.s. 4 (1993): 151–154.

Cooperman, Bernard Dov, ed. *Jewish Thought in the Sixteenth Century*. Cambridge, Mass.: Harvard University Center for Jewish Studies, 1983.

Cooperson, Michael, trans. *Impostures by al-Ḥarīrī*. New York: New York University Press, 2020.

Corriente, Federico and Angel Sáenz-Badillos, eds. *Poesía Estrófica: Actas del Primer Congreso Internacional sobre Poesía Estrófica Árabe y Hebrea y sus Paralelos Romances*. Madrid: Facultad de Filología, Universidad Complutense, 1991.

Crone, Patricia. *God's Rule*. New York: Columbia University Press, 2004.

Crone, Patricia and Shmuel Moreh, trans. *The Book of Strangers: Medieval Arabic Graffiti on the Theme of Nostalgia Attributed to Abu 'l-Faraj al-Iṣfahānī*. Princeton: Markus Wiener Publishers, 2000.

Danon, A. "Mishpeḥot sofrim." *Mizraḥ u-maʿarav* 1 (1920): 99–104, 216–226.

David, Abraham. *To Come to the Land: Immigration and Settlement in Sixteenth-Century Eretz-Israel*. Translated by Dena Ordan. Tuscaloosa and London: University of Alabama Press, 1999.

David, Abraham, ed. *In Zion and Jerusalem: The Itinerary of Rabbi Moses Basola (1521–1523)*. Translated by Dena Ordan. Jerusalem: C.G. Foundation Jerusalem Project Publications of the Martin (Szusz) Department of Land of Israel Studies of Bar-Ilan University, 1999.

Davidson, Herbert A. *Moses Maimonides: The Man and His Works*. Oxford & New York: Oxford University Press, 2005.

Davidson, Israel. *Thesaurus of Mediaeval Hebrew Poetry*. 4 vols. New York: Jewish Theological Seminary of America, 1924–1933; repr. with a new introduction by Michael Rand. Piscataway: Gorgias Press, 2017.

Davis, Joseph M. *Eliezer Eilburg: The Ten Questions and Memoir of a Renaissance Jewish Skeptic*. Cincinnati: Hebrew Union College Press, 2020.

Davis, Joseph M. "The Reception of the *Shulḥan ʿArukh* and the Formation of Ashkenazic Jewish Identity." *AJS Review* 26/2 (2002): 251–276.

Davis, Natalie Zemon. *Trickster Travels: In Search of Leo Africanus, A Sixteenth-Century Muslim Between Worlds*. New York: Hill and Wang, 2006.

de Bruijn, J.T.P. "Ḥabsiyya." *EI*² online.

Decter, Jonathan P. *Dominion Built of Praise: Panegyric and Legitimacy Among Jews in the Medieval Mediterranean*. Philadelphia: University of Pennsylvania Press, 2018.

Decter, Jonathan P. *Iberian Jewish Literature: Between al-Andalus and Christian Europe*. Bloomington: Indiana University Press, 2007.

Decter, Jonathan P. "The (Inter-religious?) Rededication of an Arabic Panegyric by Judah al-Ḥarīzī." *JAL* 51 (2020): 351–368.

Decter, Jonathan P. "The Jewish *Ahl al-Adab* of al-Andalus." *JAL* 50 (2019): 325–341.

Decter, Jonathan P. "The Rendering of Qurʾānic Quotations in Hebrew Translations of Islamic Texts." *JQR* 96 (2006): 336–358.

Decter, Jonathan P and Michael Rand, eds. *Studies in Arabic and Hebrew Letters in Honor of Raymond P. Scheindlin*. Piscataway: Gorgias Press, 2007.

de Lange, Nicholas, ed. *Hebrew Scholarship and the Medieval World*. Cambridge: Cambridge University Press, 2001.

De Looze, Laurence. *Pseudo-Autobiography in the Fourteenth Century: Juan Ruiz, Guillaume de Machaut, Jean Froissart, and Geoffrey Chaucer*. Gainesville: University Press of Florida, 1997.

Deshen, Shelomo. "Ritualization of Literacy: The Works of Tunisian Scholars in Israel." *American Ethnologist* 2 (1975): 251–259.

Diamond, James A. *Converts, Heretics, and Lepers: Maimonides and the Outsider*. Notre Dame, Indiana: University of Notre Dame Press, 2007.

Dickie, James. "The Hispano-Arab Garden, Notes Towards a Typology." In *The Legacy of Muslim Spain*, ed. Jayyusi, 1016–1035.

Diem, Werner and Marco Schöller. *The Living and the Dead in Islam: Studies in Arabic Epitaphs*. 3 vols. Wiesbaden: Harrassowitz, 2004.

Dimitrovsky, H.Z. "ʿAl derekh ha-pilpul." In *Salo Wittmayer Baron Jubilee Volume*, ed. S. Lieberman, Hebrew Section, 111–181. Jerusalem: AAJR, 1974.

Dimitrovsky, H.Z. "Rabbi Yaakov Beirav's Academy in Safed" (Hebrew). *Sefunot* 7 (1963): 41–102.

Dimitrovsky, H.Z. "Vikuaḥ sheʿavar bein maran yosef karo ve-ha-mabit." *Sefunot* 6 (1962): 71–123.

Dishon, Judith. "The Maqama of Homonyms by Joseph Ben Tanhum Hayerushalmi" (Hebrew). *Dappim: Research in Literature* 12 (1999): 25–63.

Dishon, Judith. "Ha-rofe be-reʾi ha-satirah ba-sifrut haʿivrit bisfarad bimei ha-beinayim." *Apiryon* 26–27 (1993): 26–33.

Dishon, Judith. "The Use of Homonyms in the *Maḥberet ha-Ẓimmudim* by Yosef ben Tanhum Ha-Yerushalmi" (Hebrew). *Peʿamim* 81 (1999): 19–42.

Dodds, Jerrilyn. "The Arts of al-Andalus." In *The Legacy of Muslim Spain*, ed. Jayyusi, 599–620.

Dorfman, Rivka and Ben Zion. *Synagogues Without Jews, and the Communities that Built and Used Them*. Philadelphia: Jewish Publication Society, 2000.

Dori, Zecharia. *Traditional Medicine among the Yemenite Jews*, vol. 1: *Medicinal and Aromatic Herbs* (Hebrew). Tel Aviv: Afiqim, 2003.

Dotan, Aharon. "About Pronunciation in Prayer and Torah Reading" (Hebrew). In *Sefer shivtiel*, ed. Gluska and Kessar, 68–76.

Dozy, R. *Supplément aux Dictionnaires Arabes*. 3d ed. Leiden: E.J. Brill, 1967.

Dresch, Paul. "Imams and Tribes: The Writing and Acting of History in Upper Yemen." In *Tribes and State Formation in the Middle East*, ed. P.S. Khoury and J. Kostiner, 252–287. Berkeley: University of California Press, 1990.

Dresch, Paul. *Tribes, Government, and History in Yemen*. Oxford: Clarendon Press, 1989.

Drory, Rina. "The Maqama." In *CHALAND*, 190–210.

Drory, Rina. *Models and Contacts: Arabic Literature and its Impact on Medieval Jewish Culture*. Leiden: Brill, 2000.

Druyan, Nitza. "Yemenite Jews on the Zionist Altar." In *Review Essays in Israel Studies*, ed. L.Z. Eisenberg and N. Caplan, 153–170. Albany: SUNY Press, 2000.

Dubler, C.E. "ʿAdjāʾib." *EI*² online.

Dumitrescu, Irina. "How to Read Aloud." *London Review of Books*. Vol. 42, No. 17 (Sept. 10, 2020).

Dumonceaux, Pierre. "La lecture à haute voix des œuvres littéraires au XVIIème siècle: modalités et valeurs." *Littératures classiques* 12 (1990): 117–125.

Dunbabin, Jean. *Captivity and Imprisonment in Medieval Europe, 1000–1300*. Basingstoke/New York: Palgrave Macmillan, 2002.

Duncan, Dennis. *Index, a History of the: A Bookish Adventure*. London/USA: Allen Lane, Penguin Books, 2021.

Dunn, Ross. E. *The Adventures of Ibn Battuta, a Muslim Traveler of the Fourteenth Century*. London and Sydney: Croom Helm, 1986.

Dunn, Ross. "International Migrations of Literate Muslims in the Later Middle Period: The Case of Ibn Battuta." In *Golden Roads*, ed. Netton, 75–85.

Dweck, Yaacob. *The Scandal of Kabbalah: Leon Modena, Jewish Mysticism, Early Modern Venice*. Princeton: Princeton University Press, 2011.

Edelman, H. & L. Dukes. *Ginzei Oxford* (*Treasures of Oxford*), ed. M.H. Bresslau. London, 1851; repr. Jerusalem: Kedem, 1970.

Efron, John. *German Jewry and the Allure of the Sephardic*. Princeton: Princeton University Press, 2016.

Eickelman, Dale F. and James Piscatori, eds. *Muslim Travellers: Pilgrimage, Migration, and the Religious Imagination*. London: Routledge, 1990.

Einbinder, Susan. *Beautiful Death: Jewish Poetry and Martyrdom in Medieval France*. Princeton: Princeton University Press, 2002.

Einbinder, Susan. "The Current Debate on the Muwashshaḥ." *Prooftexts* 9 (1989): 161–194.

Einbinder, Susan. "*Muʿāraḍa* as a Key to the Literary Unity of the *Muwashshaḥ*." Ph.D. dissertation, Columbia University, 1991.

Einbinder, Susan. "Prison Prologues: Jewish Prison Writing from Late Medieval Aragon and Provence." *Journal of Medieval Religious Cultures*, 38/2 (2012): 137–158.

Eisenstein, J.D. *Ozar Dinim u-Minhagim*. New York: Hebrew Publishing Company, 1938.

el-Cheikh, Nadia and C.E. Bosworth. "Rūm." *EI*² 8:601.

El-Shami, A. and R.B. Serjeant. "Regional Literature: The Yemen." In *CHALABL*, 442–468.

El-Shamy, Hasan. *Folk Traditions of the Arab World: A Guide to Motif Classification* (GMC). Bloomington and Indianapolis: Indiana University Press, 1995.

El-Shamy, Hasan. *Types of the Folktale in the Arab World: A Demographically Oriented Tale-Type Index* (DOTTI). Bloomington and Indianapolis: Indiana University Press, 2004.

El Tayib, Abdullah. "ʿAbū Firās al-Hamdānī." In *CHALABL*, 315–327.

Elad, Amikam. "The Description of the Travels of Ibn Battuta in Palestine: Is It Original?" *Journal of the Royal Asiatic Society of Great Britain and Ireland* 2 (1987): 256–272.

Elinson, Alexander E. *Looking Back at al-Andalus: The Poetics of Loss and Nostalgia in Medieval Arabic and Hebrew Literature*. Leiden/Boston: Brill, 2009.

Elior, Rachel. "Joseph Karo and Israel Baʿal Shem Tov: Mystical Metamorphosis—Kabbalistic Inspiration, Spiritual Internalization." *Studies in Spirituality* 17 (2007): 267–319.

Elman, Yaakov and Israel Gershoni, eds. *Transmitting Jewish Traditions: Orality, Textuality, and Cultural Diffusion*. New Haven: Yale University Press, 2000.

Elman, Yaakov and Israel Gershoni, eds. "Transmitting Tradition: Orality and Textuality in Jewish Cultures." In *Transmitting Jewish Traditions*, 1–26.

Elon, Menachem. *Jewish Law: History, Sources, Principles*. Translated by Bernard Auerbach and Melvin Sykes. 4 vols. Philadelphia: The Jewish Publication Society, 1994.

Enderwitz, Susanne. "Faḍāʾil." *EI*³ online.

Erder, Yoram. *The Karaite Mourners of Zion and the Qumran Scrolls*. Turnhout: Brepols, 2017.

Even-Shoshan, A. *Ha-millon he-ḥadash*. 7 vols. Jerusalem: Kiryath Sefer, 1981.

Evri, Yuval. *The Return to al-Andalus: Disputes Over Sephardic Culture and Identity Between Arabic and Hebrew* (Hebrew). Jerusalem: Magnes Press, 2020.

Evri, Yuval. "Return to al-Andalus beyond German-Jewish Orientalism: Abraham Shalom Yahuda's Critique of Modern Jewish Discourse." In *Modern Jewish Scholarship on Islam in Context*, ed. Fraisse, 337–354.

Eychenne, Mathieu. "Éléments pour une étude de la Ghouta médiévale: Les biens *ḫarāǧī* de la mosquée des Omeyyades et leur environnement rural." In *Le waqf de la mosquée des Omeyyades de Damas: Le manuscrit ottoman d'un inventaire mamelouk établi en 816/1413*, 259–292, ed. M. Eychenne, Astrid Meier, and Élodie Vigouroux, 259–291. Damas-Beyrouth: Institut français du Proche-Orient, 2018.

Fahd, T., W.P. Heinrichs, and A. Ben Abdesselem, "Sadjʿ." EI² online.

Fakhreddine, Huda. *Metapoesis in the Arabic Tradition: From Modernists to Muḥdathūn*. Leiden: Brill, 2015.

Fakhreddine, Huda and Bilal Orfali. "Against Cities: On *Hijāʾ al-Mudun* in Arabic Poetry." In *The City in Arabic Literature: Classical and Modern Perspectives*, ed. N.F. Hermes and G. Head, 38–62. Edinburgh: Edinburgh University Press, 2018.

Falck, Robert. "Contrafactum." *The New Grove Dictionary of Music and Musicians*, ed. S. Sadie, 4:700–701. London: Macmillan Publishers Limited, 1980; *Grove Music Online* https://doi.org/10.1093/gmo/9781561592630.article.06361

Falck, Robert. "Parody and Contrafactum: A Terminological Clarification." *The Musical Quarterly* 65/1 (1979): 1–21.

Farah, Cesar E. "Yemeni Fortification and the Second Ottoman Conquest." *Proceedings of the Seminar for Arabian Studies* 20 (1990): 31–42.

Fajardo, Salvador J. "The Frame as Formal Contrast: Boccaccio and Cervantes." *Comparative Literature* 36/1 (1984): 1–19.

Feldman, Emanuel. "The Rabbinic Lament." *JQR* 63/1 (1972): 51–75.

Fenton, Paul B. "Moses Shapira's Journey to the Yemen." In *Mittuv Yosef*, ed. Oettinger and Bar-Maoz, 2: lxviii–lxxxi.

Fenton, Paul B. *Philosophie et exégèse dans* Le Jardin de la métaphore *de Moïse Ibn ʿEzra, philosophe et poète andalou du XIIe siècle*. Leiden: Brill, 1997.

Fine, Lawrence. *Physician of the Soul, Healer of the Cosmos: Isaac Luria and his Kabbalistic Fellowship*. Stanford: Stanford University Press, 2003.

Fine, Lawrence. "Pietistic Customs from Safed." In *Judaism in Practice: From the Middle Ages through the Early Modern Period*, ed. L. Fine, 375–385. Princeton: Princeton University Press, 2001.

Fine, Lawrence. "Recitation of Mishnah as a Vehicle for Mystical Inspiration: A Contemplative Technique Taught by Hayyim Vital." *REJ* 141 (1982): 183–199.

Fine, Lawrence, trans. *Safed Spirituality: Rules of Mystical Piety, The Beginning of Wisdom*. New York/ Ramsey/ Toronto: Paulist Press, 1984.

Fischel, Walter J. "Azarbaijan in Jewish History." *PAAJR* 22 (1953): 1–21.

Fischel, Walter J. "Cochin in Jewish History: Prolegomena to a History of the Jews in India." *PAAJR* 30 (1962): 37–59.

Fischel, Walter J. "Garcia de Orta: A Militant Marrano in Portuguese-India in the 16th Century." In *Salo Wittmayer Baron Jubilee Volume*, ed. Saul Lieberman, English Section 1: 407–432. Jerusalem: AAJR, 1974.

Fischel, Walter J. "Goa." *EJ*² 7:651.

Fischel, Walter J. "Hormuz." *EJ*² 9:526.

Fischel, Walter J. "The Jews in Iran during the 16th–18th Centuries" (Hebrew). *Peʿamim* 6 (1980): 5–31.

Fischel, Walter J. "Maqāma ʿal ha-rambam veʾaviv." *Tarbiz* 6/3 (1935): 177–181.

Fischel, Walter J. "The Region of the Persian Gulf and its Jewish Settlements in Islamic Times." In *Alexander Marx Jubilee Volume*, English Section, 203–230. New York: Jewish Theological Seminary of America, 1950.

Fishbein, Michael and James E. Montgomery, ed. and trans. *Kalīlah and Dimnah: Fables of Virtue and Vice by Ibn al-Muqaffaʿ*. New York: New York University Press, 2022.

Fishelov, David. "From Dante's *Inferno* to Immanuel's 'Inferno'" (Hebrew). *Biqqoret ufarshanut* 27 (1991): 19–42.

Fishkin, Dana W. *Bridging Worlds: Poetry and Philosophy in the Works of Immanuel of Rome*. Detroit: Wayne State University Press, 2023.

Fishman, Talya. *Becoming the People of the Book: Oral Torah as Written Tradition in Medieval Jewish Cultures*. Philadelphia: University of Pennsylvania Press, 2011.

Fishman, Talya. "Introduction." *Regional Identities and Cultures of Medieval Jews*, ed. Castaño et al., 1–17.

Fishman, Talya. "A Medieval Parody of Misogyny: Judah ibn Shabbetai's 'Minḥat Yehudah sone hanashim.'" *Prooftexts* 8 (1988): 89–111.

Fishman, Talya. "The 'Our Talmud' Tradition and the Predilection for Works of Applied Law in Early Sephardi Rabbinic Culture." In *Regional Identities and Cultures of Medieval Jews*, ed. Castaño et al., 123–145.

Fleischer, Ezra et al., eds. *Mas'at Moshe: Studies in Jewish and Islamic Culture Presented to Moshe Gil* (Hebrew). Jerusalem: Mossad Bialik/Tel Aviv: Beit ha-sefer le-maddaʿei ha-yahadut ʿal shem Ḥayim Rosenberg, 1998.

Fleischer, Ezra. "Pilgrims' Prayer at the Gates of Jerusalem" (Hebrew). In *Mas'at Moshe*, ed. Fleischer et al., 298–327.

Fogel, Tom. "'These little girls, coming now in their thousands'—Yemeni Women and their Songs as Reflected in Studies by S.D. Goitein." Unpublished conference presentation, Ben-Zvi Institute, Sept. 3, 2018.

Fogel, Tom. "'They Have Countless Books of This Craft': Folklore and Folkloristics of Yemeni Jewish Amulets." *Jewish Folklore and Ethnology* 1 (Fall 2022): 46–64.

Footprints: Jewish Books Through Time and Place database https://footprints.ctl.columbia.edu/search/

Forni, Pier Massimo. "The Decameron and Narrative Form." In *The Cambridge Companion to Boccaccio*, ed. Guida Armstrong, Rhiannon Daniels, and Stephen J. Milner, 55–64. Cambridge University Press, 2015.

Foucault, Michel. *Discipline and Punish: The Birth of the Prison*. Translated by Alan Sheridan. Harmondsworth: Penguin, 1977; New York: Vintage Books, 1995.

Fraisse, Ottfried, ed. *Modern Jewish Scholarship on Islam in Context: Rationality, European Borders, and the Search for Belonging*. Berlin/Boston: de Gruyter, 2018.

Frances, Katherine. *Memory and Identity in the Late Medieval Prison*. Ph.D. dissertation Manchester University, 2013.

Frank, Daniel. "A Jewish Tombstone from Ra's Al-Khaimah." *JJS* 49/1 (Spring 1998): 103–107.

Frank, Daniel. *Search Scripture Well: Karaite Exegetes and the Origins of the Jewish Bible Commentary in the Islamic East*. Leiden: Brill, 2004.

Freedman, H. and M. Simon, eds. *The Midrash Rabbah* (English translation). 10 vols. London and Bournemouth: Soncino Press, 1939; repr. 1951.

Freeman, Thomas S. "The Rise of Prison Literature." *Huntington Library Quarterly* 72/2 (June 2009): 133–146.

Freimark, Peter. *Das Vorwort als literarische Form in der arabischen Literatur*. Ph.D. dissertation. Westfalische Wilhelms-Universität, Münster, 1967.

Frenkel, Miriam. "The Historiography of the Jews in Muslim Countries in the Middle Ages—Landmarks and Prospects" (Hebrew). *Pe'amim* 92 (2002): 23–61.

Frenkel, Miriam. "Travel and Poverty: The Itinerant Pauper in Medieval Jewish Society in Islamic Countries." In *Jews and Journeys*, ed. Levinson and Bashkin, 154–170.

Fudge, Bruce. "Strangers in Fiction: Knowledge, Narrative and the 'Friends of God.'" In *Tropes du voyages: Les Rencontres*, ed. Chraïbi, 175–196.

Gabrieli, F. "Adab." *EI*² 1:175–176.

Gadelrab, Sherry Sayed. "Medical Healers in Ottoman Egypt, 1517–1805." *Medical History* 54 (2010): 365–386.

Gaimani, Aharon. *The Names of Yemenite Jewry: A Social and Cultural History*. Bethesda: University of Maryland Press, 2017.

Gaimani, Aharon. "The Penetration of Rabbi Yosef Karo's Literary-Halakhic Work to Yemen" (Hebrew). *Pe'amim* 49 (1991): 120–134.

Gaimani, Aharon. "Rabbinic Emissaries and Their Contacts with Yemenite Jewry." *HUCA* 69 (1998): 101–125.

Gaimani, Aharon. "Ha-shadar rabbi david naḥmias u-maṣot teiman." *Pe'amim* 64 (1995): 39–53.

Gaimani, Aharon. "Shemot pratiyyim bi-qehillot teiman: meḥqar shemot 'al pi shetarei ketubbah." In *These Are the Names: Studies in Jewish Onomastics* (Hebrew), ed. A. Demsky, J.A. Reif, and J. Tabory 1:49–61. Ramat Gan: Bar-Ilan University Press, 1997.

Gaimani, Aharon. *Temurot be-moreshet yahadut teiman be-hashpa'at ha-shulḥan 'arukh ve-qabbalat ha-ari*. Ramat Gan: Bar Ilan University Press, 2005.

Gaimani, Aharon. "Visiting Graves of Ẓaddiqim in Yemen." *The Review of Rabbinic Judaism* 18 (2015): 281–300.

Galinsky, Judah D. and James T. Robinson. "Rabbi Jeruham b. Meshullam, Michael Scot, and the Development of Jewish Law in Fourteenth-Century Spain." *HTR* 100/4 (2007): 489–504.

Gamliel, Ophira. "Back from Shingly: Revisiting the Premodern History of Jews in Kerala." *The Indian Economic and Social History Review* 55/1 (2018): 53–76.

Gamlieli, Nissim Binyamin. *Ḥadrei teiman*. Tel Aviv: Afikim, 1978; 2d edition 2016.

Gampel, Benjamin R., ed. *Crisis and Creativity in the Sephardic World 1391–1648*. New York: Columbia University Press, 1997.

Gaon, M.D. *Yehudei ha-mizraḥ be'ereṣ yisra'el*. 2 vols. Jerusalem: By the Author, 1928–1938.

Gardiner, Noah. "Esotericist Reading Communities and the Early Circulation of the Sufi Occultist Aḥmad al-Būnī's Works." *Arabica* 64/3–4 (2017): 405–441.

Gardiner, Noah. "Forbidden Knowledge? Notes on the Production, Transmission, and Reception of the Major Works of Aḥmad al-Būnī." *JAIS* 12 (2012): 81–143.

Gavra, Moshe. "Le-foʿalo shel rabbi yiṣḥaq wannah be-sidduro 'paʿamon zahav.'" *Tema* 4 (1994): 55–65.

Gavra, Moshe. "Le-toldot nusaḥ ha-baladi ve-ha shāmi." *Tehuda* 25 (2007): 25–35.

Gavra, Moshe. *Meḥqarim be-siddurei teiman ʿim nusaḥ tiklāl es ḥayyim*. 4 vols. Bnai Brak: Ha-makhon le-ḥeqer ḥakhmei teiman, 2010.

Gavra, Moshe. *Shemot ha-mishpaḥah shel ha-yehudim be-teiman*. Bnai Brak: Ha-makhon le-ḥeqer ḥakhmei teiman, 2014.

Gavra, Moshe. *Ha-shemot ha-pratiyyim be-qerev yehudei teiman*. Bnai Brak: Ha-makhon le-ḥeqer yehudei teiman, 2016.

Gavra, Moshe. *Ha-tiklāl ha-maddaʿi ha-mehudar*. Bnai Brak: ha-Makhon le-ḥeqer ḥakhmei teiman, 2011.

Gellens, Sam I. "The Search for Knowledge in Medieval Muslim Societies: a Comparative Approach." In *Muslim Travellers*, ed. Eickelman and Piscatori, 50–58.

Geltner, Guy. *The Medieval Prison: A Social History*. Princeton: Princeton University Press, 2008.

Genette, Gérard. *Palimpsestes*. Paris: Editions du Seuil, 1981.

Genette, Gérard. *Seuils*. Paris: Editions du Seuil, 1987.

Genette, Gérard. *Paratexts: Thresholds of Interpretation*. Trans. Jane E. Lewin. Cambridge: Cambridge University Press, 1997.

George, Alain. "The Illustrations of the *Maqāmāt* and the Shadow Play." *Muqarnas* 28 (2011): 1–42.

George, Alain. "Orality, Writing and the Image in the *Maqāmāt*." *Art History* 35/1 (2012): 10–37.

Gerber, Haim. *Crossing Borders: Jews and Muslims in Ottoman Law, Economy, and Society*. Istanbul: The Isis Press, 2008.

Gerber, Jane. *Cities of Splendour in the Shaping of Sephardi History*. London: Littman Library of Jewish Civilization, 2020.

Gerber, Noah S. *Ourselves or Our Holy Books? The Cultural Discovery of Yemenite Jewry* (Hebrew). Jerusalem: Yad Izhak ben-Zvi/ The Hebrew University of Jerusalem, 2013.

Gerber, Noah S. "Jewish Studies and Its Discoveries of the Jewish Orient" (Hebrew). In *Mittuv Yosef*, ed. Oettinger and Bar-Maoz, 2:79–94.

Geries, Ibrahim. *A Literary and Gastronomical Conceit: The Boasting Debate Between Rice and Pomegranate Seeds*. Wiesbaden: Harrassowitz Verlag, 2002.

Ghersetti, Antonella, ed. *Tropes du voyage: Le voyage dans la littérature arabe*, vol. 1, Départs. *Annali di Ca' Foscari* 48/3 (2009).

Giat, Paltiel. "The Linguistic Stratum in Rabbi Isaac Wanneh's Commentary on the *Seliḥot*" (Hebrew). In *Mittuv Yosef*, ed. Oettinger and Bar-Maoz, 2:61–78.

Gil, Moshe. *Jews in Islamic Countries in the Middle Ages*. Leiden/Boston: Brill, 2004.

Giller, Pinchas. *Reading the Zohar: The Sacred Text of the Kabbalah*. Oxford: Oxford University Press, 2001.

Ginsburg, Elliot K. *The Sabbath in the Classical Kabbalah*. Albany: SUNY Press, 1989.

Ginsburg, Elliot K. *Sod ha-Shabbat: The Mystery of the Sabbath*. Albany: SUNY Press, 1989.

Ginzburg, Carlo. *The Cheese and the Worms: The Cosmos of a Sixteenth-Century Miller*. Trans. John Tedeschi and Anne Tedeschi. London and Henley: Routledge & Kegan Paul/The Johns Hopkins University, 1980.

Gittes, Katharine Slater. "The Canterbury Tales and the Arabic Frame Tradition." In *Chaucer's Cultural Geography*, ed. Kathryn L. Lynch, 152–173. New York: Routledge, 2002.

Glaser, Eduard. "My Journey Through Arḥab and Ḥāshid," trans. David Warburton. [From *Petermann's Mitteilungen* 30 (1884): 170–183; 204–213.] American Institute for Yemeni Studies, 1993.

Gluska, Isaac. "Language" (Hebrew). In *Yemen*, ed. Saadoun, 143–154.

Gluska, Isaac. "Dialectal Elements in the Hebrew Language of the Yemenite Jews" (Hebrew). *Pe'amim* 64 (1995): 22–38.

Gluska, Isaac and T. Kessar, eds. *Sefer shivtiel: Studies in the Hebrew Language and in the Linguistic Traditions of the Jewish Communities*. Ramat Gan: Ha'agudah le-ṭipuaḥ ḥevrah ve-tarbut/ Afikim/ the Shivtiel family, 1992.

Goetschel, Roland. *Meir Ibn Gabbay: le Discours de la Kabbale Espagnole*. Leuven: Peeters, 1981.

Goitein, S.D. *A Mediterranean Society*, 6 vols. Berkeley: University of California Press, 1967–1993.

Goitein, S.D. "A Yemenite Poet on Egypt of the XVIth Century." *Révue de l'histoire juive en Égypte* 1 (1947): 23–32.

Goitein, S.D. "From Aden to India," *JESHO* 23 (1979–1980): 43–66.

Goitein, S.D. *From the Land of Sheba: Tales of the Jews of Yemen*. New York: Schocken Books, 1947; new rev. ed., 1973.

Goitein, S.D. "From the Mediterranean to India: Documents on the Trade to India, South Arabia, and East Africa from the Eleventh and Twelfth Centuries." *Speculum* 29/2 (1954): 181–197.

Goitein, S.D. and M.A. Friedman. *India Traders of the Middle Ages: Documents from the Cairo Geniza*. Leiden/Boston: Brill, 2007; paperback ed. 2011.

Goitein, S.D. "Jewish Education in Yemen as an Archetype of Traditional Jewish Education" (Hebrew). In *The Yemenites: History, Communal Organization, Spiritual Life*, ed. Ben-Sasson, 241–268.

Goitein, S.D. *Letters of Medieval Jewish Traders*. Princeton: Princeton University Press, 1973; repr. 2015.

Goitein, S.D., ed. and trans. *Massaʿot ḥabshush—Ruʾyā al-yaman*. 2d ed. Jerusalem: Ben-Zvi Institute, 1983.

Goitein, S.D. "Portrait of a Medieval India Trader: Three Letters from the Cairo Geniza." *BSOAS* 50 (1987): 449–464.

Goitein, S.D., ed. *Religion in a Religious Age*. Cambridge, Mass.: Association for Jewish Studies, 1974.

Goitein, S.D. *Sidrei ḥinukh (Jewish Education in Muslim Countries, Based on Records from the Cairo Geniza)*. Jerusalem: Ben-Zvi Institute & The Hebrew University, 1962.

Goitein, S.D. "Teimanim birushalayim uve-miṣrayim bi-tequfato shel ha-rambam ve-shel beno rabbi avraham." In *Harʾel*, ed. Ratzaby and Shivtiel, 133–148.

Goitein, S.D. "The Age of the Hebrew Tombstones from Aden." *JSS* 7/1 (1962): 81–84.

Goitein, S.D. "The Support of Yemenite Jews of the Academies of Iraq and Palestine and the School of Moses Maimonides" (Hebrew). In *The Yemenites: History, Communal Organization, Spiritual Life*, ed. Ben-Sasson, 19–32.

Goitein, S.D. *The Yemenites: History, Communal Organization, Spiritual Life, Selected Studies* (Hebrew), ed. M. Ben-Sasson. Jerusalem: Ben-Zvi Institute, Yad Izhak Ben-Zvi and the Hebrew University, 1983.

Goldberg, Harvey E. "The Zohar in Southern Morocco: A Study in the Ethnography of Texts." *History of Religions* 29/3 (Feb. 1990): 233–258.

Goldberg, Jessica L. "Choosing and Enforcing Business Relationships in the Eleventh-Century Mediterranean: Reassessing the 'Maghribi Traders.'" *Past and Present* 216 (2012): 3–40.

Goldschmidt, D. "Maḥzor romania." *Sefunot* 8 (1964): 205–236.

Goldstein, David. "The Commentary of Immanuel ben Solomon of Rome on Chapters I–X of Genesis: Introduction, Hebrew Text, and Notes." Ph.D. dissertation, University College London, 1966.

Goldstein, David. *The Book of Proverbs with the Commentary of Immanuel of Rome, Naples ca. 1487*, Introduction by David Goldstein. Jerusalem: Magnes Press, 1981.

Goldstone, Jack A. "The Problem of the 'Early Modern' World." *JESHO* 41/3 (1998): 249–284.

Goldziher, Ignacz. "Mélanges Judéo-Arabes." *REJ* 43 (1901): 1–14.

Goldziher, Ignacz. *Muslim Studies*. Edited by S.M. Stern, translated by C.R. Barber and S.M. Stern. 2 vols. London: George Allen and Unwin, Ltd., 1971.

Gollancz, Hermann. *Tophet and Eden (Hell and Paradise) in Imitation of Dante's* Inferno *and* Paradiso *from the Hebrew of Immanuel Ben Solomon Romi, Dante's Contemporary*. London: University of London Press, 1921.

Goodblatt, Morris. *Jewish Life in Turkey in the XVIth Century as Reflected in the Legal Writings of Samuel De Medina*. New York, 1952.

Goodman, Martin, ed. *The Oxford Handbook of Jewish Studies*. Oxford: Oxford University Press, 2004.

Gorfinkle, Joseph I., ed. and trans. *The Eight Chapters of Maimonides on Ethics*. New York: Columbia University Press, 1912; repr. AMS Press, 1966.

Gottlieb, Ephraim. "Shem Tov Ibn Shem Tov's Path to Kabbalah" (Hebrew). In *Meḥqarim be-sifrut ha-qabbalah*, ed. Joseph Hacker, 347–356. Tel Aviv: Tel Aviv University Press, 1976.

Gould, Rebecca R. *The Persian Prison Poem*. Edinburgh: Edinburgh University Press, 2021.

Green, Arthur, ed. *Jewish Spirituality*. 2 vols. New York: Crossroad, 1986–1987.

Greenblatt, Stephen. *Marvelous Possessions: The Wonder of the New World*. Chicago: University of Chicago Press, 1991.

Greenup, A.W., ed. *Shemen ʿarev*. London, 1910.

Greidi, Shimon, ed. *Peʿilut ve-zikhron ishim 643–646 (1983–1986)*. Jerusalem: Ha-vaʿad ha-kelali lihudei teiman birushalayim, 1986.

Greidi, Shimon. "Ḥinnukh ha-yeladim be-teiman." In *Mi-teiman le-ṣion*, ed. Yishaʿyahu and Greidi, 156–165.

Greive, H. *Studien zum jüdischen Neuplatonismus: Die Religionsphilosophie des Abraham Ibn Ezra*. Berlin/ New York: Walter De Gruyter, 1973.

Griffith, Sidney H. *Hunayn Ibn Ishaq and the Kitab Adab al-falasifa: the Pursuit of Wisdom and a Humane Polity in Early Abbasid Baghdad*. Piscataway, NJ: Gorgias Press, 2009.

Griffith, Sidney H. "The Monk in the Emir's *Majlis*: Reflections on a Popular Genre of Christian Literary Apologetics in Arabic in the Early Islamic Period." In *The Majlis*, ed. Lazarus-Yafeh et al., 13–65.

Gross, Abraham. *Iberian Jewry from Twilight to Dawn: The World of Rabbi Abraham Saba*. Leiden/New York/Köln: E.J. Brill, 1995.

Grossman, Avraham. "Relations Between Spanish and Ashkenazi Jewry in the Middle Ages." In *Moreshet Sepharad: The Sephardi Legacy*, ed. Beinart, 1:220–239.

The Grove Encyclopedia of Islamic Art and Architecture, ed. Jonathan M. Bloom and Sheila S. Blair. Oxford/New York: Oxford University Press, 2009. Online.

Gruendler, Beatrice. "Originality in Imitation: Two *Muʿāraḍas* by Ibn Darrāj al-Qasṭallī." *al-Qantara* 29/2 (2008): 437–465.

Guilat, Yael. "The 'Israelization' of Yemenite-Jewish Silversmithing." In *Ascending the Palm Tree*, ed. Yedid and Bar-Maoz, 222–251.

Guilat, Yael. "The Yemeni Ideal in Israeli Culture and Arts." *Israel Studies* 6/3 (2001): 26-53.

Guo, Li. *The Performing Arts in Medieval Islam: Shadow Play and Popular Poetry in Ibn Dāniyāl's Mamlūk Cairo*. Leiden/Boston: Brill, 2012.

Guthke, Karl S. *Epitaph Culture in the West: Variations on a Theme in Cultural History*. Lewiston/Queenston/Lampeter: The Edwin Mellen Press, 2003.

Habermann, A.M. *Anshei sefer ve'anshei ma'aseh*. Jerusalem: Rubin Mass, 1974.

Habermann, A.M. "ʿAl gonvei ha-shir." In *ʿIyyunim ba-shirah u-va-piyyut*, 78–85.

Habermann, A.M. "Ha-haqdashot le-sefer 'taḥkemoni' u-reshimat tokhen maqamotav." In *ʿIyyunim ba-shirah uva-piyyuṭ*, 137–153.

Habermann, A.M. *ʿIyyunim ba-shirah u-va-piyyut shel yemei ha-beinayim*. Jerusalem: Rubin Mass, 1972.

Habermann, A.M., ed. "Rabbi Shem Tov Falaquera's *Iggeret ha-Musar*." *Qoveṣ ʿal Yad* 1 (1936): 43–90.

Habermann, A.M. *Toldot ha-defus bi-ṣfat*. Safed Museum of Printing, 1961/62.

Hacker, Joseph. "Authors, Readers, and Printers of Sixteenth-Century Hebrew Books in the Ottoman Empire." In *Perspectives on the Hebraic Book*, ed. Peggy K. Perlstein, 17–64. Washington: Library of Congress, 2012.

Hacker, Joseph. "The Intellectual Activity of the Jews of the Ottoman Empire During the Sixteenth and Seventeenth Centuries." In *Jewish Thought in the Seventeenth Century*, ed. I. Twersky and B. Septimus, 95–135. Cambridge, Mass., 1987.

Hacker, Joseph. "On the Intellectual Character and Self-Perception of Spanish Jewry in the Late Fifteenth Century" (Hebrew). *Sefunot* n.s. 2 (1983): 21–95.

Hacker, Joseph. "Jews in the Ottoman Empire (1580–1839)." In *The Cambridge History of Judaism*, vol. 7, ed. Jonathan Karp and Adam Sutcliffe, Pt. 3, 831–863. Cambridge University Press, 2017.

Hacker, Joseph. "Links Between Spanish Jewry and Palestine, 1391–1492." In *Vision and Conflict in the Holy Land*, ed. R.I. Cohen, 111–139. Jerusalem: Yad Izhak Ben-Zvi/ New York: St. Martin's Press, 1985.

Hacker, Joseph. "Ottoman Policy toward the Jews and Jewish Attitudes toward the Ottomans during the Fifteenth Century." In *Christians and Jews in the Ottoman Empire*, ed. B. Braude and B. Lewis, 1:117–126. New York: Holmes & Meier, 1982.

Hacker, Joseph. "The Sephardim in the Ottoman Empire in the Sixteenth Century." In *Moreshet Sepharad: The Sephardi Legacy*, ed. H. Beinart, 2: 109–133. Jerusalem, 1992.

Hacker, Joseph. "Shiṭat ha-surgun ve-hashpaʿatah ʿal ha-ḥevrah ha-yehudit ba'imperiya haʿuthmanit ba-me'ot ha-15–17." *Zion* 55/1 (1990): 27–82.

Hacker, Joseph. "The Sürgün System and Jewish Society in the Ottoman Empire during the Fifteenth to the Seventeenth Centuries." In *Ottoman and Turkish Jewry: Community and Leadership*, ed. A. Rodrigue, 9–65. Bloomington: Indiana University Press, 1992.

Ha-Kohen Maimon, Y.L. "Sefer ha-nimṣa la-rambam." *Sinai* 36 (1955): 201–211.

Halbertal, Moshe. *Concealment and Revelation: Esotericism in Jewish Thought and its Philosophical Implications*. Princeton: Princeton University Press, 2007.

Halevi, Raṣon, ed. *Shirat yisra'el be-teiman*. 3 vols. Kiryat Ono: Makhon mishnat ha-rambam, 1998–2003.

Halevi-Wise, Yael, ed. *Sephardism: Spanish Jewish History and the Modern Literary Imagination*. Stanford: Stanford University Press, 2012.

Halévy, Joseph. "Voyage au Nedjran." *Bulletin de la Société de Géographie de Paris* 6 (1873): 5–31, 249–273, 581–606.

Halkin, Abraham S. trans., discussions by David Hartman. *Crisis and Leadership: Epistles of Maimonides*. Philadelphia/ New York/ Jerusalem, 1985.

Halkin, Abraham S., ed. *Moses Maimonides' Epistle to Yemen: The Arabic Original and the Three Hebrew Versions*. Trans. Boaz Cohen. New York: American Academy for Jewish Research, 1952.

Hallamish, Moshe. *Hanhagot qabbaliot be-shabbat*. Jerusalem: Orḥot, 2005.

Hallamish, Moshe. *An Introduction to the Kabbalah*. Albany: SUNY Press, 1999.

Hallamish, Moshe. "Joseph Karo—Kabbalah and Halakhic Decisions" (Hebrew). *Da'at* 21 (1988):85–102.

Hallamish, Moshe. *Kabbalah: In Liturgy, Halakhah and Customs* (Hebrew). Ramat Gan: Bar-Ilan University Press, 2000.

Hallamish, Moshe., ed. *The Kabbalah in Yemen at the Beginning of the Seventeenth Century: Sefer Segulloth and Sefer Leḥem Shelomo* (Hebrew). Ramat Gan: Bar-Ilan University Press, 1984.

Hallamish, Moshe. "Ha-qabbalah be-sidduro shel rabbi yiṣḥaq wanneh." *Tema* 5 (1996): 65–82. Repr. in Hallamish, *Kabbalah*, 205–219.

Hallamish, Moshe. "Rabbi shalom ha-qorḥi ve-rabbi shelomo hakohen: pereq be-hitpatḥutah shel ha-qabbalah be-teman." *Meḥqerei yerushalayim be-maḥshevet yisrael* 2/1 (1983): 110–118.

Hallamish, Moshe. "Ha-shir bar yoḥai." In Hallamish, *Kabbalah*, 507–531.

Hallamish, Moshe. "Rabbi yiḥye ṣāliḥ veha-qabbalah." *Tema* 4 (1994): 66–92; repr. in Hallamish, *Kabbalah: In Liturgy, Halakhah and Customs*, 220–241.

Hämeen-Anttilla, Jaakko. "The Early Maqama: Towards Defining a Genre." *Études asiatiques: revue de la Société Suisse-Asie* 51/2 (1997): 577–599.

Hämeen-Anttilla, Jaakko. *Maqama: A History of a Genre*. Wiesbaden: Harrassowitz Verlag, 2002.

Hámori, András P. "Ibn 'Abd Rabbih." *EI*³ online.

Hámori, András P. "Rising to Greet You: Some Comedies of Manners." *MEL* 11/2 (2008): 205–210.

Haring, Lee. "Framing in Narrative." In *The Arabian Nights in Transnational Perspective*, ed. Ulrich Marzolph, 135–153. Detroit: Wayne State University Press, 2007.

Harris, Jay M., ed. *Be'erot Yitzhak: Studies in Memory of Isadore Twersky*. Cambridge, Mass.: Harvard Center for Jewish Studies and Harvard University Press, 2005.

Harvey, E. Ruth. *The Inward Wits: Psychological Theory in the Middle Ages and the Renaissance*. London: Warburg Institute, 1975.

Harvey, Steven. "The Author's Introduction as a Key to Understanding Trends in Islamic Philosophy." In *Words, Texts and Concepts Cruising the Mediterranean Sea*, ed. R. Arnzen and J. Thielmann, 15–32. Leuven/Paris/Dudley, MA: Peeters Publishers, 2004.

Harvey, Steven, ed. and trans. *Falaquera's Epistle of the Debate*. Cambridge, Mass.: Harvard University Press, 1987.

Harvey, Steven. "Maimonides and the Art of Writing Introductions." *Maimonidean Studies* 5 (2008): 85–106.

Hasan-Rokem, Galit. "Ecotypes: Theory of the Lived and Narrated Experience." *Narrative Culture* 3/1 (Spring 2016): 110–137.

Hassan, Waïl S. "Translator's Introduction." In Kilito, *Thou Shalt Not Speak My Language*, vii–xxvi.

Hathaway, Jane. *The Arab Lands under Ottoman Rule 1516–1800*. London: Routledge, 2019.

Hathaway, Jane. "The Forgotten Province: A Prelude to the Ottoman Era in Yemen." In *Mamlūks and Ottomans: Studies in Honour of Michael Winter*, ed. D.J. Wasserstein and A. Ayalon, 195–205. London/New York: Routledge, 2005.

Hathaway, Jane. "The Mawza Exile at the Juncture of Zaydi and Ottoman Messianism." *AJS Review* 29/1 (2005): 111–128.

Hathaway, Jane. *A Tale of Two Factions: Myth, Memory, and Identity in Ottoman Egypt and Yemen*. Albany: SUNY Press, 2003.

Havatselet, Meir, ed. and trans. *Midrash ha-ḥefeṣ: 'al ḥamishah ḥumshe torah, ḥibro Zekharyah ben Shelomoh ha-Rofe*. 2 vols. Jerusalem: Mossad HaRav Kook, 1990–1999.

Havlin, Shlomo Zalman. "On Classifications of *Pilpul*." In *"In the Dwelling of a Sage Lie Precious Treasures": Essays in Jewish Studies in Honor of Shnayer Z. Leiman*, ed. Yitzhak Berger and Chaim Milikowsky, 171–186. Brooklyn, NY: Ktav Publishing House, 2020.

Haykel, Bernard. "Dissembling Descent, Or How the Barber Lost His Turban: Identity and Evidence in Eighteenth-Century Zaydī Yemen." *Islamic Law and Society* 9/2 (2002): 194–230.

Haykel, Bernard. *Revival and Reform in Islam: The Legacy of Muhammad al-Shawkānī*. Cambridge: Cambridge University Press, 2003.

Hazan, Ephraim. "The Emissaries of Eretz Israel in the Poetry of the Jews of North Africa" (Hebrew). *Pe'amim* 24 (1985): 99–116.

Heath, Peter. "Al-Jāḥiẓ, *Adab*, and the Art of the Essay." In *Al-Jāḥiẓ: A Muslim Human-*

ist for Our Time, ed. A. Heinemann, J.L. Meloy, T. Khalidi, and M. Kropp, 133–172. Würzburg: Ergon Verlag, 2009.

Hehmeyer, Ingrid and Hanne Schönig, eds. *Herbal Medicine in Yemen: Traditional Knowledge and Practice, and Their Value for Today's World*. Leiden/ Boston: Brill, 2012.

Heinrichs, Wolfhart. "Allusion and Intertextuality." In *EAL* 1:81–83.

Heinrichs, Wolfhart. "Literary Theory: The Problem and Its Efficiency." In *Arabic Poetry: Theory and Development*, ed. G.E. von Grunebaum, 19–69. Wiesbaden: Harrassowitz, 1973.

Heinrichs, Wolfhart. "Modes of Existence of the Poetry in the Arabian Nights." In *The Heritage of Arabo-Islamic Learning*, ed. Pomerantz and Shahin, 528–537.

Heinrichs, Wolfhart. "Prosimetrical Genres in Classical Arabic." In *Prosimetrum: Cross-cultural Perspectives on Narrative in Prose and Verse*, ed. J. Harris and K. Reichl, 249–275. Cambridge, U.K.: D.S. Brewer, 1997.

Heinrichs, Wolfhart. "Rose versus Narcissus: Observations on an Arabic Literary Debate." In *Dispute Poems and Dialogues*, ed. Reinink and Vanstiphout, 179–198.

Heinrichs, Wolfhart. "Sariḳa." *EI*[2].

Heller, Marvin J. "Designing the Talmud: The Origins of the Printed Talmudic Page." *Tradition* 29/ 3 (Spring 1995): 40–51.

Heller, Marvin J. "Early Hebrew Printing from Lublin to Safed: The Journeys of Eliezer ben Isaac Ashkenazi." *Jewish Culture and History* 4/1 (2012): 81–96.

Heller, Marvin J. "A Fleeting Moment, A Short-Lived Press: Hebrew Printing in Sixteenth Century Fez." *Sephardic Horizons* 11:1 (2021). https://www.sephardichorizons.org/Volume11/Issue1/Heller.html

Heller, Marvin J. *Printing the Talmud: A History of the Earliest Printed Editions of the Talmud*. Brooklyn, NY: Im Hasefer, 1992.

Hentati, Nejmeddine. "La Prison en Occident Musulman Médiéval." *Arabica* 54 (2007): 149–188.

Hertz, J.H., trans. *Sayings of the Fathers*. New York: Behrman House, 1945.

Heyd, Uriel. "The Jewish Communities of Istanbul in the Seventeenth Century." *Oriens* 6/2 (1953): 299–314.

Hillenbrand, Robert. *Islamic Architecture: Form, Function and Meaning*. New York: Columbia University Press, 1994.

Hillenbrand, Robert. "'The Ornament of the World': Medieval Córdoba as a Cultural Center," in *The Legacy of Muslim Spain*, ed. Jayyusi, 112–135.

Hirsch, W. *Rabbinic Psychology*. London: Edward Goldston, 1947.

Hirschberg, H.Z., ed. *Mi-mizraḥ umi-maʿarav: qoveṣ meḥqarim be-toldot ha-yehudim ba-mizraḥ uva-magreb*. Ramat-Gan: Bar-Ilan University Press, 1974.

Hirschler, Konrad. *The Written Word in the Medieval Arabic Lands: A Social and Cultural History of Reading Practices*. Edinburgh: Edinburgh University Press, 2012.

Ho, Enseng. *The Graves of Tarim: Genealogy and Mobility across the Indian Ocean*. Berkeley/Los Angeles/London: University of California Press, 2006.

Hodgson, Marshall G.S. *The Venture of Islam: Conscience and History in a World Civilization*. 3 vols. Chicago: University of Chicago Press, 1974.

Hoffman, Lawrence A., ed. *The Land of Israel: Jewish Perspectives*. Notre Dame, Indiana: University of Notre Dame Press, 1986.

Hollander, A.A. et al., eds. *Paratext and Megatext as Channels of Jewish and Christian Traditions: The Textual Markers of Contextualization*. Leiden/Boston: Brill, 2003.

Holmberg, Bo. "The Public Debate as a Literary Genre in Arabic Literature." *Orientalia Suecana* 38–39 (1989–1990): 45–53.

Hopkins, J.F.P. "Geographical and Navigational Literature." In *CHALRLS*, 301–327.

Houston, Chloë, ed. *New Worlds Reflected: Travel and Utopia in the Early Modern Period*. Burlington, VT/Farnham, Surrey: Ashgate, 2010.

Hughes, Aaron. *The Art of Dialogue in Jewish Philosophy*. Bloomington: Indiana University Press, 2008.

Hughes, Aaron. *The Texture of the Divine: Imagination in Medieval Islamic and Jewish Thought*. Bloomington and Indianapolis: Indiana University Press, 2004.

Hughes, Aaron and James T. Robinson eds. *Medieval Jewish Philosophy and its Literary Forms*. Bloomington: Indiana University Press, 2019.

Huss, Boaz. "R. Joseph Gikatilla's Definition of Symbolism and Its Versions in Kabbalistic Literature" (Hebrew). In *Rivkah Shatz-Uffenheimer Memorial Volume*, ed. R. Elior and J. Dan, 1:157–176. Jerusalem, 1996.

Huss, Boaz. "*Sefer ha-Zohar* as a Canonical, Sacred and Holy Text: Changing Perspectives of the Book of Splendor between the Thirteenth and Eighteenth Centuries." *JJTP* 7 (1998): 257–307.

Huss, Boaz. *Sockets of Fine Gold: The Kabbalah of Rabbi Shimʿon ibn Lavi* (Hebrew). Jerusalem: Magnes Press/Ben Zvi Institute, 2000.

Huss, Boaz. *The Zohar: Reception and Impact*. Oxford/ Portland, Oregon: The Littman Library of Jewish Civilization, 2016.

Huss, Matti. "Criticism of Kabbala in Hebrew Rhymed Narratives" (Hebrew). *Jerusalem Studies in Hebrew Literature* 32 (2021): 325–358.

Huss, Matti. "The 'Maggid' in the Classical 'Maqama'" (Hebrew). *Tarbiz* 65/1 (1995): 129–172.

Huss, Matti. "Misogyny in the Hebrew Andalusian School of Poetry" (Hebrew). *Teʿudah* 19 (2002): 27–53.

Huss, Matti. "The Status of Fiction in the Hebrew *Maqama*: Judah Alḥarizi and Immanuel of Rome" (Hebrew). *Tarbiz* 67 (1998): 351–378.

Idel, Moshe. *Ascensions on High in Jewish Mysticism: Pillars, Lines, Ladders*. Budapest/New York: Central European University Press, 2005.

Idel, Moshe. "Encounters Between Spanish and Italian Kabbalists in the Generation of the Expulsion." In *Crisis and Creativity in the Sephardic World 1391–1648*, ed. Gampel, 189–222.

Idel, Moshe. "Hitbodedut as Concentration in Jewish Philosophy" (Hebrew). In *Shlomo Pines Jubilee Volume on the Occasion of His Eightieth Birthday*, ed. M. Idel, Z.W. Harvey, and E. Schweid, 1:39–60. Jerusalem: Mandel Institute for Jewish Studies, 1988.

Idel, Moshe. "Italy in Safed, Safed in Italy: A Chapter in the Interactive History of Sixteenth-Century Kabbalah." In *Cultural Intermediaries: Jewish Intellectuals in Early Modern Italy*, ed. David Ruderman and Giuseppe Veltri, 239–269. Philadelphia: University of Pennsylvania Press, 2004.

Idel, Moshe. "Jewish Mysticism Among the Jews of Arab/Moslem Lands." *The Journal for the Study of Sephardic and Mizrahi Jewry* 1/1 (Feb. 2007): 14–39.

Idel, Moshe. "Jewish Thought in Medieval Spain." In *Moreshet Sepharad: The Sephardi Legacy*, ed. Beinart, 1:261–281.

Idel, Moshe. "Kabbalah." EJ² 11:586–692.

Idel, Moshe. *Kabbalah & Eros*. New Haven: Yale University Press, 2005.

Idel, Moshe. *Kabbalah in Italy, 1280–1510: A Survey*. New Haven: Yale University Press, 2011.

Idel, Moshe. *Kabbalah: New Perspectives*. New Haven: Yale University Press, 1988.

Idel, Moshe. "Metamorphoses of a Platonic Theme in Jewish Mysticism." *Jewish Studies at the Central European University* 3 (2002–2003): 67–86.

Idel, Moshe. "On Mobility, Individuals, and Groups: Prolegomenon for a Sociological Approach to Sixteenth-Century Kabbalah." *Kabbalah* 3 (1998): 145–173.

Idel, Moshe. *The Mystical Experience in Abraham Abulafia*. Trans. Jonathan Chipman. Albany: SUNY Press, 1988.

Idel, Moshe. "On Paradise in Jewish Mysticism." *Journal for the Study of Religions and Ideologies* 10 (Winter 2011): 3–38.

Idel, Moshe. "Particularism and Universalism in Kabbalah, 1480–1650." In *Essential Papers on Jewish Culture in Renaissance and Baroque Italy*, ed. David Ruderman, 324–344. New York: New York University Press, 1992.

Idel, Moshe. "Printing Kabbalah in Sixteenth-Century Italy." In *Jewish Culture in Early Modern Europe: Essays in Honor of David B. Ruderman*, ed. Richard I. Cohen et al., 85–96. Cinncinnati: Hebrew Union College Press, 2014.

Idel, Moshe. "*Sefer Maʿarekhet ha-ʾElohut* and its Reverberations." In Moshe Idel, *The Privileged Divine Feminine in Kabbalah*, 67–76. Berlin/Boston: De Gruyter, 2019.

Idel, Moshe. "Some Concepts of Mishnah among Sixteenth-Century Safedian Kabbalists." In *The Mishnaic Moment*, ed. van Boxel et al., 68–86.

Idel, Moshe. "Spanish Kabbalah after the Expulsion." In *The Sephardi Legacy*, ed. H. Beinart, vol. 2. 166–178. Jerusalem: The Magnes Press, 1992.

Idelsohn, A.Z. "Ha-havarah haʿivrit." *Ha-shiloaḥ* 28 (1913): 34–42, 132–141.

Idelsohn, A.Z. "Mivṭa ha-teimanim." *Ha-safah* 1 (1912): 88–92.

Inalcik, Halil. "Bursa." *EI*² online.

Inalcik, Halil. "Bursa and the Commerce of the Levant." *JESHO* 3/2 (1960): 131–147.

Inalcik, Halil. "Istanbul." *EI*² online.

Inalcik, Halil. "Ottoman Methods of Conquest." *SI* 2 (1954): 103–129.

Irwin, Bonnie D. "What's in a Frame? The Medieval Textualization of Traditional Storytelling." *Oral Tradition* 10 (1995): 27–53.

Irwin, Robert. Review of Peter Webb, *Imagining the Arabs: Arab Identitiy and the Rise of Islam* (Edinburgh University Press, 2016). *TLS* January 11, 2017.

Itzhaki, Masha. "Abraham Ibn Ezra as a Harbinger of Changes in Secular Hebrew Poetry." In *Hebrew Scholarship and the Medieval World*, ed. de Lange, 149–155.

Ivry, Alfred. "Maimonides and Neoplatonism: Challenge and Response." In *Neoplatonism and Jewish Thought*, ed. L.E. Goodman, 137–156. Albany: State University of New York Press, 1992.

Ivry, Alfred. "Neoplatonic Currents in Maimonides' Thought." In *Perspectives on Maimonides*, ed. J.L. Kraemer, 115–140. Oxford: Oxford University Press for The Littman Library, 1991.

Jacobs, Louis. *Jewish Mystical Testimonies*. New York: Schocken Books, 1977.

Jacobs, Martin. "An Ex-Sabbatean's Remorse? Sambari's Polemics against Islam." *JQR* 97/3 (2007): 347–378.

Jacobs, Martin. "Flying Camels and Other Remarkable Species: Natural Marvels in Medieval Hebrew Travel Accounts." In *Jews and Journeys*, ed. Levinson and Bashkin, 100–115.

Jacobs, Martin. "From Lofty Caliphs to Uncivilized 'Orientals'—Images of the Muslim in Medieval Jewish Travel Literature." *JSQ* 18 (2011): 64–90.

Jacobs, Martin. "Joseph ha-Kohen, Paolo Giovio, and Sixteenth-Century Historiography." In *Cultural Intermediaries: Jewish Intellectuals in Early Modern Italy*, ed. D. Ruderman and G. Veltri, 67–85. Philadelphia: University of Pennsylvania Press, 2004.

Jacobs, Martin. *Reorienting the East: Jewish Travelers to the Medieval Muslim World*. University of Pennsylvania Press, 2014.

Jánošíková, Magdaléna. "Studying Ibn Sīnā, Performing Abulafia in a Mid-Sixteenth-Century Prison: Emotional, Medical, and Mystical Bodies between Italy and Silesia." *European Journal of Jewish Studies* 16 (2022): 5–27.

Jastrow, Marcus. *A Dictionary of the Targumim, the Talmud Babli and Yerushalmi, and the Midrashic Literature*. 2 vols. London/New York, 1886–1903.

Jayyusi, Salma Khadra, ed. *Classical Arabic Stories: An Anthology*. New York: Columbia University Press, 2010.

Jayyusi, Salma Khadra, ed. *The Legacy of Muslim Spain*, 2d ed. Leiden/New York/Köln: 1994.

Jazem, Mohammed Abdelrahim and Bernadette Leclercq-Neveu. "L'organisation des caravanes au Yémen selon al-Hamdânî (xᵉ siècle)." *Chroniques yéménites* [En ligne], 9 | 2001, mis en ligne le 07 septembre 2007.

Johnson, Barbara. "Cochin Jews and Kaifeng Jews: Reflections on Caste, Surname, 'Community' and Conversion" (Hebrew). *Peʿamim* 60 (Summer 1994): 32–48.

Jones, Alan and Richard Hitchcock, eds. *Studies on the Muwaššaḥ and the Kharja: Proceedings of the Exeter International Colloquium.* Reading: Ithaca Press, 1991.

Kahana, David. "ʿAl ha-meshorer ha-qaraʾi mosheh darʿi." *Hashiloaḥ* 13 (1904): 435–442.

Kahana, David., ed. *Rabbi Avraham Ibn Ezra: Qoveṣ ḥokhmat ha-raʾbaʿ.* Warsaw, 1894.

Kahanov, E. "Ha-tofet ve-haʿeden leʾimmanuel ha-romi, kefi she-hi mitpareshet ʿal yedei ha-komedia haʾelohit le-dante." *Maʿof u-maʿase* 6 (2000): 31–43.

Kalmar, Ivan Davidson and Derek J. Penslar, eds. *Orientalism and the Jews.* Waltham, Mass.: Brandeis University Press, 2005.

Kanarfogel, Ephraim. "Preservation, Creativity, and Courage: The Life and Works of R. Meir of Rothenburg." *Jewish Book Annual* 50 (1992–1993): 249–259.

Kanarfogel, Ephraim. "Talmudic Studies." In *The Cambridge History of Judaism*, ed. R. Chazan, 6:582–619. Cambridge University Press, 2018.

Kaplan, Lawrence. "'I Sleep But My Heart Waketh': Maimonides' Conception of Human Perfection." In *The Thought of Moses Maimonides*, ed. I. Robinson et al., 130–166. Lewiston/ Queenston/ Lampeter: Edwin Mellen Press, 1990.

Kaplan, Yosef. "Introduction." In *The Posen Library of Jewish Culture and Civilization, vol. 5: The Early Modern Era, 1500–1750*, ed. Yosef Kaplan, liv–ciii. New Haven/ London: Yale University Press, 2023.

Karah, Yechiel. "Reading Traditions Reflected in the Babylonian Talmud's Punctuation According to the Yemenite Tradition" (in Hebrew). In *Sefer shivtiʾel*, ed. Gluska and Kessar, 188–203.

Katz, Nathan. "The Judaisms of Kaifeng and Cochin: Parallel and Divergent Styles of Religious Acculturation." *Numen: International Review for the History of Religions* 42:2 (1995): 118–140.

Katz, Nathan. "Kochi." EJ[2] 12:247–250.

Katz, Nathan. *The Last Jews of Cochin.* Columbia, S.C.: University of South Carolina, 1993.

Katz, Nathan. *Who Are the Jews of India?* Berkeley and Los Angeles: University of California Press, 2000.

Katz, Nathan and Ellen S. Goldberg, "Asceticism and Caste in the Passover Observances of the Cochin Jew." *Journal of the American Academy of Religion*, 57/ 1 (Spring, 1989): 53–82.

Kaunfer, Elie G. "The History and Meaning of the 'Other' 'Lekha Dodi' Poem(s)." HUCA 79 (2008): 87–105.

Keegan, Matthew. "Before and After *Kalīla wa-Dimna*: An Introduction to the Special Issue on Animals, *Adab*, and Fictivity." JAS 8 (2021): 1–11.

Keegan, Matthew. "Commentarial Acts and Hermeneutical Dramas: The Ethics of Reading al-Ḥarīrī's *Maqāmāt*." Ph.D. dissertation, New York University, 2017.

Keegan, Matthew. "Digressions in the Islamic Archive: al-Ḥarīrī's *Maqāmāt* and the Forgotten Commentary of al-Panǧdīhī (d. 584/1188)." *IHIW* 10 (2022): 82–118.

Keegan, Matthew. "Throwing the Reins to the Reader: Hierarchy, Jurjānian Poetics, and al-Muṭarrizī's Commentary on the *Maqāmāt*." *JAS* 5 (2018): 105–145.

Kehati, Moshe. "Mi-massaʿo shel rabbi zekhariah ben seʿadya ben yaʿaqov beʾereṣ yisraʾel." *Meʾassef tsiyon* o.s. 3 (1928): 43–53.

Kelman, Tirza. "Ketuvot beʾot barzel veʿoferet bidfus: mahapekhat ha-defus viṣirat ha-ḥibbur beit yosef." *Peʿamim* 148 (2016): 9–25.

Kellner, Menachem. *Dogma in Medieval Jewish Thought: From Maimonides to Abravanel*. Oxford/Portland, OR: The Littman Library of Jewish Civilization, 2004.

Kellner, Menachem. *Maimonides' Confrontation with Mysticism*. Oxford/Portland, OR: The Littman Library of Jewish Civilization, 2006.

Kennedy, Philip F. *Abu Nuwas: A Genius of Poetry*. Oxford: Oneworld, 2005.

Kennedy, Philip F. "Abu Nuwas (circa 757–814 or 815)." In *Arabic Literary Culture, 500–925*, ed. M. Cooperson and S.M. Toorawa. Gale online, 2005.

Kennedy, Philip F, ed. *On Fiction and* Adab *in Medieval Arabic Literature*. Wiesbaden: Harrassowitz Verlag, 2005.

Kennedy, Philip F. "Islamic Recognitions: An Overview." In *Recognition: The Poetics of Narrative*, ed. Philip Kennedy and Marilyn Lawrence, 26–61. New York: Peter Lang, 2009.

Kennedy, Philip F. "The *Maqāmāt* as a Nexus of Interests: Reflections on Abdelfattah Kilito's *Les Séances*." In *Writing and Representation in Medieval Islam: Muslim Horizons*, ed. J. Bray, 153–214. London & New York: Routledge, 2006.

Kennedy, Philip F. "Reason and Revelation or A Philosopher's Squib (The Sixth Maqāma of Ibn Nāqiyā)." *JAIS* 3 (2000): 84–113.

Kennedy, Philip F. *Recognition in the Arabic Narrative Tradition: Discovery, Deliverance and Delusion*. Edinburgh: Edinburgh University Press, 2016.

Kennedy, Philip F. "Takhmīs." *EI*².

Kennedy, Philip F and Jeremy Farrell, ed. and trans. Ibn Buṭlān, *The Doctors' Dinner Party*. New York: NYU Press, 2023.

Kfir, Uriah. *A Matter of Geography: A New Perspective on Medieval Hebrew Poetry*. Leiden and Boston: Brill, 2018.

Khalidi, Tarif. "Adab Hand at Work." *TLS* 31 March 2000.

Khulūṣī, Safāʾ. "Didactic Verse." In *CHALRLS*, 498–509.

Kilito, Abdelfattah. *Arabs and the Art of Storytelling: A Strange Familiarity*, trans. Mbarek Sryfi and Eric Sellin. Syracuse: Syracuse University Press, 2014.

Kilito, Abdelfattah. *The Author and His Doubles*, trans. Michael Cooperson. Syracuse University Press, 2001.

Kilito, Abdelfattah. "Contribution à l'étude de l'écriture 'littéraire' classique: l'exemple de Hariri." *Arabica* 25/1 (1978): 18–47.

Kilito, Abdelfattah. "Foreword: In Praise of Pretense." In Cooperson trans., *Impostures by al-Ḥarīrī*, ix–xv.

Kilito, Abdelfattah. "Le Genre Séance: une introduction." *SI* 43 (1976): 25–51.

Kilito, Abdelfattah. *Les Séances: Récits et codes culturels chez Hamadhānī et Harīrī*. Paris: Sindbad, 1983.

Kilito, Abdelfattah. *Thou Shalt Not Speak My Language*, trans. Waïl S. Hassan. Syracuse University Press, 2008.

Kilpatrick, Hilary. "Adab." In EAL, 1:54–56.

Kilpatrick, Hilary. "The 'Genuine' Ashʿab: The Relativity of Fact and Fiction in Early *Adab* Texts." In *Storytelling in the Framework of Non-fictional Arabic Literature*, ed. Leder, 94–117.

Kimelman, Reuven. *The Mystical Meaning of Lekhah Dodi and Kabbalat Shabbat* (Hebrew). Los Angeles: Cherub Press/ Jerusalem: The Hebrew University Magnes Press, 2003.

Kindley, Evan. "The People We Know Best." *New York Review of Books* March 25, 2021. Accessed at https://www.nybooks.com/articles/2021/03/25/character-people-we-know-best/

Klar, Benjamin. "Arbaʿah shemot sefarim." *KS* 16 (1939–1940): 241–258.

Klein-Franke, Aviva. "Jewelry Among the Jews of Yemen—History and Artistic Development" (Hebrew). *Peʿamim* 11 (1982): 62–88.

Klein-Franke, Aviva. "Tombstones Bearing Hebrew Inscriptions in Aden." *Arabian Archaeology and Epigraphy* 16 (2005): 161–182.

Kleinschmidt, Harald. *People on the Move: Attitudes Toward and Perceptions of Migration in Medieval and Modern Europe*. Westport, CT: Praeger, 2003.

Klorman, Bat-Zion Eraqi. "'The Book of Thought' by Rabbi Saʿadyah ben Yehudah Mansurah and Messianic Expectations in the mid-Nineteenth Century" (Hebrew). In *Seʿi yona*, ed. Seri, 27–34.

Klorman, Bat-Zion Eraqi. "Jewish and Muslim Messianism in Yemen." *IJMES* 22/2 (1990): 201–208.

Klorman, Bat-Zion Eraqi. "The Jews of Yemen." Oxford Bibliographies, Jewish Studies. Online.

Klorman, Bat-Zion Eraqi. "Muslim Supporters of Jewish Messiahs in Yemen." *MES* 29/4 (1993): 714–725.

Klorman, Bat-Zion Eraqi. *Traditional Society in Transition: The Yemeni Jewish Experience*. Leiden/Boston: Brill, 2014.

Klorman, Bat-Zion Eraqi. "Yemen." In *The Jews of the Middle East and North Africa in Modern Times*, ed. R.S. Simon et al., 389–408. New York: Columbia University Press, 2002.

Kosansky, Oren. "Holy Shrines-Conceptual." *EJIW*. Brill Online.

Kozodoy, Maud. "The Jewish Physician in Medieval Iberia." In *The Jew in Medieval Iberia, 1100–1500*, ed. J. Ray, 102–137. Boston: Academic Studies Press, 2012.

Kozodoy, Maud. "Prefatory Verse and the Reception of the Guide of the Perplexed." JQR 106/3 (2016): 257–282.

Kraemer, Joel L. *Humanism in the Renaissance of Islam*. Leiden: Brill, 1986; 2d rev. ed. Leiden: E.J. Brill, 1992.

Krauss, Samuel. "The Names Ashkenaz and Sepharad" (Hebrew). *Tarbiz* 3/4 (1932): 423–435.

Kugel, James L. *In Potiphar's House: The Interpretive Life of Biblical Texts*. Cambridge, Mass./ London: Harvard University Press, 1990, 1994.

Kühn, Thomas. "Shaping and Reshaping Colonial Ottomanism: Contesting Boundaries of Difference and Integration in Ottoman Yemen, 1872–1919." *Comparative Studies of South Asia, Africa and the Middle East* 27 (2007): 315–331.

Lachter, Hartley. "Spreading Secrets: Kabbalah and Esotericism in Isaac ibn Sahula's *Meshal ha-kadmoni*." JQR 100/1 (2010): 111–138.

Landauer, S. "Die Psychologie des Ibn Sīnā." ZDMG 29 (1876): 335–418.

Lane, Edward William. *An Arabic-English Lexicon*, in 8 parts. Ed. Stanley Lane-Poole. London: Williams and Norgate, 1893; repr. Beirut: Librairie du Liban, 1968; repr. Cambridge, U.K.: The Islamic Texts Society, 1984.

Lange, Christian. *Justice, Punishment and the Medieval Muslim Imagination*. Cambridge: Cambridge University Press, 2008.

Langer, Ruth. *Cursing the Christians? A History of the Birkat HaMinim*. New York: Oxford University Press 2012.

Langer, Ruth. *To Worship God Properly: Tensions between Liturgical Custom and Halakhah in Judaism*. Cincinnati: Hebrew Union College Press, 1998.

Langermann, Y. Tzvi. "Abraham Ibn Ezra." *The Stanford Encyclopedia of Philosophy*. http://plato.stanford.edu/archives/win2016/entries/ibn-ezra/

Langermann, Y. Tzvi. "Cultural Contacts of the Jews of Yemen." In *Contacts Between Cultures* vol. 1: West Asia and North Africa, ed. Amir Harrak, 281–285. Lewiston: Edwin Mellen Press, 1992.

Langermann, Y. Tzvi. *The Jews of Yemen and the Exact Sciences* (Hebrew). Jerusalem: Misgav Yerushalayim Institute for Research on the Sefardi and Oriental Heritage, 1987.

Langermann, Y. Tzvi. "Maḥshevet hodu be-qerev yehudei teiman: ha-sefer 'Mirʾāt al-Maʿānī'" ("Indian Thought among the Jews of Yemen: *Mirʾāt al-maʿānī*"), *Alei Sefer* 22 (2011): 19–27.

Langermann, Y. Tzvi. "Manuscript Moscow Guenzburg 1020: An Important New Yemeni Codex of Jewish Philosophy." JAOS 115/3 (1995): 373–387.

Langermann, Y. Tzvi. "'Mori Yusuf': Rabbi Yosef Kafah (Qāfiḥ) (1917–2000)." *Aleph* 1 (2001): 333–340.

Langermann, Y. Tzvi. "Rabbi Yosef Qafih's Modern Medieval Translation of the *Guide*." In *Maimonides' "Guide of the Perplexed" in Translation: A History from the Thir-*

teenth Century to the Twentieth, ed. Josef Stern et al., 257–278. Chicago: University of Chicago Press, 2019.

Langermann, Y. Tzvi. "Saving the Soul by Knowing the Soul: A Medieval Yemeni Interpretation of Song of Songs." *JJTP* 12/2 (2003): 147–166.

Langermann, Y. Tzvi. "*Sharḥ al-Dalāla*: A Commentary to Maimonides' *Guide* from Fourteenth-Century Yemen." In *Traditions of Maimonideanism*, ed. C. Fraenkel, 155–176. Leiden/Boston: Brill, 2009.

Langermann, Y. Tzvi. "Some Astrological Themes in the Thought of Abraham ibn Ezra." In *Rabbi Abraham ibn Ezra: Studies in the Writings of a Twelfth-Century Jewish Polymath*, ed. I. Twersky and J.M. Harris, 28–85. Cambridge, Mass.: Harvard University Press, 1993.

Langermann, Y. Tzvi. "The Yemeni Treatise Known as *Ḥafiṣah*" (Hebrew). In *From the Collections of the Institute of Microfilmed Hebrew Manuscripts*, ed. A. David, 53–57. Jerusalem: The Jewish National and University Library, 1995.

Langermann, Y. Tzvi. *Yemenite Midrash: Philosophical Commentaries on the Torah*. San Francisco: HarperCollins, 1996.

Langermann, Y. Tzvi. "Yemenite Philosophical Midrash as a Source for the Intellectual History of the Jews of Yemen." In *The Jews of Medieval Islam: Community, Society, and Identity*, ed. D. Frank, 335–347. Leiden: Brill, 1995.

Lasker, Daniel J. "The Jewish-Christian Debate in Transition: From the Lands of Ishmael to the Lands of Edom." In *Judaism and Islam: Boundaries, Communication and Interaction: Essays in Honor of William M. Brinner*, ed. B.H. Hary, J. Hayes, and F. Astren, 53–65. Leiden: Brill, 2000.

Lasker, Daniel J. "The Jewish Critique of Christianity under Islam in the Middle Ages." *PAAJR* 57 (1990–1991): 121–153.

Lasker, Daniel J. *Jewish Philosophical Polemics Against Christianity in the Middle Ages*. New York: Ktav, 1977; 2d ed. Oxford/Portland: Littman Library of Jewish Civilization, 2007.

Lasker, Daniel J. "Karaite Mourning of Zion as an Ascetic Movement," *Jewish Thought* 3 (2021): 35–48.

Lasker, Daniel J. "Proselyte Judaism, Christianity, and Islam in the Thought of Judah Halevi." *JQR* 81/1–2 (1990): 75–92.

Latham, J.D. "Ibn al-Muqaffaʿ and Early ʿAbbasid Prose." In *CHALABL*, 48–77.

Lavi, Abraham. "A Comparative Study of al-Hariri's Maqamat and their Hebrew Translation by al-Harizi." Ph.D. dissertation, University of Michigan, 1979.

Lavi, Abraham. "The Rationale of al-Ḥarīzī in Biblicizing the Maqāmāt of al-Ḥarīrī." *JQR* n.s. 74 (1984): 280–293.

Lavon, Yaakov, ed. and trans. *My Footsteps Echo: The Yemen Journal of Rabbi Yaakov Sapir*. Jerusalem: Mishnas Rishonim/Southfield Michigan: Targum, 1997.

Lawee, Eric. "Introducing Scripture: The *Accessus ad auctores* in Hebrew Exegetical

Literature from the Thirteenth through the Fifteenth Centuries." In *With Reverence for the Word: Medieval Scriptural Exegesis in Judaism, Christianity, and Islam*, ed. J.D. McAuliffe et al., 157–179. Oxford/New York: Oxford University Press, 2003.

Lazarus-Yafeh, Hava. "Étude sur la polémique islamo-chrétienne." *Revue des études islamiques* 37/2 (1969): 219–238.

Lazarus-Yafeh, Hava. *Intertwined Worlds: Medieval Islam and Bible Criticism*. Princeton: Princeton University Press, 1992.

Lazarus-Yafeh, Hava et al., eds. *The Majlis: Interreligious Encounters in Medieval Islam*. Wiesbaden: Harrassowitz, 1999.

Lazarus-Yafeh, Hava. "Taḥrīf." *EI*² online.

Leder, Stefan. "Authorship and Transmission in Unauthored Literature: The Akhbār Attributed to al-Haytham ibn ʿAdī." *Oriens* 31 (1998): 67–81.

Leder, Stefan. "Conventions of Fictional Narration in Learned Literature." In *Storytelling in the Framework of Non-fictional Arabic Literature*, 34–60.

Leder, Stefan, ed. *Storytelling in the Framework of Non-fictional Arabic Literature*. Wiesbaden: Harrassowitz, 1998.

Lehman, Marjorie. *The* En Yaaqov: *Jacob Ibn Habib's Search for Faith in the Talmudic Corpus*. Detroit: Wayne State University Press, 2012.

Lehmann, Matthias B. *Emissaries from the Holy Land: The Sephardic Diaspora and the Practice of Pan-Judaism in the Eighteenth Century*. Stanford: Stanford University Press, 2014.

Lehmann, Matthias B. *Ladino Rabbinic Literature and Ottoman Sephardic Culture*. Bloomington: Indiana University Press, 2005.

Lehmann, Matthias B. "Rabbinic Emissaries from Palestine and the Making of a Modern Jewish Diaspora: A Philanthropic Network in the Eighteenth Century." In *Envisioning Judaism: Studies in Honor of Peter Schafer on the Occasion of His Seventieth Birthday*, ed. R.S. Boustan et al., 2: 1229–1246. Tubingen: Mohr Siebeck, 2013.

Leicester, H. Marshall Jr. "The Art of Impersonation: A General Prologue to the Canterbury Tales," *PMLA* 95/2 (1980): 213–224.

Leicester, H. Marshall Jr. *The Disenchanted Self: Representing the Subject in the Canterbury Tales*. Berkeley: University of California Press, 1990.

Lepore, Jill. "Historians Who Love Too Much: Reflections on Microhistory and Biography." *The Journal of American History* 88 (June 2001): 129–144.

Lesley, Arthur. "Shingly in Cochin Jewish Memory." *The Journal of Indo-Judaic Studies* 1/3 (2000): 7–21.

Lev, Efraim. "Eastern Mediterranean Pharmacology and India Trade as a Background for Yemeni Medieval Medicinal Plants." In *Herbal Medicine in Yemen*, ed. Hehmeyer and Schönig, 21–42.

Levi, Avivit. *Holekh tamim: morashto, ḥayyav u-foʿalo shel ha-rav yosef qāfiḥ*. Jerusalem: Yad Mahari Qāfiḥ, 2003.

Levin, Israel. *Abraham Ibn Ezra: His Life and His Poetry* (Hebrew). Tel Aviv: Hakibbutz Hameuchad, 1970; 2d. ed. 1976.

Levin, Israel, ed. *Abraham Ibn Ezra Reader* (Hebrew). New York/Tel Aviv: Israel Matz Hebrew Classics, Ltd. and I. Edward Kiev Library Foundation, 1985.

Levin, Israel. "The Concept of Plagiarism in Mediaeval Hebrew Poetry in Spain" (Hebrew). In *Peles: Studies in Hebrew Literary Criticism*, ed. Nurit Govrin, 319–377. Tel Aviv: Makhon katz le-ḥeqer ha-sifrut ha-ʿivrit/ Tel Aviv University, 1980.

Levin, Israel. *The Embroidered Coat: The Genres of Hebrew Secular Poetry in Spain* (Hebrew). 3 vols. Ramat Gan: Tel Aviv University/ Hakibbutz Hameʾuchad, 1995.

Levin, Israel, ed. *Ḥay ben mekiṣ leʾavraham ibn ʿezra*. Tel Aviv: Makhon katz le-ḥeqer ha-sifrut haʿivrit, Tel-Aviv University, 1983.

Levin, Israel. "Le-ḥeqer ben mishle shel rabbi shemuʾel ha-nagid." *Tarbiz* 29/2 (1960): 146–161.

Levin, Israel. *The Lamentation Over the Dead: A Comparative Study of a Genre in Spanish-Hebrew and Arabic Poetry* (Hebrew). Ramat Gan: Tel Aviv University/ Hakibbutz Hameʾuchad, 1973.

Levin, Israel. " ʿAl ha-naqam veʿal ha-geʾulah be-shirei ha-qodesh shel avraham ibn ezra." In *Le-zikhro shel ḥayyim schirmann*, 20–35. Jerusalem: Ha-aqademiyah ha-leʾumit ha-yisraʾelit le-maddaʿim, 1983.

Levin, Israel. "Zeman ve-tevel be-shirat ha-ḥol ha-ʿivrit bisfarad." *Oṣar Yehudei Sefarad* 5 (1962): 68–79.

Levine, David, ed. and trans. *The Bustan al-ukul* (The Garden of Wisdom). New York: Columbia University Press, 1908; repr. AMS Press, 1966.

Levine, M. Herschel, trans. *Falaquera's Book of the Seeker*. (Part I only.) New York: Yeshiva University Press, 1976.

Levinson, Joshua and Orit Bashkin, eds. *Jews and Journeys: Travel and the Performance of Jewish Identity*. Philadelphia: University of Pennsylvania Press, 2021.

Levy, Avigdor. *The Sephardim in the Ottoman Empire*. Princeton: Princeton University Press, 1992.

Levy, Isabelle and David Torollo. "Romance Literature in Hebrew Language with an Arabic Twist: The First Story of Jacob Ben Elʿazar's *Sefer ha-Meshalim*." *La Corónica* 45/2 (2017): 279–304.

Levy, Lital. "The *Nahḍa* and the *Haskala*: A Comparative Reading of 'Revival' and 'Reform.'" *MEL* 16/3 (2013): 300–316.

Liebes, Yehuda. "Bar yoḥai be-shiro shel shimʿon lavi." *Keshet ha-ḥadashah* 5 (2003): 126–142.

Liebes, Yehuda. "Ha-mashiaḥ shel ha-zohar: lidmuto ha-meshiḥit shel rabbi shimʿon bar yoḥai." In *Ha-raʿayon ha-meshiḥi be-yisraʾel: yom ʿiyyun le-regel meloʾt shemonim shanah le-gershom shalom*, 87–236. Jerusalem: Israel Academy of Sciences and Humanities, 1982.

Liebes, Yehuda. "*Zemirot lise'udot shabbat she-yasad ha'ari ha-qadosh.*" *Molad* n.s. 4 (1972): 540–555.

Liebes, Yehuda. "How the Zohar Was Written." In *Studies in the Zohar*, ed. S. Nakache, Y. Liebes, et al., 85–138. Albany: SUNY Press, 1993.

Libson, Gideon. "Hidden Worlds and Open Shutters: S.D. Goitein Between Judaism and Islam." In *The Jewish Past Revisited: Reflections on Modern Jewish Historians*, ed. D.N. Myers and D.B. Ruderman, 163–198. New Haven: Yale University Press, 1998.

Libson, Gideon. "Shlomo Dov Goitein's Research into the Relationship between the Jewish and Muslim Traditions through the Prism of His Predecessors and Colleagues." In *Modern Jewish Scholarship on Islam in Context*, ed. Fraisse, 145–180.

Livne-Kafri, Ofer. "The Muslim Traditions 'in Praise of Jerusalem' (*Faḍā'il al-Quds*): Diversity and Complexity." *AION* (*Annali dell'Università degli Studi di Napoli*) 58 (1998): 165–192.

Lobel, Diana. *Between Mysticism and Philosophy: Sufi Language of Religious Experience in Judah Ha-Levi's Kuzari*. Albany: SUNY Press, 2000.

Lobel, Diana. *A Sufi-Jewish Dialogue: Philosophy and Mysticism in Bahya ibn Paquda's 'Duties of the Heart.'* Philadelphia: University of Pennsylvania Press, 2011.

Lockhart, L. "Hurmuz." *EI*^{2}. Brill Online.

Loeffler, James. "Do Zionists Read Music from Right to Left? Abraham Tsvi Idelsohn and the Invention of Israeli Music." *JQR* 100/3 (2010): 385–416.

Loewe, Raphael. *Hebrew Poems and Translations*. Haberman Institute, Israel, 2010.

Loewe, Raphael. "Lament for a Lost Leader." *Judaism* 18/3 (1969): 343–353.

Loewenthal, A. ed. *Sefer Musre Haphilosophim Aus dem Arabischen des Honein ibn Ishak ins Hebräische übersetzt von Jehuda ben Salomo Alcharisi*. Frankfurt a. M., 1896.

Losensky, Paul E. "'The Allusive Field of Drunkenness': Three Safavid-Moghul Responses to a Lyric by Bābā Fighānī." In *Reorientations/Arabic and Persian Poetry*, ed. S.P. Stetkevych, 227–262. Bloomington/Indianapolis: Indiana University Press, 1994.

Losensky, Paul E. *Welcoming Fighānī: Imitation and Poetic Individuality in the Safavid-Mughal Ghazal*. Costa Mesa, Calif.: Mazda Publishers, 1998.

Luqman, Ali Muhammad. "Education and the Press in South Arabia." In *The Arabian Peninsula: Society and Politics*, ed. D. Hopwood, 255–268. Totowa, NJ: Rowman and Littlefield, 1972; repr. Abingdon, Oxon/New York: Routledge, 2016.

Maccoby, Hyam. *Judaism on Trial: Jewish-Christian Disputations in the Middle Ages*. East Brunswick/London/Toronto: Associated University Presses, 1982.

Mackintosh-Smith, Tim, trans. Sayyid Jamāl al-Dīn 'Alī ibn 'Abdullāh Ibn al-Qāsim, *City of Divine and Earthly Joys: The Description of Ṣan'ā'*. The American Institute for Yemeni Studies, 2001.

Mackintosh-Smith, Tim, trans. Abū Zayd al-Sīrāfī, *Accounts of China and India*, Translator's Introduction, xvii–xxx. New York: New York University Press, 2017.

Madar, Vered. "Women's Oral Laments: Corpus and Text—The Body in the Text." In *Lament in Jewish Thought: Philosophical, Theological, and Literary Perspectives*, ed. I. Ferber and P. Schwebel, 65–86. Berlin/Boston: de Gruyter, 2014.

Madar, Zecharia and Yocheved Raiany. *Nutrition and Popular Remedy: Yemenite Tradition* (Hebrew). Tel Aviv: Ministry of Defence/E'eleh beTamar, 2004.

Madelung, Wilferd. "Abū Isḥāq al-Ṣābī on the Alids of Ṭabaristān and Gīlān." *JNES* 26 (1967): 17–21.

Madelung, Wilferd. "Madjlis." *EI*² online.

Madelung, Wilferd. "Zaydiyya." *EI*² 11:477–481.

Magid, Shaul. *From Metaphysics to Midrash: Myth, History, and the Interpretation of Scripture in Lurianic Kabbala*. Bloomington: Indiana University Press, 2008.

Magné, Bernard. "Transformations of Constraint." *Review of Contemporary Fiction* 13/1 (Spring 1993):111–123.

Makdisi, George. "Autograph Diary of an Eleventh-Century Historian of Baghdad." *BSOAS* 18 (1956): 9–31, 239–260; 19 (1957): 13–48, 281–303, 426–443.

Malachi, Zvi. "'Toledot yedutun' le-nissim ibn sanchi, ḥibbur allegori me-hame'ah ha-16," *Mahut* 15 (1995): 7–41.

Malekandathil, Pius. *Maritime India: Trade, Religion and Polity in the Indian Ocean*. Revised Edition. Delhi: Primus Books, 2013.

Malekandathil, Pius. *Maritime Malabar: Trade, Culture, and Power*. New Delhi: Primus Books, 2022.

Malkiel, David. "Christian Hebraism in a Contemporary Key: The Search for Hebrew Epitaph Poetry in Seventeenth-Century Italy." *JQR* 96/1 (2006): 123–146.

Malkiel, David. "Poems on Tombstone Inscriptions in Northern Italy in the Sixteenth and Seventeenth Centuries" (Hebrew). *Pe'amim* 98–99 (2004): 121–154.

Malkiel, David. *Reconstructing Ashkenaz: The Human Face of Franco-German Jewry, 1000–1250*. Stanford: Stanford University Press, 2009.

Malkiel, David. "The Shadar-Host Economy: New Perspectives on the Travels of Emissaries from the Holy Land." *Journal of Modern Jewish Studies*, 15:3 (2016): 402–418.

Malkiel, David. *Stones Speak—Hebrew Tombstones from Padua, 1529–1862*. Leiden/Boston: Brill, 2014.

Malkiel, David. *Strangers in Yemen: Travel and Cultural Encounter among Jews, Christians and Muslims in the Colonial Era*. Berlin/Boston: de Gruyter, 2021.

Mallette, Karla. "The Hazards of Narration: Frame-Tale Technologies and the 'Oriental Tale.'" In *The Oxford Handbook of Chaucer*. Edited by Suzanne Akbari and James Simpson, 184–196. Oxford/New York: Oxford University Press, 2020.

Malti-Douglas, Fedwa. "Classical Arabic Crime Narratives: Thieves and Thievery in Adab Literature." *JAL* 19/2 (1988): 108–127.

Malter, Henry. "Personifications of Soul and Body: A Study in Judaeo-Arabic Literature." *JQR* n.s. 2 (1912): 453–479.

Mandelbaum, David G. "The Jewish Way of Life in Cochin." *Jewish Social Studies* 1/4 (1939): 423–460.

Mandelbaum, David G. "Social Stratification Among the Jews of Cochin in India and in Israel." *The Jewish Journal of Sociology* 17/2 (1975): 165–210.

Mann, Jacob. *Jews in Egypt and Palestine Under the Fāṭimid Caliphs*. New York: Ktav, 1970.

Mann, Jacob. *Texts and Studies in Jewish History and Literature*. 2 vols. New York: Ktav Publishing House, 1972.

Mansur, Otniel. *Shiṭato ha-parshanit shel rabbi yiḥye al-ḍāhirī ʿal pi perusho ṣeidah la-derekh*. Qiryat Ono: Mekhon Mishnat ha-Rambam, 2020. Front matter: https://net-sah.org/product/45004

Mansur, Otniel. "Rabbi yiḥye al-ḍāhirī: ha-ḥuṭ ha-meqashsher bein tequfot ha-filosofiya ve-ha-qabbalah be-teiman." *Tema* 16 (2019): 125–141.

Manṣura, Saadya ben Yehudah. *Sefer ha-galut ve-ha-geʾulah*. Edited by A. Yaari and Y. Ratzaby. Tel Aviv: Maḥbarot le-sifrut, 1955.

Maravall, José Antonio. *Culture of the Baroque: Analysis of a Historical Structure*. Trans. Terry Cochran. Minneapolis: University of Minnesota Press, 1986.

Marcus, Ivan G. "Beyond the Sephardic Mystique." *Orim* 1 (1985): 35–38.

Marcus, Simon. "Romaniots." *EJ*[2] 17:402–403.

Marcus, Simon et al. "Bulgaria" *EJ*[2] 4:267–275.

Margariti, Roxani E. *Aden & The Indian Ocean Trade: 150 Years in the Life of a Medieval Arabian Port*. Chapel Hill: University of North Carolina Press, 2007.

Margariti, Roxani E. "*Aṣḥābunā l-tujjār*: Our Associates, the Merchants: Non-Jewish Business Partners of the Cairo Geniza's India Traders." In *Jews, Christians and Muslims in Medieval and Early Modern Times: A Festschrift in Honor of Mark R. Cohen*, ed. A. Franklin et al., 40–58. Leiden/ Boston: Brill, 2014.

Margoliouth D.S. and C. Pellat. "al-Ḥarīrī." *EI*[2] online.

Margoliouth, G. *Catalogue of the Hebrew and Samaritan Manuscripts in the British Museum*. 4 vols. London: Department of Oriental Printed Books and Manuscripts, British Museum, 1899–1935.

Marks, Richard G. "Hinduism, Torah, and Travel: Jacob Sapir in India." *Shofar* 30 (2012): 26–51.

Marks, Richard G. "Hindus and Hinduism in Medieval Jewish Literature." In *Indo-Judaic Studies in the Twenty-First Century: A View from the Margin*, ed. N. Katz, R. Chakravarti, B. Sinha and S. Weil, 57–73. New York: Palgrave Macmillan, 2007.

Marx, Alexander. "A New Collection of Mss: A Recent Acquisition of the Library of the Jewish Theological Seminary." *PAAJR* 4 (1932–1933): 135–167.

Marzolph, Ulrich. *Arabia Ridens: Die humoristiche Kurzprosa der frühen adab-Literatur im internationalen Traditionsgeflecht*. Frankfurt am Main: Vittorio Klostermann, 1992.

Marzolph, Ulrich and Richard van Leeuwen, eds. *The Arabian Nights Encyclopedia*. Santa Barbara: ABC-CLIO, 2004.

Masarwa, Alev. *Praising Damascus: City Panegyrics as a Literary Genre and a Concept of Urbanity*. Wissenschaftliche Schriften der WWU Münster, Reihe XII, Band 35. Hildesheim: Georg Olms Verlag, 2022.

Mazuz, Haggai. "Aspects of Polemics with Islam in the Seventh Maqāma of R. Zachariah al-Ḍāhirī's Sefer ha-Mūsar" (in Hebrew). *Tema* 15 (2018): 67–80.

Mazuz, Haggai. "Tracing Possible Jewish Influence on a Common Islamic Commentary on Deuteronomy 33:2." *JJS* 67/2 (2016): 291–304.

Medina, Shalom. "Sefer hamusar, mahadurat ratzaby." *Afikim* 1/7 (1965): 8; *Afikim* 2/8–9 (1966): 11; *Afikim* 2/11–12 (1966): 9.

Medina, Shalom. "Ṣeidah la-derekh le'alḍāhirī." *Afikim* 22 (1968): 7, 10.

Meier, Astrid. "Perceptions of a New Era? Historical Writing in Early Ottoman Damascus." *Arabica* 51 (2004): 419–434.

Meisami, Julie Scott. *The Sea of Precious Virtues (Bahr al-Farā'id): A Medieval Islamic Mirror for Princes*. Salt Lake City: University of Utah Press, 1991.

Meisami, Julie Scott and Paul Starkey, eds. *Encyclopedia of Arabic Literature*. London/New York: Routledge, 1998.

Melamed, Abraham. *The Image of the Black in Jewish Culture: A History of the Other*. Trans. Betty Sigler Rozen. London/New York: RoutledgeCurzon, 2003.

Melamed, Abraham. "The Image of India in Medieval Jewish Culture: Between Adoration and Rejection." *Jewish History* 20/3–4 (2006): 299–314.

Melammed, Renée Levine and Uri Melammed. "Rabbi Asnat: A Female Yeshiva Director in Kurdistan" (Hebrew). *Pe'amim* 82 (2000): 13–78.

"Meratayyim." *Enṣiqlopedia miqra'it* 2nd rev. ed. 5:480. Jerusalem: Mosad Bialik, 1978. https://www.en.kotar.co.il/KotarApp/Viewer.aspx?nBookID=96075193#282.3776.8.fitwidth

Meri, Josef W. *The Cult of Saints Among Muslims and Jews in Medieval Syria*. Oxford/New York: Oxford University Press, 2002.

Meroz, Ronit. "Ḥavurat rabbi mosheh ben makhir ve-taqqanotehah." *Pe'amim* 31 (1987): 40–61.

Meroz, Ronit. "Spiritual Life in 16th Century Safed" (Hebrew). *Ariel* 157–158 (2002): 82–90.

Messick, Brinkley. *The Calligraphic State: Textual Domination and History in a Muslim Society*. Berkeley/ Los Angeles/ London: University of California Press, 1993.

Mezciems, Jenny. "'Tis not to divert the Reader': Moral and Literary Determinants in some Early Travel Narratives." *Prose Studies* 5/1 (1982): 1–19.

Mirsky, Aharon. "New Poems of R. Israel Nagara" (Hebrew). *Sefunot* 6 (1962): 259–302.

Mondschein, Aaron. "'Iyyunim baḥaruzot ha-petiḥah shel R. Avraham ibn Ezra le-ferusho ha'arokh le-sefer Shemot." *Shenaton le-ḥeqer ha-miqra ve-hamizraḥ ha-qadum* 21 (2012): 219–253.

Monroe, James T. *The Art of Badīʿ az-Zamān al-Hamadhānī as Picaresque Narrative*. Beirut: American University of Beirut, 1983.

Monroe, James T, ed. and trans. *Al-maqāmāt al-Luzūmīyah by Abū l-Ṭāhir Muḥammad ibn Yūsuf al-Tamīmī al-Saraqusṭī ibn al-Ashtarkūwī (d. 538/1143)*. Leiden/Boston/Köln: E.J. Brill, 2002.

Morag, Shelomo. *Mesorot ha-lashon haʿivrit ve-ha-lashon ha'aramit she-be-fi yehudei teiman*. Edited by Yosef Tobi. Tel Aviv: Afikim, 2001.

Morag, Shelomo. "A.Z. Idelsohn and the Study of the Traditional Pronunciations of Hebrew" (in Hebrew). In *The Abraham Zvi Idelsohn Memorial Volume* (= *Yuval* 5), ed. Israel Adler, Batya Bayer, and Eliyahu Schleifer, 160–168. Jerusalem: Magnes, 1986.

Moreh, Shmuel. *Live Theatre and Dramatic Literature in the Medieval Arabic World*. New York: New York University Press, 1992.

Morell, Samuel. "Ibn Abi Zimra, David (Radbaz)." *EJIW*. Brill Online.

Mourad, Suleiman A. "The *Faḍā'il* of Jerusalem Books as Anthologies." In *Approaches to the Study of Pre-modern Arabic Anthologies*, ed. Orfali and El Cheikh, 267–277.

Mourad, Suleiman A. "Jerusalem in Early Islam: The Making of the Muslims' Holy City." In *Routledge Handbook on Jerusalem*, ed. S.A. Mourad et al., 77–89. London/NY: Routledge, 2019.

Muchawsky-Schnapper, Ester. "Healing through Medicinal Plants: Old Yemenite Therapeutic Traditions and Their Application in Jerusalem Today." In *Herbal Medicine in Yemen*, ed. Hehmeyer and Schönig, 127–142.

Muchawsky-Schnapper, Ester. "Symbolic Decorations for a Woman after Childbirth in Sanʿa." *The Israel Museum Journal* 7 (1988): 61–74.

Münz-Manor, Ophir. "Imagined Journeys: Travel Narratives in Judah Alharizi's *Tahkemoni* and Zachariah Aldahiri's *Sefer Hamusar*." *JSQ* 26/1 (2019): 43–58.

Münz-Manor, Ophir. "Studies in Figurative Language of Pre-Classical *Piyyut*" (Hebrew). Ph.D. dissertation, Hebrew University, 2006.

Myers, David N. "Is There Still a 'Jerusalem School?' Reflections on the State of Jewish Historical Scholarship in Israel." *Jewish History* 23/ 4 (2009): 389–406.

Myers, David N. *Re-inventing the Jewish Past: European Jewish Intellectuals and the Zionist Return to History*. New York/ Oxford: Oxford University Press, 1995.

Myers, David N. "Was There a 'Jerusalem School'? An Inquiry into the First Generation of Historical Researchers at the Hebrew University." *Studies in Contemporary Jewry* 10 (1994): 66–92.

Naḥum, Yehuda Levi. "Tefillah le-rabbi zekhariah al-ḍahiri vidiʿot ḥadashot le-toledot mishpaḥto." In *Miyṣirot sifrutiyot mi-teiman*, ed. Tobi, 184–188.

Naḥum, Yehuda Levi. *Ḥasifat genuzim mi-teiman*. Holon: Mifʿal ḥasifat teiman, 1971.

Netton, Ian R. "Basic Structures and Signs of Alienation in the Rihla of Ibn Jubayr." In idem, ed., *Golden Roads*, 57–74.

Netton, Ian R. "Ibn Baṭṭuṭa in Wanderland: Voyage as Text—Was Ibn Baṭṭuṭa an Orientalist?" In *Orientalism Revisited: Art, Land, and Voyage*, ed. I.R. Netton, 223–251. London and New York: Routledge, 2013.

Netton, Ian R, ed. *Golden Roads: Migration, Pilgrimage and Travel in Mediaeval and Modern Islam*. London: Curzon Press, 1993.

Netton, Ian R. "*Riḥla*." EI² 8:328.

Netton, Ian R. *Seek Knowledge: Thought and Travel in the House of Islam*. Richmond: Curzon Press, 1996.

Netzer, Amnon. "The Fate of the Jewish Community of Tabriz." In *Studies in Islamic History and Civilization in Honour of Professor David Ayalon*, ed. M. Sharon, 411–419. Jerusalem: Cana; Leiden: E.J. Brill, 1986.

Neubauer, Adolph. *Catalogue of the Hebrew Manuscripts in the Bodleian Library*. 2 vols. Oxford: Clarendon Press, 1886–1906.

Neubauer, Adolph. "The Literature of the Jews of Yemen." *JQR* o.s. 3 (1891): 604–622.

Neubauer, Adolph. Review of Abraham Epstein, *Eldad ha-Dani seine Berichte über die zehn Stämme und deren Ritus in verschiedenen Versionen*, etc. (Pressburg, 1891). *JQR* o.s. 3 (1891): 541–544.

Nicholson, R.A. *A Literary History of the Arabs*². Cambridge: Cambridge University Press, 1930.

Nini, Yehuda and Maya Fruchtman, eds. *Rabbi Shem Tov Ben Izḥak Ardutiel or Don Santo De-Carrion, Maʿase-Harab* (*The Debate Between the Pen and the Scissors*). Ramat-Gan: Tel Aviv University, 1980.

Norris, H. "Shuʿūbiyya in Arabic Literature." In *CHALABL*, 31–47.

Noy, Dov. "The Folk Tale" (Hebrew). In *Yemen*, ed. Saadoun, 95–99.

Obermann, Julian. "Two Elijah Stories in Judeo-Arabic Transmission." *HUCA* 23/1 (1950–1951): 387–404.

O'Doherty, Marianne. *The Indies and the Medieval West: Thought, Report, Imagination*. Turnhout: Brepols, 2013.

Oettinger, Ayelet and Danny Bar-Maoz, eds. *Mittuv Yosef: Yosef Tobi Jubilee Volume*. 3 vols. Haifa: University of Haifa Press, 2011.

Offenberg, Adri K. "The Printing History of the Constantinople Hebrew Incunable of 1493: A Mediterranean Voyage of Discovery." *The British Library Journal* 22/2 (1996): 221–235.

Orfali, Bilal W. *The Anthologist's Art: Abū Manṣūr al-Thaʿālibī and His Yatīmat al-dahr*. Leiden/Boston: Brill, 2016.

Orfali, Bilal W. and Maurice A. Pomerantz. "The Art of the *Muqaddima* in the Works of Abū Manṣūr al-Thaʿalibī (d. 429/1039)." In *The Weaving of Words*, ed. Behzadi and Behmardi, 181–202.

Orfali, Bilal W. and Maurice A. Pomerantz. "Assembling an Author: On the Making of al-Hamadhānī's *Maqāmāt*." In *Concepts of Authorship in Pre-Modern Arabic Texts*, ed. Behzadi and Hämeen-Antilla, 107–128.

Orfali, Bilal W. and Maurice A. Pomerantz. "A Lost *Maqāma* of Badīʿ al-Zamān al-Hamadhānī?" *Arabica* 60 (2013): 245–271.

Orfali, Bilal W. and Maurice A. Pomerantz. *"Maqāmāt badīʿ al-zamān al-hamadhānī: al-naṣṣ wa'l-makhṭuṭāt wa'l-tārikh."* *Ostour* 1 (2015): 38–55.

Orfali, Bilal W. and Maurice A. Pomerantz. *The Maqāmāt of Badīʿ al-Zamān al-Hamadhānī: Authorship, Texts, and Contexts*. Wiesbaden: Reichert Verlag, 2022.

Orfali, Bilal W. "A Sketch Map of Arabic Poetry Anthologies Up to the Fall of Baghdad." *JAL* 43 (2012): 29–59.

Orfali, Bilal W. and Maurice A. Pomerantz. "Three *Maqāmāt* Attributed to Badīʿ al-Zamān al-Hamadhānī (d. 398/1008)." *JAS* 2 (2015): 38–60.

Orfali, Bilal W. and Nadia M. El Cheikh, eds. *Approaches to the Study of Pre-modern Arabic Anthologies*. Leiden/Boston: Brill, 2021.

Ossorio, Aurora Salvatierra. "Shem Tov Ibn Falaquera: From Logic to Ethics; a Redefinition of Poetry in the Thirteenth Century." *Comparative Literature Studies* 45/2 (2008): 165–181.

Ostle, Robin. "Introduction: Persons and Passions." In *Sensibilities of the Islamic Mediterranean*, ed. R. Ostle, 1–9.

Ostle, Robin, ed. *Sensibilities of the Mediterranean: Self-Expression in a Muslim Culture from Post-Classical Times to the Present Day*. London: I.B. Taurus, 2008.

Ouyang, Wen-Chin. Preface to "Utopias, Dystopias and Heterotopias: The Spatiality of Human Experience and Literary Expression." *MEL* 15/3 (December 2012): 227–231.

Ozbaran, Salih. "A Turkish Report on the Red Sea and the Portuguese in the Indian Ocean (1525)." *Arabian Studies* 4 (1978): 81–88.

Pachter, Mordechai. "Kabbalistic Ethical Literature in Sixteenth-Century Safed" (Hebrew). In *Culture and History: Ino Sciaky Memorial Volume*, ed. J. Dan, Jerusalem: Misgav Yerushalayim, 1987. English translation/adaptation in *Binah: Jewish Intellectual History in the Middle Ages*, 3:159–178. Westport, CT and London, 1994.

Pachter, Mordechai. "The Life and Personality of R. Elazar Azikri According to His Mystical Diary" (Hebrew). *Shalem* 3 (1981): 127–147.

Padva, Varda. "The Voice of the Dead in the Elegy" (Hebrew). *Jerusalem Studies in Hebrew Literature* 10–11 (Part 2) (1987–1988): 629–659.

Pagis, Dan. *Change and Tradition in the Secular Poetry: Spain and Italy* (Hebrew). Jerusalem: Keter Publishing House, 1976.

Pagis, Dan. *Hebrew Poetry of the Middle Ages and the Renaissance*. Berkeley and Los Angeles: University of California Press, 1991.

Pagis, Dan. "ʿAl mussag ha-meqoriyut ba-shirah haʿivrit mi-tequfat sefarad." *PAAJR* 37 (1969), Hebrew Section, 31–51.

Pagis, Dan. *Poetry Aptly Explained* (Hebrew). Jerusalem: Magnes, 1993.

Pagis, Dan. "The Poet as Prophet in Medieval Hebrew Literature." In *Poetry and*

Prophecy: The Beginnings of a Literary Tradition, ed. J.L. Kugel, 140–150. Ithaca & London: Cornell University Press, 1990.

Pagis, Dan. *Secular Poetry and Poetic Theory: Moses Ibn Ezra and His Contemporaries* (Hebrew). Jerusalem: Bialik Institute, 1970.

Pagis, Dan. "Variety in Medieval Rhymed Narratives." *Scripta Hierosolymitana* 27 (1978): 79–98.

Pagis, Dan. "Yesodot baroqiyim ba-shirah haʿivrit beʾitalya ʿal pi sug sifruti bilti yaduʿa." In *Poetry Aptly Explained*, 256–270. Jerusalem: Magnes, 1993.

Palmer, Philip S. "Paratextual Readers: Manuscript Verse in Printed Books of the Long Eighteenth Century." In *After Print: Eighteenth-Century Manuscript Cultures*, ed. R.S. King, 123–147. Charlottesville: University of Virginia Press, 2020.

Panofsky, Erwin. *Tomb Sculpture: Four Lectures on Its Changing Aspects From Ancient Egypt to Bernini*. New York: H.N. Abrams, 1924; repr. 1992.

Partington, Gill. "Noted Incunables: The Painstaking Labour of Producing a Renaissance Book." Review of John Boardley, *Typographic Firsts: Adventures in Early Printing*. https://www.the-tls.co.uk/articles/noted-incunables/

Paz, Yair. "Holy Inhabitants of a Holy City: How Safed Became One of the Four Holy Cities of Eretz Israel in the 16th Century." In *A Holy People: Jewish and Christian Perspectives on Religious Communal Identity*, ed. M. Poorthuis and J. Schwartz, 237–260. Leiden/Boston: Brill, 2006.

Peled, Mattitiahu. "On the Concept of Literary Influence in Classical Arabic Criticism." *IOS* 11 (1991): 37–46.

Pellat, Charles. "Fahrasa." *EI*² 2:743–744.

Pellat, Charles. "Marthiya." *EI*² online.

Pellat, Charles. "Variations sur le thème de l'adab" *Correspondance d'orient* 5–6 (1964): 19–37. Repr. in Charles Pellat, *Études sur l'histoire socio-culturelle de l'Islam*. London: Variorum Reprints, 1976.

Perec, Georges. "History of the Lipogram." In *Oulipo: A Primer of Potential Literature*, trans. and ed. Warren F. Motte Jr., 97–108. Lincoln and London: University of Nebraska Press, 1986.

Perlmann, Moshe. "The Medieval Polemics Between Judaism and Islam." In *Religion in a Religious Age*, ed. S.D. Goitein, 103–138.

Peters, Edward M. "Prison Before the Prison: The Ancient and Medieval Worlds." In *The Oxford History of the Prison*, ed. N. Morris and D. Rothman, 3–47. Oxford University Press, 1995.

Petrarch, Francis. "Letter to Posterity." In *Petrarch: A Humanist Among Princes*, ed. D. Thompson, 1–13. New York: Harper & Row, 1971.

Petrucci, Armando. *Writing the Dead: Death and Writing Strategies in the Western Tradition*. Trans. Michael Sullivan. Stanford University Press, 1998.

Petuchowski, J.J. *Theology and Poetry: Studies in the Medieval Piyyut*. London: Routledge and Kegan Paul, 1978.

Piamenta, Moshe. *Dictionary of Post-Classical Yemeni Arabic*. 2 vols. Leiden/New York/Köln: E.J. Brill, 1990.

Piattelli, Angelo M. "New Documents Concerning Bomberg's Printing of the Talmud." In *Meḥevah li-Menaḥem: Studies in Honor of Menahem Hayyim Schmelzer*, ed. S. Glick et al., English section 171–199. Jerusalem, 2019.

Pinault, David. *Story-Telling Techniques in the Arabian Nights*. Leiden/New York/Köln: E.J. Brill, 1992.

Pines, Shelomo, trans. *Moses Maimonides: The Guide of the Perplexed*. 2 vols. Chicago and London: University of Chicago Press, 1963.

Pines, Shelomo, trans. "Shīʿite Terms and Conceptions in Judah Halevi's *Kuzari*." JSAI 2 (1980): 165–251.

Pinsker, Simḥah. *Lickute Kadmoniot*. Vienna, 1860; repr. Jerusalem, 1968.

Pollock, Sheldon. *Forms of Knowledge in Early Modern Asia: Explorations in the Intellectual History of India and Tibet 1500–1800*. Durham, N.C.: Duke University Press, 2011.

Pomerantz, Maurice. "An Epic Hero in the *Maqāmāt*? Popular and Elite Literature in the 8th/14th Century." *Annales Islamologiques* 49 (2016): 1–16.

Pomerantz, Maurice. "A *Maqāmah* on the Book Market of Cairo in the 8th/14th Century: The 'Return of the Stranger' of Ibn Abī Ḥağalah (d. 776/1375)." In *Arabische Literatur und Rhetorik—Elfhundert bis Achtzehnhundert*, ed. T. Bauer and S. von Hees, 3: 179–208. Baden-Baden: Ergon Verlag, 2017.

Pomerantz, Maurice. "A Maqāma Collection by a Mamlūk Historian: Al-Maqāmāt Al-Ğalāliyya by Al-Ḥasan b. Abī Muḥammad Al-Ṣafadī." *Arabica* 61 (2014): 631–663.

Pomerantz, Maurice. "The Play of Genre: A *Maqāma* of 'Ease after Hardship' from the Eighth/Fourteenth Century and Its Literary Context." In *The Heritage of Arabo-Islamic Learning*, ed. Pomerantz and Shahin, 461–482.

Pomerantz, Maurice. "Tales from the Crypt: On Some Uncharted Voyages of Sindbad the Sailor." *Narrative Culture* 2.2 (2015): 250–269.

Pomerantz, Maurice and Aram A. Shahin, eds. *The Heritage of Arabo-Islamic Learning: Studies Presented to Wadad Kadi*. Leiden/Boston: Brill, 2016.

Pormann, Peter E. "The Physician and the Other: Images of the Charlatan in Medieval Islam." *Bulletin of the History of Medicine* 79/2 (2005): 189–227.

Pormann, Peter E. and Emilie Savage-Smith. *Medieval Islamic Medicine*. The American University in Cairo Press, 2007.

Potter, Joy H. "The Function of Framing in the *Decameron*." In idem, *Five Frames for the Decameron: Communication and Social Systems in the Cornice*, 120–151. Princeton University Press, 1982.

Qāfiḥ, Aharon. "ʿIyyunim be-fisqei ha-rav yiḥye qafiḥ." In *Mittuv Yosef*, ed. Oettinger and Bar-Maoz, 2:125–143.

Qāfiḥ, Yiḥye. *Milḥamot hashem*. Jerusalem, 1931.

Qāfiḥ, Yosef. "Arbaʿim sheʾelot u-teshuvot ba-filosofiah le-rav peraḥia b. meshullam." In *Rabbi Yosef Qafih: Collected Papers*, ed. Y. Tobi, 1:131–212. Jerusalem, 1989.

Qāfiḥ, Yosef. *Halikhot teiman: ḥayye ha-yehudim be ṣanaʿa uvenotehah*. 5th revised ed. Jerusalem: Yad Izhak Ben-Zvi and the Hebrew University of Jerusalem, 2002.

Qāfiḥ, Yosef. "Horaʾat ha-talmud be-teiman." In *Ha-rav yosef qāfiḥ: ketavim*, ed. Y. Tobi, 2:947–949. Jerusalem, 1989.

Qāfiḥ, Yosef. "Qehillat ṣanaʿa she-be-teiman." In *Ha-rav yosef qāfiḥ: ketavim*, ed. Y. Tobi, 2:861–871; reprinted from *Maḥanayim* 119 (1968):36–45.

Qāfiḥ, Yosef, ed. and trans. *Midrash ha-beʾur ʿal ḥamishah ḥumshei torah ... ḥibro Saʿadya ben David ha-mekhunneh Aldhamārī*. Qiryat Ono: Makhon mishnat ha-rambam, 1998–1999.

Qāfiḥ, Yosef, ed. and trans. *Nethanel ibn Fayyūmī, Bustan al-ʿuqūl* (*Gan ha-sekhalim*). Jerusalem, 1984.

Qāfiḥ, Yosef, ed. and trans. *Nethanel ben Yeshaʿya, Nur al-ẓalām* (*Maʾor haʾafelah*). Jerusalem, 1957.

Qāfiḥ, Yosef, ed. "*Qorot yisrael be-teiman* le-rabbi ḥayyim ḥabshush." *Sefunot*, 2 (1958): 246–286.

Qāfiḥ, Yosef, ed. and trans. *Ha-rif le-masekhet ḥulin, ʿim perush ba-safah haʿaravit leʾeḥad me-ḥakhmei yahadut teiman* etc. Jerusalem: ha-Agudah le-haṣalat ginze teman, 1960.

Qāfiḥ, Yosef. "The Ties of Yemenite Jewry with the Jewish Centers" (Hebrew). In *Yahadut teiman*, ed. Yishaʿyahu and Tobi, 29–46. Jerusalem: Yad Izhak Ben-Zvi, 1975.

Qoraḥ, Amram. *Saʿarat teiman*, ed. Shimon Greidi. 2nd rev. ed. Jerusalem, 1987.

Quinn, Josephine C. *In Search of the Phoenicians*. Princeton: Princeton University Press, 2018.

Rahman, Fazlur, ed. *Avicenna's De Anima* (*Arabic Text*), *Being the Psychological Part of Kitāb al-Shifāʾ*. London: Oxford University Press, 1959.

Rahman, Fazlur, ed. and trans. *Avicenna's Psychology: An English Translation of* Kitāb al-Najāt, *Book II, Chapter VI*. London: Oxford University Press, 1952.

Rand, Michael. *The Evolution of al-Ḥarizi's Taḥkemoni*. Leiden/Boston: Brill, 2018.

Rand, Michael. "*Shalom rav veyesha yiqrav*—Yehuda ha-Levi's Epistle to Moshe ibn Ezra: A New Edition and Commentary." *HUCA* 89 (2018): 197–220.

Rand, Michael. *Studies in the Medieval Hebrew Tradition of the Ḥarīrian and Ḥarizian Maqama: Maḥberot Eitan ha-Ezraḥi*. Leiden/Boston: Brill, 2021.

Rappel, Dov. *Ha-vikkuaḥ ʿal ha-pilpul*. Jerusalem/Tel Aviv: Dvir, 1979.

Rasaby, Isaac, ed. *Sefer rekhev elohim le-rabbi yiṣḥaq wanneh*. Bnai Brak, 1992.

Ratzaby, Yehuda. "Adab Maxims in Medieval Literature" (Hebrew). *Otsar yehudei sefarad* 4 (1961): 114–122.

Ratzaby, Yehuda. "Agudat ezov: ḥibbur bilti nodaʿ." *Areshet* 4 (1966): 202–212.

Ratzaby, Yehuda. *Bemʿagloth Temān*. Tel Aviv: By the Author, 1987.

Ratzaby, Yehuda, ed. *Bo'i Teman*. Tel Aviv: Afikim, 1967.

Ratzaby, Yehuda. "*Darde'im: minhagim u-massorot.*" *'Edot* 1 (1946): 165–180.

Ratzaby, Yehuda. "David ben yeshaʿ ha-levi, meshorer teimani ben ha-me'ah ha-shesh ʿesreh." *Yedaʿ ʿam* 15 (1971): 67–74.

Ratzaby, Yehuda. "An Historical Poem by Rabbi Saʿadia Manṣura" (Hebrew). *Peʿamim* 64 (1995): 6–21.

Ratzaby, Yehuda. "The Influence of al-Ḥariri Upon Alḍāhiri" (Hebrew), *Biqqoret u-farshanut* 11–12 (1978): 55–83.

Ratzaby, Yehuda. "ʿInyanei dat ba-pulmus bein muslimim li-yehudim be-teiman." *Yedaʿ ʿam* 14 (1970): 12–21.

Ratzaby, Yehuda. "ʿInyanei yehudim be-teiman beʿarkha'ot shel goyim." In *Ḥiqrei ʿever va-ʿarav: mugashim li-yehoshuʿa blau ʿal yede ḥaverav bi-melot lo shivʿim*, ed. H. Ben-Shammai, 515–536. Tel Aviv/Jerusalem, 1993.

Ratzaby, Yehuda. "ʿIyyunim be-hitpatḥut maḥzor-teiman." *ʿAlei sefer* 9 (1981): 99–114.

Ratzaby, Yehuda. "Lekha dodi shel ha-mequbbal rabbi shelomo alqabeṣ u-meqorotav." *Maḥanayim* 6 (1994): 162–169.

Ratzaby, Yehuda. "Le-toldot ha-maḥloqet ʿal ha-qabbalah bikhillat ṣanaʿa." *Peʿamim* 88 (2001): 98–123.

Ratzaby, Yehuda. "Limqorot ben mishlei u-ven qohelet." *Tarbiz* 25/3 (1956): 301–322.

Ratzaby, Yehuda. "Me'oṣar ha-piyyut ve-ha-shirah." *Sinai* 28 (1951): 170–180.

Ratzaby, Yehuda. "Motivim ʿaraviyyim ba-qinah haʿivrit ha-sefaradit." *Jerusalem Studies in Hebrew Literature* 10–11 (1987–1988): 737–765.

Ratzaby, Yehuda. *Oṣar leshon ha-qodesh she-livnei teiman*. Tel Aviv: By the Author, 1978.

Ratzaby, Yehuda. "Piyyutei teiman: bibliografiyah." *KS* 22 (1946): 247–261.

Ratzaby, Yehuda. "Rabbi yosef karo vihudei teiman." *Oṣar yehudei sefarad* 2 (1959): 84–88.

Ratzaby, Yehuda. "Shadarim u-minhagei teiman." *Yedaʿ ʿam* 3 (1955): 32–36.

Ratzaby, Yehuda. "Sheloshah shirim meturgamim meʿito shel rabbi zekharya al-ḍāhirī." *Tehuda* 18 (1998): 80–82.

Ratzaby, Yehuda. *Shirat Temān Haʿivrit*. Tel Aviv: ʿAm ʿoved, 1988.

Ratzaby, Yehuda. "Sifrut yehudei teiman (bibliographiyah)." *KS* 28 (1952/3): 255–278 and 394–409.

Ratzaby, Yehuda. "On the Sources of *Sefer Taḥkemoni*" (Hebrew). *Tarbiz* 26 (1957): 424–439.

Ratzaby, Yehuda. "Ṣura ve-laḥan be-shirat teiman le-sugeha." *Taṣlil* 8 (1968): 15–22.

Ratzaby, Yehuda. "Ha-talmud viyhudei teiman." *Maḥanayyim* 57 (1961): 124–129; repr. with minor bibliographical updates in *Bemʿagloth Temān*, 104–109.

Ratzaby, Yehuda. "Terufah hitulit u-musarit." *Haaretz*, 5 October 1965, p. 9.

Ratzaby, Yehuda. *Toratan she-livnei teiman: meḥabberim ve-ḥibburim*. Kiriat Ono: Mekhon Moshe, 1995.

Ratzaby, Yehuda. "Wanneh, Isaac ben Abraham." *EJ*² 20:617.

Ratzaby, Yehuda. *Yalqut ha-maqāma haʿivrit*. Jerusalem: Bialik Institute, 1974.

Ratzaby, Yehuda. "Zechariah Al-Ḍāhiri." *EJ*² 16:959.

Ratzaby, Yehuda and Yiṣḥaq Shivtiel, eds. *Har'el: qoveṣ zikkaron leha-rav refa'el alshekh*. Tel Aviv, 1962.

Ray, Jonathan. *After Expulsion: 1492 and the Making of Sephardic Jewry*. New York: New York University Press, 2013.

Ray, Jonathan. "Images of the Jewish Community in Medieval Iberia." *Journal of Medieval Iberian Studies* 1 (2009): 195–211.

Ray, Jonathan. "New Approaches to the Jewish Diaspora: The Sephardim as a Sub- Ethnic Group." *Jewish Social Studies* 15/1 (2008): 10–31.

Raz-Krakotzkin, Amnon. "The Censor as a Mediator: Printing, Censorship, and the Shaping of Hebrew Literature." In *The Roman Inquisition, the Index and the Jews*, ed. S. Wendehorst, 35–57. Leiden/ Boston: Brill, 2004.

Raz-Krakotzkin, Amnon. "Ḥaqiqah, meshiḥiyut ve-ṣenzura: hadpasat ha-shulḥan ʿarukh ke-reshit ha-moderniut." In *Tov Elem: Memory, Community and Gender in Medieval and Early Modern Jewish Societies—Essays in Honor of Robert Bonfil* (Hebrew), ed. E. Baumgarten et al., 306–335. Jerusalem: Mosad Bialik, 2011.

Raz-Krakotzkin, Amnon. "Persecution and the Art of Printing: Hebrew Books in Italy in the 1550's." In *Jewish Culture in Early Modern Europe: Essays in Honor of David B. Ruderman*, ed. Richard I. Cohen, et al., 97–108. Hebrew Union College Press/ University of Pittsburgh Press, 2014.

Raz-Krakotzkin, Amnon. "The Zionist Return to the West and the Mizrahi Jewish Perspective." In *Orientalism and the Jews*, ed. Kalmar and Penslar, 162–181.

Regev, Shaul. "The Attitude to Islam in Yemeni Jewish Philosophical Literature" (Hebrew). *Tema* 7 (2001): 17–28.

Regev, Shaul. "Najara, Israel ben Moses." *EJIW*. Brill Online.

Reichardt, Dosia. "The Constitution of Narrative Identity in Seventeenth-Century Prison Writing." In *Early Modern Autobiography: Theories, Genres, Practices*, ed. Ronald Bedford, Lloyd Davis, & Philippa Kelly, 115–129. Ann Arbor: University of Michigan Press, 2006.

Reif, Stefan C. *Judaism and Hebrew Prayer*. Cambridge/ New York: Cambridge University Press, 1993.

Reiner, Elhanan. "Bein ashkenaz li-yerushalayim—ḥakhamim ashkenazim be-ereṣ yisra'el le-aḥar ha-mavet ha-shaḥor." *Shalem* 4 (1984): 27–62.

Reiner, Elhanan. "Beʿiqvot ʿolei regel yehudim li-yerushalayim bimei ha-beinayim." *Ari'el* 83–84 (1992): 207–246.

Reinink, G.J. and H.L.J. Vanstiphout, eds. *Dispute Poems and Dialogues in the Ancient and Mediaeval Near East*. Leuven: Peeters Press, 1991.

Renan, Ernest. "Les Séances de Hariri." In *Essais de morale et de critique*, 287–302. Paris: Michel Lévy, 1859.

Reynolds, Dwight F. et al., eds. *Interpreting the Self: Autobiography in the Arabic Literary Tradition*. Berkeley: University of California Press, 2001.

Reynolds, Dwight F. "A Thousand and One Nights: a history of the text and its reception." In *CHAL-PCP*, 270–291.

Reynolds, Gabriel Said. "On the Qur'anic Accusation of Scriptural Falsification (*taḥrīf*) and Christian Anti-Jewish Polemic." *JAOS* 130/2 (2010): 189–202.

Richards, D.S. "The *Maqāmāt* of al-Hamadhānī: General Remarks and a Consideration of the Manuscripts." *JAL* 22 (1991): 89–99.

Richards, D.S. "The *Rasāʾil* of Badīʿ al-Zamān al-Hamadhānī." In *Arabicus Felix: Luminosus Britannicus: Essays in Honour of A.F.L. Beeston on his Eightieth Birthday*, ed. A. Jones, 142–162. Reading: Ithaca Press, 1991.

Richards, Jennifer. *Voices and Books in the English Renaissance: A New History of Reading*. Oxford/New York: Oxford University Press, 2019.

Richler, Benjamin. "On Editing the Catalogue of the Hebrew Manuscripts in Parma." *Materia giudaica: Rivista dell'associazione italiana per lo studio del giudaismo* VII/2 (2002): 217–221.

Richler, Benjamin. "Microfilming the Baron Guenzburg Collection of Hebrew Manuscripts in the Russian State Library in Moscow." *Judaica Librarianship* 8/1–2 (1994): 142–144.

Richter-Bernburg, Lutz. "Geographical Literature." In *EAL*, 1:244–247.

Riegler, Michael. "Benayah ha-sofer ve-ṣeʾeṣaʾav: mishpaḥat sofrim mi-teiman." *Peʿamim* 64.4 (1995): 54–67.

Riegler, Michael. "The Colophon as a Source for the History of Yemenite Books and their Scribes" (Hebrew). In *Studies in Hebrew Literature and Yemenite Culture: Jubilee Volume Presented to Yehuda Ratzaby*, ed. J. Dishon and E. Hazan, 161–179. Ramat Gan: Bar-Ilan University Press, 1991.

Riegler, Michael. "Kitvei yad ʿivriyyim mi-yemei ha-beinayyim she-hoʿatqu be-vatei kele." *Sinai* 121 (1998): 123–137.

Roberts, Alexandre M. "Being a Sabian at Court in Tenth-Century Baghdad." *JAOS* 137/2 (2017): 253–277.

Robinson, James T. "Allegorical Readings of Qohelet 7:19 in Medieval Jewish Exegesis: *The 'Ten Rulers in the City' as Body Parts, Celestial Spheres, Psychic Faculties, or Internal and External Senses*." In *Religious and Intellectual Diversity in the Islamicate World and Beyond: Essays in Honor of Sarah Stroumsa*, ed. Omer Michaelis and Sabine Schmidtke, 2:1191–1214. Leiden/Boston: Brill, 2024.

Robinson, James T. "From Digression to Compilation: Samuel Ibn Tibbon and Immanuel of Rome on Genesis 1:11, 1:14, and 1:20." *Zutot* 4 (2004): 79–95.

Robinson, James T. "Interactions between Jewish Philosophy and Hebrew Literature during the Middle Ages." Forthcoming in *The Oxford Handbook of Jewish Philosophy*.

Robinson, James T. "Maimonides, Samuel Ibn Tibbon, and the Construction of a Jewish

Tradition of Philosophy." In *Maimonides after 800 Years: Essays on Maimonides and His Influence*, ed. Jay M. Harris, 291–306. Cambridge, MA: Harvard University Press, 2007.

Robinson, James T. "'The 'Secret of the Heavens' and the 'Secret of Number': Immanuel of Rome's Mathematical Supercommentaries on Abraham Ibn Ezra in His Commentary on Qohelet 5:7 and 7:27." *Aleph* 21 (2021): 279–308.

Robinson, James T. "We Drink Only from the Master's Water: Maimonides and Maimonideanism in Southern France, 1200–1306." In *Epigonism and the Dynamic of Jewish Culture*, ed. Berger and Zwiep, 27–60.

Rodrigue, Aron, ed., *Ottoman and Turkish Jewry: Community and Leadership*. Bloomington: Indiana University Press, 1992.

Rodrigue, Aron. "The Sephardim in the Ottoman Empire." In *Spain and the Jews*, ed. E. Kedourie, 162–188. London: Thames and Hudson, 1992.

Roper, Geoffrey. "The History of the Book in the Muslim World." In *The Oxford Companion to the Book*, ed. Suarez and Woudhuysen, Ch. 38.

Roper, Geoffrey. "Maṭbaʿa." *EI*[2] online.

Rosen, Tova. "The Muwashshaḥ." In *CHALAND*, 165–189.

Rosen, Tova. "The Story of the Crooked Preacher by Jacob ben Elʿazar." In *'His Pen and Ink Are a Powerful Mirror,'* ed. Bursi et al., 231–258.

Rosen, Tova. *Unveiling Eve: Reading Gender in Medieval Hebrew Literature*. Philadelphia: University of Pennsylvania Press, 2003.

Rosen, Tova and Eli Yassif. "The Study of Hebrew Literature of the Middle Ages: Major Trends and Goals." In *The Oxford Handbook of Jewish Studies*, ed. Goodman, 241–294.

Rosen-Moked, Tova. *The Hebrew Girdle Poem* (*Muwashshaḥ*) *in the Middle Ages* (Hebrew). Haifa: Haifa University Press, 1985.

Rosenberg, Shalom. "Exile and Redemption in Jewish Thought in the Sixteenth Century: Contending Conceptions." In *Jewish Thought in the Sixteenth Century*, ed. Cooperman, 399–430.

Rosenberg, Shalom. "The Link to the Land of Israel in Jewish Thought: A Clash of Perspectives." In *The Land of Israel: Jewish Perspectives*, ed. Hoffman, 139–169. Hebrew original in *Cathedra* 4 (1977): 148–166.

Rosenthal, Abraham. "Daniel Bomberg and His Talmud Editions." In *Gli Ebrei e Venezia*, ed. G. Cozzi, 375–416. Milan: Edizioni di Comunità, 1987.

Rosenthal, Franz. "A Jewish Philosopher of the Tenth Century." *HUCA* 21 (1948): 155–173.

Rosenthal, Franz. *Knowledge Triumphant: The Concept of Knowledge in Medieval Islam*. Leiden: E.J. Brill, 1970.

Rosenthal, Franz. "Literature." In *The Legacy of Islam*, ed. J. Schacht and C.E. Bosworth, 321–349. Oxford: Clarendon Press, 1974.

Rosenthal, Franz. "The Muslim Concept of Freedom Prior to the Nineteenth Century." In *Man Versus Society in Medieval Islam*, ed. D. Gutas, 24–128. Brill, 2015.

Rosenthal, Franz. "The Stranger in Medieval Islam." *Arabica* 44/1 (1997): 35–75.

Rosenthal, Franz. *The Technique and Approach of Muslim Scholarship*. Rome, 1947.

Roth, Cecil. *Doña Gracia of the House of Nasi*. Philadelphia: Jewish Publication Society, 1948; repr. 1977.

Roth, Cecil. *The Duke of Naxos of the House of Nasi*. Philadelphia: The Jewish Publication Society, 1948.

Roth, Cecil ed. *The World History of the Jewish People*. Second Series: Medieval Period, vol. 2. Tel Aviv: Massadah Publishing Co., 1966.

Rotman, David. "Folktales/Folk Literature." *EJIW*. Brill Online.

Rotman, David. "At the Limits of Reality: The Marvelous in Medieval Ashkenazi Hebrew Folktales." *JSQ* 20/2 (2013): 101–128.

Rowson, Everett K. "The Aesthetics of Pure Formalism: a Letter of Qābūs b. Vushmgīr." In *The Weaving of Words*, ed. Behzadi and Behmardi, 131–149.

Rowson, Everett K. "Religion and Politics in the Career of Badīʿ al-Zamān al-Hamadhānī." *JAOS* 107/4 (1987): 653–673.

Rowson, Everett K. Review of Shmuel Moreh, *Live Theatre and Dramatic Literature in the Medieval Arab World*. *JAOS* 114.3 (1994): 466–468.

Rowson, Everett K. "al-Thaʿālibī." *EI*² 10:426a–427b.

Rozen, Minna. *A History of the Jewish Community in Istanbul, The Formative Years, 1453–1566*. Leiden/Boston: Brill, 2002.

Rozen, Minna. "The Position of the Mustaʿrabs in the Inter-community Relationships in Eretz Israel from the End of the 15th Century to the End of the 17th Century" (Hebrew). *Kathedra* 17 (1980): 73–101.

Rubiés, Joan-Pau. "Introduction." In *Medieval Ethnographies: European Perceptions of the World Beyond*, ed. Joan-Pau Rubiés, xiii–xxxviii. London & New York: Routledge, 2016.

Rubiés, Joan-Pau. "Travel Writing and Ethnography." In *The Cambridge Companion to Travel Writing*, ed. P. Hulme and T. Youngs, 242–260. Cambridge: Cambridge University Press, 2002.

Rubiés, Joan-Pau. "Travel Writing as a Genre: Facts, Fictions and the Invention of a Scientific Discourse in Early Modern Europe." *Journeys: The International Journal of Travel and Travel Writing* 1 (2000): 5–35.

Rubin, Nissan. "From Monism to Dualism: Relationship Between the Body and Soul in Talmudic Thought" (Hebrew). *Daʿat* 23 (1989): 33–63.

Ruderman, David B. *Early Modern Jewry: A New Cultural* History. Princeton and Oxford: Princeton University Press, 2010.

Ruderman, David B. *Jewish Thought and Scientific Discovery in Early Modern Europe*. New Haven: Yale University Press, 1995.

Ruderman, David B., ed. and trans. *A Valley of Vision: The Heavenly Journey of Abraham ben Hananiah Yagel*. Philadelphia: University of Pennsylvania Press, 1990.

Ruderman, David B. "Why Periodization Matters: On Early Modern Jewish Culture and Haskalah." *Simon Dubnow Institute Yearbook* 6 (2007): 23–32.

Ruggles, D. Fairchild. "The Gardens of the Alhambra and the Concept of the Garden in Islamic Spain." In *Al-Andalus: The Art of Islamic Spain*, ed. J. Dodds, 163–171. New York: MMA, 1992.

Saadoun, Haim, ed. *Yemen* (Hebrew). Jerusalem: Ministry of Education/Ben-Zvi Institute, 2002.

Sabar, Shalom. "Childbirth and Magic: Jewish Folklore and Material Culture." In *Cultures of the Jews*, ed. D. Biale, 670–722.

Sabar, Yona. "Arbil." *EJIW*. Brill Online.

Sabar, Yona. *The Folk Literature of Kurdistani Jews*. New Haven: Yale University Press, 1982.

Sachs, Senior. "The Riddles of Rabbi Solomon Ibn Gabirol and their Solutions" (Hebrew). *Oṣar ha-sifrut* 4 (1892): 90–111.

Sadan, Joseph. "Adāb—règles de conduite, et ādāb—dictons, maximes, dans quelques ouvrages inédits d'al-Thaʿālibī." *Revue des études islamiques* 54 (1986): 285–302.

Sadan, Joseph. "An Admirable and Ridiculous Hero: Some Notes on the Bedouin in Medieval Arabic Belles Lettres." *Poetics Today* 10:3 (Fall 1989): 471–492.

Sadan, Joseph. "Identity and Inimitability—Contexts of Inter-Religious Polemics," *IOS* XIV (1994): 325–347.

Sadan, Joseph. "Un intelectuel juif au confluent de deux cultures: Yehūda al-ḥarīzī et sa biographie arabe." In *Judíos y musulmanes en al-Andalus y el Maghreb: Contactos intelectuales*, ed. Maribel Fierro, 105–151. Madrid: Casa de Velázquez, 2002.

Sadan, Joseph. "Judah Alḥarizi as a Cultural Junction—an Arabic Biography of a Jewish Writer as Perceived by an Orientalist" (Hebrew). *Peʿamim* 68 (1996): 16–66.

Sadan, Joseph. "Kings and Craftsmen—a Pattern of Contrasts: On the History of a Medieval Arabic Humoristic Form." *SI* 56 (1982): 5–49.

Sadan, Joseph. "The 'Latrines Decree' in the Yemen versus the Dhimma Principles." In *Pluralism and Identity: Studies in Ritual Behaviour*, ed. J. Platvoet and K. van der Toorn, 167–185. Leiden/New York/Köln: E.J. Brill, 1995.

Sadan, Joseph. "Maidens' Hair and Starry Skies: Imagery System and *Maʿānī* Guides." *IOS* 11 (1991): 57–88.

Saenger, Paul. "Silent Reading: Its Impact on Late Medieval Script and Society." *Viator* 13 (1982): 367–414.

Safran, Bezalel. "Baḥya ibn Paquda's Attitude toward the Courtier Class." In *Studies in Medieval Jewish History and Literature*, ed. I. Twersky, 1:154–196. Cambridge: Harvard University Press, 1979.

Salah, Asher. "A Contextual Analysis of the Jewish Italian Elegy at the Time of the Ghettos (Sixteenth-Eighteenth Centuries)." In *Studies in Medieval Jewish Poetry: A Messenger Upon the Garden*, ed. A. Guetta and M. Itzhaki, 117–138. Leiden/Boston: Brill, 2009.

Saperstein, Marc. "The Land of Israel in Pre-Modern Jewish Thought: A History of Two Rabbinic Statements." In *The Land of Israel: Jewish Perspectives*, ed. Hoffman, 188–209.

Saperstein, Marc and Nancy E. Berg, "'Arab Chains' and 'The Good Things of Sepharad': Aspects of Jewish Exile." *AJS Review* 26/2 (2002): 301–326.

Sapir, Jacob. *Even Sapir*. 2 vols. Lyck: Mekize Nirdamim, 1866; Mainz: J. Bril, 1874.

Saitta, Gianluca. "Le genre séance au Yémen entre tradition et innovation: les *Maqāmāt hindiyya* d'Abū Bakr b. Muḥsin Bā ʿAbbūd al-ʿAlawī (xviiie siècle)." *Arabian Humanities* 3 (2014). http://journals.openedition.org/cy/2710

Saitta, Gianluca. "Notices de manuscrits de *maqāmāt* yéménites de la période postclassique, 1ère partie." *Chroniques du manuscrit au Yémen* 17 (2014) [online].

Saitta, Gianluca. "Notices de manuscrits de *maqāmāt* yéménites de la période postclassique, 2e partie," *Chroniques du manuscrit au Yémen* 18 (2014) [online].

Sassoon, D.S. *Ohel Dawid: Descriptive Catalogue of the Hebrew and Samaritan Manuscripts in the Sassoon Library*. 2 vols. Oxford University Press/London: Humphrey Milford, 1932.

Sassoon, D.S. Review of Idelsohn and Torczyner, *Shirei teiman*. *JQR* 24/4 (1934): 358–359.

Schapkow, Carsten. *Role Model and Countermodel: The Golden Age of Iberian Jewry and German Jewish Culture during the Era of Emancipation*. Lanham, MD: Lexington Books, 2016.

Schechter, Solomon. "Safed in the Sixteenth Century—A City of Legists and Mystics." In *Studies in Judaism*, Second Series, 202–285. Philadelphia: The Jewish Publication Society of America, 1945.

Scheindlin, Raymond P. "Al-Ḥarizi's Astrologer: A Document of Jewish-Islamic Relations." In *Studies in Muslim-Jewish Relations*, vol. 1, ed. Ronald L. Nettler, 165–175. Chur: Harwood Academic Publishers, 1993.

Scheindlin, Raymond P. "Asher in the Harem by Solomon Ibn Saqbel." In *Rabbinic Fantasies*, ed. Stern and Mirsky, 253–267.

Scheindlin, Raymond P. "Contrasting Religious Experience in the Liturgical Poems of Ibn Gabirol and Judah Halevi." *Prooftexts* 13 (1993): 141–162.

Scheindlin, Raymond P. "Fawns of the Palace and Fawns of the Field." *Prooftexts* 6/3 (1986): 189–303.

Scheindlin, Raymond P. *The Gazelle: Medieval Hebrew Poems on God, Israel and the Soul*. Philadelphia & New York: The Jewish Publication Society, 1991.

Scheindlin, Raymond P. "Ḥever the Pious: Some Aspects of Religion in the *Taḥkemoni* by Judah al-Ḥarīzī." In *'His Pen and Ink Are a Powerful Mirror,'* ed. Bursi et al., 282–297.

Scheindlin, Raymond P. "Ibn Gabirol's Religious Poetry and Arabic *Zuhd* Poetry." *Edebiyāt* n.s. 4 (1993): 229–242.

Scheindlin, Raymond P. "Ibn Gabirol's Religious Poetry and Sufi Poetry." *Sefarad* 54 (1994): 109–142.

Scheindlin, Raymond P. "The Love Stories of Jacob ben Elazar: Between Arabic and Romance Literature" (Hebrew). In *Proceedings of the Eleventh World Congress of Jewish Studies*, Division C 3:16–20. Jerusalem, 1993.

Scheindlin, Raymond P. "Mid-Life Repentance in a Poem by Judah Halevi." *The Maghreb Review* 29 (2004): 40–52.

Scheindlin, Raymond P. "*The Misogynist* by Judah Ibn Shabbetai." In *Rabbinic Fantasies*, ed. Stern and Mirsky, 269–94.

Scheindlin, Raymond P. "On the Poem *Adonai, Negdekha Kol Ta'avati* by Judah ha-Levi" (Hebrew). In *Studies in Hebrew Poetry and Jewish Heritage in Memory of Aharon Mirsky*, ed. E. Hazan and J. Yahalom, 227–237. Ramat-Gan: Bar-Ilan University Press, 2006.

Scheindlin, Raymond P. *The Song of the Distant Dove: Judah Halevi's Pilgrimage*. New York: Oxford University Press, 2008.

Scheindlin, Raymond P. *Wine, Women, and Death: Medieval Hebrew Poems on the Good Life*. Philadelphia: The Jewish Publication Society, 1986.

Schippers, Arie. "Hebrew Andalusian Elegies and the Arabic Literary Tradition." In *Hidden Futures: Death and Immortality in Ancient Egypt, Anatolia, the Classical, Biblical and Arabic-Islamic World*, ed. T.P.J. van den Hout, J.M. Bremer, and R. Peters, 177–194. Amsterdam University Press, 1994.

Schippers, Arie. "Muʿāraḍa." *EI*^{2} 7:261.

Schirmann, Hayyim (Jefim). "The Function of the Hebrew Poet in Medieval Spain." *Jewish Social Studies* 16 (1954): 235–252.

Schirmann, Hayyim (Jefim). *Die Hebräische übersetzung der Maqamen des Hariri*. Frankfort am Main, 1930.

Schirmann, Hayyim (Jefim). *The History of Hebrew Poetry in Christian Spain and Southern France* (Hebrew). Edited, supplemented, and annotated by Ezra Fleischer. Jerusalem: Magnes Press and the Ben-Zvi Institute, 1997.

Schirmann, Hayyim (Jefim). *The History of Hebrew Poetry in Muslim Spain* (Hebrew). Edited, supplemented, and annotated by Ezra Fleischer. Jerusalem: Magnes Press and the Ben-Zvi Institute, 1995.

Schirmann, Hayyim (Jefim), ed. *Mivḥar ha-shirah haʿivrit be'italya*. Berlin: Schocken Verlag, 1934.

Schirmann, Hayyim (Jefim). "Der Neger und die Negerin: zur Bildersprache und Stoffwahl der spanisch-hebräïschen Dichtung." *MGWJ* 83 (1939): 481–492.

Schirmann, Hayyim (Jefim). "Neqamat ha-shifḥah." *Ha'aretz* June 16, 1939.

Schirmann, Hayyim (Jefim). "Samuel Hannagid, The Man, The Soldier, The Politician." *Jewish Social Studies* 13 (1951): 99–126.

Schirmann, Hayyim (Jefim). *Ha-shirah ha-ʿivrit bi-sfarad u-ve-provans*. Jerusalem and Tel Aviv: Bialik Institute and Dvir Company, 1954–1956; 2d ed. 1960–1961.

Schirmann, Hayyim (Jefim). "Two Maqamas of Zecharia Aldahiri's Sepher Hamussar"

(Hebrew). *Studies of the Research Institute for Hebrew Poetry* 3 (Berlin, 1936): 185–210.

Schlossberg, Eliezer. "Anti-Muslim Polemics in Medieval Yemenite Midrashim" (Hebrew). *Teʿudah* 14 (1998): 205–224.

Schlossberg, Eliezer. "Hashpaʿat sifrut ha-adab ʿal rav Saʿadia gaʾon: ʿiyyun ʿal pi perusho le-sefer mishlei." *Biqqoret u-farshanut* 33 (1998): 33–48.

Schlossberg, Eliezer. "Ha-pulmus ʿim haʾislam be-midrash *Maʾor haʾafelah.*" *Tema* 3 (1993):57–66.

Schmelzer, Menahem. "Poems in Praise of Books by David Ben Joseph Ibn Yahya" (Hebrew). In *Studies in Jewish History Presented to Joseph Hacker*, ed. Y. Ben-Naeh, J. Cohen, M. Idel, and Y. Kaplan, 322–335. Jerusalem: Shazar, 2014.

Schmelzer, Menahem. "Shirei petiḥah va-ḥatimah be-sefer ʻyeḥusei tannaʾim vaʾamor-aʾimʼ le-rabbi yehudah ben qalonymus mi-shpira." In idem, *Meḥqarim be-bibliografi-ya yehudit uve-piyyuṭei yemei ha-beinayyim*, 177–187. New York and Jerusalem: The Jewish Theological Seminary, 2006.

Schmidtke, Sabine. "Biblical Predictions of the Prophet Muḥammad among the Zaydīs of Yemen (Sixth/Twelfth and Seventh/Thirteenth Centuries)." In *Muslim Perceptions and Receptions of the Bible*, ed. Adang and Schmidtke, 281–296.

Schmidtke, Sabine. "Epistle forcing the Jews [to admit their error] with regard to what they contend about the Torah, by dialectical reasoning (*Risālat ilzām al-yahūd fīmā zaʿamū fī l-tawrāt min qibal ʿilm al-kalām*) by al-Salām ʿAbd al-ʿAllām: A critical edition." In *Contacts and Controversies*, ed. Adang and Schmidtke, 73–82.

Schmidtke, Sabine. "The History of Zaydī Studies: An Introduction." *Arabica* 59/3–4 (2012): 185–199.

Schneider, Irene. "Imprisonment in Pre-Classical and Classical Islamic Law." *Islamic Law and Society* 2/2 (1995): 157–173.

Schoeler, Gregor. *The Genesis of Literature in Islam: From the Aural to the Read.* Edited and translated by Shawkat M. Toorawa. Edinburgh: Edinburgh University Press, 2009.

Schoeler, Gregor. "Muwashshaḥ." *EI*².

Scholem, Gershom. *Devils, Demons and Souls* (Hebrew). Edited by Esther Liebes. Jerusalem: Ben-Zvi Institute, Yad Izhak Ben-Zvi and the Hebrew University, 2004.

Scholem, Gershom. *Kabbalah.* Jerusalem: Keter Publishing House, 1974.

Scholem, Gershom. *On the Kabbalah and Its Symbolism.* Translated by Ralph Manheim. New York: Schocken Books, 1965.

Scholem, Gershom. "Kabbalat r. yiṣḥaq ben shlomo ben avi sahula ve-sefer ha-zohar." *KS* 6 (1927–1930): 109–118.

Scholem, Gershom. *Major Trends in Jewish Mysticism.* 3d rev. ed. New York: Schocken Books, 1954.

Scholem, Gershom. "Ha-ṣitut ha-rishon min ha-midrash ha-neʿelam." *Tarbiz* 3 (1931/32): 181–183.

Schorsch, Ismar. "Converging Cognates: The Intersection of Jewish and Islamic Studies in Nineteenth Century Germany." *Leo Baeck Institute Year Book* 55 (2010): 3–36.

Schorsch, Ismar. "The Myth of Sephardic Supremacy," in Schorsch, *From Text to Context*, 71–92.

Schorsch, Ismar. *From Text to Context: The Turn to History in Modern Judaism*. Hanover, NH: Univ. Press of New England, 1994.

Schorsch, Jonathan. *Jews and Blacks in the Early Modern World*. Cambridge/New York: Cambridge University Press, 2004.

Schorsch, Jonathan. "Mosseh Pereyra de Paiva: An Amsterdam Portuguese Jewish Merchant Abroad in the Seventeenth Century." In *The Dutch Intersection: The Jews and the Netherlands in Modern History*, ed. Y. Kaplan, 63–85. Leiden/Boston: Brill, 2008.

Schrijver, Emile. "The Transmission of Jewish Knowledge through MSS and Printed Books." In *The Oxford Companion to the Book*, ed. Suarez and Woudhuysen, Ch. 8.

Schrire, Theodore. *Hebrew Magic Amulets: Their Decipherment and Interpretation*. London: Routledge & K. Paul, 1966; repr. New York: Behrman House, Inc., 1982.

Schroeter, Daniel. Review of Yehuda Nini, *The Jews of Yemen, 1800–1914* (Harwood, 1991). *Yemen Update* 35 (1994): 28–30.

Schunck, K-D. "Benjamin." *Anchor Bible Dictionary* 1: 671–673. New York/ London/ Toronto: Doubleday, 1992.

Schwartz, Dov. "Contacts Between Jewish Philosophy and Mysticism at the Beginning of the Fifteenth Century" (Hebrew). *Da'at* 29 (1992): 41–67.

Schwarzbaum, Haim. "Le-ḥeqer arbaʿah sippurei ʿam be-sefer ha-musar le-rabbi zekharyah alḍāhiri." In *Boʾi Teman*, ed. Ratzaby, 153–164; repr. in Haim Schwarzbaum, *Roots and Landscapes, Studies in folklore chosen from his literary estate by Eli Yassif*, 183–194. Beersheva: Ben Gurion University of the Negev Press, 1993.

Schwarzbaum, Haim. Review of Yehuda Ratzaby ed., *Sefer hamusar: maḥberot rabbi zekhariah al-ḍāhirī*. *KS* 42 (1966): 32–36.

Scodel, Joshua. *The English Poetic Epitaph: Commemoration and Conflict from Jonson to Wordsworth*. Ithaca: Cornell University Press, 1991.

Segal, David Simha, trans. *The Book of Taḥkemoni: Jewish Tales from Medieval Spain*. London & Portland, OR: The Littman Library of Jewish Civilization, 2001.

Segal, J.B. "White and Black Jews at Cochin, the Story of a Controversy." *The Journal of the Royal Asiatic Society of Great Britain and Ireland* 2 (1983): 228–252.

Sellheim, R. "Kitāb." *EI*² online.

Septimus, Bernard. *Hispano-Jewish Culture in Transition: The Career and Controversies of Ramah*. Cambridge, Mass.: Harvard University Press, 1982.

Septimus, Bernard. "Linguistic Ideology and Cultural Hegemony: A Responsum of R. Samuel de Medina, Its Sources and Implications" (Hebrew). In *From Sages to Savants: Studies Presented to Avraham Grossman* (Hebrew), ed. J. Hacker et al., 293–308. Jerusalem: Zalman Shazar Center, 2010.

Septimus, Bernard. "Maimonides on Language." In *The Culture of Spanish Jewry*, ed. A. Doron, 35–54. N. p.: Levinsky College of Education, 1994.

Septimus, Bernard. "'Open Rebuke and Concealed Love': Naḥmanides and the Andalusian Tradition." In *Rabbi Moses Naḥmanides: Explorations in His Religious and Literary Virtuosity*, ed. I. Twersky, 11–34. Cambridge, Mass.: Harvard University Press, 1983.

Seri, Shalom ed. *Seʿi Yona: yehudei teiman be-yisrael*. Tel Aviv: Eʿele BeTamar/ʿAm-ʿoved, 1984.

Seri, Shalom and Israel Kessar, eds. *Halikhot qedem be-mishkenot teiman* (*Ancient Customs of the Yemenite Jewish Community*). Israel: Eʿele BeTamar Association, 2005.

Serjeant, R.B. "The Hindu Bāniyān Merchants and Traders." In Serjeant and Lewcock, eds., *Ṣanʿā: An Arabian Islamic City*, 432–435.

Serjeant, R.B. "The Interplay Between Tribal Affinities and Religious (Zaydī) Authority in the Yemen." *al-Abḥāth* 30 (1982): 11–50.

Serjeant, R.B. *The Portuguese Off the South Arabian Coast*. Beirut: Librairie du Liban, 1974.

Serjeant, R.B. "The Zaydis." In *Religion in the Middle East: Three Religions in Concord and Conflict*, ed. A.J. Arberry, 2:285–301. Cambridge: Cambridge University Press, 1969.

Serjeant, R.B and Ronald Lewcock, eds. *Ṣanʿā: An Arabian Islamic City*. London: The World of Islam Festival Trust, 1983.

Seroussi, Edwin. "From Court and Tarikat to Synagogue: Ottoman Art Music and Hebrew Sacred Songs." In *Sufism, Music and Society in the Middle East*, ed. A. Hammarlund, T. Olsson, and E. Ozdalga, 81–96. Istanbul, 2001.

Seroussi, Edwin. "Rabbi yisrael najara meʿaṣev zimrat ha-qodesh aḥarei gerush sefarad." *Asufot* 4 (1990): 285–310.

Shalem, Shimon. *Rabbi Moshe Alsheikh* (Hebrew). Jerusalem: Ben-Zvi Institute and the Hebrew University, 1966.

Shamir, Yehuda. "Allusions to Muḥammad in Maimonides' Theory of Prophecy in his *Guide of the Perplexed*." JQR 64 (1974): 212–224.

Sharʿaby, Ḥayyim. "Peraqim mi-parashat 'dor deʿah' be-teiman." In Yishaʿyahu and Zadok, eds. *Shevut teiman*, 198–211.

Sharma, Sunil. "Masʿūd-i Saʿd-i Salmān." *EI*³ online.

Sharma, Sunil. *Persian Poetry at the Indian Frontier: Masʿud Saʿd Salman of Lahore*. New Delhi: Permanent Black, 2000.

Shatzmiller, Joseph. "Les limites de la solidarité: antagonismes au sein de la société juive ancienne et moderne." In *La société juive à travers l'histoire*, ed. S. Trigano, 4:387–425. Paris, 1992–1993.

Shatzmiller, Joseph. "Travelling in the Mediterranean in 1563: The Testimony of Eliahu of Pesaro." In *The Mediterranean and the Jews: Banking, Finance and International Trade (XVI–XVIII Centuries)*, ed. A. Toaff and S. Schwarzfuchs, 1: 237–248. Ramat Gan: Bar-Ilan University Press, 1989.

Shevlin, Eleanor F. "To Reconcile Book and Title, and Make 'em Kin to One Another: The Evolution of the Title's Contractual Functions." *Book History* 2/1 (1999): 42–77.

Shinan, Avigdor and Shmuel Ettinger, eds. *Emigration and Settlement in Jewish and General History* (Hebrew). Jerusalem: The Zalman Shazar Center, 1982.

Shmuelevitz, Arye. *The Jews of the Ottoman Empire in the Late Fifteenth and the Sixteenth Centuries*. Leiden: E.J. Brill, 1984.

Shpitzer, Shelomo. "Ha'ashkenazim ba-ḥatzi ha'i ha-balkani ba-me'ot ha-15 ve-16." In *Mi-mizraḥ umi-ma'arav*, ed. Hirschberg, 1:59–79.

Shtal, Abraham. "Qeri'ah pulḥanit shel sefer ha-zohar." *Pe'amim* 5 (1980): 77–86.

Shtober, Shimon, ed. *Sefer divrei yosef*. Jerusalem: Ben-Zvi Institute, 1994.

Shulman, David. Foreword to Sanjay Subrahmanyam, *Three Ways to Be Alien: Travails and Encounters in the Early Modern World*, ix–xiii. Waltham, Mass.: Brandeis University Press/ Historical Society of Israel, 2011.

Shva, Shlomo. "Masa'ot zekhariah al-ḍāhiri." In *Ereṣ yisra'el: otobiografiyah*, 233–239. Lod: Dvir, 2001.

Simon, Rachel. "The Muslim in the Folk Literature of the Jews of Libya." In *Jews and Muslims in the Islamic World*, ed. B.D. Cooperman and Z. Zohar, 335–354. Bethesda: University Press of Maryland, 2013.

Sims, E. "Trade and Travel: Markets and Caravanserais." In *Architecture of the Islamic World*, ed. G. Michell, 80–111. London, 1978.

Sirat, Colette. "Biblical Commentaries and Christian Influence: The Case of Gersonides." In *Hebrew Scholarship and the Medieval World*, ed. de Lange, 210–223.

Sklare, David. "Responses to Islamic Polemics by Jewish Mutakallimūn in the Tenth Century." In *The Majlis*, ed. Lazarus-Yafeh et al., 137–161.

Smith, Helen and Louise Wilson, eds. *Renaissance Paratexts*. Cambridge/New York: Cambridge University Press, 2011.

Sokolow, Moshe. "Saadiah Gaon's Prolegomenon to Psalms." *PAAJR* 51 (1984): 131–174.

Sperber, Daniel. *Minhagei yisrael, meqorot ve-toledot*. Jerusalem: Mossad Harav Kook, 1994.

Stallings, A.E. Review of David Sider, ed. and trans., *Simonides: Epigrams and Elegies*. Oxford University Press, 2021. *The New York Review of Books*, October 5, 2023. https://www.nybooks.com/articles/2023/10/05/obedient-to-their-words-simonides-epigrams-and-elegies

Starn, Randolph. "The Early Modern Muddle" (Review Article). *Journal of Early Modern History* 6/3 (2002): 296–307.

Steingass, Francis. *The Student's Arabic-English Dictionary*. London: Crosby Lockwood and Son, 1884.

Steinschneider, Moritz. *Die arabische Literatur der Juden*. Frankfort am Main, 1902; repr. Hildesheim: G. Olms Verlag, 1964.

Steinschneider, Moritz. *Die hebraeischen Übersetzungen des Mittelalters und die Juden als Dolmetscher*. Berlin, 1893; repr. Graz: Akademische Druck—U. Verlagsanstalt, 1956.

Steinschneider, Moritz. "An Introduction to the Arabic Literature of the Jews." *JQR* o.s. 9/2–13/3 (1897–1901).

Steinschneider, Moritz. *Polemische und apologetische Literatur in arabischer Sprache zwischen Muslimen, Christen und Juden, nebst Anhangen verwandten Inhalts*. Leipzig, 1877; repr. Hildesheim: Georg Olms Verlag, 1966.

Steinschneider, Moritz. *Verzeichnis der hebräischen Handschriften der königlichen Bibliothek zu berlin*. 2 vols. in 1. Berlin, 1878; repr. Hildesheim and New York: Georg Olms Verlag, 1980.

Stephan, Johannes, ed. and Elias Muhanna, trans. Ḥannā Diyāb, *The Book of Travels*. 2 vols. New York: NYU Press, 2021.

Stern, David, ed. *The Anthology in Jewish Literature*. Oxford and New York: Oxford University Press, 2004.

Stern, David, ed. "Introduction." *Rabbinic Fantasies*, ed. Stern and Mirsky, 3–30.

Stern, David, ed. *The Jewish Bible: A Material History*. Seattle and London: University of Washington Press, 2017.

Stern, David and Mark J. Mirsky eds. *Rabbinic Fantasies: Imaginative Narratives from Classical Hebrew Literature*. New Haven and London: Yale University Press, 1990.

Stern, Josef. "Maimonides' Epistemology." In *The Cambridge Companion to Maimonides*, ed. Kenneth Seeskin, 105–133. Cambridge: Cambridge University Press, 2005.

Stern, S.M. "Imitations of Arabic Muwaššaḥāt in Spanish-Hebrew Poetry." *Tarbiz* 18/3–4 (1947): 166–186.

Stewart, Devin. "ʿĪsā b. Hišām's Shiism and Religious Polemic in the *Maqāmāt* of Badīʿ al-Zamān al-Hamadhānī." *IHIW* 10/1–2 (2022):11–81.

Stewart, Devin. "The Maqāma." In *CHAL-PCP*, 145–158.

Stewart, Devin. "Professional Literary Mendicancy in the *Letters* and *Maqāmāt* of Badīʿ al-Zamān al-Hamadhānī." In *Writers and Rulers: Perspectives on Their Relationship from Abbasid to Safavid Times*, ed. B. Gruendler and L. Marlow, 39–47. Wiesbaden: Reichert Verlag, 2004.

Stewart, Devin. "Of Rhetoric, Reason, and Revelation: Ibn al-Jawzī's Maqāmāt as an Anti-Parody and Sefer Taḥkemoni of Yehudah al-Ḥarīzī." *MEL* 19/2 (2016): 206–233.

Stewart, Devin. "*Sajʿ* in the Qurʾān: Prosody and Structure." *JAL* 21/2 (1990): 101–139.

Stillman, Noam (Norman). "Judaism and Islam: Fourteen Hundred Years of Intertwined Destiny? An Overview." In *The Convergence of Judaism and Islam*, ed. M. Laskier and Y. Lev, 10–20. Gainsville: University Press of Florida, 2011.

Stoetzer, W. "Rajaz." *EAL* 2:645–646.

Strack H.L. and G. Stemberger. *Introduction to the Talmud and Midrash*. Minneapolis: Fortress Press, 1996.

Strauss [Ashtor], E. "A Journey to India" (Hebrew). *Zion* 4/3 (1939): 217–231.

Stroumsa, Sarah. "The *Barāhima* in Early Kalam." *JSAI* 6 (1985): 229–241.

Stroumsa, Sarah. "Citation Tradition: On Explicit and Hidden Citations in Judaeo-Arabic Philosophical Literature." In *Heritage and Innovation in Medieval Judaeo-Arabic Culture* (Hebrew), ed. J. Blau and D. Doron, 167–178. Ramat-Gan: Bar-Ilan University, 2000.

Stroumsa, Sarah. *Freethinkers of Medieval Islam*. Leiden: Brill, 1999.

Stroumsa, Sarah. "Ibn al-Rāwandī's *sū' adab al-mujādala*: the Role of Bad Manners in Medieval Disputations." In *The Majlis*, ed. Lazarus-Yafeh et al., 66–83.

Stroumsa, Sarah. "Jewish Polemics Against Islam and Christianity in the Light of Judaeo-Arabic Texts." In *Judaeo-Arabic Studies: Proceedings of the Founding Conference of the Society for Judaeo-Arabic*, ed. N. Golb, 241–250. Amsterdam: Harwood Academic Publishers, 1997.

Stroumsa, Sarah. "The Makeover of *Ḥayy: Transformations of the Sage's Image from Avicenna to Ibn Ṭufayl.*" *Oriens* 49 (2021): 1–34.

Stroumsa, Sarah. "Prophecy *Versus* Civil Religion in Medieval Jewish Philosophy: The Cases of Judah Halevi and Maimonides." In *Tribute to Michael: Studies in Jewish and Muslim Thought Presented to Professor Michael Schwarz* (Hebrew), ed. S. Klein-Braslavy et al., 79*–102*. Tel Aviv: Tel Aviv University, 2009.

Stroumsa, Sarah. "The Signs of Prophecy: The Emergence and Early Development of a Theme in Arabic Theological Literature." *HTR* 78:1–2 (1985): 101–114.

Suarez, Michael F. and H.R. Woudhuysen, eds. *The Oxford Companion to the Book*. 2 vols. Oxford/ New York: Oxford University Press, 2010.

Summers, Joanna. *Late-Medieval Prison Writing and the Politics of Autobiography*. Oxford: Oxford University Press 2004.

Swartz, Michael D. and Joseph Yahalom. *Avodah: An Anthology of Ancient Poetry for Yom Kippur*. University Park, Pa.: Penn State University Press, 2005.

Talmage, Frank. "Apples of Gold: The Inner Meaning of Sacred Texts in Medieval Judaism." In *Jewish Spirituality*, ed. Green, 1:313–355.

Tamar, David. "Isaac Luria and Ḥayim Vital as the Messiah Son of Joseph" (Hebrew). *Sefunot* 7 (1963): 169–177.

Tamar, David. "The Messianic Expectations in Italy for the year 1575" (Hebrew). *Sefunot* 2 (1958): 61–88.

Tamari, Assaf. "The City of the Kabbalists? Sixteenth Century Safed as Center and as Periphery" (Hebrew). *Zion* 87/4 (2022): 505–547.

Tanenbaum, Adena. "The Andalusian *Seliḥah* and Its Individualistic Conception of Penitence." In *Be'erot Yitzhak*, ed. Harris, 377–398.

Tanenbaum, Adena. "Arrogance, Bad Form, and Curricular Narrowness: Belletristic Critiques of Rabbinic Culture from Medieval Spain and Provence." In *Rabbinic Culture and Its Critics: Jewish Authority, Dissent, and Heresy in Medieval and Early Modern*

Times, ed. D. Frank and M. Goldish, 57–81. Detroit: Wayne State University Press, 2008.

Tanenbaum, Adena. *The Contemplative Soul: Hebrew Poetry and Philosophical Theory in Medieval Spain*. Leiden: Brill Academic Publishers, 2002.

Tanenbaum, Adena. "Didacticism or Literary Legerdemain? Philosophical and Ethical Themes in Zechariah Aldahiri's *Sefer Hamusar*." In *Adaptations and Innovations: Studies on the Interaction between Jewish and Islamic Thought and Literature from the Early Middle Ages to the Late Twentieth Century, Dedicated to Professor Joel L. Kraemer*, ed. Y.T. Langermann and J. Stern, 355–379. Leuven: Peeters Publishers, 2008.

Tanenbaum, Adena. "Hidden Gems: The Hebrew *Maqāma* from Yemen." *IHIW* 10.1–2 (2022): 189–222.

Tanenbaum, Adena. "Nine Spheres or Ten? A Medieval Gloss on Moses Ibn Ezra's 'Beshem el asher amar.'" *JJS* 47:2 (1996): 294–310.

Tanenbaum, Adena. "Of a Pietist Gone Bad and Des(s)erts Not Had: The Fourteenth Chapter of Zechariah Alḍāhirī's *Sefer hamusar*." *Prooftexts* 23/3 (2003): 297–319.

Tanenbaum, Adena. "Sefer ha-musar le-zekhariah al-dahiri: tekhniqot sifrutiyot vetokhen." *Tema* 13 (2015): 33–41.

Tanenbaum, Adena. "The Uses of Scripture in Zechariah Alḍāhirī's *Sefer hamusar*." In *Exegesis and Poetry in Medieval Karaite and Rabbanite Texts*, ed. Joachim Yeshaya and Elisabeth Hollender, 147–184. Leiden: Brill, 2017.

Tavim, José Alberto Rodrigues da Silva. "Galut and Empire: On the Way to Final Redemption." In *The Sephardic Atlantic: Colonial Histories and Postcolonial Perspectives*, ed. S. Rauschenbach and J. Schorsch, 115–142. Palgrave Macmillan, 2018.

Tavim, José Alberto Rodrigues da Silva. "*Palli Paradesi*: Cochinese Jews, the Portuguese and Identity Reconstructions." In *India, the Portuguese and Maritime Interactions: Religion, Language and Cultural Expressions*, ed. P. Malekandathil et al., 2:3–31. Delhi: Primus Books, 2019.

Tavim, José Alberto Rodrigues da Silva. "Purim in Cochin in the Middle of the Sixteenth Century According to Lisbon's Inquisition Trials." *The Journal of Indo-Judaic Studies* 11 (2010): 7–24.

Tavim, José Alberto Rodrigues da Silva. "From Setúbal to the Sublime Porte: The Wanderings of Jacome de Olivares, New Christian and Merchant of Cochin, 1540–1571." In *Sinners and Saints: The Successors of Vasco da Gama*, ed. S. Subrahmanyam, 94–134. New Delhi, 2000.

Teplitsky, Joshua. "A 'Prince of the Land of Israel' in Prague: Jewish Philanthropy, Patronage and Power in Early Modern Europe and Beyond." *Jewish History* 29 (2015): 245–271.

Thompson, Carl. *Travel Writing*. London/New York: Routledge, 2011.

Tidhar, D. *Encyclopedia of the Founders and Builders of Israel* (Hebrew). Tel Aviv: Sifriyat Rishonim, 1947–1971.

Tietze, A. and J. Yahalom. *Ottoman Melodies, Hebrew Hymns: A 16th Century Cross-Cultural Adventure*. Budapest: akedémiai Kiadó, 1995.

Tillier, Matthieu. "Les prisonniers dans la société musulmane (IIe/VIIIe–IVe/Xe siècle)." In *Dynamiques sociales au Moyen Age en Occident et en Orient*, ed. E. Malamut, 191–212. Aix-en-Provence: Presses de l'Université de Provence, 2010.

Tillier, Matthieu. "Prisons et autorités urbaines sous les Abbassides." *Arabica* 55 (2008): 387–408.

Tillier, Matthieu. "Vivre en prison à l'époque abbasside." *JESHO* 52/4–5 (2009): 635–659.

Tirosh-Samuelson, Hava. "Philosophy and Kabbalah: 1200–1600." In *The Cambridge Companion to Medieval Jewish Philosophy*, ed. D.H. Frank and O. Leaman, 218–257. Cambridge, 2003.

Tishby, Isaiah. "Demuto shel rabbi moshe kordovero be-ḥibbur shel rabbi mordekhai dato." *Sefunot* 7 (1963): 119–166.

Tishby, Isaiah. "Ha-pulmus ʿal *sefer ha-zohar* ba-me'ah ha-sheshʿesreh be'italia." *Perakim* 1 (1967–1968): 131–182.

Tishby, Isaiah, ed. and trans. *The Wisdom of the Zohar: An Anthology of Texts*. 3 vols. Oxford/New York: Oxford University Press/ Littman Library, 1989.

Tobi, Yosef, ed. *Abraham Ben Halfon: Poems* (Hebrew). Tel Aviv: Afikim, 1991.

Tobi, Yosef. "Benayah." *EJ*[2] 3:322.

Tobi, Yosef. "Caro's *Shulhan Arukh* Versus Maimonides' *Mishne Torah* in Yemen." *The Jewish Law Annual* 15 (2004): 189–215.

Tobi, Yosef. "Challenges to Tradition: Jewish Cultures in Yemen, Iraq, Iran, Afghanistan, and Bukhara." In *Cultures of the Jews*, ed. Biale, 932–974.

Tobi, Yosef. "Conversion to Islam among Yemenite Jews under Zaydi Rule" (Hebrew). *Peʿamim* 42 (1990): 105–126.

Tobi, Yosef. "Ha-ḥeqer ha-hashva'ati shel ha-sifrut haʿamamit ha-yehudit ve-ha-muslim-it be-teiman." *Meḥqerei yerushalayim be-folklor yehudi* 24/25 (2007): 415–433.

Tobi, Yosef. "Iggeret haman u-mashal ʿal ha-tarnegol: shete paradiot mi-sifrut yehude teman." *Sheveṭ vaʿam* 6 (1971): 223–238.

Tobi, Yosef. "Information on the Jews of Yemen in Arabic Writings from Yemen" (Hebrew). *Peʿamim* 64 (1994): 68–102 and 65 (1995): 18–56.

Tobi, Yosef. *ʿIyyunim bi-megillat teman*. Jerusalem: Magnes, 1986.

Tobi, Yosef. "Jews of Yemen." In *A History of Jewish-Muslim Relations: From the Origins to the Present Day*, ed. A. Meddeb and B. Stora, 248–257. Princeton: Princeton University Press, 2013.

Tobi, Yosef. *The Jews of Yemen*. Leiden/Boston: Brill, 1999.

Tobi, Yosef. "Ketav-yad ḥadash ha-kollel ḥibbureihem shel rabbi ḥoṭer al-dhammārī ve-rabbi zekharya ha-rofé." *Tagim* 5–6 (1975): 71–88.

Tobi, Yosef. *Miyṣirot sifrutiyot mi-teiman*. Holon: Mifʿal ḥasifat ginzei teiman, 1981.

Tobi, Yosef. "Nusaḥ ha-tefillah shel yehudei teiman." *Tema* 7 (2001): 29–64.

Tobi, Yosef. "Piyyuṭ ḥadash le-rabbi yiḥye al-ḍāhirī." *Afikim* 38 (1971): 15–18.

Tobi, Yosef. "Piyyut le-rabbi moshe al-balīda." *Afikim* 48 (1973): 18.

Tobi, Yosef. "Poetry and Society in the Works of Abraham Ibn Ḥalfon (Yemen, 12th Century)." *HAR* 9 (1985): 363–372.

Tobi, Yosef. "Politics and Poetry in the Works of Shalom Shabazī." *Israel Affairs* 20/2 (2014): 240–255.

Tobi, Yosef. *Proximity and Distance: Medieval Hebrew and Arabic Poetry*. Leiden/Boston: Brill, 2004.

Tobi, Yosef. "Rabbi david ben yeshaʿ ha-levi (Yemen, 15th century)" (Hebrew). *ʿAlei sefer* 16 (1989–1990): 79–83.

Tobi, Yosef. "Rabbi yiṣḥaq wannah ve-hitḥazzqut ha-ʿissuq ba-qabbalah." *Daʿat* 38 (1997): 17–31.

Tobi, Yosef. "Šālom (Sālim) al Šabazī's (17th-century) poem of the debate between coffee and qāt." *Proceedings of the Seminar for Arabian Studies* 38 (2008): 301–310.

Tobi, Yosef. "Seder baʾashmoret ha-boqer le-rabbi yiḥye al-ḍāhirī." *Afikim* 37 (1970): 12–13.

Tobi, Yosef. "Seder qiddush leilei shabbat le-rabbi zechariah al-ḍāhirī." *Afikim* 68 (1978): 10–11.

Tobi, Yosef. "Shabazi, Shalom." *EJIW*. Brill Online.

Tobi, Yosef. "Ha-shem negdekha kol taʾavati le-alḍāhirī." *Ba-maʿarakhah* 102 (1969): 18–20.

Tobi, Yosef. "Shenei piyyutim ḥadashim le-rabbi zekharya alḍāhirī." *Afikim* 58 (1975): 9 & 22.

Tobi, Yosef. "Shir maʿaneh ʿal ʿyigdal elohim ḥayʾ le-rabbi david ben shelomoh ha-levi." *Afikim* 111–112 (1997): 40–42.

Tobi, Yosef. "Shirim ʿal ha-nefesh be-shirat teiman." *Afikim* 35 (1970): 8 and 36 (1970): 8–9.

Tobi, Yosef. "Shulḥan ʿarukh le-rabbi yosef karo leʿumat mishneh torah le-ha-rambam be-teiman." *Tema* 12 (2012): 5–30.

Tobi, Yosef. "Sifrei ha-refuʾah shel yehudei teiman." *Meḥqere yerushalayim be-folklor yehudi* 11/12 (1989–1990): 102–120.

Tobi, Yosef. "Sifrut ha-halakhah ha-zaydit ke-maqor le-toldot yehudei teiman." *Tema* 4 (1994): 93–118.

Tobi, Yosef. *Studies in Megillat Teman* (Hebrew). Jerusalem: Magnes Press, 1986.

Tobi, Yosef. *ʿAl ha-talmud be-teiman*. Tel Aviv: Afikim, 1973.

Tobi, Yosef. "Teiman ve-yerushalayim: qishrei yahadut teiman ʿim ereṣ yisrael ba-meʾot ha-7-ha-19." *Tema* 2 (1991): 5–28.

Tobi, Yosef. "*Tséré* (E vowel) and *Ḥolam* (O vowel) in Yemenite Jewish Pronunciation" (Hebrew). In *Boʾi Teman*, ed. Ratzaby, 52–57.

Tobi, Yosef. *The Yemenite Community of Jerusalem, 1881–1921* (Hebrew). Jerusalem: Yad Yiṣḥaq Ben-Zvi/ Ben-Zvi Institute, 1994.

Tobi, Yosef. *Yemenite Jewish Manuscripts in the Ben-Zvi Institute* (Hebrew). Jerusalem: The Ben-Zvi Institute, 1982.

Tobi, Yosef. "Yemenite Poetry and its Relationship with Sefardi Poetry" (Hebrew). In *Yahadut teiman*, ed. Yeshaʿyahu and Tobi, 303–332.

Toffolo, Sandra. "The Pilgrim, the City and the Book: The Role of the Mobility of Pilgrims in Book Circulation in Renaissance Venice." In *The Book World of Early Modern Europe: Essays in Honour of Andrew Pettegree*, 2:131–153. Brill, 2022.

Toorawa, Shawkat M. "Defining *Adab* by (Re)defining the Adīb: Ibn Abī Ṭāhir Ṭayfūr and Storytelling." In *On Fiction and* Adab *in Medieval Arabic Literature*, ed. Kennedy, 287–304.

Toorawa, Shawkat M. *Ibn Abī Ṭāhir Ṭayfūr and Arabic Writerly Culture: A Ninth-Century Bookman in Baghdad*. London and New York: RoutledgeCurzon, 2005.

Toorawa, Shawkat M. "Language and Male Homosocial Desire in the Autobiography of ʿAbd al-Latif al-Baghdadi (d. 629/1231)." *Edebiyât: The Journal of Middle Eastern Literatures*, n.s. 7/ 2 (1997): 251–265.

Toorawa, Shawkat M. "Travel in the Medieval Islamic World: The Importance of Patronage, as Illustrated by ʿAbd al-Latif al-Baghdadi (d. 629/1231) (and other littérateurs)." In *Eastward Bound*, ed. Allen, 53–70.

Torollo, David, ed. *Mishle he-ʿarav: la tradición sapiencial hebrea en la Península Ibérica y Provenza, s. XII y XIII*. Oxford/New York: Peter Lang, 2021.

Torollo, David, ed. "Wisdom Literature in Judeo-Arabic: *Kitāb maḥāsin al-ʾādāb* [The Book of Excellent Conduct]." *Memorabilia* 17 (2015): 90–114.

Touati, Houari. *Islam et voyage au moyen âge*. Paris: Éditions du seuil, 2000.

Tuchscherer, Michel. "Des épices au café, le Yémen dans le commerce international (XVIe–XVIIe siècle)." *Chroniques yéménites* 6 (1997), URL: http://cy.revues.org/103.

Twersky, Isadore. *Introduction to the Code of Maimonides*. New Haven & London: Yale University Press, 1980.

Twersky, Isadore. *A Maimonides Reader*. New York: Behrman House, 1972.

Twersky, Isadore. "Talmudists, Philosophers, Kabbalists: The Quest for Spirituality in the Sixteenth Century." In *Jewish Thought in the Sixteenth Century*, ed. Cooperman, 431–459.

Twersky, Isadore and George H. Williams, eds. *Studies in the History of Philosophy and Religion*. 2 vols. Cambridge, MA & London: Harvard University Press, 1973–1977.

Urbach, Ephraim E. *The Sages: Their Concepts and Beliefs*. Cambridge, Mass: Harvard University Press, 1979.

Vajda, Georges. Review of Yehuda Ratzaby ed., *Sefer Hammusar*. *REJ* 125 (1967): 445–447.

Vajda, Georges. *La Théologie ascétique de Baḥya Ibn Paquda*. Paris: Imprimerie Nationale, 1947.

van Arendonk, C. "Ḥātim al-Ṭāʾī." *EI*[1] online.

van Boxel, Piet et al., eds. *The Mishnaic Moment: Jewish Law among Jews and Christians in Early Modern Europe*. Oxford: Oxford University Press, 2022.

van der Heide, Albert. *Hebrew Manuscripts of Leiden University Library*. Universitaire Pers Leiden, 1977.

van Gelder, G.J. "Arabic Debates of Jest and Earnest." In *Dispute Poems and Dialogues*, ed. Reinink and Vanstiphout, 199–211.

van Gelder, G.J. "City Panegyric, in Classical Arabic." *EI*[3]. Brill Online.

van Gelder, G.J. "The Conceit of Pen and Sword: On an Arabic Literary Debate." *JSS* 32/2 (1987): 329–360.

van Gelder, G.J. "Didactic Literature." In *EAL*, 1:193–194.

van Gelder, G.J. "Fools and Rogues in Discourse and Disguise: Two Studies." In *Sensibilities of the Islamic Mediterranean*, ed. Ostle, 27–58.

van Gelder, G.J. "Muʿāraḍa." *EAL*, 2:534.

van Gelder, G.J. "In the Time of *al-Fiṭaḥl* When Stones Were Still Moist and All Things Spoke: Very Short Arabic Animal Fables and Just-So Stories." *JAS* 8 (2021): 12–37.

van Leeuwen, Richard. "Challenging Symbols of Power: Palaces and Castles in the *Thousand and One Nights*." In *Sensibilities of the Mediterranean*, ed. Ostle, 13–26.

van Leeuwen, Richard. "Preface: The Journey as Metaphor." In *Sensibilities of the Mediterranean*, ed. Ostle, 81–84.

van Leeuwen, Richard. *The Thousand and One Nights: Space, Travel and Transformation*. London/New York: Routledge, 2007.

van Leeuwen, Richard. "Travel and Spirituality: The Peregrinations of a Moroccan Sufi in the 16th Century." In *Tropes du voyages: Les Rencontres*, ed. Chraïbi, 157–173.

van Leeuwen, Richard. "'*Yā raḥīl*!' Reasons for Travelling in al-Ghazālī's *Ihyāʾ ʿulūm al-dīn*." In *Tropes du voyage: Départs*, ed. Ghersetti, 165–179.

Varlik, Nükhet. "Plague, Conflict, and Negotiation: The Jewish Broadcloth Weavers of Salonica and the Ottoman Central Administration in the Late Sixteenth Century." *Jewish History* 28/3–4 (2014): 261–288.

Verman, Mark. "Reincarnation (*gilgul*) and Sephardic Societies." *International Sephardic Journal* 2.1 (2005): 158–176.

Verman, Mark. "Reincarnation and Theodicy: Traversing Philosophy, Psychology, and Mysticism." In *Beʾerot Yitzhak*, ed. Harris, 399–426.

von Grunebaum, Gustave E. "Aspects of Arabic Urban Literature Mostly in Ninth and Tenth Centuries." *Islamic Studies* 8/4 (1969): 281–300.

von Grunebaum, Gustave E. "The Concept of Plagiarism in Arabic Theory." *JNES* 3 (1944): 234–253.

von Grunebaum, Gustave E. *Medieval Islam: A Study in Cultural Orientation*, 2d ed. Chicago: University of Chicago Press, 1961.

von Grunebaum, Gustave E. "On the Origin and Early Development of Arabic *Muzdawij* Poetry." *JNES* 3 (1944): 9–13.

von Grunebaum, Gustave E. *A Tenth-Century Document of Arabic Literary Theory and Criticism: The Sections on Poetry of al-Bāqillānī's Iʿjāz al-Qur'ān*. Chicago: University of Chicago Press, 1950.

von Hees, Syrinx. "The Astonishing: A Critique and Rereading of ʿAǧā'ib Literature." *MEL* 8/2 (2005): 101–120.

Verskin, Alan. *Diary of a Black Jewish Messiah: The Sixteenth-Century Journey of David Reubeni through Africa, the Middle East, and Europe*. Stanford University Press, 2023.

Verskin, Alan. *A Vision of Yemen: The Travels of a European Orientalist and His Native Guide, A Translation of Hayyim Habshush's Travelogue*. Stanford: Stanford University Press, 2018.

Wacks, David A. *Framing Iberia: Maqāmāt and Frametale Narratives in Medieval Spain*. Leiden/Boston: Brill, 2007.

Wacks, David A. "The Performativity of Ibn Al-Muqaffaʿ's 'Kalīla Wa-Dimna' and 'Al-Maqāmāt Al-Luzūmiyya' of Al-Saraqusṭī." *JAL* 34, no. 1/2 (January, 2003): 178–189.

Wagner, Mark S. "Arabic Influence on Shabazian Poetry in Yemen." *JSS* 51/1 (2006): 117–136.

Wagner, Mark S. "The Debate Between Coffee and Qāt in Yemeni Literature." *MEL*, 8/2 (2005): 121–149.

Wagner, Mark S. "The Flying Camel and the Red Heifer: Yemenite Poets in Modern Israel." *Tema* 10 (2007): 233–256.

Wagner, Mark S. "Jewish Mysticism on Trial in a Muslim Court: A Fatwā on the 'Zohar': Yemen 1914." *Die Welt des Islams*, n.s., 47/ 2 (2007): 207–231.

Wagner, Mark S. *Jews and Islamic Law in Early 20th-Century Yemen*. Bloomington: Indiana University Press, 2015.

Wagner, Mark S. *Like Joseph in Beauty: Yemeni Vernacular Poetry and Arab-Jewish Symbiosis*. Leiden/Boston: Brill, 2009.

Wasserstrom, Steven M. "Apology for S.D. Goitein: An Essay." In *A Faithful Sea: The Religious Cultures of the Mediterranean, 1200–1700*, ed. A.A. Husain and K.E. Fleming, 173–198. Oxford: Oneworld Publications, 2007.

Weber, Elka. "Sharing the Sites: Medieval Jewish Travellers to the Land of Israel." In *Eastward Bound*, ed. Allen, 35–52.

Weber, Elka. *Traveling through Text: Message and Method in Late Medieval Pilgrimage Accounts*. New York and London: Routledge, 2005.

Wehr, Hans. *A Dictionary of Modern Written Arabic*. Ed. J. Milton Cowan. 3d ed. Ithaca, N.Y.: Spoken Language Services, 1976.

Weinberger, Leon. *Jewish Poet in Muslim Egypt: Moses Darʿī's Hebrew Collection*. Leiden/Boston/Köln: Brill, 2000.

Weinberger, Leon. *Jewish Prince in Moslem Spain*. University, Alabama: The University of Alabama Press, 1973.

Weinstein, Avi trans. Joseph Gikatilla, *Gates of Light*. San Francisco: HarperCollins, 1994.

Weinstein, Roni. *Joseph Karo and Shaping [sic] of Modern Jewish Law: The Early Modern Ottoman and Global Settings*. London/New York: Anthem Press, 2022.

Werblowsky, R.J. Zwi. "A Collection of Prayers and Devotional Compositions by Solomon Alkabeṣ" (Hebrew). *Sefunot* 6 (1962): 135–182.

Werblowsky, R.J. Zwi. *Joseph Karo, Lawyer and Mystic*. Philadelphia: The Jewish Publication Society of America, 1977.

Werblowsky, R.J. Zwi. "The Safed Revival and its Aftermath." In *Jewish Spirituality*, ed. Green, 2:7–33.

Wieder, Naphtali. "Islamic Influences on the Jewish Worship." In *The Formation of Jewish Liturgy in the East and the West* (Hebrew), 659–777. Jerusalem: Ben-Zvi Institute, Yad Izhak Ben-Zvi and the Hebrew University of Jerusalem, 1998.

Wilke, Carsten L. "Dialogues of the Dead: Talking Epitaphs by Sephardi and Ashkenazi Rabbis of Hamburg." *Zutot* 5/1 (2008): 61–72.

Williams, Benjamin. "Bringing Maimonides to Oxford: Edward Pococke, the Mishnah, and the *Porta Mosis*." In *The Mishnaic Moment*, ed. van Boxel et al., 157–176.

Wolfson, Elliot R. *Abraham Abulafia—Kabbalist and Prophet: Hermeneutics, Theosophy, and Theurgy*. Los Angeles: Cherub Press, 2000.

Wolfson, Elliot R. *Along the Path: Studies in Kabbalistic Myth, Symbolism, and Hermeneutics*. Albany: SUNY Press, 1995.

Wolfson, Elliot R. "Asceticism, Mysticism, and Messianism: A Reappraisal of Schechter's Portrait of Sixteenth-Century Safed." *JQR* 106/2 (2016): 165–177.

Wolfson, Elliot R. "Beneath the Wings of the Great Eagle: Maimonides and Thirteenth-Century Kabbalah." In *Moses Maimonides (1138–1204): His Religious, Scientific, and Philosophical "Wirkungsgeschichte" in Different Cultural Contexts*, ed. G.K. Hasselhoff and O. Fraisse, 209–237. Würzburg: Ergon Verlag, 2004.

Wolfson, Elliot R. "Beyond the Spoken Word: Oral Tradition and Written Transmission in Medieval Jewish Mysticism." In *Transmitting Jewish Traditions*, ed. Elman and Gershoni, 166–224.

Wolfson, Elliot R. "Coronation of the Sabbath Bride: Kabbalistic Myth and the Ritual of Androgynisation." *JJTP* 6 (1997): 301–344.

Wolfson, Elliot R. "Forms of Visionary Ascent as Ecstatic Experience in the Zoharic Literature." In *Gershom Scholem's Major Trends in Jewish Mysticism 50 Years After*, ed. P. Schäfer and J. Dan, 209–235. Tübingen: Mohr Siebeck, 1993.

Wolfson, Elliot R. *Language, Eros, Being: Kabbalistic Hermeneutics and Poetic Imagination*. New York: Fordham University Press, 2005.

Wolfson, Elliot R. "Occultation of the Feminine and the Body of Secrecy in Medieval Kabbalah." In *Rending the Veil: Concealment and Secrecy in the History of Religions*, ed. E.R. Wolfson, 113–154. New York/ London: Seven Bridges Press, 1999.

Wolfson, Elliot R. *Through a Speculum That Shines*. Princeton: Princeton University Press, 1994.

Wolfson, Harry A. "The Internal Senses in Latin, Arabic, and Hebrew Philosophic Texts." In *Studies in the History of Philosophy and Religion*, ed. Twersky and Williams, 1:250–314.

Wolfson, Harry A. "Isaac Israeli on the Internal Senses." In *Studies in the History of Philosophy and Religion*, ed. Twersky and Williams, 1:315–330.

Wolfson, Harry A. "Maimonides on the Internal Senses." In *Studies in the History of Philosophy and Religion*, ed. Twersky and Williams, 1:344–370.

Wolfson, Harry A. "Notes on Isaac Israeli's Internal Senses." In *Studies in the History of Philosophy and Religion*, ed. Twersky and Williams, 1:331–343.

Wood, James. *How Fiction Works*. New York: Farrar, Straus & Giroux, 2008.

Worman, Ernest. "Forms of Address in Genizah Letters." *JQR* o.s. 19 (1907): 721–743.

Xavier, Angela Barrero. "Languages of Difference in the Portuguese Empire: The Spread of 'Caste' in the Indian World." *Anuario Colombiano de Historia Social y de la Cultura* 43/2 (2016): 89–119.

Yaʿakov, Doron. "Yemen, Pronunciation Traditions." In *Encyclopedia of Hebrew Language and Linguistics* online, ed. G. Khan, Leiden: Brill, 2013.

Yaakov, Efraim. *Eloha mi-teiman yavo: peraqim be-toldot ha-qabbalah be-teiman*. Ed. Meir Bar-Asher. Jerusalem: Ben-Zvi Institute, Yad Izhak Ben-Zvi and the Hebrew University, 2016.

Yaakov, Efraim. "Liqrat hahdarato shel 'Sefer haʿanaq' le-mari yiḥye al-daheri she-huva laʾaḥronah me-russya." *Tehuda* 14 (1994): 26–31.

Yaari, Abraham. *Ha-defus haʿivri beʾarṣot ha-mizraḥ*. Jerusalem: at the University Press, 1936–1940.

Yaari, Abraham. "Iggeret sheliḥut mi-yerushalayim liyehudei teiman." In *Harʾel*, ed. Ratzaby and Shivtiel, 218–225.

Yaari, Abraham. *Iggerot ereṣ yisrael*. 2d ed. Ramat Gan: Massada, 1971.

Yaari, Abraham, ed. *Massaʿ meshullam me-voltera*. Jerusalem: Bialik Institute, 1948.

Yaari, Abraham, ed. *Massaʿot ereṣ yisrael, shel olim yehudim mimei ha-beinayim veʿad reshit shivat ṣiyon*. Tel Aviv: Ha-histadrut ha-ṣionit, 1946.

Yaari, Abraham. *Meḥqerei sefer*. Jerusalem: Mosad Harav Kook, 1958.

Yaari, Abraham. "Sheliḥim meʾereṣ yisraʾel le-teiman." *Sinai* 4 (1939): 392–430.

Yaari, Abraham, ed. *Sheluḥei ʾereṣ yisraʾel, toldot ha-sheliḥut mehaʾareṣ la-golah me-ḥurban bayit sheni ʿad ha-meʾah ha-19*. Jerusalem: Mosad Harav Kook, 1951.

Yadin, Azzan. "Theosophy and Kabbalistic Writing" (Hebrew). *Peʿamim* 104 (2005): 41–64.

Yahalom, Joseph. "The Function of the Frame Story in Hebrew Adaptations of the Maqāmāt" (Heb). In *Israel Levin Jubilee Volume*, ed. R. Tsur and T. Rosen, 1:135–154. Tel Aviv: Tel Aviv University Press, 1994.

Yahalom, Joseph. "R. Israel Najarah and the Revival of Hebrew Poetry in the East After the Expulsion from Spain" (Hebrew). *Pe'amim* 13 (1982): 96–124.

Yahalom, Joseph. "A Romance Maqāma: The Place of the 'Speech of Tuvia Ben Zedeqiah' in the History of the Hebrew Maqāma" (Hebrew). *Hispania Judaica* 10 (2014): 113–128.

Yahalom, Joseph. "Tensions between Sephardic Traditions and Ottoman Influences in Jewish Literary Activity." In *Between History and Literature: Studies in Honor of Isaac Barzilay*, ed. S. Nash, 207–216. N.p.: Hakibbutz Hameuchad, 1997.

Yahalom, Joseph. *Yehuda Halevi: Poetry and Pilgrimage* (Hebrew). Jerusalem: Magnes Press, 2009.

Yahalom, Shalem. "The *Pilpul* Method of Talmudic Study: Earliest Evidence" (Hebrew). *Tarbiz* 84/4 (2016): 543–574.

Yassif, Eli. *The Hebrew Folktale: History, Genre, Meaning*. Trans. Jacqueline S. Teitelbaum. Bloomington: Indiana University Press, 1999.

Yassif, Eli. "The Hebrew Narrative Anthology in the Middle Ages." *Prooftexts* 17/2 (1997): 153–175; repr. in Stern, ed. *The Anthology in Jewish Literature*, 176–195.

Yassif, Eli. *The Legend of Safed: Life and Fantasy in the City of Kabbalah*. Trans. Haim Watzman. Detroit: Wayne State University Press, 2019.

Yassif, Eli. "Oral Traditions in a Literate Society: The Hebrew Literature of the Middle Ages." In *Medieval Oral Literature*, ed. K. Reichl, 497–517. Berlin/Boston: De Gruyter, 2012.

Yassif, Eli. "Shevarim geluḥei zaqan: ha-ma'avaq 'al ha-mithos shel ṣefat ba-yamim ha-hem, ba-zeman ha-zeh." *Mi-kan* 4 (2005): 42–79.

Yassif, Eli. "Ha-sipporet ha'ivrit be'arṣot ha-mizraḥ" *Pe'amim* 26 (1986): 53–70.

Yedid, Rachel and Danny Bar-Maoz, eds. *Ascending the Palm Tree: An Anthology of the Yemenite Jewish Heritage*. Rehovot: E'ele BeTamar, 2018.

Yellin, David. "Ginze teiman." *Ha-shiloaḥ* 2 (1897): 147–161.

Yerushalmi, Yosef Hayim. "Exile and Expulsion in Jewish History." In *Crisis and Creativity in the Sephardic World 1391–1648*, ed. Gampel, 3–22.

Yerushalmi, Yosef Hayim. "Messianic Impulses in Joseph ha-Kohen." In *Jewish Thought in the Sixteenth Century*, ed. Cooperman, 460–487.

Yeshaya, Joachim. *Medieval Hebrew Poetry in Muslim Egypt: The Secular Poetry of the Karaite Poet Moses ben Abraham Dar'ī*. Leiden/Boston: Brill, 2011.

Yeshaya, Joachim. *Poetry and Memory in Karaite Prayer: The Liturgical Poetry of the Karaite Poet Moses Ben Abraham Dar'ī*. Leiden/Boston: Brill, 2013.

Yevin, Yisrael. "'Treasures of the Yemen'—a Private Manuscript Collection in Holon" (Hebrew). In *Se'i Yona*, ed. Seri, 387–398.

Yiṣhari, Mordechai ed. *Sadoq Yiṣhari, Kakh baraḥti mi-teiman*. Rosh Ha'ayin, 1988.

Yisha'yahu, Yisrael and Aharon Zadok, eds. *Shevut teiman*. Tel Aviv: "Mi-teiman le-tziyyon," 1945.

Yishaʿyahu, Yisrael and Shimon Greidi, eds. *Mi-teiman le-ṣion*. Tel Aviv: Masadah, 1938.

Yishaʿyahu, Yisrael and Yosef Tobi, eds. *Yahadut teiman: pirqei meḥqar veʿiyyun*. Jerusalem: Yad Izhak Ben-Zvi, 1975.

Yona, Shamir and Ariel Ram Pasternak. "Concatenation in Ancient Near East Literature, Hebrew Scripture and Rabbinic Literature." *The Review of Rabbinic Judaism* 22 (2019): 46–92.

Young, Douglas C. "Preachers and Poets: The Popular Sermon in the Andalusī *Maqāma*." *JAL* 34 (2003): 190–205.

Yūsuf, May Aḥmad, ed. Ibn Abi ʿAwn, *al-Ajwibah al-muskitah*. Cairo, 1996.

Yūsuf, May Aḥmad, ed. *Das Buch der schlagfertigen Antworten*. Berlin: K. Schwarz, 1988; repr. Walter de Gruyter, 2021.

Zadock, Aharon. "R. yiḥye qāfeḥ zal—tequfato u-mifʿalo." In *Shevut teiman*, ed. Yishaʿyahu and Zadok, 166–231.

Zadock, Moshe. *Maḥshevet yisrael be-teiman: ʿal sefarim ve-ʿal sofrim*. Tel Aviv: ʿAm ʿoved, 1987.

Zadock, Moshe. "Ṣeidah la-derekh, midrash filosofi qabbali." *Ha-ṣofeh* Aug. 27, 1965.

Zakharia, Katia. *Abū Zayd al-Sarūǧī, imposteur et mystique*. Damascus: IFEAD, 2000.

Zilberberg, Gershon and Jennifer Breger. "Printing, Hebrew." *EJ*² 16:529–540.

Zim, Rivkah. "Writing Behind Bars: Literary Contexts and the Authority of Carceral Experience." *Huntington Library Quarterly* 72/ 2 (June 2009): 291–311.

Zimmels, H.J. *Ashkenazim and Sephardim: Their Relations, Differences, and Problems as Reflected in the Rabbinical Responsa*. London: Oxford University Press, 1958; repr. Gregg International Publishers Ltd., 1969.

Zumthor, Paul. "The Medieval Travel Narrative." *New Literary History* 25 (1994): 809–824.

Zunz, Leopold. *Die Ritus des synagogalen Gottesdienstes, geschichtlich entwickelt*. 2d ed. Berlin, 1919.

Zunz, Leopold. *Die Synagogale Poesie des Mittelalters*. 2d ed. Frankfurt Am Main, 1920.

Index of Hebrew Poems

Alḏāhirī, Zechariah
"ʿAl divrati sov hitnahel" 151–152
"ʿAnenei dimʿi shequdim" 121*n*239
"Asher ḥanan le-vanim haʿamusim" 306–307, 308, 318
"Asher kippat sheḥaqim lo ʿaliyyah" 211*n*162, 281–283
"Asher shat malkhuto ʿalei khol mamlekhet" 400
"Az ba-ḥalom le-rosh har ha-mor" 135–136
"Beʿeden gan elohim kol yeqarah" 401–403
"Benei ʿelyon, benei ḥokhmah, benei ish" 435
"Bereishit qedumat yomayyim" 390, 396, 411
"Be-tishrei esmeḥa liqrat penei el" 125
"Elohai pataḥ pi" 308
"Emet baqqesh ve-hashlekh ha-meradim" 121*n*239
"Ha-shoʾalim bosem be-mirqaḥat" 130
"Ha-yippale beʿein kol nediv ha-lev" 124
"Hoy nirdamim ʿuru, ʿuru" 240*n*5
"Ishim eqra me-har el har" 378–379, 422
"Leshoni eshteqad hayyetah amuṣah" 140–143
"Lifnei elohim eʿemod" 143–144
"Liqrat penei shabbat" 383, 396, 399, 405–413, 425
"Matoq le-miṣuf u-fannag" 413–415
"Nefesh yeqarah, eikh be-tokh guf tishkeni" 138, 139–140, 353–354
"Yaḥid meromam ʿal kol geviyyah" 211*n*162
"Yedidi im tivḥar le-havin sod zohar" 378, 400

Alḥarizi, Judah
"Nefesh yeqarah, eikh be-sikhlekh tivteḥi" 138, 139, 354

Alqabeṣ, Solomon
"Lekhah dodi" 383, 397, 407, 412

Ardutiel, Shem Tov
"Ribbono shel ʿolam, birʾoti baḥurotai" 429

Dato, Mordechai
"Adon ha-kol ve-ḥayy ʿolam" 397
"Boʾi kallah, boʾi kallah" 397, 412

Halevi, Judah
"Adonai negdekha kol taʾavati" 130
"Libbi ʿamod ki mi be-sod tokhen levavot yaʿamod" 145–146, 147, 152

Hanagid, Samuel
"Aḥi musar u-var torah" 83
"Asher ein lo rekhush" 83
"Ha-nimṣa be-reʿay" 454
"Leshoni eshʾalah mimmekh sheʾelah" 141
"Shemuʾel qademah yoshev keruvim" 83

Ibn Ezra, Abraham
"Az baʿalot mequṭeret mor" 133–136, 137
"Imrat yeḥidah le-yaḥid yaʾatah," 128
"Miyaldei yom al tibbahel" 148, 150, 151–152

Ibn Ezra, Moses
"Be-shem el asher amar" 84, 130
"Ḥaradah laveshah tevel" 83

Ibn Gabirol, Solomon
"Shaḥar avakeshkha" 130
"Sheḥi laʾel yeḥidah ha-ḥakhamah" 130

Ibn Lavi, Simon
"Bar yoḥai" 396, 397, 412, 413, 413*n*120

Ibn Mar Shaul, Isaac
"Elohai, al tedineni ke-maʿali" 131

Ibn Paquda, Baḥya
"Barekhi nafshi" 358*n*43

Immanuel of Rome
"Be-tishrei esmeḥa ki moʿadei el/yeʿiruni le-shorer shirei ʿagavim" 125
"Haʿovrim, hittammhu utmahu!" 444
"Roʾay ve-yodʿay lefanim/ʿalay seʾu taḥanunim!" 444, 449

Luria, Isaac
"Benei heikhala" 408–409

Najara, Israel
"Tiddad shnat 'eini" 398–399

Padova, Judah Maṣliah
'Olam hafukh 444

Unknown
"Eleh ezkerah" 434

General Index

ʿAbbāsid period 78, 80, 122, 155*n*337, 183, 200, 445
ʿAbd al-Raḥmān I 183
Abner ben Ḥeleq ha-Teimani (fictional character) 32*n*101, 64, 166, 179, 182, 229, 383
  authorial voice and 104–105
  broad learning of 254–255
  character development of 106–109
  in Damascus 65
  diction and speech patterns 90
  elegy/epitaph for Mordecai 76, 431–436
  exempla about virtuous Arabs and 327–330, 332, 335–341
  explanation of name 114–116
  folktales told by 237
  in Ḥaḍramawt 186–188
  as *ḥazzan* in Tiberias 66, 120, 212, 218, 277, 279, 280, 383–384, 385, 405, 425
  identity and disguises of 95–96, 106, 347
  imprisonment of 209, 219, 289, 295*n*11
  interaction with historical figure 101
  on "internal senses" of the soul 347–351
  kabbalism and 66, 379, 413, 420–426
  Land of Israel and 209–212
  Muslim–Jewish polemics and 300, 314, 315, 330, 332
  numeric value of name 43
  nuptials in Cochin 74, 108, 188, 195, 196
  panegyric epistles of 265–266
  as penitent 438, 441
  as pietist 358–361
  place names and 222
  poems recited by 117, 120, 121–122, 136–137, 141, 354
  as preacher 86, 120–121
  as pretender to medical knowledge 361–369
  pronunciation of Hebrew 277–285
  Rabbi Abraham Ashkenazi and 242–253
  rhetorical talent of 172–173, 355, 369, 429–430
  Sephardi elite and 274, 275, 276
  as sham mendicant preacher 371–372
  shape-shifting disguises of 203–204, 315
  as stock character 219, 321
  suffering of Yemenite Jewry and 207
  in tales involving *qāḍīs* 319–326
  Torah study and 254
  word play and 94–95
Abraham ben Ḥalfon 94, 131
Abraham ben Solomon 392*n*56
Abraham Ibn Ezra 44, 124, 130, 141, 153, 234
  audiences of 417
  auto-epitaph of 454
  Ḥayy ben Meqiṣ 176, 363–364
  liturgical *muwashshaḥāt* of 128
  piyyut (*ahavah*) of 134, 135, 136, 137, 271
  on purpose of arbitrary commandments 249*n*29
  reputation of 272
Abravanel, Isaac 267, 288
Abudarham, David ben Joseph 246, 254
Abū Nuwās 445
Abū Zayd al-Sarūjī (fictional character) 101, 112, 121, 221, 368*n*73, 371*n*79, 372
  apparent penitential turn of 440–441
  caught drinking in tavern 121
  invented biography of 61
  significance of name 112
  as trickster hero 109, 110, 111, 113
Accounts of China and India (unknown author) 169
acronyms 92–94, 242, 312*n*62, 426
acrostics 135, 210, 378, 405, 413, 439
Ādāb al-falāsifa [Apothegms of the Philosophers] (Ibn Isḥāq) 84
Adab al-kātib 79*n*118
Adab al-kātib [*Adab al-kuttāb*] (Ibn Qutayba) 87
adab culture/literature 54, 55, 61, 86, 110, 288, 441
  ʿAbbāsid courtly circles and 78–79
  adab as commodity 87
  anthologies 116
  didacticism associated with 80
  difficulty of defining 77–78
  Ḥadīth khurāfa 60
  ideal of generosity 333
  musar equivalence to 46
  oral and written 336–337
  pithy sayings 85
  prison writings and 199

as stimulus to travel 215, 216
tales of thieves and thievery 321, 326
wide variety of works encompassed by 353
See also *musar*
adam qadmon (primordial man) 377
Adanī poets 94, 131
Aden, port of 206
British colonization of (1839) 9, 163*n*362
Ottoman occupation of 6
Portuguese attack on 8
adīb ('Abbāsid courtier/gentleman) 78, 82, 83, 87
"Admirable and Ridiculous Hero, An: Some Notes on the Bedouin in Medieval Arabic Belles-Lettres" (Sadan) 336
aesthetic ideals, in *Sefer hamusar* 40
Afikim (journal) 28, 30
aggadot 249, 254, 256, 432
Agudat ezov (Isaac ha-Ezobi) 376–377
al-Aḥmar, Khalaf 445
akhbār (anecdotal narratives) 55
Alami, Solomon 346*n*2
Albo, Joseph 123, 288
Alḍāhirī, Zechariah
Arabic and Hebrew names of 23
audience of 88, 93, 137, 204
authorial sensibilities of 10–12
auto-epitaphs of 436–440
Cochini caste division and 196
conception of space 204–206
"counter-writing" and 131
didacticism and 373–374
as epigone 13–14
full name of 35
as halakhist 12, 455, 457
Hebrew printing and 16–17
imprisonment of 5*n*4, 7, 36, 38, 43, 45, 197, 203
kabbalah and 2, 15, 23, 219, 375, 385–399, 458
as member of religious/intellectual elite 252
paratexts of 122
philosophical eclecticism of 356
as polymath 1, 11
print culture and 16, 285–290
reconstructed biography of 21
as religious scholar 2, 33, 454
Torah commentary of 287
as translator 331
Alḍāhirī, Zechariah, audience of 11, 45, 88, 93, 95, 158–164, 204, 374
Abner's audience 315, 326, 328, 341, 354, 355, 357, 371, 372, 378, 380, 382, 416–417, 420, 422–424, 435–436
cultural expectations of 174–175
didacticism and 70
diversity of 11
exemplary behavior of "Arabs" and 99
kabbalism and 375, 389, 390, 415, 419, 426
limited circulation of *Sefer hamusar* and 296
Muslim-Jewish polemics and 237
tawakkul (Heb. *biṭṭaḥon*) ideal and 331–332
Alfasi, Isaac 259, 260, 262, 452
Alḥarizi, Judah 12, 13, 17, 38, 51–52, 76, 346, 419
Alḍāhirī's anti-parody and 140
Alḍāhirī's borrowing from 147
Alḍāhirī's praise of 43–44
ambivalence toward Arabic language 342
celebration of Damascus and Syria 184
denunciation of Hebrew poetry composed outside of Iberia 276
on deracination 113–114
fictional characters of 43
homonymic poems 131
on invented nature of *maqāma* protagonists 102
kabbalism and 420
relations with benefactors 123
on translation from Arabic to Hebrew 47–49
as translator 84–85
travel ambitions of 224
travel in search of patronage 180
as tutelary spirit for *Sefer hamusar* 46
use of Hebrew language 89
wanderings of 171
See also *Taḥkemoni*
allegories 49, 69, 117, 350*n*21, 430
Al mavet [The Lamentation Over the Dead] (Levin) 453
Alnadāf, Abraham 26–27

Alqabeṣ, Solomon 66, 277, 383, 397, 412
Alsheikh, Moses 386
Amir, Yehuda 36, 37
Amr Ibn Hishām 109
anadiplosis (*shirshur*) 119
anagnorisis (recognition scene) 95–97, 315, 422, 439
anagrams 28, 53, 92, 93, 208, 334
anaphora 444, 445*n*50, 447
Anatolia 166, 205, 266, 269
  Alḍāhirī's protagonists in 223, 232, 233
  Alḍāhirī's travels in 450
  as part of "Romah" 225
  Sephardi dominance in 269
  Sephardim in western Anatolia 204, 205
  See also Bursa
al-Andalus (Islamic Spain) 2, 51, 82, 85, 272, 291
  Almohad invasion 224
  courtly context of *adab* in 85
  culture of orality and performance in 155
  "Golden Age" of Jewry in 10, 273, 293
  Hebrew poets of 75, 82, 84, 127–128
  ideal of biblical classicism 89
  mythologizing of Jewish life in 273
  nostalgia for Syria and Umayyads 183–184
  slave markets in 235
  Umayyad dynasty in 183
  See also Jews, Andalusian/Iberian; Spain, Christian
animal fables 28, 61, 63, 190, 345, 458
anthropology 24, 40, 167
aphorisms 12, 79, 83, 89*n*151, 116, 215, 337–338
Arabian Nights
  See *Thousand and One Nights* (*Arabian Nights*)
Arabic language 11, 44, 46–48, 61, 297, 342, 344
  al-Ḥarīrī's expressive brilliance in 69, 91
  printing in movable type 285*n*122
  words with opposite meanings 90
  See also belles-lettres, Arabic
Arabisms 83, 89, 90, 142*n*310, 150, 320
Arabization 217, 230
Aramaic language 89, 242, 397
Ardutiel, Shem Tov 429
Ariès, Philippe 456
Aripul, Samuel 388
Aristotle 349, 350, 351*n*23, 448
ʿArussi, Raṣon 263
Ashkenazi, Rabbi Abraham b. Isaac 16, 64, 101, 206, 275
  Alḍāhirī's protagonists and 242–253, 266, 287–288
  fundraising mission to Yemen 67, 239, 287, 388
  as historical figure based in Safed 387
Ashkenazi, Eliezer 387–388
Ashkenazim 225, 232–235, 237
  intellectual revival (16th century) 199
  in Jerusalem (19th century) 256
  Talmudic study and 255, 259
ashmoret ha-boqer (kabbalistic prayer vigil) 396, 398
Association for the Rescue of the Hidden Treasures of Yemen [*Ha'agudah le-haṣalat ginzei teiman*] (Qāfiḥ) 30
astrology 79, 151
astronomy 18, 79, 229, 439, 448, 457*n*88, 458
atbash alphabetic code 93, 161
authorial voice 104–105, 314, 427
authorship 69, 114, 169, 435–436, 445
autobiography, in Arabic literary tradition 34, 449
ʿavodah (early Palestinian poetic genre) 119
Ayyūbids 5
Azikri, Eleazar 277, 386, 397

Baghdad 63, 79*n*115, 80, 82, 131, 200, 228
  Abner and Mordecai in 210, 213, 218, 228, 377
  adab culture in 82
  religious polemical debates in 299
al-Balīda, Moshe ben Yosef 10
Bar Ḥiyya, Abraham 75*n*106, 346*n*2
al-Barq al-yamānī fī 'l-fatḥ al-ʿuthmānī (al-Nahrawālī) 201–202, 293
Bar Yoḥai, Simeon (Shimon) 240, 390, 396, 406, 410, 421
Barzani, Rabbi Samuel 377
Bashirī, Yiḥye 457*n*88
Basola, Moses 178, 210*n*158, 212*n*165
Bauer, Thomas 58*n*61
Baumgarten, Eliezer 377

Bedouins 50, 100, 237, 326, 333, 343
Beeston, A.F.L. 56
Behmardi, Vahid 39*n*122
Beit Yosef (Karo) 240, 289*n*137, 357, 412*n*118
belles-lettres, Arabic 1, 2, 78, 147
  Alḍāhirī's cross-cultural borrowings from 296
  Bedouins ridiculed in 333
  travel narratives as 177
belletristic works, Hebrew 12, 68, 308, 314*n*66, 454
  kabbalism and 376, 418, 425
  medical material in 364–365
  Muslim–Jewish polemics and 316
  paucity in Yemenite Jewish literature 455
  representation of Muslims and 291, 292, 309, 318
  rhymed prose in 70, 88–89
  Sefer hamusar as 19, 32, 40, 85, 162, 375, 418, 425, 456
  tension between truth and falsehood in 427
Benaya family 285
Benjamin of Tudela 169–170, 175, 178, 235
Ben Mishlei [After Proverbs] (Samuel Hanagid) 83
Ben Qohelet [After Ecclesiastes] (Samuel Hanagid) 83
Ben Sira, apocryphal book of 338
Ben Tehillim [After Psalms] (Samuel Hanagid) 83
Benveniste, Samuel 346*n*2
Ben Zakkai, Rabbi Johanan 458, 459
Ben-Zvi Institute 29
Berakhia ha-Naqdan 99*n*179
Bertinoro, Mishnah commentary of 123, 245–246
Bialik, Hayim Nahman 28*n*85, 449*n*63
Bible, Hebrew 1, 10
  Canticles (Song of Songs) 108, 133, 134, 356, 398, 414*n*124, 436, 447*n*57
  I Chronicles 114
  Daniel 236, 335*n*110, 339, 435, 447
  Deuteronomy 267, 287, 301, 305, 306, 307–308, 313, 325, 330, 338, 339, 371, 414, 447*n*57
  Ecclesiastes 423*n*141, 447*n*57
  Esther 124, 424*n*, 447*n*57
  Exodus 38, 117*n*228, 134, 149, 274, 368, 410, 414, 447*n*57
  Ezekiel 402, 430, 447*n*56
  Genesis 29*n*89, 113, 117*n*228, 173, 186, 188, 222, 235, 249, 274, 275*n*95, 301, 305, 312, 328, 331, 333, 335*n*113, 336, 339, 380, 382, 396, 411, 422, 424, 435*n*23, 446*n*53, 447*n*57
  Habakuk 331
  Hosea 302, 305, 311, 312
  Isaiah 46, 136*n*294, 186*n*72, 234, 267, 271, 281, 314, 371, 407, 430, 431*n*7, 443, 446*n*53
  Jeremiah 134, 312*n*62, 327, 371
  Job 70, 117*n*228, 172, 173, 222*nn*197–198, 236, 274, 284, 313, 335, 339, 415, 447*n*57
  Joel 196*n*113
  Joshua 173
  Judges 113, 236, 335*n*111
  I Kings 114, 149, 329*n*96
  II Kings 172, 431*n*8
  Lamentations 70, 135, 447*n*57
  Leviticus 151, 196, 396*n*69
  Malachi 208*n*147, 293
  Micah 312*n*62, 430
  Nahum 300
  Nehemiah 277
  Numbers 117, 136, 311, 447*n*57
  Obadiah 208, 235, 293
  Proverbs 67*n*81, 75, 76, 80, 81, 87, 100, 215, 229, 235, 311, 324, 331, 336, 337, 338, 339, 344, 349, 356, 407, 432*n*13, 447*nn*55, 57
  Psalms 44, 68, 71, 114, 115, 136*n*292, 249, 311, 312, 313, 325, 327, 328, 331, 348, 353, 368, 381, 383, 436, 447*n*57
  Ruth 431, 447*n*57
  I Samuel 311, 312, 435
  II Samuel 76, 115, 324*n*90, 429, 431, 438, 443*n*44
  Zechariah 117*n*228, 364
  Zephaniah 409
Biblia Rabbinica (Bomberg, 1525) 284
biblical commentary 18, 263*n*67, 434, 446, 447*n*57, 456
binary oppositions 15, 253, 278, 408, 418
Boccaccio, Giovanni 97, 156
Boethius 198, 199
Bomberg, Daniel 247, 284

Book of Direction to the Duties of the Heart [*Al-hidāya ilā farāʾiḍ al-qulūb*] (Ibn Paquda) 82, 138, 145*n*318, 237, 358*n*43, 364
Book of Improvement of the Moral Qualities [*Kitāb iṣlāḥ al-akhlāq*] (Ibn Gabirol) 352, 364
Book of John Mandeville 168
Book of Questions on the Unity of God [*Masāʾil fī ʾl-tawḥīd*] (al-Muqammaṣ) 68*n*85
Bosworth, C.E. 54, 100*n*183
"boxing tales" 181, 182
Boyarin, Daniel 154*n*335, 255*n*42
Brann, Ross 90, 291, 292, 316, 317, 318, 436–437
Bregman, Dvora 449, 451
British Library manuscript (BL Or 11337) 73, 74, 118
Brody, Ḥayyim 22–23, 28
Buddhism 190
Bursa, city of 218, 219, 224, 377, 424
  Abner in 380, 381
  Islamic and Jewish mysticism in 379
  Jews of 225, 228, 376
  kabbalistic study in 376
  sages of 424
Bustān al-ʿuqūl (Ibn Fayyūmī) 237, 308
Buyids 299
Byzantine Empire 200, 269, 385

Cairo 63, 194, 205*n*139, 299
  Iberian Jews in 268, 269
  Jewish community of 250, 268
  Muslim–Jewish polemics in 106
Cairo Genizah 22, 177
Canaanites 192, 222, 234–235
Canterbury Tales (Chaucer) 97
caste 193, 194, 196
Castro, Rabbi Jacob de 194
Cave, Terence 97
Chaucer, Geoffrey 97
Chenery, Thomas 89
China 86, 169, 223
Christians and Christianity 68*n*85, 198–199, 200, 224, 302, 319–321
  Christian–Jewish polemics 298, 299, 300
  funerary practices 450, 451
  historical function of Christianity 303
  Jews forcibly converted to Christianity in Iberia 231
  reviled in *Sefer hamusar* 227
  See also Spain, Christian
Cochin (India), Jewish community of 188, 190
  "black" Jews 193, 195
  meshuḥrarim (those freed from bondage) 193, 194, 195
  meyuḥasim (of distinguished pedigree) 193, 194, 195, 196
  Sephardim 191, 192, 196
  sub-castes 193, 195
colonialism, European 196
Commentary on the Mishnah (Maimonides) 246*n*21, 247, 254, 284–285
Consolation of Philosophy (Boethius, c. 524) 198
Constantinople 179, 225, 235, 269, 456
  See also Istanbul
contrafaction 40, 147, 153
  as anti-parody 137–140
  counter-writing and 125–137
Cooperson, Michael 53, 91, 112
Cordovero, Rabbi Moses 37, 39, 218, 240, 386
  pre-Lurianic kabbalism and 395
  theosophy of 396
"counter-genre" 56
courtier-rabbis 272
Crone, Patricia 78, 79*n*118
cultural studies 40, 167

da Gama, Vasco 191
Daniel, tomb of 228
Dante Alighieri 442, 449
Darʿī, Moses 128, 130
Dato, Mordechai 397, 412
David ben Meʿoded 261
Davis, Natalie Zemon 18
al-Dawla, ʿAḍud 200
al-Dawlah, Sayf 200
Decameron (Boccaccio) 97, 156
Decter, Jonathan 113, 174, 223
De Looze, Laurence 31
De Medina, Samuel 270, 271, 272
dhimmī status 292*n*5, 295, 317, 325, 344, 345
  indignities of 311

medieval restrictions maintained into modern times 9
pagans unqualified for 214*n*174
diaspora, Jewish 207, 210–211
ancestral homeland in binary distinction to 212
diasporic consciousness 70
rabbinic fundraising campaigns and 242
didacticism 85, 373–374
al-Dīn, Rashīd 231*n*223
Disparition, La (Perec, 1969) 92
Divine Comedy (Dante) 442, 449
Dīwān of Hebrew and Arabic Poetry of the Yemenite Jews (Idelsohn, 1930) 23–24
dīwāns 2, 83, 120, 128, 129
collective recitation and 157, 158
ziyāda in superscriptions of 148
Yemenite 132
Dor De'ah movement 391, 458
Drory, Rina 48, 54, 57, 58*n*59, 445*n*52
on conceptualization of fiction in Hebrew *maqāmāt* 62
on introduction of fictionality into classical Arabic literature 61
on veracity in Arabic prose 60
Dunn, Ross 169

Egypt 4, 5, 10, 24, 177, 223, 245
caravans to 8
Fāṭimid 299
Ottoman conquest of 205
Eilburg, Eliezer 199
Einbinder, Susan 198–199
Ein sof (ineffable aspect of the godhead) 378, 399
Elinson, Alexander 90–91
En Yaaqov (Ibn Ḥabib) 267
Ephraim ben Gershon 236
epigrams 147, 148, 149*n*325, 150, 151, 229, 421
epistles 46, 50, 88, 102, 116, 244–245
of Abner 96, 209, 244, 251, 265, 266*n*73, 275, 281, 430
adab culture/literature and 79, 116
of Halevi 127*n*262
of al-Hamādhānī 39
of al-Ḥarīrī 49, 92
of Maimonides (to the Sages of Lunel) 257
palindromic 91
panegyric 66, 265
risāla (Mamlūk/Ottoman rhymed prose epistle) 59
Epistle to Yemen (Maimonides) 304
epitaphs
auto-epitaphs 41, 162, 440, 442, 451, 454, 456, 457, 459
fictionalized 451
Epstein, Abraham 257
eroticism 12, 134, 136, 137, 277, 365, 399, 455
eschatology 211, 353, 381, 399, 417, 424
auto-eulogies and 445
Christian 456
rabbinic 442
reinterpretation of 404, 417
Zoharic literature and 403
ethics 79, 86, 356
Ethiopia 182, 189
ethnography 23
Eurocentrism 23, 153
Even Boḥan (Kalonymus ben Kalonymus) 365–366
Even Sapir (Sapir) 22, 23, 257, 258
evil eye/evil spirits 187–188
evil inclination (*yeṣer ha-ra'*) 138, 139
exegesis 10, 11, 133, 159, 256, 267, 290
aggadic 432*n*11, 433
biblical 1, 388, 434, 446
interfaith polemics and 298
kabbalistic 353
Muslim–Jewish polemics and 303, 313
exempla 17, 77, 326–344, 373, 392
Arabs as role models 237, 297, 331
sages of Israel 337
Ezer ha-dat [Support of the Faith] (Polleqar) 316

fables 77, 190, 373
See also animal fables
faḍā'il (virtues) literature 176
faḍā'il al-buldān (Arabic literary genre) 123
Falaquera, Shem Tov 173, 316, 365, 401, 427–428
al-Faraj ba'ada al-shidda (Relief After Adversity) genre 60
al-Fāsī, David 283*n*118
al-Fayyūmī, Jacob b. Nathaniel 305
Fischel, Walter J. 24, 25
Fishman, Talya 259, 260

folklore/folktales 1, 17, 24, 50, 86, 98, 331
  about Maimonides 25, 28
  Arabic 12, 21, 296, 321
  Arabs as role models 99, 237, 296, 332
  comparative 25
  didactic 326
  framing devices and 98
  ideal of generosity in 333
  international 25, 99, 190, 237, 318*n*72, 331, 337
  interplay between Jewish and Muslim folklore 326, 331, 337
  musar and 166
  of non-Jewish provenance 87
  salacious material in 124
  Yemenite Jewish 28, 258
Frenkel, Miriam 25*n*68, 180
From the Land of Sheba (Goitein, 1947) 258
"From the Travels of Rabbi Zechariah ben Seʿadya ben Yaʿaqov in the Land of Israel" (Kehati, 1928) 26

Gaimani, Aharon 263
Galante, Moses 388
Galen 84
galut (exile) 65, 99, 135, 207, 208
  humiliation and impoverishment of 137
  lament over 104, 119
galut teiman (tribulations of Yemenite Jewry) 65, 66, 99, 208, 294, 297
Gavra, Moshe 394
gemara 248, 253, 255, 258, 264, 278
gemaṭria 92, 93
geneivat shir (poetic plagiarism) 144, 146
Genette, Gérard 70
Geniza documents 180
geography 40, 167, 223
Geonim 257, 262
George, Alain 155
Gerber, Noah 257
Gersonides (Levi ben Gershom) 249
al-Ghazālī 357*n*38
Ghaznavids, of Persia 201
gift exchange, cyclical 244
Gikatilla, Joseph 377, 378, 390, 400, 402
Ginsburg, Elliot 409
Glaser, Eduard 105–106*n*193, 392*n*54
Goa (India) 191–192, 206
Goitein, Shelomo Dov 20, 24–25
  on autobiographical quality of *Sefer hamusar* 32
  on "double bitterness" (*merataуyim*) as place name 229*n*221, 230
grammar 456, 458
Greenblatt, Stephen 167
Greidi, Shimon 29, 395*n*68
Gruendler, Beatrice 140*n*307, 152
Guenzburg, Baron David 23, 30
Guenzburg 1306 manuscript 30, 129
Guide of the Perplexed, The (Maimonides) 15, 123, 288, 418
  Zechariah ha-Rofé's commentary on 356
  on true prophecy 304

Ha-bavli, Elʿazar ben Yaʿaqov 131
Ḥabshush, Ḥayyim 20
ḥabsiyyāt (Persian prison poetry) 201
Hacker, Joseph 236, 268*n*77
Ha-dani, Eldad 257
Ḥadīth khurāfa 60
ḥadīth literature 55, 56, 61, 86, 87, 100
Ḥaḍramawt (southeastern region of Arabia) 186–188, 203, 215
Hagar (biblical maidservant) 283, 294
hagiography 198, 459
Hai Gaon 452
Hakohen, Solomon ben David 392, 393
ha-Kohen of Izmir, Elijah b. Solomon 346*n*2
halakhah/halakhic literature 10, 11, 19, 132, 194, 260, 438
  Ashkenazi 233, 234
  Alḍāhirī as halakhist 12, 455, 457
  Alḍāhirī's protagonists and 17, 18, 166, 217, 241, 249, 254–255, 279, 288, 374, 438
  Cochin Jews and 194
  exegesis and 132
  intellectual elite and 159
  Karo and 12, 348, 386, 455
  Maimonides and 260, 261–262, 264, 290
  Safed as a center of 218, 239, 376
  Sephardi norms 192, 269, 272
  Talmud and 254, 255, 261
  Yemenite 256, 257, 259, 264, 454
Halevi, David [Aluʾel] ben Yeshaʿ 10, 15, 16*n*40, 17, 392

Halevi, Judah 75, 127, 128, 129, 141, 271, 401
elegy for Moses Ibn Ezra 452
on faculties of the soul 350–351
letter to Moses Ibn Ezra 274
Muslim–Jewish polemics and 300–301, 303–304
pilgrimage to Land of Israel 177
reputation of 272
tawakkul (Heb. *biṭṭaḥon*) pietistic ideal and 237
Zionide odes of 211
Halevi, Raṣon 146*n*320
Halévy, Joseph 243*n*11, 392*n*54
Hallamish, Moshe 387, 392, 411*n*116
al-Hamādhānī, Badīʿ al-Zamān 11, 13, 50–51, 116, 223, 355
correspondence of 39, 54, 55
fictional characters of 100, 101, 109
mendicant preacher theme and 369
See also *Maqāmāt* (al-Hamādhānī)
al-Hamdānī, Abū Firās 200
Hämeen-Anttila, Jaako 51
"Handmaid's Revenge, The" (*Neqamat ha-shifḥah*) 136, 137
Haqorḥi, Shalom ben Joseph 392, 393
Ḥarāzī, Yiḥye ben Abraham 17, 160–164, 308, 428, 455
al-Ḥarīrī, Abū 'l-Ḥasan 13, 18, 43, 45, 70, 423
adab culture and 87
Alḍāhirī's borrowing from 147
Arabic language and 69
epistles with poetic constraints 92
fictional characters of 101, 109
Maqāmāt of 11, 47, 49
"Of Aleppo" (#46) 91–92
"Of Damascus" (#12) 184–185
"Of the Euphrates" (#22) 172
"Of the Maghreb" (#16) 87*n*143, 91
"Of Marāgha" or "The Diversified" (#6) 91*n*158
"Of ʿOmān" (#39) 187, 367
"Of Samarqand" (#28) 91
"The Legal" (#15) 65, 183
"The Reversed" (#17) 94
"The Spotted" (#26) 91*n*158
rhymed prose (Arabic: *sajʿ*) valued by 89
as tutelary spirit for *Sefer hamusar* 46
writing of *Maqāmāt* ascribed to fictional characters 101
al-Ḥārith Ibn Hammām (fictional character) 101, 109, 110, 111, 112, 370
Ḥarizi, Rabbi Judah
See Alḥarizi, Judah
ha-Rofé, Zechariah 10
Hathaway, Jane 5, 6, 7*n*15
Ha-yerushalmi, Joseph ben Tanḥum 131
Ḥayyāṭ, Judah 267, 384, 385, 400
Ḥayy ben Meqiṣ (Abraham Ibn Ezra) 176, 363–364
Ḥayy Ibn Yaqẓān (Ibn Sīnā) 176, 363
Ḥazmaq ha-teimani (fictional character) 161
Hebrew language 3, 46, 47, 84, 331, 343
aesthetic ideal of *ṣaḥut* 271, 274
Arabic-inflected 385, 425
Biblical 242, 252, 271, 381
epistolary and encomiastic writing 244
post-Biblical 89, 261
printing of Hebrew books 246
pronunciation of 242, 277–281
rehabilitation of the Sacred Tongue 69
as spoken language 89, 90
writing system of Iberian Jews 280
Yemenite Jews' use of classical Hebrew 88
See also rhymed prose, Hebrew
Hebrew poetry 1, 12, 272
of al-Andalus 2, 13*n*33, 40, 73
courtly 122
liturgical 18, 295
shirat ha-ḥen (esoteric verse) 277
strophic poem (*muwashshaḥ*) 88
Yemenite poetry as extension of Andalusian school 15
Hebrew printing 9, 50, 159, 391, 457
Catholic surveillance of 289*n*137
emergence of 2, 290
impact of print culture 285–290
Italy as primary center of 246, 387
in Ottoman Empire 246
in Spain 246, 247
in Venice 240*n*5
reception of kabbalah and 391
receptivity to printed books 16–17
Hebrew Printing in the East (Yaari) 387

Hebron, city of 245
ḥefeṣ as occult book 246, 366*n*65
Heinrichs, Wolfhart 78*n*112, 79, 117, 129
Heman ha-Ezraḥi (fictional character) 113, 114, 181
Ḥever ha-Keni (fictional character) 113, 361–362
al-Ḥibshi, anthologies of 19*n*50
Ḥiddushim be-ferush arbaʿim baraitot (Alḍāhirī) 263
hikāya (attributed discourse) 105
Hilkhot sheḥiṭah (Maimonides) 259
Hippocrates 84
Hirschler, Konrad 155
Historical and Ethnographic Society of Israel 26
historiography 15, 61, 153, 191*n*93, 205, 207, 241
  Islamic 33
  of Western Europe 8, 9*n*20
  Yemenite Jewish 3, 252*n*35
Ho, Enseng 186*n*73
homoeroticism 108–109
homophones 92
Hormuz, port of 187*n*76, 206, 319, 367
Ḥoṭer ben Shelomoh 10, 358*n*42
Huss, Matti 14*n*35, 445, 449

Ibn ʿAbd Rabbīhī 137
Ibn Abī Ḥajalah 111
Ibn Abi Zimra, Rabbi David 194, 268*n*76, 272
Ibn Aqnīn, Joseph 346*n*2
Ibn Baṭṭūta 169, 175, 177
Ibn Caspi, Joseph 346*n*2
Ibn Dāniyāl 157
Ibn Faḍlān 175*n*30
Ibn Fayyūmī, Nethanel 237, 308
Ibn Gabbai, Meir 377, 390
Ibn Gabirol, Solomon 130, 272, 356, 358, 389*n*42, 453
  Andalusian school and 131
  audiences of 417
  Book of Improvement of the Moral Qualities (*Kitāb iṣlāḥ al-akhlāq*) 352, 364
  elegies for Hai Gaon 452
  pietism and 358–359
  piyyutim of 271
Ibn Ḥabib, Jacob 267
Ibn Hammām, al-Ḥārith (fictional character) 370
Ibn Hassān, Yequtiel 453
Ibn Hishām, ʿIsā (fictional character) 101, 109
Ibn Isḥāq, Ḥunayn 84
Ibn Jāmiʿ, Samuel 130
Ibn Jubayr 177, 184
Ibn Lavi, Simon 131, 396, 412
Ibn Makhir 411*n*116, 412*n*118
Ibn Mar Shaul, Isaac 131
Ibn al-Muqaffaʿ 60
Ibn Nāqiyā 346
Ibn Paquda, Baḥya 82, 138, 237, 358*n*43
Ibn Qutayba 87, 200, 456
Ibn Ṣaddiq, Joseph 127
Ibn Sahula, Isaac 14*n*35, 67, 349*n*16
Ibn Ṣaqbel, Solomon 188
Ibn Shabbetai, Judah 188, 189*n*81, 436
Ibn Shāhīn, Nissim 334*n*107, 338
Ibn Sīnā 176, 350, 363
Ibn Tibbon, Judah 82, 350
Ibn Verga, Solomon 267
Ibn Yaḥya, Rabbi Jacob ben Tam 456
Ibn Zabara, Joseph 14*n*35, 338, 364
Idel, Moshe 178, 289*n*137, 391, 402, 403
Idelsohn, Abraham Tzvi 23–24
Iggeret ha-musar [Epistle of Moral Instruction] (Falaquera) 173, 346*n*2
Iggeret ha-vikuaḥ [Epistle of the Debate] (Falaquera) 316
Iggeret musar (Alami) 346*n*2
Immanuel of Rome 12, 13, 14, 68, 69, 147, 153
  on authorship and fictional characters 102–104
  auto-eulogy of 443–448, 457
  as biblical exegete 447*n*57
  epitaph poems of 450–452
  Italian Jewish literary memorialization practices and 450
  literary memorialization and 456
  poem on month of Tishrei 125
  self-glorification of 446–447
  See also *Maḥberot Immanuel*
India 7, 10, 189–190, 204, 223, 245, 454
  See also Cochin (India), Jewish community of
Indian Ocean 7, 10, 190

Initiative to Uncover the Hidden Treasures of Yemen [*Mifʿal ḥasifat ginzei teiman*] (Naḥum) 30
Institute for Microfilmed Hebrew Manuscripts 28*n*84, 29
Iran 39, 55, 86, 204
Iraq 86, 184, 245
culture of orality and performance in 155
Jewish community of 420
Irbīl (Iraq), city of 205, 218, 219, 228, 376, 419, 423
Irwin, Robert 334*n*103
Isaac ha-Ezobi 376–377, 379
Isaac Ibn Khalfon 83
al-Iṣfahāni, al-Rāghib 336
Isḥaq Ibn Krispin 75, 76*n*107
Ishmael 295*n*10, 301, 303, 306*n*45, 312
biblical sons of Ishmael 333, 334
Ishmaelites 42, 48, 76, 249, 303
Muslim–Jewish polemics and 307, 308
as prototype 294
as stand-in for Islam 313
See also Muslims, representations of
al-Iskandarī, Abū ʾl-Fatḥ (fictional character) 101, 109–110, 221
Islam 45*n*11, 110
blasphemy against 158, 297, 300
critiques of 20
historical function of 303
Ismāʿīlī 5, 175, 356
male environments of 108
penal law 199
pietism 451
role of *sajʿ* in early Islam 56
Shīʿī 5, 6, 55, 109, 200
Sunnī 5, 6, 55
See also Muslims
Islamicate culture/society 2–3, 51, 77, 186, 227, 345
Ismāʿīlī Islam 5, 175
isnād (chain of reliable authorities) 55
Istanbul 250, 376
Hebrew printing in 246, 247
Iberian Jews in 268
Ottoman policy of *sürgün* (resettlement) in 205, 236
Romaniot Jews in 236*n*239
yeshivot in 255
See also Constantinople
Italy 13, 449
Hebrew printing in 246
Inquisition prohibition on printing the Talmud 261
Renaissance 102
ʿiyyun (intensive study) 249, 254, 255

Jacob ben Eleazar 14*n*35, 67
Jacobs, Martin 168*n*12, 169–170
al-Jāḥiẓ, Abū ʿUthmān ʿAmr b. Baḥr 11, 200, 456
Jánošíková, Magdaléna 199
Jastrow, Marcus 115–116
javāb-gūʾī ("speaking in reply") 132–133
jawāb ("response") 128, 131, 133, 135–137, 139, 141, 354
implicit critique of original 152
as regular feature of Yemenite poetry 146
relationship to earlier poets and 140
Jeroḥam b. Meshullam 288, 380
Jerusalem 165, 183, 245, 256, 279
Alḍāhirī's protagonists in 165, 208, 211–212, 245, 299, 438
Ashkenazi community of 256
Christian pilgrims in 224
messianic redemption of 407
as real and symbolic place 171, 183
rebuilding of 303, 431
Schocken Library 27
Sephardi Jews in 268
Yemenite Jews (medieval) in 26, 258
See also Land of Israel (Holy Land)
"Jerusalem School" 24
Jesus of Nazareth 302, 303, 304
Jewish merchants, European 16, 179, 286
Jewish Studies 1
Jews, Andalusian/Iberian 68, 80, 153, 193, 229, 268, 269, 280
collective cultural identity of 269–270, 271, 272
cultural exceptionalism of 227
decline of 48, 224
expulsion from Iberia 266–267, 390–391
geonic-Andalusian philosophical tradition 14
"Golden Age" of 10, 273, 293

literati 82
polymaths 11
See also Sephardim
Jews, Romaniot 233, 235–238, 269, 270
Jews, Syrian 87, 228, 229, 231, 360
Jews, Yemenite 1, 3, 14, 24, 25–26, 153
affinity for Andalusian Hebrew poetry 132
dearth of records from sixteenth century about 32
deference to Jews of Land of Israel 265
deficiency in Talmudic knowledge 256
dhimmī status of 9, 292*n*5, 295, 311, 317, 325, 344, 345
in early modern period 8–10
exile of 161
as heirs of Andalusian poetic mantle 276–277
Indian Ocean trade and 190
in Jerusalem (20th c.) 25–26, 27*n*81
Mediterranean trade and 10
Muslim–Jewish polemics and 297–298
as oppressed minority 252
Orientalism in study of 23–24
punished and incarcerated by *imām* 42, 45, 293
rabbis 38
of Ṣanaʿā 4, 7
stereotyped as uncommonly gifted poets 425
Yemeni Muslim tribes and 6, 9
Joseph ben Saadya, Mori (of Jirwāḥ) 256
Judah Ibn Tibbon 82, 350
Judaism 196, 230, 302, 418*n*137
apostates from 230, 243*n*11, 304, 305, 313, 317*n*71
authenticity of Yemenite Judaism 24
freed slaves converted to 193
Islamicized 231
relation to daughter religions 303, 304*n*38
"scientific" study of 22
See also Muslim–Jewish polemics
Judeo-Arabic 22, 72, 80, 129, 304
in Genizah mss. 177
epistolary and encomiastic writing 244
Muslim–Jewish polemics and 308
Judeo-Spanish language 269
kabbalah/kabbalism 1, 9, 50, 86, 160, 162, 256, 374
Abner's kabbalistic verse 122, 405–407, 413–415
Alḍāhirī as conduit for transmission to Yemen 2, 375–376, 385–394
Alḍāhirī's discretion versus openness about 415–418
conception of paradise 95, 401–403
constrained writing and 94
doctrines and rituals associated with 11, 411
gemaṭria and 92
Italian and Spanish kabbalists 14, 384*n*26
kabbalistic chapters in *Sefer hamusar* 376–385
kabbalistic theosophy 40, 377
Lurianic 16, 178–179, 219, 376, 386, 392, 394–399
narrative elements of *Sefer hamusar* and 418–426
philosophy and 14–16
pre-Lurianic 178
recurrent themes in *Sefer hamusar* 399–418
Sabbath associated with afterlife 404–405
Sacred Marriage (*hieros gamos*) 399, 407–408, 410
Safed as a center of 240–241
Sephardi rite and 393, 394
summum bonum and 400–404, 417
travel narratives and 178, 217–218
turn toward (sixteenth century Yemen) 10
Kalīla wa-dimna (Ibn al-Muqaffaʿ) 60, 180, 190
Kalonymus ben Kalonymus 365
Kanarfogel, Ephraim 260
Kanpanton, Rabbi Isaac 255*n*42
Karaferye (Veroia) 235–237
Karaites 68, 130, 283*n*118, 298*n*20, 305*n*44
Karo, Joseph 2, 12, 37, 39*n*123, 357, 386
Abner's meeting with 101, 140, 212
Alḍāhirī's protagonists and 276, 348, 357
as halakhic authority 455
halakhic elite and 241

Immanuel of Rome's *Maḥbarot* banned by 12
kabbalistic exegesis of 353
pre-Lurianic kabbalism and 395
in Safed 240
See also *Beit Yosef*; Safed yeshivah; *Shulḥan ʿarukh*
kātib (freelance secretary) 100
Katz, Nathan 194, 195*n*107
Kehati, Moshe 26, 73
Kennedy, Philip 53, 97, 100, 110, 222
on narrative structure 340
on *takhmīs* technique 132
Ketem Paz (Ibn Lavi) 396*n*70
Keter Malkhut (Ibn Gabirol) 358–361, 389–390, 404
Kfir, Uriah 107, 131*n*277, 227
al-Khafanjī, ʿAli b. al-Ḥasan 59*n*63
Khalaṣ, Judah 346*n*2
khuṭba (religious homily or sermon) 56
Kilito, Abdelfattah 11, 50, 52, 92, 110, 441
on authorial voice 105
on "bestial" languages 345
on al-Ḥarīrī's *Maqāmāt* 373
on narrative structure of *maqāma* 309
Kimelman, Reuven 407, 412
Kimhi, David 123, 235, 288
Kitāb al-durar [The Book of Pearls] (Alḥarizi) 182, 224
Kitāb al-hidāya ilā farāʾiḍ al-qulūb [Book of Direction to the Duties of the Heart] (Baḥya Ibn Paquda) 82, 138, 145*n*318, 237, 358*n*43, 364
Kitāb al-muḥāḍarah waʾl-mudhākara [The Book of Conversation and Discussion] (Moses Ibn Ezra) 80
Kitāb al-faraj baʿda al-shidda [Relief after Adversity] (Ibn Shāhīn) 334*n*107, 338
Kurdistan, kabbalistic study in 377
Kuzarī: Kitāb al-radd waʾl-dalīl fīʾl-dīn al-dhalīl [The Book of Refutation and Proof in Defense of the Despised Faith] (Halevi) 300–301, 303–304, 350, 351

lamentation 74, 430, 433*n*17, 452, 454
Land of Israel (Holy Land) 13, 106, 177, 182, 209, 223, 238, 239–243
Alḍāhirī in 395
desire to travel to (Alḥarizi) 224
emissaries from 206, 242–253, 386–387
as focus of travels 207
Jewish "Others" in 40
language spoken by Sephardi masses in 280
Rabbi Abraham Ashkenazi as emissary from the Holy Land 242–253
redemption from exile and 210
Sephardi (*shāmī*) rite of 2, 12, 290
Talmud study and 253–268
venerated gravesites in 178
see also Sapir, Jacob
Langermann, Y. Tzvi 19, 163, 263, 350*n*21, 356, 357*n*38
Lavi, Abraham 72*n*96
Lawrence, Marilyn 97
Leder, Stefan 60
leshon kenaʿan 234–235
Levin, Yisrael 150, 453
lipograms 92, 93
live theater (*ḥikāya*) 157
Live Theatre and Dramatic Literature in the Medieval Arabic World (Moreh, 1992) 157
Losensky, Paul 132–133
al-Luğūğī, Abū Fayd (fictional character) 111–112
Luria, Isaac 277, 379, 395, 397, 408–409

maʿnā, pl. *maʿānī* (poetic themes and motifs) 127
Maʿarekhet haʾelohut 15, 377, 390
al-Maʿarrī, Abū ʿAlāʾ 92*n*162
Maʿaseh ṭuvya 163
madrikh (opening couplet of strophic poem) 133, 135
Maggid Meisharim (Karo) 357, 358*n*41
Maghreb 223
Maḥberot Immanuel (Immanuel of Rome) 12–14, 68, 69, 124, 224, 442, 445, 446, 449, 450
Alḍāhirī's familiarity with 102–103, 450
condemned and banned for eroticism in 455
cross-cultural appropriation in 449
Dante's *Divine Comedy* and 442, 449
misogyny in 189
on pretense to medical knowledge 365

Maḥberot Iti'el (Alḥarizi) 47, 72*n*96, 84–85, 113, 172–173
Maimonides (Moses ben Maimon) 2, 14, 38, 139, 207*n*145, 245, 290
commentary on the Mishnah 246*n*21, 247, 254, 284–285, 286, 403
Epistle to Yemen 304–305
folktales about 25, 28, 213–214
on historical function of Christianity and Islam 303
laws of prayer 393
legal code of 256
myth of India and 189
opposition to institutionalized rabbinate 262
on purpose of arbitrary commandments (*ṭaʿamei ha-miṣvot*) 249*n*29
rationalism of 2, 15, 418
Sefer ha-miṣvot 286
Talmud study and 257
on virtue 352, 356
See also *Guide of the Perplexed*; *Mishneh torah*
Maimonides, Abraham 358*n*42
Maimuni, Abraham 258
Malkiel, David 220
Mamlūk period 59, 111, 155, 173*n*24, 239, 385
Mandelbaum, David 194
Mansur, Otniel 29
Manṣura, Saʿadya 17, 20, 160, 161–164, 428, 455, 457–459
Manṭiq al-ṭayr [The Conference/Speech of the Birds] (Ibn Abī Ḥajalah) 111
Maqālat al-ḥadīqa fī maʿna ʾl-majāz wa ʾl-ḥaqīqa (Moses Ibn Ezra) 80, 84
maqāma literary genre 1, 3, 50–59, 62, 292
aesthetic conventions of 4
Arabic picaresque model 47
"classical" and "post-classical" 13, 58, 160
conflation of author and fictional hero in 437
difficult style of 90
eloquence versus veracity in 53
episodic form of 35, 63
fictionality in classical Arabic literature and 61
framing devices in 97–100
history of 51
layered narrative structure of 427
mendicant preachers in 369
moral conflict/ambiguity in 372–373
naming convention for chapters of 71–72
picaresque 88, 116, 124, 204, 375
pre-existing genres in 50
questionable claims to moral authority 355
recognizable character types in 105–106
relation of fiction and realism in 60–62, 241, 445
rhymed prose (Arabic: *sajʿ*) 52, 55, 88–90
stock figures of 31–33
storytelling and performance in 154–158
titles of *maqāma* collections 75–76
travel writing and 174–180
wandering/displacement theme 113, 180
"Maqāma of Baghdad" (al-Hamādhānī) 88, 360
Maqāmāt (al-Hamādhānī) 51, 54–58, 86, 182, 221, 224, 354
Maqāmāt (al-Ḥarīrī) 11, 46–47, 49, 51, 85, 182, 346
as Arabic prototype of literary *maqāma* 51, 449
author and protagonist conflated in 437
Chenery's translation of 89
critics and defenders of 61
dissimulation and fiction in 373
as literary model for Alḍāhirī 43, 295, 296, 440
Maqāmāt of al-Hamadhānī compared with 57–58
mendicancy (*kudya*) in 54
mendicant preacher in 370
oral transmission of 155
palindromes in 94
place names in 221
poems of 117, 120
prefatory apology for 455
qāḍīs portrayed in 321–322
read aloud to live audiences 154–155
structure of *Sefer hamusar* compared with 64*n*75, 65
See also *Maḥberot Iti'el* (Alḥarizi); *Maqāmāt* (al-Hamādhānī)
Maqāmāt (Ibn Nāqiyā) 346
al-Maqāmāt al-Jalāliyya (al-Ṣafadī) 111

al-Maqāmāt al-Luzūmiyya (al-Saraqusṭī) 51, 92*n*162, 111, 223, 441–442
Maqāṣid al-Falāsifa (al-Ghazālī) 357*n*38
Martyrology (Christian) 198
Mashal ʿal ha-tarnegol [Parable of the Rooster] (attrib. David ben Yeshaʿ ha-Levi) 392
Mashta school 397
maskilim 22, 37
Masoretes/Masoretic tradition 252, 283*n*118
Massaʿot (Benjamin of Tudela) 170, 235
al-Mawṣilī, al-Mubārak ibn Aḥmad 171, 224
Mawzaʿ exile (1679) 163, 393
Mecca, pilgrimage to 175, 177
Medina, Shalom 20, 29, 37, 222, 312
Meḥqerei Sefer [Studies in Jewish Booklore] (Yaari, 1958) 198
Me'ir of Rothenburg 199
Melamed, Abraham 190
Melammed, Uri 20, 29
meliṣah (elegant style) 65–66, 94, 103, 104
Mendelssohn, Moses 449*n*63
Mendes, Doña Gracia 265
Meshal ha-qadmoni (Ibn Sahula) 14*n*35, 67, 349*n*16
Meshullam of Volterra 177, 212*n*165
Messianism/messianic era 303, 317, 380
Midrash ʿaseret ha-dibberot 337
Midrash ha-gadol 263
Midrash ha-ḥefeṣ 263
midrashim 18, 19, 50, 132, 159, 295
Milḥamot hashem [The Wars of the Lord] (Qāfiḥ) 391
Minḥat yehudah (Ḥayyāṭ) 267, 384
Minḥat yehudah sone' ha-nashim (Ibn Shabbetai) 436
"mirabilia" (*ʿajā'ib*) 176
Mishlei heʿarav [Sayings of the Arabs] (unknown author) 76
Mishlei shuʿalim [Fox Fables] (Berakhia ha-Naqdan) 99*n*179
Mishnah 142, 245, 256, 289, 357, 457*n*88
  Avot 44*n*6, 136*n*293, 288, 317, 355, 370
    Maimonides' commentary on 246*n*21, 247, 254
    Obadiah of Bertinoro's commentary on 123, 246, 254
    Rabbi Abraham Ashkenazi and 249, 251
Mishneh torah (Maimonides) 123, 139*n*304, 256, 259, 260, 288, 403
  Bomberg edition 284
  interfaith polemics in 303
  Laws of Repentance (*Hilkhot Teshuvah*) 364
  reputation of 263
misogyny 63, 188–189
Misogynist, The (Ibn Shabbetai) 188, 189*n*81
Mission to the Volga (Ibn Faḍlān) 175*n*30
mi-Trani, Rabbi Moshe 39*n*123
Mocha, port of 206, 219, 239, 243, 244, 245*n*15
Modena, Leon 451
monotheism 297, 300, 302, 303
Monroe, James 55, 223, 309, 355, 357, 441
Mordecai ha-Ṣidoni (fictional character) 36*n*109, 64, 115, 123–124, 166, 172, 210
  Abner posing as doctor and 362–363, 367
  Abner as sham preacher and 369–371
  on Abner's Arabic-inflected Hebrew 277–278
  Abner's elegy/epitaph for 76, 431–436
  Abner's poetic recitations and 144, 149–150
  as alter ego of Alḍāhirī 437
  Ashkenazim and 232–235
  attitudes toward Abner's erudition 355–356
  authorial voice and 105
  character development of 106–108
  in Cochin (India) 188, 192–193, 195–196
  in Damascus 65, 165, 183–186, 212
  encounters with non-Yemenite eastern Jews 227–231
  exempla about virtuous Arabs and 334–336
  in Ḥaḍramawt 186–188
  halakhic/kabbalistic learning and 217–218
  in Hormuz 319
  identification with Sidon 222
  "inbound journey" of 438
  kabbalistic study and 378–379, 382–385, 420–425
  in Karaferye 235–236
  as merchant 212–213
  Muslim–Jewish polemics and 299–300

numeric value of name 43
preoccupation with posthumous reputation 429–430, 431
prose narration by 117
Rabbi Abraham Ashkenazi and 242–253
in Safed 137–138, 208
search for *musar/adab* and 86–87, 215–217
as stock character 100–101, 219
suffering of Yemenite Jewry and 207
in Tiberias 382–385
word play and 93, 94
Moreh, Shmuel 157
Moses (biblical) 371
Christian acceptance of 302
prophecy of 299, 332
valedictory song to Children of Israel 307
Moses de Leon, Rabbi 401*n*85
Moses Ibn Ezra 80, 83–84, 126, 127*n*262, 401
Arabicizing poetics of Andalusian school and 453
auto-elegy of 454
Halevi's letter of praise to 274
myth of India and 189
tombstone inscription for Alfasi 452
Muchawsky-Schnapper, Ester 187
mufākhara (poetic contest) 59
Muḥāḍarāt al'udabā (al-Iṣfahāni) 336–337
Muḥammad, prophet of Islam 297, 299, 301, 302, 303, 316, 332
Alḍāhirī's criticism of 306, 308
disparaging epithets applied to 305
munāẓara (poetic contest) 59, 176
al-Muqaddasī 223
muqaddima (*ṣadr*) 67–68
al-Muqammaṣ, Dāwūd 68*n*85, 189
musar 17, 46, 75–88
aḥi musar (cultivator of *musar*) 83
framing devices and 98
meanings of 77
as moral instruction 86, 369
travel and 86–87, 215–216, 229
See also *adab* culture
music/musicality 120, 131, 281, 446, 458, 459*n*92
contrafactio as musical technique 128
ethnomusicology 23
Najara's poetry and 398
of quantitative meters 116
Renaissance vocal music 126
Muslim–Jewish polemics 63, 104, 237, 297–301, 330, 344–345
Alḍāhirī's account of 306–309
authorial voice and 314
literary antecedents and 316–318
narrative structure of *Sefer hamusar* and 309–311
polemical arguments 301–305
rhetorical techniques used in 311–314
tensions between realism and fictional elements in *Sefer hamusar* 315–318
Muslims 2, 47, 100, 215, 226, 237
courtiers 199–200
traders/merchants 213–214
under Yemeni tribal authority 6
Muslims, representations of 291–297
Alḍāhirī's ambivalence 40, 216–217, 226, 227, 237, 345
Arabs and Muslims as role models in exempla 326–344
historical and imaginary figures 344–345
prototypes 294
techniques of representation 296–297
See also *qāḍīs* (Islamic religious judges)
al-Muṭahhar, Imām 4, 5, 202, 293
death of 308
ḥigger ("the lame one") epithet for 7, 295, 344
al-Mutawakkil, Imām 161

Nadāf, Ya'ish Re'uven 27
Naḥalat avot (Abravanel) 288
Nahḍa (Arabic cultural renaissance) 273
Naḥmanides, Moses 260, 404*n*95, 415
al-Nahrawālī, Quṭb al-Dīn Muḥammad 201, 202, 293
Naḥum, Yehuda Levi 30, 37
Najara, Israel 128, 259*n*52, 277, 398, 399
Nasi, Don Joseph 265
Nathan ben Yeḥiel of Rome 258
neologisms 89, 271
Neoplatonism 176, 203, 295, 353, 358
blended with Maimonidean ideas 356
kabbalah and 389, 390, 404
myth of the soul 354
Nethanel ben Yeshaʿ 308

Netivot ha-emunah [The Paths of Faith] (Ḥarāzi) 17, 160, 308, 455
Neubauer, Adolph 22, 257–258
Ne'um asher ben yehuda [Asher in the Harem] (Ibn Ṣaqbel) 188, 346
New Christians 192, 193
nisba (toponymical) names 109, 110, 113, 221, 265
notarikon 92–93, 426
numerology/*gemaṭria* 92, 426
Nur al-ẓalām [Illumination of the Darkness] (Nethanel b. Yeshaʿ) 263, 308

Obadiah of Bertinoro 123, 177, 212*n*165, 245, 246, 254
Oettinger, Ayelet 428*n*146
onomastics 109–116
On the Kabbalah and Its Symbolism (Scholem) 408
orality 154*n*335, 155
Orfali, Bilal 77–78, 364
Orientalism 23, 168, 234, 278
Ostle, Robin 220
Others/Otherness 40, 167, 175, 196, 227
Ottoman Empire 5, 13, 24, 164, 192, 205–206, 218
  Ashkenazi Jews in 233, 234*n*232
  central Yemen occupied by (1872) 9
  conflict with the Portuguese 7
  conquest of Palestine 178, 185*n*71, 205, 239
  as defenders of Sunnī Islam 6
  first occupation of Yemen (16th c.) 7
  Jews accused of collaborating with 202
  kabbalistic study in 376
  printing of Hebrew books in 246
  Sephardi dominance in 268–277
  Zaydī overthrow of Ottomans in Ṣanaʿā (1567) 1, 4, 36
Oulipo (Ouvroir de Littérature Potentielle) 92
Oxford Bodleian manuscript (Opp. Add. 8° 31 = Neubauer #2397) 71, 74, 119, 129

Paʿamon zahav ve-rimmon (Wanneh) 393
Padova, Judah Maṣliah (*ʿOlam hafukh*) 444
Pagis, Dan 436, 449, 453
paideia 10, 78, 82, 84, 255
Palestine, Byzantine 271
Palestine, Mamlūk 239, 385
Palestine, Mandatory 24, 26
Palestine, Ottoman 178, 185*n*71, 205, 239, 242, 266
palindromes 53, 91, 92, 94–95
palinodes 94, 130
Panchatantra (Indian collection of animal fables) 190
panegyrics 122, 123, 141, 143, 281
parables 50, 62, 117, 369, 421
paratext 70–71, 73, 75
Partington, Gill 286*n*128
pataḥ (in vocalic rhymes) 120
patronage 39, 50, 55, 100, 184
  competition for 79
  poetic emulation and 126
  from political élite 78
  travel in search of 175, 180
  no evidence of in *Sefer hamusar* 67, 123
  Alḥarizi's multiple dedicatees 123
  in *Maḥberot Immanuel* 103
patronymics 109, 114, 115
Peraḥia b. Meshullam 308
Perec, Georges 92–93
Pereq ḥeleq (Maimonides) 418
Persia 83, 166, 223, 230, 292
Persian poets (16th–17th c.) 132, 201
philology 23, 78
Philosophical Responsa (Peraḥia b. Meshullam) 308
philosophy 10, 17, 18, 288, 401, 448
  Abner's excellence in 255, 347, 355
  adab culture/literature and 79
  Bible commentary and 437
  citation of sources and 353
  Immanuel of Rome and 456
  Islamic 82, 176, 350, 351*n*22, 356, 357*n*38, 363
  Jewish 1, 86, 348–350, 356, 358–359
  kabbalah and 12, 418
  medicine and 362*n*52
  in prison writing 199
  rationalist 290
  spirituality and 417
  Yemenite Jews' accomplishments in 264
Phoenicians 221, 222*n*194
pietism 358–361, 451

pilgrimage 170, 175, 176, 177–178, 208, 224, 450
pilpul (sharp-witted analysis) 255, 260, 264
Pinault, David 118, 155
piyyutim 19, 20, 119, 120, 159, 261, 280
  ahavah genre 133, 134, 135
  Andalusian 132, 271
  in Byzantine Palestine 271
plagiarism 126, 127, 144
Pococke, Edward 247
Poetics (Aristotle) 96
poetry
  Andalusian school 82, 119, 276, 453
  bacchic 124
  baqqashah poems 396
  contrafaction 125–140
  elegies for lost cities (*rithā' al-mudun*) 176
  erotic 124
  European Baroque period 452
  falsehood and 427, 448
  homonymic 131, 437
  medieval love poetry (Arabic and Hebrew) 134
  metapoetic reflections 140–153
  modernist (*muḥdath*) school 122
  muʿāraḍa (emulation of another's poem) 125, 126, 128, 147, 152
  muwashshaḥāt ("girdle poems") 127, 128, 405
  poetic varieties 119–125
  prosimetrum 116–119
  shirat ha-ḥen (esoteric verse) 397
  Sufi 397
  takhmīs "fiver gloss" technique 129, 130, 145
  tokheḥah (poem of reproof) 138, 203, 353, 354
  viddui (confession for Day of Atonement) 429
  See also *piyyutim*; riddle poems
Pollack, Sheldon 8
Polleqar, Isaac 316
Pomerantz, Maurice 59, 111, 364
Portugal/Portuguese empire 7, 9, 191–192, 193, 247
  conflict with Ottomans 7, 206
  forced conversion of Jews in 268
  importance of Malabar coast to 193
  Indian Ocean trade and 206
  printing of Hebrew books in Portugal 246
postcolonial studies 167
Power in the Portrayal (Brann) 291
prayer books 2, 9, 12, 289, 389
  Andalusian *piyyutim* and 132
  baladī rite 290, 393–394
  kabbalah and 393
  printed in Italy and the Ottoman Empire 13
  shāmī rite 2, 12, 290, 393–394
  Yemenite (*takālīl*; sng. *tiklāl*) 2, 389*n*43, 393, 394
Prince and the Ascetic, The 190
print culture 9, 50, 159, 241, 245–247, 284, 285–290
  Alḍāhirī and 16
  literary memorialization and 456
  spread of 159
  See also Hebrew printing
prisons, writing from 197–204
Provence 47, 171, 270, 291*n*1, 316
Proverbios Morales (Ardutiel) 429*n*2
proverbs 17, 28, 117, 229, 337–338
puns 53, 89, 93, 96
puzzles 93
Pythagoras 84

Qabbalat shabbat 412
qāḍīs (Islamic religious judges) 292, 296, 308, 344
  in Alḥarizi's "Tale of the Astrologer" 316–317, 325
  portrayed in literature and folklore 321–324
  tale of mule and *qāḍī* 324–326
  in "Tale of Three Swindlers" 318–321
Qāfiḥ, Yiḥye 258, 286, 391–392
Qāfiḥ, Yosef 30, 45*n*11, 247*n*26, 263, 264
qamaṣ (in vocalic rhymes) 120
qaṣīdas 120, 134, 200, 201, 453
Qāsimīs 7
Qedar, as prototype 294
qinah (lament) 430, 431, 448, 452, 453
al-Qirqisānī, Yaʿaqūb 189, 283*n*118
Qoraḥ, Rabbi Amram 37, 93*n*168
Qoraḥ, Yosef 27

Quinn, Josephine 221*n*193
Qurʾān 57, 87, 297, 300, 301, 305, 306
basmala and ḥamdala invocations 67–68
Muslim–Jewish polemics and 315, 316

Rabad of Posquières 25
Rabban, Joseph 191
rabbinic literature 10, 88, 117
Rand, Michael 46*n*15, 51*n*29, 76, 127*n*262, 166, 274*nn*93–94, 428*n*146
on Alḥarizi's "telic journey" 171
on Falaquera's *Iggeret ha-musar* 173*n*25
on *Taḥkemoni* (Alḥarizi) 205, 440
Rasūlid dynasty 6
rationalism, Andalusian 234, 273
Ratzaby, Yehuda 18, 19, 20*n*54, 27–28, 74, 278, 412
index of poems 122
on Alḍāhirī and Andalusian vocalic rhymes 120
on Alḍāhirī as halakhic authority 454–455
on Alḍāhirī's borrowing from al-Ḥarīrī 65
on autobiographical quality of *Sefer hamusar* 32*n*101
on "black" Jews of Cochin 193
on chronology in *Sefer hamusar* 36, 37
on four branches of cogitation 349
on Judaizing of pre-Islamic motifs 453
on kabbalistic works 390
on language of Ashkenazim 234
on Muslim–Jewish polemics 297–298
on *Sefer hamusar* Table of Contents closing citation 75
on *Ṣeidah la-derekh* 29
on Talmud study in Yemen 260–263
on Torah study from memory 157
on Yemenite *dīwāns* 128*n*266
on reading the *Zohar* 410*n*113
Raz-Krakotzkin, Amnon 26, 289*n*137
Red Sea 7, 190, 206, 219
Refutation of al-Ḥarīrī's Maqāmāt 61
Renaissance Humanism 450
responsa literature 234*n*232, 263, 264, 279
Reuveni, David 380
Reynolds, Dwight 34
rhymed prose, Hebrew 100–101, 311*n*57, 312, 315–316, 349*n*16, 449, 457
Arabic picaresque model and 47
blurring of actual and imagined in 436
emergence of fictional narratives 51
historical context and 4, 16
"impersonated artistry" and 90
medical material in 364–365
before movable-type printing 16
Muslim–Jewish polemics in 312
Muslims represented in 90, 311*n*57
poems inserted into 315–316
precedents for 58
reality presented in fictional text 58, 62
Sefer hamusar in history of 457
See also *sajʿ* (Arabic: rhymed prose)
Richards, Donald 56–57
riddles/riddle poems 49, 63, 94, 122, 458
in elegant style of Alḍāhirī' and al-Ḥarīrī 66, 89
Greek 84
numerical 93
pre-modern Arabic readers and 53
as subgenre in *Sefer hamusar* 50
translated from Arabic 123, 381
Riḥla (Ibn Baṭṭūta) 169, 175, 177
Riḥla (Ibn Jubayr) 177, 184
risāla (as rhymed prose epistle) 59
Risāla fī'l-nafs (Ibn Sīnā) 350, 351*n*22
Roberts, Alexandre M. 200
Robinson, James 189*n*81, 288*n*133, 360*n*46
rogue hero 35, 52, 53, 97, 170
authorial voice and 105
disguise and 175
as stock character in *maqāma* 100
vagabondage of 63, 113
See also Abner ben Ḥeleq ha-Teimani (fictional character)
"Romah" [*balad al-rūm*; Rumeli] (Greco-Balkan region) 224–225, 232, 237, 327
Romaniotes
See Jews, Romaniot
Romanticism, European 24, 283*n*118
Rosen, Tova 31
Rosenthal, Franz 353
Rubiés, Joan-Pau 168
Ruderman, David 10, 163
al-Rūmī, Yāqūt 57*n*54
Rūmīyyāt (al-Hamdānī) 200

Saʿadya Gaon 44–45, 68, 77, 189, 258, 290
on complete acquisition of knowledge 349
on *musar* and *adab* 80–82
revival of Hebrew language and 271
tafsīr of 44–45, 93*n*168, 173, 235, 349
Saba, Abraham 385, 416
al-Ṣābī, Abū Isḥāq Ibrāhīm b. Hilāl 200
Sachs, Senior (Schneour) 23, 30, 257
Sadan, Joseph 126–127, 224, 333, 336
Safed, city of 13, 26, 27, 239, 245, 347
halakhic elite of 241
kabbalistic luminaries in 386
luminaries gravitating to 239–240
mystical revival in 15, 66, 137–138, 218, 277, 387
popular reputation of 347
rabbinical court 218
Talmudic mastery in 240–241
yeshivot in 106, 138, 208, 255, 354, 383
Safran, Bezalel 82
al-Ṣafadī, al-Ḥasan b. Abī Muḥammad 111
Sages of Lunel 257
Ṣahalon, Yom Tov 388
ṣāḥib kayd (artificer) 112
Said, Edward 168
sajʿ (Arabic: rhymed prose) 52, 55, 56
as narrative medium 88–95
popular oratory and 154, 155*n*337
See also rhymed prose, Hebrew
Saladin 182
Salman, Masʿūd Saʿd 201
Salonica 179, 225, 233, 246, 250, 456
Iberian Jews in 268
kabbalists from 386*n*31
yeshivot in 255
Ṣaliḥ, Yiḥye 132, 259, 377*n*3, 394*n*62, 410, 454, 457*n*88
Samuel ben Nissim of Aleppo 130
Samuel Hanagid 82–83, 141, 291, 444, 451, 453–454
Ṣanaʿā, city of 6, 15, 18, 42, 45, 187–188
Abner's imprisonment in 219
Alḍāhirī as possible resident of 37
Alḍāhirī's conception of space and 205
Benaya family of scribes 285
Beit din of 262*n*64
controversy over legitimacy of kabbalah in 391
elites' sense of superiority 252, 263*n*65
as important commercial center 206
Jewish community of 4, 5*n*4, 276
Jews deported from (1679) 163
kabbalist circles in region of 393
substitute name for 93
yeshiva of 262*n*64
Zaydī overthrow of Ottomans in (1567) 1, 4, 36
Sapir, Jacob 22, 256, 257, 259, 279, 285*n*125
al-Saraqusṭī 51, 92*n*162, 111, 223, 441, 442, 445
Sarfati, Joseph 284
Sarūj, town of 110, 372
Ṣaʿadah, city of 6, 173, 222
Alḍāhirī as possible resident of 37, 114*n*218
as center of Jewish and Zaydī learning 6*n*10
sages of 263
substitute name for 93
Sassoon, David Solomon 27, 36*n*110, 228*n*216
Sassoon 995 manuscript, former 67*n*81, 72, 73, 324*n*88
Scheindlin, Raymond 316, 317
Schirmann, Hayyim 25, 27, 31, 136, 318
Schocken Library (Jerusalem) 27
Scholem, Gershom 408, 415
Scholer, Gregor 154
Schrijver, Emile 261
Schwarzbaum, Haim 25
science 10, 17, 18
"secular" literature 19
Sefer ha-ʿanaq [Book of the Necklace] (Alḍāhirī) 2, 20, 27, 30, 131, 437
Sefer haʾapiryon (attrib. Alḍāhirī) 2*n*2
Sefer ha-ʿarukh [talmudic dictionary] (Nathan ben Yeḥiel) 258
Sefer ha-gilgulim (Vital) 379
Sefer haʿiqqarim (Albo) 123, 288
Sefer ha-maʿarekhet 267
Sefer ha-maḥshavah [The Book of Thought] (Manṣura) 17, 160, 161, 455, 457–458
Sefer ha-meshalim (Jacob ben Elazar) 14*n*35, 67
Sefer ha-mevaqqesh [Book of the Seeker] (Falaquera) 365, 427–428
Sefer ha-miṣvot (Maimonides) 286

Sefer hamusar (Alḍāhirī) 1, 160
afterlife of 41, 455
auto/biographical readings of 31–40
circulation of 20, 159, 296
conflation of author and protagonists 436–440
distinguishing features of 12–13
generic title of 346
historical context of 4–7
imagined community of readers 65
Judeocentricity in 3, 4, 185, 226, 292, 450
kabbalah and 14–16, 40
literary continuities and departures of 13–14
moral ambiguity in 85
overall structure of 63–67
periodization of 8
picaresque protagonists of 11
poems set off from prose in 118
reception and successors of 160–164
rhymed prose in Table of Contents 71–75, 131
scholarship on 3, 20–31
stimuli to travel in 212–219
title of 75–88
as unique *maqāma* 17–20
Yemenite Jewish literary canon and 20
Sefer hamusar (Alḍāhirī), Author's Introduction to 42–50, 64, 76
framing devices and 98–99
as paratext 70–71
on protagonists' relationship 107
structure of 67–70
Sefer hamusar (Alḍāhirī), epitaphs at end of 429–436
as apology or swan song 454–459
Hebrew literary antecedents of 443–454
protagonists' epitaphs as Alḍāhirī's auto-epitaphs 436–440, 446
structural function of 440–443
Sefer hamusar (Alḍāhirī), stylistic/narrative techniques
anagnorisis 95–97
authorial voice 104–105
character development 106–109
delineation of characters 105–106
fictional characters 100–104
framing devices 97–100
protagonists' names in *maqāmāt* 109–116
rhymed prose as narrative medium 88–95
Sefer ha-musar (Benveniste) 346*n*2
Sefer hamusar (Isḥaq Ibn Krispin) 75–76
Sefer ha-musar (Khalaṣ) 346*n*2
Sefer ha-musar (Moses of Modena) 346*n*2
Sefer ha-musar ha-niqra yoreh de'ah (Ibn Caspi) 346*n*2
Sefer ha-nefesh ha-ḥakhamah (Moses de Leon) 401*n*85
Sefer ha-shorashim (Kimhi) 123, 288
Sefer hegyon ha-nefesh o sefer ha-musar (Bar Ḥiyya) 346*n*2
Sefer leḥem shelomo (Solomon ben David Hakohen) 392
Sefer ma'arekhet ha-elohut [The Structure of the Godhead] (anonymous, c. 1300) 384–385, 400, 426
Sefer meisharim (Jeroḥam b. Meshullam) 288
Sefer oṣar sifrei teiman (Alnadāf, 1928) 26
Sefer segulloth (Shalom ben Joseph Haqorḥi) 392
Sefer sha'ashu'im (Ibn Zabara) 14*n*35, 338, 346, 364
sefirot (ten aspects of divinity) 377, 378, 384, 389, 390, 393, 399–400
biblical figures identified with 426
highest 414
lowest 406*n*101
Segal, David Simha 94, 423
segol (in vocalic rhymes) 120
Ṣeidah la-derekh [Provision for the Road] (Alḍāhirī) 240*n*5, 307–308, 393, 415–416, 437
on Alḍāhirī's imprisonment 38, 45*n*12
chronology in 36
on the divine name 411
on generosity 338–339
on Iberian exiles 267
kabbalah and 390, 395, 396*n*69, 424, 426
partial and fragmentary manuscripts of 29
riddling poems and 382
Sefer hamusar compared with 418–419

as Torah commentary 2, 11, 15, 29, 382, 418–419, 426, 432
Yemenite canon and 27
Sephardim 205, 233, 234
in Cochin (India) 191, 192, 196
diaspora of 398
ethnocentricity of 279
Iberian exiles 191
leading lights of Palestinian Jewry 266
Ottoman Sephardi dominance 268–277
Talmudic study and 260
See also Jews, Andalusian/Iberian
Sepher musar (Ibn Aqnīn) 346*n*2
Septimus, Bernard 270–271
ṣere (in vocalic rhymes) 120
Seridei teiman [The Remnants of Yemen] (Alnadāf, 1928) 26, 27
sermons 49, 50, 80, 96, 120, 140, 268*n*77
Ṣeror ha-mor [A Bundle of Myrrh] (Saba) 385, 416, 426
sevara (logical inference) 249, 253, 254, 255, 260, 266, 278
Shaʿarei orah [Gates of Light] (Gikatilla) 15, 377, 378, 390, 400, 402, 426
Shabbazi, Shalem 10, 15–16, 20, 146*n*320, 397, 428, 457*n*88
shadow play (*khayāl al-ẓill*) 157
Shapira, Moses (Moshe) Wilhelm 243*n*11, 257
Sharḥ al-Dalāla (Zechariah ha-Rofé) 356
Sharḥ maqāmāt al-ḥarīrī al-baṣrī (al-Sharīshī) 57
al-Sharīshī, Abū lʿAbbās 57, 112
Shekhinah 139*n*304, 240, 303, 386, 407
exile of 421
"Liqrat penei shabbat" and 410–411
See also *sefirot* (ten aspects of divinity)
Shemaʿ prayer 133, 383, 412*n*118
Shemonah Peraqim [Eight Chapters] (Maimonides) 351, 352*nn*24–25
Shemu'el ben La'el ha-Ya'iri (fictional character) 160
Shevet Musar (Elijah b. Solomon ha-Kohen of Izmir) 346*n*2
Shīʿī Islam 5, 6, 55, 109, 200
Shimon bar Yoḥai 240
shirat ha-ḥen (esoteric verse) 397
Shirat yisra'el be-teiman (Raṣon Halevi) 146*n*320
Shulḥan ʿarukh (Karo, 1565) 2, 9, 16, 50, 240, 260, 290, 455
opposition to *piyyut* in liturgy and 272
legal determinations of 393
maggid (guiding spirit) and 357
Sidon, city of 43, 124, 221–222, 370
Canaanites associated with 222
in "Greater Land of Israel" 209–210*n*158
Mordecai's travels and 86, 215
proximity to holy city of Tiberias 209
sages of 87
seafaring traders from 221–222
sifrut ha-musar (ethical literature) genre 75, 346
simanei ha'adam genre 182
Simeon ben Yoḥai, Rabbi 390, 421
Sinbad stories 59, 180
Sirāj alʿuqūl 263
al-Sīrāfī, Abū Zayd 169
slavery 235, 334*n*107
Socrates 84
Sofia (Bulgaria), city of 233
Soncino, Joshua 247
soteriology 131, 374, 400, 404
soul
"internal senses" of 347–351
moral qualities of 351–353
Neoplatonic myth of 354
threefold division of faculties 350
Spain, Christian 47, 224, 247, 316
decline of Arabic cultural influence in 48*n*20
expulsion of Jews from 191, 233, 268, 385, 390
Reconquista 274
seen as cultural wasteland 274
See also al-Andalus (Islamic Spain); Christians/Christianity
Steinschneider, Moritz 22, 76*n*107
stereotyping 101, 166, 174, 220, 425
folk tradition and 326
kabbalah and 426
Orientalism and 168
Stewart, Devin 52, 54–55, 56, 85, 91, 346
on *Maqāmāt* of al-Hamādhānī 109
on naming of fictional characters 111
on "unknown" fictional characters 101
storytelling (*qiṣṣa*) 157

Story Telling Techniques in the Arabian Nights (Pinault) 118
Stroumsa, Sarah 304*n*40
Suez Canal 9
Sufis/Sufism 175, 220, 397
Suleiman the Magnificent 4, 376–377
Sunnī Islam 5, 6, 55
al-Suyūṭī 34*n*107
Syria 86, 191, 217, 223, 245, 292, 347
  Jewish community of 87, 228, 229, 231, 360
  nostalgia for 183–184
  Ottoman conquest of 185*n*71, 205

Tabrīz (Persia) 230
Taḥkam (the Generous Arab), tale of 100, 326, 332–344
Taḥkemoni (Alḥarizi) 12, 13, 38, 85, 88, 171, 241
  adab literature and 338
  Arabic Introduction to 48
  author and protagonist conflated in 436
  author's introduction 67
  circulation and reception of 455
  cultural orbits of travel in 224
  "Dispute of the Soul with the Body and the Intellect" 138, 354
  Hebrew Introduction to 47
  Hebrew poets of East dismissed in 227
  Immanuel of Rome and 102, 103
  Judeocentricity in 226*n*212, 291
  lack of representations of Muslims in 291
  as literary model for Alḍāhirī 295, 419, 423, 440
  maqāma literary genre and 449
  memento mori motif in 451*n*68
  mendicant preacher in 371
  mercenary doctor in 361–362
  misogyny in 188
  multiple dedicatees of 123, 130, 180
  naming of protagonists in 112–113
  palindrome in 94–95
  picaresque Arabic *maqāma* and 51
  place names in 172
  Sefer hamusar as "imitation" of 21
  Sefer hamusar travel tales compared with 181
  "Tale of the Astrologer" 316–318
  title and number of *maqāmāt* in 72
  travel itineraries in 166
  as work of moral instruction 76
Ṭāhirid dynasty 6
Taʿizz, city of 6
Tales of Sendebar, The 190
Talmud 121, 173*n*24, 240, 245, 407
  Bomberg editions 247, 261–262
  burnings of (Paris 1242 and Rome 1553) 240*n*5, 260, 261, 289*n*137, 380
  early publishing history of 247
  ḥiddushim (Talmudic novellae) 263
  Rabbi Abraham Ashkenazi and 249, 251, 253–268
  study of 253–266
  Yemenite mss. in Deinard collection 258
Tamari, Assaf 241
taʾrīkh (annalistic chronicle) genre 33
tawakkul (Heb. *biṭṭaḥon*), pietistic ideal of 145, 237, 331, 352
temurah (Scripture as anagram) 93
Tetragrammaton 396, 400, 410, 411
al-Thaʿālibī, Abū Manṣūr 200
theodicy 44, 71, 415
Thousand and One Nights (*Arabian Nights*) 3, 97, 100, 117
  identity and disguise in 220
  narrative structure in 340
  oral recitations of tales comprising 155
  space and travel in 180–181
Tiberias, city of 66, 123, 179, 245, 412
  kabbalistic study in 219, 376
  sages of 248, 265
  Sephardi elite of 278
  Sephardi synagogue in 234, 424
Tiberias yeshivah 66, 101
  Abner as *ḥazzan* in 66, 120, 212, 218, 277, 279, 280
  Rabbi Abraham Ashkenazi's fundraising mission for 239, 243, 253, 265, 275
tiklāl
  See prayer books (*takālīl*; sng. *tiklāl*)
Tiklāl eṣ ḥayyim (Ṣaliḥ) 410
Tillier, Matthieu 200
Time (*ha-zeman*; *al-dahr*) 35, 122, 124
tiqqun ḥaṣot (kabbalistic prayer vigil) 396, 398, 421
Tobi, Yosef 15, 19, 30, 202*n*134, 257, 263, 392

on absence of Christians from Yemen 292*n*5
on folktales of *Sefer hamusar* 337
on funerary practices 450*n*65
on kabbalah in Yemen 392
on Talmud study in Yemen 257, 261*n*56, 263
tokheḥah (poem of reproof) 138, 203, 353, 354
Tolaʿat yaʿaqov (Ibn Gabbai) 377, 390, 426
Toldot adam ve-ḥavvah (Jeroḥam b. Meshullam) 288
Toorawa, Shawkat 55*n*47, 78–79, 108, 177*n*38
Torah 83, 121, 130, 173*n*24, 196, 249, 434
Abner's/Immanuel's illumination of 447
ahavah genre and 133
laws of marriage 142
Muslim–Jewish polemics and 300, 302, 304
Torah scrolls as *sefer* and *ḥefeṣ* 245–246
Torah study 157, 355
Zohar and 379
Torah commentary 2, 11, 15, 29, 38
See also *Ṣeidah la-derekh*
Tosafists 260
Trani, Rabbi Moses di 218, 240, 388
translations 11*n*29, 341–344
transmigration of souls 357, 379, 392–393, 415*n*127, 415*n*128
travel narratives 1, 17, 40, 165–168
Arabic and Hebrew antecedents to 175–180
attitudes toward periphery/center in 207–212
caravans and 213–214, 216
cultural orbits of travel in *Sefer hamusar* 222–225
depiction of non-Yemenite eastern Jews 224–231
diffusion of religious knowledge/practices and 218–219
encounters with "Ashkenazi" Jews 232–235
fantasy in 167
framing itineraries and embedded tales 180–183
identity and 219–221
pre-modern Arabic and Hebrew narratives 168–171
reading of travel accounts in *Sefer hamusar* 174–175
significance of place names 221–222
socio-cultural relevance of Cochin in 188–197
symbolic significance of Damascus in 183–186
toponyms and 172–175
writing from prison and 197–204
trickster stories 1, 21, 39, 53, 63, 111
Ṭuvyah ben Zeraḥ ha-Ṣeʿiri (fictional character) 160

Umayyad dynasty 5, 183
Umayyad Mosque (Damascus) 185

Vajda, Georges 170
van Leeuwen, Richard 180, 181, 221
Venice 177, 178, 179, 212*n*165, 240*n*5, 247, 276*n*98
viddui (poetic confession for Day of Atonement) 429
Vie mode d'emploi, La [Life: A User's Manual] (Perec) 92
Vital, Hayyim 379, 383*n*23

Wacks, David A. 156
Wagner, Mark 397
al-Wajīz al-mughnī [The Sufficient Compendium] (Alu'el) 15
Wanneh, Rabbi Isaac 132, 338*n*121, 377*n*3, 393, 394, 412*n*118
Wars of the Lord (Gersonides) 249
Wissenschaft des Judentums 22, 23
Wolfson, Elliot 379*n*9, 384*n*25, 417*n*135
Wolfson, Harry 348, 350, 351*n*22, 351*n*23, 356
word play 87, 91–93

Yaakov, Efraim 30, 262*n*61, 394
Yaari, Abraham 24, 25, 33–35, 198, 387, 388
Yalqut ha-maqāma haʿivrit (Ratzaby) 324*n*88
Yassif, Eli 240*n*3, 337, 357
Yatīmat al-dahr fī maḥāsin ahl al-ʿaṣr (al-Thaʿālibī) 200
Yemen 1, 179, 182, 204, 393
carceral practices in 201–202
geography of 5
Indian Ocean trade and 8, 10

isolation relative to central Islamic lands 5
meanings of name 222
Ottoman expansion into 206
Sefer hamusar scenes set in 65, 207–211
Tihāma coastal region 5, 6, 163
tribal sheikhs outside Zaydī control 201*n*128
See also Jews, Yemenite; Ṣana'ā, city of
Yemini, Ḥayyim 27
Yerushalmi, Yosef Hayim 210
Yeshaya, Joachim 128
yeshivot 211, 217, 249, 270
Babylonian 257, 261
centrality to rabbinic learning 250
Ottoman 255
rabbinic emissaries and 206
Talmud study and 253, 255
Yiḥye Ṣāliḥ 132
Yiṣhari, Mordechai 28–29, 158

Zacuto, Moses 452
Zadock, Moshe 11*n*27, 29
Zayd ben 'Alī 5
Zaydīs 6, 45, 344
Alḍāhirī imprisoned by 197
as branch of Shī'ī Islam 5
cruelty of 230, 344
imāms 5, 6, 9, 163, 202, 207
overthrow of Ottomans (1567) 1, 4, 36, 197
resistance to Ottoman rule 7
Zechariah ha-Rofé 10, 356, 357*n*38
zeidim ("wicked/arrogant") as pun on Zaydiyya 293
Zion (Hebrew historical periodical) 26
Zionism 24–25, 26, 208, 273
ziyāda (augmentation) 128–129, 130, 131, 133, 140, 143, 146
Abner's recitation of 143
to Abraham Ibn Ezra's "Miyaldei yom" 147–152
to Halevi's "Libbi 'amod" 143–147, 152
as regular feature of Yemenite poetry 146
relationship to earlier poets and 140
tosefet as Hebrew equivalent of 148
Zohar 14, 15, 240, 288, 377, 392*n*56, 408, 413, 426
as anthology or composite text 378
appearance in print 386
Heikhalot 402–403
poems in praise of 378–379, 421
Zoharic literature 178
See also kabbalah/kabbalism
Zot torat ha-behemah (Alḍāhirī) 259
zuhd motif 370
Zumthor, Paul 167

Printed in the United States
by Baker & Taylor Publisher Services